Justice, Nature and the
Geography of Difference

for Delfina

Justice, Nature and the Geography of Difference

David Harvey

First published 1996
Reprinted 1997 (twice)

Blackwell Publishers Inc
350 Main Street
Malden, Massachusetts 02148, USA

Blackwell Publishers Ltd
108 Cowley Road
Oxford OX4 1JF, UK

Library of Congress Cataloging in Publication Data
Harvey, David, 1935–
Justice, nature, and the geography of difference/David Harvey
p. cm.
Includes bibliographical references and index.
ISBN 1–55786–680–5 (alk. paper) — ISBN 1–55786–681–3 (pbk.:alk. paper)
1. Social justice. 2. Social change. 3. Social values.
4. Global environmental change. 5. Cultural relativism. 6. Space and time. I. Title.
HM216.H26   1996   96–961
303.3'72—dc20   CIP

British Library Cataloguing in Publication Data
A CIP catalogue record for this book is available from the British Library

Typeset in 10 on 12pt Garamond
Printed and bound in Great Britain by MPG Books Ltd, Bodmin, Cornwall

This book is printed on acid-free paper

Contents

Thoughts for a Prologue

Here is a map of our country:
here is the Sea of Indifference, glazed with salt
This is the haunted river flowing from brow to groin
we dare not taste its water
This is the desert where missiles are planted like corms
This is the breadbasket of foreclosed farms
This is the birthplace of the rockabilly boy
This is the cemetery of the poor
who died for democracy   This is a battlefield
from a nineteenth-century war the shrine is famous
This is the sea-town of myth and story   when the fishing fleets
went bankrupt   here is where the jobs were   on the pier
processing frozen fishsticks   hourly wages and no shares
These are other battlefields   Centralia   Detroit
here are the forests primeval   the copper   the silver lodes
These are the suburbs of acquiescence   silence rising fumelike
        from the streets
This is the capital of money and dolor whose spires
flare up through air inversions whose bridges are crumbling
whose children are drifting blind alleys pent
between coiled rolls of razor wire
I promised to show you a map you say but this is a mural
then yes let it be   these are small distinctions
where do we see it from is the question

Adrienne Rich *An Atlas of the Difficult World*

Acknowledgments

The lines from "An Atlas of the Difficult World," from *An Atlas of the Difficult World: Poems 1988–1991* by Adrienne Rich. Copyright © 1991 by Adrienne Rich. Reprinted with permission of the author and W.W. Norton & Company, Inc.

Introduction

In recent years I have frequently found myself speaking at conferences on "globalization." The conference at Duke University in November, 1994, was by far the most interesting. It brought together diverse people not only from many disciplines and walks of life but also from many different countries. It was a welcome change to listen to academics, activists, and representatives from the arts from countries like South Korea, China, India, Russia, and Egypt as opposed to the rather repetitive and sterile discussions of globalization (increasingly dubbed by cynics "globaloney") that all too often occur in university settings in the United States or Europe. But the atmosphere of the conference was frequently tense and arguments often hard to follow, illustrative of the inroads that hypercritical currents of thought like poststructuralism, postmodernism, deconstruction, and the like have made throughout the world.

But what truly rendered the occasion memorable for me was my stay in the Omni Hotel in Durham, North Carolina. The hotel was full of *families* – of a very distinctive sort. The men wore either slightly baggy suits, or blazers and flannels, usually embellished with a jolly necktie. The children were remarkably well behaved, the boys typically dressed in blazers and flannels and the girls for the most part in frilly dresses. And the women all wore ankle-length dresses and, most distinctive of all, had long hair, the only permissible deviation apparently being to loop it up into a bun. This was definitely not Levi, Calvin Klein or even Benetton territory (though Laura Ashley could have made it) – not a pair of jeans in sight. And everyone was remarkably friendly, bestowing beaming "hellos" and "good-days" to obvious deviants from the sartorial norm such as myself.

I was curious enough to follow this distinctive crowd whither it was headed and soon found myself in the midst of the Southeastern Regional Meeting of Evangelical Pentecostal Preachers. I was intrigued enough to stay. An evening of participant observation taught me a lot. I could not help contrasting, for example, the incredible enthusiasm, joy, and vigor of the Pentecostal meeting with the angst and competitive tension at the globalization conference. While the Pentecostal meeting was very much led from the front by white male preachers (no concern here to balance the program according to criteria of gender or race), the levels and degree of enthusiastic audience participation were extraordinarily high, compared to the heard-it-all-before incredulity and resentful passivity of the campus audience. Furthermore, for the Pentecostals it was an orchestration of emotions and passions rather than of intellect that was being sought and the ends and objectives of the orchestration were clear. I wondered what the parallel objective of the globalization conference might be. I had a hard time finding any strong or coherent answer to that question.

The preacher who opened the ceremonies that evening did so with the following invocation. "Through these four days," he said, "we have come to understand the foundational beliefs that keep us firmly on the rock." *Foundational beliefs!* I wondered what on earth would happen if I started to talk about foundational beliefs in the globalization conference. The deconstructionists would go to work with icy precision, the relativists would callously sneer, the critical theorists would rub their hands and say "this simply will not do" and the postmodernists would exclaim "what a dinosaur!" And I myself agree that all foundational beliefs should be scrutinized and questioned. But what troubled me was the thought that when a political group armed with strong and unambiguous foundational beliefs confronts a bunch of doubting Thomases whose only foundational belief is skepticism towards all foundational beliefs, then it is rather easy to predict who will win. Which led me to the following reflection: the task of critical analysis is not, surely, to prove the impossibility of foundational beliefs (or truths), but to find a more plausible and adequate basis for the foundational beliefs that make interpretation and political action meaningful, creative, and possible.

In this book, I try to define a set of workable foundational concepts for understanding space–time, place, and environment (nature). The critical search for such foundational concepts is, of course, no trivial or easy task. It requires nothing short of establishing a metaphysical basis for enquiry. But it is dangerous in academia these days to confess to being *meta* about anything, for to do so is to suggest a longing for something mystically outside of us (or sometimes within us) to which we can appeal to stabilize the flood of chaotic images, ephemeral representations, contorted positionings, and multiple fragmentations of knowledge within which we now have our collective being. But metaphysics in its traditional sense is precisely about the kind of critical enquiry that allows for the free interplay of passions, emotions, rationality, and intellect rather than their restrictive compartmentalizations. That balance is not always easy to strike. If, for example, the Pentecostals were unduly high on charged emotions and the collective orchestration of passions and desires for highly restrictive ends, then we academics surely err in being far too highly captivated by the cerebral and highly disciplined (in every sense, both positive and negative, of that word) qualities of our own individualistic, professionally defined, fragmented, and often egotistically driven enterprises. Metaphysics at its best also seeks general principles to understand but never repress the evident complexity of physical, biological, and social life. Enquiry of this sort is never easy going and during the writing of this book I have often found myself longing for the easy simplicities of faith of the Pentecostals, the certitudes of positivism or the absolutes of dogmatic Marxism.

As the evening with the Pentecostals wore on, it became evident that there was a very particular political target for the occasion. And that target was racism. The blood of Jesus, it was said, will wash away all signs of racial distinction. Racial discrimination within the church was construed as a barrier to the expansion of its powers and in the midst of extraordinary scenes preacher after preacher exhorted the assembled whites to embrace their black brethren with joy, humility, and understanding. And so it was that an audience that in the context of the US south would be traditionally thought hostile to racial integration came to embrace (on the surface at least) not only the black brethren present but also the ideal of racial equality in the eyes of the church and of the Lord. Now I happen to be in favor of almost anything that mitigates the destructive, degrading, and debilitating practices of racism in the United States and it certainly seemed to me that more may have been accomplished on that score in one evening of Pentecostal preaching than in two decades of lip-service paid in my own university to ideals of affirmative action. There was, however, a hitch. Evil has, apparently, to reside somewhere and the denunciation of the traitorous Jews, the murderers of Jesus Christ, hovered over the Pentecostal proceedings making me wonder how much the politics of the occasion was also dominated by an attempt to wean away actual or potential African–American supporters of Farrakhan's "Nation of Islam."

On my way out of the meeting I found myself confronted not only with a whole battery of preachers dying to tell me what appalling sinners they once had been and how wondrous it was to rediscover the ways of the Lord, but a set of booths selling everything from religious icons and books to T-shirts. A particular T-shirt caught my eye and I could not resist buying it. Produced by *Righteous Wear*, a *Jesus Christ Centered Company*, it proclaimed in startling colors:

GET RIGHT
OR
GET LEFT

Deconstructionists could have a field day with that one, I thought. Authority for the logo was located, however, in Ecclesiastes 10:2 and Matthew 25:33–4. Being in the Omni Hotel, I had instant access to *Gideon*'s Bible and, on repairing to my room, I checked the two citations. Ecclesiastes merely stated that God placed wisdom on His right hand and foolishness on His left. I didn't mind that since being of the political left I have long recognized that it takes a little foolishness to change anything. But the passage from Matthew was much more bothersome. God separates the nations as a shepherd separates the sheep from the goats. And the sheep were placed on His right hand from whence they inherited the kingdom and the goats were placed on His left hand and condemned to "the eternal fire prepared for the devil and his angels." Now it is a standing joke among many of his friends that God is not a leftist sympathizer, but condemnation to such total damnation seemed a bit too much.

So why, exactly, were the goats condemned to the eternal fire? The reason given is that:

> I was hungry and you gave me no food, I was thirsty and you gave me no drink, I was a stranger and you did not welcome me, naked and you did not clothe me, sick or in prison and you did not visit me.

The goats protest that they did not see Him hungry, thirsty, naked, sick, or in prison. God notes that they have met such people all around them on a daily basis and says "if you did it not to the least of these, you did it not to me."

Now these happen to be rather old-fashioned, traditional, and, dare I say it, "foundational" values for a socialist politics. So what has happened to those concerns? Why was there so little take up on such questions in the globalization conference? And how come the religious "right" now claims these concerns as their own? On this last point I immediately had a provocative thought. If God is located somewhere in space then maybe what appears to be on His left is actually to our right! This turns out to be a far from trivial point: Leibniz, whose ideas I will often invoke (particularly in chapter 10), contested Newton's theories of absolute space and time and insisted upon a relational theory of space–time on the theological grounds that the absolute theory diminished God's powers by making it seem as if He was located in (rather than creator and Lord of) space and time. In the Leibnizian view it would be impossible to talk of God having a left or right hand because God is an omnipresent power throughout the universe and not to be construed as someone who sits somewhere in space and time surveying all that happens.

What seems like an arcane seventeenth-century theological controversy has a contemporary echo. In the current rush to provide "cognitive maps" of everything going on in art, politics, the humanities, literary, and social theory, etc. (*Mapping the West European Left, Mapping Ideology,* or *Locating Culture* to cite some recent book titles), the question of the relative location of various political groupings, stances, ideas, and movements has become a major criterion of evaluation and judgment. The discussion unfortunately evades the problem that mapping requires a map and that maps are typically totalizing, usually two-dimensional, Cartesian, and very undialectical devices with which it is possible to propound any mixture of extraordinary insights and monstrous lies. Mathematicians (like Euler and Gauss) long ago proved, for example, that it is impossible to map even the spherical surface of the earth on a flat piece of paper without distortion, and the history of map projections (including those of a topological variety) indicates an infinity of possible mapping systems making it possible to transform left into right or both into nowhere, depending upon the particular projection chosen. This is not to say that maps are useless – far from it (and I shall frequently appeal to them in what follows). But the mapping metaphor subsumes (and sometimes obscures) the problematics of representation within an often unquestioned choice to employ one particular projection (and I deliberately use the term in both its mathematical and psychological sense) rather than some other. For myself, I think the whole rhetoric of left versus right (radical versus reactionary, progressive versus conservative; revolutionary versus counterrevolutionary) is less than helpful these days since all sorts of different meanings are being assigned to those terms (often depending upon the unspecified map deployed). If I generally resort in what follows to the binary of pro- or anti-capitalist (socialist) then it is partly out of an urge to come up with somewhat clearer terms of discussion, even though, I hasten to concede, even that binary is confused enough.

But weaseling out of God's damning judgment through such arcane arguments (theological or otherwise) hardly seemed the point. I needed to reflect upon how the conference on globalization (myself included), ostensibly "radical" and "leftist" (though not remarkably anti-capitalist) in its orientation, might help to feed the hungry, clothe the naked, minister to the sick, and generally pursue the foundational aims of socialist/anti-capitalist politics. It is not sufficient, I concluded, to explore the metaphysical groundings, the foundational beliefs, that might be applied to understanding abstract terms as well as the concrete politics of space, time, place, and environment (nature) in isolation. Such explorations should simultaneously pursue a political commitment to feed, nourish, clothe and sustain the hungry, the poor, and the weak. Concerns about social justice (and how to understand and operationalize foundational beliefs about that contested term) thereby intertwine with the question of how to understand foundational geographical concepts.

At the intersection of all these arguments lies the question of the *just production of just geographical differences*. We need critical ways to think about how differences in ecological, cultural, economic, political, and social conditions get produced (particularly through those human activities that we are in a position in principle to modify or control) and we also need ways to evaluate the justice/injustice of the differences so produced. While, like most socialists, I have a certain attachment to the principle of equality, for example, this plainly cannot mean the erasure of all forms of geographical difference (even presuming such erasure would be feasible in a world that includes Nepal, Nicaragua, Finland, Italy, Saudi Arabia, and the United States). Indeed, the equality principle could just as easily imply the *proliferation* of geographical differences of a certain benign sort (leading immediately to the question of how to construe what is or is not "benign"). *Uneven geographical development* is a concept deserving of the closest elaboration and attention. Furthermore, any historical–geographical materialist worth his or her salt, must surely recognize that radically different socio-ecological circumstances imply quite different approaches to the question of what is or is not just. The baseline argument I shall therefore adopt – an argument which I suspect many will now be happy to concede – is that spatial and ecological differences are not only *constituted by* but *constitutive of* what I shall call *socio-ecological and political–economic processes*. This includes the difficult prospect that such processes are constitutive of the very standards of social justice that may be used to evaluate and modify their own operation. It is my foundational aim to provide a solid conceptual apparatus to enquire into the justness of such relations and how the sense of justice in turn gets historically and geographically constituted. Coincidentally, I also consider this work to be an enquiry into the foundational principles for an adequate historical–geographical materialism in the Marxist tradition.

A number of general themes intertwine in the chapters that follow. I want here to lay some of these out in advance as guiding threads or signposts.

The Problem of Dialectics

I try to develop a dialectical and relational approach to the general topic at hand. The nature of dialectics is often misunderstood and there are, in addition, many forms of dialectics that can reasonably claim our attention. I therefore thought it wise to set out (in chapter 2) some initial principles of dialectics (as I interpret them) as a guide to the theoretical and conceptual practice that follows. To some, of course, the very mention of the word dialectics sounds unpromising and unduly complicated, though to others, such as those working in literary theory, dialectical formulations are now so commonplace as to be old hat. Resistance to this way of thinking has been much stronger in the social sciences for obvious reasons (even laying aside the political implications, it challenges standard applications of statistical methods and mathematical modeling procedures, not so much in terms of actual practices but in terms of interpretations and meanings). In this regard I find myself siding with literary theory and arguing strongly *against* that very large segment of social theory and of the physical, biological, and engineering sciences that sits comfortably and often unquestioningly in a positivist or simple empiricist mode of thought and work. I would like to persuade my colleagues in these fields that an understanding of dialectics can deepen our understanding of socio-ecological processes in all manner of ways, without entirely refuting or abandoning findings arrived at by other means. In particular, I want to offer a dialectical way to emphasize relations and totalities, as opposed to isolated causal chains and innumerable fragmented and sometimes contradictory hypotheses proven statistically correct at the 0.5 percent level of significance. Part of the work of the dialectician is, then, to translate and transform other bodies of knowledge accumulated by different structures of enquiry and to show how such transformations and translations are revealing of new and often interesting insights. There are, however, limits to that process leaving a residue of problems and issues for which translation is hard if not impossible. These are most clearly evident in the way fundamental understandings are derived concerning foundational concepts such as *space, time,* and *nature.* Since I concentrate for the most part on these foundational topics, the difference that dialectical argument and praxis makes will be very much in evidence throughout.

The Problem of Historical–Geographical Materialism

While dialectics is relatively weakly implanted in the social, physical, biological, and engineering sciences, it is a familiar mode of thought in some segments of the humanities, becoming particularly powerful with the wave of philosophizing in literary theory and the pervasive influences of Hegel, Marx, Heidegger, Derrida, and a host of others. The relational dialectics I adopt has made headway, for example, in feminist theory for interesting reasons. According to Friedman (1995), "cultural narratives of relational positionality" have permitted feminists to move beyond the confines of what she calls "scripts of denial, accusation and confession" that rest on simple binaries and often upon essentialist categories (e.g., women/good: men/bad). Within a relational framework, "identities shift with a changing context, dependent upon the point of reference" so that there are no essences or absolutes. "Identities are fluid sites that can be understood differently depending on the vantage point of their formation and function." I strongly support this way of thinking. But here my argument also moves gently in contra-flow (recalling, perhaps, the power of the simple binaries of those evangelical preachers).

The reduction of everything to fluxes and flows, and the consequent emphasis upon the transitoriness of all forms and positions has its limits. If everything that is solid is always instantaneously melting into air, then it is very hard to accomplish anything or even set one's mind to do anything. Faced with that difficulty the temptation is strong to go back to some simple foundational beliefs (whether these be a fetishism of the family on the right or of something called "resistance" on the left) and dismiss the process-based arguments out of hand. I believe such a maneuver would be fundamentally wrong. But while I accept the general argument that process, flux, and flow should be given a certain ontological priority in understanding the world, I also want to insist that this is precisely the reason why we should pay so much more careful attention to what I will later call the "permanences" that surround us and which we also construct to help solidify and give meaning to our lives. Furthermore, while it is formally true that everything can be reduced to flows – including, as A.N. Whitehead says, Cleopatra's Needle and the Sphinx – we are in daily practice surrounded by things, institutions, discourses, and even states of mind of such relative permanence and power that it would be foolish not to acknowledge those evident qualities. There is, I believe, little point in asserting some sort of "dissolution of all fixity and permanence" in the famous "last instance" if, as far as we human beings are concerned, that last instance is nowhere in sight. The "solid rock" of historical–geographical materialism is here used to say that dialectical argumentation cannot be understood as outside of the concrete material conditions of the world in which we find ourselves; and those concrete conditions are often so set in literal concrete (at least in relation to the time and space of human action) that we must perforce acknowledge their permanence, significance, and power.

All of this has political import. Consider, for example, Derrida's extraordinary fantasy in *Specters of Marx* in which immersion in the flows is thought somehow to be radical and revolutionary in itself. The move that makes this possible is to separate "dialectics" from all tangible sense of historical–geographical conditions as well as from any rootedness in a tangible and organized politics. Derrida can then envisage a "New International without status, without title and without name . . . without party, without country, without national community." This is, as Eagleton (1995: 37) remarks, "the ultimate post-structuralist fantasy: an opposition without anything as distastefully systemic or drably 'orthodox' as an opposition, a dissent beyond all formulable discourse, a promise which would betray itself in the act of fulfillment, a perpetual excited openess to the Messiah who had better not let us down by doing anything as determinate as coming."

We need not only to understand but also to create permanences – organization, institutions, doctrines, programs, formalized structures, and the like – in order to change anything in any kind of meaningful or directed way. And it is at this point that I part company with that genre of relational dialectics that has become pure idealism. I seek a far firmer grounding to politics in the concrete historical and geographical conditions in which human action unfolds. In this regard, therefore, I find myself writing *against* an emerging trend, grounded in dialectical and relational ways of thinking, producing what might be called "a new idealism" in which thought and discourse are believed to be all that matter in powering the historical geography of socio-ecological and political–economic change.

The Problem of Theorizing

There is a great deal of talk these days about practices of "theorizing" and of "getting the theory right." These are concerns that I share but I hasten to add that it is not always easy to understand what is meant by theorizing and theory. It stands to reason that these terms take on very special meaning when I assume a dialectical (relational), historical–geographical, and materialist approach to knowledge and that the rules of theorizing are here quite different from how they might be construed in, say, an analytic or positivist approach. The knowledges and theories produced by such difference means are not wholly incompatible with each other. But nor are they directly assimilable to each other. The general stance I take is that a dialectical, historical–geographical and materialist theory, because it deals with totalities, particularities, motion, and fixity in a certain way, holds out the prospect of embracing many other forms of theorizing within its frame, sometimes with only minimal loss to the integrity of the original (though in other instances the losses may be substantial). I am not concerned to justify that argument here. But there is one line of thought that is so fundamental to what follows that it is worth broaching in advance.

The insertion of spatial considerations into most forms of social theorizing (dialectical and nondialectical) often turns out to be profoundly disruptive of how the theory can be specified and put to work. Social theoretic meta-narratives (such as those provided by Marx and Weber) usually concentrate on processes of temporal change, keeping spatiality constant. If spatiality typically disrupts received theory and dominant metanarratives, then those who, for whatever reason, want to disrupt them can most easily do so by invoking some sort of spatiality. This accounts, I suspect, for the extraordinary eruption of spatial metaphors in poststructuralist and postmodernist work (the work of Foucault being quite explicit on the point).

But here, too, I find myself in a somewhat odd position. For while I welcome on the one hand the explosion of interest (again, much of it in literary rather than social theory) in things spatial and a proliferation of texts and arguments that wrestle with what spatiality might be all about, it has never been my intention to use such a conceptual apparatus to attack meta-theory *per se*. My concern is, rather, with trying to rebuild Marxian meta-theory in such a way as to incorporate an understanding of spatio-temporality (and socio-ecological issues) within its frame. This has me writing *against* those uses of spatiality and of spatial metaphor whose sole purpose seems to be to take unreconcilable difference, incommunicability, particularity, and irreducible individualism and fix them in stone.

It has never been my point to argue that spatiality makes theory impossible: I want to reconstruct theory with space (and the "relation to nature") clearly integrated within it as foundational elements. The only way to do that is to theorize what might be meant by "the production of space" in particular or, more generally, "the production of nature." Such a project is not without its difficulties (as the length and intricacy of some of the argument in this book illustrates). But we should and, I think, do end up with a very different kind of understanding of how theory should be construed and what a "meta-theory" should look like. I believe it possible, on this basis, to construct a general theory of dialectical and historical geographical materialism.

The Question of Values and the Nature of Justice

Situating oneself in the full flood of all the fluxes and flows of social change makes appeal to any permanent set of values with which to animate collective or well-directed social action suspect. This is not a new thought. Sometime towards the end of the second century, camped along the misty, ague-plagued regions of the Danube, the Emperor Marcus Aurelius, trying vainly to hold back the barbarian hordes that threatened the borders and the permanence of the Roman Empire, wrote in his *Meditations*:

> One thing hastens into being, another hastens out of it. Even while a thing is in the act of coming into existence, some part of it has already ceased to be. Flux and change are for ever renewing the fabric of the universe. ... In such a running river, where there is no firm foothold, what is there for a man to value among all the many things that are racing past him?

It is not hard in these times to empathize with the question. But the question cannot be evaded, not despite but because of all the manifest insecurities and volatilities in the political economy of daily life and the parallel preoccupation in radical segments of the humanities and the arts with emphasizing (even hypostasizing) the instabilities of fluxes and flows. It is in this realm of "values" that conservative and religious thought has its strongest appeal, precisely because the presumption of permanence (in culture) or of eternal truths (in religion) gives a stability to values that radical thought finds hard to acknowledge. But meaningful political action (and, for that matter, even meaningful analysis) cannot proceed without some embedded notions of value, if only a determination as to what is or is not important to analyze intellectually let alone to struggle for politically.

In some forms of enquiry, of course, the distinction between "facts" and "values" is held to be sacrosanct. To permit values to enter into the domain of scientific objective enquiry, for example, is often seen to taint all evidence and results and render them suspect or useless. In the dialectical/relational view, the separation of facts and values is impossible to achieve (except by sleight of hand or within certain strictly limited domains where it may reasonably be held that values are or can be held constant). In some areas of science, as we shall see, this dialectical/relational view of the inevitable fusion of facts and values has undergone a revival of sorts, as multiple contestations have arisen over, for example, how to interpret quantum theory.

The answer to these difficulties, it seems to me, is to replace the fixed idea of "values" with an understanding of "processes of valuation." Once we come to appreciate how such processes operate, we can also better understand how and why certain kinds of "permanence" get constructed in particular places and times so as to form dominant social values to which most people willingly subscribe. In what follows, therefore, there is a constant preoccupation with processes of valuation, how they operate and to what degree some set of relatively permanent values can be or have been constructed as pivots for diverse forms of socio-ecological action. The reader will doubtless notice, for example, the "perpetual return" to considerations of money as a dominant symbol of a process of valuation that affects us all. I had at one point toyed with the idea of taking all the passages that dealt with money and assembling them into one chapter. But, in the end, it seemed more appropriate to let the question of money permeate the various chapters in much the same way that it permeates almost every facet of socio-ecological, personal, and collective life in the world we have now constructed. The process of money valuation is, it transpires, simultaneously a process defining space, time, environment, and place and I shall endeavor to unravel that connection in some detail.

But money is not the only way in which the process of valuation can be understood. The relatively permanent configurations of values around family, gender, religion, nation, ethnic identity, humanism, and various ideals of morality and justice, indicate the existence of quite different and sometimes antagonistic processes of valuation. How these different processes can be reconciled is in itself a major topic of enquiry (and not a little bemusement, as the Evangelical Pentecostal example of selling "righteous wear" through a "Jesus Christ Centered Company" illustrates). The power of money, for example, can be used to support other processes of valuation. But it can also undermine them and come into conflict with them. In what follows, such conflicts will be the occasional focus of attention. And if I ultimately converge on the value "social justice" as a central concern it is only in part for personal historical reasons (it allows me to revisit the terrain of my first "Marxist" work, *Social Justice and the City*, written more than two decades ago). I also firmly believe that this is the best terrain of valuing upon which the anti-capitalist struggle can take its stand (no matter whether that struggle is weakly reformist as in the "Blairism" of the British Labour Party or more revolutionary as implied by the environmental justice movement).

While, therefore, it may be true, as that old reprobate Lawrence Durrell once remarked, that "life consists of perpetual choosing and the perpetual reservation of judgement," a political movement has to make its choice and not reserve its judgment. This was, I believe, the central difference between the Evangelical Pentecostals and the globalization conference – the former had no reservations of judgment whereas finding and expressing such reservations is the name of the game in many intellectual modes of thought and practice. All values, like the Sphinx, will ultimately dissolve and it is particularly hard given the swift-flowing currents of change to settle on any particular set of core values for very long. But we have no option except to articulate values and stick by them if emancipatory change is to be produced. Values inhere in socio-spatial processes, furthermore, and the struggle to change the former is simultaneously a struggle to change the latter (and vice versa). And it is precisely at this point that the human imaginary has to be deployed to its full force in the quest for progressive socio-ecological and political–economic change.

The Politics of Possibility

One of the viruses of a dialectical/relational approach is that it opens up all sorts of possibilities that might otherwise appear foreclosed. It does so in the first instance in the realms of thought and discourse and for this reason it can be the fount for all manner of Utopian schemes and fantasies (of the sort that Derrida has recently offered). But I also regard it important, theoretically and politically, to root the sense of those possibilities in the mass of constraints that derive from our embeddedness in nature, space–time, place and a particular kind of socio-ecological order (capitalism) that regulates the material conditions of daily life.

This is no remote or arcane issue. For just as the Evangelical Pentecostal preachers were building a political force by appeal to religious conviction to build the city of God here on earth, so we find a variety of pro-capitalist political movements animated by articulation of some sort of Utopian vision. I turn, for example, to a report in the *New York Times* (August 23, 1995) on a conference on "Cyberspace and the American Dream." Alvin Toffler, author of *The Third Wave*, was an important presence at the conference. He argues that a "third wave" information-based revolution is replacing "second wave" industrialism and is now in the process of forming a "civilization with its own distinctive world outlook, its own ways of dealing with time, space, logic, and causality." This in itself is an interesting theme; but if Toffler is right, then the processes and rules producing historical–geographical difference are also presumably undergoing a revolutionary shift. Now it so happens that Toffler is a widely read "postindustrial" and "Utopian" thinker. He is also politically influential: Newt Gingrich, Republican leader of the US House of Representatives, has adopted Toffler as one of his "gurus" and has evolved a revolutionary rhetoric in which the dismantling of the institutional structures of the regulatory and welfare state is seen as an imperative prelude to the liberation of emancipatory "third wave" forces now supposedly hemmed in by the institutions, practices, and decrepit power structures of a fading era of "second wave" industrial capitalism. The press report in the *New York Times* continues by stating that a new coalition of forces (from both left and right of the political spectrum) is organizing "to harness the brightest minds of high technology and use their collective brainpower to assist Mr Gingrich as he tries to reshape the nation's political and economic landscape in preparation for the information revolution." And there are many who now believe that an emancipatory revolution in political economy, in social relations, in the explorations of identity, semantic worlds, and artistic forms is being born out of the capacity to create a "virtual" reality in cyberspace. Gingrich wonders, furthermore, if it might be possible to distribute laptop computers to every child in America as a solution to all social and economic ills and a columnist in the *Baltimore Sun* argues that the way out of the long-term structural unemployment and confinement of human talents in the desolate public housing projects of the inner city is through access to the entrepreneurial possibilities of the Internet.

There is more than a hint of an oft-criticized and, some would say, quite "vulgar" Marxist view of history in all of this: only liberate the contemporary "productive forces" (technologies) from their socio-economic and political chains (government regulation) and let the liberties of the market take command, the argument runs, and all will be well with the world. Much of the revolutionary power and widespread appeal of the hegemonic pro-capitalist version of this Utopian argument derives, I suspect, from the beguiling simplicity of this vulgar Marxist formulation (particularly when articulated with the clarity and conviction of someone like Margaret Thatcher or Newt Gingrich).

The connection between this "right-wing Utopianism" and political power and practice is significant. Even if it is a far from dominant argument (even within the right) it is a potent pro-capitalist weapon with which to go to work against a whole array of forces that would, in the name of equality, justice, morality, or just plain political–economic and ecological common sense, seek to curb, regulate, and diminish all the manifest excesses for which capitalism is justly infamous. The connection also highlights the difficulty of anti-capitalist politics. Unable to deploy its own Utopian vision (though there are plenty of mini-versions), anti-capitalist politics lacks the power to animate and mobilize a mass movement on a global basis. That was not true of *The Communist Manifesto*, but, as I think Marx would himself be the first to appreciate, we cannot seek the poetry of our future in the particular poetry of that past, however appealing it still may be. And while it may seem insulting to include Derrida and Toffler in the same sentence, both provide Utopian visions but the latter, in part by his simplicity, clarity and seeming rootedness in the materiality of the world, is proving far more effective at changing it.

In view of Marx's well-known antipathy to Utopian thinking, it may seem strange to include him in a discussion of this sort. But Marx produced a certain kind of Utopianism that he was most anxious to keep separate from other varieties. When he writes in *Capital* that "what separates the worst of architects from the best of bees" is that "the former erects his structure in imagination before giving it material form" he opens a creative space for the human imagination to play both a constructive and a key role. When he writes in the *Eighteenth Brumaire*, that each revolutionary movement has to create its own poetry particularly in those situations where the "content" (the process of revolutionary change) outstrips "the phrase" (the capacity to represent what is happening), then he indicates a task for the revolutionary imagination that it is essential to fulfill. This raises the question for all of us: what kind of architecture (in the broadest possible sense of that term) do we collectively want to create for the socio-ecological world in which we have our being? Not to pose that question is to evade the most crucial task confronting all forms of human action. It is with this in mind that I struggle to find foundational concepts for the human imaginary to contemplate our embeddedness in space, time, nature, and place.

I have struggled in what follows to write as clearly as simply as I can often on difficult and complicated subjects. But we can never write (to paraphrase Marx) under historical or geographical conditions of our own making. As the conference on globalization indicated, the proliferating influence of what are loosely called "poststructuralist" and "postmodernist" ways of thinking and writing makes it particularly hard these days to find anything as mundane as a common language for expression, particularly in academia. Yet the highly specialized and distinctive languages that have been evolved these last 30 years often have something very important to say. I have therefore often found myself forced (sometimes with good effect) to take up such languages and terms, if only to give due consideration to what are serious arguments worthy of equally serious scrutiny. And in some instances I have found it useful to internalize within my own text certain specialized languages as privileged modes of expression of particular but important standpoints. Partly for this reason, I decided to devote a whole chapter to the topic of "discourse" in order to clarify my own discursive strategies while trying to position the role of the rapidly proliferating modes of representation in processes of socio-ecological and political–economic change. In other instances, most particularly in the development of the relational theory of space and time in chapter 8; I had no option except to engage with metaphysics at a fairly high level of abstraction. Foundational concepts do not come easily and, as Marx commented in one of his many prefaces to *Capital* the difficulties that arise cannot easily be brushed aside. This is, he went on to remark:

> a disadvantage I am powerless to overcome, unless it be by forewarning and forearming those readers who zealously seek the truth. There is no royal road

to science, and only those who do not dread the fatiguing climb of its steep paths have a chance of gaining its luminous summits.

I hope that those who climb the path will find the summit as illuminating as I do.

Not all historical and geographical conditions of existence are inhibiting to the production of new ways of thinking. I want to acknowledge the peculiarly favorable conditions that have allowed my own work to proceed. One of the great privileges of university life is to set up and co-teach courses in such a way as to be able to learn from a variety of very talented people working in diverse fields. I want to thank G.A. Cohen, Andrew Glyn, Neil Hertz, Bill Leslie, Kirstie McClure, Emily Martin, Erica Schoenberger, Erik Swyngedouw, Katherine Verdery, Gavin Williams, and Reds Wolman for providing an opportunity for extended dialogue through such a format. It is a similar privilege to work with some extraordinarily talented graduate students who struggle gamely to educate me in matters that I might otherwise be deeply resistant to. They will doubtless throw up their hands in frustration at my failure to take on board everything they have said, but my work has been immeasurably strengthened by their contributions. I include here the Oxford contingent of Clive Barnett, Maarten Hajer, Argyro Loukaki, Andrew Merrifield, Adrian Passmore and Mike Samers, and Felicity Callard, Lisa Kim Davis and Melissa Wright in Johns Hopkins. Over the years I have been able to present my ideas in innumerable seminars, meetings, and workshops and I want to thank all of those – and there were many of them – who on such occasions responded with tough and fair-minded questions and criticisms. Some of the materials presented here have also been published (in whole or in part) in books and journals and the many editorial comments received have also been helpful. Working with Sallie Davies of the BBC on a series of radio programs also proved to be a great learning experience. Among my close colleagues and friends, some of whom have at various times looked at and commented on the work in progress, I want to thank Kevin Archer, Patrick Bond, Mike Johns, Vicente Navarro, Ric Pfeffer, Bertell Ollman, Erica Schoenberger, Erik Swyngedouw, and Dick Walker. I most particularly want to thank Neil Smith for rescuing the whole project from oblivion with his patient encouragement when days became very dark and prospects for closure very bleak and John Davey of Blackwell Publishers for his patience, encouragement, and lively interest in the project. These may not be the best of times, but friends and colleagues of this caliber make absolutely certain that it is not the worst of times either. Finally, all my love goes to Haydee and Delfina with whom it has been possible to explore ways of thought and feeling that are immeasurably richer than those I could ever hope to achieve on my own.

PART I

Orientations

TWENTY YEARS ON?

American Tourist. "PARDON, ME, SIR, BUT CAN YOU PUT ME WISE TO THE NAME OF THIS THRIVING INDUSTRIAL BURG?"
Mr. Punch. "I REGRET TO SAY, SIR, THAT THIS IS OXFORD."

[A Trust has been formed to protect the beauties of Oxford and its environs, and has appealed for a sum of £250,000 to purchase the land required for this purpose. Donations should be sent to the account of the Oxford Preservation Trust, Barclay's Bank, High Street, Oxford.]

Twenty Years On, *Punch*, August 8th, 1928. The Mansell Collection.

1
Militant Particularism and Global Ambition

I. Local Militancy and the Politics of a Research Project

In 1988, shortly after taking up a position in Oxford, I became involved in a research project concerning the fate of the Rover car plant in that city. Oxford, particularly for outsiders, is usually imagined as a city of dreaming spires and university grandeur, but as late as 1973 the car plant at Cowley in east Oxford employed some 27,000 workers, compared to less than 3,000 in the employ of the university. The insertion of the Morris Motors car plant into the medieval social fabric of the city early in the century had had enormous effects upon the political and economic life of the place, paralleling almost exactly the three-stage path to socialist consciousness set out in *The Communist Manifesto*. Workers had steadily been massed together over the years in and around the car plant and its ancillary installations, had become conscious of their own interests and built institutions (primarily the unions) to defend and promote those interests. During the 1930s and again in the 1960s and early 1970s, the car plant was the focus of some of the most virulent class struggles over the future of the industrial relations in Britain. The workers' movement simultaneously created a powerful political instrument in the form of a local Labour Party that ultimately assumed continuous control of the local council after 1980. But by 1988 rationalizations and cut-backs had reduced the work force to around 10,000; by 1993 it was down to less than 5,000 (as opposed to the 7,000 or so then in the employ of the university). The threat of total closure of the car plant was never far away.

A book on the Cowley story, *The Factory and the City: The Story of the Cowley Auto Workers in Oxford*, edited by Teresa Hayter and myself was published late in 1993. It originated in research work conducted in support of a campaign against closure that began in 1988, when British Aerospace (BAe) acquired the Rover car company in a sweetheart privatization deal from the Thatcher government. Partial closure and rationalization at the plant was immediately announced and the prospect of asset-stripping or even total closure loomed. Land values in Oxford were high and BAe, with the property boom in full flood, acquired a property development company specializing in the creation of business parks (Arlington Securities) in 1989. The fear was that work would be transferred to Longbridge (Birmingham) or, worse still, to a greenfield nonunion site in Swindon (where Honda was already involved in co-production arrangements with Rover) releasing the Oxford land for lucrative redevelopment that would offer almost no prospects for employment to a community of several thousand people that had evolved over many years to serve the car plant. BAe's subsequent profitable sale of Rover to BMW (while Arlington retained the released land) shows the fears were not groundless.

An initial meeting to discuss a campaign against closure drew representatives from many sectors. It was agreed to set up a research group to provide information on what was happening and what the effects of any moves by BAe might be on the work force and on the Oxford economy. The Oxford Motor Industry Research Project (OMIRP) was formed and I agreed to chair it. Shortly thereafter, the union leadership in the plant withdrew its support for both the campaign and the research, and most of the Labour members on the city council followed suit. The research was then left to a small group of independent researchers mainly based in the Oxford Polytechnic (now Oxford Brookes University) and Oxford University, aided by dissident shop-stewards or ex-workers from Cowley.

For personal reasons I was not active in the campaign nor did I engage much with the initial research. I did help to publicize the results and to mobilize resources for the research project which the union leadership and the majority of the local Labour Party actively tried to stop – they did not want anything to 'rock the boat' in their 'delicate negotiations' with BAe over the future of the plant and the site. Fortuitously, OMIRP produced a pamphlet, *Cowley Works*, at the very moment when BAe announced another wave of rationalizations that would cut the work force in half and release half of the land for redevelopment. The history of the plant together with the story of the struggle to launch a campaign and the dynamics of the subsequent run-down are well described in the book.

Teresa Hayter, the coordinator of OMIRP, received a research fellowship at St Peter's College in 1989 to pull together a book about the history of Cowley, the failed campaign, and the political problems of mobilizing resistance to the arbitrary actions of corporate capital. The book involved the formation of a broad-based group. Each contributor produced a chapter (or chapters) on topics with which they were most familiar. Each chapter was read by others and comments went back and forth until a final version was arrived at. I agreed, partly for purposes of making the book more attractive to prospective publishers, to be a co-editor of the book with Teresa Hayter. This meant that in addition to the one chapter I co-authored, I spent quite a lot of time, along with Hayter, editing, commissioning new segments to ensure full coverage, and generally trying to keep the book as a whole in view while attending to the parts.

The book is a fascinating document. It brings together radically different positionalities – varying from an unnamed shop-steward in the plant, others who had worked there or who had been long-term residents of east Oxford, as well as academics, planners and independent leftists. The language differs radically from chapter to chapter. The activist voice emanating from the plant experience contrasts with the more abstract judgments of the academics, for example, while the perspective from the community reads differently from the perspective of the production line. In the preface we argued that the hetero- geneity of voices and of styles was a very particular strength of the book.

It was early evident, however, that the many contributors had quite different political perspectives and interpretations. Initially, these differences were negotiated through; everyone trod warily through a minefield of differences in order to get to the other side with a completed book. The difficulties arose with the conclusion. I proposed two conclusions, one by Hayter and one by myself, so that readers might get a better handle on the political differences and be left to judge for themselves. This was rejected. And so I drafted a conclusion based on various ideas put forward by several members of the group. That draft conclusion succeeded in exploding almost every mine that had been negotiated in the writing of the book. Matters became extremely tense, difficult, and sometimes hostile between Hayter and me, with the group to some degree polarized around us.

In the midst of these intense arguments, I recall a lunch in St Peter's College at which Hayter challenged me to define my loyalties. She was very clear about hers. They lay with the militant shop-stewards in the plant, who were not only staying on and laboring under the most appalling conditions but daily struggling to win back control from a reactionary union leadership so as to build a better basis for socialism. By contrast, she saw me as a free-floating Marxist intellectual who had no particular loyalties to anyone. So where did my loyalties lie?

It was a stunning question and I have had to think about it a great deal since. At the time I recall arguing that while loyalty to those still employed in the plant was important, there were many more people in east Oxford who had been laid off or who had no prospects for employment (for example, alienated and discontented young people some of whom had taken to joy-riding bringing criminalization and police oppression for the whole community in their wake) who deserved equal time. All along, I noted, Hayter had treated my concerns for the politics of community as a parallel force to the politics of the workplace with scepticism. I further thought that some consideration should be given to the future of socialism in Oxford under conditions in which the working-class solidarities that had been built around the plant were plainly weakening and even threatened with elimination. This meant the search for some broader coalition of forces both to support the workers in the plant and to perpetuate the socialist cause. I also thought it would be disloyal not to put a critical distance between us and what had happened in order to better understand why the campaign had failed to take off. Hayter refused to countenance anything that sounded critical of the strategy of the campaign and likewise rejected any perspective that did not accept as its basis the critical struggle for power on the shop-floor of the plant.

But all sorts of other issues divided us. Deteriorating work conditions in the plant, for example, made it hard to argue unequivocally for the long-term preservation of what were in effect "shit-jobs," even though it was plainly imperative to defend such jobs in the short-run because there were no reasonable alternatives. The issue here was not to subordinate short-term actions to long-term pipe-dreams, but to point out how difficult it is to move on a long-term trajectory when short-term exigencies demand something quite different. I was also concerned about the incredible overcapacity in the automobile industry in Britain as well as in Europe in general. Something was going to have to give somewhere and some way had to be found to protect workers' interests in general without falling into the reactionary politics of the "new realism" then paralyzing official union politics. But across what space should that generality be calculated? Britain? Europe? The world? I found myself arguing for at least a European-wide perspective on adjustments in automobile production capacity, but found it hard to justify stopping at that scale when pressed. There were also important ecological issues to be considered deriving not only from the plant itself (the paint shop was a notorious pollution source) but also from the nature of the product. Making Rover cars for the ultra rich and so contributing to ecological degradation hardly seemed a worthy long-term socialist objective. The ecological issue ought not to be ducked, I felt, even though it was plain that the bourgeois north Oxford heritage interests would likely use it to get rid of the car plant altogether if given the chance. The problem of time-horizon and class interests needed to be explicitly debated rather than buried. Furthermore, while I would in no way defend the appalling behavior of BAe, I did think it relevant to point out that the company had lost about one-third of its stockmarket value in the first few months of 1992 and that its hopes for a killing on the property market had been seriously diminished in the property crash of 1990. This posed questions of new forms of public or community control over corporate activity (such as BAe's turn to property speculation as an alternative to production) that would not repeat the bitter history of nationalization (such as the disastrous rationalizations and reordering of job structures already suffered by Rover, when it was British Leyland in the 1970s).

I felt it would be disloyal to the conception of socialism not to talk about *all* of these issues in the conclusion. Not, I hasten to add, with the idea that they could be resolved, but because they opened a terrain of discussion implicit in the materials assembled in the book. Such a conclusion would keep options open and help readers consider active choices across a broad terrain of possibilities while paying proper attention to the complexities and difficulties. But Hayter felt, even though she partially agreed on the long-term significance of such ideas, that discussing them would dilute the immediate struggle to keep jobs in Cowley and prevent their transfer to a greenfield nonunion site in Swindon. The issues I wanted to raise could be attended to, she held, only when the work force and the progressive stewards had regained their strength and power in the workplace.

I was operating, it became plain, at a different level and with different kinds of abstraction. But the impetus for the campaign, the research, and the book did not come from me. It arose out of the extraordinary strength and power of a tradition of union militancy emanating from the plant. This tradition had its own version of internationalism and presumptions to universal truth, although a case could be made that its capture and ossification by a rather narrow Trotskyist rhetoric was as much a part of the problem as the more fundamental conflict between Hayter's and my perspective. But it would be wrong to depict the argument in sectarian terms. For the issue of a purely plant-based versus a more-encompassing politics was always there. I could not abandon my loyalty to the belief that the politics of a supposedly unproblematic extension outwards from the plant of a prospective model of a total social transformation is fundamentally flawed. The view that what is right and good from the standpoint of the militant shop-stewards at Cowley, is right and good for the city, and by extension, for society at large is far too simplistic. Other levels and kinds of abstraction have to be deployed if socialism is to break out of its local bonds and become a viable alternative to capitalism as a working mode of production and social relations. But there is something equally problematic about imposing a politics guided by abstractions upon people who have given of their lives and labor over many years in a particular way in a particular place.

So what level and what kinds of abstraction should be deployed? And what might it mean to be loyal to abstractions rather than to actual people? Beneath those questions lie others. What is it that constitutes a privileged claim to knowledge and how can we judge, understand, adjudicate, and perhaps negotiate through different knowledges constructed at very different levels of abstraction under radically different material conditions?

II. Raymond Williams and the Politics of Abstraction

These were questions that preoccupied Raymond Williams, erupting frequently in his work, though, for reasons that will shortly become apparent, they are far better articulated in his novels than in his cultural theorizing. My purpose here is not, I should make plain, to hold up Williams as some paragon of virtue on these matters. Indeed, I accept the criticism that the nearer he steers to what might be called "cultural holism" – the view that culture must be understood as a "whole way of life" and that social practices have to be construed as "indissoluble elements of a continuous social material process" – the closer he comes to an organicist view of the social order; a 'community' characterized by a certain "structure of feeling" as a "total way of life" that cannot help but be exclusionary with respect to outsiders and in some respects oppressive for insiders too. The critical interventions of Said (1989) and of Gilroy (1987) strongly point out the difficulty with respect to outsiders, the latter accusing Williams of complicity with a metropolitan colonialism and imperialism by virtue of his situatedness within the "structures of feeling" that were associated with working-class support for the British Empire. A purely organicist view makes it equally difficult to examine multiple forces of oppression and domination within a cultural configuration. Williams, it is generally acknowledged, is nowhere near sensitive enough on the gender issue, for example, though, again, he felt he handled such questions much more firmly in his novels than in his theorizing. Roman's (1993) sympathetic and constructive critique of some of the pitfalls into which Williams sometimes seems to fall is exemplary in exposing some of the dangers as well as the opportunities that Williams creates from both a feminist and a more racially sensitive perspective. There is no doubt either, that Williams' reluctance to let go of "lived experience" leads him to accept, as Hall (1989: 62) has remarked, a rather "empiricist notion of experience" as if there is nothing problematic about taking daily experience as a direct basis for theory construction. Williams' reticence in this regard has even led some, like Snedeker (1993), to conclude, erroneously I believe, that Williams made no real theoretical contributions at all, save giving Gramsci's notions of hegemony a new and somewhat more nuanced lease of life. Yet there is a certain paradox at work here for it is also true, as Snedeker (1993: 113) concedes, that Williams' influence, in spite of all his supposed defects, "remains powerful in contemporary cultural studies, with their emphasis on the counter hegemonies of feminist, Third World, and working class movements."

I will not try either to defend or offer a systematic critique of Williams in the controversial stances he took on politics and culture [see the edited collections by Eagleton (1989) and Dworkin and Roman (1993) for extended discussions]. But there are two crucial points concerning his work that help explain why so many of his most trenchant critics find themselves returning so often to his formulations. The first concerns the dialectical way in which his concepts get formulated. Consider, for example, the following passage:

> In most description and analysis, culture and society are expressed in an habitual past tense. The strongest barrier to the recognition of human cultural activity

is this immediate and regular conversion of experience into finished products. What is defensible as a procedure in conscious history, where on certain assumptions many actions can be definitively taken as having ended, is habitually projected, not only into the always moving substance of the past, but into contemporary life, in which relationships, institutions and formations in which we are still actively involved are converted, by this procedural mode, into formed wholes rather than forming and formative processes. Analysis is then centred on relations between these produced institutions, formations, and experiences, so that now, as in that produced past, only the fixed explicit forms exist, and living presence is always, by definition, receding. (Williams, 1977: 128–9)

Williams is not immune from the tendency to produce alienated conceptions that instanciate "formed wholes" as dominants over "forming and formative processes." But certainly in this passage he declares a strong preference for dialectical readings that prioritize the understanding of processes over things, so that any organicist notion of community, for example, is necessarily tempered by the knowledge of the complicated flows and processes that sustain it. Williams here charts a terrain of *theoretical* possibilities in which the reduction of relations between people into relations between concepts can be as continuously challenged as can our understanding of relationships, institutions, and forms be brought alive by focusing attention on the processes at work producing, sustaining, or dissolving them.

The second point is that the manner of "embeddedness" [as contemporary sociologists – such as Granovetter (1985) – like to refer to it] of political action in what anthropologists like to term "intimate culture" (Lomnitz-Adler, 1991) is simultaneously empowering and problematic. But it also follows that the abstractions to which we appeal cannot be understood independently of whatever it is that political and theoretical activity is embedded in, and whatever it is that social life is being intimate about. A study of some of Williams' formulations can here be extremely helpful, since he both uses and systematically questions the notion of embeddedness and intimate culture throughout his work. In what follows, I shall pay particular attention to the way Williams treats *environment, space* and *place* as framing concepts that help define what these ideas might mean.

III. The Novel as Environmental History

Press your fingers close on this lichened sandstone. With this stone and this grass, with this red earth, this place was received and made and remade. Its generations are distinct but all suddenly present. (*People of the Black Mountains*, Vol. 1, p. 2)

So ends the opening statement of Williams' last and unfinished novel. The story begins in 23,000BC and passes across periods of vast environmental and social change. The second story, for example, is set at the edge of the great ice sheet that surrounded the Black Mountains at the maximum point of glaciation in 16,000BC. Subsequent episodes take up the advent of settled agriculture, writing, and other key moments of transformation of both the physical and social environment through human action. The earlier reconstructions draw heavily on archeological, paleological, and environmental history (the list of sources furnished at the end of volume 2 is extensive indeed) while the later periods lean much more heavily on the works of economic, social, and cultural historians, making this a fictional account deeply rooted in those material realities identified through research across a wide range of disciplines. In episode after episode, the people who have traversed and struggled in that place are imagined into life.

So why was one of Britain's most eminent socialist thinkers, in the very last fictional work he undertook, writing the social and environmental history of the Black Mountains?

One partial answer to that question presumably lies in Williams' insistence that social beings can never escape their embeddedness in the world of nature and that no conception of political action could, in the final analysis, afford abstractions that did not encompass the fact. "Nature" was a key word for Williams (1983b: 219) – perhaps "the most complex word in the language" since the idea of it "contains, though often unnoticed, an extraordinary amount of human history ... both complicated and changing, as other ideas and experiences change" (Williams, 1980: 67). An enquiry into environmental history as well as into changing conceptions of nature therefore provided a privileged and powerful way to enquire into and understand social and cultural change. Williams construes the social and environmental dialectically, as different faces of the same coin. Close attention to the environmental side was, however, bound to throw into relief certain features that might otherwise be missed. His materialism and critical realism always see to it that work (or what he elsewhere calls "livelihood") – broadly understood as simultaneously life-giving and culturally creative activity – is the fundamental process through which our relation to and understanding of the world of nature gets constituted. "Once we begin to speak of men mixing their labour with the earth, we are in a whole world of new relations between man and nature and to separate natural history from social history becomes extremely problematic" (Williams, 1980: 76). Such a dialectical and transformative view of how specific social relations connect to new ways of mixing labor with the land, is not unique to Williams. It echoes, for example, the views of Marx and Engels that "as long as men exist, the history of nature and the history of men are mutually conditioned" because by "acting on the external world and changing it, [we] at the same time change [our] own nature" (Marx, 1967: 173). William Cronon (1983: 13–14), the doyen of the contemporary movement to create a distinctively environmental form of history, makes a similar argument:

> An ecological history begins by assuming a dynamic and changing relationship between environment and culture, one as apt to produce contradictions as continuities. Moreover, it assumes that the interactions of the two are dialectical. Environment may initially shape the range of choices available to a people at a given moment but then culture reshapes environment responding to those choices. The reshaped environment presents a new set of possibilities for cultural reproduction, thus setting up a new cycle of mutual determination. Changes in the way people create and re-create their livelihood must be analysed in terms of changes not only in their *social relations* but in their *ecological* ones as well.

But the environmental history of the Black Mountains is not something that evolves purely in place. The novel records waves of migration and colonization which situate the history of the Black Mountains in a matrix of spatiality, constituted by the flows and movements pulsing across Europe and beyond. The distinctiveness, or what Williams affectionately calls the "sweetness of the place" gets constructed through the working out in that place of interventions and influences from outside. The three themes of place, space, and environment are tightly interwoven in this particular novel as inseparable elements in complex processes of social and environmental transformation.

But why choose the novel as a vehicle to explore these themes? Why not write straight environmental history, or rest content with the abundant source materials upon which Williams draws? I think there are two reasons.

The first is explicitly laid out in the novels as key characters reflect on the nature of the knowledge and understandings they hold. In *People of the Black Mountains* (Vol. 1, pp. 10–12) we find Glyn – the person through whom the voices and tales of the past become historically present – reflecting on disciplinary knowledges of the place:

> Yet the kinds of scrutiny that were built into these disciplines had their own weaknesses ... They would reduce what they were studying to an internal procedure; in the worst cases to material for an enclosed career. If lives and places were being seriously sought, a powerful attachment to lives and to places was entirely demanded. The polystyrene model and its textual and theoretical equivalents remained different from the substance they reconstructed and simulated ... At his books and maps in the library, or in the house in the valley, there was a common history which could be translated anywhere, in a community of evidence and rational inquiry. Yet he had only to move on the mountains for a different kind of mind to assert itself: stubbornly native and local, yet reaching beyond to a wider common flow, where touch and breadth replaced record and analysis; not history as narrative but stories as lives.

This is a familiar theme in Williams' novel (and it presages the move within the discipline of history of a shift from narrative to story form). In *Border Country* (p. 10) we similarly encounter Matthew Price, like Williams, Cambridge-educated son of a railway signalman from a rural Welsh community, but now fictionally placed as a university lecturer in economic history in London. His work on population movements in Wales in the nineteenth century has hit an impasse. The data are all there but something is missing:

> The techniques I have learned have the solidity and precision of ice cubes, while a given temperature is maintained. But it is a temperature I can't really maintain: the door of the box keeps flying open. It's hardly a population movement from Glynmawr to London, but it's a change of substance, as it must have been for them, when they left their villages. And the ways of measuring this are not only outside my discipline. They are somewhere else altogether, that I can *feel but not handle, touch but not grasp.* [my italics]

The implication is clear enough and applies with great force to Williams' own work. Concerned with the lived lives of people, the novel form allows him to represent the daily qualities of those lives in ways that could not be handled or grasped by other means. So while on the one hand Williams insists that his novels should not be treated as separate from his cultural theorizing, he also freely admits that he found some themes far easier to explore in his novels than in his theoretical work (Williams, 1989a: 319).

But there is another reason behind the choice of a novel form. He wants to emphasize the ways in which personal and particular choices made under given conditions are the very essence of historical–geographical change. The novel is not subject to closure in the same way that more analytic forms of thinking are. There are always choices and possibilities, perpetually unresolved tensions and differences, subtle shifts in structures of feeling all of which stand to alter the terms of debate and political action, even under the most difficult and dire of conditions. Williams greatly admired Brecht's theater. Brecht, he says, discovered "ways of enacting genuine alternatives: not so much as in traditional drama, through the embodiment of alternatives in opposing characters, but by their embodiment in one person, who lives through this way and then that and invites us to draw our own conclusions" (Williams, 1961: 157). This means "there is no imposed resolution – the tension is there to the end, and we are invited to consider it." All of Williams' central characters live that tension. The stories of the people of the Black Mountains are precisely about that also. Politically this allows Williams to remind us of the way in which these peoples, by virtue of the choices they made and the ways they lived their lives, are "all historically present." His aim is empowerment in the present through celebrating the strength and capacity to survive in the past. But there is something else at work too:

The crisis which came to me on the death of my father, who was a socialist and a railway worker – I haven't been able to explain this to people properly, perhaps I explained it partly in my novel *Border Country* – was the sense of a kind of defeat for *an idea of value*. Maybe this was an unreasonable response. All right, he died, he died too early, but men and women die. But it was very difficult not to see him as a victim at the end. I suppose it was this kind of experience which sent me back to the historical novel I'm now writing, *People of the Black Mountains*, about the movements of history over a very long period, in and through a particular place in Wales. And this history is a record of ... defeat, invasion, victimization, oppression. When one sees what was done to the people who are physically my ancestors, one feels it to be almost incredible ... The defeats have occurred over and over again, and what my novel is then trying to explore is simply the condition of anything surviving at all. It's not a matter of the simple patriotic answer: we're Welsh, and still here. It's the infinite resilience, even deviousness, with which people have managed to persist in profoundly unfavourable conditions, and *the striking diversity of beliefs in which they've expressed their autonomy. A sense of value which has won its way through different kinds of oppression of different forms ... an ingrained and indestructible yet also changing embodiment of the possibilities of common life.* (Williams, 1989a: 321–2) [my italics]

The embeddedness that Williams celebrates is the ability of human beings, as *social* beings, to perpetuate and nurture in their daily lives and cultural practices the *possibility* of common values in the midst of a striking heterogeneity of beliefs. The maintenance of such values depends crucially, however, upon a certain kind of interpersonal relating that typically occurs in particular places.

IV. The Dialectics of Space and Place

So what were people building in the Black Mountains? It was *place* that was being "received and made and remade." But what did "place" mean to Williams? It is not one of his key words (though "community" which is generally given a place-bound connotation in his work is). Nevertheless:

A new theory of socialism must now centrally involve *place*. Remember the argument was that the proletariat had no country, the factor which differentiated it from the property owning classes. But place has been shown to be a crucial element in the bonding process – more so perhaps for the working class than the capital-owning classes – by the explosion of the international economy and the destructive effects of deindustrialization upon old communities. When capital has moved on, the importance of place is more clearly revealed. (Williams, 1989a: 242)

The embeddedness of working-class political action is, according to this account, primarily in "place." In his novels, however, the meaning of place becomes particularly clear. The processes of place creation and dissolution – again a very dialectical conception as compared to the formed entity of an actual place – are active moments in the action. But the constitution of place cannot be abstracted from the shifting patterns of space relations. This principle is constantly reiterated in *People of the Black Mountains* and it also informs the incredibly rich literary analysis of *The Country and the City*. It is rendered even more vivid in the strike episode in *Border Country*: political consciousness in a rural Welsh village community, traversed by a railway line along which goods and information flow, gets transformed by virtue of its relation to the miners' strike in South Wales, only in the end to be sold out by decisions taken in London. In an essay on the general strike of 1926 Williams (1989a: 105–6) makes clear how the episode in *Border Country* was shaped only after long conversations with his father. He then reflects on the structure of the problem as follows:

> These men at that country station were industrial workers, trade unionists, in a small group within a primarily rural and agricultural economy. All of them, like my father, still had close connections with that agricultural life. ... At the same time, by the very fact of the railway, with the trains passing through, from the cities, from the factories, from the ports, from the collieries, and by the fact of the telephone and the telegraph, which was especially important for the signalmen, who through it had a community with other signalmen over a wide social network, talking beyond their work with men they might never actually meet but whom they knew very well through voice, opinion and story, they were part of a modern industrial working class.

The strike episode shows how something special is achieved in that place – in this case a realization of class consciousness and an understanding of the *possibility* (and this word is always lurking in the margins of all Williams' discussions) of a real alternative. But this possibility is arrived at through the internalization within that particular place and community of impulses originating from outside. How external impulses were transformed into a very local "structure of feeling" is a crucial part of the story. Something very special occurred in the fictional Glynmawr (the strike, he narrates, had raised the prospects of common improvement" to an extraordinary practical vividness" – *Border Country*, p. 153) and the actual Pandy to give a meaning to socialism that was of a peculiarly high order, thus making the tragedy of its sell-out from afar particularly devastating.

But there is a counterflow at work here. After the collapse of the strike, one of its dynamic leaders, Morgan Prosser, takes to doing business deals until he ultimately becomes the biggest businessman in the valley, only in the end to be bought out by corporate capital. Says Morgan:

> "this place is finished, as it was. What matters from now on is not the fields, not the mountains, but the road. There'll be no village, as a place on its own.

There'll just be a name you pass through, houses along the road. And that's where you'll be living, mind. On a roadside." (*Border Country*, p. 242)

While Morgan always professes his willingness to give up his business ways if another genuine alternative for common betterment can be found, he pushes home relentlessly the view that the only choice is either to "settle" in place and take what comes or to internalize whatever can be had from the external forces at play and use them to particular, personal, or place-bound advantage.

In *The Fight for Manod*, this local internalization of capitalistic values becomes even more apparent. Says Peter Owen, the radical sociologist coopted to look at what a new town built in the rural backwater of Manod in Wales might mean, "the actual history is back there in the bloody centre: the Birmingham–Dusseldorf axis, with offices in London, Brussels, Paris, Rome." "What always breaks us up is this money from outside" complains a local resident Gwen (p. 140). As the tale of secret land company procurements comes to light, we see how a faceless capitalism exercises a deeply corrupting influence on everyone in the place:

> The companies. And then the distance, the everyday obviousness of the distance, between that lane in Manod, all the immediate problems of Gwen and Ivor and Trevor and Gethin and the others: the distance from them to this register of companies, but at the same time the relations are so solid, so registered. The transactions reach right down to them. Not just as a force from outside but as a force they've engaged with, are now part of. Yet still a force that cares nothing about them, that's just driving its own way. (*Fight for Manod*, p. 153)

What follows for Matthew is the bitter realization that:

> to follow what seems our own interests, as these farmers are doing in Manod, isn't against [this process] but is part of it; is its local reproduction.

All of this poses acute problems of political identity depending upon the spatial range across which political thought and action is construed as possible:

> "This is Tom Meurig," Peter said. "He lives in Llanidloes or in Europe, I can't remember which." Tom Meurig laughed. ...
> He can't make up his mind," Peter said, "whether to proclaim an immediate federation of the Celtic Peoples, with honorary membership for the Basques, or whether simply to take over Europe, with this new communal socialism they've been dreaming up in the hills."
> "Either of those," Meurig said, "or the third possibility: getting one of our people on to the District Council." (*Fight for Manod*, p. 133)

The humor of that exchange conceals an incredible tension. It turns out that the internalization of these external forces in Manod depends crucially upon a farmer on the district council having privileged knowledge of plans being hatched else-where. The relevant place and range of political action (as well as action in the novel) cannot get resolved outside of a particularly dialectical way of defining loyalties to place across space. And within such loyalties we will always find a pecu-liar tension between resistance and complicity to dominant social processes.

V. The Place of Socialist Politics

Williams tries to incorporate "place" more directly into socialist theorizing. The key phrase here is what Williams calls "militant particularism." I want to pay particular attention to this idea since it captures something very important about both the history and prospects for socialism. Williams (1989a: 249; 115) reflects as follows:

> The unique and extraordinary character of working class self-organization has been that it has tried to connect particular struggles to a general struggle in one quite special way. It has set out, as a movement, to make real what is at first sight the extraordinary claim that the defence and advancement of certain particular interests, properly brought together, are in fact the general interest.

Ideals forged out of the affirmative experience of solidarities in one place get generalized and universalized as a working model of a new form of society that will benefit all of humanity. This is what Williams means by "militant particularism" and he sees it as deeply ingrained into the history of progressive socialism in Britain as well as "a most significant part of the history of Wales." It is not hard to generalize the point, even though Williams himself was reluctant to let go of the particularities and specificities of actual places as the fundamental basis for his thinking. The French revolutionaries, after all, proclaimed doctrines of "the rights of man"; the international workers move-ment proclaimed the global transition to socialism for the benefit of all; the civil rights movement in the United States articulated a politics of universal racial justice; certain wings of contemporary feminism and the ecology move-ment project their militant particularism as the basis for a wide-ranging social reconstruction that will advantage, if not save, us all.

Williams appears to suggest that many if not *all* forms of political engage-ment have their grounding in some kind of militant particularism (such as that which I encountered in Cowley). But the difficulty is:

> That because it had begun as local and affirmative, assuming an unproblematic extension from its own local and community experience to a much more general movement, it was always insufficiently aware of the quite systematic obstacles which stood in the way. (Williams, 1989a: 115)

Such obstacles could only be understood through abstractions capable of confronting processes not accessible to direct local experience. And here is the rub. The move from tangible solidarities understood as patterns of social life organized in affective and knowable communities to a more abstract set of conceptions that would have universal purchase involves a move from one level of abstraction – attached to place – to another level of abstraction capable of reaching out across space. And in that move, something was bound to be lost. "In came," Williams ruefully notes, "necessarily, the politics of negation, the politics of differentiation, the politics of abstract analysis. And these, whether we liked them or not, were now necessary even to understand what was happening." Even the language changes, shifting from words like "our community," and "our people" in the coalfields to "the organised working class," the "proletariat" and the "masses" in the metropolis where the abstractions are most hotly debated (*Loyalties*, p. 293).

The shift from one conceptual world, from one level of abstraction to another, can threaten the common purpose and values that ground the militant particularism achieved in particular places:

> This was my saddest discovery: when I found that in myself ... that most crucial form of imperialism had happened. That is to say, where parts of your mind are taken over by a system of ideas, a system of feelings, which really do emanate from the power centre. Right back in your own mind, and right back inside the oppressed and deprived community there are reproduced elements of the thinking and the feeling of that dominating centre. ... If that negative politics is the only politics then it is the final victory of a mode of thought which seems to me the ultimate product of capitalist society. Whatever its political label it is a mode of thought which really has made relations between men into relations between things or relations between concepts. (Williams, 1989a: 117)

This tension between the different levels and kinds of abstractions to which individuals necessarily appeal in order to understand their relation to the world, is particularly vivid in his novels, often internalized within the conflicting emotions of the protagonists. In *Border Country*, Matthew takes the name given by his father into the wider world, but in Glynmawr he is always known as Will, the name his mother wanted. The duality of that identity – who is he, Matthew or Will? – is perpetually at work throughout the novel. Caught in that duality it becomes almost impossible to find a language with which to speak:

> He was trained to detachment: the language itself, consistently abstracting and generalizing, supported him in this. And the detachment was real in another way. He felt, in this house, both a child and a stranger. He could not speak as either; could not speak really as himself at all, but only in the terms that this pattern offered. (*Border Country*, p. 83)

The tension is registered even in the way in which a familiar landscape gets remembered:

> It was one thing to carry its image in his mind, as he did, everywhere, never a day passing but he closed his eyes and saw it again, his only landscape. But it was different to stand and look at the reality. It was not less beautiful; every detail of the land came up with its old excitement. But it was not still, as the image had been. It was no longer a landscape or a view, but a valley that people were using. He realized as he watched, what had happened in going away. The valley as landscape had been taken, but its work forgotten. The visitor sees beauty: the inhabitant a place where he works and has friends. Far away, closing his eyes, he had been seeing this valley, but as a visitor sees it, as the guide book sees it: this valley, in which he had lived more than half his life. (*Border Country*, p. 75)

This distinction between a "tourist gaze" and lived lives in place is vital to Williams. Lived lives and the sense of value that attaches thereto are embedded in an environment actively molded and achieved through work, play, and a wide array of cultural practices. There is a deep continuity here between the environmental ambience of *Border Country* and the more explicit environmental history of *People of the Black Mountains*. Only at the end of the former novel can Matthew/Will come together, perhaps to reconcile the different structures of feeling that arise through the mind that asserts itself walking on the mountain and the knowledge achieved through the "polystyrene models and their theoretical equivalents":

> now it seems like the end of exile. Not going back, but the feeling of exile ending. For the distance is measured, and that is what matters. By measuring the distance, we come home. (*Border Country*, p. 351)

Again and again, this same duality erupts in Williams' novels. The battle between different levels of abstractions, between distinctively understood particularities of places and the necessary abstractions required to take those understandings into a wider realm, the right to transform militant particularism into something more substantial on the world stage of capitalism – all of these elements become central lines of contradiction and tension that power the story line of the novels. *Loyalties* turns crucially on such tensions. And in that novel we get a far profounder exploration of political dilemmas than comes from any of the theoretical work.

VI. A Question of Loyalties

The story of *Loyalties* begins with a meeting in 1936 between Welsh miners and Cambridge University students on a farmstead in Wales to work out common means to fight fascism in Spain. Out of that meeting comes a brief passionate liaison between a Welsh girl, Nesta, who has striking artistic talents, and Norman, a young Cambridge student from an upper-class background. The question of their distinctive places, both materially and in the structure of society, is raised immediately. She maintains that the place – Danycapel – has made her what she is; he graciously concedes that it must therefore be a good place but then urges her not to get stuck in it. She remains for the rest of her life there – the woman embedded in the particular place that has both nurtured her and which she continues to nurture – while he, the man, returns to a more cosmopolitan, internationalist, and seemingly rootless world of international political intrigue and scientific enquiry. Though the two never talk again after their brief initial encounters, the novel turns on the continuance of the tension between them primarily in the figure of Gwyn, the son born out of wedlock between two class and gender positions – the one closely place-bound and the other ranging more widely across space – within a supposedly common politics defined largely through the Communist party. Gwyn, like Matthew Price in *Border Country* internalizes the tension: raised in that place where Nesta dwells, he eventually goes to Cambridge to study, in part at the insistence of Norman's sister, who performs a crucial link role nurturing a familial connection to Gwyn that Norman broadly ignores.

The place-bound politics arising out of the experience of class solidarities and gender relations in Wales in radically different from the more abstract conceptions held by academics and party leaders. The difference is not, it should be noted, between parochialism and universalism. The miner, Bert, who ultimately marries Gwyn's mother and becomes Gwyn's real father, fights in Spain alongside other workers and students. When the student, who was close to Norman at Cambridge, is killed in action, Bert acquires his binoculars (a symbolic terrain of vision?) only on his deathbed to hand them on to Gwyn. Bert also fights in World War II (billed as "the ultimate war against fascism"), and suffers a hideous injury in Normandy that permanently disfigures his face – Bert forever carries the marks of his internationalist commitments on his body.

Norman, Gwyn's biological father, dwells in a different world and fashions loyalties to the party and to the cause in a radically different way. Perhaps modeled on Burgess, Maclean, Philby, and Blunt (the Cambridge group who became Soviet agents during the 1930s), Norman, an accomplished scientist, is involved in passing on scientific knowledge to the Communist powers, suffering interrogation, perpetual mental pressures acquiring internal mental scars as he anguishes over whether to sustain loyalties contracted in one era when they made sense, in a cold war world where conscience might dictate another course of action. Williams does not, interestingly, condemn Norman, though Bert's bitter deathbed judgment is powerfully registered against these "runaways from their class" – "they used us ... we know now we got to do it by ourselves." Gwyn echoes this judgment – Norman and his ilk were the very worst "because they involved in their betrayal what should have been the alternative: their own working class party, their socialism."

But Gwyn's final angry confrontation with Norman (see below) is paralleled by an extraordinary outburst directed against Gwyn by his mother Nesta. The occasion arises when she reveals to him two sketch portraits she has hidden away – one of the young Norman, fair-haired and ethereal and the other of a now-deceased Bert, drawn after his return from the war, a portrait that "was terrible beyond any likeness, as if the already damaged face was still being broken and pulled apart." Gwyn is deeply moved but can only say how "intensely beautiful" the latter portrait is:

> She was staring at him angrily. Her face and body seemed twisted with sudden pain. He was bewildered because he had never seen her in even ordinary anger. She had been always so contained and quiet and pleasant, always younger than her age, self-possessed and slightly withdrawn.
> "*It is not beautiful!*" she screamed, in a terrible high voice.
> "Mam, please, I didn't mean that," Gwyn struggled to say.
> "Do you understand nothing?" she screamed. "Do you know nothing? Have you learned nothing?"
> "Mam, all I meant –"
> "It is not beautiful!" she cried again. "It's ugly. It's destroying! It's human flesh broken and pulped!"
> "Yes. Yes in him. But the truth, that you saw the truth –"
> "It's ugly, it's ugly!" she screamed now past all control. (*Loyalties*, pp. 347–8)

This violent clash of sensibilities, of "structures of feeling" as Williams puts it, says it all. The problem here is not only the level of abstraction at which the world view of socialist politics gets constituted, but of the very different structures of feeling that can attach to those different levels of abstraction. Gwyn has acquired the distance to look upon the portrait of Bert as a work of art, as a thing of beauty precisely because it can capture and represent the awfulness of disfigurement with an elemental truth. But for Nesta it is not the representation that matters, but what is being represented; the sheer pain of that always remains fundamental and elemental.

The difficulties posed by the search for *any* kind of critical distance then come more clearly into focus. In *Border Country*, for example, Matthew/Will takes to climbing the nearby mountain, the Kestrel, and admiring the view from on high. Looking at "the patch" where he had been raised, he knew it:

> was not only a place, but people, yet from here it was as if no one lived there, no one had ever lived there, and yet, in its stillness, it was a memory of himself.
> ... The mountain had this power, to abstract and to clarify, but in the end he could not stay here: he must go back down where he lived.

And then:

> On the way down the shapes faded and the ordinary identities returned. The voice in his mind faded and the ordinary voice came back. Like old Blakely asking, digging his stick in the turf. What will you be reading, Will? Books, sir? No better not. History, sir. History from the Kestrel, where you sit and watch memory move, across the wide valley. That was the sense of it: to watch, to interpret, to try and get clear. Only the wind narrowing the eyes, and so much living in you, deciding what you will see and how you will see it. Never above, watching. You'll find what you're watching is yourself. (*Border Country*, pp. 291–3)

But it is not only the *level* of abstraction at which different representations operate that is vital here. There is something else going on in these interchanges that derives from the *kind* of abstraction achievable given different ways of acquiring knowledge of the world. There is a polarization in Williams' argument. Ingold (1993: 41), in a rather different context, describes the opposition as that between a vision of the world as a sphere which encompasses us or as a globe upon which we can gaze:

> the local is not a more limited or narrowly focused apprehension than the global, it is one that rests on an altogether different *mode* of apprehension – one based on an active, perceptual engagement with components of the dwelt-in world, in the practical business of life, rather than on the detached, disinterested observation of a world apart. In the local perspective the world is a sphere ... centred on a particular place. From this experiential centre, the attention of those who live there is drawn ever deeper *into* the world, in the quest for knowledge and understanding.

Both Bert and Nesta seem always to be reaching out from their centered place – Danycapel – whereas Norman always tries to understand the world in a more detached way *en route* to his political commitments. Gwyn internalizes both perspectives and is given with conflicting thoughts and feelings. Yet, Williams seems to be saying, we cannot do without both kinds of abstraction any more than we can do without the conflicting modes of representation that necessarily attach to them. Williams tries to define a complementary, even dialectical relation between the two visions, though I think it is evident on what side of that opposition he feels most comfortable. We should, he again and again insists, never forget the brute ugliness of the realities of lived experience for the oppressed. We should not estheticize or theorize those lived realities out of existence as felt pains and passions. To do so is to diminish or even to lose the raw anger against injustice and exploitation that powers so much of the striving for social change. The formulaic view that "truth is beauty," for example, deserves to be treated with the wrath that Nesta metes out.

The question of loyalties is defined, then, both by the *level* and *kind* of abstraction through which political questions are formulated. As an affective and emotive political force, loyalties always attach to certain definite structures of feeling. The richest characters in all of Williams' novels are precisely those who internalize different and conflicting loyalties to radically different structures of feeling – Gwyn in *Loyalties* or Matthew Price in *Border Country* and Owen Price in *Second Generation*. And it is no accident that Williams turns to the novel to explore the tensions. The Brechtian strategy is everywhere apparent and suggests not only that the tensions can never be resolved but that we should never expect them to be so. By perpetually keeping them open, we keep open a primary resource for the creative thinking and practices necessary to achieve progressive social change.

This is a telling formulation of a problem that many must recognize. I recognize it not only as someone who, like Williams, went from an English state school to a Cambridge education, but also more immediately in the contested politics of the Cowley project. Where did my loyalties lie? Williams' warnings are salutary. The possibility of betrayal looms, in our heads as well as in our actions, as we move from one level of abstraction or from one kind of epistemology to another. The dissident shop-stewards in the Cowley car plant probably said unkindly words about me of exactly the sort that Bert said of "the class runaways" in *Loyalties*. Interestingly, Hayter inserted into the conclusion the very strong words of a shop-steward in the plant: "Betrayal is a process, not an individual act, and it is not always conscious." While the comment was not directed at me, it could well have been in the light of our discussions.

But betrayal is a complex as well as a bitter term. Let me go back to the fictional account in *Loyalties* (pp. 317–19). Here is how Norman's close associate defends him to Gwyn:

> "There are genuine acts of betrayal of groups to which one belongs. But you have only to look at the shifts of alliance and hostility, both the international shifts and within them the complex alliances and hostilities of classes, to know how dynamic this definable quantity becomes. There are traitors within a class to a nation, and within a nation to a class. People who live in times when these loyalties are stable are more fortunate than we were."
> "Not only in times. In places," Gwyn said.

In any case, Norman was involved in scientific research that had a completely different domain of reference. This entailed:

> a dynamic conflict within a highly specialized field. It was vital to prevent it, through imbalance, reaching that exceptionally dangerous stage in which, by its own logic, it passed beyond nations and classes and beyond all the loyalties that any of us had known. Except, perhaps, in the end, a simple loyalty to the human species.

Nothing of such moment was involved in the Cowley case of course. Although there is one minor twist at the end of *Loyalties* that would make the connection. Norman, allowed to retire without disgrace, has bought in a wood to save it from development. In the face of Gwyn's accusation of class betrayal of "the morality of shared existence" that underlies the militant particularism of a community like Danycapel, Norman argues:

> You abuse what you call my class but what you are really abusing is knowledge and reason. By the way the society is, it is here, with us, that ideas are generated. So it has been with socialism: at once the good ideas and the errors. Yet we have begun to correct them, and this is all that can be done. In reason and in conscience our duty now is not to something called socialism, it is to conserving and saving the earth. Yet nothing significant for either is generated among what you call your fellow countrymen. Indeed, that is, precisely, their deprivation. It is also their inadequacy, and then what are you asking of me. That I should be loyal to ignorance, to shortsightedness, to prejudice, because these exist in my fellow countrymen? That I should stay still and connive in the destruction of the earth because my fellow countrymen are taking part in it? And that I should do this because of some traditional scruple, that I am bound to inherit a common inadequacy, a common ignorance, because its bearers speak the same tongue, inhabit the same threatened island? What morality, really, do you propose in that?

Gwyn's response is sharp enough:

> What you thought about communism, what you now think about nature, is no more than a projection of what suited you. The fact that for others each belief is substantial merely enabled you to deceive them. (*Loyalties*, p. 364)

The argument in *Loyalties* is not, of course resolved. And I think Williams' point is to insist that it can never be. Loyalties contracted at one scale, in one place and in terms of a particular structure of feeling, cannot easily be carried over without transformation or translation into the kinds of loyalties required to make socialism a viable movement either elsewhere or in general. But in the act of translation something important gets lost leaving behind a bitter residue of always unresolved tension.

VII. Loyalties, Identities, and Political Commitments

Accepting this leads to some uncomfortable political reflections. Let me depict them at their starkest. The socialist cause in Britain has always been powered by militant particularisms of the sort that Williams described in Wales and I encountered in Cowley. A good deal of historical evidence could, I believe, be assembled in support of that argument. A recent volume of essays on *Fighting*

Back in Appalachia (Fisher, 1993) documents the point brilliantly within the United States. But those militant particularisms – even when they can be brought together into a national movement – as they have been at various historical moments by the Labour Party in Britain – are in some senses profoundly conservative because they rest on the perpetuation of patterns of social relations and community solidarities – loyalties – achieved under a certain kind of oppressive and uncaring industrial order. While ownership may change (through nationalization, for example), the mines and assembly lines must be kept going for these are the material bases for the ways of social relating and mechanisms of class solidarity embedded in particular places and communities. Socialist politics acquires its conservative edge because it cannot easily be about the radical transformation and overthrow of old modes of working and living – it must in the first instance be about keeping the coal mines open and the assembly lines moving at any cost (witness the tangles of industrial policy of successive British Labour governments in the 1960s and 1970s). Should the struggle at Cowley be to keep the increasingly oppressive jobs in the car plant going, or to seek out different, better, healthier, more satisfying jobs in some quite different and more ecologically sensitive system of production? At a time of weakness and no alternatives, the Cowley struggle necessarily focused on the former objective, but I had the distinct impression that even in the long-run and under the best of circumstances it would always be thus for those working on the shopfloor, for those most strongly imbued with the militant particularism associated with working in the plant.

There is another way of putting this. Can the political and social identities forged under an oppressive industrial order of a certain sort operating in a certain place survive the collapse or radical transformation of that order? The immediate answer I shall profer is "no" (and again I think a good deal of evidence can be marshalled to support that conclusion). If that is so, then perpetuation of those political identities and loyalties requires perpetuation of the oppressive conditions that gave rise to them. Working-class movements may then seek to perpetuate or return to the conditions of oppression that spawned them, in much the same way that those women who have acquired their sense of self under conditions of male violence return again and again to living with violent men.

That parallel is instructive here. It is, as many feminists have argued and many women have shown, possible to break the pattern, to come out of the dependency. Working-class movements can similarly retain a revolutionary impulse while taking on new political identities under transformed conditions of working and living. But it is a long hard process that needs a lot of careful work. Williams recognizes this difficulty explicitly in his discussion of the ecological issue:

> It is no use simply saying to South Wales miners that all around them is an ecological disaster. They already know. They live in it. They have lived in it for

generations. They carry it with them in their lungs. ... But you cannot just say to people who have committed their lives and their communities to certain kinds of production that this has all got to be changed. You can't just say: come out of the harmful industries, come out of the dangerous industries, let us do something better. Everything will have to be done by negotiation, by equitable negotiation, and it will have to be taken steadily along the way. (Williams, 1989a: 220)

The worry at the end of that road of negotiation, is that socialist parties and governments will only succeed in undermining the social and political identities and loyalties that provide the seed-bed of their own support (again, quite a bit of evidence can be marshalled for that proposition in western Europe since World War II). Socialism, it could be argued, is always about the negation of the material conditions of its own political identity. But it so happens that capitalism has fortuitously taken a path these last 20 years towards the elimination of many of the militant particularisms that have traditionally grounded socialist politics – the mines have closed, the assembly lines cut back or shut down, the ship-yards turned silent. We then either take the position that Hayter voiced to me – that the future of socialism in Oxford depended on the outcome of a struggle to get mass employment in car production back into Cowley (a view I could not accept) or else we have to search for new combinations of both old and new forms of militant particularism to ground a rather different version of socialist politics. I see no option except to take the latter path, however difficult and problematic it may be. This does not entail the abandonment of class politics for those of the "new social movements," but the exploration of different forms of alliances that can reconstitute and renew class politics. Put pragmatically, class politics in Oxford could survive the total closure of the Cowley plant, but only if it secures a new basis.

There is still another dimension to all this, which has to do with the question of spatial scale and temporal horizon. With respect to the former, Neil Smith (1992: 72–3) has recently remarked how we have done a very bad job of learning to negotiate between and link across different spatial scales of social theorizing and political action. He emphasizes what I see as a central confusion in contemporary constructions of socialism arising out of "an extensive silence on the question of scale":

> The theory of geographical scale – more correctly the theory of the production of geographical scale – is grossly underdeveloped. In effect, there is no social theory of geographical scale, not to mention an historical materialist one. And yet it plays a crucial part in our whole geographical construction of material life. Was the brutal repression of Tianamen Square a local event, a regional or national event, or was it an international event? We might reasonably assume that it was all four, which immediately reinforces the conclusion that social life operates in and constructs some sort of nested hierarchical space rather than a

mosaic. How do we critically conceive of these various nested scales, how do we arbitrate and translate between them?

Capitalism as a social system has managed not only to negotiate but often to actively manipulate such dilemmas of scale in its forms of class struggle. This has been particularly true of its penchant for achieving uneven sectoral and geographical development so as to force a divisive competitiveness between places defined at different scales. But where does "place" begin and end? And is there a scale beyond which "militant particularism" becomes impossible to ground let alone sustain? The problem for socialist politics is to find ways to answer such questions, not in any final sense, but precisely through defining modes of communication and translation between different kinds and levels of abstraction.

VIII. On Conclusions

I conceded that Hayter write the conclusion to *The Factory and the City*. The book, after all, was largely the result of her efforts. The result reads very oddly. Broadly "workerist" assertions that focus exclusively on the struggle to regain radical control in the plant are ameliorated here and there by questions about overcapacity, community involvement, and the environment. The effect is strange since it fails to identify any productive internalized tension. This is a pity: there was an opportunity here not to seek closure of an argument but to use the materials in the book to reflect upon and learn from what had happened, to open up a terrain of discussion and debate. I cannot help contrasting our effort with the far more thoughtful conclusion – largely focusing upon the tension between class-based and plant-based Marxist perspectives on the one hand and neo-populist communitarian perspectives on the other – provided by Stephen Fisher in *Fighting Back in Appalachia*, an edited collection of incidents of struggle and conflict in Appalachia that has many parallels in terms of the multiple voices it incorporates.

Our failure helps explain, I think, why Williams resorted to the novel to explore certain dilemmas. The closure that we often seem compelled to search for in a piece of cultural or political economic research can more easily remain perpetually open for reflection in the novel form, even when, as happens to Matthew Price, some sort of reconciliation becomes possible once "the distance is measured." Dual conclusions to the Cowley book would have kept issues and options open, the tensions alive, at the same time as it would have highlighted the question of the different levels and kinds of abstractions.

In view of all this, I was quite startled to read Williams' novel *Second Generation*, sometime after the Cowley book was finished. This novel was published in 1964 and set in Oxford at around that time. It revolves around the tensions between a university-based socialism on the one hand and the contested politics within the car plant on the other. The opening paragraph sets the scene for the problem of socialist politics in a divided city:

> If you stand, today, in Between Town Road, you can see either way: west to the spires and towers of the cathedral and colleges; east to the yards and sheds of the motor works. You see different worlds, but there is no frontier between them; there is only the movement and traffic of a single city. (*Second Generation*, p. 9)

Kate Owen, a local Labour Party organizer and wife of a union leader in the plant is torn between loyalty to family and community and the sexual freedom that beckons from the other side of the class divide within a university-based socialism. Peter Owen, her son, is likewise caught in between. He is studying for his doctorate in industrial sociology at an Oxford college at the same time as a violent shopfloor struggle is wearing his father down and down in Cowley. All the themes Williams develops elsewhere concerning the contested knowledge that it is possible to acquire and hold are richly developed here, including the interplays of gender and class within "structures of feeling" embedded in socialist politics worked out in different places.

Many of the substantive issues that arose in the work on the Cowley project actually crop up, without resolution, in *Second Generation*. Had I read it before rather than after becoming associated with the Cowley research, my approach might have been different. I would on the one hand have insisted on the Brechtian strategy of keeping the conclusions open. But on the other I would have taken more notice of Williams' (1989a: 220) injunction that "everything will have to be done by negotiation, equitable negotiation, and it will have to be taken steadily along the way."

IX. Evaluations and Possibilities

The three words "space," "place," and "environment" encompass much of what geographers do. Their meaning has been contested within geography over the years in fierce debates (particularly in the radical journal *Antipode*) over, for example, how and why localities and places might be said to matter and how properly to view relations between place and space (see, for example, Agnew and Duncan, 1989; Cooke, 1989, 1990; Massey, 1991; Pred, 1984; Smith, 1987; Swyngedouw, 1989, 1992a). And in the course of this discussion, the question of level of abstraction and scale has again and again been raised (see Cox and Mair, 1989; Cooke, 1989; Duncan and Savage, 1989; Horvath and Gibson, 1984, Merrifield, 1993; Swyngedouw, 1992b; as well as Smith, 1990, 1992). But geographers are not the only ones to deal in such matters. In recent years the meanings to be attributed to space, place, and nature have become a crucial matter of debate in social, cultural, and literary theory (see, for example, Carter et al., 1993) – a debate in which geographers have certainly participated (see Bird et al., 1993; Gregory and Urry, 1985; Keith and Pile, 1993). These sorts of concerns and interests have been impelled in part by the question of the relations between what appears to be an emergent global capitalist culture on the one hand and the reassertion of all sorts of reactionary as well as potentially progressive "militant particularisms" based in particular places on the other, coupled with a seemingly serious threat of global environmental degradation. But the concerns have also in part been produced by a burgeoning tradition of cultural studies that Raymond Williams helped to define, with its emphasis upon structures of feeling, values, embeddedness, difference, and the particularities of the counterhegemonic discourses and social relations oppositional groups construct.

Williams thought a great deal about questions of space, place, and environment and evidently worried as to how they might be brought into play both in his cultural theory and in his views on socialism. Transformations of space, place, and environment are neither neutral nor innocent with respect to practices of domination and control. Indeed, they are fundamental framing decisions – replete with multiple possibilities – that govern the conditions (often oppressive) over how lives can be lived. Such issues cannot be left unaddressed in struggles for liberation. Furthermore, such struggles necessarily internalize a certain reflexivity, if not an unresolvable tension, concerning both the levels and kinds of abstractions they inevitably embrace as part and parcel of their working tools for practical action.

The fact that Williams' dealings and concerns over space, place, and environment are voiced primarily in his novels suggests, however, a certain hesitancy if not an outright difficulty in getting this tripartite conceptual apparatus into the heart of cultural theory. The conclusion is not, however that space, place, and environment cannot be incorporated into social and cultural theory, but that practices of theorizing have to be opened up to the possibilities and dilemmas that such an incorporation requires. By treating Williams at his word, and seeing his novels and his critical cultural theory as complementary, we identify a field of theorizing far richer than that which many of the high theorists of contemporary culture currently envision. Theory is never a matter of pure abstraction. *Theoretical practice* must be constructed as a continuous dialectic between the militant particularism of lived lives and a struggle to achieve sufficient critical distance and detachment to formulate global ambitions. The problematic that consideration of Williams' works as a whole defines is universal enough to bring its own rewards. It indicates the crucial importance of building a critical materialist and thoroughly grounded (in the literal sense) understanding of place, space, and environment into cultural and social theory. The stakes in such a project are high. Theory cannot be brought to bear upon the world of daily political practices without finding ways to embed in it the materialities of place, space, and environment. Such embedding cannot be achieved by confined metaphorical and idealist allusions to such phenomena (as occurs, for example, in the work of Foucault when he appeals to a spatial concept of *heterotopia* as a field for radical action). My ambition in the chapters that follow, is to provide such a materialist framework for analysis and thereby integrate space, place, and environment into theories of the social process as well as into thinking about practical politics.

2

Dialectics

Raymond Williams chose to handle the complex issues of place, space, and environment by resort to the "possible worlds" of fiction. But was this a necessary rather than a contingent feature of his explorations in cultural theory? In this chapter I begin upon the task of showing that such a move is in no way necessary. I hope to show that historical materialist enquiry infused with dialectical understandings can integrate themes of space, place, and environment (nature) into both social and literary theory. Most such theory has not in the past taken such a project seriously. And this in spite of abundant mention and appeal to spatio-temporal, place-bound, and environmental metaphors (such as Althusser's "continents of knowledge," Jameson's "cognitive mapping," Foucault's "heterotopia," and a host of studies with titles like the "geography of the imagination," "the space of literature," and the like). There seems to be a world of difference, as Smith and Katz (1993) observe, between invocation of space, place, and environment (nature) as convenient metaphors on the one hand and integrating them as historical and geographical realities into social and literary theory on the other. I shall also hope to show that such a theoretical project not only has a transformative effect upon the terrain of theory, but also opens up a terrain of political possibilities.

The first step down this road is to provide some sort of grounding in dialectics. Williams was, of course, deeply imbued with dialectical ways of thinking. Consider, once again, the following passage:

> In most description and analysis, culture and society are expressed in an habitual past tense. The strongest barrier to the recognition of human cultural activity is this immediate and regular conversion of experience into finished products. What is defensible as a procedure in conscious history, where on certain assumptions many actions can be definitively taken as having ended, is habitually projected, not only into the always moving substance of the past, but into contemporary life, in which relationships, institutions and formations in which we are still actively involved are converted, by this procedural mode, into

formed wholes rather than forming and formative processes. Analysis is then centred on relations between these produced institutions, formations, and experiences, so that now, as in that produced past, only the fixed explicit forms exist, and living presence is always, by definition, receding. (Williams, 1977: 128–9)

But Williams did not or could not put this mode of thought to work in confronting issues of place, spatio-temporality, and environment directly in his cultural theory. He has not been alone in this. In geography and the social sciences, the craft of dialectical reasoning is not well understood, so the lack of dialectical treatment of space, place, and environment is not surprising. In literary theory, however, dialectical modes of thought have become dominant in recent years, thanks in part to the resurgent influence of Hegel, Marx, Heidegger, Althusser, Foucault, Ricoeur, Derrida, and many others trained in the traditions of European philosophy. As literary theory permeates social theory, the stage is set for strong confrontations between broadly positivist, empiricist, and historical materialist traditions on the one hand and a vast array of phenomenological, hermeneutic, and dialectical traditions on the other. It is then very likely that nondialectical readings, however well intentioned, of dialectically constructed arguments will generate widespread misinterpretations. Within the recent history of geography, for example, Duncan and Ley's (1982) Cartesian and positivist reading of dialectical work has played havoc (possibly designedly so) with the general understanding of dialectics. For this reason, I think it important to set out, as simply as possible, the general principles of dialectics, to explore its epistemological and ontological underpinnings and to illustrate by way of examples how it might operate at the interfaces of social, geographical, and literary theory.

I begin with a caveat. There is, of course, much Marxist thought that is either nondialectical or (as in the case of analytical Marxism) overtly hostile to dialectics, and a whole tradition of dialectical thinking (most strongly influenced by Leibniz, Hegel, Heidegger, and Derrida, though its origins go back at least to the Greeks) that is by no means Marxist. Furthermore, there are divergent interpretations of dialectics within the Marxist tradition [Bhaskar (1993) lists several of them] and parallel strains of thought such as "process-based philosophy" and "organic" lines of argument advanced by, for example, A.N. Whitehead, David Bohm, and a variety of contemporary ecologists such as Naess and Capra, that bear some sort of kinship to Marx's dialectics. Compare, for example, the statement from Williams cited above and that of Whitehead (1985: 90):

nature is a structure of evolving processes. The reality is the process. It is nonsense to ask if the colour red is real. The colour red is ingredient in the process of realisation.

Or Bohm (1983: 48):

> The notion that reality is to be understood as process is an ancient one, going back at least to Heraclitus, who said that everything flows. ... I regard the essence of the notion of process as given by the statement: Not only is everything changing, but all is *flux*. That is to say, *what is* is the process of becoming itself, while all objects, events, entities, conditions, structures, etc. are forms that can be abstracted from this process.

Then compare these statements with Ollman's (1993: 11) formulation of Marx's position:

> Dialectics restructures our thinking about reality by replacing the common sense notion of "thing," as something that *has* a history and *has* external connection with other things, with notions of "process," which *contains* its history and possible futures, and "relation," which *contains* as part of what it is its ties with other relations.

In what follows I shall occasionally take up these parallel ways of thinking in order to illustrate the broader frame of reference within which Marx's version of dialectics lies. So while I try to situate myself firmly in the Marxist tradition, I shall try to take due cognisance of the richness of the dialectical tradition as a whole.

I. The Principles of Dialectics

Marx chose never to write out any principles of dialectics for a very good reason. The only way to understand his method is by following his practice. This suggests that the reduction of dialectics to a set of "principles" might be self-defeating. The dialectic is a process and not a thing and it is, furthermore, a process in which the Cartesian separations between mind and matter, between thought and action, between consciousness and materiality, between theory and practice have no purchase. The long-standing debate, for example, over whether the dialectic is an ontological statement about the nature of reality or a convenient epistemology for understanding nature is, from this standpoint, as spurious as the Cartesian separation between mind and matter. Yet the debate does have significance. The debate over what constitutes a "dialectical mode of argumentation" is, Ollman argues, a debate over how to abstract from the phenomena we encounter in everyday life. Setting down the principles of dialectics provides an opening gambit for further enquiry, a preliminary discussion of how to formulate such abstractions. Marx, of course, had the example of Hegel's logic and method before him and without careful study of it, he probably could not have arrived at the dialectical practices embedded in

Capital, the apparatus of conceptual abstractions that allowed him to understand the world in the way he did, nor could he have formulated his political strategies and practices.

To write out "the principles of dialectical argumentation" is like going back to Hegel as a prelude to doing something much more Marxist. It is a necessary "going back" but only a means to go forward onto a terrain of action on which the principles themselves, in the fashion of Marx, disappear into a flow of theoretical and political practices. I shall not evoke Hegel's particular formulation here, but try to summarize as simply as I can some of the basic theses about dialectics that can be distilled not only from Marx's practices but also from those who have in recent years been drawn back to reflect on what dialectics might mean.

The principles of dialectics can be summarized in 11 propositions.

1. Dialectical thinking emphasizes the understanding of processes, flows, fluxes, and relations over the analysis of elements, things, structures, and organized systems. The citations already given are quite explicit on that point. There is a deep ontological principle involved here, for dialecticians in effect hold that elements, things, structures, and systems do not exist outside of or prior to the processes, flows, and relations that create, sustain, or undermine them. For example, in our contemporary world, flows of capital (goods, and money) and of people give rise to, sustain, or undermine places such as factories, neighborhoods, and cities understood as things. Epistemologically, the process of enquiry usually inverts this emphasis: we get to understand processes by looking either at the attributes of what appear to us in the first instance to be self-evident things or at the relations between them. We typically investigate flows of goods, money, and people by examining relationships between existing entities like factories, neighborhoods, and cities. Newton, likewise, did not start with gravity, but with the apple, his head, the earth, and the moon. This method only really allows us, however, to compare the state of relations between such entities at different points in time (a confining method called "comparative statics"). On this basis we may infer something about the processes that have generated a change of state but the idea that the entities are unchanging in themselves quickly leads us to a causal and mechanistic way of thinking. Dialectical reasoning holds, however, that this epistemological condition should get reversed when it comes to formulating abstractions, concepts, and theories about the world. This transforms the self-evident world of things with which positivism and empiricism typically deals into a much more confusing world of relations and flows that are manifest as things. Consider, for example, the definition of "capital." In classical political economy and in neoclassical economics it is typically defined as a stock of productive assets of a certain value (a set

of things) out of which a flow of services can be generated. But in Marx's definition, capital is constituted as *both* the process of circulation of value (a flow) *and* the stock of assets ("things" like commodities, money, production apparatus) implicated in those flows. In so far as workers become embedded in that process (as inputs to production and as consumers of finished products) so they too become "appendages" of and thereby a particular manifestation of "capital" ("variable capital" in Marx's terminology). "Money" similarly takes on all manner of "thing-like" forms but those "things" (like coins or entries on a computer screen) only have meaning in terms of the processes of social production and exchange that validate them. Without the processes continually working to support it, money would be meaningless.

This way of thinking is rather more widespread than is generally realized. Quantum theory, for example, has the same entity (e.g., an electron) behaving "under one set of circumstances as a wave, and in another set of circumstances as a particle" (Bohm and Peat, 1987: 40). Since matter (thing-like substances) and energy (a flow) are interchangeable, neither one nor the other can be prioritized as an exclusive focus of enquiry without serious loss of insight and understanding. Electrons thus appear as both "things" and as "flows." Yet it took many years for physicists to recognize that these two conceptions were not incommensurable or mutually exclusive. Only when they overcame this barrier, could modern quantum theory begin to take shape. It has likewise proven very difficult for social scientists to abandon what Ollman (1993: 34) calls the "common sense view" – erected into a philosophical system by Locke, Hume, and others – that "there are things and there are relations, and that neither can be subsumed in the other."

2. Elements or "things" (as I shall call them) are constituted out of flows, processes, and relations operating within bounded fields which constitute structured systems or wholes. A dialectical conception of both the individual "*thing*" and the *structured system* of which it is a part rests entirely on an understanding of the processes and relations by which thing and structured system are constituted. This idea is not intuitively self-evident since we are surrounded by "things" that seem to have such a permanent and solid character that it is difficult to imagine them as somehow in flux. We cannot downplay, therefore, the significance of what Whitehead (1985: 137) calls "permanences" – the innumerable "practically indestructible objects" that we daily encounter in the world and without which physical and biological life would not and could not exist as we now know it. But, he went on to observe, even something as solid and long lasting as an Egyptian pyramid is constituted out of matter in motion. Dialectics forces us always to ask the question of every "thing" or "event" that we encounter: by what process was it constituted and how is it sustained?

3. The "things" and systems which many researchers treat as irreducible and therefore unproblematic are seen in dialectical thought as internally contradictory by virtue of the multiple processes that constitute them. I am, for purposes of social theory, considered an individual within a social system and for certain restricted forms of enquiry such a supposition might appear entirely reasonable. But further inspection shows that I am a rather contradictory and problematic "thing" created by all sorts of processes. My body contains a variety of life-supporting organs such as the heart, lungs, liver, and digestive system "whose functioning is more or less automatic, and required by the fact that the body ... is involved in the perpetual process of internal self-reconstruction" (Ingold, 1986: 18). The metabolic processes which permit that internal self-reconstruction to proceed entail exchanges with my environment and a whole range of transformative processes which are necessary for the maintenance of my bodily individuality. If the processes change, then the body is either transformed or ceases to exist. My sociality (for example, the acquisition of language and symbolic skills) is likewise built up through my capturing of certain powers which reside in social processes. Continuous reconstitution of those powers (with respect to mental faculties and symbolic skills, for example) is a process which is as perpetual as my life is long (we all know what it means to "keep sharp" or "get rusty" at what we do). To put the matter this way is not to view the "thing" (or the system) as a passive product of external processes (I certainly do not view myself that way). What is remarkable about living systems is the way they capture diffuse (and often high entropy) energy or information flows and assemble them into complex but well-ordered (low entropy) forms. Human individuals, furthermore, have a remarkable capacity to capture and reorganize energy and information flows in ways which are creative rather than passive. But the fact that they do so in no way challenges the ontological proposition that "things" and systems are perpetually constituted and reconstituted (like the places set up in Williams' novels) out of processes.

4. "Things" are always assumed "to be internally heterogeneous [i.e., contradictory] at every level" (Levins and Lewontin, 1985: 272). This follows from the first two propositions but is worth stating explicitly. There are four major points to be made here:

(*a*) Any "thing" can be decomposed into a collection of other "things" which are in some relation to each other. For example, a city can be considered as a "thing" in interaction with other cities, but it can also be broken down into neighborhoods or zones which can in turn be broken down into people, houses, schools, factories, etc. which can in turn be broken down *ad infinitum*. The *ad infinitum* clause is very important because it says that there are no irreducible building blocks of "things" for any theoretical reconstruction of how the world works. It then follows that what looks like a system at one level of analysis (e.g., a city) becomes a part at another level, e.g., a global network of world cities. This idea has become very important in contemporary quantum physics where a fundamental guiding principle is that "whatever we say a thing or structure is, it isn't" because "there is always something more than what we say and something different" (Bohm and Peat, 1987: 141–2). There is, as Levins and Lewontin (1985: 278) put it, "no basement" since experience shows that "all previously proposed undecomposable 'basic units' have so far turned out to be decomposable, and the decomposition has opened up new domains for investigation and practice." It is legitimate to investigate "each level of organization without having to search for fundamental units." The other implication, taken seriously in the dialectics of deconstruction, is that all fixed and frozen categories are capable of dissolution. Critical practice in the humanities is very much guided these days, perhaps overly so, by concerns to dissolve fixed categories within conflicting fields and fluxes of socio-linguistic and representational practices.

(*b*) If all "things" are heterogeneous by virtue of the complex processes (or relations) which constitute them, then the only way we can understand the qualitative and quantitative attributes of "things" is by understanding the processes and relations they internalize. Ollman (1976) has been very explicit about this in constructing his arguments concerning internal relations. But such arguments are now advanced in much of the ecological literature (see Eckersley, 1992: 49–55; Naess, 1989: 79; Zimmerman, 1988). The only way we can understand the (contradictory) qualitative and quantitative attributes of "things" is by understanding the processes and relationships which constitute them and which they internalize. I, as an individual, cannot be understood except by way of the metabolic, social, and other processes which I internalize. This implies, however, that I necessarily internalize heterogeneity and a bundle of associated contradictions. Contradiction is here understood in the sense given to the term by Ollman (1990: 49), as "a union of two or more internally related processes that are simultaneously supporting and undermining one another." This is a sentiment that Whitehead (1985: 155), always preferring the word "event" to thing because it captures the dynamism involved, characterizes as follows:

> the concept of internal relations requires the concept of substance as the activity synthesising the relationships into its emergent character. The event is what it is, by reason of the unification in itself of a multiplicity of relationships.

[Cf., here also, Maurice Wilkins' (1987) discussion of the operation of principles of complementarity in microbiology and other spheres of science and creative endeavor.]

(*c*)   There is, however, a limitation to be put upon this argument. I as an individual, do not in practice internalize everything in the universe, but absorb mainly what is relevant to me through my relationships (metabolic, social, political, cultural, etc.) to processes operating over a relatively bounded field (my ecosystem, economy, culture, etc.). There is, however, no fixed or *a priori* boundary to this system. Where my relevant environment begins and ends is itself a function of the ecological, economic, and other processes which are relevant to me. Relevance is dependent, furthermore, on my own actions (the atmosphere relevant to my breathing, to take a trivial example, depends on whether I stay indoors all day, take a hike in the country, or fly to Los Angeles).

(*d*)   Setting boundaries with respect to space, time, scale, and environment then becomes a major strategic consideration in the development of concepts, abstractions, and theories. It is usually the case that any substantial change in these boundaries will radically change the nature of the concepts, abstractions, and theories. In geography we often encounter this problem in the form of the paradoxes generated by different scales of ecological correlation. We will frequently encounter this scale problem in what follows.

5. Space and time are neither absolute nor external to processes but are contingent and contained with them. There are multiple spaces and times (and space–times) implicated in different physical, biological, and social processes. The latter all *produce* – to use Lefebvre's (1991) terminology – their own forms of space and time. Processes do not operate *in* but *actively construct* space and time and in so doing define distinctive scales for their development. This is a complicated problem; it will be the subject of enquiry in part III.

6. Parts and wholes are mutually constitutive of each other. "Part *makes* whole, and whole *makes* part" (Levins and Lewontin, 1985). This is a principle that Giddens (1984) promotes in some of his writings on structuration theory (agency makes structure and structure makes agency) and it is, of course, a fundamental principle which operates across the whole breadth and range of Marx's work. To say that parts and wholes are mutually constitutive of each other is to say much more than that there is a feedback loop between them. In the process of capturing the powers that reside in those ecological and economic systems which are relevant to me, I actively reconstitute or transform them within myself even before I project them back to reconstitute or transform the system from which those powers were initially derived. To take a couple of trivial but important examples; I breath in, I reconstitute myself by virtue of the oxygen I gain but in the process transform the chemistry of the air within me, and I breath out and in so doing transform the atmosphere around me or, I take in ideas and thoughts through listening and reading. I gain

a sense of selfhood thereby but in the process reformulate and transform words and in projecting them back into society change the social world. Reductionist practices "typically ignore this relationship, isolating parts as preexisting units of which wholes are then composed" while some holistic practices reverse the preferential treatment.

7. The interdigitation of parts and wholes entails "the interchangeability of subject and object, of cause and effect" (Levins and Lewontin, 1985: 274). Organisms, for example, have to be looked at as both the subjects and the objects of evolution in exactly the same way that individuals have to be considered as both subjects and objects of processes of social change. The reversibility of cause and effect renders causally specified models (even when endowed with feedback loops) inappropriate. Precisely by virtue of its embeddedness in and representation of the flow of continuous processes, dialectics makes limited appeal to cause and effect argument and then only as a particular limiting case. Causal argumentation necessarily rests, for example, upon absolute not relational conceptions of space and time. There can be, argues Whitehead (1920: 53), "no explanation" of "nature as process" or the passing of time. "All that can be done is to use language which may speculatively demonstrate [them]."

8. Transformative behavior – "creativity" – arises out of the contradictions which attach both to the internalized heterogeneity of "things" and out of the more obvious heterogeneity present within systems. Heterogeneity, as Ollman and Levins and Lewontin (1985: 278) insist, means more than mere diversity: "the parts and processes confront each other as opposites, conditional on the wholes of which they are parts." Out of these oppositions, themselves constituted out of the flow of process, creative tensions and transformative behaviors arise. Becoming, to appropriate Hegel's language, arises out of the opposition between being and not-being. Or, to cite Whitehead (1969: 28), the "principle of process" is that "being is constituted by becoming." In the dialectical view, opposing forces, themselves constituted out of processes, in turn become particular nodal points for further patterns of transformative activity. Matter and not-matter, positive and negative charges, repulsion and attraction, life and death, mind and matter, masculine and feminine, capital and labor, etc. are constituted as oppositions around which congeal a whole host of transformative activities that both reproduce the oppositions and restructure the physical, biological, and social world

9. "Change is a characteristic of all systems and all aspects of systems" (Levins and Lewontin, 1985: 275). This is perhaps the most important of all dialectical principles and one which Ollman (1990, 1993) puts above all others. The implication is that change and instability are the norm and that the appearance of stability of "things" or systems is what has to be explained. In Ollman's (1990: 34) words, "given that change is always a

part of what things are, [our] research problem [can] only be *how, when,* and *into what* [things or systems] change and why they sometimes appear not to change." Levins and Lewontin make a similar point

> The dialectical view insists that persistence and equilibrium are not the natural state of things but require explanation, which must be sought in the actions of the opposing forces. The conditions under which the opposing forces balance and the system as a whole is in stable equilibrium are quite special. They require the simultaneous satisfaction of as many mathematical relations as there are variables in the system, usually expressed as inequalities among the parameters of that system.

Nature, says Whitehead (1969: 33) is always about the perpetual exploration of novelty. Since transformative action – and I here think primarily of creative rather than routine action – arises out of contradiction, it follows that it can in principle be found anywhere and everywhere in the physical, biological, and social world (see chapter 5). To put it this way does not imply, however, that all moments within some continuous process are equally significant as creative points of transformative activity. The theoretical and empirical research task is to identify those characteristic "moments" and "forms" (i.e., "things") embedded within continuous flows which can produce radical transformations or where, conversely, "gatekeeping" or other mechanisms might be constructed so as to give a "thing" or a system (such as a person, a city, a region, a nation state) qualities of identity, integrity, and relative stability. If, as is intuitively obvious, the physical world around us appears to be constituted by what Whitehead (1969: 241–8) calls "permanences" – relatively stable configurations of matter and things – then the issue of how such permanences are maintained yet also integrated into a dynamic world of processes becomes a critical subject of analysis. Again, this tension is the focus of contradiction. "If the opposites, static and fluent," writes Whitehead (1969: 408), "have once been so explained separately to characterize diverse actualities, the interplay between the thing which is static and the things which are fluent involves contradiction at every step in its explanation." The question of "agency" in social and biological as well as in physical systems has to be formulated broadly in such terms.

10. Dialectical enquiry is itself a *process* that produces *permanences* such as concepts, abstractions, theories, and institutionalized structures of knowledge which stand to be supported or undermined by continuing processes of enquiry. A certain relationship is implied between the researcher and the researched, a relationship which is not construed in terms of an "outsider" (the researcher) looking in on the researched as an object, but one between two active subjects each of which necessarily internalizes something from

the other by virtue of the processes that connect them. Observation of the world is, Heisenberg argued, inevitably intervention in the world, in much the same way that deconstructionists will argue that the reading of a text is fundamental to its production. Marx similarly insists that only by transforming the world can we transform ourselves; that it is impossible to understand the world without simultaneously changing it as well as ourselves. Formal dialectical logic cannot, therefore, be presupposed as an ontological quality of nature: to do so would be to superimpose a particular mental logic on the world as an act of mind *over* matter. The dialectical unity of mental and material activities (expressed by Marx as the unity of theory and praxis), can never be broken, only attenuated or temporarily alienated.

11. The exploration of "possible worlds" is integral to dialectical thinking. In some ways this idea goes back to Aristotle, broadly rejected by seventeenth-century science, that "the becoming of a natural being is a constant process of actualization of its potentiality" (Leclerc, 1986: 21). The exploration of potentialities for change, for self-realization, for the construction of new collective identities and social orders, new totalities (e.g., social ecosystems), and the like is a fundamental motif in Marxian dialectical thinking. Bookchin likewise argues that *education* (the exploration of possibilities) rather than deduction (spinning out the implications of known truths) or induction (discovering the general laws regulating what already exists) is the central motif of dialectical praxis as well as the primary purpose of knowledge construction. When the location theorist August Lösch (1954), in his opening argument proposed that our task "is not to explain our sorry reality, but to improve it" and concluded with his vision of a science which "like architecture rather than architectural history, creates rather than describes," he was bringing to bear a dialectical (albeit Hegelian) sense of creative science as the exploration of more rational and equitable spatially ordered worlds. It is in this sense that his (infamous) statement that if "the model does not conform to reality then it is reality that is wrong" has to be understood.

   Dialectical enquiry necessarily incorporates, therefore, the building of ethical, moral, and political choices (*values*) into its own process and sees the constructed knowledges that result as discourses situated in a play of power directed towards some goal or other. Values and goals (what we might call the "teleological" as well as the "Utopian" moment of reflexive thought), are not imposed as universal abstractions from outside but arrived at through a living process (including intellectual enquiry) embedded in forms of praxis and plays of power attaching to the exploration of this or that potentiality (in ourselves as well as in the world we inhabit). The rise of a distinctively "green-value theory" in recent years, is an excellent case study of how an intersection of socio-ecological processes and plays of power can generate a new vision of possibilities. The search for *possibilities* was, of course, always central to Raymond Williams' work: recall how he repeatedly invokes that "sense of value which has won its way through different kinds of oppression of different forms ... [as] an ingrained and indestructible yet also changing embodiment of the possibilities of a common life" (Williams, 1989a: 321–2). The search for those possibilities is, given the dialectical rules of engagement, contained *within*, rather than articulated before or after social practices, including those of the research process. It is never, therefore, a matter of choosing between different applications of neutral knowledge, but always an embedded search for possibilities that lies at the very heart of dialectical argumentation.

II. Dialectical Concepts, Abstractions, and Theories

There is a long-standing debate over whether the world is inherently dialectical or whether the dialectic is simply one convenient set of assumptions or logic to represent certain aspects of physical, biological, and social processes. The former view, which I shall call the strong version of dialectical argumentation, was powerfully promoted by Engels, most particularly in *The Dialectics of Nature* and *Anti-Duhring*. While Marx made no general statement on the subject, he certainly held that social processes at work under capitalism were inherently dialectical. This strong view has come in for considerable criticism in part because of its association with ideas of teleology and doctrines of emergence and immanence which appear almost deterministic in their evolutionary implications. The meaning of this controversy depends in part on how dialectics is represented in the first place. The rather mechanical rendering of Hegel's dialectic as just a matter of thesis, antithesis, and synthesis certainly suggests, when set down synchronically, a rather simplistic teleology (class struggle under capitalism necessarily gives rise to a classless socialism). Engels, for example, looked to the logical and idealist conception of dialectical argumentation set out in Hegel as his model as what was truly dialectical. So although Engels again and again insisted on the strong view that the natural and social world is inherently dialectical, he in fact imposed a particular logical and mental conception (Hegel's) of what that dialectics was on the natural and social world. Marx, on the other hand, though he starts with Hegel, achieved a radical materialist transformation of Hegel's views (cf. Bhaskar, 1989: chapter 7). The effect is to dissolve the dialectic as a logic into a flow of argument and practices. The way I have here tried to specify dialectics, by focusing on the relationships between processes, things, and systems, avoids many of the problems which Engels bequeathed and readies abstract discussion of dialectics as a set of principles for dissolution into a flow of argument. This seems to be much more in accord with Marx's own practice. I therefore see no reason to abandon the strong version of dialectics when formulated in this way. The *least* that can be said of it is that there is as much evidence for the argument that processes constitute things and systems in the natural and social world as there is evidence for any alternative proposition.

There is, however, an acute epistemological problem of how to present, codify, abstract, and theorize the vast amount of information of seemingly incomparable status generated out of the kind of research program which a dialectical stance mandates. The principles of dialectical enquiry as enunciated above (entailing multiple changes of scale, perspective, orientation, and the like, while internalizing contradictions, oppositions, and heterogeneity at every level), *should* generate a perpetual state of motion in our concepts and our thoughts. But the negative side of this flexibility and openness is that it appears to have little chance of producing anything except a vast panoply of insecure and shifting concepts and findings (of the sort that much of literary theory is showing itself all too adept at producing these days). For those unfamiliar with dialectical thinking, the seeming slipperiness of dialectical concepts elicits a good deal of scepticism, impatience, and distrust. If, as Pareto argued (in a passage that Ollman makes much of), Marx's words are like bats, simultaneously having the character of birds and mice, then it seems possible to see anything one wants to in any particular situation. The purpose of multiple and relational approaches to phenomena is, as Ollman points out in his commentary on this passage, to try to identify a restricted number of very general underlying processes which simultaneously *unify and differentiate* the phenomena we see in the world around us. This was very much the focus of Whitehead's concerns. In this sense, dialectics does seek a path towards a certain kind of ontological security, or reductionism – not a reductionism to "things" but to an understanding of common generative processes and relations. In this way we can conceive, for example, of a common process of capital circulation giving rise to an infinite variety of physical city landscapes and social forms.

This commitment to parsimony and generality with respect to processes (though not to things or systems) is common across a variety of fields, which range from David Bohm's work in quantum theory and its implications for physical, biological, social, and esthetic forms (see Bohm, 1983; Hiley and Peat, 1987; Bohm and Peat, 1987), Wilkins' (1987) pursuit of principles of complementarity and the union of opposites in fields as diverse as physics, molecular biology, psychology, music, and the visual arts, Levins and Lewontin's work on dialectical biology, as well as Marx's dialectical materialism. Perhaps one of the most interesting findings from such studies is that singular processes can give rise to highly diversified and highly complex as well as often quite unpredictable results. There are precedents for this kind of finding in spatial analysis. August Lösch, for example, in searching for both a normative and positive theory of geographical location of human activities, started with a very simple set of generative principles concerning the maximization of profit by individual agents subject to monopolistic competition and economies of scale. From these principles he generated landscape patterns of remarkable spatial complexity (I note in passing how many geographers misinterpret his work to be about geometrical patterns directly when it is really about the variety of geographical patterns that can be produced out of a simple set of generative principles). Work on fractals, chaos theory, and the like, illustrates how generative orders of even greater complexity can be developed out of simple rules of process. Bohm and Peat (1987: 157) argue, furthermore, that the whole idea of such generative orders "is not restricted simply to mathematics but is of potential relevance to all areas of experience." They apply it to painting, musical composition, novel writing:

> In all this activity, what is crucial is that in some sense the artist is always working from the generative source of the idea and allowing the work to unfold into ever more definite forms. In this regard his or her thought is similar to that which is proper to science. It proceeds from an origin in free play which then unfolds into ever more crystallized forms.

In setting the generative principles to work in this way, Bohm and Peat embrace a dialectical view of human creativity, one that unifies art and science in a certain complementarity of opposites. In so doing, they come close to embracing (apparently without knowing it) Adorno's interpretation of the work of art as a "dialectical image" understood as "crystallizations of the historical process" and as "objective constellations in which the social condition represents itself" (cited in Williams, 1977: 103).

None of this means that underlying generative processes are easy to identify or specify. Indeed, the immense complexity of "things" and systems which we encounter makes it particularly hard, given the epistemological problem that we must always start with "things" and systems as they are, to identify underlying processes and to specify them exactly right. Furthermore, different processes intersect and intertwine – capital circulation and ecological processes intersect, for example, to create complex forms of environmental transformation; this requires either a reformulation of the idea of process under consideration or finding ways to describe how different processes can and do intersect. The emphasis on prioritizing process which I have here outlined suggests, however, that the search for order which has traditionally characterized western science since the Renaissance is itself transformed from a search to classify and categorize things and the relations between things, into a search for generative principles which produce orders (i.e., things and systems with definable quantitative and qualitative attributes) of different types.

III. Relations with Other Systems of Thought

Dialectical thinking (and I now concentrate on its mental and representational side alone) is one out of several possible modes of approach to understanding and representing the human condition and the world in which human life unfolds. It is in many respects intuitively appealing, if only because we experience life as process (rather than as a "thing" or as an amalgam of "things" and relationships between them), and because we are constantly having to cope with the problem of keeping the process going even in the very act of producing the many "things" with which we surround ourselves. Furthermore, we are all acutely aware of what it means to become committed to the process of maintaining, developing, or letting go of the "things" we create (such as dwellings, machines, money, skills). Academics surely also will recognize that how we learn is very different from what we write and that the written word often returns to haunt us as the power of a fixed "thing," an alien force, that can rule our lives even no matter how hard we strive to go beyond it. But intuitive appeal has never provided the only or even the main justification for accepting any particular set of epistemological or ontological assumptions as *the* basis for generating knowledge. Indeed, much of the success of western science has been based upon the construction of counter-intuitive ways of thinking.

A primary opposing system of thought is given by the Cartesian rationality which was built into classical physics and has since become the basis of theorizing in many of the other natural sciences, in engineering, medicine, the social sciences, and philosophy (particularly of the analytic variety). Levins and Lewontin (1985: 269) categorize this mode in terms of "four ontological commitments, which then put their stamp on the process of creating knowledge." These four commitments are:

> There is a natural set of units or parts of which any whole system is made.

> These units are homogeneous within themselves, at least insofar as they affect the whole of which they are parts.

> The parts are ontologically prior to the whole; that is, the parts exist in isolation and come together to make wholes. The parts have intrinsic properties, which they possess in isolation and which they lend to the whole. In the simplest cases the whole is nothing but the sum of its parts; more complex cases allow for interactions of the parts to produce added properties of the whole.

> Causes are separate from effects, causes being the properties of subjects, and effects the properties of objects. While causes may respond to information coming from effects (so-called "feedback loops"), there is no ambiguity about which is causing subject and which is caused object. (This distinction persists in statistics as independent and dependent variables.)

This Cartesian view is widespread and it, too, has a certain intuitive appeal. We encounter "things" (e.g., individuals) and systems (e.g., transport and communication nets) which appear to have a stable and self-evident existence so that it appears perfectly reasonable to build knowledge upon categorizations of them and upon the pattern of causal relations between them. From the dialectical point of view, however, this is to look at matters in an unduly restrictive and one-sided way. Levins and Lewontin go on, correctly in my view, to characterize the Cartesian view as an "alienated" form of reasoning because it depicts a world in which "parts are separated from wholes and reified as things in themselves, causes separated from effects, subjects separated from objects." Whitehead's (1969: 8–9) objections take a slightly different but equally interesting tack. Descartes' separation between mind and matter is fundamentally incoherent, he argues, since no reason can be found for the distinction. So while the Cartesian system "obviously says something that is true ... its notions are too abstract to penetrate into the nature of things." Worse still, the separation induces "a curious mixture of rationalism and irrationalism" into the method of natural science so that "its prevalent tone of thought has been ardently rationalistic within its own borders and dogmatically irrational beyond those borders." Marx (1967: 352) voiced a similar objection that the "weak points in the abstract materialism of natural science, a materialism that excludes history and its process, are at once evident from the abstract and ideological conceptions of its spokesmen, whenever they venture beyond the bounds of their own speciality."

Marx was in general highly critical of the "common sense" view which whenever "it succeeds in seeing a distinction it fails to see a unity, and where it sees a unity it fails to see a distinction" and so "surreptitiously petrifies" distinctions to the point where they become incapable of generating new ideas let alone new insights into how the world works (cited in Ollman, 1990: 44). He would, doubtless, be equally scathing about the atomistic and causative reasoning which dominates in contemporary economics and sociology, the methodological individualism which pervades much of current political philosophy, and the like.

But it would be wrong to view Cartesian and dialectical conceptions as fundamentally incompatible in *all* senses, as someone like Capra (1982) and to some degree Levins and Lewontin (1985) tend to do. Cast in a more complementary light they can provide a fecund source of new ideas. In theoretical physics what were seen in the nineteenth century as radically incommensurable propositions "that matter is in its essence of a particle nature, or that it is of a wave nature," were ultimately treated as a unity under the conception in quantum theory. Here, too, there is an intuitive rendition which makes for a common sense reading. We all know what Heraclitus meant when he said that we cannot step into the same river twice, but we also all know that there is a sense in which we can return again and again to the banks of the same river. At this point, however, there may indeed arise some sort of claim for the superiority of the dialectical view, precisely because it allows for an understanding of "things" and systems as if they are real and stable as a special case of the proposition that processes are always at work creating and sustaining "things" and systems. The converse proposition appears not to hold, however. Cartesian thinking has a hard time coping with change and process except in terms of comparative statics, cause and effect feedback loops, or the linearities built into examination of experimentally determined and mechanically specified rates of change (as represented in differential calculus). This was the sort of realization that led the anthropologist Anthony Leeds (1994: 32), towards the end of a very active career, to begin to shift perspective:

> In earlier years I thought of society ... as a structure of positions, roles, statuses, groups, institutions, and so on, all given shape ... by the cultures on which they draw. Process, I saw as "forces," movement, connection, pressures, taking place in and among these loci or nodes of organization, peopled by individuals .... Although this still seems largely true to me, it has also come to seem a static view – more societal order than societal becoming. ... Since it does not seem inherent in nature ... that these loci exist, it seems unacceptable simply to take them as axiomatic; rather we must search for ways to account for their appearances and forms. More and more, the problems of becoming ... have led me to look at society as continuous process, out of which structure or order precipitates in the forms of the loci listed above. ...

Ollman's (1990: 32) argument is particularly strong on exactly this same point:

> In the view which currently dominates the social sciences, things exist *and* undergo change. The two are logically distinct. History is something that happens to things; it is not part of their nature. Hence the difficulty of examining change in subjects from which it has been removed at the start.

Marx, on the other hand, abstracts "every historical form as in fluid movement, and therefore takes into account its transient nature *not less* than its momentary existence."

IV. Dialectical Applications – Marx's Conception of Capital

I want here to look more closely at Marx's particular use of dialectical thinking. My purpose is not to argue whether he was right or wrong, but to illustrate *how* he puts dialectical thinking to work to understand capitalism as a social system defined and bounded by a process of capital circulation. His language in *Capital* directly signals adherence to a materialist dialectics in which the priority of process over thing and system is everywhere apparent. This is captured by his statement, cited above, that he aims to abstract "every historical social form as in fluid movement" so as to take into account "its transient nature not less than its momentary existence." The prior commitment to process rather than to "thing" or system could not be more plainly stated. Capital is directly conceptualized, therefore, as a *process* or as a *relation* rather than as a "thing". It is viewed, in its simplest incarnation, as a flow which at one "moment" assumes the "form" of money, and at another assumes the "form" of commodities or the "form" of productive activity. "Value," Marx (1967: 152–3) writes, "is here the active factor in a process, in which, while constantly assuming the form in turn of money and commodities, it at the same time changes in magnitude, differentiates itself by throwing off surplus value from itself. ... Value therefore now becomes value in process, money in process and, as such, capital." This process definition differs radically from that typically incorporated into neoclassical economics where capital is treated as an unproblematic (i.e., noncontradictory) stock of assets (of things) with certain qualitative and quantitative attributes which, when set in motion by human agency, embody causative powers (e.g., capital investment creates unemployment). Marx's point is not that there is no such thing as a stock of assets, but that we cannot understand what those assets are about, what they are worth or how they might be used without understanding the process in which they are embedded, in particular the process which gives rise to, reconstitutes, maintains, devalues, or destroys them. When Marx argues that "capital does" or "capital creates" he is *not* arguing that a thing called capital has causal power, but that the process of capital circulation, understood as a whole, is at the center of vital social transformations and for that reason has to be looked upon as embodying a powerful generative principle affecting social life.

We can understand this argument more generally by examining the following statement drawn from the *Grundrisse* (pp. 99–100):

> The conclusion we reach is not that production, distribution, exchange and consumption are identical, but they all form members of a totality, distinctions within a unity. Production predominates not only over itself, in the antithetical definition of production, but over other moments as well. The process always returns to production to begin anew. That exchange and consumption cannot be predominant is self-evident. Likewise, distribution as distribution of products; while as distribution of the agents of production it is itself a moment of production. A definite production thus determines a definite consumption, distribution and exchange as well as *definite relations between these different moments.* Admittedly, however, *in its one-sided form*, production is itself determined by the other moments. For example if the market, i.e. the sphere of exchange, expands, then production grows in quantity and the divisions between its different branches become deeper. A change in distribution changes production, e.g. concentration of capital, different distribution of the population between town and country, etc. Finally, the needs of consumption determine production. Mutual interaction takes place between the different moments. This is the case with every organic whole.

Those unfamiliar with dialectical ways of thinking will, quite reasonably, regard such a statement as obscure if not incredibly tautological (the obscurity in part derives from the fact that this was written as notes for Marx's own guidance and not as a definitive text designed to persuade a sceptical public). But if we track back to my initial representation of dialectical thinking, it becomes plain enough what Marx is saying. The reproduction of social life is being treated as a continuous process operating within certain bounds which define a totality or a whole. Under capitalism (as well as in certain other kinds of society) this process becomes internally differentiated so as to contain distinctive "moments" of production, exchange, distribution, and consumption. When we look closely at any one of these "moments" we find that it cannot be understood independently of the process as a whole which passes through all the other moments. Production, therefore, necessarily *internalizes* impulses and pressures emanating from consumption, exchange, and distribution. But to think of production only in those terms is to think of it "one-sidedly." We also have to recognize that production internalizes influences from itself (i.e., it is internally heterogeneous and contradictory – this is why Marx says that production is "antithetical" to itself) and that creative and transformative powers with respect to the process as a whole potentially reside within its domain. But that potentiality presumably resides elsewhere also. If we understand production in a broad sense to mean *any* transformative activity (no matter where it occurs), then plainly we are by definition asserting the "predominance" of production over everything else. But Marx also insists that the point of maximum leverage, the point of maximum transformative capacity and, in the famous last instance, the "moment" which exercises a "determin- ant" transformative power over the system as a whole lies within rather than without the domain of production. Transformative activities in other domains then only have relevance for the process as a whole when they are internalized within the production moment.

Now if we read this passage in Cartesian terms, we might interpret Marx as saying that production as an independent entity causes changes in consump- tion, exchange and distribution. But this is exactly what Marx is *not* saying. He cannot say it, precisely because production, according to his conception, internalizes relations with all the other moments (and vice versa). Yet he *is* saying (and I am not concerned whether he was right or wrong) that *the* trans- formative moment in the whole process resides at the moment of production and that it is there where we have to concentrate our attention if we wish to understand the creative mechanisms by which the process (in this case the circulation of capital) is reconstituted, transformed, or enhanced. How, in short, are the powers that reside in this process of capital circulation mobilized at the moment of production in such a way as to transform the system of which it forms but a fleeting and inherently unstable moment? This seems a perfectly reasonably question to ask. It is in principle no different from asking how does any one individual internalize certain powers that reside in their environment, creatively transform them and thereby change the course of history or of evolution?

In effect, the question can be answered only through a detailed historical materialist enquiry into the process of internalization that produces capital at the point of production itself. What Marx seeks to establish beyond any shadow of doubt is that it is the appropriation of the form-giving fire of the labor process, the appropriation of all manner of creative possibilities and powers of the laborer (mental and cooperative capacities, for example) that allows capital to "be" in the world at all. But the internalization of these powers of labor as powers of capital at the point of production entails the transformation of the laborer into an appendage of capital, not only within production but in all spheres of mental, social, and physical activity. The figure of the "cyborg," now given such currency by Haraway's (1990) remarkable manifesto on the subject, enters upon the historical stage with the colonization of production by capitalist powers and the internalization of the powers of labor within the figure of capital itself.

There are all sorts of things to be said pro or contra the Marxian (or more broadly, the dialectical) view, of course. It may be, for example, that there are other "moments" (such as reproduction and all that this entails) which ought to be incorporated in the schema or that his stress on the significance of *labor* in production as *the* radical point of departure for the transformation of both social relations and the relation to nature is overemphatic. But the fundamental point I want to insist on here is that critique of Marx (and of those Marxists who follow his dialectical procedures) should at least recognize what he is doing and how he is doing it and not read him or (mis)represent him unthinkingly through Cartesian, positivist, or analytic lenses.

But let us suppose, for illustrative purposes, that Marx correctly captured the general process of capital circulation through his abstractions. It is then important to see how such a theoretical formulation is (*a*) elaborated upon and specified and (*b*) put to work as an "explanatory" device.

With respect to (*a*) we find Marx building more and more specific versions of his argument concerning the process of circulation of capital in general by recognizing that different processes attach to different kinds of capital, such as industrial, money (finance), merchant, landed and even state capital (borrowings and taxation). Differences can also be specified according to the physical form of the capital (whether it is fixed, large scale, embedded in the land, etc.) as well as according to different organizational forms (joint stock companies, small businesses, land tenure conditions in agriculture, and the like). And the uncertain dynamics of class differentiation and struggle is a major source of uneven development, internalized contradiction and instability. The process of capital circulation in general is modified by disaggregation into more and more specific though intersecting conditions of circulation. Capital in general now has to be considered not as an undifferentiated unity but as something which is heterogeneous and often internally contradictory. The discovery of which of these internal differentiations has primacy or significance depends on the historical, geographical, and theoretical interrogation of material circumstances (this is why Marx's dialectics have to be considered as coupled with a certain conception of materialism). For example, the often fraught relations between financiers ("finance capital") and the industrial interest ("industrial capital") have periodically erupted into crises of considerable magnitude for the whole system of capital circulation.

To elaborate on the theory in this way is not, however, to introduce a mass of *external* contingencies. The organization of firms or of nation states, to take just a couple of examples, is not an external event that interferes with a pure circulation process of capital. In each case, we attempt to understand a social form (a particular kind of entity or organizational form, such as a corporation or a government) as arising out of the circulation process and commanding a particular "moment" in the circulation of capital. That entity (a corporation, for example) has a shaping influence by virtue of the powers it internalizes and the creativity of the transformations (social as well as material) which it accomplishes. But its existence is embedded in the continuous flow of the process of which it is a part and, like any other entity, it internalizes contradictions, is heterogeneous, and inherently unstable by virtue of the complex processes which support, reconstitute, or develop it. The recent history of both firms and nation states would, I think, broadly justify such a view of their status. Lewontin (1982), incidentally, provides a similar interpretation for the mediating role of the organism (in the context of genetic mutations and environmental adaptations) in evolution: organisms through their productive activities transform the environments to which they subsequently adapt in exactly the same way that firms actively transform the social and economic environments to which they must perforce then adapt.

The work of elaboration, further specification, and better articulation of the theory is on-going and can never be complete, if only because the world is always changing, in part *because of* the creative thoughts and activities generated by dialecticians as well as others (Cartesians in particular!). Theorizing, like any other process, is as continuous and transformative, as heterogeneous and as contradictory, as any other process which dialecticians confront. There is always plenty more to do "something more to be said" and innumerable points of theoretical intervention to be examined and acted upon. The process of dialectical thinking and its application to human affairs has also to be produced, sustained, developed. The aim and objective of my own work (e.g. *The Limits to Capital*) has in part been given over to identifying (dialectically) extensions to the theory and better specifying its operation with respect to time and space. But I would also want to better define the domains within which certain kinds of capitalistic processes operate and with what effects and consider what kinds of transformative opportunities thereby arise to change the trajectory of social life.

As an explanatory device, the theory does not operate as a simple predictor of events (states of things). It has to be viewed more as a set of generative and transformative principles, embedded in continuous processes, which, by virtue of internalized heterogeneity and contradiction, reveals the possibility to create all kinds of new but always transient states of things. Here, too, we encounter a major source of misunderstanding. To explain phenomena in terms of the circulation of capital certainly does not imply that all phenomena that lie within its domain have to be or are the same. Limiting and quite extraordinary situations could arise where this was indeed the case, but the generative and transformative principles embedded in the circulation processes are such as to give rise to as many shapes and forms of social life (of commodities, of capitalist cities, of consumption habits, for example) as someone like Mandelbrot can generate through fractal methods. Yet there is an underlying unity to the production of such differences and that underlying unity sets limits on the nature of the differentiations which can be generated. Socialist social relations cannot, for example, be produced out of capitalistic generative principles.

The purpose of materialist enquiry is not to *test* in some positivistic or formal sense whether or not capital circulation exists (we know it does) but to show in what forms, over what domains (within what bounds) and with what effects it operates and what transformative possibilities exist. Can we show, for example, that what is usually referred to as "cultural production" lies within its domain or not? Are there circumstances in, for example, the circulation of capital through built environments or in the production of space which require us to re-think the specification of the process? Can we track the circulation of capital through state apparatuses and functions and what does this mean for our conception of the limits and potentialities of state power? What happens if capital circulation is barred from direct operation in certain sectors (e.g., health care or education) or if it is suddenly liberated to flow into arenas formerly denied to it (like the former Soviet bloc)? In what ways and in what directions is social change promoted by capital circulation and in what respects can this be regarded as a stable rather than as an inherently unstable process?

In the instance of capital circulation (itself a loosely bounded domain of Marxist enquiry) the problem is to explore the forms and domains of operation, the *how* of generative and transformative principles at work. This implies a particular materialist research strategy. Treating nation states, for example, as homogeneous entities and examining their behaviour and performance according to a set of economic indicators is of limited value. The principles of dialectical thinking would suggest that the focus of enquiry should be on *how* nation states internalize powers (or lose their grip on such powers), in what ways they are heterogeneous and internally contradictory, and in what ways these internalized tensions result in the kind of creativity or self-destructiveness which leads to new configurations of activity. And how, finally, do such activities transform social life?

The charge that Marxists "read off" from theory to reality is from this perspective sadly misplaced. This is not to claim that all Marxist enquiry of this sort is error free. Generative principles can get distorted, domains of operation can be imagined rather than substantiated, and materialist studies of actual processes are just as liable to get lost in a thicket of detail as any other kind of research. Through construction of generative principles and theories, Marxists themselves seek, of course, to change the world. But this does not imply that the results of enquiry will always be appropriate or that they can never be confused and destructive. Marxist argumentation cannot, any more than any other way of thinking, escape the dilemmas described by Bohm and Peat (1987: 57) as follows:

> We cannot impose any worldview we like and hope that it will work. The cycle of perception and action cannot be maintained in a totally arbitrary fashion unless we collude to suppress the things we do not wish to see while, at the same time, trying to maintain, at all costs, the things that we desire most in our image of the world. Clearly the cost of supporting such false vision of reality must eventually be paid.

And, it is fair to comment, many have paid the cost of such a false vision on the part of Marxism. But then no other processes of thought can claim a mantle of untarnished virtue.

3
The Leibnizian Conceit

Throughout much of this argument, I have invoked the idea of "internal relations" as being fundamental to dialectics. I shall now try to clarify this idea, in order to avoid some of the confusions and substantial errors that can arise. For Ollman dialectics are inherently radical, materialist, and Marxist. From this it might be erroneously concluded (though Ollman certainly does not do so) that the notion of internal relations leads down the same path. Since, in subsequent chapters, I shall have recourse to the figure of Leibniz (a precursor of thinking on internal relations whose influence Ollman acknowledges) as proposing a relational view of space and time, I shall here briefly take up his particular version of internal relations: the problem being, of course, that Leibniz is generally considered a deeply conservative theoretician in political matters as well as a foundational figure in the rise of that German idealist tradition against which Marx rebelled.*

In the *Monadology*, written towards the very end of his life, Leibniz proposes a metaphysics founded on the concept of a monad that internalizes everything there is. Each monad mirrors the universe: a principle of "correspondence" internally constitutes each monad as that mirror of the universe. Leibniz restricts this correspondence principle in two respects. First, each monad has a distinctive position and perspective in relation to the universe and its mirror-

---

*For those interested in the history of geographical thought, it is worth noting that Gunnar Olsson and I were both equally impressed with Ollman's book on *Alienation* and its emphasis on internal relations when it was first published in 1972, but that the linguistic and idealist direction in which Olsson subsequently took the idea is in all other respects quite at odds with my own work in historical–geographical materialism. Perhaps for similar reasons Bhaskar (1993), in laying out his own version of dialectical realism in a book of intimidating difficulty and intensity, notes both a certain convergence between his own work and that of Ollman's, while criticizing Ollman for tending to treat dialectics as pure epistemology rather than as a powerful ontological position. Such controversies are not easy to sort out but fundamental to how the notion of internal relations connects to dialectical argumentation.

ing therefore emphasizes certain proximate regions and perspectives rather than others. Secondly, monads vary in the quality of the mirroring they achieve – some sharper and others more blurry.

But if I am a monad and I internalize everything there is then all I need to understand the universe is to contemplate my own inner self. To be sure, what I learn will be conditioned by my positionality and perspective as well as by the acuity of my mirroring capacity. But it is still reasonable to argue, as Leibniz indeed did, that "I am the measure of all things" and that deep reflection on my own internal conditions is all that is required to achieve full knowledge of the universe. Let me, for purposes of identification, call this the "Leibnizian conceit." It poses some very important problems as well as possibilities and I shall have reason to come back to it again and again in subsequent chapters.

Let me first comment on the conditions that were associated with Leibniz's formulation of this thesis. Most recent presentations on Leibniz focus purely on his writings and his metaphysics as a set of ideas. I have to go back to a work first published in 1948 by Meyer (translated in to English in 1952) to find an argument that attempts to weave together Leibniz's derivation of metaphysical principles and the circumstances of his world. That world was torn with strife and controversy, religious wars and violence, pestilence and plague, political intrigue and chaotic fragmentations, and all manner of unsettling discoveries (geographical, scientific, etc.). And Leibniz was deeply engaged in the politics of that world, trying to find solutions, to establish harmonies where there were none, to negotiate rational outcomes, to reconcile ideas about God's perfection with the obvious imperfections in daily life as well as with the extraordinary advances then occurring in science (particularly Newton's work) and in philosophy (particularly Descartes). He was also an active participant in contemporary geopolitical struggles and practices. Meyer seeks to understand how Leibniz's ideas grew out of his experience of that world. And, most crucially, he interprets the theses arrived at in the *Monadology* as registering a moment of failure:

> In his later life Leibniz becomes fully convinced that he has found a solution to the problem of relating the individual to the universal. ... The *ultima thule* of monadological reflection is complete retreat into the isolated Self; biographic-ally speaking, freedom and commitment cease to be related in any stable manner, until at the very end of Leibniz's life they break out into fatal conflict. At the point where Leibniz advances the self-conscious claim of raising the essence of his own individuality to a universal law lies the distinction between his critical and his speculative philosophy; and at this point the philosopher becomes isolated from the rest of the world. He flees the noisy, chaotic controversy of the contemporary scene in order to listen to the distinct, quasi-mathematical voice of his inner monologue; for only now can he find the two fundamental principles of his monadological system, the principles of "uncontradicted truth" and of "sufficient reason." (Meyer, 1952: 9)

Meyer's commentary is not without relevance and force with respect to a wide range of contemporary theorizations. I shall briefly take up two examples. Consider, first, Derrida's resort to something akin to the Leibnizian conceit in his discussion of self – other relations as he examines how the "european subject" (an entity that Leibniz was also crucially concerned with) constitutes itself on the inside through the construction of an "other" – the colonial subject. Spivak (1988: 294), in her interesting commentary on the whole problem of how the colonized other can speak, attacks the "first world intellectual masquerading as the absent nonrepresenter who lets the oppressed speak for themselves" and approvingly cites Derrida's strategy as follows:

> To render thought or the thinking subject transparent or invisible seems ... to hide the relentless recognition of the Other by assimilation. It is in the interest of such cautions that Derrida does not invoke "letting the other(s) speak for himself" but rather invokes an "appeal" to, or "call" to the "quite-other" ... of "rendering delirious that interior voice that is the voice of the other in us."

The dangers in such a gesture are obvious. If the only way in which the "other" can be represented is through "rendering delirious" the voices that I have internalized in the process of discovering myself, then very soon the identities of "l'autre c'est moi" become as surely planted as did the thesis of "l'etat c'est moi." And this is exactly where Meyer felt the fatal contradiction lay in Leibniz's strategy:

> Leibniz claims that the observation of the essence of things is nothing else but an observation of the essence of our own spirit. ... The intellectual individuality of man, informed by an entirely new ethos of intellectual achievement, becomes the measure of all human existence. In this doctrine of personalist absolutism – which is essentially the same as Louis XIV's doctrine of political absolutism – no real community is possible. And at this point Leibniz's conception of man's sovereign spirit comes to contradict his own idea of toleration. The commonwealth becomes a mere "aggregate of monads", and the aesthetically significant concept of "*harmonia mundi*" can no longer bridge the gulf between individual men, states, or nations.

The second example is drawn from the frequent appeal on the part of deep ecologists not only to dialectics but also to a version of the philosophy of internal relations that echoes the Leibnizian conceit. Arne Naess, the founder of the deep ecology movement, was a serious student of Spinoza and evidently used this philosophical training to great effect. In deep ecology it becomes the task of the Self (understood as something transcendental to the egotistical "self") to become the medium for "rendering delirious" (to appropriate Derrida's phrase) that interior voice that is the voice of that great other – "nature" – within us (see chapter 7). Through self-discipline we can render our vision of nature less blurry and hope, by virtue of the "correspondence rules": we internalize, to arrive at an understanding of the external world by erecting a monadic Self into the measure of all things.

I am not seeking here to discredit the Leibnizian conceit entirely. Strategies of this sort have been of enormous importance throughout history and presumably will continue to play a role. But, left to itself, not only does it run into the fatal contradiction of the sort that beset Leibniz [is this why Derrida (1994) has returned to Marx?], but it also begets a cacophony of "inner monologues" (of the sort that Derrida, for one, is particularly adept at producing) on the part of philosophers and literary theorists who have all too clearly retreated from "the noisy chaotic controversy of the contemporary scene," withdrawn into an isolated self, and thereby severed any connection between freedom and political commitment.

In any case, the Leibnizian conceit precisely underlies that form of philosophical idealism which Marx, through his dialogue with Hegel, rejected. Whitehead (1985: 193–4), while acknowledging how much his own doctrines owe to Leibniz, voices a number of parallel objections. Leibniz, he argues, had on his hands:

> two distinctive points of view. One was that the final real entity is an organising activity, fusing ingredients into a unity, so that this unity is the reality. The other point of view is that the final real entities are substances supporting qualities. The first point of view depends upon the acceptance of internal relations binding together all reality. The latter is inconsistent with the reality of such relations. To combine these two points of view, his monads were therefore windowless: and their passions merely mirrored the universe by the divine arrangement of a pre-established harmony.

Thus there can be "no concrete reality of internal relations" in the sense of actual processes of internalization open to investigation: God (or what Hegel later chose to call "spirit") has to function as the *Deus ex machina* for the whole system to work.

While Leibniz may have furnished a foundation stone for "the great achievements of German philosophy" he leaves behind some awkward problems as to how to use the doctrine of internal relations in practical affairs. There are three main difficulties. The first, dealt with at some length in Ollman (1976: appendix A), is that if everything is about flows then how are we to speak of any particulars or individuals at all? If *individuation,* the identification of *individuals* or of what Strawson (1965) calls *particulars* is considered dependent on spatial–temporal location then shifting the grounds for defining space and time, which, as we shall see in chapter 10, is indeed the necessary implication of the relational view, shifts the grounds for how individuals, particulars, and entities (such as "things" and "bodies") are to be identified and understood.

The conception of the fundamental elements or individuals of which the world is composed is then perpetually open to question. Strawson (p. 119) states, for example "that no system which does not allow for spatial or temporal entities can be a system which allows for particulars at all." And in advancing his views on how particulars and entities are to be established, he uses Leibniz's arguments as a foil to construct what he considers a more coherent and comprehensive way to individuate phenomena. Leibniz's monads are entity-like enough, it turns out, to provide easy means to rebut Strawson's objections, but they are unsatisfactory as a general argument for the reasons Whitehead correctly advances. The answer here, given by writers as diverse as Ollman, Whitehead, and Bohm, is that there is no particular barrier to construing things and entities as "permanences" or even as relatively autonomous entities provided we recognize how those things and entities are constituted, sustained and ultimately dissolved in flows and how all entities are relationally defined with respect to others.

To this Whitehead (1985: 203) perceptively adds two other objections. He first observes:

> The difficulty which arises in respect to internal relations is to explain how any particular truth is possible. Insofar as there are internal relations, everything must depend upon everything else. But if this be the case, we cannot know about anything until we equally know everything else. Apparently, therefore, we are under the necessity of saying everything at once. This supposed necessity is palpably untrue. Accordingly it is incumbent on us to explain how there can be internal relations, seeing that we admit finite truths.

We will encounter this difficulty again in chapter 12, where I take up some of the groundings of identity politics. If I internalize everything (including every "otherness") there is, then I am under the necessity to speak for everyone there is which is equivalent to saying nothing particular at all. Equally serious, is that "the doctrine of internal relations makes it impossible to attribute 'change' to any actual entity" (Whitehead, 1969: 74). If all monads internalize everything there is, then under what impulses can they change except by their own internal volition? Put another way, to say that flux and change is everywhere is equivalent to saying that it is also nowhere in particular.

This may all seem to be a rather arcane and erudite issue, so let me illustrate its more practical and political–economic importance by a return to Marx's conception of capital as outlined earlier. The argument, recall, is that production, consumption, exchange, and distribution are separate moments of a process (a flow of value), that each moment internalizes the conditions of the others, but that the moment of production is regarded in some sense as fundamental. A common Marxist reading of this is that we only have to revolutionize (or to study) the moment of production to change (or understand) the whole world because all else is internalized there. But this is nothing less than the idealist view of internal relations imported into Marxism in the name of historical materialism. From this standpoint some of the criticisms launched against "foundationalist" and "economistic" forms of Marxism in which production is treated as the only relevant category, have some justification. Such arguments become even more Leibnizian (and idealist) to the degree that "production" is construed as a hermetically sealed ("windowless") moment – albeit characterized by a "correspondence principle" through which everything else is internalized within it – rather than as an open moment in the continuous flow of social and political life. But things look very different if the notion of internal relations is situated not in a world of monadic entities (which appear as "permanences") but as continuous transformations and internalizations of different "moments" (events, things, entities) within the overall process of political–economic reproduction.

Production, consumption, exchange, and distribution, to go back to Marx's formulation, are all relevant moments within the social process, each internalizing effects of the others. Bohm (1983: 297) makes a parallel criticism of Leibniz, albeit while exploring how what Bohm calls "the implicate order" provides a common ground for understanding both consciousness and matter conjointly within the wholeness of becoming:

> We propose ... that the basic element be a *moment* which, like the moment of consciousness, cannot be precisely related to measurements of space and time, but rather covers a somewhat vaguely defined region which is extended in space and has duration in time. The extent and duration of a moment may vary from something very small to something very large... . As with consciousness, each moment has a certain explicate order, and in addition it enfolds all the others, though in its own way. So the relationship of each moment in the whole to all the others is implied by its total content: the way in which it "holds" all the others enfolded within it. In certain ways this notion is similar of Leibniz's idea of monads, each of which "mirrors" the whole in its own way, some in great detail and others rather vaguely. The difference is that Leibniz's monads had a permanent existence, whereas our basic elements are only moments and are thus not permanent. Whitehead's idea of "actual occasions" is closer to the one proposed here, the main difference being that we use the implicate order to express the qualities and relationships of our moments, whereas Whitehead does this in a rather different way."

There are, plainly, different versions of how to understand internal relations. My own preference (and it has been a fairly consistent feature of much of my previous work) is to treat of "moments" within processes rather than to take the monadic view of, say, production as *the* element for sole consideration. Consumption, exchange, distribution must be considered as moments in their own right precisely in order to understand the process of internalization as it occurs in production. Marx produced strong arguments to support his view that the moment of production was more crucial than the others to explaining how capitalism works and how socialism might be achieved, but this does not in any way justify neglect of the other moments – indeed, working on those other moments (such as consumption) is a fruitful way towards internalizing specific and desired forms of change within production (the most obvious case is when consumer boycotts affect production activities). To the degree that Ollman fails to make such distinctions clear enough (though I suspect he agrees with me), he leaves open the possibility for both a conservative and idealist doctrine of internal relations as well as a purely "productivist" version of Marxian political economy.

This still leaves the thorny question of where change comes from in particular, in a world construed in terms of internal relations. Why might certain agents for change (such as an organized working class) be considered as more fundamental than others? This is perhaps the foremost question to be answered and it will be a major preoccupation in later chapters. For the moment, all that I need record is that critical assessment of doctrines of internal relations places that as a metaphysical as well as a political issue of paramount importance. Leibniz's particular solution, arrived at in the *Monadology*, was founded on failures of political practice that made retreat into the windowless world (his study) of an intellectual monad engaging in extensive correspondence with the outside world a particularly attractive proposition. Hardly surprisingly, the political failures of the left in the last two decades have rendered a similar retreat into a windowless Leibnizian world of internalized relations, as for example in the case of Deleuze (1993), a rather attractive option. It has been facilitated in many respects by the perfection of computer technologies [another innovation of Leibniz who, as Heim (1991) points out, developed not only the first calculating machine but also the binary arithmetic – a universal calculus that "would compile all human culture, bringing every natural language into a single shared data base" – to go with it]. The picture of the monadic individual, locked onto a computer screen connected by modem into a vast world of correspondence in cyberspace in many respects is a fulfillment (repetition) of the Leibnizian dream. "Monads have no windows, but they do have terminals" writes Heim, going on to describe a cyberworld in which Leibniz's "monadological metaphysics" underpin both the logic and "erotic ontology" of cyberspace. And there are many who now regard intensive exploration of this new space as a form of radical and revolutionary action. I will return to this topic in chapter 10.

The "new radical idealism," as I shall call it, rests largely on such a withdrawal and it is something which in itself the pure doctrine of internal relations is powerless to prevent, except by embedding it deeply in the political commitments [or, as Bhaskar (1993) prefers it, in the "liberatory axiology"] that gave Marx's dialectics and his historical materialism so much of its power. Otherwise the severance between freedom and political commitment becomes just as fatal a contradiction for contemporary dialectical work as it ultimately became for Leibniz. Dialectics, with its focus on change, has a strong claim to be at least one of the key modes of enquiry. But, as Bhaskar (1993) notes, there are various strains within that tradition and it is important to be as explicit as possible concerning how dialectics can operate and what it might mean to bring some rather than other dialectical principles to bear upon any form of enquiry. Treating different modes of thought dialectically (a kind of meta-dialectic if you will) as complementary though antagonistic rather than as mutually exclusive and unrelated can, for this reason, yield creative insights. This is an ancient principle that the Greeks understood well. "The finest harmony is born from differences," said Heraclitus, and "discord is the law of all becoming." Marx, likewise held that "one-sided" representations are always restricting and problematic and that the best way to proceed was always "to rub together conceptual blocks in such a way that they catch fire." Perhaps a little rubbing in the right way can chart creative ways to think about socio-geographical and environmental change, and how to bring spatio-temporality, place, and environment (nature) within the frames of social and literary theory. In the chapters that follow, I shall try to put such a mode of argument to work to see what it can yield. In the process I shall try to dissolve dialectics as an abstract set of principles into a flow of argumentation and theoretical practices.

4

The Dialectics of Discourse

Writing is a form of discourse. When I engage in it I am bound by its rules. We use discourses to persuade ourselves and others to a certain way of understanding (and often acting towards) a subject matter we regard as important. There has been a profound wave of reflection recently on the nature and role of discourses, exploring their multiplicity and heterogeneity, their inherent limitations as well as their expressive capacities. This reflection is itself bound by rules of discourse.

The capacity to both reflect through discourse on what we think and do, and to reflect discursively on the nature of the discourses we construct, has important implications. It opens up the creative possibility for critical reflection. But it also poses dangers of circularity. It can lead into a labyrinth in which multiplying discursive reflections become so interwoven that it becomes impossible to discern anything of substance.

There has also been much salutary discussion recently on the "subject positionality" or the "standpoint" embedded in particular discourses. Attention has been drawn to the hidden positionalities and power plays that lie buried within even the most seemingly innocuous and ethically neutral discourses. It is difficult now to advance any claims to "truth" or even "relevance" or "politics" without providing some initial grounds (including declarations of "subject positionality") upon which to base such claims. This mandatory initial gesture opens the flood gates for a lot of personal self-indulgence as well as useful critical reflection. As Professor Paik Nak-chung, a prominent member of the oppositional South Korean writer's union recently observed, he would normally feel embarrassed to talk about himself, but when visiting the United States he had discovered a thoroughly respectable way to do that: it was called "revealing one's subject positionality."

My concern is to examine the term "discourse" and try to position its role, capacities, and powers in relation to nondiscursive aspects of social life, including those that might enter into the definition of subject positionality. This step is necessary to the overall argument because I need to understand how the discursive construction of fundamental terms to be taken up later – *environment, nature, space–time, place,* and *justice* being key words – might operate in relation to the nondiscursive realities to which such terms supposedly allude. To this end, I construct a "dialectical cognitive map" to represent the flow of social processes and then use that map to situate what discourse might be about and to better understand what social and literary theories are about. I am not, I should emphasize, trying to design some meta-theory of the social process – maps are far too unreliable for that. My aim is far more modest: to create an initial map to assess the form, the power, the creative possibilities as well as the limitations inherent in different theorizations (including my own).

I. The Basic Framework

I begin by defining six distinctive "moments" to the social process (figure 4.1). These are basic markers to chart much of what goes on in social and literary theory. They also lay a ground work for the substantive investigations to follow. I use the term "moment" in order to avoid, as far as possible, any sense of prior crystallization of processual activities into "permanences" – things, entities, clearly bounded domains, or systems. I present the moments in no particular order of significance.

(*a*) The moment of *language/discourse* can roughly be defined as the moment of resort to the vast panoply of coded ways available to us for talking about, writing about, and representing the world.

(*b*) Discourses are manifestations of *power.* The moment of *power* is itself both internally heterogeneous and complex, but power relations (political, economic, symbolic, military, etc.) and pressures are fundamental within the social process and some conception of how they work is therefore crucial for understanding social processes.

Discourse/language	
Power	Beliefs/values/desires
Social relations	Institutions/rituals
Material practices	

Figure 4.1 "Moments" in a Cognitive Map of the Social Process.

(*c*) We all possess beliefs, fantasies, values, and desires about how the world is (ontologies), how better understandings of the world might be achieved (epistemologies), and how I/we want to "be" in the world. This complex interior world I shall designate as the moment of *thought, fantasy, and desire* (the "imaginary") recognizing that such terms are scarcely adequate for what I mean to say and that the separation between them may mislead (the thought–body dichotomy implied cannot easily be justified, for example).

(*d*) The moment of *institution building* broadly refers to the organization of political and social relations between individuals on a more or less durable basis. We here recognize that human thoughts and desires can become collectively manifest and reified as cultural rituals (such as those of religion, authority, and deference) or, more obviously, as seemingly permanent social institutions (such as those of law, the state, politics, science, education, religion, the academy, the professions, the military, and the market place).

(*e*) The moment of *material practices* focuses on the material embeddedness of human life. Material practices are the sensuous and experiential nexus – the point of bodily being in the world – from which all primary knowledge of the world ultimately derives. But material practices also instantiate and objectify human desires in the material world, not only through the reproduction of self and bodily being but also through modifications of surrounding environments encompassing everything from the microtechnologies of the living and the workplace through to the built forms and created environments of cities, agrarian landscapes, and globally modified ecosystems.

(*f*) The moment of *social relations* describes the various forms of sociality human beings engage in, and the more or less durable orderings of social relations to which this sociality may give rise. It focuses on the way human beings relate to each other – "modes of social relating" – as they live their lives, produce together, communicate, etc. Cooperative structures, divisions of labor, social hierarchies of class, race, age, and gender, or differentiated individual or group access to material and symbolic activities and social power, are some of the issues encompassed within this moment.

I am here reducing a vast array of activities to six fundamental moments of social life. The social process, as I conceive of it, flows in, through and around all of these moments and the activities of each and every individual embrace all of the moments simultaneously. While this highly schematic (and very Cartesian) representation has the advantage of immediate clarity, it is liable to lead to egregious error left in such a raw form. So I offer some immediate clarifications, building on the dialectical way of thinking outlined in chapter 2.

1. The analytics I want to work with are *dialectical.* Each moment is constituted as an *internal relation* of the others within the flow of social and
material life. Discourses internalize in some sense everything that occurs at
other moments (thus giving credence to Derrida's foundational statement
that "there is nothing outside of the text" or Foucault's foundational view
that discourse *is* power). Discourses express human thought, fantasy, and
desire. They are also institutionally based, materially constrained, experi-
entially grounded manifestations of social and power relations. By the same
token, discursive effects suffuse and saturate all other moments within the
social process (affecting, for example, beliefs and practices as well as being
affected by them).

    But to privilege discourse above other moments is insufficient, mislead-
ing, and even dangerous. The theory of internal relations has to be used in
a way that avoids the trap of "monadic idealism" and the pitfalls of the
"Leibnizian conceit." Errors arise when examination of one "moment" is
held sufficient to understand the totality of the social process. Again and
again we will find slippages of the sort that convert a dialectically correct
statement like "there is nothing outside of the text" into false statements
that "everything can be understood through texts" (or, worse still, "everything *is* a text and can be understood as such") and equally false practices
that seek to use, say, the deconstruction of texts as the privileged (and
sometimes the only) pathway to understanding.

2. Internal relations are shaped through an activity of *translation* from one
moment to another. But translation from, say, what is being desired to what
is being said, done, institutionalized, etc., is fraught with dangers and
difficulties. Something, and sometimes a great deal, gets lost. Translations
from one language to another are difficult enough, but translation from,
say, power as physical force to power as discourse is often a slippery business.
A gap always exists between the different moments so that slippage, ambiguity and unintended consequences inevitably occur. Hegemonic discourses
can be policed by a repressive apparatus of political–economic power (such
as that in the former Soviet Union) without seriously invading deeply held
beliefs, fantasies, and desires about racial, ethnic and gender differences or
the existence of God, nation, and the supernatural. The power of certain
kinds of political discourse (Thatcherism, Peronism, fascism, the religious
right in the United States in the 1990s) may, on the other hand, derive from
the uncanny capacity of those seeking political–economic power to both
mobilize and subtly promote certain deeply held beliefs, fantasies, fears, and
desires against others and utilize that mobilization to sustain and promote
a certain configuration of power relations. So although each moment
internalizes forces from all of the others, the internalization is always a
translation or metamorphosis of those effects rather than an exact replica
or perfect mimesis. This makes the question of how to construe the

"correspondence rules" operative across moments crucial for how we understand the social process to work.

3. Each moment internalizes heterogeneity largely by way of a variety of conflicting effects from all the other moments (an idea that Althusser sought to capture through use of the term "overdetermination"). Power relations are not homogeneous, for example. We cannot know *a priori* whether we should appeal to authoritative versus economic, gender-based versus class-based, symbolic versus raw physical dimensions of power (just to take a few examples of categories that are deployed). Contestation over deeply held beliefs, desires, and values is likewise everywhere evident, frequently pitting different fantasy worlds in the form of Utopian desires and strivings against each other in severe internalized traumas or bitter external polemical/political conflicts. Heterogeneity of beliefs and incoherent ways of desiring and valuing can be found within each and every one of us, generating plenty of inner turmoil and moral torments. Racist, elitist, and sexist thoughts surface in surprising ways even among those who dedicate their lives to campaigning against such phenomena, in exactly the same way that new material social practices designed to achieve a change in power relations can become unglued by subtle shifts of emphasis that reinstate old power relations within, for example, new material practices and divisions of labor.

4. I have so far construed the relations between "moments" as flows, as open processes that pass unhindered from one moment to all others. But flows often crystallize into "things," "elements," and isolable "domains" or "systems" which assume a relative permanence (and sometimes even acquire limited causal powers) within the social process. Reifications of free-flowing processes are always occurring to create actual "permanences" in the social and material world around us. Examples might be material landscapes (such as cities), social institutions that seem almost impossible to transform by virtue of the solid way they have been constructed, divisions of labor that are so routinized and organized through an infrastructure of factory and machinery that they seem impossible not to replicate, socially constructed discourses that tightly constrain and regulate behaviors (for example, discourses about time and space outlined in part III), and even discourses which become so widely accepted and reified, that they themselves become part of a landscape of knowledge seemingly impermeable to change. This problem of how "things" crystallize out of processes preoccupied Adorno. Coles (1993: 232) writes:

> For Adorno the world is thoroughly relational. Each thing is a "crystallization" of its relation with others. Yet the language of "crystallization" is as important here as that of "relation". The relational world is not one of pure fluidity and harmony, but one where things crystallize into highly dense, infinitely specific, and often very recalcitrant entities that resist the surrounding world in which

they are born. One could say that for Adorno, the first movement toward a dialogical understanding of freedom lies in a recognition of both this relational quality and this recalcitrance.

My argument is not that permanences, power structures, and rigidities of discourse are irrelevant or weak in relation to the fluid processes that constitute them. I do want to insist, however, that analysis should confront how such permanences can occur, how fluid internal relations can be converted into social causation and how the internalization of forces operating at other moments might limit or undermine the permanences and the social causation with which they are associated. The nation state, a relatively recent product of concentrated power in human history, has just such an air of a permanence precisely because it successfully internalizes a wide range of desires and beliefs, discourses, social relations, and institutional and material practices and has thereby become an entity endowed with causal powers. It would be silly to deny that the nation state operates as a causative agent. But, as the case of the Soviet Union so well demonstrates, it would be equally silly to accept those causal powers as permanently given, independent of how social processes produce entities.

So although I am explicitly *not* proposing here a causal or circular model (of the sort that says, for example, that those in power set up discourses that shape beliefs, fantasies, and desires so as to regulate practices of institution building that set the stage for material production and reproduction activities that in turn construct social relations that finally return to ensure the perpetuation of power), I do want to recognize that situations may arise in which it seems as if such a causal (and circular) logic is at work. It is undoubtedly the dream (and sometimes illusion) of those who hold power that matters can be or are regulated in such a circular causative manner. Such situations often appear desperately difficult from the standpoint of any oppositional movement precisely because it seems impossible to break out of the circularity. So even though the basic argument concerns internal relations rather than causality, the crystallization of causal structures (permanences) out of such a dialectical system of internal relations can and frequently does occur, posing problems not only for analysis but also for how the social process works. In the evaluation of social and literary theories, close attention has to be paid to shifts in language from free flowing processes to a crystallized causal schema.

5. The importance of discourse is that it is the moment of communicative persuasion or discussion *between persons* regarding certain lines of action and belief. Acts of communication have a certain spatial field of operation as well as a temporality, both of which depend upon the socially constructed and technologically mediated capacities for communication over space and time. The games played within discourses are extraordinarily complicated so that

the discursive moment becomes indistinguishable, as Foucault argues, from the exercise of power itself. But this is precisely what is meant by internalization: the discursive moment *is* a form of power, it *is* a mode of formation of beliefs and desires, it *is* in itself an institution, a mode of social relating, a material practice, a fundamental moment of experience. Discourses can never be pure, isolated or insulated from other moments in social life, however abstract and seemingly transcendent they become. Nor can they be insulated and separated from those doing the discoursing. Human beings (both individually and collectively) are the bearers of discourses. On the other hand, discourses, though humanly produced, have the awkward habit of assuming a certain power over how individuals think and behave. In this, as in many other facets of the social process, human beings can imprison themselves in systems and things of their own construction. This does not detract from the ineluctable fact that discourse is always social relating between people. But it does pose the thorny question of what kind of social relating is going on. And this can best be approached by examining the relation of language to discourse and the determinative power of both in relation to social being.

II. The Moment of Language (Discourses)

The words "discourse" and "language" are often used interchangeably. While there are evident overlaps, it is, I think, useful to treat language as in some sense more fundamental, as one of the key raw materials out of which specific discourses, understood as bounded (sometimes strictly so) ways of representing the world, get shaped.

Debates over the powers of language have taken all sorts of twists and turns in the twentieth century. To begin with, important distinctions have been suggested that lead to different definitions of language, the most celebrated being Saussure's distinction between "langue" (language as a structure of internal relations, grammatical rules, word positionings) and "parole" (common, everyday speech). Some view language as an objective and fixed structure of possibilities (perhaps genetically coded) that human beings use, albeit in diverse ways, while others see language as either a subjective or broadly historical construction. Those of the latter persuasion broadly divide over the question as to whether changes in language lead or follow changes in material practices, institutional forms, social and power relations, beliefs, and the like. This relates to the controversy over the relation between language and that to which it supposedly refers – reflection theories of language (the idea that words are mimetic of the realities they describe) here butt heads with constructivist ideas (the view that our understanding of the "real" is constructed through words). And there are all sorts of intermediate positions and synthetic dialectical formulations that bridge or mediate these simple binaries.

I cannot resolve these controversies (I doubt anyone ever will) but the position I take on them has a role to play in the subsequent analysis. If, for example, the conceptions of space and time, of nature and the environment, of place and justice, differ both between and within different social formations and cultural configurations (as I shall later argue), then I need some way to interpret both how differences in languages and meanings arise and what significance must be attached to the existence and perpetuation of distinctive meanings.

Consider, for example, the implications of accepting what is known as the Whorf–Sapir hypothesis. This view arose out of anthropological studies of native-American cultures and the realization that there was a radical difference in how native-Americans and Europeans perceived, understood, and acted towards the "same" reality. Space and time, for example, had quite different and unassimilable meanings from the standpoint of native-Americans (this point will be taken up later). This led Sapir to argue that "no two languages are ever sufficiently similar to be considered as representing the same social reality," and that, therefore, "the worlds in which different societies live are different worlds, not the same world with different labels attached."

This leads, when taken too literally, to some kind of linguistic determinism, in which language differences are seen to lie at the root of different perceptions, understandings and constructions of reality and, hence, of different behaviors, practices, and beliefs. The implications are highly relativistic (each culture has its own incommunicable structure of feeling and understanding of the world) at the same time as they are deeply anti-Eurocentric (the idea that there is one and only one superior – for example, scientific – mode of representing and understanding the world is denied). But there are some nuances in the Whorfian view.

Whorf's argument is usually represented in terms of the different way words relate to things in different cultural circumstances – the famous example being that of the Eskimo who has a vast array of different words to describe what we generically and simplistically refer to as "snow," and who therefore perceive and act upon the world in ways to which Europeans remain oblivious precisely because of linguistic impoverishment. But Whorf was much more interested in grammatical constructions rather than nouns and this has great relevance to my own argument. Time, for example, is constructed grammatically through, in the European case, an elaborate system of past tenses that simply does not exist in many native-American languages. We learn fundamental ideas about time, without being particularly aware of it, simply by learning our grammar. Just as important is the grammatical distinction between nouns (things) and verbs (processes). Whorf here used the example of "fire" which in native American languages is usually treated as a verb (a process) rather than a noun (a thing). But in most European languages "fire" is a noun and we have a tendency, therefore, to think of it as a "thing" rather than as a "process." This example of Whorf's is useful for it sheds light on how dialectical formulations emphasizing processes can so easily be translated into relations between things almost without noticing it, simply through the medium of language. But as this example illustrates, there is nothing "deterministic" about this. I can, and do, take issue with the conversions of dialectical process arguments (about capital, for example) into causal-relations-between-things arguments. It is possible to avoid the tricks that language can play in the same way as we can learn a variety of terms to describe snow. The point here is to be aware of the significance of language differences and linguistic limitations, while conceding what seems an irrefutable proposition: that language has a vital role to play in constructing understandings of and mediating action in the world. But why do such differences in language exist? Here it is perfectly feasible to answer that the reason the Eskimos have multiple names for "snow" is because their social and material practices of reproduction require it in exactly the same way that we now have multiple names for different metallic alloys for which the generic term "steel" used to be sufficient.

The issue of the determinate power of language over social life cannot so easily be dismissed, however. "Man acts as though *he* were the shaper and master of language while in fact *language* remains the master of man," says Heidegger (1971: p. 146) and a wide range of commentators and theorists concur with him in this judgment. In recent years, what Palmer calls "the descent into discourse" has consequently become more and more hegemonic in social and literary theory. We have fallen victim, Palmer (1990: 3) argues, to the illusory premise/promise:

> that language, broadly conceived as systems of signification that extend well beyond mere words to include symbols and structures of all ways of communicating (from the articulated to the subliminal), is the essential ground within which social life is embedded. Language thus constructs being: it orders the relations of classes and genders, ever attentive to specific hierarchies; it is the stage on which consciousness makes its historical entrance and politics is scripted. As its own master, moreover, language is nonreferential, and there can be no reduction of its beginnings and meanings "to some primal anterior reality."

Palmer's objections to this move are strongly voiced. "In the current fixation on language," he argues (p. 5), "a materialist understanding of the past is all too often sacrificed on the altar of an idealized reading of discourse and its influence." What then gets lost "is the centrality of the question: How are texts and interpretations used within the interactions of institutions? How do they generate and participate in the relations of power and ordering?" (p. 45). Palmer does not argue that the moment of language (discourse) is neutral or passive in the social process, but that serious losses of understanding arise when it occupies a hegemonic and determinate place.

The place of language in the social process is a matter of acute political contestation. Consider, for example, the intensive debate within feminism, lucidly summarized by Cameron (1992), over the role of language as a vehicle for the oppression of women. At one end of the spectrum there are those, like Dale Spender, who see language as entirely "man made," encoding a male point of view, a patriarchal symbolic order of meaning, that so thoroughly defines women's reality as to imprison both men and women within an "iron cage" of sexist language. The political antidote is to build an alternative language that encodes feminine meanings that define autonomy, self-determination, and the emancipation of women. The difficulty here is that if meanings within language are entirely self-referential then there would be no way to escape or even to identify the problem. For this reason, some of the most creative contributions of feminist theory have come from a consideration of how the "prisonhouse of language," the evident patriarchy of the dominant symbolic order, can be disrupted only by appeal to some relation between the moment of language and the "psychoanalytic" moment of fantasy and desire and/or the moment of bodily practices. Some influential feminist theorists – Irigaray and Kristeva being the most prominent – have made use of (and to some degree reworked) Lacanian psychoanalysis precisely because it dwells upon the relational moment of insertion and socialization of the body into a symbolic order where the phallus reigns supreme (Cameron, 1992: 119, 169). But, as Cameron goes on to suggest, this cannot be construed in isolation from other moments in the social process:

> Language, though the socially produced means of thought, is not socially controlled. Increasingly control over the development of language and its use is held by state institutions, including mass media and monopolistic private enterprise as in journalism and advertising. ... The semiologists have sometimes failed to appreciate the possibility and existence of class or other minority control over language.

It is impossible to probe far into the role of language from any standpoint, including feminism, without encountering the question of its relation to the other moments of the social process. As Cameron (1992: 220) concludes:

> While language is certainly a political issue for the repressed peoples of the world, I think it would be wise to think long and hard about the politics of blaming oppression solely or primarily on language. For the powerful, after all, there is much to recommend this account: it deflects attention from the fact that poor, Black and female speakers are disadvantaged because they are poor, Black and female. ... If language is detached from the context of social relations, blown up to occupy the whole picture instead of appearing as a piece of the picture, it loses its connection to the struggle as a whole.

Any consideration of the moment of language (and of discourse) that attempts to isolate it from the other "moments" of the social process is doomed to myopia. And this, I take to be the heart of the arguments advanced under the name of historical materialism. Here, for example, is Palmer's version:

Historical materialism has no difficulty in accommodating an appreciation of the materiality of texts and the importance of discourse. ... It can accept that discourse plays a role in constructing social being, just as it can appreciate the importance language plays in the politics of labour and the process of revolutionary transformation. The opposition between discourse and materialism hardens into a this versus that countering of interpretive choices at the very point where discourse demands recognition of the totalizing discursive determinations of language, writing and texts, elevating itself to an all-encompassing authority that is both everywhere and nowhere.

But Palmer here adds another wrinkle to the argument that deserves consideration. "To be sure," he writes, "in this process the 'text' is often conceived so broadly as to include virtually everything, from words, to institutions, to social relations of authority." In geography, for example, we now find cities, landscapes, bodies, and cultural configurations being interpreted purely as texts. Even the institutions, powers, social relations, and material practices at work in producing, say, urban life get reduced to texts in a totalizing gesture that is both extraordinary and startling given the anti-totalizing rhetoric of many of those engaging in the reduction. It is – and I make the point again in order not to be misunderstood – one thing to say that texts (discourses) internalize everything there is and that meaningful things can be said by bringing deconstructionist tactics to bear both upon actual texts (histories, geographies, novels) as well as upon a wide range of phenomena in which the semiotic moment has clear significance (such as movies, paintings, sculptures, buildings, monuments, landscapes, dress codes, and even a wide range of events such as religious rituals, political ceremonies, and popular carnivals). But it is quite another to insist that the whole world is nothing other than a text needing to be read and deconstructed. This is the fatal error to which someone like Baudrillard succumbs as he reduces the life process to something that occurs upon a cinema screen and nothing else (bizarrely claiming, in one of his most recent works, that the Gulf War did not "really" take place). Henri Lefebvre (1991: 7, 72, 143) attacked such a totalizing and reductionist gesture (a "willful dalliance with nihilism" is how he depicted even Baudrillard's earlier works):

Semiology raises difficult questions. ... When codes worked up from literary texts are applied to spaces – to urban spaces, say – we remain, as may easily be shown, on the purely descriptive level. Any attempt to use such codes as a means of deciphering social space must surely reduce that space itself to the status of a message, and the inhabiting of it to the status of a reading. This is both to evade history and practice. ... Space was *produced* before being *read*; nor was it produced in order to be read and grasped, but rather in order to be *lived* by people with bodies and lives in their own particular urban context. [italics in the original]

The position I am here converging on is close to that defined by the historical materialism of Raymond Williams that builds, to some degree, upon the pioneering work of Volosinov. "A definition of language," Williams writes, "is always, implicitly or explicitly, a definition of human beings in the world." Language is, Williams insists, "constitutive" of that way of being, but it is so not in any one-way determinative sense such that material practices dictate language or vice versa. Language is, he insists (1977, p. 29) "an indissoluble element of human self-creation." As such, it has to be understood as a historical–geographical creation. While it acquires a formal structure (and structuralist linguistics have revealed a great deal about what that might be), it cannot ever, in the final analysis, be treated as autonomous from the broader flow of historical–geographical change. "Language has then to be seen as a persistent kind of creation and re-creation: a dynamic presence and a constant regenerative process" (p. 31). Usable signs are:

> living evidence of a continuing social process, into which individuals are born and within which they are shaped, but to which they then actively contribute in a continuing process. ... We then find not a reified "language" and "society" but an active social language. Nor ... is this language simply a "reflection" or "expression" of "material reality." What we have, rather, is a grasping of this reality through language, which as practical consciousness is saturated by and saturates all social activity, including productive activity. ... Language is the articulation of this active and changing experience, a dynamic and articulated social presence in the world. (Williams, 1977: 37–8)

The sense that language internalizes from all moments in the social process is very strong here, but Williams does not allow that internalization to rule the game. In this he follows Volosinov who insisted that

> the word-sign was less a fixed, neutral, nonreferential, arbitrary unit than it was an active, historically changing, constantly modified component of communication, its meaning conveyed by tones and contexts that were themselves always products of struggles and conflicts among classes, social groups, individuals, and discourses. (Palmer, 1990: 23)

III. The Internal Heterogeneity of Discourses

Let me elaborate on what I mean by "heterogeneity internalized within each moment" by reference to the moment of discourse.

Discourses vary from the expert discourses of science, medicine, and the professions, the particular working discourses that attach to institutions or divisions of labor in material production and reproduction, through to those more general discourses about society, self, and nature including those of parody, humor as well as of religion, nationhood and political identity. Such discourses are always porous with respect to each other and in the normal course of events we find ourselves switching from one discursive mode to another often without noticing it. Analysis reveals that such shifts imply all sort of slippages, ambiguities, and incoherences. But such slippages occur not only as we perform discursive and communicative acts with children, partners, the teacher, the doctor, the police officer, the gas-station attendant, or the boss. Slippages occur just as manifestly even within settings that in other respects seem relatively stable as regards the discursive rules that are supposed to operate. Scientists suddenly resort to metaphors drawn from sexual experience to code their understandings of supposedly objective facts, lawyers turn to literary narratives to substantiate their cases, and philosophers use the language of the market place to substantiate their metaphysical claims. Such slippages are, I shall argue particularly in chapters 7 and 13, particularly strongly manifest in environmental debates where conflicting metaphors of nature abound and where cool-headed scientists suddenly slip into a metaphorical market language about how "we may be running out of time" (an odd idea when one reads Stephen Hawking on "a short history" of that commodity) and passionately engaged nature romanticists and deep ecologists suddenly invoke the scientific authority of Lovelock's model of Gaia, quantum mechanics or the mathematical discourse of chaos theory as if it is all the same to them.

As a consequence it is not hard to see how contestation is always internalized within the discursive moment. Counter-hegemonic and dissident discourses (feminism, anti-racism, ecologism, postcolonialism, and the sexual subject are some of the contemporary favorites of the avant-garde in academia, for example) erupt to challenge hegemonic forms and it is out of such contestation that social change may flow. Intertextual analysis can illustrate how discursive effects mark out a complex "trace" across a variety of seemingly independent discursive domains, sometimes presaging disruptive effects but in other instances offering hidden supports to pervasive ideologies. Supposedly neutral scientific discourses, as we shall see in chapter 7, offer silent but strong support to capitalist free market and sexist ideologies, for example.

But fiercely fought struggles within the discursive moment do not necessarily carry over unmodified to other moments. Feminists may effectively change discourses about women, gender, and sexuality within academia (or, more likely, in limited domains such as history and the humanities, leaving the sciences broadly untouched) without seriously affecting deeply held fantasies, desires, and beliefs, material social practices (around child-rearing and housework for example), or the fundamentals of power relations. A mere change of words does little if the connotations and associations build back into identical configurations of meaning. "Niggers" have changed their appellation to "negroes" to "blacks" to "African-Americans" within the United States without removing racial prejudices. This does not mean that the struggle to change discourse is redundant, merely that such struggles function as a necessary but not sufficient moment for changes to occur elsewhere.

The internalization of heterogeneity within the moment of discourse creates abundant opportunities to sow confusion as well as enlightenment. Discourses can obfuscate, hide, and misrepresent relations to other "moments" within the flow of social life. I am not talking solely here about the technique of "the big lie," for there are all sorts of means by which a discourse can so limit or constrain vision (sometimes unwittingly) so as to prevent discussion of serious problems. Class discourses may hide serious gender and race issues and vice versa. And when under attack, we may defend ourselves by disrupting discourse deliberately as a means to defray power. Marx wrestled with this difficulty primarily under the rubric of "fetishism." But the objectification and reification of fluid social processes, the conversion of relations between people into relations between concepts as Williams so aptly put it, also have their part to play. This use of discourse to confuse rather than to enlighten, primarily attaches to the drive to defend some entrenched power position (practices, beliefs, institutions) or some space of resistance by preventing issues from being identified and articulated. In the recent debate over health care in the United States, for example, poll after poll of popular opinion showed a belief that universal coverage was desirable, that discriminatory practices against the sick and the infirm were unjust and that something had to be done to contain medical costs. The difficulty was to define a set of institutions and practices that could match up to that belief and here those who held a lot of political–economic power – insurance companies, hospitals, doctors, and the like – were in a position to launch a discursive offensive that so confused issues that nothing of moment was done. The discursive thrust was to block change – to use discourses as a means for nondecision-making – rather than to facilitate it.

Two issues arise out of what Foucault calls "the radical pluralism" and heterogeneity of discourses. First, how do different discourses relate to each other, if at all? Is there a common enough language to make any kind of common politics possible? Foucault correctly attacks the idea of some sort of "spirit of the age" or "weltanschauung" as far too simple-minded. He shows how different institutional power bases generate quite distinctive discourses appropriate to their own circumstances and disciplinary aims. But the identification of difference does not deny the possibility of identity, leaving the issue of what kind of identity, what kind of common language, might be possible in the midst of difference. I shall return to this question in what follows because if, for example, discursive differences over what is meant by "nature" and the "environment" are irreconcilable, then no common politics towards the environment are possible, leaving the whole question of our relation to "nature" as an effect of whatever discourse happens to be hegemonic in a particular time and place.

The second question is this: how can we reflect discursively on the power and value of the variety of theoretical discourses available within social and literary theory? The "dialectical map" of the social process proposed at the outset of this chapter can facilitate that sort of exercise and I now want to explore that map in somewhat greater detail.

IV. The General Character of Social Theories

Volosinov, in moving to a conclusion of his remarkable tract on *Marxism and the Philosophy of Language*, touches upon virtually all aspects of the six-point schema that I began by outlining:

> Without a way of revealing itself in language, be it only in inner speech, personality does not exist either for itself or for others. ... Language lights up the inner personality and its consciousness; language creates them and endows them with intricacy and profundity – and it does not work the other way. Personality is itself generated through language, not so much, to be sure, in the abstract forms of language, but rather in the ideological themes of language. Personality, from the standpoint of its inner, subjective content, is a theme of language, and this theme undergoes development and variation within the channel of the more stable constructions of language. Consequently, *a word is not an expression of inner personality; rather, inner personality is an expressed or inwardly impelled word.* And the word is an expression of social intercourse, of the social interaction of material personalities, of producers. The conditions of that thoroughly material intercourse are what determine and condition the kind of thematic and structural shape that the inner personality will receive at any given time and in any given environment... . The inner personality is generated along with language, in the concrete and comprehensive sense of the word, as one of its most important and profound themes. The generation of language, meanwhile, is a factor in the generative process of social communication, a factor inseparable from that communication and its material base. The material base determines differentiation in a society, its sociopolitical order; it organizes society hierarchically and deploys persons interacting within it. Thereby are the place, time, conditions, forms and means of verbal communication determined and, by the same token, the vicissitudes of the individual utterance in any given period in the development of language, the degree of its inviolability, the degree of differentiality in perceptions of its various aspects, the nature of its ideational and verbal individualization. ... (pp. 152–3)

Volosinov here locates the role of language (discourse) within some sort of "directionality of determination." In this instance, the directionality runs from social and material practices through language to personality and beliefs, making an otherwise incoherent inner life of the subject broadly responsive to external social forces and material activities. This is an excellent illustration of how fluid dialectical formulations (of the sort that Volosinov is generally committed to) get metamorphosed, often through the tricks of language itself, into more simplified causal schemas. But it also squarely faces up to the issue of *determination.* Where is the leveraging point for social change? A philosophy of internal relations left entirely to itself evades the question.

Within the history of social theory the long debate over where the true leverage point for social change might lie has frequently been reduced to the search for causal structure. The unthinking crystallization of fluid, dialectical, and dynamic formulations into causal schemas can, however, generate serious misunderstandings on the part of both critics and acolytes alike. Foucault, in his search for an emancipatory politics of the body, is said to concentrate on the nexus between discourses and power as the prime cause of whatever social change there is. Derrida, while arguing (correctly, in my view) that the text internalizes all, appears to suggest (or at least many of his acolytes do) that textual deconstructions (in the narrow sense) are inherently revolutionary. Weber is thought to focus on the relation between beliefs (primarily religious) and institution building, and Marx is usually read as treating everything else, at least in the celebrated "last instance," as derivative of material practices (productive forces). In each case one moment is converted into some sort of entity endowed with independent causal powers.

Each major theorist, it is true, tends to appeal to a particular structure of "permanences" (elements) that transfix relations between the various "moments" to give a structured order to a society. And there is often some sort of privileging of one or other moment as the locus of social change. Such a structured system seems to imprison the social process in an iron cage of reproductive circular causality (such as Marx's "logic of capital," Weber's "bureaucratic–technocratic rationality" or Spender's "prisonhouse of language"). The dilemma of social change is then typically posed in terms of how this system perpetuates itself through circular and cumulative causation and how it might break down, either under the weight of its own internal contradictions (Marx) or through some kind of voluntaristic eruption or erosion at the margins. In either case, we can reasonably ask where is the agency (the locus of power) that can transform the structure and liberate the social process from the permanences it has achieved?

But these causal versions, for which plenty of textual evidence can be found, entail serious misreadings of the much more complex arguments of most major theorists. The more dialectically minded simultaneously keep open an entirely different level of theorizing. In Marx's case, for example, much of the argument is precisely about how dynamic and fluid processes get transformed historically into "structured permanences" such as those inscribed within the political economy of capitalism and the logic of capital accumulation. And in looking for the locus of social change, Marx clearly states that it is in the realms of discourses and beliefs that we become conscious of political issues and "fight them out." Furthermore, this "fighting out" necessarily entails institution building (be it trade unions, political parties, state powers, hegemonic institutions that promote and regulate hegemonic discourses, etc.) as a fundamental moment on the path towards transformed material practices and social relations. The search for alternative forms of political–economic power operates in Marx's thought and practice across all the "moments" of social action. Marx, in both his analytic work and politics moves freely from one moment to another. The famous "last instance" of the material practices of production and reproduction, then operates, as it were, as both the *starting point* and the *measuring point* of achievement – the point where we can tangibly judge what has been accomplished (much as money operates as the measuring rod of achievement for the circulation of capital through its various metamorphoses as money, commodities, and production). Material practices occupy their key position because Marx believes that sensual interaction with the world is the privileged grounding for all forms of human knowledge and for all under-standings of what it means to "be" in the world. And Marx is not alone in this belief – it grounds much of western science, for example. Material practices are the measuring point precisely because it is only in terms of the sensual interaction with the world that we can re-figure what it now means to "be" in the world.

But does this imply that the moment of material practices is the sole locus of meaningful social change? This would appear to be a fundamental tenet of Marx's historical materialism. Did he not explicitly argue, along with Engels in *The German Ideology*, that the materialist conception of history:

> relies on expounding the real process of production – starting from the material production of life itself – and comprehending the form of intercourse connected with and created by this mode of production, i.e. civil society in its various stages, as the basis of all history; describing it in its action as the state, and also explaining how all the different theoretical products and forms of conscious-ness, religion, philosophy, morality, etc., etc., arise from it, and tracing the process of their formation from that basis; thus the whole thing can, of course, be depicted in its totality (and therefore, too, the reciprocal action of these various sides on one another).

The internal tension in this passage is obvious enough. What begins as a one-way causal schema starting with the material base is converted into reciprocal action of different "moments" within the totality in the parentheses. And with this totality the moment of language has a key role to play. Here is Marx in the *German Ideology*:

> Only now, after having considered four moments, four aspects of the funda-mental historical relationships, do we find that man also possesses "conscious-ness"; but even so, not inherent, not "pure" consciousness. From the start the "spirit" is afflicted with the curse of being "burdened" with matter, which here

makes its appearance in the form of agitated layers of air, sound, in short of language. Language is as old as men, and for that reason is really beginning to exist for me personally as well; for language, like consciousness, only arises from the need, the necessity of intercourse with other men."

And in the *Eighteenth Brumaire*, Marx depicts the relation between the imaginary and language as vital to political action:

> Men make their history, but not of their own free will; not under circumstances they themselves have chosen but under the given and inherited circumstances with which they are directly confronted. The tradition of the dead generations weighs like a nightmare on the minds of the living. And, just when they appear to be engaged in the revolutionary transformation of themselves and their material surroundings, in the creation of something which does not yet exist, precisely at such epochs of revolutionary crisis they timidly conjure up spirits of the past to help them; they borrow their names, slogans and costumes so as to stage a new world-historical scene in this venerable disguise and borrowed language. Luther put on the mask of the apostle Paul; the Revolution of 1789–1814 draped itself alternatively as the Roman republic and the Roman empire; and the revolution of 1848 knew no better than to parody at some points 1789 and at others the revolutionary traditions of 1793–5. In the same way, the beginner who has learned a new language always retranslates it into his mother tongue: he can only be said to express himself in it freely when he can manipulate it without reference to the old, and when he forgets his original language while using the new one.

This preoccupation with language is a persistent theme in Marx's work as he probes the fetishistic conceptions of bourgeois political economy and seeks to substitute an entirely different language of political–economy. Through a deconstruction of the monetized language of the commodity and of profit and the creation of an alternative language that emphasizes exploitation, Marx evidently hoped to use the power of language, and of naming, to a political end. His purpose is to make us stare into the abyss of capitalism's contradictory and destructive logic as an economic system, while understanding how its political–economic power is replicated not only by social material practices of production–distribution–consumption, but also by its hegemonic powers with respect to ideology (discourses), institutions (the state apparatus but also institutions of learning, law and religion). Marx moves freely between "moments" in both his theoretical works (like *Capital*) and his more overtly political writings. Material practices are not the only leverage for change, but they are the moment upon which all other effects and forces (including those within material practices themselves) must converge in order for change to be registered as real (experiential and material) rather than remain as imagined and fictitious. A nonmechanical and dialectical reading of Marx thus reveals a rather different understanding of his argument compared to readings seeking causal structure.

Foucault is similarly liable to misinterpretation when reduced to a causal schema. At first sight, he does seem to dwell on the determinative power of discourses as a privileged moment in his scheme of things. But his more general argument seems to be that "power" operates through discursively informed and institutionally based social practices that are primarily organized as disciplinary powers exerted on the body. Discourses form through these relations between power, social practices, and institutions, internalizing their forms and powers from these other moments in the social process. The moment of discourse gains its seemingly autonomous disciplinary powers with respect to social life to the degree that there is amnesia with respect to the processes that both form and reinforce it. The function of discourse is to create "truths" that are in fact "effects of truth" within the discourse rather than the universal truths they claim to be. Such "effects of truth" become particularly pernicious, in Foucault's view, precisely because they emanate from institutions (the asylum, the hospital, the prison) which operate as incarnations of power. His main aim is to undermine these "effects of truth" and to show how truth in discourse is always an internalized effect of other moments in the social process. The appeal of this argument lies in the way it moves from one moment to another showing how each moment internalizes effects of others. Nor are references to the moment of desires/beliefs/values lacking in his work, though he preferred (perhaps out of deference to Lacan) in his historical studies to produce an "archeology" of knowledge on the grounds that it was impossible ever to rediscover essential truths about desires. Like Marx, he accepts that we are always confined to the world of material effects, though he broadens the notion of materiality to incorporate past discourses. So while there are innumerable passages in which it is possible to discern in Foucault a tendency towards "discursive determinism" of the sort that says we are forever imprisoned by the discourses available to us, the passages where he makes such arguments invariably contain more than casual hints of ambiguity, in part through his insistence on a radical pluralism, an internalized heterogeneity, within the discursive moment itself, but also by appeal to some moment that is, as it were, outside of any logic of determination at all.

5
Historical Agency and the Loci of Social Change

How do predominantly anti-humanistic theories, of the sort that Foucault and Marx advance, account for the directionality and form of social change? Some sort of agency, residing somewhere within the social process, must exist that can disrupt the seemingly automatic reproduction of the repressive social orders typically depicted in social theory.

I. On Residuals and Marginality

Most social theories and an important subset of literary theories adopt a resolutely anti-humanist tone, frequently making it appear as if the "subject" (the individual person) has little or no autonomy outside of the system of socially and historically constituted internal relations that forms that subject. While the underlying explanation of the directionality and patterning of change may vary from one theorist to another, the overall sense of imprisonment of the individual within the socializing process is very strong. Faced with this situation, theorists have frequently been forced by the logic of their own arguments to identify what I shall call a "residual" or a "surplus" within some moment(s) of the social process, that somehow escape the dominant logic, the disciplinary apparatus, the dead weight of history, the problematics of linguistic incarceration, or whatever. Recall, for example, Williams' recounting of Glyn's thoughts as he roams the Welsh mountains:

> At his books and maps in the library, or in the house in the valley, there was a common history which could be translated anywhere, in a community of evidence and rational inquiry. Yet he had only to move on the mountains for a different kind of mind to assert itself: stubbornly native and local, yet reaching beyond to a wider common flow, where touch and breadth replaced record and analysis; not history as narrative but stories as lives.

Williams was hardly the archetypal anti-humanist. But his concerns with determination, and particularly with the power of historically constituted language put him on the borderland (always, it seems, his preferred position) between the humanistic and the anti-humanistic traditions. But what is important in this passage (and there are many such in Williams' writing), is the insistence that there is something that cannot be captured within the dominant forms of a moment (in this case language). This "something" is "stubbornly" resistant to being absorbed into any structured logic of relational determinations. Adorno advances a similar idea. For him, according to Coles (1993: 232), magic and myth:

> tend to open up a space beyond the immediately given for the acknowledgement of non-identity, of more than we currently grasp. The world ceases to be an immutable force pressing upon the self, and the self's grasp of the world ceases to have the character of an immutable and exhaustive cage as myth acknowledges a surplus that transcends our experience, into which both the self and the world might move.

Perhaps the most telling example is that of Foucault, whose resolute anti-humanism is hardly in doubt, but who located the residual and open point of resistance as bodily pleasures, while simultaneously depicting the political history of "the distinctive ways in which various successive power/knowledge regimes institute the body as an object within their respective techniques and practices" (Fraser, 1989: 61). The effect is to make the body the primary site of contestation in the social order, the implication being that there is always something residual in the politics of the body that is outside of the regimes of control that are applied to it, no matter how totalizing and how draconian those regimes may be. The particular choice of the body as a site of resistance derived in large degree from Foucault's personal preoccupations, but by the same token, much of the influence of his argument derives from a widespread sympathy with the view that repressions on the body deserve to be resisted and that the politics of the body is where revolutionary action may well reside.

Kristeva, to take another example, argues her way out of the determinacy of the symbolic order of the father (the phallus), by appeal to the realm of the semiotic, which attaches to the pre-Oedipal maternally oriented phase of a child's life. That phase is ungendered and, precisely for that reason, exists as the only ground for real as opposed to superficial challenges to the symbolic order. While women have privileged access to that realm by virtue of their maternal functions, the realm is not closed to men (they, too, had a pre-Oedipal phase). Traces of this semiotic moment persist as a permanent subterranean challenge to the symbolic order. Kristeva locates them in, for example, the poetry of Mallarmé and Rimbaud, as well as in feminist theory itself. It is only out of this semiotic realm, she argues, that truly revolutionary consciousness can arise.

Phenomenologists, on the other hand, tend to locate the moment of indeter-

existential moment of experience itself. While Heidegger saw language as master of us, the experiential moment of what he called "presencing" – appropriating some facet of the world into one's own being – was the potential site of that surplus which could be the source of an alternative way of being in the world, outside of the technical–scientific–economic rationality that was otherwise threatening to rule over the lifeworld of the individual.

There is, however, a difficulty with this approach. The suspicion lurks that what is actually being talked about is a way to escape from the power of particular theorizations rather than anything that has to do with the processes of social change occurring in actual historical–geographical situations. Antihumanistic theorists, it appears, dig themselves out of the difficulties they have themselves created by finding some convenient corner of "freedom" that is outside of their own system of determination. There are, thus, some readings of Marx (Gouldner's being by far the most explicit) that see two distinctive Marxisms – that of imprisonment in the logic of capital and that of voluntaristic revolutionary action. If this is the case, then a serious question arises as to whether the locus of change (in Marx's case in organized working-class action) is really there or simply a necessary fiction that attaches to the theoretical argument. I shall later provide grounds for refuting this interpretation, but the question of locating agency is so pervasive that we must perforce cover all bases. In addition, the turn to a "residual" or "surplus" within some moment also has the unhappy habit of itself becoming the sole cause, the sole locus of agency for change within the social system. Let me illustrate with two case studies.

1. The Case of the Lacanian Residual

The first case is drawn from that most difficult of all "moments" in the flow of sociality: that which concerns the realms of human belief, desires, fantasies, fears, dreams, and values. Since Freud, this has become the privileged terrain of psychoanalysis. A psychoanalytic understanding of desire and its realization/ denial/repression is now frequently privileged as an irreducible "moment" of freedom and as, therefore, the "true" locus of change.

Consider, for example, Zizek's (1993) Lacanian analysis of the unexpected revival of nationalism in eastern Europe in the wake of the collapse of Communist rule. The fundamental thesis of Lacan, Zizek holds (p. 118)

> is that what we call "reality" constitutes itself against the background of ... an exclusion of some traumatic Real. This is precisely what Lacan has in mind when he says that fantasy is the ultimate support of reality: "reality" stabilizes itself when some fantasy frame of a "symbolic bliss" closes off the view into the abyss of the Real. Far from being a kind of dreamlike cobweb that prevents us from "seeing reality as it effectively is," fantasy constitutes what we call reality: the most common bodily "reality" is constituted via a detour through the cobweb

of fantasy. In other words we pay a price to gain access to "reality": something – the real of the trauma – must be "repressed."

Two immediate conclusions are adduced. First, "reality" is always framed by a fantasy, i.e., for something real to be experienced as part of "reality" it must "fit the preordained coordinates of our fantasy space" (p. 43) and secondly, discursive activity is meaningless independent of its fantasy support (p. 213). Zizek insists that fantasy constitutes a "hard kernel" that resists reduction either to the symbolic orders of discursive activities or to any supposedly "objective" qualities of reality. "The Real," says Zizek, in a passage that echoes Williams is "a surplus, a hard kernel which resists any process of modeling, simulation, or metaphoricization."

A strong distinction is invoked here between three "moments" in the social process – realities of experience and of discourses and the fantasy beliefs that support them. Zizek pursues these differences to look at how the ideology of nationhood, the formation of an entity called nation, occurs:

> This paradoxical existence of an entity which "is" only insofar as subjects believe (in the other's belief) in its existence is the mode of being proper to ideological causes: the "normal" order of causality is here inverted, since it is the Cause itself which is produced by its effects (the ideological practices it animates). Significantly, it is precisely at this point that the difference between Lacan and "discursive idealism" emerges most forcefully: Lacan does not reduce the (national, etc.) Cause to a performative effect of the discursive practices that refer to it. The pure discursive effect does not have enough "substance" to compel the attraction proper to a Cause – and the Lacanian terms of the strange "substance" which must be added so that a Cause obtains its positive ontological consistency, the only substance acknowledged by psychoanalysis, is of course *enjoyment* (as Lacan states it explicitly in *Encore*). A nation *exists* only as long as its specific *enjoyment* continues to be materialized in a set of social practices and transmitted through national myths that structure these practices. To emphasize in a "deconstructionist" mode that Nation is not a biological or transhistorical fact but a contingent discursive construction, an overdetermined result of textual practices, is thus misleading: such an emphasis overlooks the remainder of some real, nondiscursive kernel of enjoyment which must be present for Nation *qua* discursive entity-effect to achieve its ontological consistency.

There is a lot going on in this passage. Note first how the construction of the "institution" of nationhood understood as a ritualized "entity" (or permanence) is linked to social practices that materialize a specific relation between discourse and fantasy/belief/desire. At least four of the "moments" identified in figure 4.1 are invoked. Social relationships (class and gender hierarchies, lateral distinctions, divisions of labor) are ignored, however, and the population is treated as homogeneous when it plainly is not. The weak justification for such an assumption rests on the statement that nationhood is about subjects' beliefs in other subjects' beliefs. The parallel to Anderson's (1983) interpretation of nation as an "imagined community" is striking. Power is likewise missing from the argument, but then Zizek's point is that it was precisely at the moment of revolution, in 1989, that power (understood psychoanalytically as a "master signifier") appeared to be vacated (even though, as Zizek is quick to admit, it "really" was not); the question he tries to answer is how that empty space of the "missing master signifier" got to be filled by nationalism. These are all fascinating questions.

The final step in the argument is where the difficulties begin. It is one thing to identify a "stubbornly recalcitrant" residual in the psychoanalytic "moment," but quite another to deny any such power to any other moment (such as discourse or material practices). What then follows is a reductionist psychoanalytic interpretation of resurgent eastern European nationalism based on "enjoyment" as an expression of human fantasy and desire. The forces internalized within this one particular "moment" in the social process become the locus of social determination. Posed primarily as an alternative to other theorizations, Zizek's argument appears primarily as a means to escape from them, rather than as a cogent analysis of how a nationalist politics – its institutions and practices, its discourses and power relations, its social relations, as well as its "fantasy space" – is actually taking root in daily life.

2. Voices from the Margins

One of the least admirable traits of political argument in recent times has been the romantic turn in radical politics towards "voices from the margins" as somehow more authentic, less corrupt, and therefore more revolutionary. The idea is that there are those who are so radically "other," so radically outside of the dominant systems of determination, so marginal in relation to the iron cage of circular and cumulative causation, that they and only they have the capacity to see through the fetishisms that fool the rest of us. They and only they have the capacity to generate radical change.

In part this romantic turn to the marginalized "other" for political salvation derives from a certain frustration at the inability of traditional movements (such as those of the working class) to foment radical change. The thesis some now advance is that the fantasy space of the working classes is so thoroughly occupied by the imaginaries superimposed by capitalist commodification, the discursive field of working-class political culture is so dominated by a ruthlessly exploitative mass media, and the institutions of potential political resistance so bureaucratized and beholden to and incorporated within capitalist interests, that the working class (even if such a collective entity is conceived to exist any more) has become nothing more than an appendage of capitalist accumulation in its culture, its politics and its subjectivity. Its capacity to be an agent of revolutionary change, so the argument goes, has been severely compromised if not totally eviscerated. *Ergo*, the search for an alternative agent of historical change. While this is an argument I do not share, it is not one that can be dogmatically dismissed.

But there are other reasons for the romantic turn towards voices from the margins as a vehicle for political salvation at the center. Zizek suggests, for example, that the Christian tradition of believing that authentic nobility of purpose somehow attaches to conditions of total degradation (such as those that put Christ on the cross) carries with it the presumption that it is only the impoverished, the marginalized, and the repressed who have the capacity to transcend their state, tell us plain truths, and lead us into the promised land. "Transcendence" is the operative word here as is the vision that true nobility can exist only in the midst of degradation. It then comes as a bitter disappointment to discover that the impoverished, the marginalized, and the oppressed often lack that extraordinary and moving nobility that can occasionally be found and that they often aspire not to a radically different social order, but to one that gives them a piece of what the privileged already have. Movements of marginalized "others" are often held to a far higher standard of moral purpose and political commitment than are those of political activism at the center.

But there are more solid reasons to take seriously the question of marginality as a point of escape from imprisonment in dominant discourses. Raymond Williams (see chapter 1) actively used his positionality on "the border" as a fundamental resource with which to challenge dominant ideas. Says Di Michele (1993: 27):

> one gets the impression that Williams did always live *on* the border, in a sort of metaphorical "border country" of his own which allowed him to look deep inside, with great advantage, both at England and at Wales. He could look, as it were, from *there* and from *here* simultaneously at his two worlds, which never appeared to him as two landscapes or places; they were in fact landscapes "with figures," living worlds and authentic communities, where people were socially and culturally present with their various types of fulfillment and despair, with their crises and successes, with their myths and beliefs, with their "full rich life." From that privileged "border country" experience, Williams ... could conceive the idea of a multifaceted world-view which let him discover significant relations between people, which are not naturally "given" but have to be consciously pursued and brought out on the surface by tenacious, even harmful search and effort. These relationships must be lived and felt, in the first place; they must be worked out by the impartial and neutral observer, in the second place.

What is at work here is a crucial ability (attached to the thesis of militant particularism in dialogue with universalizing politics) to use what we now call "standpoint" (and Williams frequently resorted to that term) and location (place) to create a critical space from which to challenge hegemonic discourses, including even, as we saw in chapter 1, those discourses about the "proletariat" and "socialism" that were dedicated to the emancipation of a marginalized and disempowered working class. But the borderland space that Williams defined for himself had rather more complex functions in his life, work, and thought. It was in part an actual material place of refuge (either as recorded in memory or in day-to-day active experience), partially outside of the embrace of overwhelmingly powerful social processes and social relations. This experiential realm underpinned a "metaphorical" point of resistance outside of the language of dominant and hegemonic discourses. Such a location provides a unique point of resistance beyond the reach of some all-embracing and determinate theory (a unique "structure of feeling" outside of external forces of determination). Here was the ultimate refuge of a counter-hegemonic politics that could never be taken away, the residual place that could never be tamed (in much the same fashion that Foucault appealed to the human body). This was the space from which alternative discourses, politics, imaginaries, could emanate.

Bell Hooks (1990) resorts to a similar line of argument. In a poignant essay on "Choosing the Margin as a Space of Radical Openness," Bell Hooks traces her "journey from small town Southern black life," overcoming the repressions of home and community ("mama and daddy aggressively silencing me ... the censorship of black communities") to arrive at the university, all along the way being forced to struggle against "efforts to silence my coming to voice." Along the way she had to confront the repressions of language:

> I was just a girl coming slowly into womanhood when I read Adrienne Rich's words, "This is the oppressor's language, yet I need it to talk to you." This language that enabled me to attend graduate school, to write a dissertation, to speak at job interviews, carries the scent of oppression. Language is also a place of struggle.... Dare I speak to oppressed and oppressor in the same voice? Dare I speak to you in a language that will move beyond the boundaries of domination – a language that will not bind you, fence you in, or hold you?

She learned to transgress boundaries, and to push against oppressions "set by race, sex, and class domination." It was a journey full of pain. "Coming to voice" entailed "intense personal emotional upheaval regarding place, identity, desire:"

> Everywhere we go there is pressure to silence our voices, to coopt and under-mine them. Mostly, of course, we are not there. We never "arrive" or "can't stay." Back in those spaces where we come from, we kill ourselves in despair, drowning in nihilism, caught in poverty, in addiction, in every postmodern mode of dying that can be named. Yet when we few remain in that "other" space, we are often too isolated, too alone. We die there too. Those of us who live, who "make it," passionately holding on to aspects of that "downhome" life we do not intend to lose while simultaneously seeking new knowledge and experience, invent spaces of radical openness. Without such spaces we would not survive.... For me this space of radical openness is a margin – a profound edge.

It is from this space in the margin – "a site of creativity and power" – that Bell Hooks shapes a radical intervention:

> This marginality [is] a central location for the production of a counter-hegemonic discourse that is not just found in words but in habits of being and in the way one lives. As such, I was not speaking of a marginality one wishes to lose – to give up or surrender as part of moving into the center – but rather of a site one stays in, clings to even, because it nourishes one's capacity to resist. It offers to one the possibility of radical perspective from which to see and create, to imagine alternatives, new worlds.

But what kinds of new worlds? Resistance to what? The oppressions of race, gender, and class? To a monetized economy and a commoditized culture? To the thousand and one postmodern ways of dying? To a superimposed and alienating way of life? To hegemonic discourses (including those proclaiming the emancipation of blacks and women)? The answer surely has to be all of the above. As with Williams, the focus on language is powerfully connected to the way life gets lived and things get done, the way social relations are experienced and power gets exercised. Language (discourse) is a place of struggle. But discursive struggles waged in isolation from the historical geography of lived lives and dominant power relations are meaningless. "This is not," Bell Hooks insists, "a mythic notion of marginality. It comes from lived experience." The margin is not simply a metaphor, but an imaginary that has real underpinnings. From that location a powerful condemnation of supposedly emancipatory discourses shaped at the center can be launched:

> I am waiting for them to stop talking about the "other," to stop even describing how important it is to be able to speak about difference. ... Often this speech about the "other" is also a mask, an oppressive talk hiding gaps ... [it] annihilates, erases: "No need to hear your voice when I can talk about you better than you can speak about yourself. No need to hear your voice. Only tell me about your pain. I want to know your story. And then I will tell it back to you in a new way. Tell it back to you in such a way that it has become mine, my own. Re-writing you, I write myself anew. I am still author, authority. I am still the colonizer, the speaking subject, and you are now at the center of my talk.

Confronted with such colonizing discourses, it is not hard to imagine Bell Hooks, like Spivak, preferring Derrida's resort to the Leibnizian conceit of "rendering delirious the voice of the other within oneself." But Bell Hooks here challenges hegemony in discourse by appeal to an experiential nexus (of material practices, rituals, social, and power relations) in which dreams and desires find expression outside of that permitted by some dominant discourse:

Stop. We greet you as liberators. This "we" is that "us" in the margins, that "we" who inhabit marginal space that is not a site of domination but a place of resistance. Enter that space. ...

The internalization of these effects, mobilized and constructed at the margin, within discourse is what makes language a place of struggle. The idea of standpoint, of location, and of place is very strong here:

I had to leave that space I called home to move beyond boundaries, yet I needed also to return there. ... Indeed, the very meaning of "home" changes with the experience of decolonization, of radicalization. At times, home is nowhere. At times, one knows only extreme estrangement and alienation. Then home is no longer just one place. It is locations. Home is that place which enables and promotes varied and everchanging perspectives, a place where one discovers new ways of seeing reality, frontiers of difference.

The transitions at work in this passage need elucidation. Is there a movement from a real "space" one might call "home" (a secure but in some ways restrictive environment in which to grow and become according to strict rules) to a metaphorical "place" that is to open to a different kind of becoming, open to the multiple forces pulsating throughout the world? And if so, how is this metaphorical place constituted? There are two dangers. The first is to slide into the Leibnizian conceit in the name of radical openness, to transform that metaphorical place into a windowless space supposedly sufficient unto itself because it internalizes effects from outside [cf. Deleuze's (1993) considerations on Leibniz]. The second is to slide into acceptance of a postmodern world of fragmentation and unresolvable difference, to become a mere point of convergence of everything there is as if openness is by definition radical. Bell Hooks appears to head in that direction: "one confronts and accepts dispersal and fragmentation as part of the construction of a new world order that reveals more fully where we are, who we can become, an order that does not demand forgetting."

The purpose of these two brief considerations on Zizek and Bell Hooks is first to examine how the idea of a "residual" or a "surplus" somehow outside of or beyond the hegemonic rules of determination gets set up. Once located, that surplus is used to identify the locus of agency, of resistance, of an organizing force that can change the hegemonic directionality of historical–geographical change. In recent years this free point from which to resist dominant practices has increasingly been located "on the margins." Voices from the margin – and in this regard Bell Hooks' chosen location is emblematic – become those to whom we are urged to pay the closest attention as the harbingers of serious social change. So where *is* the locus of agency to give change direction and how is it that spatiality is in some form or other increasingly invoked in the argument?

II. The Locus of Change

The simplest answer to the first question – where is the locus of agency? – is everywhere. This is not as unhelpful an answer as it might at first seem. To begin with, the presumption from a dialectical/process-based and historical materialist view of the world is that it is not change *per se* that has to be explained, but the forces that hold down change and/or which give it a certain directionality. There is no single moment within the social process devoid of the capacity for transformative activity – a new imaginary; a new discourse arising out of some peculiar hybrid of others; new rituals or institutional configurations; new modes of social relating; new material practices and bodily experiences; new political power relations arising out of their internalized contradictions. Each and every one of these moments is full to the brim with transformative potentialities. Since divisions of labor attach unevenly across the different moments, individuals with special expertise in, say, the discursive realm or the political institutional realm, always have the possibility to exercise some kind of agency for change even within their own limited situations.

But several interesting questions then follow:

1. How are all of these diverse potentialities and possibilities controlled and disciplined to produce permanences, the circular causal structures and systems that we daily encounter in that entity we call society? How do the stabilities of a historically and geographically achieved social order crystallize out from within the flux and fluidity of social processes? Historical materialism does address that question. Marx's *Grundrisse* is an extraordinary exercise in such a form of enquiry, looking in detail, for example, at how money arises out of exchange and capital out of the circulation of money. He did not complete that analysis but others, following in his footsteps and broadly using the method that he pioneered, have told a far more detailed story of capitalism's origins.

2. How are "correspondence rules" established between the different moments to guarantee the stability of a given social order? Marx's general argument is particularly strong on this point, even though it is susceptible to a rather misleading mechanical and causal interpretation. Discourses, imaginaries, powers, social relations, institutions, and material practices must become differentiations within the totality of capitalism understood not as a thing, but as an on-going social process that traverses all moments of the social process. Marx's beginning point was material practices and the experiential world of daily life and labor. But he then delves into the necessary relations between all the different moments that help keep the social order stable (stable here does not mean changeless, for capitalism reproduces itself only through change, though only of a certain sort).

3. Are there internal contradictions within this process such that tensions between and within the moments become a point of leverage for change? Marx certainly thought this was the case within capitalism. Such contradictions automatically turn capitalism into an internal battleground of conflicting forces whose balance of powers can never exactly be predicted, leaving the trajectory of historical change open. The class contradiction between capital and labor, the tendency to produce crises of over-accumulation/devaluation of capital (coupled with the disintegration of a global capitalism into warring geopolitical blocs), the need to guarantee freedom of speech and enquiry as part of a need to preserve entrepreneurial creativity and initiative, while repressing dissident voices ... these are all major contradictions within capitalism. The task of historical materialist enquiry is then to establish where the main contradictions lie in particular historical–geographical situations and how they might be interlinked. In the *Eighteenth Brumaire*, for example, Marx looks at the way certain contradictions become salient only to become buried within other contradictions – the overaccumulation/devaluation crisis of 1847–8 reveals the central capital–labor contradiction only to be displaced by state repressions into an internalized crisis of bourgeois legality, legitimacy, and institutions.

4. Marx was deeply suspicious of any idea of a "surplus" or a "residual" *outside of* the overall flow of determination within social processes. Because of the contradictions, there are innumerable leverage points *within* the system that can be seized upon by dissident groups or individuals to try to redirect social change down this or that path. There are always weak links. Historical materialist enquiry seeks to understand how weak links formed and were exploited in the past to bring the social system into its present state, where weak links in the edifice of societal reproduction might now exist, and how they might be used by certain kinds of agents for what kinds of social ends.

5. So who and where are the agents of social change? Again, the simplest answer is everyone, everywhere. Everyone who lives, acts, and talks is implicated. This is precisely Williams' point concerning the perpetual reconstitution of language through use by individuals. But why do certain individuals or groups come to view the social order as unduly repressive and requiring radical change? This is a more restrictive question. And how do they get mobilized individually or collectively to affect the trajectory of change? These are far more difficult questions. The purpose of historical materialist analysis is to try and understand how individuals and groups came to understand themselves and their reality and act in accordance with that understanding. There is much that is fortuitous and contingent in this, precisely because of the contradictions in which all agents find themselves embroiled and the resultant heterogeneity in how to understand oneself and one's reality. The effect is to make political–economic change an unpredictable (and far from mechanical) affair.

The dance of historical change becomes as vulnerable to the sexual whims and fantasies of aging dictators, for example, as it does to coherent mass movements. And even when mass movements are at work, the determination of what contradictions are seen as primary is always up for grabs. Politics must engage with *all* moments of the social process simultaneously, establishing its own counter-coherences within and correspondence rules between discourses, institutions, social relations, power politics, and the imaginary and material practices. Given the slippages that can occur between these moments, and the difficulties of translation that I earlier invoked there is nothing automatically predictable about these relations either. It is, therefore, just as important to engage with the imaginary of the worker as with the experiential world of life and labor. Struggle can never locate itself exclusively or even primarily at one moment within the social process.

All of this must sound, and in some respects is, profoundly at odds with traditional views of Marx's historical materialism. Yet it seems to me the only conceivable way to view the question of agency and locus of change in a genuinely dialectical and historical materialist manner. So what remains is the problem of how to reconcile these views with some of the more obvious features of Marx's argument – in particular the commitment to revolutionary class struggle – that on the surface appear so incompatible with them.

The problem for Marx is not to explain change because change is the norm and stability the rare occurrence. Nor is Marx's general problem one of explaining how particular groups, interests, and powers "seize the time" and turn this or that aspect of the social process to their own advantage or lose out in a particular high stakes game (as happened in France between 1848 and 1852, for example). What Marx was interested in was *revolution.* He was concerned to understand how the *totality* of the social ordering that constituted capitalism could change; how, in short, capitalism might be overthrown. But that also meant understanding how capitalism as a social ordering could preserve itself through changes (technological, administrative, discursive) and through all sorts of struggles (wars, civil rights movements, colonial encounters, ethnic conflicts, etc.). This converges directly on the single most important question: what are the necessary and sufficient conditions to transform the structure of capitalist social ordering to produce an alternative kind of society called "socialist" or "Communist"? Marx's conclusion was quite simple and, I think, indubitably correct: the only way to transcend capitalism was through a class struggle waged against capitalist class and their associated interests across all moments of the social process.

So the question for Marx is not who is going to be an historical agent because all of us are. But how can one kind of collective agent crystallize out as an overwhelming political force that can accomplish this revolutionary task. The question of agency is defined in terms of a political commitment. But why should we commit ourselves to that politics rather than some other? The answer is simple enough. The structure of permanences and internalized relations secured within the capitalist social order is, in Marx's view, extraordinarily damaging to the lives of untold millions; it is immoral and unjust, at the same time as it is life-threatening to the human species and a travesty of denial of our species potential. There is more than a little romanticism incorporated in that answer (particularly evocation of a species potential), but without that sort of imaginary as an alternative, the reality of human destitution, impoverishment and degradation in the midst of plenty becomes unbearable.

There are, of course, all sorts of arguments to be set against Marx. The class opposition has never properly constituted itself as a coherent force and even when it has achieved some modicum of power it has not radically transformed matters. Even if there were historical periods and geographical places where class opposition to capitalism congealed it has now effectively been dissipated. Above all, the single-minded pursuit of class questions does not allow of a proper consideration of other important historical oppressions on the basis of gender, sexual preference, lifestyle, racial, ethnic, or religious identities and affiliations, geographical region, cultural configuration, and the like. There are certain truths to all of these objections and many circumstances in which the intertwining of, say, racial, gender, geographical, and class issues creates all sorts of complexities that make it imperative for several sets of oppressions to be addressed.

But the converse complaint must also be registered: those who reject Marx's political commitment and the notion of class agency that necessarily attaches to it in effect turn their backs on his depiction of the human destitution, degradation and denial that lie at capitalism's door and become complicitous as historical agents with the reproduction of the particular set of permanences that capitalism has tightly fashioned out of otherwise open, fluid, and dynamic social processes.

Put that bluntly, the force of Marx's political commitment makes many people nervous. Foucault (1984: 46) probably speaks for many when he writes:

> This work done at the limits of ourselves must, on the one hand, open up a realm of historical enquiry, and, on the other, put itself to the test of reality, of contemporary reality, both to grasp the points where change is possible and desirable, and to determine the precise form this change should take. This means that the historical ontology of ourselves must turn away from all projects that claim to be global or radical. In fact we know from experience that the claim to escape from the system of contemporary reality so as to produce the overall programs of another society, of another way of thinking, another culture, another vision of the world, has led only to the return of the most dangerous traditions.

The warning is salutary and deserves to be taken seriously. But the turning away from all projects that claim to be global or radical is deeply damaging. It leads

Foucault to prefer projects that are "always partial and local" but then hope these realize generality in a different way. All of which brings us back close to Williams' idea of militant particularism and the second general question I earlier posed: how is it that "the partial and the local" – spatiality (in some guise or other) – is now so frequently appealed to as the locus of residual forces that can exercise real power over the trajectory of social change?

III. Towards a Theory of Historical–Geographical Materialism

In recent years, the extraordinary, but now quite widespread claim, has been advanced that "space" defines the realm of difference, of otherness, the uncontrolled, the unpredictable, the unexpected, and, hence, the locus of agency and the leveraging point for emancipatory politics. Space defines the untamable residual to all metatheories of the social process. These are very strong claims that deserve critical scrutiny. They presage the question of how to understand the geography of difference, the spatiality of theorizations, in relation to the issues of agency and social determination. Here, for example, is Knorr-Cetina's (1994) description of those movements within sociology that "imply a rupture with Enlightenment thinking" and "a negation of many of the definitive features that have been associated with the modern." These movements center on microanalysis as:

> a detailed description of social episodes through means such that ethnography, discourse analysis or visual methods. ... Most importantly, microanalyses have discovered, emphasized and described the *local* nature of modern life; the whole body of microanalytic research rests on localizing concepts, epitomized by terms such as "local order" and "indexicality" in ethnomethodology, "situation", "setting" and the "stage" metaphor in symbolic interactionism, "province" of meaning and "situatedness" in phenomenology, etc. The whole microanalytic revolution is a revolution not about what is small, but about the *spatialization of experience.*

This same sentiment can be arrived at from a quite different direction. When Foucault (1984: 56) argues that the dialectic is "a way of evading the always open and hazardous reality of conflict by reducing it to a Hegelian skeleton," he invokes a version of the dialectic that cannot "distinguish among events" and "differentiate the networks and levels to which they belong." Escape from the teleologies of Hegel and Marx can then most readily be achieved by appeal to the particularities of spatiality (network, levels, connections). This accords with the rather widespread view, which Ross (1988: 8) attributes to Feuerbach, that time is "the privileged category of the dialectician, because it excludes and subordinates where space tolerates and coordinates." Within geography we also find advocates of this view. Sayer (1985), for example, argues that time is the realm of necessity (and hence the quite properly privileged domain of the abstractions of social theory) whereas space is the realm of contingency (and therefore quite properly the privileged domain of particularist empirical geographical enquiry).

Let me put my cards on the table. I am resolutely opposed to the claim that "space" is outside of social determination or theorization and even more emphatically that it is somehow outside of the dialectic. Nor do I accept – at least without considerable qualification – the political equivalent; the idea that "spaces on the margin" are *the* sites of radical openness and revolutionary possibility. This is not to say that liberated spaces are impossible to construct, that social constructions of spatiality cannot be used, in either a real or metaphorical sense, as strategic elements within revolutionary politics. Nor, most emphatically, does it mean that "voices from the margin" are not worth listening to or irrelevant to political struggle against capitalist domination. Indeed, as I shall later hope to show, a spatializing of political strategies (geopolitics) is crucial for any form of emancipatory politics. But I do challenge the turn to the supposed *indeterminacy* of spatiality as the moment of freedom, the site of resistance, and therefore the seedbed of social change. To think in such terms is, I shall later argue (see part III), to fundamentally misconstrue how space is itself constituted through the social process.

My arguments here in part derive from experience. I entered academic geography in an era when the belief in uniqueness of place supposedly put the discipline "outside of theory." This exceptionalist claim became a matter of fierce debate in the 1960s and I, for one, have spent much of my academic life subsequently seeking to refute that proposition and to discover the ways in which topics like space, place, and environment might be understood both theoretically and practically. Apart from changing political commitments, my intellectual turn to historical materialism and to dialectics derives in large degree from the conclusion that this was the best way to explore such questions. I therefore find it odd that so many contemporary academics, in their haste to escape the confines of what they see as an imprisoning set of meta-theories, might want to return to an exceptionalist style of argumentation that produced, in the geography of the 1950s, a dull, listless, fragmented, unenlightening, and unproductive style of work in which theoretical presumptions and prejudices (in 1950s academic geography these had to do with imperialism and understanding the world as a field for capital accumulation) hid behind exceptionalist claims. Of course, it might reasonably be argued that the theoretical sophistication now achieved makes the production of such a dismal style of work unlikely. But even as knowledgeable a commentator as Spivak (1988: 280) worries about the political implications of too hasty a retreat from meta-theory:

> However reductionistic an economic analysis might seem, the French intellectuals forget at their peril that this entire overdetermined enterprise was in the

interest of a dynamic economic situation requiring that interests, motives (desires), and power (of knowledge) be ruthlessly dislocated. To invoke that dislocation now as a radical discovery that should make us diagnose the economic (conditions of existence that separate out "classes" descriptively) as a piece of dated analytic machinery may well be to continue the work of that dislocation and unwittingly to help in securing "a new balance of hegemonic relations."

But there are important reasons why beliefs about the contingency of spatiality are so widespread. To begin with, the insertion of spatiality, and even more particularly the insertion of some notion of the dynamic and fluid construction of spatiality as a product of material and social processes, typically disrupts many social theories. Consider the case of neoclassical economics, where theory crucially depends upon showing how equilibrium prices form in competitive environments. What Koopmans and Beckmann showed, was that equilibrium was impossible to achieve in even a relatively simple spatial location/allocation problem. This "paradox" (which played a role in the award of a Nobel prize to Koopmans) has never been resolved, leaving neoclassical economic theory to elaborate its arguments on a foundation of shifting sand. The same can be said of certain kinds of class analysis (which stumble on spatializations such as neighborhood, network, community, city, and nation), much of analytical Marxism (the theorizations of Roemer and Wright, for example), versions of the Hegelian dialectic (including its recent resurrection in bowdlerized form in Fukuyama's "end of history") and some renditions of historical materialism that have worked out their theoretical schemas as if spatial ordering and the changing production of space was of no importance.

Many social theories have ignored space (or, more accurately, assumed a stable and unchanging spatial structure of entities and permanences). Many of the propositions advanced or deduced from those theories fall apart when spatiality is reintroduced. The assault on such theories using spatiality as a means to undercut them has therefore been both correct and salutary. But the inference that there can be no theory of the production of space or that the search for any sort of general or meta-theory must be abandoned, is plainly wrong.

But how, then, can a theoretical discourse about spatiality be constructed and how can historical materialism be made more explicitly geographical? Later chapters will take up those questions in much greater detail. Here I shall simply confine myself to some preliminary remarks on what a discourse about "historical–geographical materialism" must address.

1. The discursive activity of "mapping space" is a fundamental prerequisite to the structuring of any kind of knowledge. All talk about "situatedness," "location" and "positionality" is meaningless without a mapping of the space

in which those situations, locations, and positions occur. And this is equally true no matter whether the space being mapped is metaphorical or real.

2. Mapping is a discursive activity that incorporates power. The power to map the world in one way rather than another is a crucial tool in political struggles. Power struggles over mapping (again, no matter whether these are maps of so-called "real" or metaphorical spaces) are therefore fundamental moments in the production of discourses.

3. Social relations are always spatial and exist within a certain produced framework of spatialities. Put another way, social relations are, in all respects, mappings of some sort, be they symbolic, figurative, or material. The organization of social relations demands a mapping so that people know their place. Revolutionary activity entails a re-mapping of social relations and agents who no longer acknowledge that place to which they were formerly assigned. From this it follows that the production of spatial relations (and of discourses about space relations) is a production of social relations and to alter one is to alter the other.

4. Material practices transform the spaces of experience from which all knowledge of spatiality is derived. These transformative material practices in part accord with discursive maps and plans (and are therefore expressing of both social relations and power) but they are also manifestations of symbolic meanings, mythologies, desires. The spatialities produced through material practices (be they frameworks for living, for communication, for work, for symbolic activities and rituals, for enjoyment) also constitute the material framework within which social relations, power structures, and discursive practices unfold.

5. Institutions are produced spaces of a more or less durable sort. In the most obvious sense they are territorializations – territories of control and surveillance, terrains of jurisdiction, and domains of organization and administration. But they also entail the organization of symbolic spaces (monuments, shrines, walls, gates, interior spaces of the house) and the spatial orchestration of semiotic systems that support and guide all manner of institutional practices and allegiances. Insertion into the symbolic spatial order and learning to read the semiotics of institutionalized landscapes is an effect of power upon the individual that has a primary role in guaranteeing subservience to the social order.

6. The imaginary (thoughts, fantasies, and desires) is a fertile source of all sorts of possible spatial worlds that can prefigure – albeit incoherently – all manner of different discourses, power relations, social relations, institutional structures, and material practices. The imaginary of spatiality is of crucial significance in the search for alternative mappings of the social process and of its outcomes. The structures of many social and literary theories are, in this regard, often secret mappings of otherwise intractable processes and events by appeal to a certain imaginary. The secrecy is often a deliberate

masking of the presuppositions of power and of social relations that lie behind the perpetuation of institutions. The moment of conversion of these imaginaries into discourses is therefore critical, not in the sense that it is determinate, but because it is at that relational moment that the impositions of and revulsions against institutions, power, and social relations become most apparent.

This schematic overview of some of the general orientations of a historical–geographical materialism with respect to handling spatiality leaves a great deal out. In what follows I shall attempt to flesh out this schema, not only with respect to space, but also with respect to cognate terms such as time, place, and environment. But historical–geographical materialism is a form of discourse and it, too, has its positionality within the social process. It helps understand the world in rather different ways to those given by more conventional social and literary theories. But as Marx long ago argued, our task is not only to understand the world but also to change it. But change it into what? Here the question of political commitment is crucial. So if, like Marx, I believe the fundamental contradiction we have to confront is that of the destructive logic of capital, then historical–geographical materialism has to be regarded as a discursive moment in relation to that political objective. But, as I began by remarking, the writing of a book is an engagement within the realm of discourse and inevitably bound by its rules and limitations. Discourse and language may be a vital locus of struggle. But they are not the only or even necessarily the most important places of struggle. In writing a book I am confined there. Nevertheless, the critical capacity to use discourse to reflect on the nature of the discourses we construct can have an important political role to play. And that is what the rest of this book is about.

PART II

The Nature of Environment

Part II Prologue

Around "Earthday" 1970, I recall reading a special issue of the business journal *Fortune*. It celebrated the rise of the environmental issue as a "non-class issue" and President Nixon, in an invited editorial, opined that future generations would judge us entirely by the quality of environment they inherited. On "Earthday" itself, I attended a campus rally in Baltimore and heard several rousing speeches, mostly by middle class white radicals, attacking the lack of concern for the qualities of the air we breathed, the water we drank, the food we consumed and lamenting the materialist and consumerist approach to the world which was producing all manner of resource depletion and environmental degradation. The following day I went to the Left Bank Jazz club, a popular spot frequented by African-American families in Baltimore. The musicians interspersed their music with interactive commentary over the deteriorating state of the environment. They talked about lack of jobs, poor housing, racial discrimination, crumbling cities, culminating in the claim, which sent the whole place into paroxysms of cheering, that their main environmental problem was President Richard Nixon.

What struck me at the time, and what continues to strike me, is that the "environmental issue" necessarily means such different things to different people, that in aggregate it encompasses quite literally everything there is. Business leaders worry about the political and legal environment, politicians worry about the economic environment, city dwellers worry about the social environment and, doubtless, criminals worry about the environment of law enforcement, and polluters worry about the regulatory environment. That a single word should be used in such a multitude of ways testifies to its fundamental incoherence as a unitary concept. Yet, like the word "nature," the idea of which "contains, though often unnoticed, an extraordinary amount of human history ... both complicated and changing, as other ideas and experiences change" (Williams, 1980: 67), the uses to which a word like environment is put prove instructive. The "unnoticed" aspect of this poses particular difficulties. Lovejoy (1964: 7–14) comments:

It is largely because of their ambiguities that mere words are capable of independent action as forces in history. A term, a phase, a formula, which gains currency or acceptance because one of its meanings, or of the thoughts which it suggests, is congenial to the prevalent beliefs, the standards of value, and tastes of a cetain age, may help to alter beliefs, standards of value, and tastes, because other meanings or suggested implications, not clearly distinguished by those who employ it, gradually become the dominant elements of signification. The word "nature," it need hardly be said, is the most extraordinary example of this.

The contemporary battleground over words like "nature" and "environment" is a leading edge of political conflict, precisely because of the "incompletely explicit *assumptions,* or more or less *unconscious mental habits,*" which surround them. And it is, of course, primarily in the realms of ideology and discourse where "we become conscious of political matters and fight them out."

The fight in part arises because words like "nature" and "environment" convey a commonality and universality of concern that can all too easily be captured by particularist politics. "Environment" is, after all, whatever surrounds or, to be more precise, whatever exists in the surroundings of some being that is *relevant to* the state of that being at a particular place and time. The "situatedness" of a being and its internal conditions and needs have as much to say about the definition of environment as the surrounding conditions themselves, while the criteria of relevance can also vary widely. A Los Angeles police officer standing at the corner of Normandie and Figueroa just after the Rodney King verdict came in, will hardly be thinking about the ozone hole, any more than the scientist studying the development of that hole in the nether regions of the Antarctic will be thinking deeply about an uprising in Los Angeles. Conditions, needs, desires, and situation are rarely stable for long, rendering the idea of some stable definition of environmental problems moot.

Yet each and every one of us is situated in an "environment" and all of us therefore have some sense of what an "environmental issue" might be. In recent years, however, a rough convention has emerged, which circumscribes "environmental issues" to a particular subset of possible meanings, primarily focusing on the relationship between human activity and well-being, on the one hand and (*a*) the condition or "health" of the biome or ecosystem which supports human life, (*b*) specific qualities of air, water, soil, and landscapes, and (*c*) the quantities and qualities of the "natural resource base" for human activity, including both reproducible and exhaustible assets. But even mildly biocentric interpretations would quite properly challenge the implicit division between "nature" and "culture" in this convention. The consequent political/philosophical division between "environmentalists" who adopt an external and often managerial stance towards the *environment* and "ecologists" who view human activities as embedded in *nature* (and who consequently construe the notion of human health in emotive, esthetic as well as instrumental terms) is becoming politically contentious (see Dobson, 1990). In any case, there is increasing public acceptance of the idea that much of what we call "natural," at least as far as the surface ecology of the globe and its atmosphere is concerned, has been significantly modified by human action (Marsh, 1965; Thomas, 1956; Goudie, 1986; Turner et al., 1990). The distinction between built environments of cities and the humanly modified environments of rural and even remote regions then appears arbitrary except as a particular manifestation of a rather long-standing ideological distinction between the country and the city (Williams, 1973). We ignore the ideological power of that distinction at our peril, however, since it underlies a pervasive anti-urban bias in much ecological rhetoric.

In what follows I shall try to establish a theoretical position from which to try and make sense of what are generally called "environmental issues." In so doing, I want to connect those issues to questions of social change and the way in which "nature" or "environment" is valued. I seek to show that all proposals concerning "the environment" are necessarily and simultaneously proposals for social change and that action on them always entails the instantiation in "nature" of a certain regime of values. Ultimately, by putting environmental and social change into a dialectical and historical–geographical frame of thinking, I hope to derive constructive ways to confront the dilemmas of what so often appear to be contradictory and often mutually exclusive *social* definitions of environmental problems.

6

The Domination of Nature and its Discontents

I. The Issue

I begin with two quotations.

> We abuse land because we regard it as a commodity belonging to us. When we see land as a community to which we belong, we may begin to use it with love and respect. (Aldo Leopold, *The Sand County Almanac*)

> Where money is not itself the community, it must dissolve the community. ... It is the elementary precondition of bourgeois society that labour should directly produce exchange value, i.e. money; and similarly that money should directly purchase labour, and therefore the labourer, but only insofar as he alienates his activity in the exchange. ... Money thereby directly and simultaneously becomes the *real community*, since it is the general substance for the survival for all, and at the same time the social product of all. (Karl Marx, *Grundrisse*, pp. 224–6)

From Marx's perspective the land ethic that Leopold has in mind is a hopeless quest in a bourgeois society where the community of money prevails. Leopold's land ethic would necessarily entail the construction of an alternative mode of production and consumption to that of capitalism. The clarity and self-evident qualities of that argument have not, interestingly, generated a rapprochement between ecological/environmentalist and socialist politics; the two have by and large remained antagonistic to each other and inspection of the two quotations reveals why. Leopold defines a realm of thinking and action outside of the narrow constraints of the economy; his is a much more biocentric way of thinking. Working-class politics and its concentration on revolutionizing political economic processes appears to perpetuate rather than resolve the problem as Leopold defines it, because it offers at best an instrumental and managerial approach to nature. At its worst, socialism pursues "Promethean" projects in which the "domination" of nature is presumed both possible and desirable.

In what follows I shall try to see if there are ways to bridge this antagonism and turn it into a creative rather than destructive tension. Can a progressive ecological politics be invented that does not in some way or other invoke some sense of superior understanding, dominion, and even domination? Is there or ought there to be a place for a distinctively "ecological" angle to progressive socialist politics? And, if so, what should it be? And how did we arrive at this seeming impasse in which the struggle for emancipation from class oppressions appears so antagonistic to the struggle to emancipate human beings from a purely instrumental relation to nature?

II. The Domination of Nature

Contemporary ecological thought often traces the origins of such questions, as well as many of our contemporary environmental ills, back to the hubris and wrong-headedness of Enlightenment acceptance of the thesis that nature was there for the using and that the domination of nature was a feasible project. This argument is badly in need of scrutiny.

Philosophical arguments favoring the domination, "mastery," control, or "humanization" of nature, though they may have had ideological taproots in the Christian doctrine of dominion (White, 1967), came strongly into their own during the seventeenth and eighteenth centuries. Francis Bacon vigorously propounded such views and in a celebrated passage in the *Discourse on Method* Descartes argued that the "general good of all mankind" could best be pursued not by resort to speculative philosophy but by the attainment of "knowledge that is useful in life" so as to "render ourselves the masters and possessors of nature." Such views were implicated in the development of modern science and the rise of distinctively instrumental and capitalistic values with respect to the human use of the "natural" world. Descartes and Bacon, Marx (1967: 368) argued, "saw with the eyes of the manufacturing period." Animals were no longer viewed as living assistants as they were in the Middle Ages and construed instead as machines. This "anticipated an alteration in the form of production and the practical subjugation of Nature by Man as a result of the altered methods of thought." While Marx's judgment is a bit formulaic, I nevertheless think it important to see the articulation of ideas of domination as part of an overall package of thought, beliefs, sensibilities, attitudes, and practices which gained ascendancy in the political economy of western European society during the seventeenth and eighteenth centuries (see Cassirer, 1968; Leiss, 1974; Merchant, 1983).

The particular role of the "domination of nature" thesis can best be understood in relation to the twin Enlightenment ideals of *human emancipation* and *self-realization. Emancipation* addressed a whole range of issues starting with problems of material wants and needs, physical, biological, and social insecurities, passing through varieties of oppression of the individual by state, dynastic, or class privileges and powers, through to emancipation from superstition, false consciousness, organized religion, and all-manner of supposedly irrational beliefs. *Self-realization* was an even vaguer proposition, but it certainly called for the release of the creative and imaginative powers with which humans are individually endowed and the opening up of entirely new vistas for individual human development, whether it be through production, consumption, artistic, scientific and cultural output, politics, or law. It was also accompanied by what Taylor (1994: 29) calls "the massive subjective turn of modern culture, a new form of inwardness in which we come to think of ourselves as being with inner depths." The "voice of nature within us" becomes a key component of action and understanding. Plainly, this massive subjective turn poses acute dangers when coupled with any philosophy of internal relations – it produces the very worst forms of what I have already dubbed "the Leibnizian conceit." But it also facilitates that useful though dangerous separation between "I" and "it" that grounds modern scientific enquiry into the processes at work "in nature." That separation was the key to unlocking the secrets of nature so as to facilitate emancipation and self-realization.

The twin aims of emancipation (often a collective project) and self-realization (for the most part individualized) were inseparable but frequently contradictory. Since the thesis of domination of nature attached to both, it, too, internalized contradictions. But it took time for them to become apparent. Initially, emancipation in the public sphere was quite properly viewed as a precondition for self-realization, while individual self-realization was viewed as a proper means to collective emancipatory ends. And it was presumed that reason could always unite the two. But:

> The whole eighteenth century understands reason ... not as a sound body of knowledge, principles, and truths, but as a kind of energy, a force which is fully comprehensible only in its agency and effects. What reason is and what it can do, can never be known by its results but only by its function. And its most important function is to bind and to dissolve. It dissolves everything merely factual, all simple data of experience, and everything believed on the evidence of revelation, tradition, and authority; and it does not rest content until it has analyzed all these things into their simplest component parts and into their last elements of belief and opinion. Following this work of dissolution begins the work of construction. Reason cannot stop with the dispersed parts; it has to build from them a new structure, a true whole. (Cassirer, 1968: 13)

The outcome of this *process of creative destruction*, "of doubting and seeking, tearing down and building up" (Cassirer, 1968: ix) was by no means as homogeneous as many now depict it. But Enlightenment thought did share the belief that the secrets of nature – including human nature – stood to be revealed and that knowledge – and self-knowledge – could be used not only to make human beings more at home with and comfortable in the world but also to open up a terrain of conscious political choice as to the trajectory of collective human development. The Enlightenment attributed to critical thought, furthermore, "not merely an imitative function but the power and task of shaping life itself" (Cassirer, 1968: vii). It is, Foucault (1984: 42) suggests, this critical attitude rather than any body of doctrinal elements that still binds us so strongly to Enlightenment practices. But the Enlightenment also tended to share a particular view of how the secrets of nature and human nature were to be uncovered. It departed in certain key respects from the grand systematic and deductive systems of the seventeenth century – as represented in the work of Descartes, Leibniz, and Spinoza – and looked to Newton (and Locke) as its guide. The beginning point of enquiry is phenomenal experience – *observation* – and the method applied to the data so acquired is *analysis* with the objective of uncovering the *universal principles and laws* embedded in the facts without recourse to any kind of transcendental explanation (such as the universal harmonies presumed by Leibniz as a manifestation of God's wisdom). It was only through discovery of the "true laws" of nature that we could learn "to work with nature as nature does" in ways beneficial to our species being.

These Enlightenment principles have powerfully shaped attitudes to the natural world in ways that have lasted to this day. They were, and continue to be, riddled, however, with their own particular "irrationalities." Presumptions were built into how the world was to be understood that could not themselves be subject to rational or inductive proof. We have already considered (see chapter 2) how Cartesian rationality, which continued in some respects to ground Enlightenment thought, was mired at a certain level in serious contradictions. And we will later take up (chapter 10) how Newton's conceptions of absolute space and time similarly entailed unwarranted *a priori* conceptions. Newton and his followers presumed there were universal laws governing the material world waiting to be uncovered and given their proper logical/mathematical expression. Hume exposed the transcendent presumptions in that and, in typical Enlightenment fashion tore apart Newton's mathematical empiricism to build up his own version of sceptical empiricism. Hume also reworked Descartes mind–body dualism in important ways such that Callicott (see chapter 7) can now appeal to it to ground ecological ethics. As the eighteenth century wore on, the conceptual tension between the mechanical systems that preoccupied Newton and the study of biological organisms and their history also became more and more apparent, in some ways presaging the more contemporary conflicts between philosophies of organism (such as those of Whitehead) and philosophies of mechanical systems. And the application of natural scientific method to the study of society produced a variety of schisms that persist to this day.

Enlightenment thinking was, in fact, remarkably heterogeneous. Vico and Rousseau, for example, supported the general view of emancipation and self-realization but differed radically from Descartes, Locke, Voltaire, and the encyclopedists on what to seek and how to get there. Both cast radical doubt upon the power of scientific knowledge to understand the meaning of nature (Vico insisted that this was outside of us and therefore impossible to understand whereas we could understand society because we had made it). While the twin aims of emancipation and self-realization might command broad support among all the dissenting classes and revolutionary-minded elements in society, the exact meaning attached to each differed markedly from place to place and group to group. Enlightenment thought was in fact riddled with practical biases with respect to race, gender, geography, and class. But beyond these obvious and very damaging blind spots, radically different choices of preferred means (and their ultimate embedding in social practices) had, furthermore, strong implications both for the definition of preferred objectives and for the developmental path actually proposed.

Classical political economy, child of the Enlightenment in the hands of Locke, Hume, and Adam Smith and further elaborated on by Ricardo and Mill, looked to the freedom of the market as well as its hidden hand – a hidden hand which forced technological change and the mobilization of science to the art of production – as a means to couple the increasing productivity which would free society from want and need, with a capacity for individualized self-realization through market choice. This is not to imply that *any* kind of production or consumption would do, for it was the profound belief and hope of more than just marginal thinkers within this tradition that freedom of choice in consumption would be accomplished by a refinement of taste, a cultivation of leisure and civilized values and behavior, that would endow society with a degree of civilization heretofore unknown (this continued to be a fervent belief even as late as John Maynard Keynes). Freedom from excessive state interference, from aristocratic and dynastic privileges, were powerful elements in liberal rhetoric. Yet it remained either silent or troubled with respect to the dispossessed peasantry and the working classes which were flooding into urban centers across Europe, as well as with respect to the fates of women and colonized peoples. This liberal strain of thinking is, of course, still with us, both philosophically and practically in terms of the vast flood of privatization schemes and free-market rhetoric that now dominates economic reform programs (for example, in what once used to be the Soviet bloc). Let the market do its work and emancipation and self-realization will follow, is the philosophy of most of the world's major capitalistic powers and institutions (such as the World Bank and the IMF).

This tends, however, to breed a highly instrumental view of nature as consisting of capital assets – as resources – available for human exploitation. One side-effect of eighteenth century political economy was that the domination of nature was viewed as a necessary prerequisite to emancipation and self-realization. Sophisticated knowledge of nature was required in order to manipulate the natural world to human purposes, to exploit it for market exchange, even to humanize it (and sell its qualities) according to human design. But the thesis of domination never deliberately embraced the destruction and despoliation of the natural world. Prudence would require the protection and enhancement of natural assets as a form of capital except under conditions of such abundance that free and unchecked depletion made rational sense. If destruction and depletion could be found, then it was a sign of such immense abundance that it did not matter. When it mattered the price system would adjust to indicate a condition of scarcity that required attention. And if gross despoliation could be found, then the fault lay with the imprudent practices of a rapacious and uncaring merchant and agrarian capitalism that came into its own during this period, rather than with Enlightenment thought itself.

Enlightenment thinkers embraced, however, a vaster panoply of proposals than those voiced by the liberal theorists. Some of these were so perverse and oppositional that there is room to debate whether they deserve to be even looked upon as part of the Enlightenment corpus *sensu strictu.* They included the specific views of self-realization and emancipation set out by the Marquis de Sade as well as those of Jacobean revolutionaries like Babeuf. But if there is one other major attractor within this chaos of possibilities, it lies in the communitarian tradition which always saw, and continues to see, emancipation and self-realization as a collective rather than individualistic concern. Communitarians of all sorts, Utopian socialists, anarchists, and proto-Communists, as well as a host of democratic moral theorists had at least this in common: that the free market cannot provide the appropriate means for emancipation and self-realization for the mass of the population either in part or in whole and that some alternative form of political–economic organization – a truly public realm or a "moral economy" of some sort – must be found to deliver on Enlightenment promises. From this perspective, it is even possible to see the doctrine of self-realization now made so much of by deep ecologists such as Naess (and implicitly articulated by Aldo Leopold) as a particular version of the Enlightenment impulse projected across a conception of community which embraces the whole biosystem in which human life is embedded (see chapter 7).

Marx's nineteenth-century version of the Enlightenment project is in polar opposition to that of liberal theory, yet it is also at odds with most versions of communitarian doctrines. He was, of course, just as deeply interested in questions of emancipation and self-realization as his opponents and in this sense fully subscribed to Enlightenment aims. But in *Capital* he shows how freedom of the market, the hidden hand, necessarily delivers equality in the realm of exchange but oppression and exploitation of the working class in production and it is therefore a fatally flawed mechanism for making good on

Enlightenment promises. The emancipation of the working class has as its precondition at the very least strict social and political control over market operations and, if possible, the radical transformation of power relations in the realm of production as well as in the discursive and institutional spheres. Marx argued that self-realization should be detached entirely from individual selfishness and greed and be seen as a project of realization of self through relations with others in collective or communistically organized society. Emancipation from social want in general led Marx certainly to accept that some version of the idea that the domination of nature was a necessary condition for human emancipation and in this regard he, too, accepts a broadly instrumentalist, anthropomorphic and controlling attitude towards natural environmental conditions. The realm of freedom, he wrote (Marx, 1967: Vol. 3, p. 820), consists:

> in socialized man, the associate producers, rationally regulating their interchange with nature, bringing it under their common control, instead of being ruled by it as a blind power, and achieving this with the least expenditure of energy and under conditions most favorable to, and worthy of, their human nature.

But the exact meaning of this is, as Grundmann (1991b) has recently noted, somewhat ambiguous in part because of the peculiarly dialectical way in which Marx conceptualized the interaction between the social and natural worlds, but also because Marx's politics of self-realization rested strongly on the recapture of an unalienated relationship not only to fellow human beings but also to that creative and sensuous experience of nature which capitalist industry had rendered so distant and opaque. Exactly what the conditions were that rendered the relation to nature "most worthy" of our human nature remains unspecified. And how this was to be done in the face of modern science, technology, and industrial organization poses a whole host of practical difficulties for the Marxian theory.

Some way had to be found to achieve the aims of emancipation and self-realization without abandoning the Enlightenment view that modern science, industry, and technology provide the means to emancipate human beings from the natural limits which confined them to a state of perpetual want, insecurity of life-chances and absence to the full belly so necessary for the exercise of creative powers. These are significant conundrums to which I shall subsequently return. For the moment I simply want to establish that Marx in no way objected to overall Enlightenment aims, including a particular version of the domination of nature thesis, but that he did have wide-ranging and strong objections to the way in which the liberal and communitarian theorists of the day interpreted those aims and by what means. He also meant something rather special when he connected the ideas of domination, science, and progressive liberation of the productive forces to achieve foundational goals of a future communistic society. For Marx what really mattered was the development of conscious powers for the continuous production of nature in ways that would undermine class privileges and oppressions and liberate the creative powers of individuals to produce themselves through the production of nature.

If liberal and Marxian theory accept albeit conflicting versions of the domination of nature thesis as fundamental to their emancipatory projects, then two of the major currents of thought which have shaped politics over the past two centuries appear to have at least this common base. Dissent from the domination view has not been lacking, however, and the main lines of dissent were already well-defined within the Enlightenment itself. It was, to begin with, entirely possible that "nature's laws" would ultimately show that human beings were prisoners of nature rather than masters of it. This formed, as we shall see, the Malthusian basis for opposition to Enlightenment Utopianism as regards the perfectibility of "man." But there were a number of other ways in which uncovering "nature's laws" had troubling consequences for Enlightenment optimism.

1. Montesquieu in his famous text on *The Spirit of the Laws* applied something loosely akin to scientific method to the comparative study of societies. He set out to uncover the fundamental causes that underlie the seeming chaos of human history and the enormous diversity of governmental forms. And one of the fundamental causes identified was soil and climate. "If it is true," he wrote, "that mentalities and passions are extremely different in different climates, then the laws must correspond to the difference of passions and to the difference in mentality." This environmental foundation to the geography of difference did not lead him to pure environmental determinism, for it was the task of good government to bring about an adjustment of laws, and of moral order, to prevailing physical circumstances (Cassirer, 1968: 214; Glacken, 1967: 572–81). But this meant that laws and systems of governance must vary according to environmental constraints, thus opening up the whole question of environmental influences on human behavior as well as the Pandora's box of cultural and moral relativism based on environmental difference. Rousseau followed down this path, recognizing that law "should recognize local cultural environmental conditions." While this plainly challenged the idea of any simple or easy domination of nature, it also laid the groundwork for later theories of environmentally based racial difference and environmentally determined cultural superiority. Rousseau likewise argued that "despotism is suited to hot climates, barbarism, to cold, and good government, to temperate regions" (cited in Glacken, 1967: 592).

2. If the Enlightenment proposed an attack upon enslavement through a certain scientific "disenchantment" of the world (as Max Weber was later to put it), then there was an immediate response of searching for "re-enchantment." The sense of a loss of contact with the natural world – alienation from

nature – produced a variety of responses across the spectrum of the class system. Those being divorced from access to their means of production – land – launched movements of protest that became widespread (the eighteenth-century diggers and levelers in England being a classic case). Similar movements continue to be found in peasant societies throughout the world, indicative of an intense resistance to the idea that the penetrations of the free market and of modern science are the only vehicles for emancipation and self-realization. Those in the upper classes of a more traditional frame of mine increasingly sought what Weber (1991: 142) called "redemption from the intellectualism of science in order to return to one's own nature and therewith to nature in general." The "romantic reaction" had its roots in the eighteenth century – with the Rousseau of the second Discourse and the Nouvelle Helloise pioneering the way. The "voice of nature within us" that Rousseau released when coupled with the "massive subjective turn" had all manner of consequences for how nature was to be construed and thereby rendered conflictual the relationship between an ideology of domination on the one hand and a politics of emancipation and self-realization on the other. This spawned a tradition – incorporating later figures like Wordsworth, Schiller, and Thoreau – that is powerfully present, particularly in the deep ecology movement.

3. Even in the absence of clear protest movements of this sort, Enlightenment thinkers had to confront clearly the question of exactly what "the humanization of nature" might mean and to exactly what effect the newly found powers of science and rational enquiry, of autonomous moral judgment, might be used. This question became a central preoccupation of esthetic theory, also a child of Enlightenment thought. Baumgarten, drawing heavily upon Leibniz, led the way in Germany and the Earl of Shaftesbury pushed an analogous project in Britain. The effect was to move towards a definition of "culture" and "the relation to nature" which would have been quite extraordinary to preceding generations. The transformation of nature – its humanization through landscape gardening, for example – became one privileged means of not only regaining what seemed to be lost elsewhere, but of defining a future for humanity in which self-realization could only be achieved by liberating the human senses to the sublime and transcendental experience of being at one with the world. But if the liberation of the senses became a crucial aspect of the Enlightenment project through the rise of esthetics, then the effect was not only to achieve what Eagleton (1990: 42, 49) calls "a massive introjection of abstract reason by the life of the senses" but to produce an internal opposition to the very provenance of reason itself:

Reason, having spun off with Baumgarten the subaltern discourse of aesthetics, now appears to have been swallowed up by it. The rational and the sensuous, far from reproducing one another's inner structure, have ended up wholly at odds.

So while it was Baumgarten's ambition to bring the understanding of poetry, art, landscapes within the realm of reason, such a project defied the techniques of reduction that played such a key role in science. To reduce the impact of the color red upon our senses to its purely physical concept was to lose something in exactly the same way that the reduction of a landscape's meaning to a description of its geological components was to lose the essence of what esthetic experience was about. Esthetics therefore had to remain at the level of surface appearance, immediate impact and, most important of all, at the level of the totality. And esthetic knowledge was very hard to come by without resort to something akin to the Leibnizian conceit. The result was to transform the concept of domination of nature:

> It was Baumgarten who made the pregnant and happy statement that dominion over all inferior powers belongs to reason, but that this rule must never degenerate into tyranny. The subject shall not be deprived of its own nature, nor shall it renounce its peculiar character; it is rather to be understood and protected in both these aspects. (Cassirer, 1968: 347)

4. Finally, there is the question of the nature of the human nature for which self-realization is meaningful. Even at its very inception, Enlightenment thinking was plagued with the question of the supposed "natural goodness" and "perfectability" of "man" and those who ventured too simplistically down that path met a chorus of dissenting voices. Rousseau (1973: 60), for example, while he conceded the vigorous power of self-improvement saw this as a double-edged virtue lying at the source of "[man's] discoveries and his errors, his vices and his virtues, makes him at length a tyrant both over himself and over nature." He began to sound much more like other conservative political commentators of his period when he argued that too much liberty, like too much good wine, could all too easily:

> ruin and intoxicate weak and delicate constitutions to which they are not suited. People once accustomed to masters are not in a condition to do without them. If they attempt to shake off the yoke they will more estrange themselves from freedom, as, by mistaking it for unbridled licence to which it is diametrically opposed, they nearly always manage, by their revolutions, to hand themselves over to seducers, who only make their chains heavier than before. (pp. 33–4)

This was, of course, the fear that led Edmund Burke to argue passionately against the French revolution. The conservative case tended to the view that the inherent baseness and evil in human beings could be constrained only by the strictest of institutional arrangements and that, in the absence of such arrangements, all forms of society and civility would disintegrate. The problem was, then, to find ways to create good out of inherent evil and it was Adam Smith's genius to suggest (quite plausibly) that the base instincts of greed and avarice could be mobilized into a social system that would operate to the benefit of all only in a free market in which the "hidden hand" would guide society as a whole in profitable directions. And what if (and this was perhaps Marx's main contribution) human nature was itself malleable, transformable, and, hence, an unstable set of qualities that were there for the making? The aims of self-realization and emancipation could not then be held as stable trajectories based on an essentialist reading of human wants, needs, capacities and powers. Deprived of such essentialist readings the whole idea of "alienation from nature" becomes suspect.

In all of these respects, Enlightenment thought uncovered contradictions within itself and raised issues that permeate current environmental debate. We should, Foucault (1984: 43) correctly argues:

> refuse everything that might present itself in the form of a simplistic and authoritarian alternative: you either accept the Enlightenment and remain within the tradition of its rationalism ...; or else you criticize the Enlightenment and then try to escape from its principles of rationality (which may be seen ... as good or bad). And we do not break free of this blackmail by introducing "dialectical" nuances while seeking to determine what good and bad elements there may have been in the Enlightenment.

There has probably never been a historical period and geographical concentration of such free discursive play of the human imaginary as that which the Enlightenment produced. To be sure, many of the discursive adventures bore little relation to existing political–economic practices but that disjuncture was as inevitable as it was deliberate. The science of nature as of society was meant to reveal not just what existed but what stood to be created. If thought was supposed "no longer to imitate but to acquire the power and task of shaping life itself," then the exploration of possible worlds and of the limits to human possibilities became a mandatory aspect of what all discourses were supposed to be about. And there is no doubt that all of this discursive ferment had its role to play in the tumultuous politics that led into the American and French revolutions.

But it was in another not entirely disassociated respect that Enlightenment thought began to find a more material basis for its discursive exercises. As market relations and monetization consolidated their hold, that aspect of Enlightenment thought that created the liberal theory to accompany market exchange began to make inroads into political power and institutional forms. Eighteenth-century political economy, inspired above all by

Locke, was constantly seeking a rapprochement between state policies and politics (particularly with respect to the currency and foreign trade), the production of wealth, and the proper valuation of whatever political economists of the period understood as the primary sources of all wealth – bullion, labor, and the land being the prime candidates. But this meant that the domination of nature, as well as the domination of human nature (particularly in the figure of the laborer) became subsumed within the logic of the market. The genius of eighteenth-century political economy was this: that it mobilized the human imaginary of emancipation, progress, and self-realization into forms of discourse that could alter the application of political power and the construction of institutions in ways that were consistent with the growing prevalence of the material practices of market exchange. It did so, furthermore, while masking social relations and the domination of the laborer that was to follow, while subsuming the cosmic question of the relation to nature into a technical discourse concerning the proper allocation of scarce resources (including those in nature) for the benefit of human welfare.

III. Political Economy, Environment, and Saccard's Dream

The practice and theory of capitalistic political economy with respect to the environment has consequently become hegemonic in recent world history. Within that history, it has been capital circulation that has made the environment what it is. The complex dialectic in which, as Marx has it, we make ourselves by transforming the world, gets radically simplified into a rather simple one-track affair, even allowing for the ways in which esthetic judgments, romantic reactions, nature tourism, vegetarianism, animal rights movements, and monetized protections of nature through wilderness and habitat preservation surround the crass commercialism of our use of nature and so give it a veneer of accountability and respectability. The prevailing practices dictate profit-driven transformation of environmental conditions and an approach to nature which treats of it as a passive set of assets to be scientifically assessed, used and valued in commercial (money) terms.

It is not fashionable these days, of course, to evoke directly a triumphalist attitude to nature. But I think it important to understand that this is what both the theory and practice of capitalistic political economy entails. This is what daily practice is all about, whether we care to acknowledge it or not, whenever the circulation of capital is let loose upon the land. It has also been the focus of Utopian visions. In the 1830s the Saint-Simonians announced, for example, the end of exploitation of man by man by virtue of the associated capitals of the world undertaking the rational exploitation of the globe: the exploitation of "external nature becomes henceforth the sole end of man's physical activity" (cited in Leiss, 1974: 82). The consequent radical simplification of the dialectic through which we make ourselves by making our world, does not, as is sometimes thought, reduce the capitalist approach to nature to an unimaginative or bloodless affair, in which cold calculation drives out worldly passions. Indeed, the evidence suggests that it is precisely the power of money to give vent to all manner of human passions that gives such extraordinary power to the capitalistic approach to and over nature. As Simmel (1978: 251) notes, "money enlarges the diameter of the circle in which our antagonistic psychic drives flourish," and it often does so to the degree that money dissolves "into pure desire for it." Here, for example, is how Saccard, Zola's nineteenth-century anti-hero in his novel *Money*, sees the issue as he builds his Universal Bank to finance innumerable projects for the transformation of the Levant:

> "Look here," cried Saccard ... "you will behold a complete resurrection over all those depopulated plains, those deserted passes, which our railways will traverse – Yes! fields will be cleared, roads and canals built, new cities will spring from the soil, life will return as it returns to a sick body, when we stimulate the system by injecting new blood into exhausted veins. Yes! money will work these miracles. ..." (Zola, 1991)

Zola's language here is instructive. The circulation of money is assimilated to the circulation of the blood and the biological metaphors of the circulation of the blood and sexual desire are then put to work so strongly that it seems less and less to be metaphor than expressive of a deep continuity:

> You must understand that speculation, gambling, is the central mechanism, the heart itself, of a vast affair like ours. Yes, it attracts blood, takes it from every source in little streamlets, collects it, sends it back in rivers in all directions, and establishes an enormous circulation of money, which is the very life of great enterprises.

> Speculation – why, it is the one inducement that we have to live; it is the eternal desire that compels us to live and struggle. Without speculation, my dear friend, there would be no business of any kind. ... It is the same as in love. In love as in speculation there is much filth; in love also, people think only of their own gratification; yet without love there would be no life, and the world would come to an end.

Saccard's vision, his love of life, seduces all around him. Even Mme Caroline, the cautious sister of the engineer who will be the practical agent of Saccard's schemes (and who will in the end be ruined by them), is seduced by both Saccard and his vision. She, who knows the Levant well, is struck by the desolate and unharmonious present state of the land in relation to human potentialities:

She became angry, and asked if it was allowable that men should thus spoil the work of nature, a land so blest, of such exquisite beauty, where all climates were to be found – the glowing plains, the temperate mountain-sides, the perpetual snows of lofty peaks. And her love of life, her ever-buoyant hopefulness, filled her with enthusiasm at the idea of the all-powerful magic wand with which science and speculation could strike this old sleeping soil and suddenly reawaken it. ... And it was just this that she saw rising again – the forward, irresistible march, the social impulse towards the greatest possible sum of happiness, the need of action, of going ahead, without knowing exactly whither ... and amid it all there was the globe turned upside down by the ant-swarm rebuilding its abode, its work never ending, fresh sources of enjoyment ever being discovered, man's power increasing ten-fold, the earth belonging to him more and more every day. Money, aiding science, yielded progress.

That formula – "money, aiding science, yielding progress" – has ever been at the center of capitalist culture and its Promethean historical geography of environmental transformations. And Zola was not inventing: he based his whole novel on the activities of the Pereire brothers, finance capitalists *extraordinaire*, who schooled in the principles of Saint-Simonian thought converted that Utopian vision into a practical politics of financial monopolization, speculation, and construction that dominated Second Empire France until their bankruptcy in 1867 engineered by the opposition of Rothschild (the model for the "bloodless jew" Gundermann in Zola's novel).

IV. The Frankfurt School Critique of Domination

While there were plenty of currents of thought (romanticism, organicism, Darwinian biology, Nietzschian philosophy, to name a few) opposed to the core ideas of the Enlightenment we owe the frontal assault upon the ideology of domination of nature to the Marxists of the Frankfurt School. The distinctive train of thought has subsequently been kept very much alive (though in a transformed state) by some feminists, particularly of an eco-feminist persuasion as well as by a variety of thinkers in the ecological movement. And even though many now hold that the Frankfurt School's analysis failed, it opened up a proliferating trail of thought that has been both persistent and influential.

The story of the Frankfurt School has been thoroughly told and evaluated elsewhere (Jay, 1973; Leiss, 1974, Eckersley, 1992). It sought to replace the Marxist emphasis on class struggle as the motor of history with what it saw as the far larger conflict "between man and nature both without and within." This was viewed as "a conflict whose origins went back to before capitalism and whose continuation, indeed, intensification, appeared likely after capitalism would end" (Jay, 1973: 256). The Enlightenment was considered a key moment in the history of that conflict, a moment of reformulation of beliefs, practices, and discourses in which the idea of domination and mastery of nature became paramount. In *The Dialectics of the Enlightenment* Horkheimer and Adorno undertook a dialectical analysis of the consequences of the shifting terms of the struggle between "man and nature." Sharing as they did the Enlightenment objectives of emancipation and self-realization, the question they clearly posed was this: how is it that those objectives have been frustrated ("negated" was their preferred term) by the very philosophical and political–economic shifts and practices designed to realize them? Given the rise of fascism and totalitarianism this was a pressing political problem rather than an abstract concern. The continuing elaboration and proliferation of weapons and delivery systems of mass destruction keeps that concern very much alive. Horkheimer and Adorno chose not to see such negative politics as an aberration or betrayal of Enlightenment principles but as a distinctive product of the contradictions implicit in Enlightenment thoughts and practices.

In formulating their argument they appealed to a particular version of the theory of internal relations. Descartes had construed nature as "the other" and in so doing reified nature as a thing – a purely external other – entirely separate from the world of thought. While Descartes himself still clung strongly to religious meanings, the effect was to make it seem as if nature had no meaning in itself. Deprived of any autonomous life force, nature was open to be manipulated without restraint according to the human will. Nature became, as Heidegger later complained, "one vast gasoline station" for human exploitation. What this analysis elided, according to the Frankfurt School, was the dialectics of internal relations in which nature was both "something external to man but also an internal reality" (Jay, 1973: 267). Domination of the external "other" could and would become internalized, Horkheimer (1947: 94) argued, creating "a dialectical reversal of the principle of domination by which man makes himself a tool of that same nature which he subjugates." Mastery over external nature required and produced an oppressive mastery over internal nature. Worse still:

> Mastery over nature inevitably turns into mastery over men. A vicious circle results, imprisoning science and technology in a fateful dialectic of increasing mastery and increasing conflict. The attractive promises of mastery over nature – social peace and material abundance for all – remain unfulfilled. The real danger that the resulting frustration may be turned against the instruments of mastery themselves (science and technology) must not be underestimated. As integral factors in the ascending spiral of domination over internal and external nature, they are bound to an irrational dynamic which may destroy the fruits of their own civilizing rationality. (Leiss, 1974: 194)

What Horkheimer and Adorno called "the revolt of nature" (the return of the repressed and a rebelliousness manifest as "violent outbreaks of persistently repressed instinctual demands") was not necessarily a positive force for change. The effect may be "to fetter rather than to free nature," with fascism – "a satanic synthesis of reason and nature" – seen as one distinctive outcome (Jay, 1973: 272).

> The purpose of mastery over nature is the security of life – and its enhancement – alike for individuals and the species. But the means presently available for pursuing these objectives encompass such potential destructiveness that their full employment in the struggle for existence would leave in ruins all the advantage so far gained at the price of so much suffering. (Leiss, 1974: 163–4)

It is not my purpose here to undertake any deep elaboration, critique or defense of the Frankfurt School's achievements. But I do think it important to distill from their critique of the domination of nature some key questions for environmental–ecological politics:

1. The role of scientific enquiry as a liberatory force is called into question. Horkheimer and Adorno did not abandon science (though they did provide a reasonably compelling way to understand why so many in the ecological movement – particularly the nature romanticists – do). They took it as the key task of critical enquiry to reform science itself, to try and recapture some sense of humanity and purpose and to internalize within science itself some effort at a "re-enchantment" with the world (sometimes depicted as over-coming "alienation from nature") as opposed to the "disenchantment" embedded in that creation of nature as "other" in Enlightenment thought. They fought against positivism and the scientific method as usually construed in Newtonian/Cartesian terms but held open the possibility for the construction of an alternative science.
2. This question was tightly coupled with considerations of rationality/ irrationality. The Frankfurt School challenged the hegemony of instru-mental rationality and sought in its place an alternative rationality that had the power to give a deeper sense of meaning to life, to recuperate a sensuous and open dialogical relation between human beings and external nature without giving in to what they saw as the blind forces of romantic fury, religious ideology, nature idolatry and satanic myth. How to do that is still, of course, a very open question.
3. To do this, the Frankfurt School chose to pay very close attention to the esthetic tradition. But what kind of esthetic was possible after Auschwitz, asked Adorno? That question is also put to the test and the answer is as nuanced as it is problematic. It is all very well to liberate the life of the senses to foster the return of all that had been repressed by instrumental rationality and Enlightenment reason. But what if the result was fascism? What if it was a dynamic but thoroughly banal mass culture of consumerism in which

every fetishism under the sun was put up for sale? What kind of esthetic was possible after Henry Ford as well as after Auschwitz? Adorno's response was to construct a legendary elitism and purism on the esthetic front. Purity in art was the only guarantee against cooption and corruption. But this was all too easy to construe as a noble but futile gesture that in any case brought the esthetic appreciation of nature very close to traditional bourgeois taste and in some ways reinforced the idea of art for art's sake. Adorno, it is tempting to argue, withdrew into his own version of the Leibnizian conceit in the face of the "noisy chaos" and distressing circumstances of the political world in which he found himself. But even if the esthetic gesture of the Frankfurt School's most respected esthetic analyst is found wanting, the question broached of what kind of esthetic and in whose name is a persistent refrain within ecological/environmental arguments.

4. None of these questions could be answered without at some point turning to psychoanalysis and the issue of human repressions, desires, and needs. The confrontation between Marx and Freud was conjoined in Frankfurt School analysis, sometimes with positive but more often with confusing results. But here, too, the Frankfurt School broached a terrain of discussion that simply will not go away, both in the sense of understanding how, for example, sexual drives and repressions, maternal longings and macho desires (everything, in short, that we construe as "human nature") become built into arguments for a certain relation to nature (including that expressed in Saccard's vision). Put more broadly, who is this "self" that is struggling to be realized and which of the innumerable struggles that result can be understood as emancipatory and in what way?

5. While they called into question the separation between "man and nature" and sought to reintegrate the two sides via appeal to a dialectics of internal relations, the Frankfurt School nevertheless instanciated rather than undermined the simple binary division "man/nature." In ecological circles it is a standard line of criticism of them that they never rose above the anthropomorphism of that separation and could not therefore move towards a genuinely ecocentric viewpoint (see Eckersley, 1992: chapter 5). They replicated Descartes in the very act of criticizing him. But this is a rather more general problem than many ecological thinkers presently recognize. While the dialectical formalism (Hegelianism) of the Frankfurt School in the end got in the way of its powers of historical materialist analysis, thus illustrating the limits of a certain kind of application of the philosophy of internal relations, the question of how and under what circumstances it is valid to resort to such a binary form of analysis (as opposed to submerging everything in some ecocentric soup) has to be confronted. For while it is very much the case that the "man–nature" dichotomy has no fixed boundary and that it is, as Haraway (1990, 1991) again and again argues, being transgressed all the time in modern science and technology as well as in

our daily practices, we end up in our discourses speaking to and trying to persuade only that part of the ecological world to which we distinctively belong. And this is true for even the most wildly ecocentric analyst.

6. The internal relation between the domination of nature as "other" and the domination of "others" opened up by the Frankfurt School is a continuing concern. This is a theme that has been extremely important within feminist politics since the mid-1960s. The thesis that the domination of nature (usually construed as a woman) is inherently connected to the domination of women has been converted by ecofeminists [such as Shiva (1989)] into a politics that rests upon the idea that nurturing the environment depends upon rescuing the feminine principle as paramount in human affairs. Only in that way, the argument goes, could the rapaciousness of, say, Saccard's sexual drive to dominate and possess the world be counteracted. The depiction of nature as feminine, however, did not only license an oppressive male politics of domination and oppression. It also connected, as Soper (1995) observes, to a rather more complicated set of masculine emotions varying from that of desire for outright possession (rape) through patriarchal benevolence and Oedipal guilt to longing to return to the womb-like comfort of a nurturing mother earth. So while, in the highly gendered and oppressive metaphorics of Francis Bacon, abundant evidence could be culled for the linkage between domination of nature and domination of women, and while, in the colonial literature (particularly of geographic discovery) abundant support can be found for the domination of nature being rendered equivalent to the domination of "natives" (usually depicted as very "natural" beings), the straight equation of such attitudes to all forms of masculine desire is suspect. Nevertheless, a cogent argument supported by abundant evidence can be constructed that connects a certain kind of masculinity with certain forms of scientific enquiry and technological practices of domination, mastery and control both of external and internal "nature."

But this connection between the domination of nature and the domination of others has a further dimension. "Nature-transforming" projects of any sort have distributional consequences and the patent inequity of many of these has been the source of powerful conflicts. These are now the focus of struggle in the environmental justice movement and within a polyglot group of movements known as "the environmentalism of the poor" (see chapter 13). This was not a theme that the Frankfurt School explicitly explored, but it is always latent in their critical analysis. And some of these conflicts take a curious turn. There is little ambiguity when, say, massive ecological destruction is visited on an impoverished population – such as that of Bhopal – through the breakdown of a modern industrial technology that has all the hallmarks of the domination of nature imprinted on it. But when the World Wildlife Fund presses to create a nature reserve in a developing country and insists on the eviction of indigenous populations who have long used that habitat as their resource base, then this suggests that the World Wildlife Fund has acquired just as severe and draconian ideal of the domination of nature in all of its senses as anyone in the World Bank or, for that matter, in the Enlightenment ever did. Is it ever possible, then, entirely to avoid some version of the dominion/domination/control thesis and, if not, is it ever possible for that not to convert into some version of the dominion/domination/control over others? That question is never far from the heart of all ecological politics.

The failings of the Frankfurt School's approach reflect in certain respects the fecundity of the questions opened up. While it opens up a terrain of investigation into "repressed nature" it does so by hypothesizing "instinctual urges" (a thoroughly essentialist idea) for which it is very hard to find independent evidence outside of the very technologies of enquiry which are being subjected to criticism. While it draws attention to the potential for rebellion against the instrumentalities of domination of nature (and of human nature) including the techniques of consumerism and management of mass culture, against the processes of globalization and colonization of the life world by a homogenizing instrumental rationality and market commodification, it provides very little vision as to how such rebelliousness might channel into productive and emancipatory directions as opposed to self-destructive nihilism.

But in all of this, there are two specific lines of difficulty that are of particular import for my own enquiry. The first concerns the limits and power of a philosophy of internal relations. To varying degrees, the Frankfurt School appealed to this mode of thought and Adorno's work was particularly strong in this regard – his *Negative Dialectics*, as we have seen, was a particularly trenchant exploration of the power of internal relations as a revelatory device. But Whitehead's critique of a mode of analysis in which "everything relates to everything else" so as to lead to nothing is here appropriate. Indeed, Habermas' judgment that "negative dialectics leads nowhere" is cast in the same mold. In effect, the danger always inherent in application of a dialectics of internal relations is precisely that everything so mirrors everything else that there is no room for radical change, no moment of leverage that permits an exit from processes of domination that totally occupy beliefs, discourses, institutions, power structures, material practices, and social relations.

Secondly, there is the related problem of agency. Having laid aside the working class as the agent of contemporary history, the Frankfurt School had difficulty in finding an alternative locus of action. To be sure, several of them found some sort of alternative – Marcuse put his faith in youthful rebellion (powered by Eros) and Habermas in new social movements dedicated to the construction of an ethics of communicative action. But for the most part the Frankfurt School could not identify any coherent or meaningful agency of social change that was not already thoroughly corrupted, coopted, and trapped in the mechanics of domination of nature, self, and others. Here, too, a more open conception of internal relations across diverse moments of the social process (as outlined in chapter 4) could have helped open up the dialectical form of analysis into a more historical and less purely logical mode.

It was for these two fundamental reasons that the reputation of "pessimism" became firmly attached to the work of the Frankfurt School. But there were far more powerful and persuasive arguments for pessimism available within the main currents of western thought and these did not in any way require coming to terms with Marxism, dialectics, or internal relations. For if ever there was a cause for pessimism as regards our relation to nature, it surely lay with Parson Malthus and his doctrines.

V. Ecoscarcity and Natural Limits: The Malthusian Tradition

Initially formulated at the end of the eighteenth century as a straight antidote to Enlightenment optimism, the Malthusian and neo-Malthusian arguments concerning ecoscarcity and natural limits have operated as a perpetual jeremiad refrain within the dominant progressive humanism of the western pro-capitalist tradition. Passion between the sexes (a self-realization argument) produced population growth beyond the natural capacities of the earth's larder and emancipation from poverty, war, and disease was necessarily frustrated as a result. The drive for self-realization automatically thwarted any hopes for emancipation from material want. But the ecoscarcity argument has, as Glacken (1967) also shows, a long pre-history, that includes a whole series of eighteenth-century thinkers, confronted as they all were with the obvious facts of periodic famines and deadly epidemics. And while most hoped that the domination of nature might cure such ills, there were many who recognized that this had to be in clear acknowledgement of what the limits in nature were. The perpetual return of that argument, and its periodic ascendency, now even within some currents of Marxism, testifies to the grumbling persistency of the problem of ecoscarcity.

Benton (1989: 55) argues that "the basic ideas of historical materialism can without distortion be regarded as a proposal for an ecological approach to the understanding of human nature and history." The difficulty, he asserts, is that there is a hiatus, "internal to" the mature writings of Marx between this general commitment and Marx's political–economic conception of the labor process. I want to propose that a more dialectical reading of Marx, in which the labor *process* is seen as "a form-giving fire" perpetually modifying other *processes* while passing through and giving rise to distinctive "*things*," eliminates much of that hiatus. Not only does it then become possible to explore the commonalities and conflicts between Marx's project and some sectors of contemporary ecological thinking, but it also allows us to begin to construct more adequate languages with which to reflect upon the nature of socio-ecological activities and projects.

The danger here is of accepting, often without knowing it, concepts that preclude radical critique. One of the most pervasive and difficult to surmount barriers, as I shall show in later chapters, is that which insists on separating out "nature" and "society" as coherent entities. What is surprising here, is that even the deepest and the most biocentric of ecologists at some level accepts this distinction (or worse still directly appeals to it by depicting society, for example, as a "cancer" let loose upon the planet). By insisting upon a prior dissolution of the problem into freely flowing socio-ecological processes, I do not mean to imply that the particular kind of "permanence" we call "society" has no meaning discursively or practically or that situations do not arise in which it makes sense to isolate that particular permanence for analysis. But I do want to insist that radical critique keep open precisely the way in which this entity (if such it is) gets constituted out of socio-ecological processes.

To press home this point, I shall examine the role played by ideas of "natural limits" and "ecoscarcity" (and its cognate term of "overpopulation") in contemporary debate. In ecological thinking the issue of natural limits is often in the forefront of discussion. Lee (1989), for example, creates a narrative in which it seems that the rules of human behavior should be derived from the second law of thermodynamics and the inherent sustaining power of ecosystems. Anything that violates these two principles is unsustainable and thereby doomed to produce ecocatastrophe. We must, therefore, learn to live within the limits of these two natural laws. The difficulty here, of course, is that neither principle is helpful at all in explaining the shifting history of human social organization, or even the genesis of life itself. It is one thing to argue that the second law of thermodynamics and the laws of ecological dynamics are necessary conditions within which all human societies have their being, but quite another to treat them as sufficient conditions for the understanding of human history. To propose the latter would imply that the whole of human history is an exercise in unsustainability in violation of natural law. This is so grand an assertion as to be pointless.

Benton (1989, 1992) has insisted that even Marxists, who have traditionally been hostile to the idea, should clearly recognize the "natural limits" to human potentialities while Perelman (1993), even more bravely, asserts that a close study of Marx's writings shows that he was much more of a Malthusian than he cared to admit. This is a sufficiently serious argument to warrant a return to its origins in the work of Malthus himself.

It is sometimes forgotten that Malthus wrote his first *Essay on the Principle of Population* in 1798 as a political tract against the Utopian socialist anarchism of Godwin and Condorcet and as an antidote to the hopes of social progress embodied in Enlightenment thought as well as in the French revolution. In his introduction, Malthus lays down principles of enquiry which ought, he argues, to govern discourse concerning such an important subject as the perfectibility of man:

> A writer may tell me that he thinks a man will ultimately become an ostrich. I cannot properly contradict him. But before he can expect to bring any reasonable person over to his opinion, he ought to show that the necks of mankind have been gradually elongating, that the lips have grown harder and more prominent, that the legs and feet are daily altering their shape, and that the hair is beginning to change into stubs of feathers. And till the probability of so wonderful a conversion can be shown, it is surely lost time and lost eloquence to expatiate on the happiness of man in such a state: to describe his power, both of running and flying, to paint him in a condition where all narrow luxuries would be condemned, where he would be employed only in collecting the necessaries of life, and where, consequently, each man's share of labour would be light, and his portion of leisure ample.

Malthus engages in two tactics here. One is to insist that all discussion of future possible social orders be subjected to the rules of sceptical empirical enquiry into existing reality. The second is to float easily across the social–biological divide so as to use the latter as a means to confound the former. Yet the first edition of the *Essay* is strongly colored by deduction from *a priori* universal principles: namely that food is necessary to the existence of man and that the passion between the sexes is necessary and constant. He places these two postulates in the context of a world of finite resources and deduces the famous "natural law" in which population growth (a geometric series) places pressure on the means of subsistence (an arithmetic expansion) inevitably producing poverty, disease, famine, war, and a general tendency towards "overpopulation." In subsequent editions of the *Essay* Malthus sought to give much more empirical substance and scientific respectability to his deductive arguments by furnishing as much empirical information as he could muster. He also went on to elaborate somewhat on the preventive checks (delay of marriage, for example) through which population is kept in balance with the means of subsistence, without resort to the violence of famine, disease, and war. The subsequent evolution in Malthus' ideas on the subject is too well known to warrant repetition here, as is the neo-Malthusian "adjustment" in which it is understood that technological change and social adaptation can create a dynamic balance in what still remains a fundamental race between population growth (society) and the availability of resources "in nature." But what is usually forgotten is the class character of Malthus' argument. And since this particularly pernicious aspect of his argument is still very much with us it deserves careful consideration.

Malthus (1970: 82) recognizes that "misery" has to fall somewhere and maintains that the positive checks of famine, disease, and poverty will necessarily be the lot of the lower classes. Their miserable condition is the result of a natural law which functions "absolutely independent of all human regulation." Their distress is to be interpreted as "an evil so deeply seated that no human ingenuity can reach it" (Malthus, 1970: 101). On this basis Malthus arrives, "reluctantly," at a set of policy recommendations: providing welfare to the poor merely increases the aggregate of human misery because freeing the lowest classes from positive checks only results in an expansion of their numbers, a gradual reduction in their standard of living, a decline in the incentive to work, and a diminished contribution to wealth creation as waged laborers. Increasing subsistence levels to "a part of society that cannot in general be considered as the most valuable part diminishes the shares that would otherwise belong to more industrious and worthy members, and thus forces more to become dependent" (Malthus, 1970: 97). From this Malthus draws a moral:

> Hard as it may appear in individual instances, dependent poverty ought to be held disgraceful. Such a stimulus appears to be absolutely necessary to promote the happiness of the great mass of mankind, and every general attempt to weaken this stimulus, however benevolent its apparent intention, will always defeat its own purpose. ... I feel no doubt whatever that the parish laws of England have contributed to raise the price of provisions and to lower the real price of labour. They have therefore contributed to impoverish that class of people whose only possession is their labour. It is also difficult to suppose that they have not powerfully contributed to generate that carelessness and want of frugality observable among the poor, so contrary to the disposition to be remarked among petty tradesmen and small farmers. The labouring poor, to use a vulgar expression, seem always to live from hand to mouth. Their present wants employ their whole attention, and they seldom think of the future. Even when they have an opportunity of saving, they seldom exercise it, but all that is beyond their present necessities goes, generally speaking, to the ale-house. The poor laws of England may therefore be said to diminish both the power and the will to save among the common people, and thus to weaken one of the strongest incentives to sobriety and industry, and consequently to happiness.

This argument sounds all too familiar. Substitute welfare for the poor laws, drugs for the ale-house, teenage pregnancy for carelessness and want of frugality, and we here find written the familiar litany of complaints that has increasingly dominated the discussion of welfare policies towards the lower classes in Britain and the United States these last 20 years.

But this must all be offset by Malthus' approach to the upper classes – principally those of the industrial and landed interests whose roles are more closely analyzed in *The Principles of Political Economy*. Here, he recognizes a difficulty in accounting for the continued accumulation of capital in society. The capitalist saves, invests in productive activity, sells the product at a profit, ploughs back the profit as new investment, and commences the cycle of accumulation once more. But the capitalist has to sell the product to someone if a profit is to be had and the capitalist is saving rather than consuming. If the capitalist saves too much and the rate of capital accumulation increases too rapidly, then long before subsistence problems are encountered, the capitalist will find expansion checked by the lack of effective demand for the increased output. Consequently, "both capital and population may at the same time, and for a period of great length, be redundant, compared to the effective demand for produce" (Malthus, 1968: 402). Malthus' solution to this effective demand problem (a problem that was to be central to Keynes' reformulation of the theory of capitalist crises in the 1930s) is to rely upon the proper exercise of the power to consume on the part of those unproductive classes – the landlords, state functionaries, etc. – who were outside of the production process. Malthus took pains to dissociate himself from any direct apologetics for conspicuous consumption on the part of the landed gentry. All he wanted to do was to pin down where the effective demand might come from that would keep capital accumulation stable:

> It is unquestionably true that wealth produces wants; but it is a still more important truth that wants produce wealth. Each cause acts and reacts upon the other, but the order, both of precedence and importance, is with the wants which stimulate industry. The greatest of all difficulties in converting uncivilized and thinly peopled countries into civilized and populous ones, is to inspire them with the wants best calculated to excite their exertions in the production of wealth. One of the greatest benefits which foreign commerce confers, and the reason why it has always appeared an almost necessary ingredient in the progress of wealth, is its tendency to inspire new wants, to form new tastes, and to furnish fresh motives for industry. Even civilized and improved countries cannot afford to lose any of these motives. (Malthus, 1968: 403)

Effective demand, located in the unproductive classes of society and stimulated by need creation and foreign trade (the contemporary arguments around GATT and NAFTA are exemplary in this regard) plays a vital role in stimulating both the accumulation of capital and the expansion of employment. Labor, it may then be argued, will be unemployed if the upper classes fail to consume as much as possible or if there are any restrictions on foreign trade (again, put in contemporary terms, the United States does a favor to the world by redistributing spending power to the affluent classes, consuming to the hilt, and insisting upon open world trade).

This theory of effective demand does not sit easily with the theory of population. For one thing it appears illogical (if not downright obscene) to assert that the power to consume be withheld from the lowest classes in society in the name of controlling the pressure of population on resources, while asserting via the theory of effective demand that the upper classes should consume as much as possible. Within the advanced capitalist countries this obscenity is now rampant as we find "consumer confidence" (and the penchant for debt financing of consumption) of the upper classes depicted as fundamental to sustaining the accumulation of capital, while all forms of welfare for the lower classes are slashed because they are regarded as a pernicious drain on growth. Internationally, this same opposition arises as advanced capitalist countries preach to the rest of the world about how the latter's population growth is putting pressure on resources while urging their own upper classes on to an orgy of conspicuous consumption as a necessary contribution to "sustainable" growth.

Malthus was (unlike many contemporary analysts) at least aware of the contradiction. He sought to resolve it by arguing that the upper classes do not increase their numbers according to natural law but regulate their numbers by prudent habits generated out of a fear of decline in their station in life. Only the lower classes are caught within the immutable law of nature such that they imprudently breed. The law of population is in effect disaggregated into one law for the poor and another law for the rich. But Malthus also has to explain why an effective demand cannot be generated by an increasing power to consume on the part of the laboring classes. Such a possibility is dismissed as illogical because "no one will ever employ capital merely for the sake of the demand occasioned by those who work for him" (Malthus, 1968: 404), which is another way of saying that profit necessarily arises out of the exploitation of the working classes.

But if production is controlled by capitalists, then is it not also possible that "the laws of private property, which are the grand stimulants to production, do themselves so limit it as always to make the actual produce of the earth fall very considerably short of the power of production?" (Malthus, 1970: 245). To this question Malthus replies with a qualified "yes" quickly finding a moral rationale:

> It makes no difference in the acute rate of increase in population, or the necessary existence of checks to it, whether the state of demand and supply which occasions an insufficiency of wages to the whole of the labouring classes be produced prematurely by a bad structure of society, and an unfavourable distribution of wealth, or necessarily by a comparative exhaustion of the soil. The labourer feels the difficulty in the same degree and it must have nearly the same result, from whatever cause it arises.

So the property-owning classes do the laborers a favor by creating artificial scarcity before natural scarcities hit home. The control of effective demand by the propertied interest prevents the visitation of misery on all sectors of mankind, the premature exhaustion of resources, and "secures to a portion of society the leisure necessary for the progress of the arts and sciences" – a phenomenon that "confers on society a most signal benefit." Thus is the Enlightenment project reserved for a small elite while everyone else is condemned to live by natural law. This is an appalling instance of that awful habit of denying one section of our species the right to be considered human.

Classical political economy frequently invoked natural scarcity and diminishing marginal returns as the root cause of crises and persistent poverty. Ricardo, for example, adopted much of what Malthus had to say about overpopulation and ecoscarcity, attributing the falling rate of profit under capitalism to diminishing returns on land (or on all resources) to the point where the rent on increasingly scarce resources would absorb all profit. This prompted Marx to observe that when faced with a crisis all Ricardo could do was to take refuge in organic chemistry. Marx, of course, would have no truck with the ecoscarcity argument. Poverty and lack of well-being as well as the crisis tendencies of capitalism had to be explained through the internal dynamics of the capitalist mode of production rather than by resource scarcities or by so-called "natural laws" of population. What Marx comes up with is a thorough explanation of the production of impoverishment, of unemployment, of misery and disease among the lower classes as a necessary outcome of how *laissez-faire* free-market capitalism works, no matter what the rate of population growth. There is a specific rule of overpopulation under capitalism that relates to the need to produce an industrial reserve army, a relative surplus population, for the expansionary dynamics of a capitalist mode of production.

Yet Marx also recognized that resource endowments had a key role to play in generating *wealth* (a concept quite different from value), insisting by resort to a highly gendered metaphor that the earth was its mother and labor its father (1967: 50). He also insisted that the "metabolism" with nature was a universal and perpetual condition of human labor (1967: 50) and that disruption of that metabolism for any reason (and he saw capitalism providing abundant causes for complaint) could spell disaster. Furthermore, we could only ever work with nature through nature's own laws. It is hard to read this without inferring that Marx, at least, had a profound respect for the qualities of nature and the relational–dialectical possibilities inherent within it as well as within ourselves. Furthermore, his more detailed discussions on Malthus indicate that he thought there were many situations in which population dynamics might have either positive or negative relations to the reproduction of a particular mode of production. Capitalism, he argued, requires a growing population as a real foundation for capital accumulation (see Harvey, 1982: 161). "Very complicated and varying relations" of production to population could be found in different epochs and places. Even the category of overpopulation could sometimes make sense:

> In different modes of social production there are different laws of the increase of population and of overpopulation. ... Thus what may be overpopulation in

one stage of social production may not be so in another, and their effects may be different. ... The amount of overpopulation posited on the basis of a specific production is thus just as determinate as the adequate population. Overpopulation and population, taken together, are *the* population which a specific production basis can create. (*Grundrisse*, pp. 604–5)

The Marxist tradition subsequently paid most attention to his outright rejection of the ecoscarcity arguments of Malthus and Ricardo. And it sometimes went on to draw the unwarranted implication that all forms of the overpopulation or ecoscarcity argument are merely a product of apologetic bourgeois reasoning. Even worse, it was sometimes assumed that nature could be dominated by society and totally transformed to meet human needs, and that the humanization of all nature was an unproblematic project in principle (though fraught with technical and economic difficulties). Stalin took over not only a simplistic language of the "mastery" of nature but, in his celebrated support of Lysenko, gave such an exhibition of hubris towards the natural world that even some otherwise convinced Marxists shuddered. It was only when it became clear that Lake Baikal was turning into an ecological disaster to parallel Lake Erie that serious questions began to be raised concerning the proper ecological perspectives to be built into socialism.

As Grundmann complains, Marx, at times, seems to assume that growth of productive forces implies an increasing power to dominate nature, when "there may be productive forces which do *not* lead" in that direction "but, rather, to an increasing uncertainty, risk, and uncontrollability as well as to unnecessary oppression in the production process." This does not imply that concern for the natural environment is incompatible with a Promethean view. Indeed, "anthropocentrism and mastery over nature, far from *causing* ecological problems, are the starting-points from which to address them." Nevertheless, Marx's expectation that "science and technology would create an intelligible and controllable world as well as the expectation that only capitalist relations stand in the way" of a rational regulation of our metabolism with nature, have to be questioned. And this implies a challenge to some of the presumptions of historical–geographical materialism.

It is in this context that some Marxists have returned to the ecoscarcity and natural limits argument as being in some sense far more fundamental than Marx (or more importantly Marxists) have been prepared to concede. Unfortunately, the manner of that return by Benton (1989, 1992), Perelman (1993), and O'Connor (1988) often appears as a sad capitulation to capitalistic arguments. Not, of course, that any of them would in any way support the class distinctions that Malthus used (and latterday neo-Malthusians continue to use) to such vicious effect. But the universality of "natural limits" and the deeper appeal to "natural law" as inherently limiting to the capacity to meet human desires, is now increasingly treated as an axiomatic limiting condition of human existence. So what, then, would a dialectical–relational formulation of the problem look like?

Consider, to begin with, a key term like "natural resources." In what sense can we talk about them as being "limited" and in what ways might we reasonably say they are "scarce?" The definition of these key terms is evidently crucial, if only for the whole science of economics which usually defines itself as "the science of the allocation of scarce resources." So let me offer a relational definition of the term "natural resource" as a "cultural, technical and economic appraisal of elements and processes in nature that can be applied to fulfill social objectives and goals through specific material practices." We can unpack the terms in this definition one by one. "Appraisal" refers to a state of knowledge and a capacity to understand and communicate discursively that varies historically and geographically. The long history of capitalism itself shows that technical and economic appraisals can change rapidly and the addition of the cultural dimension makes for even greater fluidity and variability in the definition. Social objectives and goals can vary greatly depending upon who is doing the desiring about what and how human desires get institutionalized, discursively expressed, and politically organized. And the elements and processes in nature change also, not only because change is always occurring (independent of anything human beings do), but because material practices are always transformative activities engaged in by human beings operating in a variety of modes with all sorts of intended and unintended consequences. What exists "in nature" is in a constant state of transformation. To declare a state of ecoscarcity is in effect to say that we have not the will, wit, or capacity to change our state of knowledge, our social goals, cultural modes, and technological mixes, or our form of economy, and that we are powerless to modify either our material practices or "nature" according to human requirements. To say that scarcity resides in nature and that natural limits exist is to ignore how scarcity is socially produced and how "limits" are a social relation within nature (including human society) rather than some externally imposed necessity.

Even the short history of capitalism surely proves that resources are not fixed, that all of them are dynamic and changing. It is one thing to say that capitalism in a given state is encountering a condition of ecoscarcity and overpopulation of its own distinctive making. Indeed, it can be argued with some force, *pace* Marx, that capitalism as a mode of production necessarily must always do that, so that to translate this particular circumstance into a set of universal limitations is to completely elide the political–ecological point. In this regard at least, Benton (1989: 77), after pursuing the holy grail of natural limits to its own limit, has it right:

> What is required is the recognition that each form of social/economic life has its own specific mode and dynamic of interrelation with its own specific contextual conditions, resource materials, energy sources and naturally mediated

unintended consequences (forms of "waste", "pollution" etc.). The ecological problems of any form of social and economic life ... have to be theorized as the outcome of this specific structure of natural/social articulation.

But many of the terms used in contemporary environmental debate incorporate capitalistic values without knowing it. Consider, for example, the most favored term in much contemporary discussion – "sustainability." That term means entirely different things to different people (see Redclift, 1987), but it is very hard to be in favor of "unsustainable" practices so the term sticks as positive reinforcement of policies and politics by giving them the aura of being environmentally sensitive. The general drift of the term's use (and in particular its promotion through the Brundtland Report on *Our Common Future*) situates it against the background of sustaining a particular set of social relations by way of a particular set of ecological projects. It is not hard to satirize that idea:

> *Imagine a highly simplified ecological–economic situation (along the lines of Love-lock's Daisyworld on Gaia) in which New York City has two species, international bankers and cockroaches. The ecosystem is quite symbiotic since bankers produce masses of waste paper (now the primary physical export of New York City) and that is the favored food of cockroaches. International bankers are the endangered species and so "sustainability" gets defined in terms of organizing the use of the earth (e.g. organizing "sustainable" agriculture in Malawi to facilitate debt repayments) to keep them in business.*

The model, though far-fetched, is illuminating, since it indicates why and how it is that international finance, via the World Bank, is these days so interested in ecological sustainability. The duality of ecological and social projects (see chapter 8) here takes some interesting twists for while it is true that debt repayment, as ecologists argue, is at the root of many ecological problems it is precisely the threat of debt default that forces international finance to recognize that such ecological problems exist. What is then evident is that all debate about ecoscarcity, natural limits, overpopulation, and sustainability is a debate about the preservation of a particular social order rather than a debate about the preservation of nature *per se*.

Ideas about environment, population, and resources are not neutral. They are political in origin and have political effects. Once, for example, connotations of absolute limits come to surround the concepts of resource, scarcity, and subsistence, then an absolute limit is set on population. And the political implications of a term like overpopulation can be devastating. Somebody, somewhere, is redundant and there is not enough to go round. Am *I* redundant? Of course not. Are *you* redundant? Of course not. So who is redundant? Of course! It must be *them*. And if there is not enough to go round, then it is only right and proper that they, who contribute so little to society, ought to bear the brunt of the burden. And if we are told that there are certain of us who, by virtue of our skills, abilities, and attainments, are capable of "conferring a signal benefit upon mankind" then it is our bounden duty to protect and preserve ourselves for the sake of all mankind, for the sake of civilization.

Whenever a theory of overpopulation seizes hold in a society ruled by a dominant class, then the subservient classes invariably experience some form of material, political, economic, and social repression. This was, of course, a result entirely predictable in the terms set up by the Frankfurt School. The difference, however, is that we here arrive at an understanding of the same outcome directly through class analysis.

VI. Conclusion

Western discourses regarding the relation to nature have frequently swung on a pendulum between cornucopian optimism and triumphalism at one pole and unrelieved pessimism not only of our powers to escape from the clutches of naturally imposed limits but even to be autonomous beings outside of nature-driven necessities at the other pole. It is, I think, a standing and deep embarrassment within the tradition of western thought that so few indications can be found of escaping from the stasis of a swinging pendulum of opinion and converting that motion into a learning spiral. To reject all talk of dominion, of "powerful understanding," and of scientific rationality is as foolish as to accept the wilder propositions of some Enlightenment thinkers. We are, whether we like it or not, inheritors of the Enlightenment tradition and the only interesting question is what we make of it and what we do with it. The positive side of the Frankfurt School contribution lay, I think, in its Utopianism, its belief that somewhere, somehow it might be possible to have "dominion without tyranny," rationality that was something more than purely instrumental and a science that was of higher order than that which we have currently constructed. What it could not come to terms with (and here its understandable obsessions with fascism coupled with its commitments to a Hegelian dialectics got in the way), were the class forces and powers that have kept and continue to keep the pendulum of thought swinging in ways convenient to the day-to-day and hence short-term perpetuation of class privilege and power. There is, in short, nothing more ideologically powerful for capitalist interests to have at hand than unconstrained technological optimism and doctrines of progress ineluctably coupled to a doom-saying Malthusianism that can conveniently be blamed when, as they invariably do, things go wrong.

7

Valuing Nature

The history of how human beings have valued their natural world is long and intricate. The diverse arguments on the matter that now preoccupy many segments of society (and which have become the focus of much ecological thinking) form a discursive point of potential leverage from which to break out of that capitalistic-imposed pendulum-swing between optimism and pessimism of which I complained in chapter 6. Whether it is possible to do so in part depends on coming to terms with dominant modes of valuation that were initiated practically with the development of capitalism and discursively developed through Enlightenment political economy.

I. Money and the Valuation of Nature

Bourgeois political economy – child of eighteenth-century thought – articulated the view of nature as "resource" and attributed to itself the prime theoretical task of determining the rational allocation of resources that were scarce. To this end it appealed to the theory of markets, to the goals of maximizing utility, and to the centrality of money as the common means to measure heterogeneities of human desires, of use values and of elements and processes "in nature." There are four arguments in favor of money valuations of "nature."

1. Money is *the* means whereby we all, in daily practice, value significant and very widespread aspects of our environment. Every time we purchase a commodity, we engage with a train of monetary and commodity transactions across space through which money values are assigned to natural resources or significant environmental features used in production, consumption, and exchange.
2. Money is the only well-understood and *universal* yardstick of value that we currently possess. We all use it and possess both a practical and intellectual understanding (of some sort) as to what it means. It serves to communi-

cate our wants, needs, desires as well as choices, preferences, and values, including those to be put specifically upon "nature," to others. The comparability of different ecological projects (from the building of dams to wildlife or biodiversity conservation measures) depends on the definition of a common yardstick (implicit or acknowledged) to evaluate whether one is more justifiable than another. No satisfactory or universally agreed upon alternative to money has yet been devised for making comparative decisions on a rational basis. Money, as Marx noted, is a leveler and cynic, reducing a wondrous multidimensional ecosystemic world of use values, of human desires and needs, as well as of subjective meanings, to a common objective denominator which everyone can understand.

3. Money in our particular society is *the* basic (though by no means the only) form of social power. It is therefore a means to achieve, liberate, and even emancipate human desires. Its neutral and universal qualities as a mere thing can be put to use in an infinite number of ways for purposes that may be judged good or bad as the case may be. The lack of any moral judgment inherent in the money form itself, can liberate the individual from direct repressive social constraints (though whether with good or bad effects may be debated). This leads to the powerful argument that the market is by far the best mechanism yet devised to realize human desires with a maximum of individual freedom and the minimum of socio-political restraints.

4. To speak in money terms is always to speak in a language which the holders of social power appreciate and understand. To seek action on environmental issues often requires that we not only articulate the problem in universal (i.e., money) terms that all can understand, but also that we speak in a voice that is persuasive to those in power. The discourse of "ecological modernization" (see chapter 13) is precisely about trying to respond to environmental issues by way of profitable enterprise. Environmental economics is also a useful and pragmatic tool for getting environmental issues on the agenda. I cite here E.P. Odum's struggle to gain wetland protection legislation in his home state of Georgia, which fell upon deaf ears until he put some plausible but rather arbitrary money values on the worth of wetlands to the state economy (see Gosselink et al., 1974). This persuaded the legislature to formulate, at a relatively early date, extensive wetland protection legislation. There are enough parallel instances (e.g., Margaret Thatcher's sudden conversion to a shade of green politics in 1988) to make it quite evident that political clout attaches to being able to articulate environmental issues in raw money terms.

Exactly how to do that poses difficulties. Pearce et al. (1989), for example, operationalize the widely accepted Brundtland Report (1987) view that "sustainable" development means that present actions should not compromise the ability of future generations to meet their needs, by arguing that the value of the total stock of assets, both humanly produced (e.g., roads and fields and factories) and given in "nature" (e.g., minerals, water supplies, etc.), must remain constant from one generation to another. But how can this stock be quantified? It cannot be measured in noncomparable physical terms (i.e., in actual or potential use values), let alone in terms of inherent qualities, so money values (exchange values) provide the only common (universal) denominator.

The difficulties with such a procedure are legion.

1. What, for example, is money? Itself dead and inert, it acquires its qualities as a measure of value by means of a social process. The social processes of exchange which give rise to money, Marx concluded, show that money is a *representation* of socially necessary labor time and price is "the money name of value." But the processes are contradictory and money is therefore always a slippery and unreliable representation of value as social labor. Debasement of the coinage, extraordinary rates of inflation in certain periods and places, speculative rages, all illustrate how money can itself be seriously unstable as a representation of value. Money, we say, "is only worth what it will buy" and we even talk of "the value of money" which means that we vest in whatever is designated as money some social qualities inherent in everything else that is exchanged. Furthermore, money appears in multiple guises – gold and silver, symbols, tokens, coins, and paper. Should we use dollars, pounds sterling, yen, cruzeros, deutschmarks? Moneys of this sort are only as credible as the credit and power of the state that backs them. There have, furthermore, been historical instances when formal moneys have been so discredited that chocolate, cigarettes, or other forms of tangible goods become forms of currency. To assess the value of "nature" or "the flow of environmental goods and services" in these terms poses acute problems that have only partial recompense by way of sophisticated methods of calculation of "constant prices," "price deflators," and noble attempts to calculate constant rates of exchange in a world of remarkable currency volatility.

2. It is difficult to assign anything but arbitrary money values to assets independently of the market prices actually achieved by the stream of goods and services which they provide. As Sraffa long ago observed, this condemns economic valuation to a tautology in which achieved prices become the only indicators we have of the money value of assets whose independent value we are seeking to determine. Rapid shifts in market prices imply equally rapid shifts in asset values. The massive devaluation of fixed capital in the built environment in recent years (empty factories, warehouses, and the like) to say nothing of the effects of periodic property market crashes illustrates the intense volatility of asset valuation depending upon market behaviors and conditions. This principle carries over into valuing "natural" assets in market economies (consider the value of a Texas oilwell during the oil scarcity of 1973–5 versus its value in the oil glut of 1980). No matter how

sophisticated the method for valuing "natural assets" (even assuming the distinction between natural and humanly created can be made), the accounts necessarily depend on arbitrary assumptions. The attempt to hand on a constant stock of capital assets (both humanly constructed and naturally occurring) measured in such money terms as is arbitrary as the assumptions.

3. Money prices attach to particular things and presuppose exchangeable entities with respect to which private property rights can be established or inferred. This means that we conceive of *entities* as if they can be taken out of any ecosystem of which they are a part. We presume to value the fish, for example, independently of the water in which they swim. The money value of a whole ecosystem can be arrived at, according to this logic, only by adding up the sum of its parts, which are construed in an atomistic relation to the whole. This way of pursuing monetary valuations tends to break down when we view the environment as being construed organically, ecosystemically, or dialectically (Norgaard, 1985; see also chapter 2) rather than as a Cartesian machine with replaceable parts. Indeed, pursuit of monetary valuations commits us to a thoroughly Cartesian–Newtonian–Lockeian and in some respects "anti-ecological" ontology of how the natural world is constituted (see below). If we construe the world, in the manner of deep ecology, as "networks or fields of relations in which things participate and from which they cannot be isolated" (Naess, 1989: 49), then the money valuation of things in themselves becomes impossible.

4. Money valuations presume a certain structure to time as well as to space. The temporal structure is defined through the procedure of discounting, in which present value is calculated in terms of a discounted flow of future benefits. There are no firmly agreed-upon rules for discounting and the environmental literature is full of criticism as well as defenses of discounting practices in relation to environmental qualities. Volatility in actual interest rates and the arbitrariness of interest rates assigned on, for example, public projects make valuation peculiarly difficult. Such valuation, furthermore, only makes sense if assets are exchangeable so that discounting the future value of, say, the state of energy fluxes in the ocean or the atmosphere is totally implausible. The multiple and often nonlinear notions of time which attach to different ecological processes also pose deep problems. While, for example, it might be possible to discover something about human time preferences (or at least make reasonable assumptions about them), the multiple temporalities at work in ecosystems are often of a fundamentally different sort. McEvoy (1988: 222) cites the case of the (nonlinear) reproductive cycle of sardine populations in California waters – the sardines adapted to "ecological volatility" by individually "living long enough to allow each generation to breed in at least one good year." The stock suddenly collapsed when fishing "stripped the stock of its natural buffer." Of course, sensible policies and practices with respect to risk and uncertainty

might have avoided such an outcome, but the point remains that the temporality defined by such ecological behaviors is antagonistic to the linear, progressive, and very Newtonian conception of time we characteristically use in economic calculation. "Natural fluctuations" in insect, animal, or fish populations can be idiosyncratic and occasionally catastrophic and matching such a wayward temporality with the temporality of markets and capital accumulation even under stable capital availability conditions is often impossible. But even supposing some sort of valuation can be arrived at, profound moral questions remain concerning current rights versus the treatment of future generations. For this, and other reasons, "green value theory" [as Goodin (1992) calls it] is deeply antagonistic to discounting practices as registered in the market. "The concern for the future should add up towards infinity," writes the deep ecologist Naess (1989: 127). The difficulty with this irresponsible kind of statement, all too typical of the radical ecologists, is that it condemns us to a joyless present in the form of a rate of consumption close to the bare minimum of physical existence. But on this score the rhetoric of sustainability directs public policy concerns beyond the temporality possible in the market to a temporality of inter-generational transfers of wealth-creating possibilities (de-Shalit, 1995).

5. Property arrangements can be of various sorts. They look very different under conditions of, say, strong wetland preservation or land-use controls. It is the task of much of contemporary environmental policy to devise a regulatory framework with which to cajole or persuade those holding private property rights to use them in environmentally benign ways, perhaps even paying attention to rather longer time horizons than those which the market discount rate dictates. Challenging though this theoretical, legal, and political problem may be, it still presumes the environment has a clear enough structure so that some kind of cost–benefit argument concerning the relation between social environmental goods and individualized property rights can be constructed. Appeal to money valuations condemns us, in short, to a world view in which the ecosystem is viewed as an "externality" to be internalized in human action only via some arbitrarily chosen and imposed price structure or regulatory regime. This is precisely the mode of thinking which allowed Hardin (1968) to articulate the thesis of "the tragedy of the commons" in which individual users of some common resource, seeking to maximize their individual utility, ultimately destroy that resource through overuse. Persuasive though that parable is on the surface, it breaks down not only when the presumption of individual utility maximizing behavior is inappropriate, but also as soon as the sharp dichotomy between internal and external disappears, as occurs within ecosystems as well as in societies in which what we now rather patronizingly call "respect for nature" is internalized in customary usages, religious beliefs, taboos, and the like (McCay and Acheson, 1987).

6. It is hard in the light of these problems not to conclude that there is something about money valuations that makes them inherently *anti-ecological,* confining the field of thinking and of action to instrumental environmental management. While the point of environmental economics (in both its theory and its practice) is to escape from a too-narrow logic of resource/environmental valuations and to seek ways to put money values on otherwise unpriced assets, it cannot escape from the confines of its own institutional and ontological assumptions (which may well be erroneous) about how the world is ordered as well as valued.

7. Money as a form of social power has a certain asymmetry to it – those who have it can use it to force those who do not to do their bidding. This power asymmetry in social relations ineluctably connects to the inequities in environmental relations in exactly the same way that the project to dominate nature necessarily entailed a project to dominate people (Leiss, 1974). Excessive environmental degradation and costs, for example, can be visited upon the least powerful individuals or even nation states as environmental hazards in the workplace as well as in the community. Ozone concentrations in large cities in the United States affect the poor and "people of color" disproportionately and exposure to toxins in the workplace is class-conditioned. From this arises a conflation of the environmental and the social justice issues, leading many to argue that the solution to the latter is a necessary prerequisite to any attack upon the former (see chapter 13).

8. Money, lastly, hardly satisfies as an appropriate means to represent the strength or the manifold complexity of human wants, desires, passions, and values, even though it has the capacity to liberate desires from social constraints. "We see in the nature of money itself something of the essence of prostitution," says Simmel (1978: 377) and Marx (1973) concurs. Freud took things even further, picking up on our penchant to describe money as something dirty and unclean ("filthy lucre" and "filthy rich" are common expressions). "It is possible the contrast between the most precious substance known to men and the most worthless ... has led to the specific identification of gold with faeces," he wrote, and shocked his Victorian readers by treating gold as transformed excrement and bourgeois exchange relations as sublimated rituals of the anus. Money, wrote his friend Ferenzci, "is nothing other than odorless, dehydrated filth that has been made to shine" (Borneman, 1976: 86). We do not have to go so far as Freud and Ferenzci to recognize that there is something morally or ethically questionable or downright objectionable to valuing human life in terms of discounted lifetime earnings and "nature" (for example, the fate of the grizzly bear and the spotted owl as species) in monetary terms. This is the negative underside to the power of money to press for liberation.

Capitalism is, from this last standpoint, beset by a central moral dilemma: money supplants all other forms of imagery (religion, traditional religious authority, and the like) and puts in its place something that either has no distinctive image because it is colorless, odorless, and indifferent in relation to the social labor it is supposed to represent, or, if it projects any image at all, connotes dirt, filth, excrement, and prostitution. The effect is to create a moral vacuum at the heart of capitalist society – a colorless self-image of value that can have no purchase upon collective as opposed to individual social identity. It cannot provide an image of social bonding or of community in the usual sense of that term (even though it is the *real* community in the sense that Marx meant it) and it fails as a central value system to articulate human hopes and aspirations in collective terms. Money is what we necessarily aspire to for purposes of daily reproduction and the realization of individual desires, wants, and needs. In this sense money does indeed become the community; but a community emptied of any particular moral passion or of humane meanings even though it engages human passions in furious and obsessive ways.

At this point, the critic of money valuations, who is nevertheless deeply concerned about environmental degradation, is faced with a dilemma: eschew the language of daily economic practice and political power and speak in the wilderness, or articulate deeply-held nonmonetizable values in a language (i.e., that of money) believed to be inappropriate or fundamentally alien. The deeper dilemma is that though money may lack moral meaning in itself, it becomes the vehicle through which human desires and passions get mediated and measured. Zola caught the problem directly when he has Caroline say:

> Money was the dung-heap that nurtured the growth of tomorrow's humanity. Without speculation there could be no vibrant and fruitful undertakings any more than there could be children without lust. It took this excess of passion, all this contemptibly wasted and lost life to ensure the continuation of life. ... Money, the poisoner and destroyer, was becoming the seed-bed for all forms of social growth. It was the manure needed to sustain the great public works whose execution was bringing the peoples of the globe together and pacifying the earth. ... Everything that was good came out of that which was evil.

Although the ultimate moral of Zola's novel is that acceptance of that thesis leads to speculative farce and personal tragedy, no less a theorist than Max Weber sternly and quite properly warned that it was an egregious error to think that only good could come out of good and only evil out of evil. Money may be profoundly inadequate, soulless, and "the root of all evil," but it does not necessarily follow that social and by extension all ecological ills result from market coordinations in which private property, individualism, and money valuations operate. On the other hand, we also have sufficient evidence concerning the unrestrained consequences of what Kapp called *The Social Costs of Private Enterprise* to know that it is equally illusory to believe the Adam Smith thesis that social good automatically arises out of the necessary evils of the hidden hand of market behaviors. Left to its own devices, Marx (1967: 474–5) argued, capitalistic progress "is a progress in the art, not only of robbing the laborer, but of robbing the soil."

The conclusion is, then, rather more ambiguous than many might want to accept. First, all the time we engage in commodity exchanges mediated by money (and this proposition holds just as firmly for any prospective socialist society) it will be impossible in practice to avoid money valuations. Secondly, valuations of environmental assets in money terms, while highly problematic and seriously defective, are not an unmitigated evil. To judge how good or bad they are presumes, however, the existence of other modes of valuation against which money valuations can be compared and critically judged. So how else can nature be valued?

II. Do Values Inhere in Nature?

There has been a long history within bourgeois life of resistance to and search for an alternative to money as a way to express values. Religion, community, family, nation, have all been proferred as candidates, but the particular set of alternatives I here wish to consider are those which see values residing in nature – for romanticism, esthetics, environmentalism, and ecologism all have strong elements of that ethic built within them. And the idea is not foreign to Marxism either (at least in some of its renditions). When Marx (1972) argued in "On The Jewish Question" that money has "robbed the whole world – both the world of men and nature – of its specific value" and that "the view of nature attained under the dominion of private property and money is a real contempt for and practical debasement of nature," he comes very close to endorsing the view that money has destroyed earlier and perhaps recoverable intrinsic natural values.

The advantage of seeing values as residing in nature is that it provides an immediate sense of ontological security and permanence. The natural world provides a rich, variegated, and permanent candidate for induction into the hall of universal and permanent values to inform human action and to give meaning to otherwise ephemeral and fragmented lives (cf. Goodin, 1992: 40). Writes Leopold (1968: 223–4):

> It is inconceivable to me that an ethical relation to land can exist without love, respect and admiration for the land, and a high regard for its value. By value, I of course mean something far broader than mere economic value; I mean value in the philosophical sense so that a thing is right when it tends to preserve the integrity, stability, and beauty of the biotic community. It is wrong when it tends otherwise.

But how do we know and what does it mean to say that "integrity, stability and beauty" are qualities that inhere in nature?

This brings us to the crucial question: if values reside in nature, then how can we know what they are? The routes to such an understanding are many and varied. Intuition, mysticism, contemplation, religious revelation, metaphysics, and personal introspection have all provided, and continue to provide, paths for acquiring such understandings. On the surface, at least, these modes of approach contrast radically with scientific enquiry. Yet, I shall argue, they all necessarily share a commonality. All versions of revealed values in nature rely heavily upon particular human capacities and particular anthropocentric *mediations* (sometimes even upon the charismatic interventions of visionary individuals). Through deployment of highly emotive terms such as love, caring, nurturing, responsibility, integrity, beauty, and the like, they inevitably represent such "natural" values in distinctively humanized terms, thus producing distinctively human *discourses* about intrinsic values. For some, this "humanizing" of values in nature is both desirable and in itself ennobling, reflecting the peculiarities of our own position in the "great chain of being" (Lovejoy, 1964). "*Humanity is nature becoming conscious of itself*" was the motto that the anarchist geographer Reclus adopted, clearly indicated that the knowing subject has a creative role to play at least in translating the values inherent in nature into humanized terms. But if, as Ingold (1986: 104) notes, "the physical world of nature cannot be apprehended as such, let alone confronted and appropriated, save by a consciousness to some degree emancipated from it," then how can we be sure that human beings are appropriate agents to represent all the values that reside in nature?

The ability to discover intrinsic values depends, then, on the ability of human subjects endowed with consciousness and reflexive as well as practical capacities to become *neutral* mediators of what those values might be. This often leads, as in religious doctrines, to the strict regulation of human practices (e.g., asceticism or practices like yoga) so as to ensure the openness of human consciousness to the natural world. This problem of anthropocentic mediations is equally present within scientific enquiry. But here too the scientist is usually cast in the role of a knowing subject acting as a *neutral* mediator, under the strictest guidelines of certain methods and practices (which sometimes put to shame many a Buddhist), seeking to uncover, understand, and represent accurately the processes at work in nature. If values inhere in nature, then science by virtue of its objective procedures should provide one reasonably neutral path for finding out what they might be. Hence arises the long history of a connection between the observation of nature and the search for foundational moral principles and values.

How neutral this exercise turned out to be has been the subject of considerable debate. Consideration of three examples provides some insight into the nature of the difficulty.

1. The Fable of the Sperm and Egg

Feminist work has, over the years, revealed widespread resort to gendered metaphors in scientific enquiry. The effect is often to write social ideas about gender relations into scientific representations of the natural world and thereby make it appear as if those social constructions are "natural." Merchant (1983) highlights, for example, the gendered imagery with which Frances Bacon approached nature (in essence as a female body to be explored and a female spirit to be dominated and tamed by ruse or force) in his foundational arguments concerning experimental method (an imagery which sheds great light on what is happening in Shakespeare's *The Taming of the Shrew*). These are not, however, isolated or singular examples. Haraway (1989), in an insightful essay on "Teddy Bear patriarchy" in the New York Museum of Natural History, points out how "decadence – the threat of the city, civilization, machine – was stayed in the politics of eugenics and the art of taxidermy. The Museum fulfilled its scientific purpose of conservation, preservation, and the production of permanence in the midst of an urban world that even at the turn of this century seemed to be on the border of chaos and collapse." It opposed to this world of troubled sociality a visual technology of exhibits deployed in part as a means to communicate to the outside world a sense of the true organicism of the natural order (founded on hierarchy, patriarchy, class, and family) which ought to be the foundation of stability for any social order. In so doing, it explicitly used and continues to use primatology as a means to produce or promote race, class and gender relations of a certain sort.

Martin's (1991) example of the fable of the egg and sperm as depicted in the extensive medical and biological literature on human fertility is particularly instructive. Not only is the female reproductive process (particularly menstruation) depicted as wasteful compared to the immensely productive capacity of men to generate sperm, but the actual process of fertilization is depicted in terms of a passive female egg, tracked down, captured, and claimed as a prize by an active, dynamic, and thrusting male sperm after a difficult and arduous journey to claim its prize. The sperm sounds oddly like an explorer looking for gold or an entrepreneur competing for business (cf. Zola's parallel image cited above of financial speculation as the wasteful lust necessary to produce anything). It transpires, however, that the metaphor deployed in scientific studies of human fertility was fundamentally misleading; the sperm is by no means as directed, energetic, and brave as it was supposed to be (it turns out to be rather listless and aimless when left to itself) and the egg turns out to play an active role in fertilization. But it took time for researchers to lay their gendered predilections aside, and when they did so it was mainly by turning the egg into the equivalent of the aggressive femme fatale who snares, entraps, and victimizes the male (sperm) in an elaborate spider's web as "an engulfing, devouring mother." New data, Martin (1991: 498) suggests, "did not lead scientists to eliminate gender stereotypes in their descriptions of egg and sperm. Instead, scientists simply began to describe egg and sperm in different, but no less damaging terms." We plainly cannot draw any inferences whatsoever as to the values inherent in nature by appeal to investigations and enquiries of this sort.

2. Darwin's Metaphors

Consider, as a second example, the complex metaphors that play against and alongside each other in Darwin's *The Origin of Species*. There is, firstly, the metaphor of stock breeding practices (about which Darwin was very knowledgeable by virtue of his farm background). This, as Young (1985) points out, took the artificial selection procedures which were well understood in stock breeding and placed them in a natural setting, posing the immediate difficulty of who was the conscious agent behind natural selection. There is, secondly, the Malthusian metaphor which Darwin explicitly acknowledged as fundamental to this theory. Entrepreneurial values of competition, survival of the fittest in a struggle for existence then appeared in Darwin's work as "natural" values to which social Darwinism could later appeal and which contemporary "common sense" continues to deploy. Todes (1989) in a detailed examination of how Darwin's ideas were received in Russia shows, however, that the Russians almost universally rejected the relevance of the Malthusian metaphor and downplayed intraspecific struggle and competition as an evolutionary mechanism:

> This unifying national style flowed from the basic conditions of Russia's national life – from the very nature of its class structure and political traditions and of its land and climate. Russia's political economy lacked a dynamic pro-laissez faire bourgeoisie and was dominated by landowners and peasants. The leading political tendencies, monarchism and a socialist-oriented populism, shared a cooperative social ethos and a distaste for the competitive individualism widely associated with Malthus and Great Britain. Furthermore, Russia was an expansive, sparsely populated land with a swiftly changing and often severe climate. It is difficult to imagine a setting less consonant with Malthus's notion that organisms were pressed constantly into mutual conflict by population pressures on limited space and resources. ... This combination of anti-Malthusian and non-Malthusian influences deprived Darwin's metaphor of commonsensical power and explanatory appeal. ... (Todes, 1989: 168)

Though a great admirer of Darwin, this aspect of his work was not lost on Marx. "It is remarkable," he wrote to Engels, "how Darwin recognizes among beasts and plants his English society with its divisions of labor, competition, opening up of new markets, inventions and Malthusian 'struggle for existence' " (Marx and Engels, 1965: 128).

Had Darwin (and Wallace) not been so struck, as were many Englishmen of that era, by the extraordinary fecundity of tropical environments and oriented their thinking to the sub-Arctic regions, and if they had been socially armed with images of what we now call "the moral economy of the peasantry," they might well have downplayed, as the Russian evolutionists of all political persuasions did, the mechanisms of competition. They might have emphasized cooperation and mutual aid instead. When Kropotkin arrived in London from Russia, armed with his theories of mutual aid as a potent force in both natural and social evolution, he was simply dismissed as an anarchist crank (in spite of his impressive scientific credentials), so powerful was the aura of social Darwinism at the time.

But there is another interesting metaphor at work in Darwin's argument, to some degree antagonistic to that of competition and the struggle for existence. This had to do with species diversification into niches. The guiding metaphor here seems to have been the proliferation of the divisions of labor and the increasing roundaboutness of production occurring within the factory system, about which Darwin was also very knowledgeable given that he was married to Emma, the daughter of industrialist Josiah Wedgwood. Increasing specialization and diversification of species into noncompetitive environmental niches here ameliorates a story that would otherwise surely end up in one species dominant over all.

In all of these instances, the interplay of socially grounded metaphors and scientific enquiry is such as to make it extremely difficult to extract from the scientific findings any socially untainted information on the values that might reside in nature. It is not surprising, therefore, to find Darwin's influential and powerful scientific views being appropriated by a wide range of political movements as a "natural" basis for their particular political programs (see Gerratana, 1973). Nor should we be surprised that others, such as Allee and his ecologist colleagues at the University of Chicago in the inter-war years, could use their scientific work on (in this case) animal ecology as a vehicle to support and even promote their communitarian, pacifist, and cooperative views (Mitman, 1992).

3. The Territorial Imperative

Animal ethology in the hands of Ardrey, Lorenz, and Morris suggested that territoriality in animals was about exclusive control over localized resources and the inference was carried over that social systems necessarily have as their basis competitive struggles for control of territories (from the micro-scale of private property and local "turf" wars to geopolitical struggles between nation states). Territorial exclusions and competitive struggles were then presumed to be natural. This is an issue of considerable importance to the argument on place and community advanced in chapter 11, so it is useful to provide here a provisional comment on its validity. Ingold (1986: 143), after careful examination of the extensive anthropological evidence on territorial behavior among hunters and gatherers, concludes that territoriality is rarely competitive or exclusionary. It:

> furnishes a mode of reciprocal communication, conveying information about the locations of people and resources which is of mutual benefit to all parties. By the same token, it has nothing whatsoever to do with the maintenance, through active defense, of exclusive access to resources by a social group. ... [It] is a means of effecting cooperation over an extensive but common range in an ecological situation (the exploitation of dispersed fauna or flora) which precludes regular face to face contact between cooperating units in the course of extractive activities. Quite simply, it prevents adjacent groups, ignorant of each others' positions, from traversing the same ground and thereby spoiling the success of their respective exploitative operations ... *territorial compartmentalization may be perfectly compatible with the collective appropriation of nature.* (Ingold, 1986: 143)

Territorial stakeouts, according to this account, are as much about mutual cooperation between members of a species as about competition. Indeed, the distinction between competition and cooperation collapses into a dialectical relation in which one can become the other and vice versa under certain conditions. Exclusionary territoriality, Ingold points out, is solely a function of property rights of a settled and exclusionary sort and such rights are a product of society not inherent in nature. And this was, of course, a point long ago understood by Rousseau (1973: 84):

> The first man who, having enclosed a piece of ground, bethought himself of saying "This is mine," and found people simple enough to believe him, was the real founder of civil society. From how many crimes, wars, and murders, from how many horrors and misfortunes might not anyone have saved mankind, by pulling up the stakes, or filling in the ditch, and crying to his fellows: "Beware of listening to this imposter; you are undone if you once forget that the fruits of the earth belong to us all, and the earth itself to nobody."

III. The Nature of Metaphors

The conclusion to be drawn from these three examples is, it seems to me, inescapable. If values reside in nature we have no scientific way of knowing what they are independently of the values implicit in the metaphors deployed in mounting specific lines of scientific enquiry. Even the names we use betray the depth and pervasiveness of the problem. "Worker bees" cannot understand the *The Communist Manifesto* any more than the "praying mantis" goes to church; yet the terminology helps naturalize distinctive social power relations and practices (cf. Bookchin, 1990a). The language of "the selfish gene" or "the blind watchmaker" provide equally vivid social referents of scientific arguments and Dawkins (1989), most persistent popularizer of these views, quite unself-consciously uses the metaphor of survival conditions for Chicago gangsters as a convenient metaphor to explain the basic logic of genetic selection. Rousseau (1973: 65), interestingly, spotted the trick long ago (while, in his character-istic way, making active use of it) when he wrote of "the blunder made by those who, in reasoning on the state of nature, always import into it ideas gathered in a state of society." Ecologists concerned, for example, to articulate concep-tions of equilibrium, plant succession, and climax vegetation as properties of the natural world, have reflected as much about the human search for permanence and security as the quest for an accurate and neutral description or theorization of ecological processes. And the idea of harmony with nature not as a human desire but as a nature-imposed necessity likewise smacks of the view that to be natural is to be harmonious rather than conflictual and contradictory both of which are quickly dubbed as artificial, the result of "disturbance" and the like. We have loaded upon nature, often without know-ing it, in our science as in our poetry, much of the alternative desire for value to that implied by money.

But the choice of values lies within us and not in nature. We see, in short, only those values which our value-loaded metaphors allow us to see in our studies of the natural world. Harmony and equilibrium; beauty, integrity and stability; cooperation and mutual aid; ugliness and violence; hierarchy and order; competition and the struggle for existence; turbulence and unpredict-able dynamic change; atomistic causation; dialectics and principles of comple-mentarity; chaos and disorder; fractals and strange attractors; all of them can be identified as "natural values" not because they are arbitrarily assigned to nature, but because no matter how ruthless, pristine, and rigorously "objective" our method of enquiry may be, the framework of interpretation is given in the metaphor rather than in the evidence. From contemporary reproductive and cell biology we will learn, for example, that the world is necessarily hierarchically ordered into command and control systems that look suspiciously like a Fordist factory system while from contemporary immunology we will conclude that the world is ordered as a fluid communi-cations systems with dispersed command–control–intelligence networks which look much more like contemporary models of flexible industrial and commercial organization (Martin, 1992).

When, therefore, it is claimed that "nature teaches," what usually follows, Williams (1980: 70) remarks, "is selective, according to the speaker's general purpose." The solution, here, cannot be to seek scientific enquiry without metaphors. Their deployment (like the parallel deployment of models) lies at the root of the production of all knowledge. It is the primary means whereby the human imaginary gets mobilized to gain understandings of the natural and social worlds and we can no more dispense with that imaginary than we can live without breathing. The qualities of that imaginary, as Osserman (1995) so brilliantly demonstrates in his enchanting book on the history of mathematical understandings of the universe, were fundamental to erecting more and more adequate representations of all sorts of intricate physical processes. Max Black (1962: 242) reflects "perhaps every science must start with metaphor and end with algebra; and perhaps without metaphor there would never have been any algebra." "Metaphoric perception," Bohm and Peat (1987: 35–41) concur, is "fundamental to all science" both in extending existing thought processes as well as in penetrating into "as yet unknown domains of reality, which are in some sense implicit in the metaphor." And if this argument holds for those branches of knowledge, such as physics and biology, which are generally held to be characterized by a certain "purity" of scientific method, then it holds even more so, as Timpanaro (1970) and Williams (1978) agree, with the contested and often arbitrary and tendentious findings of psychoanalysis. This latter field is in particular plagued by intertwining of terms that have a double character "in that they are internally held to be 'findings' from empirical evidence and yet at the same time are quite rapidly diffused in forms of discourse usually dependent on concepts founded in a more 'normal' linguistic mode, in the development of a language in social and historical experience" (Williams, 1978: 14).

But to put it this way does not mean that the metaphors are purely products of the human imaginary, unalloyed and untainted by any exposure to material practices, power relations, and the like. Kuhn (1988: 12) thus holds that all theories of metaphor presuppose a theory of literal meanings and considers that tropes like metaphor would be unimaginable "except within a community whose members had previously assimilated their literal use." Literal meanings do not derive directly from something called "reality" in the sense usually accorded that term as something entirely and exclusively outside of thought. But metaphors do derive their power from the social and material practices and experiences of the world to which literal meanings always attach.

We can, therefore, only reflect critically upon the dialectical properties (internalizations) of the metaphors in use and watch carefully as human beings amass scientific and other evidence for a particular "naturalized" set of values. And then we find that the values supposedly inherent in nature are properties of the metaphors, of the human imaginary internalizing and working on the multiple effects of other moments in the social process, most conspicuously those of material social practices. "We can never speak about nature," says Capra (1975: 77) "without, at the same time, speaking about ourselves."

IV. Deep Ecology, Self-realization and the Leibnizian Conceit

The connection that Capra makes has not gone unrecognized in ecological thinking and attempts to rescue some ideal of intrinsic or inherent values on its basis are legion. Callicott, for example, accepts that any concept of *intrinsic* value as objective and independent of any valuing consciousness is untenable. But something called *inherent* value, he argues, can be naturally grounded and to bolster his argument he goes back to Hume, modified by Darwin. Hume suggests that the values you project onto objects are not arbitrary, but arise spontaneously in you because of the "constitution of your nature." From Darwin Callicott (1989: 182) gets the idea that the "affective constitution of human nature is standardized by natural selection" so that:

> certain sentiments were naturally selected in a social environment which permitted and facilitated growth in the size and complexity of society. The social sentiments, however, though fixed by natural selection, are open-ended. There is more than just a little room for the cultural determination of their objects. Thus, just what is of value, either instrumentally or inherently is partly determined by what Hume called "reason," but what might be better called "cultural representation." Aldo Leopold masterfully played upon our open social and moral sentiments by representing plants and animals, soils and waters as "fellow members" of our maximally expanded "biotic community." Hence, to those who are ecologically well-informed, nonhuman natural entities are inherently valuable – as putative members of one extended family or society. And nature as a whole is inherently valuable – as the one great family or society to which we belong as members or citizens.

What is at work here is "the biologization of ethics" and that brings us uncomfortably close, as Callicott acknowledges, to the sociobiology of E.O. Wilson (1978: 5–6):

> [Morality] evolved as instinct. If that perception is correct, science may soon be in a position to investigate the very origin and meaning of human values, from which all ethical pronouncements and much of political practice flow [Morality] resides in the deep emotional centers of the brain, most probably within the limbic system, a complex array of neurons and hormone-secreting cells located just beneath the "thinking" portion of the cerebral cortex.

More recently, Wilson has pursued what he calls the "biophilia hypothesis" which maintains that:

> eons of evolution, during which humans constantly and intimately interacted with nature, have imbued Homo sapiens with a deep, genetically based emotional need to affiliate with the rest of the living world. Meeting this need ... may be as important to human well-being as forming close personal relationships. (Stevens, 1993: C1; Wilson and Kellert, 1993)

But there are those, such as Ross (1993), who strongly and rightly "dispute the whole idea behind the 'genetic' way of looking at the world that is rapidly becoming second nature" and challenge "the growing reliance on the authority of 'nature' to deal with problems that are primarily social in origin and development." In part the objection to Wilson rests on the reductionism: the idea that the whole of human endeavor (including attitudes and behaviors) can be reconstructed simply on the basis of genetic information. But it is plainly wrong to replace one form of reductionism with another, by, for example, rejecting all material and biological conditions of human behavior as irrelevant in favor of a triumphalist mode of thought in which human history, economy, and culture reign supreme. This is, therefore, an issue that will be taken up more directly in chapter 8. For the moment, I shall rest my argument on the objection that the metaphors and patterns projected onto nature (and thought therefore to be coded in our genes) are derived precisely from the human social institutions that thereby become "naturalized" through biological enquiry.

If discourses about values are established and communicated through the mediating powers of language, institutions, social relations, and the like, then there seems no way to attribute anything intrinsic to external nature in them. To rescue his argument from this difficulty, Callicott shifts his terrain from Darwinian biology to quantum theory. In so doing, he makes a move that is quite common in modern environmental philosophy: pursuing an active connection between seemingly analogous lines of thought in ecology and contemporary physics. Quantum theory, he argues, has had to abandon the Cartesian distinction between facts and values and since some version of the Cartesian dualism underlies Hume's and even Leopold's line of thought, a radical reconceptualization of the intrinsic argument is required. If, in quantum theory, there is no reason to distinguish arbitrarily between mind and matter, facts and values, consciousness and materiality, then physics and ethics are "equally descriptive of nature." This conclusion, as Zimmerman (1988: 10) rightly argues, is open to dispute since there are at least six different interpretations of quantum physics (see Bell, 1989) and by no means all of them are antagonistic to Descartes [see, for example, Lockwood's (1989) active defense of the Cartesian view from within quantum theory]. But

> Callicott claims that quantum physics views the universe as an internally related cosmic "web." The dualistic view of the "I" as residing inside of a skin bag and thus separate from everything else has been undermined by the insight of contemporary physics (and ecology) that in some sense the world is my body: I and the world interpenetrate. Since we have traditionally assumed that the "I" is internally related to all of nature, then we can arguably regard nature, too, as intrinsically valuable. (Zimmerman, 1988: 4)

Callicott (1989: 174) himself concludes:

Since nature is the self fully extended and diffused, and the self, complementarity concentrated and focused in one of the intersections, the "knots", of the web or life or in the trajectory of one of the world lines in the four-dimensional space–time continuum, nature is intrinsically valuable, *to the extent* that the self is intrinsically valuable.

This is nothing less than a resurrection of what I earlier termed "the Leibnizian conceit:" the (monadic) self internalizes natural values. But through what kind of conception of "self" can we, or ought we, construe our relation to that "other" which we call "nature?" This is the question at which Callicott arrives and it is one that has preoccupied deep ecology.

Naess (1989: 79), the leading figure in deep ecology, insists on a *relational* answer: "a human being is not a thing in an environment, but a juncture in a relational system without determined boundaries in time and space." This is an extremely important definition that has a significant bearing on my whole argument. To begin with, it picks up on the process philosophy of Whitehead and the dialectical conceptions of internal relations (see chapter 2) and specifically incorporates the view that "whole and part are internally related" (Naess, 1989: 59). It also challenges conventional views of time and space (see chapters 9 and 10). In effect, Naess is arguing that the individual cannot be construed as a bounded entity, a kind of box unto him or herself, but rather like a *point* (which is geometrically defined as something that has no dimensions) formed by innumerable vectors of influences and relations converging at the same junction. Relationalism:

> makes it easy to undermine the belief in organisms or persons as something that can be isolated from their milieux. Speaking of interactions between organisms and the milieux gives rise to the wrong associations as an *organism is interaction*. Organisms and milieux are not two things – if a mouse were lifted into absolute vacuum, it would no longer be a mouse. Organisms presuppose milieux. Similarly, a person is a part of nature to the extent that he or she is a relational junction within the total field. The process of identification is a process in which the relations which define the junction expand to comprise more and more. The "self" grows towards the "Self." (Naess, 1989: 56)

Getting away from "certain conceptions of the status of things" and emancipating ourselves from "strong atomistic or mechanistic trends in analytical thought" are therefore vital steps towards a redefinition of intrinsic value through a process of *Self-Realization*. Fox (cited in Naess, 1989: 19) explains:

> The appropriate framework of discourse for describing and presenting deep ecology is not one that is fundamentally to do with the value of the non-human world, but rather one that is fundamentally to do with the nature and

possibilities of the self, or, we might say, the question of who we are, can become and should become in the larger scheme of things.

The word "should" suggests that value norms arise relationally with respect to the broader biotic community of which we are a part, but the means by which we discover them depend fundamentally on the human capacity for "Self-Realization" (as opposed to the narrower sense of "ego fulfillment" or "self-realization" as understood in bourgeois society). The "deep ecology" literature here tacitly appeals to the notion of a "human essence" or a "human potentiality" (or in Marx's language, a "species being" whose qualities have yet to be fully realized) from which humanity has become fundamentally alienated (both actually and potentially) through separation from "nature." The desire to restore that lost connection (severed by modern technology, commodity production, a Promethean or utilitarian approach to nature, the "community" of money flows, and the like) then lies at the root of an intuitive, contemplative, and phenomenological search for "Self-Realization." If values are "socially and economically anchored," Naess (1989: 45) argues, then the philosophical task is to challenge those instrumental values which alienate. Through "elaboration of a philosophical system" we can arrive at a "comprehensive value clarification and disentanglement," so as to spark a collective movement that can achieve "a substantial reorientation of our whole civilization."

This philosophical system rests on the individual application of the Leibnizian conceit to the understanding of the values that reside in nature. Naess' appeal is that we work hard at sharpening our conceptual understanding while opening ourselves up to the innumerable flows that bind us to the world of nature. The discourse that results is uncompromisingly hostile to that of environmental management (hence the distinction between "deep" and "shallow" ecology) or even to environmental ethics (understood in the narrow sense as the extension of humanly based ethical systems to the animal world). It abhors all talk of money valuations and the market and places itself fundamentally at odds with hegemonic forms of political power and all of the dominant institutions of market-based as well as socialistically organized societies. It is thoroughly revolutionary in its implications, but sees that collective revolution being accomplished through the realm of changing individual practices deriving fundamentally from the processes of Self-Realization. But it does, as we shall see, make gestures towards communities of resistance and communitarian forms of practical organization as an element of its strategy for defining entirely new ecological practices.

All sorts of philosophical, metaphysical, and religious "clarifications" of deep ecology are available. Naess appeals to Spinoza, but figures like Heidegger also offer considerable sustenance to this style of thinking (Steiner, 1992: 136; Foltz, 1995). Instead of nature becoming a "gigantic gasoline station," Heidegger (1971) argues, nature must be seen as "the serving bearer, blossoming and fruiting, spreading out in rock and water, rising up into plant and animal." Mortals, Heidegger concludes, "dwell in that they save the earth" but "saving does not only snatch something from danger. To save really means to set something free into its own presencing." The slogans of *Earth First* (e.g., "set the rivers free!"), while they derive directly from the complex character of William Abbey (whose egotistical devotion to the Leibnizian conceit – without knowing it – is arrogantly transparent) parallel those of the far more philo-sophically respectable Heidegger. The key concept for Heidegger is *presencing*, which translates into internalizing within the self the "authentic" qualities of the external world (again, a very Leibnizian tactic). And this presupposes learning how to *dwell* properly and affectively on earth. If we are to recover the art of dwelling with nature, we must learn, however, to build, dwell, and liberate *place*. Since the question of "place" will be taken up in chapter 11, I will not pursue it further here except to comment on how much deep ecological thinking echoes Heidegger's quest for what Naess (1989: 61) calls "a geographical sense of belonging" or "of being at home" in place. The relationship proposed here is active not passive:

> To "only look at" nature is extremely peculiar behavior. Experiencing of an environment happens by doing something in it, by living in it, meditating and acting. (Naess, 1989: 63)

The activity of place construction, precisely because that is where we can achieve our own geographical sense of belonging, here becomes of vital signif-icance to any process of Self-Realization and, for this reason, Naess (1989: 63) argues, "the local community is the starting point for political deliberation" on ecological questions. This takes us out of the realm of the purely personal – a realm that many deep ecologists, being deeply attached to the Leibnizian conceit, seem to have difficulty escaping from – to the sociality of any project of Self-Realization.

V. The Moral Community and Environmental Values

Naess' and Heidegger's ideas are paralleled by movements in North America towards a bioregional ethic, in which Leopold's recommendation that we enlarge the boundaries of community "to include soils, waters, plants, and animals, or collectively: the land," is taken quite literally as a program for living with nature in place. The ideals of a place-bound environmental identity are strong and lead to principles of how to dwell in the land in a Heideggerian sense. Berg and Dasmann (cited in Alexander, 1990: 163) say this means:

> learning to live-in-place in an area that has been disrupted and injured through past exploitation. It involves becoming native to a place through becoming aware

of the particular ecological relationships that operate within and around it. It means understanding activities and evolving social behavior that will enrich the life of that place, restore its life-supporting systems, and establish an ecologically and socially sustainable pattern of existence within it. Simply stated it involves becoming fully alive in and with a place. It involves applying for membership in a biotic community and ceasing to be its exploiter.

Bioregionalism as a cultural movement therefore:

> celebrates the particular, the unique and often indescribable features of a place. It celebrates this through the visual arts, music, drama and symbols which convey the *feeling* of place. (Mills, cited in Alexander, 1990)

We arrive here at the core of what Goodin (1992: chapter 2) calls a *green theory of value*. It is a set of sentiments and propositions which provides a "unified moral vision" running, in various guises, throughout almost all ecological and green political thinking. It has radical, liberal and quite conservative manifestations as we shall shortly see. And by virtue of its strong attachment of moral community to the experience of place, it frequently directs environmental politics towards a preservation and enhancement of the achieved qualities of particular places.

But the notion of a moral community also proves problematic. Consider, for example, how it plays in the work of Sagoff (1988). While individuals often act as purely self-interested and atomistically constituted economic agents selfishly pursuing their own goals, he argues, they not only can but frequently do act in completely different ways as members of a "moral community" particularly with respect to environmental issues (hence legislation to protect endangered species). In the American case he concludes that:

> Social regulation most fundamentally has to do with the identity of a nation – a nation committed historically, for example, to appreciate and preserve a fabulous natural heritage and to pass it on reasonably undisturbed to future generations. This is not a question of what we *want*; it is not exactly a question of what we *believe in*; it is a question of what we *are*. There is no theoretical way to answer such a question; the answer has to do with our history, our destiny, and our self-perception as a people. (Sagoff, 1988: 17)

There are a variety of points to be made here. First, this is a strongly communitarian version of the "Self-Realization" thesis advanced by Fox (see above). Secondly, it has as much to say about the construction of a nation's identity as it does about the environment. And here we immediately hit upon a difficulty with the moral suasion and political implications of distinctively green values. For they are inevitably implicated in the construction of particular kinds of "moral community" that can just as easily be nationalistic, exclusionary, and in some instances violently fascistic as they can be democratic, decentralized, and anarchist. Bramwell (1989), for example, points out the Nazi connection, not only via Heidegger (whose role is more emblematic than real) but also via the building of a distinctively fascist tradition around German romanticism, themes about "blood and soil" and the like, incidentally noting the extensive and often innovative conservation and afforestation programs that the Nazis pursued (see also Ferry, 1995: chapter 5). Even if Bramwell overstates the case, it is not hard to see how distinctive attitudes to particular environments can become powerfully implicated in the building of any sense of nationalist or communitarian identity. Sagoff's insensitivity in using the term America when he means the United States and his tendency to depopulate the continent of indigenous peoples and to ignore its class, gender, and racial structure in his account of the nation's encounter with the environment contains many of the same disturbing exclusions.

Environmental politics then becomes caught up in handing down to future generations a sense of national identity grounded in certain environmental traits. Put the other way round, nationalism without some appeal to environmental imagery and identity is a most unlikely configuration. If the forest is a symbol of German nation, then forest die-back is a threat to national identity. This association played a key role in sparking the contemporary German green movement but it has also posed considerable difficulty for that movement because it reveals how contemporary ecological sensibilities have their roots in traditions that also prompted the Nazis to be the first "radical environmentalists in charge of a state" (Bramwell, 1989: 11; see also Ferry, 1995: 91–107). Even an ecological radical like Spretnak (1985: 232) is then forced to recognize that "the spiritual dimension of Green politics is an extremely charged and problematic area in West Germany."

It is relatively easy, of course, to pillory the environmentalist excesses of Nazism, so let me take the difficulty onto a much more respectable terrain, namely that of Aldo Leopold himself. In formulating his land ethic, Leopold was keenly aware of the role that the encounter with the frontier was supposed to have played in the creation of national character and political identity in the United States. The closing of the frontier, as Frederick Jackson Turner had argued, changed radically the conditions under which democracy in the United States had been achieved and therefore posed a threat to the continuation of those democratic frontier traditions. Leopold's emphasis upon the preservation of wilderness, even of the authentic hunting ethos, had strong political meanings that can only be understood against the background of the importance of the conception of wilderness to American cultural identity and political ideology (see Nash, 1989).

The point here is not to see *all* ideas about "moral community," bioregionalism or place-bound thinking (e.g., nationalism and imagined community) as necessarily exclusionary or neo-Nazi. Raymond Williams (see chapter 1), builds elements of such thinking into his socialism. In his novels the whole contested terrain of environmental imagery, place-bound ideals, and the disruption of both by contemporary capitalism become meaningful arguments about the roots of alienation and the problematics of the human relation to nature. The task, then, is to try and articulate the social, political, institutional, and economic circumstances that transform such place-bound sentiments concerning a special relation to "nature" into exclusionary and sometimes radical neo-Nazi directions. The evocation of the Nazi connection by Bramwell (though itself a manifestation of conservative hostility to the greens as "new authoritarians antagonistic to free-market liberalism") is here very helpful, since it raises the question of the degree to which strong leanings towards reactionary rather than progressive trajectories might always in the last instance be implicated in green theories of value. In any case, it quickly becomes apparent that environmental values drawn from a moral community have as much to say about the politics of community as they do about the environment. From this standpoint the extraordinary efflorescence of community-based (if not communitarian) movements as a means to resolve environmental difficulties and to achieve a more ecological way of life (see, for example, Rajan, 1993) is deserving of appreciative but also deeply critical scrutiny. By the same token, the vast cottage industry of thinking that goes under the name of "environmental ethics" deserves critical and appreciative scrutiny for the way in which it proposes universal moral principles for the regulation of "our" relation to nature while hiding as hastily and completely as it can any trace of the militant particularisms from which it usually derives much of its inspirational power.

VI. The Languages of Nature

Consider, for a moment, the multiple languages – scientific, poetic, mythic, moral and ethical, economistic and instrumental, emotive and affective – in which ecological issues and value are typically articulated. Some argue that a transdisciplinary language is required to better represent and resolve ecological problems and that the very existence of these multiple languages is a fundamental part of the problem. But there is also a deep reluctance to try to cram everything we want to say about "nature" and our relation to it into one singular and homogeneous language. A limited case can be made for both positions.

The heterogeneity of discourses about "nature" has to be accepted as not only an inevitable but also a very constructive and creative feature of ecological argumentation, provided that it is read not as fragmented and separate modes of thought and action embedded in isolated communities, but as the internalized heterogeneity, the play of difference, which all of us surely feel and experience in our interaction with "others" in both the human and nonhuman world. This is particularly apparent in the diversity of "values" instanciated in nature through social action. In capitalist society these values are primarily (and necessarily) instrumental and utilitarian, dependent upon the monetary calculus and the market. But an intuitive sense of intrinsic natural value is also widespread, partly in recognition of the idea that "Self-Realization" (whether it be in a narrow, egotistical, or "deep" sense) is not outside of some sort of intimate relation of self to nature. The search for moral values and an environmental ethic evokes community politics and brings the environmental issue fully within the frame of cultural politics. It also brings it within the purview of bureaucratic opinion and the regulatory/legal/administrative discourse of institutions. All of the forms of value that I earlier described are to be found at work both discursively and all of them internalize demonstrable effects within practical politics, social relations, and material practices.

Yet there is in this eclecticism an omnipresent danger. Not only do different discourses lie uneasily side by side so that it becomes hard to spot the unity within the difference. But the careful analysis of the way power relations get embedded in distinctive discourses suggests that the vast conceptual muddle and cacophony of discourses is far from innocent in the reproduction of capitalism. Critical engagement with that is no trivial political task.

I began by arguing that the definition of "environment" is so confused as to make it difficult if not impossible to develop any clear conception of what it is we mean by it without first defining the positionality of the subject being environed and having some understanding of the lines of action either being engaged upon or contemplated by that subject. We now find that the concept of "nature" – while all important for the reasons that Williams outlined – embodies a similar set of difficulties. Soper (1995: 2) puts it this way:

> Nature refers us to the object of study of the natural and biological sciences; to issues in metaphysics concerning the differing modes of being of the natural and the human; and to the environment and its various non-human forms of life. The natural is both distinguished from the human and the cultural, but also the concept through which we pose questions about the more or less natural or artificial quality of our own behavior and cultural formation; about the existence and quality of human nature; and about the respective roles of nature and culture in the formation of individuals and their social milieu. Nature also carries an immensely complex and contradictory symbolic load; it is the subject of very contradictory ideologies; and it has been represented in an enormous variety of differing ways.

The "contradictory ideologies" may be, however, less contradictory than they seem once statements are contextualized, positioned, and evaluated in relation to certain kinds of action. Discourses about "nature" and the "natural" become less confusing when taken as moments in a social process in which conflicting forms of social power struggle to gain command of institutions, social relations and material practices for particular purposes. This is not necessarily to suggest that dominant power structures promote one and only one discourse rather than another (though the dominant utilitarianism and Prometheanism – modified by a dose of convenient Malthusianism – that attaches to corporate capitalism and the modern state is hardly in doubt). Rather, it indicates a situation in which different conceptions of nature get evoked for quite different political and substantive purposes within the overall flow of conflictual social action.

But this also means that discourses about nature internalize a whole range of contradictory impulses and conflictual ideas derived from all of the other moments in the social process. And from that standpoint, discussion of the discourses of nature has much to reveal, if only about how the discourses themselves conceal a concrete political agenda in the midst of highly abstract, universalizing, and frequently intensely moral argumentation.

If, as I shall argue in chapter 8, all socio-political projects are ecological projects and vice versa, then some conception of "nature" and of "environment" is omniprescent in everything we say and do. If, furthermore, concepts, discourses, and theories can operate, when internalized in socio-ecological practices and actions, as "material forces" that shape history (cf. Lovejoy, 1964; Ollman, 1976: 23–4), then the present battles being waged over the concepts of "nature" and of "environment" are of immense importance (as we shall see more concretely in chapter 13). All critical examinations of the relation to nature are simultaneously critical examinations of society. The incredible vigor with which ruling interests have sought to contain, shape, mystify, and muddy the contemporary debate over nature and environment [for the most part within discourses of "ecological modernization," (see chapter 11), "sustainability," "green consumerism," or the commodification and sale of "nature" as a cultural spectacle testifies to the seriousness of that connection.

What this in effect means, is that dominant systems of power can advance and protect a hegemonic discourse of efficient and rational environmental management and resource allocation for capital accumulation (and to some degree even construct policies, institutions, and material practices that draw upon such discourses). But they can also strive discursively as well as institutionally to manage the heterogeneity of discourses (even those of radical opposition) to their own advantage. Sophisticated discursive strategies are now in place, for example, to absorb and defray the different imaginaries that typically root much of radical ecological thinking. Bourgeois institutions have a long history of exercising "repressive tolerance" and the current state of environmental/ecological debate, over goals, values and requirements, appears more and more as an excellent case study of how a limited articulation of difference can play exactly such a sustaining role for hegemonic and centralized control of the key institutional and material practices that really matter for the perpetuation of capitalist social and power relations. The task of critical reflection and discursive interventions must surely then be to confront head on the question of how to find a language to make radical ecology truly radical.

8
The Dialectics of Social and Environmental Change

1. Political Values and Environmental–Ecological Issues

One of the more interesting exercises to undertake in enquiring into the environmental–ecological debate, is to inspect arguments not for what they have to say about the environment or nature, but for what it is they say about political–economic organization. In so doing, an impressive array of alternative social forms are invoked as seemingly "necessary" to solve the issues at hand, along with an extraordinary display of disparate culprits and villains needing to be overthrown if our present ecodrama is to have a happy rather than tragic ending. "Environmentalists," notes Paehlke (1989: 194), not only "occupy almost every position on the traditional right-to-left ideological spectrum," but also can adapt to diverse political positions while simultaneously claiming they are beyond politics in the normal sense. Again and again, "the authority of nature and her laws" is claimed either to justify the existing condition of society or "to be the foundation stone of a new society that will solve ecological problems" (Grundmann, 1991b: 114). What is often at stake in ecological and environmentalist arguments, Williams (1980: 71) suggests, "is the ideas of different kinds of societies."

Part of the problem here is that environmental–ecological arguments, precisely because of their diversity and generality, are open to a vast array of uses to which environmentalists and ecologists would almost certainly object. Their rhetoric gets mobilized for a host of special purposes, ranging from advertisements for Audi cars, toothpastes and supposedly "natural" flavors (for foods) and "natural" looks (mainly for women) to more specific targets of social control and investment in "sustainable development" or "nature conservation." But the other side of that coin is that ecologists and to some degree even environmentalists of a more managerial persuasion, tend to leave so many loopholes in their arguments, litter their texts with so many symptomatic silences, ambiguities, and ambivalences that it becomes almost impossible to pin down their socio-political programs with any precision even though their aim may be "nothing less than a non-violent revolution to overthrow our whole polluting, plundering and materialistic industrial society and, in its place, to create a new economic and social order which will allow human beings to live in harmony with the planet" (Porritt and Winner, cited in Dobson, 1990: 7).

My intention in what follows is not to provide some firm classification or indeed to engage in critical evaluation of any particular kind of politics (all of them are open to serious objections), but to illustrate the incredible political diversity to which environmental–ecological opinion is prone.

Authoritarianism

Ophuls (1977: 161) writes: "whatever its specific form, the politics of the sustainable society seem likely to move us along the spectrum from libertarianism towards authoritarianism" and we have to accept that "the golden age of individualism, liberty and democracy is all but over." Faced with escalating scarcities, Heilbroner (1974: 161) likewise argues, there is only one kind of solution: a social order "that will blend a 'religious' orientation and a 'military' discipline [that] may be repugnant to us, but I suspect it offers the greatest promise for bringing about the profound and painful adaptations that the coming generations must make." While their personal commitments are overtly liberal (and in Heilbroner's case social democratic) both authors reluctantly concede the necessity of some kind of centralized authoritarianism as a "realistic" response to natural resource limits and the painful adaptations that such limits will inevitably force upon us. In the case of the strongly Malthusian wing of the ecological movement, and Garrett Hardin is probably the best representative, the appeal to authoritarian solutions is explicit as the only possible political solution to the "tragedy of the commons." Most of the writing in this genre presumes that resource scarcities (and consequent limits to growth) and population pressure lie at the heart of the environmental–ecological issue. Since these issues were paramount in the early 1970s, this style of argument was then also at its height. In recent years, however, "authoritarian solutions to the environmental crisis have been abandoned by the movement" (Dobson, 1990: 26). But there is almost always an authoritarian edge somewhere in ecological politics.

Corporate and State Managerialism

A weak version of the authoritarian solution rests upon the application of techniques of scientific–technical rationality within an administrative state armed with strong regulatory and bureaucratic powers in liaison with "big" science and big corporate capital. The centerpiece of the argument here is that our definition of many ecological problems (e.g., acid rain, the ozone hole, global warming, pesticides in the food chain, etc.) is necessarily science led and that solutions equally depend upon the mobilization of scientific expertise and corporate technological skills embedded within a rational (state-led) process of political–economic decision making. "Ecological modernization" (Hajer, 1992; Weale, 1992: chapter 3) is the ideological watchword for such a politics. Conservation and environmental regulation (at global as well as at national scale) would here be interpreted as both rational and efficient resource management for a sustainable future. Certain sectors of corporate capital, particularly those which stand to benefit from providing the technology necessary for global monitoring of planetary health, find the imagery of global management or "planetary medicine" very attractive, for example (see below, chapter 13).

Pluralistic Liberalism

Democratic rights and freedoms (particularly of speech and opinion) are sometimes regarded as essential to ecological politics precisely because of the difficulty of defining in any omnisicient or omnipotent way what a proper environmental–ecological policy might be and what particular values should be brought to bear in discussing environmental issues. Open and perpetual negotiation over environmental–ecological issues in a society where diverse pressure groups (such as Greenpeace) are allowed to flourish is seen as the only way to assure that the environmental issue is always kept on the agenda. Whoever wants to speak for or about "nature" can, and institutions are created (such as environmental impact statements and environmental law) to permit contestation over the rights of trees and owls. Consensus about environmental issues, and therefore the best bet for environmental protection, can best be reached only after complex negotiation and power plays between a variety of interest groups. But consensus is at best only a temporary moment in a deeply contested and pluralistic politics concerning the values to be attributed to nature and how to view ecological change.

Conservatism

In some of the ecological literature on the principle of prudence and respect for tradition plays a leading role. Human adaptations to and of natural environments have been arrived at over centuries and should not be unnecessarily disturbed. Conservation and preservation of existing landscapes and usages, sometimes argued for by explicit appeal to esthetic judgments, give such a framework a conservative ring (see, for example, Collingwood, 1960). But arguments of this sort have a radical edge. They can be strongly anti-capitalistic (against development) and, when placed in an international setting, they can also be strongly anti-imperialistic. Tradition ought presumably to be respected everywhere, so that all-out modernization is always regarded as problematic. Considerable sympathy can then be extended towards, say, indigenous peoples under seige from commodification and exchange relations. All of this has its romantic side, but it can also produce a hard-headed politics of place that is highly protective of a given environment. The issue is not nonintervention in the environment, but preservation of traditional modes of social and environmental interaction precisely because these have been found to work, at least for some (usually but not always elite) groups. The preservation of the political power and values of such groups is just as important here, of course, as environmental considerations.

Moral Community

The complex issues which arise when ideals of "moral community" are invoked have already been examined. Many "communities" evolve some rough consensus as to what their moral obligations are with respect to modes of social relating as well as to ways of behaving with respect to the "rights of nature" (see Nash, 1989). While often contested, by virtue of the internal heterogeneity of the community or because of pressures towards social change, these moral precepts concerning, for example, the relation to nature (expressed increasingly in the field of "environmental ethics") can become an important ideological tool in the attempt to forge community solidarities (e.g., nationalist sentiments) and to gain empowerment. This is the space, *par excellence* of moral debate (see, for example, Attfield, 1991) on environmental issues coupled with the articulation of communitarian politics and values that center on ideals of civic virtues. A virtuous relation to nature is closely tied to communitarian ideals of civic virtues.

Ecosocialism

While there is a definite tendency in socialist circles to look upon environmentalism as a middle class and bourgeois issue and to regard proposals for zero growth and constraints on consumption with intense suspicion (see Benton, 1989: 52, for a good summary) there are enough overlaps in enough areas to make ecosocialism a feasible political project (though it is still a relatively minor current within most mainstream socialist movements). Some environmental issues, such as occupational health and safety, are of intense concern to workers, while many ecological groups accept that environmental problems can be "traced back to the capitalist precept that the choice of production technology is to be governed solely by private interest in profit maximization of market share" (Commoner, 1990: 219). "If we want ecological sanity," assert Haila and Levins (1992: 251), "we have to struggle for social justice." This means social control of production technology and the means of production, control over capitalistic "accumulation for accumulation's sake, production for production's sake" which lies at the root of many environmental issues, and a recognition that "the future of humanity simply cannot build on pleasant life for a few and suffering for the majority" (Haila and Levins, 1992: 227). This places the environmental issue firmly within the socialist orbit. Those socialists (see O'Connor, 1988; Foster, 1994) who accept that there is an ecological crisis, then argue that a second route to socialism is available; one that highlights the contradiction between the social organization of production and the (ecological) conditions of production, rather than class contradictions. The necessity for socialism is then in part given because only under socialism can thorough, enduring, and socially just solutions be found to the environmental problems.

Ecofeminism

The nature–nurture controversy has been nowhere more thoroughly debated than in the feminist movement and in ecofeminism we find a diverse set of opinions on how to connect the environmental–ecological issue with feminist politics (see Plumwood, 1993; Shiva, 1989 for quite different presentations). In radical ecofeminism, for example, the devaluation and degradation of nature is seen as deeply implicated in the parallel devaluations and degradation of women under a system of patriarchal oppression. One line of political response is to celebrate rather than deny the web-like interrelations between women and nature through the development of rituals and symbolism as well as an ethic of caring, nurturing, and procreation. An alternative line of argument resists the essentialism implicit in such an argument and defines a "feminist environmentalism" in which the "link between women and the environment can be seen as structured by a given gender and class (/caste/race) organization of production, reproduction, and distribution" (Agarwal, 1992: 119). In both equations, the feminism is as prominent, if not more so, than the ecology and solutions to ecological problems are seen as dependent upon the acceptance of certain kinds of feminist principles.

Decentralized communitarianism

Most contemporary ecological movements, Dobson (1990: 25) argues, eschew authoritarian solutions on principle and "argue for a radically participatory form of society in which discussion takes place and explicit consent is asked for and given across the widest possible range of political and social issues." Their politics generally derive inspiration from "the self-reliant community modelled on anarchist lines" (O'Riordan, 1981: 307) and writers like Bookchin, Goldsmith, and a host of others (including the German green party) have tried to articulate the form of social relations which should prevail within such self-reliant communities that could become, by virtue of their scale, "closer" to nature. Egalitarianism, nonhierarchical forms of organization, and widespread local empowerment and participation in decision-making are usually depicted as the political norm (Dauncey, 1988). Decentralization and community empowerment, coupled with a certain degree of bioregionalism, is then seen as the only effective solution to an alienated relation to nature and alienation in social relationships.

The positions I have here outlined are by no means mutually exclusive and all kinds of cooptations from one line of thought to another can be observed. The World Bank's concern with "sustainability" (both ecological and financial) has led to a cooptation of ecofeminist arguments to place women in the forefront of development projects. Decentralized green politics likewise seeks to coopt some of the findings if not some of the personnel from within a highly centralized science of global environmental management.

The array of ecological politics I have here outlined must also be supplemented, by an even vaster and much more complex array of special pleading, in which environmental–ecological issues or requirements are invoked for very particular social purposes. Scientists, for example, hungry for funding as well as for attention, may create environmental issues that reflect as much about the political–economy and sociology of science as they do about the condition of the environment. Robert May (1992), a Royal Society research professor writing on the evident urgency of taking measures to conserve biological diversity, focuses, for example, as much on the underfunding of taxonomy (relative to physics) as on how to define the importance of or deal with the issue. While on the one hand scientific ignorance is clearly a barrier to proper identification of what the relevant issues or solutions might be, the perpetual claims for more funding sometimes deservedly provoke scepticism.

Jacks and Whyte (1939: 261–2) provide another and even more insidious example. Writing in 1939, these two highly respected soil scientists, deeply concerned about soil erosion in Africa, argued that:

> A feudal type of society in which the native cultivators would be to some extent tied to the lands of their European overlords seems the most generally suited to meet the needs of the soil in the present state of African development. Africa cannot be expected to accept feudalism without a struggle; in parts of British Africa it would mean jettisoning the promising experiment of Indirect Rule, everywhere it would mean denying to the natives some of the liberty and opportunities for material advancement to which their labors should entitle them. But it would enable the people who have been the prime cause of erosion and who have the means and ability to control it to assume responsibility for the soil. Self-interest, untrammelled by fears of native rivalry, would ensure that the responsibility was carried out in the ultimate interests of the soil. At present, humanitarian considerations for the natives prevent Europeans from winning

the attainable position of dominance over the soil. Humanity may perhaps be the higher ideal, but the soil demands are dominant, and if white men will not and black men cannot assume the position, the vegetation will do so, by the process of erosion finally squeezing out the whites.

Both blunt and startling, this statement illustrates how, in the name of the environment, all kinds of restrictions should be put upon the rights of "others" while conferring rights (and obligations) on those who supposedly have the knowledge and the high technology to control the problem. While few would now dare to be so blatant, there is a strong strain of this kind of thinking in World Bank arguments and even in such a seemingly progressive document as the Brundtland Report. Control over the resources of others, in the name of planetary health, sustainability or preventing environmental degradation, is never too far from the surface of many western proposals for global environmental management. Awareness of precisely that potentiality stimulates a good deal of resistance in developing countries to any form of environmentalism emanating from the west.

Similar issues arise whenever the environmental–ecological issue gets converted into a purely esthetic question. The special issue of *Fortune* devoted to the environment in 1970, for example, contained a strong argument for the redevelopment of the downtowns of the United States along what we would now call "postmodern" lines, invoking environmental quality (usually depicted as user-friendly and as tree-lined or waterfront spaces) as its primary goal. The whole contemporary "culture of nature" as Wilson (1992) calls it, is a very cultivated and hard-sold taste, that preys upon environmental quality through commercial cooptation.

A cynical observer might be tempted to conclude that discussion of the environmental issue is nothing more than a covert way of introducing particular social and political projects by raising the specter of an ecological crisis or of legitimizing solutions by appeal to the authority of nature-imposed necessity. I would want, however, to draw a somewhat broader conclusion: all ecological projects (and arguments) are simultaneously political–economic projects (and arguments) and vice versa. Ecological arguments are never socially neutral any more than socio-political arguments are ecologically neutral. Looking more closely at the way ecology and politics interrelate, then becomes imperative if we are to get a better handle on how to approach environmental/ecological questions.

II. Historical–Geographical Materialism and the Political–Economy of Socio-ecological Projects

There is an extraordinarily rich record of the historical geography of socio-ecological change that sheds much light on the ways in which socio-political and ecological projects intertwine with and at some point become indistinguishable from each other. The archive of such materials from archeology (see, for example, Butzer, 1982), anthropology (see, for example, Bennett, 1976; Ellen, 1982; Ingold, 1986), geography (Thomas, 1956; Goudie, 1986; Turner et al., 1990), and more recently history (cf. the debate in *Journal of American History*, 1990) is extensive indeed. Yet much of the contemporary debate on environmental–ecological issues, for all of its surface devotion to ideals of multidisciplinarity and "depth," operates as if these materials either do not exist or, if they do, exist only as a repository of anecdotal evidence in support of particular claims. The debate remains at the purely discursive level and fails to integrate itself with what we know about the historical–geography of material practices. Systematic work is relatively rare and that which does exist (e.g., Butzer, 1982) has not been anywhere near as central to discussion as it should. The debate now arising within Marxism – between, for example, Benton (1989, 1992) and Grundmann (1991a, b) – operates at a level of historical–geographical abstraction that is most un-Marxist.

The difficulty in part derives from the tendency in discursive debates to homogenize the category "nature" (and discuss its social meaning and constitution as a unitary category) when it should be regarded as intensely internally variegated – an unparalleled field of difference. In much the same way that the formal debate over "language" (see chapter 3) loses sight of the multiple languages at work in the world, so the general debate over the society/nature relation loses sight of the incredible degree of ecosystemic variation. As much attention should then be paid to the production of difference as to the relational meaning of nature in general. So where does all this difference come from?

An impressionistic survey illustrates well how societies strive to create ecological conditions and environmental niches for themselves which are not only conducive to their own survival but also manifestations and instanciations "in nature" of their particular social relations. Since no society can accomplish such a task without encountering unintended ecological consequences, the contradiction between social and ecological change can become highly problematic, even from time to time putting the very survival of the society concerned at risk. This latter point was made as long ago as 1864, by that extraordinary pioneer in the study of the historical–geography of environmental change, George Perkins Marsh. While Marsh recognized that it was often hard to distinguish between anthropogenic and nonanthropogenic changes, he regarded it as "certain that man has done much to mould the form of the earth's surface" in ways that were by no means always destructive to human interests. Nevertheless, we have long forgotten that the earth was given to us "for usufruct alone, not for consumption, still less for profligate waste." The net effect of human interventions is that "the harmonies of nature are turned to discords because the intentional changes pale "in comparison with the contingent and unsought results which have flowed from them." Engels, without much in the way of evidence, made the same point:

> Let us not, however, flatter ourselves overmuch on account of our human victories over nature. For each such victory nature takes its revenge on us. Each victory, it is true, in the first place brings about the results we expected, but in the second and third places it has quite different, unforeseen effects which only too often cancel the first. ... Thus at every step we are reminded that we by no means rule over nature like a conqueror over a foreign people, like someone standing out of nature – but that we, with flesh, blood, and brain, belong to nature, and exist in its midst, and that all our mastery of it consists in the fact that we have the advantage over all other creatures of being able to learn its laws and apply them correctly.

This implies the sheer necessity of *always* taking the duality of social and ecological change seriously (cf. Cronon's "dialectical" views cited in chapter 6) or, as Marx and Engels' (1975: 55) put it, recognizing that the "antithesis between nature and history is created" only when "the relation of man to nature is excluded from history."

Putting that relation back into history reveals a lot. Cronon (1983), for example, shows how a New England environment that was the product of more than 10,000 years of Indian occupation and forest use (promoting, through burning, the forest edge conditions which tend to be so species diverse) was misread by the settlers as pristine, virginal, rich, and underutilized by indigenous peoples. The implantation of European institutions of governance and property rights (coupled with distinctively European aspirations towards accumulation of wealth) wrought an ecological transformation of such enormity that indigenous populations were deprived of the ecological basis for their particular way of life. The annihilation of that way of life and the social orderings that constructed it (and thereby of Indian peoples themselves) was as much an ecological as a military or political event. In part this had to do with the introduction of new disease regimes (smallpox in particular) but changes in and on the land also made it impossible to sustain a nomadic and highly flexible indigenous mode of production and reproduction.

One path towards consolidation of a particular set of social relations, therefore, is to undertake an ecological transformation which requires the reproduction of those social relations in order to sustain it. Worster (1985a) doubtless exaggerates in his flamboyant projection onto the American West of Wittfogel's theses on the relation between large-scale irrigation schemes and despotic forms of government, but his basic argument is surely correct. Once the original proposals for a communitarian, decentralized, "bio-regional," river-basin-confined settlement system for the US west, drawn up by the geologist John Wesley Powell at the end of the nineteenth century, were rejected by a congress dominated by large-scale corporate interests (Powell being thoroughly vilified in the process), those interests sought to assure their own reproduction through construction of dams, mega-water projects of all sorts and vast transformations of the western ecosystem. Sustaining such a grandiose ecological project came to depend crucially upon the creation and mainten-ance of centralized state powers and certain class relations (the formation and perpetuation, for example, of large-scale agribusiness and an oppressed landless agrarian proletariat). The consequent subversion of the Jeffersonian dream of agrarian democracy has ever since created intense contradictions in the body politic of states like California (see, for example, Gottlieb, 1988 or Polanski's film *Chinatown*). But here another implication (notably absent in much of Cronon's work) follows: contradictions in the social relations entail social contradictions on the land and *within* ecosystemic projects themselves. Not only do the rich occupy privileged niches in the habitat while the poor tend to work and live in the more toxic or hazardous zones (see chapter 13), but the very design of the transformed ecosystem is redolent of its social relations. Conversely, projects set up in purely ecological terms – one thinks of the so-called "green revolution" for example – have all manner of distributive and social consequences (in the green revolution case the concentration of land holdings in a few hands and the creation of a landless agrarian proletariat).

Created ecosystems tend to both instanciate and reflect, therefore, the social systems that gave rise to them, though they do not do so in noncontradictory (i.e., *stable*) ways. This simple principle ought to weigh much more heavily than it does upon all angles of environmental–ecological debate. It is a principle which Lewontin (1982: 162) argues has been forgotten as much in biology as in social science:

> We cannot regard evolution as the "solution" by species of some predetermined environmental "problems" because it is the life activities of the species themselves that determine both the problems and solutions simultaneously. ... Organisms within their individual lifetimes and in the course of their evolution as a species do not *adapt* to environments; they *construct* them. They are not simply *objects* of the laws of nature, altering themselves to the inevitable, but active *subjects* transforming nature according to its laws.

The effect is to say that what separates Pakistan from the US west is not so much differences in something called "natural environmental conditions" (important though these may be) but the historical geography of struggles over the social process (incorporating all of its moments) through which environ-ments have been transformed. This implies that we cannot somehow abandon in a relatively costless way the immense existing ecosystemic structures of, say, contemporary capitalism in order to "get back close to nature." Such construct-ed ecosystems are a reworked form of "second nature" that cannot be allowed to deteriorate or collapse without courting ecological disaster not only for the social order that produced it, but for all species and forms that have become dependent on it. The proper management of constituted environments (and in this I include their long-term socialistic or ecological transformation into something completely different) may therefore require transitional political institutions, hierarchies of power relations, and systems of governance that could well be anathema to both ecologists and socialists alike. This is so because, in a fundamental sense, there is nothing *unnatural* about New York city and sustaining such an ecosystem even in transition entails an inevitable compromise with the forms of social organization and social relations which produced it.

To term New York city a "created ecosystem" may sound somewhat odd. But human activity cannot be viewed as external to ecosystemic projects. To view it so makes no more sense than trying to study pollination without bees or the precolonial ecosystem of the northeastern United States without the beaver. And it is particularly odd to find many otherwise dedicated ecological thinkers excluding the massive transformations of urbanization from their purview while insisting in principle that in an ecological world everything relates to everything else. The long history of urbanization is, after all, one of the most significant of all the processes of environmental modification that have occurred throughout recent world history. In the last century that process has become explosive, creating a set of global ecological conditions that have never been seen before. And environmental issues have emerged that are wholly specific to the ecologies our urbanizing activities have created. We will surely pay a severe price for the discursive habit of excluding urban historical geography from the overall thrust of environmental historical geography (see chapter 14). We have, Gottlieb (1993) correctly insists, to shift environmental analysis "from an argument about protection or management of the natural environment to a discussion of social movements in response to the urban and industrial forces of the past hundred years." The created environments of an urbanizing world, their qualities and particular difficulties, their proneness to new configurations for the development and transmission of new diseases, their extraordinarily difficult problems of sustainability (in whatever sense) have to move to the center of our attention relative to much of the contemporary preoccupation with wilderness, peripheral peasant movements, preservation of scenic landscapes, and the like.

Human beings, like all other organisms, are "active *subjects* transforming nature according to its laws" and are always in the course of adapting to the ecosystems they themselves construct. It is fundamentally mistaken, therefore, to speak of the impact of society *on* the ecosystem as if these are two separate systems in interaction with each other. The typical manner of depicting the world around us in terms of a box labelled "society" in interaction with a box labelled "environment" not only makes little intuitive sense (try drawing the boundary between the boxes in your own daily life) but it also has just as little fundamental theoretical or historical justification. Money flows and commodity movements, for example, have to be regarded as fundamental to contemporary ecosystems (particularly given urbanization), not only because of the past geographical transfer of plant and animal species from one environment to another (see Crosby, 1986), but also because these flows formed and continue to form a coordinating network that keeps contemporary ecological habitats reproducing and changing in the particular way they do. If those money flows ceased tomorrow, then the disruption within the world's ecosystems would be enormous. And as the flows shift and change their character, as is always the case given the uneven geographical development of capitalism, so the creative impulses embedded in any socio-ecological system will also shift and change in ways that may be stressful, contradictory or salutary as the case may be. Here, too, Cronon's (1991) consideration of Chicago as a city operating as a fundamental exchange point between and transformative influence within the ecosystems of North America provides an interesting case study. It in effect translates and extends Smith's theses (see Smith, 1990) concerning "the production of nature" through commodity exchange and capital accumulation into a detailed historical–geographical narrative. The category "environmental or ecological movement" may also for this reason be a misnomer particularly when applied to resistances of indigenous peoples to ecological change. Such resistances may not be based, as many in the west might suppose, upon some deep inner need to preserve a distinctive and unalienated relation to nature or to keep intact valued symbols of ancestry and the like, but upon a much clearer recognition that an ecological transformation imposed from outside (as happened in the colonial New England or as has more recently happened to rubber tappers in the Amazon) will destroy indigenous modes of production. Guha (1989: xii), for example, in his study of the Chipko "tree-hugging" movement in the Himalayas against commercial logging and high-tech forest yield management, shows (contra Shiva's well-known interpretation) that "the most celebrated 'environmental' movement in the Third World is viewed by its participants as being above all a *peasant* movement in defence of traditional rights in the forest and only secondarily, if at all, an 'environmental' or 'feminist' movement." Yet, to the degree that a "homogenizing urban–industrial culture" is generating its own distinctive forms of ecological and cultural contradictions and crises, the Chipko, precisely by virtue of their ecological practices, "represent one of the most innovative responses to the ecological and cultural crisis of modern society" (Guha, 1989: 196).

Indigenous groups (including those peasant women made so much of in ecofeminist writings) can, however, also be totally unsentimental in their ecological practices. It is largely a western construction, heavily influenced by the romantic reaction to modern industrialism, which leads many to the view that they were and continue to be somehow "closer to nature" than we are (even Guha, it seem to me, falls into this trap). Faced with the ecological vulnerability often associated with such "proximity to nature," indigenous groups can transform both their practices and their views of nature with startling rapidity. Furthermore, even when armed with all kinds of cultural traditions and symbolic gestures that indicate deep respect for the spirituality in nature, they can engage in extensive ecosystemic transformations that undermine their ability to continue with a given mode of production. The Chinese may have ecologically sensitive traditions of Tao, Buddhism, and Confucianism (traditions of thought which have played an important role in promoting an "ecological consciousness" in the west) but the historical geography of deforestation, land degradation, river erosion, and flooding in China contains not a few environmental events which would be regarded as catastrophes by modern-day standards. Archeological evidence likewise suggests that late ice-age hunting groups hunted many of their prey to extinction while fire must surely rate as one of the most far-reaching agents of ecological transformation ever acquired, allowing very small groups to exercise immense ecosystemic influence (Sauer, 1956).

The point here is not to argue that there is nothing new under the sun about the ecological disturbance generated by human activities, but to assess what exactly is new and unduly stressful, given the unprecedented rapidity and scale of contemporary socio-ecological transformations. But historical–geographical enquiries of this sort also put in perspective those claims typically advanced by some ecologists that once upon a time "people everywhere knew how to live in harmony with the natural world" (Goldsmith 1992: xvii) and to view with skepticism Bookchin's (1990a: 97) equally dubious claim that "a relatively self-sufficient community, visibly dependent on its environment for the means of life, would gain a new respect for the organic interrelationships that sustain it." Much contemporary "ecologically conscious" rhetoric pays far too much attention to what indigenous groups *say* without looking at what they *do*. We cannot conclude, for example, that native-American practices are ecologically superior to ours from statements such as those of Luther Standing Bear that:

> We are of the soil and the soil is of us. We love the birds and the beasts that grew with us on this soil. They drank the same water as we did and breathed the same air. We are all one in nature. Believing so, there was in our hearts a great peace and a welling kindness for all living, growing things. (Cited in Booth and Jacobs, 1990: 27)

The inference of "better and more harmonious ecological practices" from statements of this sort would require belief in either some external spiritual guidance to ensure ecologically "right" outcomes, or an extraordinary omniscience in indigenous or pre-capitalistic judgments and practices in a dynamic field of action that is usually plagued by all manner of unintended consequences. "The possibility of over-exploitation of a resource is perfectly compatible with our notion of peoples living close to nature, observing and acting accordingly" (Haila and Levins, 1992: 195). Furthermore, "comparative studies have suggested that all high civilizations that incorporated intensification strategies were metastable and that their growth trajectories can be interpreted as those of accelerating energy extraction, to the point that both the ecosystem and the socioeconomic structures were stretched to capacity, with steady or declining absolute caloric productivity and input–output ratios" (Butzer, 1982: 320). All societies have had their share of ecologically based difficulties and, as Butzer goes on to assert, we have much to learn from studying them.

Indigenous or pre-capitalist practices are not, therefore, necessarily superior or inferior to our own just because such groups possess discourses that avow respect for nature rather than the modern "Promethean" attitude of domination or mastery (see Leiss, 1974). Grundmann (1991a) is surely correct in his argument contra Benton (1989; 1992) that the thesis of "mastery over nature" (laying aside its gendered overtones for the moment) does not necessarily entail destructiveness; it can just as easily lead to loving, caring, and nurturing practices. It was, as we have already noted, precisely the intent of the esthetic tradition to assert "mastery without tyranny" with respect to the natural world. Uncritical acceptance of "ecologically conscious" sounding statements can, furthermore, be politically misleading. Luther Standing Bear prefaced the thoughts cited above with the very political argument that "this land of the great plains is claimed by the Lakota as their very own." Native-Americans may well have strong claims to land rights, to the use of the landscape as a mnemonic upon which to hand their sense of historical identity, but the creation of an "ecologically conscious" rhetoric about a privileged relation to the land to support them is, as we have already argued, an all-too-familiar and dangerous practice.

Inspection of the historical–geographical record reveals much about why words like "nature" and "environment" contain "such an extraordinary amount of human history" (Williams, 1980: 67). The intertwinings of social and ecological projects in daily practices as well as in the realms of ideology, representations, esthetics, and the like are such as to make every social (including literary or artistic) project a project about nature, environment, and ecosystem, and vice versa. Such a proposition should not, surely, be too hard for those working in the historical materialist tradition to swallow. Marx argued, after all, that we can discover who and what we are (our species potential, even) only through transforming the world around us and in so doing put the dialectics of social and ecological change at the center of all human history. But is there some way to create a general enough language to capture that dialectical evolutionary movement?

III. Towards an Evolutionary View

We badly need a much more unified language than we currently possess for exercising the joint responsibility towards nature that resides with the social and biological/physical sciences. The question of the unity of science has, of course, been broached many times – not least by Marx (1964). But serious problems have arisen on the social theory side whenever a biological basis has been invoked (familiar examples include the way social Darwinism founded Nazism, the profound social antagonisms generated in the debate over socio-biology and the dismal history of the eugenics movement particularly as applied to racial categories). The response on the social science side has often been to retreat from any examination of the ecological side of social projects and act as if these either did not matter or as if they had to be construed as something "external" to enquiry. I want to argue that this is not satisfactory and that ways have to be found to create if not a common language, then means to translate across discursive domains. This is, however, dangerous territory – an open field for organicist or holistic rather than dialectical modes of thinking – and it may require deep shifts in ontological and epistemological stances on both the social and natural scientific sides, if it is to succeed.

But the territory cannot be left empty of all thought about how to approach the problem. With this in mind let me propose a dialectical and relational schema for thinking through how to understand the dialectics of social–environmental change. The simplest schema is to break down the evolutionary process into four distinctive facets:

1. Competition and the struggle for existence (the production of hierarchy and homogeneity).
2. Adaptation and diversification into environmental niches (the production of diversity).
3. Collaboration, cooperation, and mutual aid (the production of social forms).
4. Environmental transformations (the production of nature).

I want to treat these as relational categories rather than mutually exclusive processes and thereby to insist that each internalizes effects of the others. Thus socio-biologists are correct when they argue that cooperation ("reciprocal altruism" is their preferred term) is in some sense an adaptive form of competition. The difficulty is that they make the competitive moment the shaping moment of all else (always a convenient gesture given the ideological struggle to "naturalize" capitalism) and use adaptation to absorb collaboration within the competitive framework. This is an excellent example of that habit analyzed in chapter 4, of converting internal relations among moments into hierarchical causal structures almost without noticing it. But from a relational point of view competition can just as easily be seen as a form of cooperation. The example of territoriality examined in chapter 7, is an interesting case in point. But is it not also a fundamental tenet of the liberal theory of capitalism that rampant competition between individuals produces a collaborative social effect called "society?" Adaptation and diversification of species and activities into special niches is also a form of both competition *and* collaboration and the effect is to transform environments in ways that may make the latter more rather than less diverse. Species may diversify further creating more diversified niches. The production of a more diversified nature in turn produces greater diversity of species.

The example of the liberal theory of capitalism, however weakly implanted it is in practice and however ideological its content, can be pressed further into service here to alert us to something else important. For within that theory it is not simply competition that matters, but the particular *mode* of competition, the rules and regulations that ensure that only one sort of competition – that within freely functioning markets respecting property rights and freedom of contract – will prevail. From this perspective it seems as if the normal causal ordering implied in socio-biology gets reversed because it is only through the collaborative and cooperative structures of society (however coerced) that competition and the struggle for existence can be orchestrated to do its work. But the point here is not to change the causal ordering and thereby to make it seem as if society (the mode of cooperation) has in some way contained nature (competition, adaptation, and environmental change). It is much more appropriate to suggest that competition is always regulated in important ways by the effects internalized within it of cooperation, adaptation, and environmental transformations. Thinking in these terms allows us better to see how a particular kind of environmental transformation (such as the great water projects of the US west) affects both the mode of competition (within society as well as between species) and the mode of collaboration/adaptation. Capitalistic competition consequently means something quite different in the agribusiness sector in California compared to, say, dairy producers in Wisconsin, because the forms of environmental transformation have been so radically different in the two places.

I will not elaborate much further on this idea, but it should be apparent that there are different modes of competition, adaptation, cooperation, and environmental transformation. Given the relational/dialectical theory advanced in chapters 2–4, it should also be plain that each facet of the overall process internalizes a great deal of heterogeneity within itself. Such heterogeneity is a source of contradiction, tension, and conflict, sparking intense struggles for stability, hegemony, and control. A mode of production, in Marx's sense, can then be construed as a particular regulated unity of these different modalities. The transition from one mode of production entails transformations in all modalities in relation to each other, including, of course, the nature of the nature produced.

What I am proposing here is a way of depicting the fundamental physical and biological conditions and processes that work through all social, cultural, economic projects to create a tangible historical geography and to do it in such a way as not to render those physical and biological elements as a banal and passive background to human historical geography. But my purpose is also to specify these conditions and processes in such a way as to understand the possibilities for collective human activity in negotiating through these fundamental elements to generate significantly diverse outcomes of the sort that a Marxist theory of historical–geographical development envisages. Given, for example, the four "moments" in the biological evolutionary process, then organisms of any sort (most particularly the human species) can work with the moments of competition, adaptation, cooperation, and environmental modification in a variety of ways to produce radically different outcomes (such as quite different modes of production). "No natural laws can be done away with," Marx wrote in a letter to Kugelman in 1868, but "what can change, in historically different circumstances, is only the form in which these laws operate." What we have to pay attention to, therefore, is the particular way in which organisms (again, of any sort) work with these quite different possibilities in dynamic and interactive ways. And to do that requires that somehow the artificial break between "society" and "nature" must be eroded, rendered porous, and eventually dissolved.

While my language here is highly abstract and general, I do not find it hard to set this style of thinking into motion, to differentiate it further, to capture some of the ways in which the natural and social flow into each other without falling back into the typical reductionism of socio-biology. And there are plenty of hints that this is not necessarily an isolated way of looking at the problem. When, for example, Callon (1986) analyzes the difficulties of developing the domestication of scallop fishing in St Brieuc Bay, he treats the scallop as an active agent in the whole process, thereby breaching the common protocol that says the question of agency is confined within the social sphere. And in so doing he opens up the fluid way in which competition, collaboration (alliance formation), adaptation, and environmental transformation all run into each other as part of a more general process of socio-environmental change. Bateson (1988) likewise points out the different ways in which all species (including human beings) can affect subsequent evolution through their behavior. Animals make active choices and by their behavior change the physical and social conditions with which their descendants have to cope. They also modify their behavior in response to changed conditions and by moving expose themselves to new conditions that open up different possibilities for evolutionary change. Lewontin (1982) likewise argues for understanding a whole set of processes in which organisms "are not simply *objects* of the laws of nature, altering themselves to bend to the inevitable, but active *subjects* transforming nature according to its laws." Through efforts such as these, the uneasy boundary between the social and the natural worlds will surely be dissolved, as indeed it must, and analysis brought to the point where we might lose our fears of "biological determination" by recognizing, as Fuss (1989) so powerfully argues in her discussion of essentialism in feminism, that the distinction between biological essentialism and social constructionism is itself a false construction that thoroughly deserves to be dissolved. Haraway (1995) has produced some exemplary work on the practical and material dissolution of this boundary in social and scientific practices. But she also pays careful attention to how strictly that boundary gets policed in our thoughts, in our disciplines, and in our courses and provides food for thought as to what configurations of corporate and state power have most to gain from that policing. And it is through a critical understanding of how such power relations play out in political–ecological debates that we can arrive at a deeper conception of what ecosocialist politics might be all about.

IV. Towards an Ecosocialist Politics

Defining a proper ground for a socialist approach to environmental–ecological politics has proven a peculiarly difficult problem. In part this has to do with the way in which the socialist–Marxist movement took over from capitalism a strongly productivist ethic and a broadly instrumental approach to a supposedly distinct natural world and sought a transformation of social relations on the basis of a further liberation of the productive forces. It has subsequently proven hard to wean Marxism away from a rather hubristic view of the domination of nature thesis. In addition, Marxism has shared with much of bourgeois social science a general abhorrence of the idea that "nature" can control, determine, or even limit any kind of human endeavor. In so doing it has either avoided a definition of any foundational view of nature altogether, or resorted to a rather too simplistic rhetoric about "the humanization of nature" backed by a dialectical and historical materialism that somehow absorbed the problem by appeal to a set of epistemological/ontological principles. And in those rare cases when Marxists have taken the material biological and physical conditions of existence as foundational to their material-ism, they have either lapsed into some form of environmental determinism (as in the case of Wittfogel, 1953) or into a damaging materialist pessimism (Timpanaro, 1970; Benton, 1989). The effect has been to create a polarity within Marxism between "materialist triumphalism and materialist pessimism" (Williams, 1978: 9) that uncomfortably reflects the bourgeois habit of taking the triumphalist path when all goes right and invoking Malthusian limits when things go wrong.

So while there have been numerous principled writings in the Marxist tradition on the question of nature, beginning with Engels' *The Dialectics of*

Nature and continuing through works such as Schmidt's *Marx's Concept of Nature*, Smith's exploration of the idea of the "production of nature" in *Uneven Development*, and, most recently, Grundmann's examination of *Marxism and Ecology*, the armory of Marxism–socialism to counter the rhetoric and politics of a rising tide of ecological movements has not been well stocked. The response has been either to reject environmental–ecological politics as a bourgeois diversion (as, indeed, much of it patently is) or to concede in part to environmental–ecological rhetoric and try to rebuild Marxism–socialism on rather different theoretical and practical foundations from those that traditionally grounded working-class political projects and political action. And in some formulations a noble attempt has been made to do both, with not particularly felicitous results.

Consider, for example, a book by John Bellamy Foster, published with all the Marxist credibility of the Monthly Review Press, entitled *The Vulnerable Planet: A Short Economic History of the Environment.* Foster strongly argues that "the crisis of the earth is not a crisis of *nature* but of *society*." He goes on to discuss how accumulation for accumulation's sake in the west and production for production's sake in what was the Communist world have had devastating effects upon the world's environment since World War II, setting the stage for a contemporary condition of planetary ecological crisis. There is much that is persuasive and telling in the account but there are two central failings in the analysis. First, the postulation of a planetary ecological crisis, the very idea that the planet is somehow "vulnerable" to human action or that we can actually destroy the earth, repeats in negative form the hubristic claims of those who aspire to planetary domination. The subtext is that the earth is somehow fragile and that we need to become caring managers or caring physicians to nurse it back from sickness into health. This leads to Foster's extraordinarily hubristic conclusion that "the conscious and collective organization of the entire planet in the common interest of humanity and the earth has become a necessity if we are to prevent the irreparable despoliation of the earth by forces of institutionalized greed." Against this it is crucial to understand that it is materially impossible for us to destroy the planet earth, that the worst we can do is to engage in material transformations of our environment so as to make life less rather than more comfortable for our own species being, while recognizing that what we do also does have ramifications (both positive and negative) for other living species. It is vital, furthermore, to disaggregate "the environmental issue" into a tangible set of problems that exist at quite different scales, varying from the global issues of ozone, climate warming, and biodiversity to regional problems of soil depletion, desertification, and deforestation to the more localized questions of water quality, breathable air, and radon in the basement. Politically, the millenarian and apocalyptic proclamation that ecocide is imminent has had a dubious history. It is not a good basis for left politics and it is very vulnerable to the arguments long advanced by Simon (1981) and now by Easterbrook (1995), that conditions of life (as measured, for example, by life expectancy) are better now than they have ever been and that the doomsday scenario of the environmentalists is far-fetched and improbable. Furthermore, as Foster's conclusion all too clearly indicates, there is nothing in the argument that cannot be made broadly compatible with a segment of corporate capital's concerns to rationalize planetary management in their own interests. But then this is precisely what happens when the class content of the whole environmental–ecological argument gets subordinated to an apocalyptic vision of a planetary ecological crisis.

The second failing (which connects powerfully to the first) lies in the specification and interpretation of four ecological laws [largely drawn from Barry Commoner (1990), whose dedication to progressive left and ecological issues has been long-standing]. They are "(1) everything is connected to everything else, (2) everything must go somewhere, (3) nature knows best, and (4) nothing comes from nothing." The first is an important truism which has very little meaning without recognizing that some things are more connected than others. It is precisely the task of ecological analysis to try and identify unintended consequences (both short- and long-term, positive and negative) and to indicate what the major effects of actions are. Without such under-standings there is little that can be said for or against specific forms of environmental modification on the basis of this law. The second law properly indicates that there is no solution to active pollution problems except to move them around (a version of Engels' comment on how the bourgeoisie handles its housing problem – see chapter 13). The fourth law properly points out the cautionary principle (based on the laws of thermodynamics) that energy in usable form for human beings can indeed be depleted (though never destroyed). The third law is where the real problem lies. For to say "nature knows best" is to presume that nature can "know" something. This principle, as I showed in chapter 6, then dissolves either into the (once more hubristic) idea that someone is somehow in a privileged position to know what nature knows or into the conservative view that our environmental transformations should be as limited as possible (the "tread lightly on the surface of the earth" injunction favored by many ecologists). Foster thus accepts uncritically Commoner's argument that "any major man-made change in a natural system is likely to be detrimental to that system." To which I would want to reply "I hope so" leaving open the question as to whether the changes are favorable or detrimental to social or other forms of life and what meaning such changes might have for social relations, life chances of individuals, ecological beings, and the like.

Foster uses these laws to arrive at a thorough and convincing condemnation of capitalism in which the market, not nature, knows best, the only connection that matters is the cash nexus, it doesn't matter where something goes as long as it doesn't re-enter the circuit of capital and goods in nature are considered a free gift. All of this is reasonably true and Foster does a good job of explaining how destructive the consequences can be. But the difficulties begin when these same ecological laws are applied to socialism. I hope it would be true that socialists, rather than nature, will know best. Indeed, the only persuasive reason for joining the socialist (as opposed to the fascist, libertarian, corporate capitalist, planetary management) cause is precisely that socialists know best how to engage in environmental–ecological transformations in such a way as to realize long-term socialist goals of feeding the hungry, clothing the poor, providing reasonable life-chances for all, and opening up paths towards the liberation of diverse human creativities.

But ecosocialist politics cannot avoid the vital analytic point that much of what happens in the environment today is highly dependent upon capitalist behaviors, institutions, activities, and power structures. The sustainability of contemporary environments heavily depends upon keeping capitalism going. To put things this way is not to argue for continuation of the capitalist system of environmental transformation, but to recognize that the task of socialism is to think through the duality of ecological–social transformations as part of a far more coherent project than has hitherto been the case. To paraphrase Marx, we can collectively hope to produce our own environmental history, but only under environmental conditions that have been handed down to us by way of a long historical geography of capital circulation, the extraction of surplus values, monetized exchange, and the circulation of commodities.

On the one hand, therefore, we cannot afford to limit options by internalizing a capitalistic logic in which concepts of sustainability, ecoscarcity, and overpopulation are deeply implicated. But on the other hand, we cannot avoid the problem of conversion of capitalistic ecosystems, in which, for example, the circulation of money and the extraction of surplus values have become primary ecological variables. The task is, then, to both define and fight for a particular kind of ecosocialist project that extricates us from the peculiar social oppressions and contradictions that capitalism is producing through its highly specific ecological projects. Marx hinted at this dilemma:

> In our days, everything seems pregnant with its contrary. Machinery, gifted with the wonderful power of shortening and fructifying human labor, we behold starving and overworking it. The new-fangled sources of wealth, by some strange weird spell, are turned into sources of want. The victories of art seem bought by the loss of character. At the same pace that mankind masters nature, man seems to become enslaved to other men or to his own infamy. Even the pure light of science seems unable to shine but on the dark background of ignorance. All our invention and progress seem to result in endowing material forces with intellectual life, and in stultifying human life into a material force. (Cited in Grundmann, 1991b: 228)

It is then tempting, but not sufficient, to cite Engels' path towards an effective resolution to ecological as well as social dilemmas:

> by long and often cruel experience and by collecting and analyzing historical material, we are gradually learning to get a clear view of the indirect, more remote, social effects of our production activities and so are afforded an opportunity to control and regulate these effects as well. ... This regulation, however, requires something more than mere knowledge. It requires a complete revolution in our hitherto existing mode of production, and simultaneously a revolution in our whole contemporary social order.

I say this is insufficient because it leaves unresolved far too many dilemmas concerning the actual direction any ecosocialist might take. And here the debate between Marxists and ecologists of all stripes has much to offer. That debate has hitherto largely been a matter of articulating fixed positions, but there are other, more dialectical ways, to go about reading it, perhaps even "to rub together conceptual blocks in such a way that they catch fire." In that spirit I will conclude with the five key areas in which such a "rubbing" might help ecosocialist conceptual politics catch fire.

1. Alienation, Self-realization and the Esthetics of Development

Ideals of "self-realization" are widespread in the ecological literature. They parallel in certain ways Marx's concerns, particularly in *The Economic and Philosophic Manuscripts of 1844* but also in later works such as the *Grundrisse*, for human emancipation and self-development through the working out of our creative powers. In the Marxist tradition, however, quite properly concerned as it has been with impoverishment and deprivation, the liberation of the productive forces came to be seen as the privileged and to some degree exclusive means towards the broader goal of human self-realization (see Grundmann, 1991b: 54). As such, it became a goal in itself.

The ecological critique of socialist "productivism" is here helpful, since it forces Marxists to re-examine the problematics of alienation (see, for example, Meszaros, 1970; Ollman, 1976). Under capitalism, private property, class relations, wage labor, and the fetishisms of market exchange separate and alienate us from any sensuous and immediate contact (except in those fragmented and partial senses achievable under class-ordered divisions of labor) from "nature" as well as from other human beings. But if "man lives on nature" then "that nature is his *body* with which he must remain in continuous interchange if he is not to die." The health of that body is fundamental to our health. To "respect" nature is to respect ourselves. To engage with and transform nature through work is to transform ourselves. This forms one side of Marx's theses. But estrangement from immediate sensuous engagement with nature is an essential moment in consciousness formation. It therefore is a step on a path towards emancipation and self-realization (cf. Ingold, 1986, cited above). But herein lies a paradox. This never-ending estrangement of consciousness permits reflexivity and the construction of emancipatory forms of knowledge (such as science); but it also poses the problem of how to return to that which consciousness alienates us from. How to recuperate an unalienated relation to nature (as well as unalienated forms of social relations) in the face of contemporary divisions of labor and technological–social organization, then becomes part of a common project that binds Marxists and ecologists ineluctably together.

The secular version of the romantic tradition was, in the first instance, heavily esthetic in its orientation, taking the view that too high a price was paid for material emancipation in relation to our sensuous capacities to appropriate nature, but in more recent years, particularly in the advanced capitalist countries, the criticism has also been on ascetic grounds, revolting against the quality of life developed under the aegis of mass consumerism (including the mass tourist trade and the organized consumption of "nature") and seeking for a quite different set of nonmaterial values. The religious versions and secular versions look rather different and yet they all have in common that proximity to God or proximity to the self (and therefore realization of the self) depends on the construction of a certain attitude to nature. The young Marx, influenced by romanticism and esthetic concerns, was very sympathetic to such a viewpoint and there is some evidence that he never abandoned this sympathy though it became much less explicit in his later writings.

Where these sentiments split asunder is exactly where a recuperation might be sought. For Marxists, there can be no going back, as many ecologists seem to propose, to an *unmediated* relation to nature (or a world built solely on face-to-face relations), to a pre-capitalist and communitarian world of nonscientific understandings with limited divisions of labor. The only path is to seek political, cultural, and intellectual means that "go beyond" the mediations such as scientific knowledge, organizational efficiency, technical rationality, money, and commodity exchange, while acknowledging the significance of such mediations. The emancipatory potential of modern society, founded on alienation, must continue to be explored. But this cannot be, as it so often is, an end in itself for that is to treat alienation as the end point, the goal. The ecologists' and the early Marx's concern to recuperate though "in higher form" the alienation from nature (as well as from others) that modern-day capitalism instantiates must be a fundamental goal of any ecosocialist project. The quest for meaningful work as well as meaningful play (making sure, for example, that "victories of art" are not brought by "loss of character") becomes a central issue through which the labor movement can grasp the nettle of ecological argumentation concerning alienation from nature, from others and, in the last instance, from ourselves. The idea of "re-enchantment" with the sensuous world through a more sensitive science, more sensitive social relations and material practices, through meaningful labor processes, provides a better language than that of alienation with all of its essentialist overtones. But here we hit another problem: re-enchantment with nature is already a consumer item and a central aim of the commodification and Disneyfication of our experience of nature. In what ways, then, can we differentiate between an "authentic" and an "alienated" (commodified and "disneyfied") re-enchantment with our natural world?

This does not deny the relevance or power of phenomenological approaches in exploring the potentialities of more intimate and immediate relations to nature or to others (usually with particular emphasis upon an intimate knowledge of *place* – see chapter 11). The depth and intensity of feeling implicit even in Heidegger's approach is not irrelevant, any more than is the search for adequate poetic languages, representations, symbolic systems. Sartre's existentialism owes as much, after all, to Marx as to Heidegger. The danger arises when such modes of thought are postulated as the sole basis of politics (in which case they become inward-looking, exclusionary, and even neo-fascistic), when it was surely Marx's intent to search for the unity within the duality of *existential* and *mediated* experiences of the world. Exploring that duality has to be at the center of ecosocialist politics, implying an uncomfortable but instructive duality of values between the purely instrumental (mediated) and the existential (unmediated).

2. Social Relations and Ecological Projects

Explorations of our "species potential" and our capacity for "self-realization" require that we take cognizance of the relation between ecological projects and the social relations needed to initiate, implement, and manage them. Nuclear power, for example, requires highly centralized and nondemocratic power relations coupled with hierarchical command and control structures if it is to work successfully. Objections to it therefore focus as much on the social relations it implies as on the ecological problems of health and long-term hazardous wastes. The nature of many of the ecological projects undertaken in the Soviet Union likewise required social relations that were fundamentally at odds with the theoretical project of constructing a new society founded on egalitarianism and democracy. But this sort of critique is the easy part. For if we turn the equation around, and state that the only kinds of ecological projects to be undertaken are those which are consistent with nonhierarchical, decentralized, highly democratic, and radically egalitarian social relations, then the range of possible ecological projects becomes highly restricted, perhaps even life-threatening for substantial numbers of people. Adoption of such a stance certainly does not accord with the open exploration of our species potentiality and would probably militate against the alleviation of the tangible material misery in which much of the world's population lives.

There is, here, no resolution to what will always be a contradictory situation, save that of recognizing fully the nature of the tension and seeking political ways to live with its effects. More immediately, we have also to recognize the effects that arise from the instanciation "in nature" of certain kinds of social relations. If, for example, we view, as I think we must, contemporary eco-systems as incorporating the built environments of cities and the capital and commodity flows that sustain them, and if these ecosystems are instanciations of capitalist social relations, then what feasible (as opposed to catastrophically destructive) social and ecological transformations are available to us? This is by no means an easy question to answer, but here, too, the typically glib and simplistic answers on offer from much of the ecological movement simply will not do (see chapter 13).

3. The Question of Technology

"Technology discloses man's mode of dealing with Nature, the process of production whereby he sustains his life, and thereby also lays bare the mode of formation of his social relations, and of the mental conceptions that flow from them" (Marx, 1967: 352). While it is plainly wrong to attribute any technological determinism to Marx ("discloses" cannot be read as "deter-mines"), the centrality of technology and of technological choices in embed-ding social relations in ecological projects (and vice versa) means that careful attention has to be paid to this issue. Grundmann (1991b) is here, surely on very strong grounds when he points to some of the deep tensions in Marx's own approach. If, for example, machinery employed by capital not only dispossess workers of their surplus value but also deprives them of their skill and virtuosity while mediating their relations to nature in alienating ways, then self-realization (however much we insist on the collectivity of the project and the potential for authentic "re-enchantment") may be in jeopardy for technological reasons. Some kinds of technologies run counter even to the aim of exercising greater control over nature since they incorporate high environmental risks and minimal social benefits. But the problem goes even deeper. The technological mixes that capitalism bequeaths us (with its particular mixes of socio-ecological projects) either have to be roundly rejected (as many ecologists now suggest) or gradually transformed in ways that better accord with socialist social relations, and of the mental conceptions (such as those concerning the relation to nature) that flow from them. Arguments over "appropriate technology" and "small-is-beautiful" here come into play, not as necessary technological principles or trajectories for the construction of social-ism, but as a set of question marks over the future technological organization of a socialist society (cf. Commoner, 1990). How to sift through technological choices that minimize as opposed to accentuate risks in the metabolic relation to nature is then a key part of the social and political problem to be resolved.

4. The Dialectics of Commonality and Difference

Since much of the radical ecological critique now in vogue has its roots in anarchism, it has typically taken the path of emphasizing community, locality, place, proximity to "nature," particularity, and decentralization (deeply antagonistic to state powers) as opposed to the more traditional socialistic concerns with the universality of proletarian struggles and the overthrow of capitalism as a world-historical system of domination. Any ecosocialist project has to confront that opposition. Here I think a more *geographical* historical materialism, one that is more ecologically sensitive, has much to offer, both in terms of analysis as well as in terms of prospective transformations. The *general* struggle against capitalist forms of domination is always made up of *particular* struggles against the specific kinds of socio-ecological projects in which capitalists are engaged and the distinctive social relations they presuppose (against commercial forestry and timber management in the Himalayas as against large-scale water projects in California or nuclear power in France). The articulation of socialist principles of struggle therefore varies greatly with the nature and scale of the socio-ecological project to be confronted. And by the same token, the nature of the socialist transformation sought depends crucially upon the socio-ecological possibilities that exist in relation to particular projects, looking very different in Nicaragua or Zimbabwe from how it looks in Sweden and very different in terms of multinational finance from how it looks in terms of medical wastes dumped next to housing projects. But it is at this point that the *general* presumptions of the transition to socialism deserve to be reflected upon. Socialism is not necessarily about the construction of homogeneity. The exploration of our species potentiality can presumably also be about the creative search for and exploration of diversity and heterogeneity. Socio-ecological projects, much more in tune with confronting questions of alienation (and re-enchantment) and opening up diverse possibilities for self-realization, can be regarded as fundamentally part of some socialist future. The failures of capitalism to produce anything other than the uneven geographical development of bland, commoditized, homogeneity is, surely, one of the most striking features of its failures.

The radical ecological literature that focuses on place construction, bioregionalism, and the like here has something creative to offer, partly as an excellent ground for critique of capitalism's production of waste (do we really need to ship British beer to Australia and Australian beer to Britain?) as well as its production of serial conformity in urban design and the like. Mumford wishfully depicted the region, for example, "like its corresponding artifact, the city, [as] a collective work of art" not found "as a finished product in nature, not solely the creation of human will and fantasy." Embedded in a socialist project of ecological transformation, such a way of thinking turns on the "production of nature" as diverse localized works of art coupled with the creation of ecosystemic differences which can respect diversity of culture, places, and ecosystems. The richness of human capacity for complexity and diversity in a context of the free exploration of the richness, complexity, and diversity encountered in the rest of nature can become a vital part of any ecosocialist project. "Each of us," says a bioregionalist like Berg (cited in Alexander, 1990: 170) "inhabits a 'terrain of consciousness' determined in large part by the place we dwell in, the work we do, and the people with whom we share our lives." And there is absolutely no reason not to follow him in arguing that "the re-creation of caring and sustainable human cultures" ought to become "part of the 'real work' of our time." In so doing he is echoing something that derives as much from Raymond Williams as from Heidegger.

But we also hit here the point of departure of ecosocialism from pure bioregionalist, place, and local communitarian politics. The problem is that there is more than a hint of authoritarianism, surveillance, and confinement in the enforced localism of such a decentralized politics and a naive belief that (1) respect for human diversity is compatible with the belief that all decentralized societies will necessarily construct themselves "upon the (*enlightenment!*) values of democracy, liberty, freedom, justice and other such like *desiderata*," (Sale, 1985) rather than in terms of slavery, sexual oppression, and the like (see Dobson, 1990: 122), (2) that the "impoverishment" which often attaches to communal autarky and strong restrictions on foreign trade can be overcome, and (3) that restrictions on population movements coupled with exclusions of disruptive "foreigners" can somehow be squared with ideals of maximizing individual freedoms, democracy, and openness to "others." Young's (1990a) salutary warnings (see chapter 12) concerning the nightmare of communitarian politics in which community is defined as *against* others and therefore formulated in an entirely exclusionary, chauvinistic, and racist way, is not that easily avoided. When Goldsmith condescendingly writes (cited in Dobson, 1990: 97), for example, that "a certain number of foreigners could be allowed to settle," but that they would not "partake in the running of the community until such time as the citizens elected them to be of their number," the leaning towards a politics of exclusion that is neofascist becomes rather too close for comfort. The "ecologism" of the right-wing Lombardy Leagues in northern Italy, for example, shares exactly such a perspective not only with respect to the immigration of non-Italians but also with respect to movements from southern Italy. Furthermore, there is in this thinking a presumption that bioregions are given, by nature or by history, rather than that they are *made* by a variety of intersecting processes operating at quite different temporal and spatial scales. In other words, bioregions get thought about, in a most undialectical fashion, as the things rather than as unstable products of shifting processes. This then provokes the question: at what scale should a *bioregion, place, or human community* be defined?

Ecosocialist politics must, we can conclude, pay attention to a politics in which "universality" has a dual meaning. This is best expressed in Young's (1990a: 105) rule that "universality in the sense of the participation and inclusion of everyone in moral and social life does not imply universality in the sense of adoption of a general point of view that leaves behind particular affiliations, feelings, commitments, and desires." The perpetual negotiation of the relation between those two senses of universality, whether read across differences of gender, ethnicity, or other social affiliation or across the diversity of socio-ecological projects that might be explored under socialism, must therefore remain at the heart of ecosocialist thinking.

5. The Question of Temporal and Spatial Scales

At first sight, the question of scale appears as a purely technical matter. Where, for example, do ecosystems (or socio-ecological projects) begin and where do they end, how does a pond differ from the globe, how is it that processes which operate with profound effect at one scale become irrelevant at another? "Issues of appropriate scaling," Haila and Levins (1992: 236) argue, "are among the fundamental theoretical challenges in the understanding of society–nature interactions." There is, they say, "no single 'correct' way" to define temporal and spatial scales: these are constituted by the organisms considered so that different scales are simultaneously present at any particular site in nature (see chapter 10). If, as is in the dialectical view (see chapter 2), there are no basic units to which everything can be reduced, then the choice of scale at which to examine processes becomes both crucial and problematic. The difficulty is compounded by the fact that the temporal and spatial scales at which human beings operate as ecological agents have also been changing. Cronon (1983: 99) notes, for example, how even before colonial settlement began in New England, long-distance trade from Europe was bringing two hitherto largely isolated ecosystems into contact with one another in such a way as to commercialize the Indians' material culture and dissolve their earlier ecological practices. If we think these days of the scale defined by the commodity and money flows that put our breakfasts upon the table, and how that scale has changed over the last hundred years, then immediately it becomes apparent that there is an instability in the definition of scale which arises out of practices of capital accumulation, commodity exchange, and the like (see chapters 9 and 10).

Yet, as Smith (1992: 72) remarks, "the theory of the production of geographical scale" (to which I would add also the production of temporalities) – "is grossly underdeveloped." It seems to imply the production of a nested hierarchy of scales (from global to local) leaving us always with the political–

ecological question of how to "arbitrate and translate between them." The ecological argument is incredibly confused on exactly this point. On the one hand the Gaian planetary health care specialists think globally and seek to act globally, while the bioregionalists and social anarchists want to think and act locally, presuming, quite erroneously, that whatever is good for the locality is good for the continent or the planet. But at this point the issue becomes profoundly political as well as ecological, for the political power to act, decide upon socio-ecological projects and to regulate their unintended consequences has also to be defined at a certain scale (and in the contemporary world the nation states mostly carved out over the last hundred years maintain a privileged position even though they make no necessary politico-ecological sense). But this also says something very concrete about what any ecosocialist project must confront. On the one hand there will presumably be continuing transformations in human practices that redefine temporal and spatial scales, while on the other hand political power structures must be created that have the capacity to "arbitrate and translate between" the different scales given by different kinds of projects. Here, too, it seems that an ecosocialist perspective has an enormous import for socialist thinking on how human potentialities are to be explored and what kinds of political institutions and power structures can be created that are sensitive to the ecological dimensions of any socialist project.

V. Epilogue

"At the end of every labor process," Marx (1967: 174) once observed, "we get a result that already existed in the imagination of the labourer at its commencement." The purpose of the kind of labor that I have here engaged in, is to try and produce conceptual clarifications that might enter into the political practices of a critique of capitalism and the construction of socialism. But to be realized, as Eckersley so acutely points out, the aspirations released by analyses of this sort "must be critically related to one's knowledge of the present, thereby uniting desire with analysis and [lead on] to informed cultural, social, and political engagement." To bring my argument full circle, that means developing ways to conceptualize and represent ecological issues in ways that speak to the aspirations of the working-class movement, certain segments of the women's and ecologists' movement, as well as to those African-Americans who, in the Left Bank Jazz Club in Baltimore more than 20 years ago, quite correctly defined their main environmental problem as the presidency of Richard Nixon.

PART III

Space, Time, and Place

Need to shift a lot of space quickly?

In background Canary Wharf. 10 million sq. ft. Approx £4 billion. Foreground Audi 100 2.8E Estate. 50 cubic ft. £23,735. And, with a 174 bhp V6 engine, we all know which one is going to go faster.

Part III Prologue

There is a good deal of historical–geographical evidence for the thesis that different societies (marked by different forms of economy, social and political organization, and ecological circumstance) have "produced" radically different ideas about space and time. This thesis can be taken further. A seeming consensus can be constructed from these multiple enquiries to the effect that time and space are social constructs.

But behind this seeming consensus, there lurk innumerable and potentially damaging confusions. While, for example, it is now almost conventional to accept as an article of faith in social science that space and time are constituted by, as well as constitutive of, social relations and practices, there is often a slippage in actual accounts into a much more prosaic presentation in which social relations occur *within* some preconstituted and static framework of space and time. Such slippage is all the more remarkable for passing almost unnoticed, suggesting that there is something radically amiss in the way relations between spatio-temporality and sociality are construed at the very outset. It is not at all clear, for example, whether or not it is permissible or even possible to treat space and time as separate qualities. The number of books that concentrate on time alone (even a whole journal is now devoted to *Time and Social Theory*) suggests that the separation is widely accepted but little serious consideration is given to the grounds for or consequences of such a separation. Aveni's (1989) fascinating account of different *Empires of Time* abstracts entirely from questioning the nature of space, even though the spatializations necessary to construct time (as, for example, in all calendars and clocks) litter the text on almost every page. Does the social construction of space and time, furthermore, imply that they are mere social conventions devoid of any material basis? If space and time are judged to be material qualities then by what means, outside of imagination or intuition, can these qualities be established? And then what are we to make of all those plainly nonmaterialist metaphorical uses of concepts of space and time by means of which we speculate (through novels or fantasy) about who or what we are, or might be, and how the world in general works? And if, finally, the boundary between material and metaphorical uses is judged irrelevant, as some now claim, then does this mean that the virtual reality of cyberspace now under construction is both just as real and just as fictional as anything yet constructed?

The answers to these questions are important because space and time are foundational concepts for almost everything we think and do. The conclusions we reach will have far reaching implications for how we understand the world to be and how we might theorize about it. In what follows, therefore, I shall first try to distill from a rather wide-ranging historical, geographical, and anthropological literature some sense of what exactly it might mean to speak of the social construction or "production" of space and time. I will then seek in chapter 10 a general metaphysical foundation – a relational theory of space–time – that seems appropriate to interpret the historical–geographical findings.

Concepts of space and time affect the way we understand the world to be. And they also provide a reference system by means of which we locate ourselves (or define our "situatedness" and "positionality," to use the language of chapter 3) with respect to that world. It is therefore impossible to proceed far with a discussion of space and time without invoking the term "place." This in turn has implications for how we "place" things and how we think of "our place" in the order of things in particular. But the word "place" also carries a surfeit of meanings. To begin with, there are all sorts of words such as milieu, locality, location, locale, neighborhood, region, territory, and the like, which refer to the generic qualities of place. There are other terms such as city, village, town, megalopolis, and state which designate particular kinds of places and still others, such as home, hearth, "turf," community, and nation, which have such strong connotations of place that it would be hard to talk about one without the other. "Place" (like space and time) also has an extraordinary range of metaphorical meanings. We talk about the place of art in social life, the place of men in society, our place in the cosmos, and we internalize such notions psychologically in terms of knowing our place or feeling we have a place in the affections or esteem of others. We express norms by putting people, events, and things in their "proper" place and seek to subvert norms by struggling to define a new place ("on the margin" or "on the border," for example) from which the oppressed can freely speak. Place has to be one of the most multi-layered and multipurpose keywords in our language.

While this immense confusion of meanings makes any theoretical concept of place immediately suspect, I regard the generality, the ambiguity, and the multiple layers of meanings as advantageous. It suggests some underlying unity (or process of internalization) which, if we can approach it right, will reveal a great deal about social, political, and spatial practices in interrelation with each other over time. So although I shall concentrate mainly on the territorial and material qualities of place, the very looseness of the term lets me explore the inner connections to other meanings. I shall suggest, for example, that while the collapse of certain kinds of spatial barrier has undermined older and seemingly secure material and territorial definitions of place (such as "home" and "nation"), the very fact of that collapse (the reality or even threat of "time–space compression" or the construction of cyberspace) has put renewed emphasis upon the interrogation of metaphorical and psychological meanings which, in turn, generate material practices that give new material definitions of place. Fear of the "other" who now seems so threateningly close everywhere around the globe can, for example, lead to all sorts of exclusionary territorial behavior. Explorations of this sort should help clarify the thorny problem of "otherness" and "difference" because territorial place-based identity, particularly when conflated with race, ethnic, gender, religious, and class differentiation, is one of the most pervasive bases for both progressive political mobilizations (militant particularism) as well as for reactionary exclusionary politics. When people write about "the power of place" it seems they are either engaging in a straight fetishism of endowing a thing with power or talking about a certain social process of place construction that has momentum, meaning, and political–economic implications for how our world will be. Getting behind the concept of place in a manner consistent with the social constitution of space and time is, therefore, an important project for any foundational understanding of the principles of historical–geographical materialism. But within that foundational understanding we will also find empirical as well as theoretical support for the view that the triumvirate of space–time–place can only be fully appreciated in relation to the processes of socio-ecological transformation examined in part II.

9

The Social Construction of Space and Time

There, where the power-house of all time and space – call it brain or heart of creation – activates every function; who is the artist who would not dwell there?

Paul Klee

I. The Spaces and Times of Social Life

Durkheim pointed out in *The Elementary Forms of the Religious Life* (1915) that space and time are social constructs. The writings of anthropologists such as Hallowell (1955), Lévi-Strauss (1963), Hall (1966) and, more recently Bourdieu (1977), Munn (1986), Hugh-Jones (1979), Gell (1992) and Moore (1986) confirm this view: *different societies produce qualitatively different conceptions of space and time.* Sorokin (1937–41) in his extraordinary treatise put the idea firmly onto the agenda of sociology, Yi-Fu Tuan (1977), Sack (1980), Parkes and Thrift (1980), and Carlstein et al. (1978) provide geographical accounts and historians such as Gurevich (1985), Le Goff (1980), and Braudel (1974) have elaborated on historical changes in conceptions of space and time in considerable detail. Literary theorists and art historians have, of course, long embraced the relativism of space and time (see, for example, Ross, 1988) and, more recently, feminists (Spain, 1992) have made it an important facet in their arguments. Space and time, it is generally agreed, are social constructs.

But all sorts of confusions and misconceptions attach to this conclusion. So I begin with four points of clarification.

1. Social constructions of space and time are not wrought out of thin air, but shaped out of the various forms of space and time which human beings encounter in their struggle for material survival. For example, night and

day, the seasons, lifecycles in the animal and plant world, and the biological processes which regulate human reproduction and the body, are typical encounters with various kinds of temporality. But each of these stands to be modified or even transcended as we harness sources of energy to turn night into day, as we use an international division of labor to put fresh produce into our shops at all times of the year, as we speed up the lifecycles of chickens and pigs through genetic engineering and as human life expectancy rises with improved living standards and medical knowledge. The discovery of the varying properties of time and space in the material world (through the study of physics, ecology, biology, geology, etc.) is therefore fundamental. Such knowledge permits a social choice as to which particular process or processes shall be used to construct space and time. The swing of the pendulum or the pace of radioactive decay are now used, whereas in other eras it may have been the cyclical motions of the planets and the stars or the migrations of animal populations. To say that time and space are social constructs does not deny their ultimate embeddedness in the materiality of the world:

> Time is "in" the universe; the universe is not "in" time. Without the universe, there is no time; no before, no after. Likewise, space is "in" the universe; the universe is not "in" a region of space. There is no space "outside" the universe. (Hewitt, 1974: 515)

2. Conceptions of space and time depend equally upon cultural, metaphorical, and intellectual skills. The rise of a doctrine of "deep time" (the idea that "there is no sign of a beginning and no prospect of an end" in the famous formulation of the geologist James Hutton, writing in 1788) from the mid-seventeenth through the early nineteenth centuries was as much fueled by metaphorical visions as it was by any observation of rocks and outcrops:

> The interplay of internal and external sources – of theory informed by metaphor and observation constrained by theory – marks any major movement in science. We can grasp the discovery of deep time when we recognize the metaphors underlying several centuries of debate as a common heritage of all people who have ever struggled with such basic riddles as direction and immanence. (Gould, 1988: 7)

Time and space may be "facts of nature" but, as with "values in nature" (see chapter 5) we cannot know what those facts are outside of our own cultural embeddedness in language, belief systems, and the like.

3. Social constructions of space and time operate with the full force of objective facts to which all individuals and institutions necessarily respond. To say that something is socially constructed is not to say it is personally

subjective. There are, Gurevich (1985: 14) argues, certain "universal concepts and representations which are canonical for the society as a whole, and without which no theories, no philosophical, esthetic, political or religious ideas or systems can be constructed." Once accepted, foundational concepts like space and time become pervasive; "the obligatory nature of these categories upon all members of the society" does not "mean that the society consciously imposes these norms upon its members by requiring them to perceive the world and react to it in this particular way; society is unaware both of the imposition and of the acceptance, the 'absorption', of these categories and images by its members." For example, in modern societies we accept clock time, even though such time is a social construct, as an objective fact of daily life. It provides a commonly held standard, outside of any one person's influence, to which we turn to organize our lives and to assess and judge all manner of social behaviors and subjective feelings. Even when we do not conform to it, we know very well what is being rebelled against.

4. Social definitions of objective space and time are implicated in processes of social reproduction. Bourdieu (1977) shows, for example, how in the case of the north African Kabyle, temporal and spatial organization (the calendar, the partitions within the house, etc.) serve to constitute the social order through the assignment of people and activities to distinctive places and times. The group orders its hierarchies, its gender roles, and divisions of labor, in accordance with a specific mode of spatial and temporal organization. Its choice of material embeddedness for social constructs of space and time internalizes social relations (as well as institutional and social power). The role of women in Kabyle society is, for example, defined in terms of the spaces occupied at specific times. A particular way of *representing* (as opposed to using) space and time guides social practices in ways which secure the social order. Hugh-Jones (1979) in her study of spatial and temporal processes in northwest Amazonia, underscores that argument by establishing the relationship between the space–time principles which structure the Pira-parana Indian cosmos and the building of basic units of social structure, families, and patrilineal groups, through marriage and procreation: the space–time principles articulated in the structure of the Indian cosmos operate as both "an imaginary projection of present experience" and "a projection which both controls present experience and forms an integral part of it." Representations of space and time arise out of the world of social practices but then become a form of regulation of those practices: which is why, as we shall see, they are so frequently contested.

In what follows I use two studies, by Gurevich and Munn, to tease out some fundamental underlying questions and principles on the social construction of space and time.

II. Gurevich and *The Categories of Medieval Culture*

Gurevich (1985) contrasts pre-Christian, Christian, and early modern conceptions and practices with respect to space and time so as to illuminate connections to social relations and modes of establishing values concerning "self," "other," "nature," and the like. He argues that "our modern categories of space and time have very little in common with the time and space perceived and experienced by people in other historical epochs." In the early medieval period space and time were not understood:

> as a set of neutral coordinates, but rather as mysterious and powerful forces, governing all things. ... Hence both space and time are axiologically and emotionally charged: time and space can be good or evil, beneficial for certain kinds of activity, dangerous or hostile to others; there is sacral time, a time to make merry, a time for sacrifice, a time for re-enactment of the myth connected with the return of "primordial time"; and in the same way there exists a sacral space, there are sacred places or whole worlds subject to special forces. ... Medieval man [was] aware of himself as the unity of all those elements from which the world was created. ... In the particle the whole was subsumed; the microcosm was a replica of the macrocosm.

This had profound implications for how the "self" and the "body" (primary constituents of identity) were thought to relate to the world:

> Man's dependence on the natural environment, and his incapacity to apprehend it as an object upon which he could act from outside, finds its cultural reflection in the idea of the inner analogy between man the "microcosmos" and world the "megacosmos" which have the same structure and consist of the same elements; and also in the image of the "cosmic" human body – incomplete, not clearly differentiated from the surrounding world into which it merges, open to this world and absorbing it into itself. (p. 32)

The understanding of space and time was bound up with self-evaluation (p. 85). The "characteristic traits of the medieval popular culture and, accordingly of the popular imagination" were constituted by "the levelling of all barriers between the body and the world, the fluidity of transition between them" (p. 54). Nothing could be more "natural" therefore, than to make "man the measure of all things" because "man" was thought to be inseparable from nature and to internalize all things. We here encounter the medieval origins of what later became the "Leibnizian conceit" (see chapter 3).

If, furthermore, the distinction between individuals or groups (families, clans, communities) and the earth was regarded as highly porous and blurred, then human beings could use their place, their farmstead for example, "as a model of the universe" (pp. 45–7). The effect was to produce a conception of "dwelling in the land" that comes very close to that which Heidegger (see chapter 9) was later to articulate with great force. Says Gurevich of the pre-Christian medieval period:

> The site of the dwelling has "grown together" with its owners so intimately that neither is conceivable without the other. Just as the man possessed the farmstead, so it in turn "possessed" him and put its own stamp on his personality. ... Scandinavian topography is not based on purely geographical coordinates: it is saturated in emotional and religious significance, and geographical space represents at the same time religious–mythological space. The one passes effortlessly into the other. (pp. 48–9)

The medieval way of looking at space and time was *relational* and *dialectical* rather than absolute. Space and time did not exist "outside and before experience; they were given only in experience itself, of which they formed an indissoluble part, which could not be detached from the living fabric" (p. 102). This defined a particular sense of situatedness and of positionality of human beings in relation to the world. But:

> with the transition from paganism to Christianity, medieval man's conception of space underwent a radical structural transformation. Cosmic space, social space and ideological space were all given hierarchic structure.

Spatio-temporality became indissolubly bound up with religious and moral concepts such that positive knowledge became so saturated with biblical meanings that "religious and ethical values are superimposed on and overrule the purely cognitive values." Christianity broke the cyclic world view of time and substituted a more eschatological view in which there was a beginning, a culmination, and an end, such that time became "linear and irreversible" (p. 111). The Christian awareness of "time as drama" in which "earthly life and the whole of history are seen as the arena of a struggle between good and evil" rendered the moment of internal freedom of choice as critical to the historical process. Nevertheless, such acts could not be abstracted from daily routines. The result was a variety of spatio-temporal conceptions deriving from different modes of experience (agricultural, political, ecclesiastical, military, etc.). But these disparate spatio-temporal conceptions were subordinated to an over-arching Christian conception. The quest for self-realization and redemption "was understood as movement in space: the saint could be taken into paradise, just as the sinner could be thrown into hell" (p. 74). Since space beyond the bounds of Christendom "lost its positive qualities," the extension of Christian space became part of an often violent struggle to wrest space from the forces of evil. Geographical space, the revolving stage of a temporal drama, thereby "expands and increases in complexity" at the same time as there is "a progressive annexation of the inner space of the human soul, revealing hitherto unsuspected riches." So we see, concludes Gurevich, that neither space nor time were conceived as forms "prior to matter"; both are "just as real as the rest of God's creatures."

III. Munn on *The Fame of Gawa*

Nancy Munn's study, *The Fame of Gawa* (1986), deals with value formation through spatio-temporal practices found on a small atoll (population not many more than 500) within the chain of islands that constitute the Massim off the northeast of Papua New Guinea. Munn (1986: 121) places the three concepts of *space*, *time*, and *value* at the heart of a "relational nexus" that acts as "a *template* or a *generative schema* ... for constructing intersubjective relations in which value is both *created* and *signified*." She introduces her study with the assertion that socio-cultural practices "do not simply go on in or through time and space," but they also "constitute (create) the spacetime ... in which they go on." Actors are, therefore "concretely producing their own spacetime."

Munn tracks the formation of symbolic systems of meanings – of *values* – through the socio-cultural practices which socially construct space and time. Different forms of space–time derive from different social practices. This means that space–time in Gawan society is multidimensional and hierarchical depending upon the sorts of social practices being looked at. The effect is to generate a "complex interplay of the incommensurable spacetimes of different trans-actions," rather than "any homogeneous spacetime defined by determinate calendric frames." But incommensurable does not mean unconnected. A lot of Gawan activity is precisely about linking one domain of space–time and value formation to another.

Munn looks at a variety of practices in this light. The house and garden forms one sphere of socio-cultural practices and space–time construction which is highly gendered as the domain of women, and holds its own distinctive template for the construction of symbolic meanings and values. Relations between household units, primarily defined by marriage and exchanges between groups (in which the exchange not only of produce and cooked food but also the highly significant gifts of canoes), forms another level and both of these together form the basis for the construction of a much broader sphere of valuation structured around the offering of hospitality to males from other islands and the reciprocal male search for hospitality from other islands. This latter extends the range of individual space–time relations – "giving food away to overseas visitors for their own consumption is perceived as initiating a spatiotemporally extending process" which allows "food to be converted into fame." Conversely, consumption of food in the domestic sphere by oneself is perceived as negative value because of the contraction of space–time implied.

These hospitality relations among the male islanders create a spatio-temporal world founded in interpersonal contacts and relationships which ground the sense of value (fame) in a limited orbit.

The exchange of kula shells, however, is much less limited and "constitutes the widest regional network of their island world" in which males can make connections "with more distant contemporaries with whom they have few or no face-to-face relationships." The circulation of shells, and of names attached to shells, frees them from locality and makes them "the topic of discourse through which they become available in other times and places." Kula exchange constructs an intersubjective space–time at a completely different (spatio-temporal) value level to that achieved through offering (and receiving) hospitality to (or from) other men. In both hospitality and kula exchange relations, however, the value acquired, while primarily registered through male activity, also has a strong female basis: "at the base of the male power for controlling and transforming spacetime is the female control level, which forms the dynamic grounds and precondition of the masculine level of the process" (p. 160).

Munn's analysis implies that "the evaluative rendering of the self by significant others," is "intrinsic to the value-production process" and "in producing a given level of spatiotemporal extension beyond the self, actors produce their own value" (p. 15). "Sociocultural spacetime" is, then, the relevant measure of value, which is characterized "in terms of an act's relative capacity to extend or expand what I call intersubjective spacetime – a spacetime of self–other relationships formed in and through acts and practices" (p. 9). Value thereby becomes "general and relational, rather than particular and substantive" (p. 8). From the standpoint of Gawan society as a whole, this means that its "*internal* viability" depends entirely upon "its positive evaluation by *external* others" which depends upon the constitution of "a mode of spacetime formed through the dynamics of action." This is a very relational conception of space–time.

Munn's account raises several issues. While "the mode of spacetime formed in a given type of practice is also a formation of the actors' selves," there is an important distinction between *direct constructions* arrived at through the activities within the garden or the giving of hospitality on the one hand and the *indirect constructions* generated by exchange of kula shells on the other. This distinction affects how value (meaning) gets formed and expressed. While both constructions produce symbolic mediations (including specific ways of talking – discourses – and symbolic spatial representations), indirect constructions such as the exchange of kula are much more dependent upon abstraction and generalization of the notions of space–time and value and, as such, they require the formation of specific socio-cultural discourses *about* space–time and value if they are to be sustained. Naming, memory, language all become caught up in this process.

This poses the problem of how translations are made from one domain of spatio-temporal practices (as well as associated discourses and symbols) to another, for we are not dealing with completely separate worlds, but with interlocking constructions that take us from the gardens and houses to the expanded space–time of kula shell exchanges. "The exchange of canoes for armshells," she argues, "effects a transformation *across* these different value levels of spacetime" (p. 150). As one moves from garden produce to canoes and kula shell exchanges, canoes appear as crucial "spatiotemporal intermediates" between the internal space–time of Gawan exchanges "and the maximal circulation of kula armshells and necklaces in the inter-island world." The canoes, constructed by households and internally transmitted from one marriage group to another, not only enable travel from island to island, but as gifts they allow someone to break into the kula circle itself.

Once they are set up, however, these intersecting abstractions and discourses affect and regulate social practices (this conclusion is common also to Bourdieu and Hugh-Jones). The body, the house, gender relations of reproduction as well as gender roles, Munn shows, all become caught up in a wider symbolism constructed around space, time and value. For example, bodily space–time serves in the Gawan case "as a condensed sign of the wider spacetime of which it is a part" (p. 17), while the expansions of intersubjective space–time created through hospitality and kula exchanges affect the dialectic of hierarchy and equality within the community as a whole (p. 20).

If the expansion of space–time lies at the heart of value construction, then the contraction of space–time (or simply failure to expand it) amounts to a loss of value or "negative value." When Gawans eat their own food instead of giving hospitality to others they in effect destroy values. But the most important negating mechanism is witchcraft, constituted as a hidden world that "dissolves and disorders the overt, visible spatiotemporal order, crystallizing a latent, negative significance, and even subverting the apparent positive value potentials of transmissive acts into negative, destructive value" (pp. 13–14). It is through witchcraft that fame gets subverted, communities become "defamed," while individuals suffer from heaviness, illness, death.

Valuation and devaluation consequently form a binary and dialectically constituted couplet within the Gawan world of spatio-temporal practices. The negative moment has important social consequences. Witchcraft, by attacking those who individually deviate or accumulate, serves on the one hand to reinforce the "fundamental egalitarian premises of the society, especially as these premises are embedded in acts of giving as opposed to keeping or consuming oneself." On the other hand, the witch also attacks the polity as a whole to make it nonviable, thus provoking forms of collective action. "This evaluative dialectic – the formulation, in effect, of positive and negative discourses about the Gawan self" Munn (1986: 271) concludes:

is intrinsic to the transformational process of value production. Indeed, without these evaluative discourses Gawa cannot produce value for itself, inasmuch as it is through their operation that Gawans define and bring into consciousness their own value state or the general state of viability of the community. (p. 271)

IV. Preliminary Theoretical Reflections

So what general points can be distilled from these two accounts?

First, from Gurevich I would emphasize the *relational and dialectical* view of space and time that pervades the medieval account, both pagan and Christian. But Christianity superimposed a hierarchical and linear (bounded space with an end to time) viewpoint on top of (and without eliminating) the more heterogeneous, diversified and localized conceptions of barbarian societies (a difference mainly associated in Gurevich's view with differences in the scale of economic and political organization). Munn advances the same relational and dialectical view but provides a much more sophisticated and detailed account of how, in Gawan society, different constructions of space and time attach to different domains (typically gendered) while also providing ways to understand the transformative practices that allow movement from one domain (that of production within the household which is largely the domain of women, for example) to another (such as the exchange of kula shells as a spatio-temporal practice confined to men). The ultimate unity and multiplicity of space–times insisted upon as a general principle by Gurevich are in Munn's account rendered as different spatio-temporalities tangibly linked through specific social practices.

Secondly, from Gurevich I would emphasize the way in which both space and time were understood in the premodern medieval world view not as abstractions (of the sort with which we are all now familiar), but as "*an indissoluble attribute of being, as material as life itself*" (p. 310). While Munn does not make such a claim in that form, the material qualities of space and time are omnipresent even when, as in symbolic activities or in the case of witchcraft, the actual spatio-temporal relations are hidden from view. Munn (1986: 268) also does a better job in demonstrating the indissoluble link, generally presumed in Gurevich, between space and time, arguing again and again that "since the basic form of social (or sociocultural) being is intrinsically spatiotemporal, it follows that space–time should not be abstracted from the analytical concept of the sociocultural." If this is generally and theoretically the case, then it would follow that all those accounts that concentrate either solely on space or on time must fail. Munn signals her own allegiance to this view by dissolving the pair space *and* time into *space–time*.

Thirdly, the porosity of the human body and self in relation to the surrounding world is worthy of note in both accounts because it frames "self–other" relations (including the relation to "nature") in a very particular way. It does not mean that the "individual" and "individualism" do not exist, but that individuals were construed to exist (and to large degree practiced that existence) in ways quite different from modern conceptions and practices. The self was believed to internalize all there is (a strong doctrine of internal relations of the sort outlined in chapter 2) but the reverse therefore also holds – because the self internalizes all things then the self can be the measure of all things. This idea, that goes back to Protagoras and the Greeks, allows the individual to be viewed as some kind of decentered center of the cosmos, or, as Munn (1986: 14, 17) prefers to put it "bodily spacetime serves as a condensed sign of the wider spacetime of which it is a part." Hence "the mode of spacetime formed in a given type of practice is also a formation of the actors' selves (as well as of the specific self–other relations by which these selves are being defined)." The effect is to make "the intersection of the problem of value signification and that of the constitution of the subject (more) apparent."

This relational conception of the self deserves some further analysis. Strathern (1988: 135) provides some further clues:

> The socialized, internally controlled Western person must emerge as a *microcosm of the domesticating process* by which natural resources are put to cultural use. ... The only internal relation here is the way a person's parts "belong" to him or herself. Other relationships bear in from outside. A person's attributes are thus modified by external pressure, as are the attributes of things, but they remain intrinsic to his or her identity. ... Extrinsic modification thus transforms or controls intrinsic attributes but does not challenge their status as the definitive property of the entity in question. The refractions of this commodity metaphor suggest an image of persons standing in respect of their own selves as original proprietors of themselves.

By contrast, the "Melanesian person is a living commemoration of the actions which produced it" (p. 302):

> persons are the objectified form of relationships, and it is not survival of the self that is at issue but the survival or termination of relations. Eating does not necessarily imply nurture; it is not an intrinsically beneficiary act, as it is taken to be in the Western commodity view that regards the self as thereby perpetuating its own existence. Rather, eating exposes the Melanesian person to all the hazards of the relationships of which he/she is composed. ... Growth in social terms is not a reflex of nourishment; rather, in being a proper receptacle for nourishment, the nourished person bears witness to the effectiveness of a relationship with the mother, father, sister's husband or whoever is doing the feeding. ... Consumption is not simple matter of self-replacement, then, but the recognition and monitoring of relationships. ... The self as individual subject exists ... in his or her capacity to transform relations.

The relational conception of self, individual, and, consequently, of political identity indicates a world that parallels not only the insights of dialectical argumentation and the philosophy of internal relations (see chapter 2) but also that of deep ecologists (such as Naess examined in chapter 7). It constitutes a rejection of the world view traditionally ascribed to Descartes, Newton, and Locke and indicates a relational conception of spatio-temporality. It also entails a dissolution of the fact–value and matter–mind dualities that pervade so much of western thought. We will later take up the consequences of such a world view.

What is missing from Gurevich's account (apart from its lack of concern for gender), however, is some notion of how self–other relations and values connect to the specific ways in which space–time came to be socially constructed both in the realms of discourse as well as in the realms of practices, social relations, beliefs, institutions, and political–economic power. Although Gurevich *asserts* that all the categories of medieval culture were mutually intertwined (p. 290) he nevertheless chooses to treat questions of wealth, labor, money, and value separately from questions of space–time. While he insists that it was the way all of these foundational concepts worked together that constituted the "parameters of the medieval human personality, the guidelines of its world view and of its behavior patterns, as ways in which human beings came to be aware of themselves" (p. 298), he fragments the pieces of the puzzle in ways that make it difficult to reconstitute the whole. This problem in Gurevich's account is handled better by Munn and there are three particular points of her elaboration to which I want to draw attention.

First, relations become embodied in things – food, canoes, kula shells – thus posing the general enigma that Marx addressed under the rubric of "the fetishism of commodities" or, as Mauss (1990: 3) prefers to formulate it in his opening question in *The Gift*: "What power resides in the object that causes its recipient to pay it back?" Mauss, in pursuing an answer to the riddle of gift relationships recognizes that the thing given "itself possesses a soul" and that "to make a gift of something to someone is to make a present of some part of oneself." One must, therefore, give back to others what is really part and parcel of themselves:

> that thing coming from the person is not only morally, but physically and spiritually, that essence, that food, those goods, whether movable or immovable, those women or those descendents, those rituals or those acts of communion – all exert a magical or religious hold over you. Finally, the thing given is not inactive. Invested with life, often possessing individuality, it seeks to return to ... its "place of origin," or to produce ... an equivalent to replace it.

The effect is to create a "mixture of spiritual ties between things that to some degree appertain to the soul, and individuals, and groups that to some extent treat one another as things." The parallel here to Marx's celebrated fetishism thesis in which commodity market exchange transforms relations between people into relations between things while similarly investing things with social values is obvious. But there is something lacking in Mauss's explanation of how objects become active in relation to people.

Munn's (1986: 109) answer is in part to insist on the spatio-temporality of the valuing process that requires things (food, canoes, kula shells) as mediators that can, as it were, bear the message of one's fame across space and time. But she also shows that this development depends on language:

> When a young man who wishes to advance in kula is starting out, he must not only develop his own kula speech skills, but also listen to the discussions of more senior men, learning the path histories, metaphors, names, and so on, pertinent to kula.

The *discourse* about the thing, or *evaluative* discourses more generally, are fundamental to the spatio-temporal *practices* of valuing both the thing and the person. Without naming, memory, discourses, and the like, the whole process of constituting a mediated world of space–time relations would fall apart. The oral circulation of the names of men, shells, and islands "is an exponential aspect of the emergent spacetime of kula":

> Fame models the spatiotemporal expansion of self effected by acts of influence by recasting these influential acts (moving the mind of another) into the movement or circulation of one's name. ... The circulation of names frees them, detaching them from these particularities and making them the topic of discourse through which they become available in other times and places. (p. 117)

The circulation of information and the construction of discourses about things (if only what Marx calls "the language of money") then and there, as here and now, becomes a vital facet not only in the construction of space–time relations but also the constitution of the value, however fetishized, of both people and things. The power of objects and things over us, the fact that they seem to have a life of their own and to possess value on their own account depends entirely on the way discourses of value envelop them and invest them with symbolic meaning.

Here I find it useful to recapitulate the general conceptualization laid out in chapter 4. Discourses are, I there argued, internalized as beliefs, embedded within material practices and modes of social relating within institutionalized frames, and operate as forms of political economic power. By the same token, discourses *internalize* events, experiences, structures, and power relations, but not as a mere reflection. They act to constitute the world by virtue of the multiple translations and transformations which link them to these other domains of action understood as a whole. If things seem to have a life of their own, then it is only because those things which are handled in the realm of material practices are considered to internalize discursive effects of political economic power and spatio-temporal relations. Only in such terms can we unpack the composite problem of how it is that things become imbued with social relations and operate with such full force as to appear to govern us (as, for example, money typically does) more ruthlessly than any political dictator could ever hope to do. This in turn may explain why the one singular power dictators lack is the power to change the fundamentals of language.

But Munn's account also reveals a dialectic of *valuation* and *devaluation* as means to control inequality and to secure some kind of communitarian social solidarity. The negation of value is just as important as its production. When Mauss remarks on how "madly extravagant" potlatch can become (a phrase that Derrida treats as revelatory of the underlying madness of economic reason), he is pointing to a system that negates values as fast as it creates them. Like potlatch, witchcraft on Gawa negates values and so prevents concentrations of wealth, enforcing a certain kind of egalitarian democracy.

The dynamics of all of this then becomes a crucial question. Here Munn's account is notably lacking for she makes it seem as if Gawans live in a self-contained process of constructing intersubjective space times. Her studies of Gawa proceed, for example, as if the islanders were entirely free from colonial influences.

But this is patently not the case and here Gurevich's broad conception of shifting conceptions of space and time across the barbarian, Christian and into the early modern period yields a rather better sense of at least the breadth and depth of potential changes. So how can we think about these dynamics?

V. External Force and the Social Construction of Space and Time

Societies change and grow, they are transformed from within and adapt to pressures and influences from without. Objective but socially given conceptions of space and time must change to accommodate new material practices of social reproduction, new ways of assigning value.

How are such shifts accomplished? In certain instances the answer is simply given. New concepts of space–time and value have been imposed by main force through conquest, imperial expansion or neocolonial domination. The European settlement of North America imposed quite alien conceptions of time and space upon indigenous populations, for example, and in so doing altered forever the social framework within which the reproduction of these peoples could, if at all, take place (see, for example, Hallowell, 1955). Cronon's

(1983: 50) account of the impact of colonial settlement on the New England Indians is again relevant. A conflict arose over the different ways in which spatio-temporality and value were constructed:

> Whereas Indian villages moved from habitat to habitat to find maximum abundance through minimal work, and so reduce their impact on the land, the English believed in and required permanent settlements. ... English fixity sought to replace Indian mobility; here was the central conflict in the ways Indians and colonists interacted with their environment. The struggle was over two ways of living and using the seasons of the year, and it expressed itself in how two peoples conceived of property, wealth, and boundaries on the landscape. (p. 53)

And while each Indian village held sovereign rights that defined a village's political and ecological territory, the rights were never individual rights nor were they "forever." People owned what they made with their own hands, but there was "little sense either of accumulation or of exclusive use" precisely because "the need for diversity and mobility" led them "to avoid acquiring much surplus property." Mobility meant that they had no permanent rights to the land. They possessed rights of use only which did not "include many of the privileges Europeans commonly associated with landownership: a user could not (and saw no need to) prevent other village members from trespassing or gathering nonagricultural food on such lands and had no conception of deriving rent from them." Nor did Indians "own any other kind of land: clam banks, fishing ponds, berry-picking areas ... and here too the concept of usufructury right was crucial, since different groups of people could have different claims on the same tract of land depending on how they used it." Property rights, "in other words, shifted with ecological use" (Cronon, 1983: 63). The "sale" of land by Indians to the colonizers was conceived on the Indian side as a compact to share the land and its use rather than alienating it. "As the English understood these transactions, what was sold was not a bundle of usufruct rights, applying to a range of different 'territories,' but the land itself, an abstract area whose bounds in theory remained fixed no matter what the use to which it was put" and such lands were, moreover, alienated "forever." To the abstraction of legal boundaries alienated "in perpetuity" was added the abstraction of price (and land rent), a measurement of property's value assessed on a unitary scale. "More than anything else, it was the treatment of land and property as commodities traded at market that distinguished English conceptions of ownership from Indian ones." The value system of the colonizers was set in a matrix of socially constructed space–time which was radically at odds with that of the Indian community.

The urban order has been equally subject to superimposed change. The imposition of a mathematically rational spatial order in the house, the classroom, the village, the barracks and even across the city of Cairo itself were, for example, centerpieces of a late nineteenth-century project to bring Egypt into line with the disciplinary frameworks of European capitalism. Colonizing, Mitchell (1991: ix) observes, "refers not simply to the establishing of a European presence but also the spread of a political order that inscribes in the social world a new conception of space, new forms or personhood, and the new means of manufacturing the experience of the real."

Such impositions were not necessarily well received. The spread of a capitalist value system and its associated sense of intersubjective space–time has often entailed a fierce battle to socialize different peoples into the common net of time–space discipline implicit in industrial organization and into a respect for partitions of territorial and land rights specified in strictly Cartesian terms. While rearguard actions against such impositions abound, public definitions of time and space throughout much of the contemporary world have largely been imposed through capitalist development. Mitchell (1991: xii) characterizes their qualities as follows:

> The precise specification of space and function that characterize modern institutions, the coordination of these functions into hierarchical arrangements, the organization of supervision and surveillance, the marking out of time into schedules and programmes – all contribute to constructing a world that appears to consist not of a complex of social practices but of a binary order: on the one hand individuals and their activities, on the other an inert structure that somehow stands apart from individuals, preexists them, and contains and gives a framework to their lives. Such techniques have given rise to the peculiar metaphysics of modernity, where the world seems resolved into the two-dimensional form of individual versus apparatus, practice versus institution, social life and its structure – or material reality and its meaning.

If such a characterization is correct (and I shall have cause to return to its prevalence shortly), then the porosity and fluidity of, for example, the body in space and time identified by Gurevich and Munn here gives way to the western conceit of the individual as a preformed entity within a set of absolute structures of space and time.

VI. Contesting the Social Construction of Space and Time

The public sense of time and space is frequently contested from within the social order. This in part arises out of individual and subjective resistance to the absolute authority of the clock and the tyranny of the cadastral map. Modernist and postmodernist literature and painting are full of signs of revolt against simple mathematical and material measures of space and time, while psychologists and sociologists have revealed, through their explorations, a highly complicated and often confused world of personal and social representations which depart significantly from public practices. Personal space and time do not automatically accord, then, with the dominant public sense of either and, as Hareven (1982) shows, there are intricate ways in which "family time" can be integrated with and used to offset the pressing power of the "industrial time" of deskilling and reskilling of labor forces and the cyclical patterns of employment. More significantly, the class, gender, cultural, religious, and political differentiation in conceptions of time and space frequently become arenas of social conflict. New definitions of what is the correct time and place for everything as well as of the proper objective qualities of space and time can arise out of such struggles. A few examples of such conflict or negotiation are perhaps in order.

1. Class Struggle and the Definition of Space–Time

In the chapter in *Capital* on "The Working Day," Marx (1967: 233–5) sets up a fictitious conversation between capitalist and worker. The former insists that a fair-day's work is measured by how much time a worker needs to recuperate sufficient strength to return to work the next day and that a fair-day's wage is given by the money required to cover daily reproduction costs. The worker replies that such a calculation ignores the shortening of his or her life which results from unremitting toil and that the measure of a fair-day's work and wage looks entirely different when calculated over a working life. Both sides, Marx argues, are correct from the standpoint of the laws of market exchange, but different class perspectives dictate different time-horizons for social calculation. Between such equal rights, Marx argues, force decides. The history of struggle over the working day, the working week, the working year (vacation with pay rights) and the working lifetime (retirement and pension rights) has subsequently been writ large in the whole historical geography of class struggle (Thompson, 1967; Roediger and Foner, 1989). Marx noted how capitalists stretched and warped notions of time to their own ends. When the state sought to regulate child labor, "capitalist anthropology" decided "the age of childhood ended at 10 or at the least 11." When the working day was timed the factory clock moved fast and slow as required. When ideas about night and day were important in defining conditions of contract, then the judiciary fixed appropriate meanings to those terms. When mealtimes were set up, the machinery was still kept running.

Such time discipline crucially depended upon the construction of distinctive spaces of surveillance. Here Marx anticipates Foucault as he cryptically quotes from the bourgeois apologists of the eighteenth century:

> for "extirpating idleness, debauchery and excess," promoting a spirit of industry ... capital proposes this approved device: to shut up such labourers as become dependent on public support, in a word, paupers, in "an *ideal workhouse*." Such an ideal workhouse must be made a "House of Terror," and not an asylum for

the poor, "where they are to be plentifully fed, warmly and decently clothed and where they do little work." In this "House of Terror," this "ideal workhouse, the poor shall work 14 hours a day, allowing proper time for meals, in such a manner that there shall remain 12 hours of neat-labour. ... The "House of Terror" for paupers of which the capitalistic soul of 1770 only dreamed, was realized a few years later in the shape of a gigantic "Workhouse" for the industrial worker himself. It is called the Factory. And the ideal this time fades before the reality. (Marx, 1967: 262–3)

The struggle over spatio-temporality in the labor process is fierce and carried into every niche and corner of production:

these minutiae, which, with military uniformity regulate by stroke of the clock the times, limits, pauses of the work, were not at all the products of Parliamentary fancy. They developed gradually out of the circumstances as natural laws of the modern mode of production. Their formulation, official recognition, and proclamation by the State were the result of a long struggle of classes. (Marx, 1967: 268)

Read as an account of the constitution of spatio-temporality within a given mode of production and value creation, Marx's chapter on "The Working Day" is as prescient as it is fecund, spawning a host of later studies and commentaries.

2. Gender Struggles and the Definition of Space–Time

The gendering of "Father Time" yields a second example. Under capitalism time gets construed quite differently according to gender roles through the curious habit of defining valued working time as only that taken up in selling labor power directly to others. But, as Forman (1989) points out, the long history of confinement of a woman's world to the cyclical times of nature has had the effect of excluding women from the linear time of patriarchal history, rendering women "strangers in the world of male-defined time." The struggle, in this case, is to challenge the traditional world of myth, iconography, and ritual in which male dominion over time parallels dominion over nature and over women as "natural beings." This is an issue which Kristeva (1986) addresses directly in terms of a female subjectivity which is linked, she argues, in one of her most important essays, to *cyclical times* (repetition) and *monumental time* (eternity), while being excluded from the *linear time* of history, of projects, "teleology, departure, progression and arrival." The last is very much about *production* whereas the former relates primarily to *reproduction*, "survival of the species, life and death, the body, sex and symbol." When evoking "the name and destiny of women, one thinks," she argues, "more of the *space* generating and forming the human species than of *time*, becoming or history" (p. 190). When William Blake insisted, for example, that "Time and Space are Real Beings. Time is a Man, Space is a Woman, and her mascu-line Portion is Death" (quoted in Forman, 1989: 4), he was articulating a widespread allegorical presumption that has strong contemporary echoes. The inability to relate the time of birthing (and all that this implies) to the mascu-line preoccupation with death and history is, in Forman's view, one of the deeper psychological battlegrounds between men and women as well as within the feminist movement, the latter dividing according to Kristeva between streams that seek a place alongside men in history (equality, civil and political rights, etc.), a separate feminine identity with their own distinctive sense of time–space (as do the ecofeminists) or, as a third wave, seek a place of maternal love and suffering (and spatio-temporal sense that goes with that) in an attempt to revolutionize the dominant notions of intersubjective space–time and value.

Discursive arguments of this sort are internalized in social practices. Wigley provides an interesting case study through consideration of the architectural principles and practices laid out in Alberti's foundational renaissance texts. Alberti, Wigley (1992: 342) argues, took from Xenophon, the idea that the sexuality of the woman cannot be self-controlled "because her fluid sexuality endlessly overflows and disrupts" her own boundaries as well as the bound-aries of men, "disturbing ... if not calling it into question" the latter's identity (note the relational dialectic of flow and permanence). The control and bounding of the woman is vital to male identity:

> the role of architecture is explicitly the control of sexuality. ... In Xenophon, the social institution of marriage is naturalized on the basis of the spatial division of gender. ... Marriage is the reason for building a house. The house appears to make a space for the institution. But marriage is already spatial. It cannot be thought outside the house that is the condition of its possibility before its space.

Within the house, under the male's protection, the woman learns her "natural" place "by learning the place of things" and commanding the spaces of the household, thus "internalizing the very spatial order that confines her." This spatial order, Xenophon proposed, "is itself a thing of beauty ... more beautiful than any of the possessions it orders."

There are two important points here. First, the woman's otherwise fluid social identity is constrained by her insertion into a bounded space – the house. Secondly, the ordering of space – considered as beauty – is more important than what it orders, creating an esthetic mask for a highly gendered social relation.

Alberti extends Xenophon's argument in two ways. First, the "closeting off" and control of all bodily functions helps secure a boundary of the isolated body, establishing spaces of purity and individuality that are protected from the porosity that characterized, for example, Gurevich's account of the medieval self. Secondly, the privatization of sexuality within the household (the interior space of bedrooms) becomes important:

Alberti's design should not be understood as the privatization of a preexisting sexuality as that-which-is-private. The body that is privatized is newly sexualized. Indeed, it is a new body. The new sexuality is produced at the very moment of its privatization. All of the ensemble of strategic mechanisms that define and constitute the house are involved in the production of this sexuality as such. (p. 346)

The production of space is the production of sexuality and of gender roles. But in Alberti's work as well as subsequently, that equation is masked and rendered opaque, often through appeal to abstract principles of beauty of the sort that Xenophon proposed. This "masking" in representation and discourse is connected, Wigley holds, with the insertion of a truly private and individualized male space – the study – into the house. An intellectual space beyond sexuality and the power of the woman, it was the space of an isolated male identity engaged in writing, the production of diaries (e.g., that of Pepys) and memoirs, the protection of genealogical records, legal documents, and the "serious" side of financial affairs. It was from that kind of space that a certain kind of "monadic" discourse became possible (Leibniz probably had a study of this kind), signaling a withdrawal from the "chaos of daily life" and the shaping of knowledge and identity through the production of texts produced in enclosed, secure, and very private spaces. The materiality of the body and the textuality of the perceiving self became separable (as in the work of Descartes) and therefore constantly in tension with each other. "Such changes in the social economy of both the body and the subject," reports Stone (1991: 100), "very smoothly serve the purposes of capital accumulation." The production of "a privatized body and of a subject removed from the public sphere" constructs an isolated social monad open to manipulation.

If Wigley is right, discursive forms (such as memoirs, diaries, and private thoughts of individuals) cannot be separated from the constructed and gendered spaces in which they occur (such as the secluded study, the privatized bedroom, and the woman's dressing room) any more than they can be separated from the power and social relations (such as those of gender) and the institutional forms (such as the family economy) instanciated in the "beautiful" ordering of domestic spaces within the bourgeois household. Women's revolt against both the discourses and spatio-temporal practices that contain and control them is, then, part and parcel of the on-going struggle over the values with which spatio-temporal practices are imbued.

Alberti's proposals remained broadly drawing board propositions throughout much of the Renaissance, but became a much stronger reality from the nineteenth century onwards in Britain and the United States. The particular mix of gendered authority, subjugation, and disempowerment that went with the organization of interior domestic space and housing design in the nineteenth century is well documented (Blumin, 1989: 179–91; Cott, 1977;

Douglas, 1977), as is the struggle on the part of some women to define alternative spatial orderings of domestic space to realize an entirely different conception of gender roles (see Hayden, 1981). But, as Marion Roberts (1991) so ably shows, the reorganization of London after 1945, inspired by the Abercrombie Plan, explicitly built spatio-temporal principles of social reproduction and gender relations into both the interior design of the housing as well as into the spatial organization of the whole city: the effect was to make it difficult for women to escape from the stereotyped gender role assigned to them of stay-at-home housewife, mother, and commander-in-chief of the domestic space. Alberti's ideas had become reality. But then it was also from that space of entrapment and marginalization that Betty Friedan in *The Feminine Mystique* (1963) launched her powerful feminist attack upon "the problem that had no name" precisely because its location had been so occluded.

3. Ecological Versus Market Definitions of Spatio-Temporality

Imagine a conversation between an economist and a geologist over the space–time horizon for optimal exploitation of a mineral resource. The former holds that the appropriate time horizon is set by the interest rate and market price, but the geologist, holding to a very different conception of time, argues that it is the obligation of every generation to leave behind an aliquot share of any resource to the next. There is no logical way to resolve that argument. It, too, is resolved by force. The dominant market institutions prevailing under capitalism fix time horizons by way of the interest rate and in almost all arenas of economic calculation (including the purchase of a house with a mortgage), that is the end of the story. We here identify the potentiality for social conflict deriving entirely from the time horizon over which the effect of a decision is held to operate. While economists often accept the Keynesian maxim that "in the long run we are all dead" and that the short-run is the only reasonable time horizon over which to operationalize economic and political decisions, environmentalists insist that responsibilities must be judged over a far longer time horizon within which all forms of life (including that of humans) must be preserved. The opposition in the sense of time is obvious (see chapter 7). If the practices are capitalistic, then the time horizon cannot be that to which environmentalists cleave. The purpose of the rhetoric of sustainability is to direct public policy towards thinking about time horizons well beyond those encountered in the market.

Spatial usages and definitions are likewise a contested terrain between ecologists and economists, the former tending to operate with a much broader conception of the spatial domain of social action, pointing to the spillover effects of local activities into patterns of use that affect global warming, acid rain formation, and global despoliation of the resource base. Such a spatial conception conflicts with decisions taken with the objective of maximizing land rent at a particular site over a time horizon set by land price and the interest rate (see chapter 13). What separates the ecological movement from environmental management (and what in many respects makes the former so special and so interesting) is precisely the variety of conceptions of time and space which it brings to bear on questions of social reproduction and organization.

The intricacy of social control by spatial ordering (and, conversely, the complex ways in which social orders get challenged by the transgression of spatial boundaries) requires sophisticated analysis. Symbolic spaces and the semiotics of spatial orderings, for example, create texts that have to be read in social terms. The internal spatio-temporal organization of the household, of workplaces, of cities, is the outcome of struggles to stabilize or disrupt social meanings by opposed social forces. The fixing of spatiality through material building creates solidly constructed spaces that instanciate negotiated or imposed social values (as in the case with all forms of environmental transformation, cf. chapter 8). The spatialized control of unwanted groups – the homeless, gypsies, "New Age" travelers, the elderly – and spatial stigmatization is as widespread a phenomenon in contemporary society as it was in the medieval world (Sibley, 1995). But by the same token, the search for emancipation from social control instills the desire, the longing and in some instances even the practices of searching for a space "outside" of hegemonic social relations and valuations. Spaces "on the margin" become valued spaces for those who seek to establish differences (see chapter 5). That metaphorical longing has often been translated into action through the formation of Utopian communities, communes in far-away lands, migration. The search for what Foucault calls "heterotopia" – a space of liberty outside of social control – becomes a living proof of how vital spatial ordering is to the actual practices and institutions of a power-laden social process.

Sit-ins, street demonstrations, the storming of the Bastille or the gates of the US embassy in Teheran, the striking down of the Berlin Wall, the occupation of a factory or a college administration building are all signs of attack against an established social order. The initiation of some new social order requires a radical change in spatio-temporality. To separate themselves off from the past, the victors of the French revolution not only devised an entirely new calendar (see Zerubavel, 1985): they also broke open all the old spaces of privilege and constructed a new set of ceremonial spaces consistent with their revolutionary aims (Ozouf, 1988: 126–37). The Parisian communards, to take another example, readily put aside their pressing tasks of organizing for the defense of revolutionary Paris in 1871, to tear down the Vendôme column. The column was a hated symbol of an alien power that had long ruled over them; it was a symbol of that spatial organization of the city that had put so many segments of the population "in their place," by the building of Haussmann's boulevards and the expulsion of the working class from the central city.

Haussmann imposed an entirely new conception of space into the fabric of the city, a conception appropriate to a new social order based on capitalistic (particularly financial) values and state surveillance. The transformation of social relations and daily life envisaged in the 1871 revolution entailed, or so the communards felt, the reconstruction of the interior spaces of Paris in a different nonhierarchical image. So powerful was that urge that the public spectacle of toppling the Vendôme column became a catalytic moment in the assertion of communard power over the city's spaces (Ross, 1988). The communards tried to build an alternative social order not only by reoccupying the space from which they had been so unceremoniously expelled but by trying to reshape the objective social qualities of urban space itself in a nonhierarchical and communitarian image. The subsequent rebuilding of the column was as much a signal of reaction as was the building of the Basilica of Sacré Coeur on the heights of Montmartre in expiation for the commune's supposed sins. The latter (as I have shown elsewhere – see Harvey, 1989c) was an attempt on the part of the forces of reaction to shape memory through the construction of a certain place and, thereby, to put revolutionary Paris "in its place."

The point of these examples is to illustrate how social space, when it is contested within the orbit of a given social formation, can begin to take on new definitions and meanings. This occurs because the social constitution of spatio-temporality cannot be divorced from value creation or, for that matter, from discourses, power relations, memory, institutions, and the tangible forms of material practices through which human societies perpetuate themselves. The interlinkages are there, always to be observed.

VII. Historical Materialist Perspectives on the Social Constitution of Space and Time

If space and time are both social and objective, then it follows that social processes (often conflictual) define their objectification. How, then, can these processes be studied? In the first instance, objectifications of space and time must be understood, not by appeal to the world of thoughts, ideas and beliefs (though study of these is always rewarding) but from the study of material processes of social reproduction. Let me illustrate. I often ask beginning geography students to consider where their last meal came from. Tracing back all the items used in the production of that meal reveals a relation of dependence upon a whole world of social labor conducted in many different places under very different social relations and ecological conditions of production. That dependency expands even further when we consider the materials and goods used indirectly in the production of the goods we directly consume. Yet we can in practice consume our meal without the slightest knowledge of the intricate geography of production and the myriad social relationships embedded in the spatio-temporal system that puts it upon our table. The spatio-temporality of my experience when I go to work, stop off at the bank, shop in the supermarket, cook, eat, and sleep at home, is very different from that embodied in the production and exchange of the commodities I buy. Decisions that seem reasonable from the former standpoint are not necessarily appropriate from the latter. Which set of experiences best captures the spatio-temporality of capitalism? The answer is "both" because both are equally material and equally historically constructed. And it is here that the unity (that Munn, for example, advocates) between phenomenological and political–economic perspectives comes into play, signaling the continuing dialogue (rather than rupture) between the "young" and the "mature" Marx. But there is also another way to look at the unity: it is through the mediation of a thing called "money" that the two spheres relate. Cronon (1991: 378–84) puts it this way:

> Living in the city means consuming goods and services in a market place with ties to people and places in every corner of the planet, people and places that remain invisible, unknown and unimagined as we consume the products of their lives. The market fosters exchange relationships of almost unimaginable complexity, and then hides them from us at the very instant they are created, in that last moment when cash and commodity exchange hands and we finally consume the things we have purchased.

Cronon (1991: 263–6) builds his whole analysis of the development of Chicago in the nineteenth century around an examination of changing commodity flows and the new spatio-temporalities and value systems they defined. Yet the paradox of Chicago:

> was that the same market that brought city and country ever closer together, giving them a common culture and fostering ever more intimate communication between them *also concealed the very linkages it was creating. The geography of capital produced a landscape of obscured connections.* The more concentrated the city markets became and the more extensive its hinterland, the easier it was to forget the ultimate origins of the things it bought and sold. (Cronon, 1991: 340) [My italics].

This was the condition that Marx (1967: 71–83) picked upon in developing one of his most telling concepts – *the fetishism of commodities.* He sought to capture by that term the way in which markets conceal social (and, we should add, geographical) information and relations. We cannot tell from looking at the commodity whether it has been produced by happy laborers working in a cooperative in Italy, grossly exploited child laborers working under conditions of slave labor in Pakistan, or wage laborers protected by adequate labor legislation and wage agreements in Sweden. The grapes that sit upon the supermarket shelves are mute, we cannot see the fingerprints of exploitation upon them or tell immediately what part of the world they are from. By further enquiry, the veil can be lifted on this geographical and social ignorance and we can become aware on these issues, as happens with consumer boycotts of commodities produced under particularly inhumane conditions. But in so doing it is necessary to go beyond what the market reveals. This was Marx's agenda: to get behind the veil, the fetishism of the market, in order to tell the full story of social reproduction through commodity production and exchange.

For Cronon (1991: 384–5), remaining ignorant of these "nearly infinite" interrelations is "to miss our moral responsibility for the ways they shape each other's landscapes and alter the lives of people and organisms within their bounds." If the "others" who put breakfast on our table are judged, as they surely must be, "significant," then what kinds of intersubjective space–time and what kind of valuation schema is being constructed thereby and how does this affect our sense of self, of moral and political identity? If, for example, we consider it right and proper to show moral concern for those who help put dinner on the table, then this implies an extension of moral responsibility (and values) throughout the whole intricate geography and sociality of intersecting markets. We cannot reasonably go to church on Sunday, donate copiously to a fund to help the poor in the parish, and then walk obliviously into the market to buy grapes grown under conditions of appalling exploitation. We cannot reasonably argue for high environmental quality in the neighborhood while still insisting on living at a level which necessarily implies polluting the air somewhere else. We need to know how space and time get defined by the quite different material processes which give us our daily sustenance.

But that idea deserves deeper scrutiny. Munn showed how different spatio-temporalities are defined by different social practices in different domains and that space–time in Gawan society is multidimensional and hierarchical depending upon the sorts of social practices being looked at. But she also shows the complex interplay of seemingly incommensurable space–times and that all sorts of social mechanisms exist that translate and transform from one spatio–temporality to another. Those social mechanisms rest on social relations mediated by things (food, canoes, kula shells). Munn's account is complicated in its details, even for a relatively homogeneous population of no more than 500 people living on one small island. The possibility exists that a similar or, perhaps, far greater complexity and heterogeneity of spatio-temporalities might be found within contemporary capitalism. If so, we need to identify the modes of translation and transformation from one spatio-temporality to another, paying particular attention to the mediating role of things.

But spatio-temporality within capitalism is usually characterized as a binary structure, contrasting the various intricately interwoven spatio-temporalities to be found in the "lifeworld" of individuals (such as the gendered spatio-temporalities encountered within the household) and the abstract "rationalized" spatio-temporalities attributed to modernity or capitalism (such as those that emerge from a discussion of market exchange). This is how Mitchell (see the citation above) depicts it. Such a duality also seems to be implied in Marx's analysis of the fetishism of commodities, and it is a general feature to be found in writers as diverse as Lefebvre, Heidegger, and Habermas. Is this dualism appropriate? The answer to that can be found through consideration of that "thing" – money – which has the greatest power to mediate across these different domains.

VIII. The Spatio-temporality of Moneys

Money, in contemporary society, is by far the most important "thing" in which social relations become invested, values articulated, and social powers incorporated. It poses the mystery, already partially addressed, of how a *thing* can appear to have such a life of its own as to rule and regulate our actions. Money, as a paramount expression of value, internalizes some kind of spatio-temporality – it conveys values over time and space while expressing values achieved through certain spatio-temporal activities. The thesis I shall advance is that the heterogeneity of spatio-temporalities under capitalism is closely mirrored through the heterogeneity of money and its uses.

Marx advances the thesis in the *Grundrisse* (pp. 221–5) that "where money is not itself the community, it must dissolve the community" and so "directly and simultaneously" become "the real community." But he nuances this argument by distinguishing three roles of money, only the last of which entails complete dissolution of "traditional" society.

1. As an *embodiment of wealth* money has a certain substantial and material form (such as gold). Such moneys are not generally used for exchange, but stay within the social unit (individual, family, kin, social order) as symbols of wealth, status, and prestige. They may be converted into jewelry, altar-pieces, icons, symbolic artefacts, and the like, which can become the bearers of long-term memory and symbols of the continuity of social meanings (within families – "the family silver" – as well as within larger social units). They remain within the social unit, unless exchanged as gifts, tributes, ritualized "commerce" of the kula sort or as "blood money" (compensation for crimes or sins committed). They can also be appropriated by main force. The space–time constituted through such money forms is usually spatially circumscribed and long-lasting [unless, as Gurevich (1985: 218) reports of the Norseman, the moneys though highly prized and sought-after are then sunk at sea].

2. Money used as a *medium of exchange* does not stay in place but circulates, more or less freely. It can operate alongside barter and gift structures and even be implicated in them (see Parry and Bloch, 1989). Such moneys can assume diverse forms varying from gold to coins and tokens to paper credits,

and the like. Furthermore the intentionality of the exchange depends entirely upon the conception of *wealth* involved – the sale of indulgences and the purchase of other ways to appease the gods or enter into heaven (in Greek mythology it took gold to get ferried across the River Styx into Hades) is just as important as the use of money to buy goods. The spatio-temporality defined by such practices depends in part upon the intentionality or use. For example, religious tribute in medieval Europe flowed to Rome which consequently became the site of assembly of a vast stock of embodied wealth. Such moneys also depend, however, upon the *trust* and *faith* to be put in the relation between the signifier (money) and the signified (wealth) and that depends upon the ability of persons to *credit* others (see Anderlini and Sabourian, 1992). Credit, therefore, lies at the origin of the money form even though the credit *system* is a much later construction. Money forms a signifying system internalizing a wide range of distinctive practices, discourses, beliefs, institutions, and political–economic powers. This system sometimes threatens to become free-floating and even self-referential, relative to what the signifiers are supposed to signify – hence the distinctive history of monetary crises. The question of credit, trust, and faith in the money form affects how money can operate to mediate social relations in space and time (Caffentzis, 1989). Given some trusted representation of wealth (e.g., Maria Teresa dollars), value relations between participants can break free from ritually circumscribed places and spaces to become part of a more integrated spatio-temporal world of exchange. A coin can travel carrying its representative powers with it through many anonymous hands over many years and over extensive spaces – provided credit, faith, and trust in both the signifier and the persons doing the signifying is built into the structuring of spatio-temporal relations.

3. As a *form of social power,* money acquires another distinctive function. Those who have it can use it for all sorts of creative purposes including exercising control over the access of others to social wealth. The control over a thing converts into control over people. Money is a means for men to control women, for lords to control their vassals, for emperors to control their territories and for capitalists to control laborers. But such forms of social control via money power presume some sort of social ordering in which access to wealth (however defined) cannot be procured by other means (e.g., peasants and serfs cannot move out to unclaimed untilled land, women cannot make their own way in the world, laborers are deprived of the means of production which have become privatized, etc.). Money as social power therefore depends critically upon it being a *privileged* means to control access to wealth. While money as a representation of value can circulate freely, as social power it depends on some sort of territorial configuration and socio-political system (a state apparatus, in short) that renders that particular form of social power hegemonic rather than occasional and dispersed.

The three roles of money that Marx identifies do not replace each other. They all remain copresent (gold is still meaningful as an embodiment of wealth, for example). But the use of money as an individualized and exclusionary form of social power is a central feature of capitalism. Marx then focuses on that particular use by capitalists of the social power of money to control laborers in order to make more money. This analysis rests on a sharp distinction between *wealth* (the physical command over use values of whatever sort) and *value* (the expression of generalized social labor through exchange, itself a historical product). As an expression of labor values, money operates as both measure and as medium of circulation of those values. The (abstract) *exchange value* differs from but internalizes the (concrete) *use value* aspects of money. Only a portion of the total money is used directly as capital (though most money at some time or another is brought within its orbit). But the story does not stop there. Merchants, bankers, landlords and rentiers of all kinds can each use their money power *vis-à-vis* each other as well as with respect to the direct producers to procure some share of the surplus value produced by laborers [see Harvey (1982: chapters 9–11) for an exegesis of Marx's argument]. Affluent workers control poorer, men control women, parents control children, the state controls society, and political parties or corporations control the state apparatus (to cite just a few examples). Money stands to be used in all manner of different ways to control all manner of social relations.

The diverse uses of money have not been well analyzed. In practice, Zelizer (1994: 202) observes, individuals have "invented an extensive array of currencies, ranging from housekeeping allowances, pin money, and spending money to money gifts, gift certificates, remittances, tips, Penny Provident savings, mothers' pensions, and food stamps." They have "differentiated and segregated their monies, setting food money apart from rent money, school money, or charity money as well as funds for burial, weddings, Christmas, or recreation." How they do this is often the focus of struggle and is strongly affected by family structures, cultural predilections, habits, gender, and class position. The creation of "earmarked" moneys illustrates the complex web of social and space–time relations out of which moneys arise and within which money uses are embedded. When, for example, money is earmarked within a household unit for burials, weddings, vacations, remittances, old age, college education, or whatever, it is set aside for a certain purpose each of which has a certain spatio-temporality attached to it.

Zelizer unfortunately ignores the spatio-temporalities created by these different uses while Hareven, in analyzing the different forms of "family time," similarly ignores the diverse uses of money. Conjoining the two analyses provides a rather more complex but unified picture of how different fields of social action connect. While some currencies (such as promises exchanged among family members) may never escape restricted spatio-temporal domains, by far the most interesting circumstance is when a "promissory note" verbalized in one domain is realized through action in another, as happens, for example, when a child is promised a reward for clearing up the playroom and that reward is taken in the form of an ice cream purchased from the store. This seemingly trivial example illustrates the sorts of daily practices whereby "currencies" operative in one domain are constantly being translated into another, acquiring quite different spatio-temporal characteristics as they go. We here encounter the contemporary version of the ways in which different domains of valuation on Gawa were interlinked through practices that wove together separate threads of spatio-temporality at different spatial scales into a coherent social world.

Since this is not an altogether easy idea to grasp, let me illustrate with an example – the creation of so-called "green money." In response to widespread unemployment on Vancouver Island in the 1980s, people in the town of Courtenay constructed a Local Employment and Trade System (LETSystem) based upon a new kind of local money "immune from international recession, debt charges, supply problems, theft, scarcity, and currency fluctuations" (Dauncey, 1988: 51).

> A number of people who live locally and who want to work and trade together get together, agree to the LETSystem rules, and give themselves account numbers. Each person then makes out two lists, one of "wants" and one of "offers," with prices attached (following normal market prices). A joint list is made up and circulated to everyone. Then the members look down the list and phone whoever has what they want, and start trading. ... The limits of one to one barter are eliminated, as you can now trade with the people in the system as a whole: barter is now a collective proposition.

The money in this case is reduced to a positive or negative entry on each individual's trading account. Such a system has to be spatially confined (probably no more than 5,000 people in a geographical area local enough for everyone to know each other personally, Dauncey suggests) and is heavily dependent upon both trust in the others involved and adequate information (including on the reliability of the trading partner). The system is self-regulating through local relationships, friendships, and personal trust and even helps to build those qualities rather than undermining them as often happens with conventional monetary exchange. The money is created "in a natural, organic way – by someone creating something of real value, and trading it with someone else." This encourages personal, local and creative initiatives in ways that build self-esteem and self-reliance both individually as well as within the community as a whole. Finally:

> In the ordinary economy, there is no commitment to the local community built into the patterns of trading. In return, it offers the freedom of the global market, which is also important. The LETSystem does not deny the value of the global economy or of free global trading – it is a complementary, not an alternative

system. It simply says that if a local economy becomes too dependent on such trading, it becomes very vulnerable to the vagaries of international trade winds, and that too much global trading undermines community stability and sustainability. (p. 63)

The LETSystem is an interesting example of a set of social practices set in motion by individuals to create a certain kind of money that embodies a different kind of spatio-temporality to that experienced on the world market. There are several historical examples of note (the town of Worgl in Austria used its own money from 1932–5 and recessionary conditions in Britain spawned some 400 or so such organizations by 1991).

The general point is this: different social practices of valuation (varying from family-based valuations of self, to local trading systems to positionality in the world market) occur in different spatio-temporal domains (varying from the household to locality to global financial markets) but are built into a singular system under the relational umbrella of the money form. Something similar to (though much more elaborate than) the interlocking system of spatio-temporalities that Munn identified on Gawa exists within contemporary capitalism. Though each concrete money use defines a particular spatio-temporality, it does so in some relation to the spatio-temporal processes regulating the abstract qualities of money on the world market. This dialectic between use (often local and particular) and exchange value (simultaneously local and global) must be kept in view if the riddles posed by the connection between different spatio-temporalities and different moneys in contemporary society are to be unravelled.

IX. The Historical Geography of Space and Time under Capitalism

The construction of new dominant mental conceptions and material practices with respect to space and time were fundamental to the rise of capitalism. The conceptions that arose from the Middle Ages in Europe onwards were associated with new ways of establishing values; in particular the rise of money as a means of exchange and a distinctive and exclusionary form of social power to be used in pursuit of further capital accumulation. Money became a central mediator in the valuation of all exchanges (strongly differentiating them from gift and barter) as well as in the valuation of social labor. "Things" had to be individuated, particularized, and isolated as elements over which private property rights to buy and sell could be clearly established. Money came to measure socially necessary labor *time* through coordinating the trading of values over *space*. The new processes of valuation made the Cartesian–Newtonian conceptions of absolute space and time more practical from the standpoint of commerce; they provided unambiguous means for establishing identities (be it of individuals, things, properties, collectivities such as nation states as territorial units, and the like).

Le Goff (1980, 1988) shows how the transition from feudalism to capitalism entailed a fundamental redefinition of concepts of space and time which then served to reorder the world according to quite new social principles. The hour was an invention of the thirteenth century, the minute and the second became common measures only as late as the seventeenth (and we now find ourselves concerned with nanoseconds and even smaller divisions). While the first of these measures had a religious origin (illustrating a deep continuity between the Judeo-Christian view of the world and the rise of capitalism), the spread of adequate measures of time keeping had much more to do with the growing concern for efficiency in production, exchange, commerce, and administration. It was an urban-based revolution "in mental structures and their material expressions" and it was "deeply implicated," according to Le Goff (1980: 36), "in the mechanisms of class struggle." "Equal hours" in the city, Landes (1983: 78) confirms, "announced the victory of a new cultural and economic order." Gurevich (1985: 28–33) likewise argues that "our modern categories of space and time have very little in common with the time and space perceived and experienced by people in other historical epochs." The Renaissance, he goes on to state, signaled "a transition to another way of perceiving the world, and to man's new awareness of himself (individualism, and the conception of the human body as something 'exclusive', 'alienated' from the world)." But the victory was partial and patchy, leaving much of even the western world outside of its reach until at least the mid-nineteenth century.

The history of cartography in the transition from feudalism to capitalism has, like the history of time-keeping, been very much about refinement of spatial measurement and representation according to clearly defined mathematical principles. Here, too, the interests of trade and commerce, of property and territorial rights (of the sort unrecognizable in the feudal world) were of paramount importance in reshaping mental structures and material practices. When it became clear that geographical knowledge was a vital source of military and economic power, then the connection between maps and money, as Landes (1983: 110) shows, followed not far behind. The introduction of the Ptolemaic map into Florence in 1400 and its immediate adoption there as a means to depict geographical space and store locational information, was arguably the fundamental breakthrough in the construction of geographical knowledge as we now know it. Thereafter it became possible in principle to comprehend the world as a global unity.

The political significance of this cartographic revolution deserves consideration. "Rational" mathematical conceptions of space and time were, for example, a necessary condition for Enlightenment doctrines of political equality and social progress. One of the first actions of the French revolutionary assembly was to ordain the systematic mapping of France as a means to ensure equality of political representation [though once more I note with interest that historical sociologists, like Zerubavel (1985: 82–100) prefer to concentrate their attention on the republican calendar as a key symbol rather than cadastral mapping]. This is such a familiar constitutional issue in the democracies of the world (given the whole history of gerrymandering) that the intimate (and often contested) connection between democracy and mapping is now taken for granted. But imagine attempting to draw up an egalitarian system of representation armed only with the Mappa Mundi! On the other hand, the Cartesian grid also has its defects. The peculiar-looking (and now hotly contested) shapes of constituencies that have to be drawn up for the US congress in order to ensure adequate political representation of minority interests is a contemporary case in point. The Jeffersonian land system, with its repetitive mathematical grid that still dominates the landscape of the United States, sought the rational partitioning of space so as to promote the formation of an agrarian individualistic democracy. In practice this proved admirable for capitalist appropriation of and speculation in space, subverting Jefferson's aims, but it also demonstrates how a particular definition of objective social space facilitated the rise of a new kind of social order.

Accounts of the sort which Le Goff and Landes provide illustrate how concepts of space and time connect to capitalistic practices. Helgerson (1986) points out, for example, the intimate connection between the fight with dynastic privilege and the Renaissance mapping of England (by Speed, Norden, Caxton, and the others) in which the political relation between individual and nation became hegemonic. The new means of cartographic representation allowed individuals to see themselves in terms that were more in accord with these new definitions of social and political relations. In the colonial period, to take a much later example, the maps of colonial administrations had very distinctive qualities that reflected their social purposes (Stone, 1988).

Capitalism is, however, a revolutionary mode of production, always restlessly searching out new organizational forms, new technologies, new lifestyles, new modalities of production and exploitation and, therefore, new objective social definitions of time and space. Periodical reorganizations of space relations and of spatial representations have had an extraordinarily powerful effect. The turnpikes and canals, the railways, steamships and telegraph, the radio and the automobile, containerization, jet cargo transport, television and telecommunications, have altered space and time relations and forced new material practices as well as new modes of representation of space. The capacity to measure and divide time has been revolutionized, first through the production and diffusion of increasingly accurate time pieces and subsequently through close attention to the speed and coordinating mechanisms of production (automation, robotization) and the speed of movement of goods, people, information, messages, and the like. The material bases of objective space and time have become rapidly moving rather than fixed datum points in human affairs.

Why this movement? Since I have explored its roots in greater detail elsewhere (Harvey, 1982, 1989a) I simply summarize the principal argument. Time is a vital magnitude under capitalism because social labor is the measure of value and surplus social labor time lies at the origin of profit. Furthermore, the turnover time of capital is significant because speed-up (in production, in marketing, in capital turnover) is a powerful competitive means for individual capitalists to augment profits. In times of economic crisis and of particularly intense competition, capitalists with a faster turnover time survive better than their rivals, with the result that social time horizons typically shorten, intensity of working and living tends to pick up and the pace of change accelerates. The same occurs with the experience of space. The elimination of spatial barriers and the struggle to "annihilate space by time" is essential to the whole dynamic of capital accumulation and becomes particularly acute in crises of capital overaccumulation. The absorption of surpluses of capital (and sometimes labor) through geographical expansion into new territories and through the construction of a completely new set of space relations has been nothing short of remarkable. The construction and reconstruction of space relations and of the global space economy, as Henri Lefebvre (1974) acutely observes, has been one of the main means to permit the survival of capitalism into the twentieth century.

The general characteristics (as opposed to the detailed where, when and how) of the historical geography of space and time which results are not accidental or arbitrary, but implicit in the very laws of motion of capitalist development. The general trend is towards an acceleration in turnover time (the worlds of production, exchange, consumption all tend to change faster) and a shrinking of space horizons. In popular terms, we might say that Toffler's (1970) world of "future shock" encounters, as it were, Marshall McLuhan's (1966) "global village." Such periodic revolutions in the objective social qualities of time and space are not without their contradictions. It takes, for example, long-term and often high-cost fixed capital investments of slow turnover time (like computer hardware) to speed up the turnover time of the rest, and it takes the production of a specific set of space relations (like a rail network) in order to annihilate space by time. A revolution in temporal and spatial relations often entails, therefore, not only the destruction of ways of life and social practices built around preceding time–space systems, but the "creative destruction" of a wide range of physical assets embedded in the landscape. The recent history of deindustrialization is amply illustrative of the sort of process I have in mind.

The multiple spatio-temporalities at work within western capitalism do not always cohere. If, as is the case, the temporal and spatial world of contemporary Wall Street is so very different from that of the nineteenth-century stock exchange and if both depart from that of rural France (then and now) or of Scottish crofters (then and now), then this must be understood as a particular set of responses to a pervasive aggregate condition shaped by the rules of commodity production and capital accumulation. Furthermore, it is frequently the case that tensions arise within capitalism as the spatio-temporality of financial markets outstrips and confuses the spatio-temporalities of production, consumption, urbanization, and the like.

X. Time–Space Compression

Rapid changes in the objective qualities of social space and time are both confusing and disturbing. The nervous wonderment at it all is excellently captured in the *Quarterly Review* for 1839:

> Supposing that our railroads, even at our present simmering rate of travelling, were to be suddenly established all over England, the whole population of the country would, speaking metaphorically, at once advance *en masse*, and place their chairs nearer to the fireside of their metropolis. ... As distances were thus annihilated, the surface of our country would, as it were, shrivel in size until it became not much bigger than one immense city. (Cited in Schivelbusch, 1978: 32).

The poet Heine likewise recorded his "tremendous foreboding" on the opening of the rail link from Paris to Rouen:

> What changes must now occur, in our way of looking at things, in our notions! Even the elementary concepts of time and space have begun to vacillate. Space is killed by the railways. I feel as if the mountains and forests of all countries were advancing on Paris. Even now, I can smell the German linden trees; the North Sea's breakers are rolling against my door. (Cited in Schivelbusch, 1978: 34).

George Eliot was so taken with such sentiments that she chose to introduce her complex tale of shifting social relations in Britain in *Felix Holt, The Radical* with an extraordinary description of changing space–time conditions that included the following observations:

> Posterity may be shot, like a bullet through a tube, by atmospheric pressure from Winchester to Newcastle; that is a fine result to have among our hopes; but the slow old-fashioned way of getting from one end of the country to the other is the better thing to have in the memory. The tube-journey can never lend much to picture and narrative; it is as barren as an exclamatory O! Whereas the happy outside passenger seated on the box from the dawn to the gloaming gathered enough stories of English life, enough of English labours in town and country, enough aspects of earth and sky, to make episodes for a modern Odyssey.

The German theater-director Johannes Birringer (1989: 120–38) records a similar sense of shock (though with a good deal more hyperbole) in a contemporary setting. On arrival in Dallas and Houston he felt an "unforseen collapse of space," where "the dispersion and decompositions of the urban body (the physical and cultural representation of community) have reached a hallucinatory stage." He remarks on "the unavoidable fusion and confusion of geographical realities, or the interchangeability of all places, or the disappearance of visible (static) points of reference into a constant commutation of surface images." The riddle of Houston, he concludes, "is one of community: fragmented and exploded in all direction ... the city impersonates a speculative disorder, a kind of positive unspecificity on the verge of a paradoxical hyperbole (global power/local chaos)."

I have called this sense of overwhelming change in space–time dimensionality "time–space compression" in order to capture something of Heine's sense of foreboding and Birringer's sense of collapse. The experience of it forces all of us to adjust our notions of space and time and to rethink the prospects for social action. This rethinking is embedded in all manner of political–economic struggles. Failure to rethink can be the prelude to disaster. Cronon (1991: 105–8, 318–7) provides us with the telling example of John Burrows, a successful merchant operating out of Davenport, Iowa in the 1840s who perfected business methods to deal with the uncertainties of trading in agricultural products, battling seasonal transportation uncertainties across the badly organized space that stretched between St Louis to New Orleans. Burrows had to have the fixed capital to warehouse large and often unpredictable surges of commodities as well as the cash reserves and credit capacity to handle large surges of income and expenses. But by 1857 he is bankrupt, "a victim of the new economic regime", cast aside and left to die a lonely and bitter old man. What drove him under was the coming of the railroad from the hitherto inaccessible Chicago and the new orderings of space and time that it imposed. "The opening of the Chicago & Rock Island Railroad rather bewildered me," he wrote. The coming of the railroad changed all the rules. The differences between seasons, between night and day as well as vulnerability to the weather were radically transformed and regularity of connection coupled with reasonably accurate timetables placed merchants in a very different operating milieu. Merchants with very little capital or credit could operate out of Chicago opportunistically on low profit margins but rapid capital turnover. Burrows, who had much of his capital tied up in fixed investments that had stood him in good stead in the 1840s simply could not compete nor find an adequate response. The time–space compression wrought by the coming of the railroad squeezed him out, but it did so in part because, "the new structural conditions created by the railroad and by Chicago's metropolitan market were simply too alien to his familiar way of doing business"; his *identity* as a "man of affairs" was so wrapped up with a certain form of spatio-temporality that he could not devise a competitive strategy to carry him into a quite different spatio-temporal world. He tried to operate, in other words, with a value system that was inconsistent with the new modes of valuation imposed by the new spatio-temporality of the railroad.

It has long been observed, of course, that changes in the transport network favor some locations (like Chicago in the nineteenth century) over others. But what is interesting in Cronon's account is that business identities also had to change to embrace the new spatio-temporal regime. This general point is taken up in considerable detail in Schoenberger's (1996) account of recent failures of corporate leaders in the United States to adapt their strategies to changed spatio-temporal conditions of competition. The *identity* of the players and the *culture of the corporation*, acquired under a certain regime of spatio-temporality prevents doing what obviously ought to be done in order to survive under another.

But changing spatio-temporal orderings have also been the focus of intense cultural, esthetic, and political debate. Reflection on this idea helps us understand some of the turmoil that has occurred within the fields of cultural and political production in the capitalist era. Consider, glancing backwards, that complex cultural movement known as modernism (against which postmodernism is supposedly reacting). There is indeed something special that happens to writing and artistic representation in Paris after 1848 and it is useful to look at that against the background of political–economic transformations occurring in that space and at that time. Heine's vague foreboding became a dramatic and traumatic experience in 1848, when for the first time in the capitalist world, political–economy assumed an unlooked for simultaneity. The economic collapse and political revolutions that swept across the capitals of Europe in that year indicated that the capitalist world was interlinked in ways that had hitherto seemed unimaginable. The speed and simultaneity of it all was deeply troubling and called for some new mode of representation through which this interlinked world could be represented. Simple narrative structures simply could not do the job (no matter how brilliantly Dickens ranged across space and time in a novel like *Bleak House*).

Baudelaire (1981) took up the challenge by defining the modernist problematic as the search for universal truths in a world characterized by (spatial) fragmentation, (temporal) ephemerality and creative destruction. The complex sentence structure in Flaubert's novels and the brushstrokes of Manet defined totally new modes of representation of space and time that allowed for new ways of thinking and new possibilities for social and political action. Kern's (1983) account of the revolution in the representation of space and time that occurred shortly before 1914 (a period of extraordinary experimentation in fields as diverse as physics, literature, painting, and philosophy) emphasizes how time–space compression generates experiences out of which new conceptions arise. The avant-garde movements in the cultural field in part reflected but in part also sought to impose new definitions of space and time upon a western capitalism in the full flood of violent transformation.

The recent complex of movements known as "postmodernism" is likewise connected in the writings of authors as diverse as Jameson (1984), Berman (1982), and Daniel Bell (1976) to some new experience of space and time. I have elsewhere sought to see how far postmodernism can be understood simply by relating it to the new experiences of space and time generated in response to the political–economic crisis of 1973 (Harvey, 1989a). Much of the advanced capitalist world was at that time forced into a major revolution in production techniques, consumption habits and political–economic practices. Strong currents of innovation led to speed-up and acceleration of turnover times. Time-horizons for decision making (now a matter of minutes in international financial markets) shortened and lifestyle fashions changed rapidly. And all of this has been coupled with a radical reorganization of space relations, the further reduction of spatial barriers, and the emergence of a new geography of capitalist development. These events have generated a powerful sense of time–space compression affecting all aspects of cultural and political life. Whole landscapes have had to be destroyed in order to make way for the creation of the new. Themes of creative destruction, of increased fragmenta-tion, of ephemerality (in community life, of skills, of lifestyles) have become much more noticeable in literary and philosophic discourse in an era when restructuring of everything from industrial production techniques to inner cities has become a major topic of concern. The transformation in "the structure of feeling" which the move towards postmodernism betokens has much to do with the shifts in political–economic practices that have occurred over the last two decades. It seems to refract in particular the way in which means of communication have been dematerialized. The erasure of the distance between the signifier and the signified (a familiar postmodern idea), for example, is most emphatically achieved in cyberspace, a world in which "the ballast of materiality" has largely been cast away:

> the major step being taken here, technologically, is the transition, wherever advantageous, from information transported physically, and thus against inertia and friction, to information transported electrically along wires, and thus effectively without resistance or delay. Add to this the ability to store information electromagnetically ... and we see yet another significant and evolutionary step in dematerializing the medium and conquering – as they say – space and time. (Benedikt, 1991: 9)

A closer look at the contradictions built into these cultural and political movements illustrates how deeply they are embedded in capitalist political economy. Consider the cultural response to the recent speed-up and accelera-tion of capital turnover time. The latter presupposes a more rapid turnover in consumption habits and lifestyles which consequently become the focus of capitalist social relations of production and consumption. Capitalist penetration of the realm of cultural production becomes particularly attractive because the lifetime of consumption of images, as opposed to more tangible objects like autos and refrigerators, is almost instantaneous. In recent years, a good deal of capital and labor has been applied to dominating, organizing, and orchestrating so-called "cultural" activities. This has been accompanied by a renewed emphasis upon the production of controlled spectacles (such as the Olympic Games) which can conveniently double as a means of capital accumulation and of social control (reviving political interest in the old Roman formula of "bread and circuses" at a time of greater insecurity).

The reactions to the collapse of spatial barriers are no less contradictory. The more global interrelations become, the more internationalized our dinner ingredients and our money flows, and the more spatial barriers disintegrate, so more rather than less of the world's population cling to place and neighborhood or to nation, region, ethnic grouping, or religious belief as specific marks of identity. Such a quest for visible and tangible marks of identity is readily understandable in the midst of fierce time–space compression. No matter that the capitalist response has been to invent tradition as yet another item of commodity production and consumption (the reenactment of ancient rites and spectacles, the excesses of a rampant heritage culture), there is still an insistent urge to look for roots in a world where image streams accelerate and become more and more placeless (unless the television and video screen can properly be regarded as a place). The foreboding generated out of the sense of social space imploding in upon us (forcibly marked by everything from the daily news to random acts of international terror or global environmental problems) translates into a crisis of identity. Who are we and to what space/place do we belong? Am I a citizen of the world, the nation, the locality? Can I have a virtual existence in cyberspace and what will that mean for the constitution of self, of value and of the ability to identify place, community, and the like? Not for the first time in capitalist history, if Kern's (1983) account of the period before World War I is correct, the diminution of spatial barriers has provoked both an increasing sense of exclusionary nationalism and localism, and an exhilarating sense of the heterogeneity and porosity of cultures and personal–political identifications.

The evident tension between place and space echoes a tension within capitalist political economy; it takes a specific organization of space to try and annihilate space and it takes capital of long turnover time to facilitate the more rapid turnover of the rest. These tensions can be examined from yet another standpoint. Multinational capital should have scant respect for geography these days precisely because weakening spatial barriers open the whole world as its profitable oyster. But the reduction of spatial barriers has an equally powerful opposite effect; small-scale and finely graded differences between the qualities of places (their labor supply, their infrastructures, and political receptivity, their resource mixes, their market niches, etc.) become even more important because multinational capital is in a better position to exploit them. Places, by the same token, become much more concerned about their "good business climate" and inter-place competition for development becomes much more fine-tuned. The image-building of community (of the sort which characterizes Baltimore's inner harbor) becomes embedded in powerful processes of inter-urban competition (Harvey, 1989b). Concern for both the real and fictional qualities of place increases in a phase of capitalist development in which the power to command space, particularly with respect to financial and money flows, has become more marked than ever before. The geopolitics of place tend to become more rather than less emphatic. Globalization thus generates its exact opposite motion into geopolitical oppositions and warring camps in a hostile world. The threat of geopolitical fragmentation in global capitalism – between geopolitical power blocks such as the European Union, the NAFTA, and the Japanese trading empire – is far from idle.

It is for these reasons that it is imperative to come to terms with the historical geography of space and time under capitalism. The dialectical oppositions between place and space, between long- and short-term time horizons, exist within a deeper framework of shifts in time–space dimensionality that are the product of underlying capitalist imperatives to accelerate turnover times and to annihilate space by time. The study of how we cope with time–space compression illustrates how shifts in the experience of space and time generate new struggles in such fields as esthetics and cultural representation, how very basic processes of social reproduction, as well as of production, are deeply implicated in shifting space and time horizons. The production of spatio-temporalities is both a constitutive and fundamental moment to the social process in general as well as fundamental to the establishment of values. And that principle holds cross-culturally as well as in radically different modes of production and significantly different social formations. How and why that is necessarily the case now needs theoretical explication.

10

The Currency of Space–Time

It is hardly more than a pardonable exaggeration to say that the determination of the meaning of nature reduces itself principally to the discussion of the character of time and the character of space.

Alfred North Whitehead

I. Bodies in Space

The conception of the human body (and of all that goes with it – conceptions of self, subjectivity, identity, value, and social being) depends upon definitions of space and time. If the latter are relational rather than absolute, then it follows that conceptions of the body and the conceptions of spatio-temporality are mutually constitutive of each other. That same conclusion can be arrived at from an entirely different direction. If, as Whitehead argues, it is bodily sensation that provides the primary locus for all of our experience of space and time, then it is through the sensations of the human body that our common sense notions of space and time initially get constructed. In *Process and Reality*, Whitehead (1969: 98–9) writes:

> sense-perception of the contemporary world is accompanied by perception of the "withness" of the body. It is this withness that makes the body the starting point for our knowledge of the circumambient world. We find here our direct knowledge of "causal efficacy." ... But we must – to avoid "solipsism of the present moment" – include in direct perception something more than the presentational immediacy [for] even this presentational immediacy begins with sense-presentation of the contemporary body. The body, however, is only a peculiarly intimate bit of the world. Just as Descartes said, "this body is mine;" so he should have said "this actual world is mine." My process of "being myself" is my origination from my possession of the world.

On this starting point, at least, the staid and conservative Whitehead finds common ground with the youthful and rebellious Marx, who vehemently argued in the *Economic and Philosophical Manuscripts of 1844*:

> *Sense perception* must be the basis of all science. Only when science starts out from sense perception in the dual form of *sensuous* consciousness and *sensuous* need – i.e. only when science starts out from nature – is it *real* science. (Cited in Eagleton, 1990: 197).

But whereas Marx was concerned to show how "the human body, through those extensions of itself we call society and technology, comes to overreach itself and bring itself to nothing" (Eagleton, 1990: 198), Whitehead had the more mundane but equally significant aim of coming to terms with how the body might ground science. If, for example, the body primarily experiences the world in terms of entities bound together in a system of causal efficacy, then that working model of causality lends immediate credibility to absolute notions of space and absolute notions of time as well as to the view that space and time are clearly separable and quite different from each other. Such views of space and time stand, of course, to be modified by what Whitehead calls "the sense-presentation of the contemporary body" by which I presume he means the way in which symbolic orders, memory, power relations, and the like operate to define that "withness" of the body that grounds experience. Hence, the mutual constitution of the "withness" of the body and of the experience of space and time cannot be understood without reference to those social practices, such as those found on Gawa, of valuation of the body, the self, and the social being. In the capitalist social order we inhabit, these social practices are powerfully mediated through the circulation of different forms of money, the placing of meaning on money itself and the "sense-presentation" of the body in everything from contemporary science and the media through to the esthetics of the body and its care that connects to the presentation of self in everyday life. These are rather difficult matters to sort out, and we must here venture to rather difficult theoretical terrain.

To this end, I shall begin by exploring the ideas of Leibniz and Whitehead on relational aspects of space and time as a counter to the absolute views of Newton as well as to the hegemonic views of Kant. Leibniz was deeply opposed (as evidenced by the famous Clarke–Leibniz correspondence) to the Newtonian absolute conceptions that have typically grounded views of the body throughout much of the history of modern capitalism. As I shall hope to show, the relational approach to spatio-temporality best captures the typical ways of thought of medieval and precapitalistic societies about space and time (such as those described by Gurevich and Munn). Though it has taken a back seat in comparison to absolute (and more recently relativistic) conceptions in advanced capitalistic societies, the relational view has never entirely disappeared. It finds a strong, and in some regards more advanced champion than

Leibniz in the figure of Alfred North Whitehead and strong traces of it are to be found not only in Marx but in a wide range of other thinkers. I advocated the relational view in *Social Justice and the City* more than 20 years ago and have broadly held to it since, but I neglected then as well as in the intervening years to explicate its meaning. I now believe that a proper consideration of it can enliven and enlighten discussion of the sociality of being in the contemporary world.

II. Leibniz on Space and Time

Leibniz, though a dead white European male, occupied a particularly interesting space–time location. Temporally he shared the modernist passion for science and reason but mixed it with a medieval ontology of how the universe is constructed. Geopolitically, he is at the center of European scientific endeavors and political–theological controversies (see chapter 3), yet he also explored, through his contacts with Jesuit priests, eastern philosophical and mathematical systems, leading Needham to suggest [probably incorrectly according to Mungello (1977)] that he derived calculus as well as binary arithmetic and modal logic (the foundations of contemporary computer languages) from his studies of the *I Ching*. It was from this particular situatedness that he evolved distinctive views on the meanings to be assigned to space and time. His views have not been held in great esteem by many philosophers (particularly after Bertrand Russell's strong critique), but there are some signs (see Brown, 1990) of serious reconsideration of his metaphysics while many of his contributions in the fields of science, mathematics, and logic are now clearly recognized as foundational for a wide range of contemporary practices (he is now regarded as the metaphysician of cyberspace, for example). Given Leibniz's resolutely anti-materialist metaphysics, simple adoption of his arguments poses certain difficulties for any Marxian view (see chapter 3). But these are not insurmountable, depending upon the conception of dialectics involved.

Leibniz, as was shown in chapter 3, was a strong proponent of the idea of internal relations. In the *Monadology* (1991: 24) he summarized his position thus:

> Now this interlinkage or accommodation of all created things to each other, and of each to all the others, brings it about that each simple substance has relations that express all the others, and is in consequence a perpetual living mirror of the universe.

It was from this standpoint of internal relations that he opposed the Newtonian view that space and time existed in their own right, that they were content-neutral containers indifferent with respect to whatever it was that was placed within them. He argued instead that space was always contingent on substance or matter, not, however, in the way understood in relativity theory or by geographers when they use the term "relative space" to indicate how space gets bent or warped depending on the matter being traversed. He developed instead a relational view in which space and time "are nothing apart from the things 'in' them," and "owe their existence to the ordering relations that obtain among things" (Rescher, 1979: 84). For Leibniz, space and time were not real or material or even ideal in and of themselves, but took on a "secondary" or "contingent" (albeit a "well-grounded" and thoroughly material) existence derivative entirely from the substances and processes they contain. So how, then, are space and time to be construed? Consider the following statements culled from his writings:

> And as one and the same town viewed from different sides look altogether differ-ent, and is, as it were, perspectively multiplied, it similarly happens that, through the infinite multitude of simple substances, there are, as it were, just as many different universes, which however are only the perspectives of a single one according to the different points of view of each monad. (Leibniz, 1991: 24)

This defines what I will call the first version of spatio-temporality: the idea that situatedness, positionality and condition provide a multiplicity of temporal and spatial perspectives on a single actual universe. It contrasts with a second view in which Leibniz explores with the tools of logic, a multiplicity of possible universes of radically different spatio-temporalities:

> ... there could exist an infinity of other spaces and worlds entirely different [from ours]. They would have no distance from us (nor other special relations to us) if the spirits inhabiting them had sensations not related to ours. Exactly as the world of the space of dreams differs from our waking world, there could even be in such a world quite different laws of motion. (Leibniz, cited in Rescher, 1979: 94)

> ... it cannot be denied that many stories, especially those called novels, may be regarded as possible, even if they do not actually take place in this particular sequence of the universe which God has chosen – unless someone imagines that there are certain poetic regions in the infinite extent of space and time where we might see wandering over the earth King Arthur of Great Britain, Amadis of Gaul, and the fabulous Dietrich von Bern invented by the Germans. A famous philosopher of our century does not seem to have been far from such an opinion, for he expressly affirms somewhere that matter receives all the forms of which it is capable (Descartes, Principles of Philosophy, Part III, Art 47). This opinion cannot be defended, for it would obliterate all the beauty of the universe and all choice. (Leibniz, cited in Rescher, 1981: 91–2)

Technically, Leibniz argued, space like time, in no matter what universe (for all universes have some sort of spatio-temporality) is nothing more than "a structure of relations of an appropriate sort." In particular:

> space is the order of *coexistence* – that is, the order among the mutually contemporaneous states of things; while time is the order of *succession* – that is, the order among the various different mutually coexisting states of things which (because they are mutually) coexisting – must, of course, have some sort of "spatial" structure. (Rescher, 1979: 86–7)

This brings us to what I consider the first virtue of the Leibnizian system: space and time are "mutually coordinate in such a way that neither is more fundamental than the other" (Rescher, 1979). They are coordinate as ordering principles of substances such that *both* are contingent [this opposes Feuerbach's view that time is the privileged domain of the dialectic as well as Sayer's (1985) more recent argument that time is the realm of necessity and space the realm of the contingent].

If, however, space is "an order of coexisting substances, then every world has its own space" and "distinct individuals in distinct worlds that do not coexist with one another" are held to be spatially disjoint or "spatially *unrelated* – somewhat like the dream-worlds of different people" (Rescher, 1981: 86). Potentially, then, "every possible world has its own space as it has its own laws." This does not imply that any world can be spaceless, but that the ordering of space "is necessarily different in different worlds since different worlds contain different (and incompatible) substances and these substances internalize such differences. Hence, a difference in things brings a difference in spaces in its wake, even as it carries with it a difference of laws." This I hold to be the second virtue of Leibniz's formulation: that it allows of a "plurality of distinct spaces as opposed to a single all-comprehending superspace with many distinct sectors or subspaces" (Rescher, 1981: 88–9). More particularly, "a space is individuated as a single space through the mutual relatedness and connectedness of its parts, and where these elements of mutual relation and interconnection are absent, the warrant for speaking of a single space is lacking."

Leibniz's reasoning was both theological and metaphysical. In practice, the physical world which we encounter has only one unique ordering of space and time so that the possible existence of a plurality of spaces and times is not directly troublesome for materialist science. The appearance of different spatial and temporal orderings can come about in such a world only in the sense of the multiple perspectives on the same reality set out in *The Monadology*. But Leibniz is concerned with God's creativity and perfection. He thought that the Newtonian view placed God *in* space and time as if either God's actions were predetermined or even as if the properties of space and time preceded God. The discussion of a plurality of spaces and times within multiple possible worlds (each with its own laws of motion) recognizes that the physical world we occupy is an expression of God's creative choice and will. For Leibniz, God's perfection delivers "the best of all possible worlds." The exploration of quite different possible orderings of space and time is meant to illuminate the particular qualities of God's choice.

The breakthrough into capitalist modernity, many now hold, entailed the secularization of thinking about space and time. Even Whitehead (1969: 61), who maintained a conception of God as fundamental to his works, regarded Leibniz's formulation of the best of possible worlds as "an audacious fudge produced in order to save the face of a Creator constructed by contemporary, and antecedent, theologians." If, however, we secularize matters entirely, then the question of which of the multiple possible spatio-temporal worlds we inhabit becomes a matter of secular social choices rather than an imposition of God's singular will. I consider this to be the third virtue of Leibniz's argument: that space and time can be viewed as ordering systems inherent within social practices and activities that are in some sense "chosen" (perhaps "arrived at" would be a better phrase) rather than given. It is, for example, a relatively short step from the idea that "every possible world has its own characteristic spatial structure" (Rescher, 1979: 93) to the idea that each distinctive social formation has its own characteristic spatial-temporal structure and its own distinctive laws of motion. And this will be so because it is "the difference in *things*" (or, as I would prefer it, the difference in social practices and processes) which "brings a difference in *spaces* in its wake, even as it carries within it a difference of laws" (Rescher, 1981: 88).

Leibniz's emphasis upon creativity of the spatiality of coexistence and the temporality of succession opens up other lines of argument which become most apparent by consideration of his own illustrations of multiple possible spatial worlds. The world and space of dreams, and even of novels and poetry, differ from that of daily experience and may have their own laws of motion. But here we hit a conundrum. How do we *know* that such spatial worlds are separate from each other as opposed to being different perspectives on the same universe as proposed in *The Monadology*? Leibniz's own view (cited in Rescher, 1981: 90) is that "whoever asks whether another world, or another space, can exist is asking to this extent whether there are minds that communicate nothing to us." The extreme postmodern view of fragmentation and separated spatial worlds then depends crucially, if we follow the logic of Leibniz's argument, upon (*a*) inhabitants experiencing sensations radically different from ours and (*b*) incommunicability between those spatially and temporally ordered worlds. Leibniz presumed (largely for theological reasons) that the actual material world in which we lived was a harmoniously ordered universe upon which multiple monads might develop infinitely different perspectives. In this respect, Leibniz conformed to the view of a single universe, but his manner of argumentation opens up a variety of troubling questions as well as intriguing possibilities, particularly given the way he sought to impose a metaphysical unity in the face of political–economic fragmentation and political chaos (see chapter 3). If we accept the transformation I am here proposing and drop the theological idea of a singular creative deity and accept social choice and creativity with respect to the orderings of space and time, then the issue of how these different social choices are arrived at and whether or not they are embedded in entirely separate worlds of sensation and incommunicable language (as opposed to the multiplication of perspectives on a single universe) becomes central to the contemporary discussion around postmodern versus modernist perspectives.

There is, perhaps, another way to put this. Leibniz made a strong distinction between *possible* and *compossible* worlds. While the former embraces an infinite variety of potential creative choices, the latter restricts the spatial relations internalized within a particular choice set (e.g., the actually-existing monads in Leibniz's argument) to the orderings of coexistence actually found within that public space (or common universe) which all monads perceive. To be in that common world is to share given qualities of space and time by virtue of the "mutual relatedness and connectedness of its parts." Putting this in the context of the materials assembled on the social construction of space and time in chapter 9 entails that, while the social choice with respect to spatial and temporal ordering is potentially infinite, the actual social choice once made, condemns all "mutually related and connected" members of that social world to an existence within a common experiential framework of public space and time. This, of course, is the fundamental point upon which Gurevich for one insists (see p. 212). But here, too, there arises another difficulty: for if different social formations can arise out of each other, then there has to be some way of transforming the frameworks of space and time (as well as the laws of motion) which in turn implies that a plurality of spaces and times (as well as conflicting laws of motion) must at some time or other coexist, even if only temporarily, within a common universe. Incommunicability, of the sort that characterized the negotiations over land sales between colonial settlers and Indian groups in the early stages of colonization of New England, then becomes part of the clash of different social definitions of spatio-temporality.

The emphasis upon communicability is important here. It prefigures in an interesting way Habermas's (1987: 322) treatment of spatio-temporality within his theory of communicative action. If reason is "by its very nature incarnated in contexts of communicative action," he writes, then speech acts connect the plans and actions of different actors "in historical time and across social space." But although there is always a "transcendental moment of universal validity" that "bursts every provinciality asunder" so that "the validity claimed for propositions and norms transcends spaces and times, 'blots out' space and time, the acceptance, promulgation and above all contestation of such claims can never escape the 'here and now' of specific contexts." The parallel here with

Williams' analysis of the dilemmas of "militant particularism" is startling and in itself suggests a convergence of thought about how spatio-temporalities, once constituted, frame political action. And there is a strong link, as we shall later see (chapter 12) to the idea of "situated knowledge." To contest a dominant notion of spatio-temporality is to contest the process that produced it and to redefine, in thought, alternative possible worlds of being.

Such contestations are ruled out in Leibniz's own theory. But it is ruled out by the assumption of God's attachment to principles of *harmony*. A secularized version of Leibniz's argument can and evidently should dispense with such an assumption in favor of a more conflictual model of social relations incorporating ideas of class, gender, colonial and other forms of struggle. Even under conditions of a common universe, therefore, there can be more than just different perspectives on that commonality, but contradictions and oppositions of the sort described in chapter 9 which imply that we internalize a plurality of ordering principles of space and time and find ourselves often internally conflicted as to which ordering perspective to adopt (a simple example would be the conflicting spatio-temporal views I internalize from activities of parenting on the one hand and from professional life as an academic on the other).

Let me summarize the nature of the argument I am here making. I could be interpreted as saying that there is a singular actually existing framework of space and time and that social variations arise only by virtue of our varied perspectives ("situatedness" as we now typically refer to it) on a common universe. This view, while in itself plausible and full of insights regarding different modes of human behavior in space and time, appears inconsistent with the examples which Leibniz gives of different possible worlds – the worlds of dreams and of novels. These are alternative possible worlds in some sense fundamentally different from each other. Such possible worlds are not entirely outside of human experience, though Leibniz might reasonably claim that in some sense the worlds they depict are outside of the material world of sense perception. Leibniz's findings on multiple possible worlds of space and time are purely logical constructs. But they can be used as a means to look more closely at the differentiation of actual spatial and temporal orderings within and between different modes of production and social formations. A secularized and social understanding of relational space and time on a Leibnizian foundation provides, in short, a strong theoretical and logical framework capable of representing the variegated social practices of construction of space and time laid out in chapter 9. It also permits the exploration of alternative modes of production in terms of the production of different possible worlds of spatio-temporality.

III. Whitehead's Relational Theory of Space and Time

Alfred North Whitehead proposed a relational theory of space and time. Curiously, he never discussed Leibniz's views in detail (perhaps out of deference to his friend and collaborator Russell who mounted such a devastating attack against Leibniz's metaphysics while learning greatly from his mathematical logic) though he did occasionally acknowledge both similarities and differences. The differences are important. To begin with, Whitehead, as befits someone raised in the traditions of British empiricism, pushed for a realist rather than a logical version of the relational view. He thereby counters Leibniz's tendency to veer off into unalloyed idealism. He also had the advantage of writing after Einstein published the general theory of relativity. While he disputed Einstein's interpretations (thereby opening a gap between the relative and relational views) he never doubted the importance or veracity of Einstein's discoveries. Whitehead consequently provides a much stronger metaphysical basis for the kind of materialist dialectical understanding of spatio-temporality for which I am searching. Unfortunately, his lack of interest in the dialectical tradition *per se* (he recognized Hegel's importance, for example, but confessed he never managed to read more than a page or two of him) denied him some of the insights that Leibniz provides.

Whitehead published a paper entitled "La Théorie Relationniste de l'Espace" in 1914. Judged poorly written and overlong by his primary expositor and biographer Victor Lowe (1962: 178), it nevertheless occupied a pivotal transitional role between the early Whitehead that collaborated with Russell on *Principia Mathematica* and the later Whitehead that expounded upon a philosophy of process and organism. In it, Whitehead argued that we ought not to consider physical bodies as if they are first in space and then act upon each other. Bodies are in space, rather, only because they interact, so that space is "only the expression of certain properties of their interaction" (Lowe, 1962). Space and time are not, therefore, independent realities, but relations derived from processes and events. Put in Whitehead's own words:

> The fundamental order of ideas is first a world of things in relation, then the space whose fundamental entities are defined by means of those relations and whose properties are deduced from the nature of these relations.

This reconceptualization of spatio-temporality led Whitehead to the intriguing terrain of how to devise an adequate language with which to capture process, motion, flux, and flow without abandoning the obvious common-sense idea that we are surrounded with things possessing relative stability and definable properties. Once on that terrain, as Fitzgerald (1979: 74) observes, it became obvious to Whitehead that it was extremely difficult "to explain change within the confines of Newton's philosophy of nature" and particularly within the confines of any absolute conception of space and time. "Change at a durationless instant is a very difficult conception. How can one explain velocity without referring to the past as well as the future?" In searching to answer that question, Whitehead was forced to construct a new and quite radically different philosophy of space and time (Fitzgerald, 1979: 74).

Once Whitehead (1985: 53) came to believe that "nature is a process," he found himself working at odds with most conceptions of science. The usual answer to the question "what is nature," for example, "is couched in terms of stuff, or matter, or material – the particular name chosen is indifferent – which has the property of simple location in space and time, or, if you adopt the more modern ideas, in spacetime." It then followed that "as soon as you have settled, however you do settle, what you mean by a definite place in space–time, you can adequately state the relation of a particular material body to space–time by saying that it is just there, in that place; and so far as simple location is concerned, there is nothing more to be said on the subject" (Whitehead 1985: 61–9). This was, of course, the famous mechanistic theory of nature with which science had broadly remained content since the seventeenth century, mainly because it worked so well across a broad terrain of technological practices. But this doctrine of matter:

> is the outcome of uncritical acceptance of space and time as external conditions for natural existence. By this I do not mean that any doubt should be thrown on facts of space and time as ingredients of nature. What I do mean is "the unconscious presupposition of space and time as being that within which nature is set." (Whitehead, 1920: 20)

Whitehead (1920: 153–4) was led to deny the "usual indeed universal" doctrine that "spatio-temporal relationships are external" and instead proposed a theory based "upon the doctrine that the relatedness of an event are all internal relations." He went on to observe that:

> The conception of internal relatedness involves the analysis of the event into two factors, one the underlying substantial activity of individualization, and the other, the complex of aspects – that is to say, the complex of relatednesses as entering into the essence of the given event – which are unified in the individual activity. In other words, the concept of internal relations requires the concept of substance as the activity synthesizing the relationships into its emergent character.

The language here is rather special and requires some exegesis. Whitehead's starting point was to criticize the concept of simple location. "I shall argue that among the primary elements of nature apprehended in our immediate experience, there is no element whatever which possesses this character of simple location." It does not follow that Newtonian science is wrong: "by a particular process of constructive abstraction, we can come up with the Newtonian formulation." But this is only one abstraction out of a field of radically different possibilities and we cannot understand it without "reference to that from which it has been extracted." In other words, an understanding of process must precede or parallel an understanding of space and time.

Whitehead's ultimate objective is to replace the Newtonian mechanistic view with "a philosophy of organism" and in *Science and the Modern World* (1985: 80ff) he opens the way to that project through a reconsideration of the status of space and time. He observes that things are both *separated* and *bound together* in space and time. He calls these characters the "separative" and the "prehensive" characters of space–time. *How* things are separated and bound together then becomes the focus of attention because it is precisely this *how* that is captured in any definition of space and time. A third characteristic is what Whitehead terms the "modal" character of space–time within which – and only within which – a version of simple location can be defined because "everything which is in space receives a definite limitation of some sort." In other words, individuation and the definition of *things, particulars or events* always occurs in space–time. But which space–time? It is only the modality of the definition that is interesting and that modality is, for Whitehead, always relational. The effect is to eliminate the idea of simple location as a grounding principle entirely. Space and time are now construed as "simply abstractions from the totality of prehensive unifications as mutually patterned in each other ... space–time is nothing else than a system of pulling together of assemblages into unities." The word "event" is then defined to mean "one of these spatio-temporal unities." What is interesting here, of course, is the actual process of pulling together assemblages into unities so as to define spatio-temporalities. Three general aspects to his argument stand out.

1. Whitehead, unlike Leibniz, allows that time can be differentiated from space. In his earlier writings he saw this differentiation only occurring "at a somewhat developed stage of the abstractive process" (Whitehead, 1920: 37). But in developing his philosophy of organism he later came to see the differentiation as a product of the whole process of pulling together assemblages into organic forms that persisted over duration:

   > it is in this endurance of pattern that time differentiates itself from space ... each enduring object discovers in nature and requires from nature a principle discriminating space from time ... the importance of space as against time, and of time as against space, has developed with the development of enduring organisms. (Whitehead, 1985: 150)

   The implication is that the evolution of any organism, including that of society itself (and Whitehead was not averse to considering society as an organism of some sort though he never deigns to specify the meaning), is to some degree predicated on a particular separation of time and space, such as that so prevalent in the social theory that attaches to capitalist modernity. But we can at least now think of the separation as the product of a process. The effect is to open up an aperture for critical discussion of those particular processes that imply such a separation within social theory itself.

2. Multiple processes generate multiple *real* as opposed to Leibniz's ideal differentiation in spatio-temporalities. This, Whitehead recognized, was one of the most difficult of all propositions to accept or understand:

> These different measure systems with their divergencies of time reckoning are puzzling, and to some extent affront our common sense. It is not the usual way in which we think of the Universe. We think of one necessary time-system and one necessary space. According to the new theory, there are an indefinite number of discordant time-series and an indefinite number of distinct spaces.

Furthermore, the separation of space and time makes it possible for space–time to be stratified in many different ways by different time systems:

> It is at first sight somewhat of a shock to think that other beings may slice nature into time-sections in a different way to what we do. ... Our whole geometry is merely the expression of the ways in which different events are implicated in different time systems." (Whitehead, 1922: 336)

Concentrating as he does on the physics of organisms, Whitehead argues in an aside that luckily "differences among ourselves" on this matter "are quite imperceptible." But it is not hard to broaden the point to understand the social dimension to this argument. Nevertheless, the existence in principle of a multitude of spaces and times is brought back down to earth by Whitehead's (1920: 111) empiricist approach to interlinked processes at work within nature:

> amid the alternative time-systems that nature offers there will be one with a duration giving the best average cogredience for all the subordinate parts of the percipient event. This duration will be the whole of nature which is the terminus posited by sense-awareness. Thus the character of the percipient event determines the time-system immediately evident in nature.

In other words, we can through observation and reflection understand which of the multiplicities of spatio-temporalities is primarily at work both in nature as well as in the experiential world of a moving observer. And in so doing we come to recognize the importance of "cogredience"

(Whitehead here parallels Leibniz's conception of compossibility) – the way in which multiple processes flow together to construct a single consistent, coherent, though multifaceted time–space system.

Since this is an important idea to which I will occasionally return in what follows I offer an example, taken from chapter 9, as to what "cogredience" might mean. Money, I there argued, has multiple uses and it is quite possible for each use to define a different spatio-temporality. Yet money is, in the end, just money so the term operates as a kind of umbrella to indicate a wide range of "compossible" or "cogredient" uses of a consistent and coherent entity endowed with certain qualities. The fact that some of these uses may be contradictory *vis-à-vis* other uses in no way detracts from the overarching coherence of the money concept.

3. Whitehead discusses at great length the problem of how the "permanences" of the organism are ever arrived at and how spatiality is crucial to the bounding of each "permanence" for the duration of its existence. But he is always acutely aware of the process of dissolution that can take even something so seemingly permanent as Cleopatra's needle and ultimately dissolve it. Indeed, Whitehead often held that it was his focus on processes of dissolution that differentiated him from many other process philosophers that had preceded him. And in a few striking sentences Whitehead (1985: 165–7) unpacks some of the correlative features of what I have elsewhere called "time–space compression":

> it is possible that certain species of primates are apt to go to pieces under conditions which lead them to effect changes of space–time systems ... accordingly, an unfavorable environment leading to rapid changes in its proper space–time system, that is to say, an environment jolting it into violent accelerations, causes the corpuscles to go to pieces and dissolve into light-waves of the same period of vibration.

So how, then, can we summarize Whitehead's contribution? The argument mounted against Newton by Leibniz was, Cassirer (1943) points out, really an argument at cross-purposes between two radically different philosophical traditions. It was the logical skills and metaphysical attachments of Leibniz versus the practical philosophy of nature practised by Newton. Whitehead's criticisms arise, however, from within the Newtonian tradition itself. They do not rely on the logical exploration of possible worlds in the fashion of Leibniz, but on the study of relational possibilities of actual processes at work in nature, in so far as human beings can experience and describe them. While Whitehead does diverge from the abstract materialist tradition of natural science by insisting that the bifurcation of nature into facts and values, mind and matter, materiality and consciousness is false, he keeps firmly within the empiricist orbit by hinging his arguments always on the "withness" of human bodily experience. The effect is to convert the multiplicity of possible spatio-temporal worlds proposed by Leibniz into an empirical problem of how to unravel the multiple spatio-temporalities at work within a variegated world of intersecting processes. To the degree that the materials assembled in chapter 9 by historians, anthropologists, geographers, social scientists, and the like, do each in their own way unravel part of the general problematic that Whitehead sets out, then it seems reasonable to conclude that some sort of theoretical basis can be forged for all of that diverse information through the relational theory of space and time that Whitehead proposed.

IV. Towards a Relational Theory of Space, Place, and Environment

Can the relational theory of space and time be used to understand the dialectics of space and place? If so, can it be extended in some way to construct a dialectical understanding of the *space–place–environment* triad? There are strong grounds for answering "yes" to both questions.

Leibniz (1968: 220–3) considers how we arrive at concepts of space and place. We typically observe entities changing locations and speak of one entity "taking the place" of another. From this we infer that there are absolute qualities of places through and across which entities move. Space then appears as all places taken together. But Leibniz's aim is to show how such an inference is misleading and that place, like space, has no "absolute reality." It is he insists, only a relation. Whitehead goes further. "An entity merely known as spatially related to some discerned entity is what we mean by the bare idea of 'place'," he writes. So place is a site of relations of one entity to another and it therefore contains "the other" precisely because no entity can exist in isolation. But relations are not all equally present because "the concept of place marks the disclosure in sense-awareness of entities in nature known merely by their spatial relations to discerned entities" (Whitehead, 1920: 52).

Whitehead's doctrine of "permanences" firms up the idea. A "permanence" arises as a system of "extensive connection" out of processes. Entities achieve relative stability in their bounding and their internal ordering of processes creating space, for a time. Such permanences come to occupy a piece of a space in an exclusive way (for a time) and thereby define a place – their place – (for a time). The process of place formation is a process of carving out "permanences" from the flow of processes creating spaces. But the "permanences" – no matter how solid they may seem – are not eternal: they are always subject to time as "perpetual perishing." They are contingent on the processes that create, sustain and dissolve them.

Whitehead's views on this matter roughly correspond, interestingly, to the recent formulation given by de Certeau (1984: 117) in which place is understood as "an instantaneous configuration of positions," implying "an indication of stability":

> A space exists when one takes into consideration vectors of direction, velocities and time variables. Thus space is composed of intersections of mobile elements. Space occurs as the effect produced by the operations that orient it, situate it, temporalize it. ... In contradistinction to the place, it has thus none of the univocity or stability of a "proper." In short, space is a practised place. Thus the street geometrically defined by urban planning is transformed into a space by walkers. ...

Place is, then, the site of the inert body, reducible to the "being there" of something permanent, in contrast to the instabilities of motions creating space. But a strategic "calculus of force-relationships" arises "when a subject of will and power (a proprietor, an enterprise, a city, a scientific institution) can be isolated from an environment." The achievement of permanences alters the calculus of action in so far as they become "subjects of will and power."

The import of all this for interpretation of a relational theory of space, time, and place is considerable, provided, of course, we are prepared to accept the homology between Whitehead's "permanences" and de Certeau's "subjects of will and power." The difference is that de Certeau extends the idea of permanences into the realm of a dialectic of space and place with "subjects of will and power" (such as the nation state) capable of elaborating external strategies and internal orderings (including surveillance structures) that have much to do with the maintenance of their own permanences (their boundaries and internal integrity).

Consider a simple example. States have been carved out as entities historically (for most of the world between 1870 and 1925) from the flow of multiple intersecting spatial processes. They are bounded and isolated as entities from their environments and acquire a certain permanence through institutions that assure their character and internal integrity. They can be construed as a "victory of space over time," enabling strategies to be formulated within their confines to assure internal discipline and legitimacy while pursuing external geopolitical strategies. But they also engage in geopolitical strategies (including, for example, the development of military technologies of surveillance and communication over space) that produce space as an effect of the strategies they pursue, while simultaneously being perpetually undermined by the very processes of space creation that enabled them to be constituted as permanences in the first place (flows of information, of money, of capital, of immigrants, of cultural habits, of ideologies, etc.). "In our societies," remarks de Certeau (1984: xx), "as local stabilities break down, it is as if, no longer fixed by a circumscribed community, tactics wander out of orbit ... [introducing] a Brownian movement into the system." The changing status of the state, the undermining of seemingly powerful permanences (such as the Soviet Union) then become much more readily understood as the inevitable outcome of a place–space dialectic that not only undermines the supposed "rationality" of politics, economics, and science, but also pits the strategic world of places against the wayward trajectories of multiple spatialities defined by often divergent processes. It is for this reason that we can reasonably speak of "spaces of liberation" and "oppositional" spaces, even give practical meaning to Foucault's idea of a "heterotopia" (a space beyond and outside of the instrumentalities of surveillance).

This then leaves the whole question of environmental qualities and processes to be resolved. Since spaces, times and places are relationally defined by *processes*, they are contingent upon the attributes of processes that simultaneously define and shape what is customarily referred to as "environment." We cannot talk about the world of "nature" or of "environment" without simultaneously revealing how space and time are being constituted within such processes:

> The things which are grasped into a realised unity, here and now, are not the castle, the cloud, and the planet simply in themselves; but they are the castle, the cloud, and the planet from the standpoint, in space and time, of the prehensive unification. ...

The bringing together (or "prehensive unification") of diverse processes (physical, biological, social, cultural) defines space, place, and environment. No part of that can be construed without the other:

> It is not the substance which is in space, but the attributes. What we find in space are the red of the rose and the smell of the jasmine and the noise of the cannon. We have all told our dentists where our toothache is. Thus space is not a relation between substances, but between attributes. (Whitehead, 1920: 21)

Place is defined as the site of relations between attributes. If so, then the argument for any kind of independent spatial science, in Whitehead's case geometry and in my case geography, falls away entirely. Whitehead regarded geometry as a branch of physics in much the same way that I regard the kind of geometricized spatial science that has evolved in geography as a general branch of the study of socio-environmental processes. Certainly, the idea that spatio-temporality can be examined independently of those processes evoked in environmental and ecological work cannot be sustained. From this perspective the traditional dichotomies to be found within the geographical tradition between spatial science and environmental issues, between systematic and regional (place-bound) geographies appear totally false precisely because space–time, place, and environment are all embedded in substantial processes whose attributes cannot be examined independently of the diverse spatio-temporalities such processes contain. The implications for the philosophy of geographical thought are immense, but I do not here have the space or time to make a place to explore them in any detail.

V. Individuation, Identity, and Difference

Why, exactly, are such considerations of importance? The answer is as startling as it is profound.

To begin with, space and time, once they are set, are a primary means to individuate and identify objects, people, relations, processes, and events. *Location* and *bounding* are important if not vital attributes for the definition of the objects, events, and relationships existing in the world around us. To choose one ordering principle rather than another is to choose a particular spatio-temporal framework for describing the world. The choice is not neutral with respect to what we can describe. The absolute theory of space and time always forces us into a framework of mechanistic descriptions, for example, that conceal from view important properties of the world (such as those of living organisms) that stand only to be revealed by a relational view. To choose the wrong framework is to misidentify elements in the world around us.

Space and time appear, however, not to be of equal significance to individuation. Many individuals can occupy the same moment in most social (as opposed to personalized) accounts of time, but none of us can occupy exactly the same space at that moment of time without becoming "the other." If the difference of horizons and perspectives between two people is annihilated, notes Bakhtin (1990: 23), then those two people would have "to merge into one, to become one and the same person." The relations between "self" and "other" from which a certain kind of cognition of social affairs emanates is always, therefore, a spatio-temporal construction. This is a crucial issue for understanding how identities (personal and political) get formed. Changes in spatio-temporal frame affect self–other relations (by, for example, either dissolving the self–other distinction entirely or redefining who are or are not significant others in assigning value to the self).

The power to individuate within a given spatio-temporal frame is associated within the power to name; and naming is a form of power over people and things. Cronon (1983: 65) notes, for example, how the mobile Indian communities of New England named the land in such a way as to tell "where plants could be gathered, shellfish collected, mammals hunted and fish caught." Furthermore the same places could have different names depending on the time of year. The purpose of such names "was to turn the landscape into a map which, if studied carefully, literally gave a village's inhabitants the information they needed to sustain themselves." But the Indian practice of naming is much more than that: by attaching stories to the land through naming, Native-Americans embed their history in the landscape. "Geographical features," notes Basso (1984: 44):

> have served the [Western Apache] for centuries as indispensable mnemonic pegs on which to hang the moral teachings of their history. ... The Apache landscape is full of named locations where time and space have fused and where, through the agency of historical tales, their intersection is "made visible for human contemplations." It is also apparent that such locations, charged as they are with personal and social significance, work in important ways to shape the images that Apaches have – or should have – of themselves.

This Indian practice contrasted radically with that of the settlers who, in stealing the land also stole Indian identity. In New England, the colonists had a Cartesian vision of fixed property rights, of boundaries in abstract space, and they "created arbitrary place-names which either recalled localities in their homeland or gave a place the name of its owner." To the Indians the English spatio-temporal system and the placenames it generated were essentially useless and to the English the Indian placenames were equally so. The clash between these two social and ecological systems was a clash over naming as well as over the relevant conceptions of space and time to be deployed in the definition of value (see also Mignolo, 1994).

Political struggles over the meaning and manner of such representations of place and identity abound, most particularly over the way in which places, their inhabitants and their social functions get located, named and discursively represented. As Edward Said (1978) so brilliantly demonstrates in his study of *Orientalism*, the identity of variegated peoples can be collapsed, shaped, and manipulated through the connotations and associations imposed as outsiders name places and peoples. Said may have erred in placing the practices of naming too strongly as a purely western imposition (not giving sufficient recognition to the practices of resistance, complicity, and cooptation practiced by indigenous peoples), but he was surely right to draw attention to the power of naming as a power over others as well as over things. To this day, terms like Middle and Far East indicate a view from Buckingham Palace (or, more precisely, from the Greenwich meridian) that centers power literally as well as figuratively within a one-dimensional spatial grid.

The assignment of *place* within some socio-spatial structure indicates distinctive roles, capacities for action and access to power. Locating things (both physically and metaphorically) is fundamental to activities of valuing as well as identification. *Placing*, and the *making of places* are essential to social development, social control, and empowerment in any social order. The processes of place construction therefore interrelate (in ways to be taken up in chapter 11) with the social construction of space and time.

All forms of explanation and theorizing are dependent upon (*a*) the individuation of phenomena and events and (*b*) on the establishment of some mode of connection across space and time between phenomena and events. Yet very little critical attention has been paid to how such relations should be constructed. By default, they become a matter of convention. Within the Marxian tradition, for example, the tendency to prioritize time over space has been very strong, still largely undented by the critical interventions of Lefebvre and, more recently, by geographers in the English-speaking world. E.P. Thompson (1967: 21), for example, rightly holds that under the social relations of capitalism "time is now currency: it is not passed but spent," but errs in ignoring Marx's (1973: 534) insistence that the product only becomes a commodity through locational movement and that the value-form only becomes meaningful when exchange between communities and across space becomes "a normal social act" (Marx, 1967: 91). Indeed, a plausible argument can be constructed (see below) that the value system built into *any* social formation is indissolubly linked to the specific character of its spatio-temporal ordering of both social relations and working relations to the physical world.

The hidden political significance of all this needs highlighting. Academic disciplines constitute their distinctive objects of enquiry through a particular spatio-temporal framing of the world. This framing is political precisely because it defines a certain and restricted set of "self–other" relations for examination (if only between the investigator and the investigated): the choice of spatio-temporality is not innocent with respect to the social relations (including those of domination and of power) that are highlighted or, just as significantly, rendered invisible (such as the spatio-temporality of many women's lives, of sexuality, of colonized subjects and the like). Acceptance of a conventional spatio-temporal frame then amounts to acceptance of existing patterns of social relations, without even necessarily knowing it. Put another way, a certain mode of social construction of space and time arising out of certain social processes of domination and oppression can become in turn embedded in the way academic disciplines constitute their objects of enquiry: the effect is to make those disciplines complicitous with the perpetuation of those processes of domination.

But there is one sense in which the conventional prioritization of time over space in social theory and research is badly formulated. The whole argument could profitably be cast the other way round. Bergson argued that the human intellect "spatializes the universe" and it does so, Whitehead (1969: 242) suggests, because "spatialization is the shortest route to a clear cut philosophy expressed in a reasonably familiar language." Descartes, who "gave an almost perfect example of such a system of thought" effectively hid the potential fluidity of spatialization behind a fiction of static categories, entities and things between which temporal–causal relations could be examined. Spatiality is not ignored, but particular and unchanging assumptions of spatiality are embedded in the very foundations for all thinking, theorizing, and practical research. Williams (1977: 39) spotted this problem when he complained of the way the spatial fixity of the signs we use to communicate privileged a synchronic form of analysis that reduced real processes occurring in time to "a secondary or accidental character." Gupta and Ferguson (1992: 7), likewise complain of the way that space "disappears from analytical purview" while functioning "as a central organizing principle in the social sciences." It is the very stationarity of spatially determined categories that allows the study of movement in time to be highlighted in the way it is. Space may be forgotten as an analytical category open to questioning, but it is omnipresent as an unquestioned category in everything we do.

My point is not (see chapter 2) that the spatialized Cartesian–Kantian formulations that dominate our thinking are wrong. For certain purposes they are perfectly reasonable approximations. But they *are* approximations and in some very important arenas of research and thinking potentially misleading. The purpose of formulating an alternative relational metaphysics, a dialectic of space, place, time, and environment, is to argue for an alternative way of thought through which to question the limits of Cartesian–Kantian thinking. And if I give the last word to Whitehead (1969: 241) on this, it is because I think he has struck upon the most felicitous formulation of the problem. He reflects on the opening lines of a famous hymn thus:

> Abide with me;
> Fast falls the eventide
>
> Here the first line expresses the permanences, "abide," "me" and the "Being" addressed; and the second line sets these permanences amid the inescapable flux. Here at length we find formulated the complete problem of metaphysics. Those philosophers who start with the first line have given us the metaphysics of "substance"; and those who start with the second line have developed the metaphysics of "flux." But, in truth, the two lines cannot be torn apart in this way; and we find a wavering balance between the two is a characteristic of the greater number of philosophers. ...

The relational theory not only helps explain why so many of us find ourselves wavering on the frontiers between, for example, space and place or thing and flow, it also helps identify what it is we might be wavering about.

VI. Relational Space in Social and Literary Theory

The "wavering" of which Whitehead speaks can be found throughout the natural and social sciences as well as within literary theory. It can be found in the texts of Derrida, Foucault, and Haraway, or in the work of the humblest positivist sociologist who wonders out loud at the end of an extended but routine statistical enquiry whether or not her categories of enquiry were right or if there might be disruptive feedback effects which make the entities that seemed meaningful at the beginning of a process seem far less so at the end. The "wavering" often comes down more heavily on one or other side of the divide, leaving the positivist urban sociologist or urban economist bemused when confronted with, say, the writings of de Certeau or Lefebvre on the production of spaces in the city.

While I have concentrated on the theories of Leibniz and Whitehead as foundational arguments, the ease with which it is possible to cite other writers, such as de Certeau, suggests that the relational view has a strong though often subterranean presence. Consider, for example, how Simmel (1994) in a brilliant and perceptive essay on "Bridge and Door" sets up the problem:

> The image of external things possesses for us the ambiguous dimension that in external nature everything can be considered to be connected, but also as separated. The uninterrupted transformations of materials as well as energies brings everything into relationship with everything else and make one cosmos out of all the individual elements. On the other hand, however, the objects remain banished in the merciless separation of space; no particle of matter can share its space with another and a real unity of diversity does not exist in spatial terms. And by virtue of this equal demand on self-excluding concepts, natural existence seems to resist any application of them at all.

Simmel goes on to discuss how human activities of bridge-building (connecting and bringing phenomena into a "prehensive unity" to use Whitehead's terms) and house and door construction (cutting out a portion of "the continuity and infinity of space" and arranging this "into a particular unity in accordance with a *single* meaning" such that "a piece of space was thereby brought together and separated from the whole remaining world") reach across the divide in such a way as to operate as contradictory determinations of social life. "Viewed in terms of the opposing emphases that prevail in their impression," he concludes, "the bridge indicates how humankind unifies the separatedness of merely natural being, and the door how it separates the uniform, continuous unity of natural being." This is Whitehead's theory in action.

Interestingly, Heidegger (1971: 154–5) reflects on an almost identical theme. Spaces receive their being from locations and not from "space," he argues:

> The location is not already there before the bridge is. Before the bridge stands, there are of course many spots along the stream that can be occupied by something. One of them proves to be a location, and does so because of the bridge. Thus the bridge does not first come to a location to stand in it; rather a location comes into existence only by virtue of the bridge.

For this reason, he argues, the activity of "building is closer to the nature of spaces and to the origin of the nature of 'space' than any geometry and mathematics." Heidegger here in effect enunciates his own particular version of a relational theory of space and time, seeking to relate the world of flux and change to that of permanences.

Similar relational views have in fact been articulated by a wide variety of thinkers in diverse traditions – religious, ecological, and sometimes conservative, as well as radical and Hegelian–Marxist. This diversity should not be surprising since any recourse to a philosophy of dialectics or internal relations leads, either explicitly or implicitly, to a relational view on space and time. Furthermore, the fact that the two strongest explorations of the relational view are Leibniz and Whitehead (both of whom had marked theological interests tinged with considerable political conservativism) indicates that it is by no means necessarily connected with radical politics, any more than attachment to a dialectical philosophy of internal relations brings radicalism in its wake (see chapter 3). But the relational view has radical potentiality; it is a necessary condition for theorizing any large-scale emancipatory changes. Some hints as to what exactly that might mean can be gleaned from a brief look at the way internal relations and an associated relational view of spatio-temporality play in the work of a variety of writers in the Hegelian–Marxist tradition.

1. Bakhtin

Bakhtin, in his early text on *Art and Answerability*, articulates a theory of value and meaning entirely dependent upon the space–time relations between the "I" and the "other." Bakhtin accepts the primacy of individual sense experience and uniqueness (i.e., elements, things, and bodies already have existence) but insists that this can in no way imprison us in subjectivism. As Holquist (1990: xxv) points out in his introduction:

> a first implication of recognizing that we are all unique is the paradoxical result that we are therefore fated to need the other if we are to consummate ourselves. Far from celebrating the solipsistic "I", Bakhtin posits uniqueness of the self as precisely that condition in which the necessity of the other is born.

This dialogic and relational conception of the self (the necessary dialectic of self and otherness) operates in space and time. And as Bakhtin (1981: 81) in his later writings on the "chronotope" makes clear, there is "an intrinsic connectedness of temporal and spatial relationship" such that the two are as inseparable in literature as they are in life. Holquist summarizes Bakhtin's argument this way:

> As a body that was born into the world at a particular time and place, and that will pass away in an equally specific time and place, I literally embody a unique

slice of time/space. As the means, therefore, of particularizing the otherwise infinitely general aspects of time/space, I become the instrument for assigning specific value to abstract time and space. In themselves, space and time have neither meaning nor value, for value is always for someone: "Strictly speaking, geography knows no far or near, here and there. ... And history, likewise, knows no past, present, and future. ... The time of history is itself nonreversible, of course, but within it all relations are fortuitous and relative (and reversible), for there is no absolute center of value (of the kind provided by the situatedness of the individual subject)."

Individuals necessarily produce their own valuation of space and time by virtue of their situatedness in the world. From this Bakhtin derives the purely "perspectival" angle that Leibniz earlier identified. Bakhtin writes:

> When I contemplate a whole human being who is situated outside and over against me, our concrete, actually experienced horizons do not coincide. For at each moment, regardless of the position and the proximity to me of this other human being whom I am contemplating, I shall always see and know something that he, from his place outside and over against me, cannot see himself; parts of his body that are inaccessible to his own gaze (his head, his face, his expression), the world behind his back, and a whole series of objects and relations, which in any of our mutual relations are accessible to me but not to him. As we gaze at each other, two different worlds are reflected in the pupils of our eyes ... but in order to annihilate this difference completely, it would be necessary to merge into one, to become one and the same person. (1981: 22–3)

But value is not only conditional on the relation between the "I" and the "other" in space and time; it also changes according to social practices and social/power relations. The perspectival view then merges into a more general relational view of space and time by virtue of the continuous shifts of social practices that put value upon both the "I" and the "others" by creating a particular space–time nexus between them. There is a similarity here to Munn's arguments (see chapter 9) concerning the production of value through spatio-temporal practices which open a new time/space of self–other relations through hospitality and kula shell exchanges. Bakhtin also explores the complexities of "value," "exchange," "otherness," and various forms of alienation that so preoccupied Marx. But he does so in a way that brings the social construction of space and time to the forefront of understanding value in ways that are only tangentially alluded to in Marx. "Everything of value, everything that is valorized positively, must achieve its full potential in temporal and spatial terms" (Bakhtin, 1981: 167). Both Marx and Bakhtin agree that the human being "is about the production of meaning" and that meaning is "the articulation of values" (Holquist, 1990: xii). They also agree that "it is at the level of social relations that the true meaning of value and exchange must be sought." Like Marx, Bakhtin also insists on the materiality of these processes arguing that what separates him from the Kantian conception of space and time is that he does not regard them as in any sense transcendental, "but as forms of the most immediate reality" (Bakhtin, 1981: 85). This view aligns Bakhtin with Whitehead rather than Leibniz. But Bakhtin does emphasize the individuality and the space–time conditions of social relating and in so doing moves towards a relational view of space and time that will ultimately shape profoundly his understanding of language, the body, and all systems of representation (particularly those set up in literature). His theory of the chronotope, resting as it does on the inseparability of space and time in literary texts, derives entirely from a relational view.

2. Ollman

Ollman situates Marx's dialectics against the background of the tradition which derives from Leibniz, Spinoza, and Hegel and sees Marx's work as a materialist rendition of a philosophy of internal relations. Ollman's argument proceeds roughly as follows. All of Marx's categories – such as capital, labor, nature, the state, commodity, and money – are relational. "Such relations are internal to each factor (they are ontological relations), so that when an important one alters, the factor itself alters; it becomes something else: (1976: 15). It then becomes impossible to understand a category like "money" without examining the way it internalizes all sorts of other meanings such as commodity, labor, gender, status, memory, capital, and the state.

In the two appendices to *Alienation*, Ollman provides some interesting insights into how objections to a philosophy of internal relations might work. He recognizes the force, for example, of Strawson's objections that particulars, individuals, etc. are impossible to identify given the relational theory, but notes that Strawson's work "both begins and ends with the assertion that people believe the world is composed of particular things ('objective particulars') and that he conceives it his task to find reasons to support this view" (pp. 256–7). In so doing, Strawson is open to the accusation of "an *a priori* anthropology" which presumes that the world has never been (nor ever can be) conceived in any other way than that given in contemporary common sense. More importantly, Ollman reformulates his views on the philosophy of internal relations with "special stress on the dialectical conception of identity" as follows:

> If Marx takes account equally of identity and difference, their order in his thinking is identity first and then difference. As part of his way of viewing the world, Marx took identity for granted. It is the relation between mutually dependent aspects of a whole before differences are noted. The aspects yet unnamed because unspecified, are identical in containing through their internal relations with each other the same whole. (p. 266)

In the Aristotelian view, identity and difference are mutually exclusive, but the philosophy of internal relations allows us not only a radically different conception of totality from that set out in atomistic or formalist readings (see chapter 2), but it also permits us "to see identity where [there are] differences and vice versa" and to escape from the "either/or" logic of the Strawson variety. *Difference* is given in this scheme of things by the *perspective* on the totality not by supposing some clearly defined, isolated entity that is a totality in itself. This ontological shift has, of course, huge implications for the contemporary debate on identity and difference. But a strong case can, I think, be made that it is only by way of such an ontological shift that we can begin to establish a truly dialectical way of understanding how capitalism (or any other social system) works.

Ollman recognizes that his own work is itself relational, constructed from a particular perspective, and that it cannot therefore be construed as a full representation of any totality. If the relational view "admits as many totalities (structured wholes) as there are take-off points for analysis" (p. 266), all theories must then be seen "as so many one-sided (in the sense of uni-dimensional and therefore incomplete) versions of the same system." We must then learn to "interpret each theory in a manner that is compatible with the others." The multiple "windows" through which we can look upon the world, generate multiple theoretical perspectives (as Leibniz well knew) which are not necessarily mutually exclusive. Standpoint theory, of the sort which Haraway (1991) and Hartsock (1983) advance, has some of the same qualities to it, as I shall later show.

But Ollman neglects to consider the relational qualities of space and time. This is odd given the key role the conceptions of space and time play in Strawson's account of particulars and Strawson's explanation as to why the relational view (and he treats Leibniz's views as a convenient foil) must fail. We are therefore in danger of reading Ollman's account as a matter of internal relations operating within a Kantian framework of space and time when it seems to me that the true spirit of any dialectical account lies with a relational view of space and time. For this reason it appears useful to parallel consideration of Ollman's account with an examination of Lefebvre's *Production of Space*.

3. Lefebvre

In the *Production of Space* Lefebvre situates himself firmly in the tradition of thought we have here been examining:

> A new concept, that of the production of space, appears at the start; it must "operate" or "work" in such a way as to shed light on processes from which it cannot separate itself because it is a product of them. Our task, therefore, is to employ this concept by giving it free rein without for all that according it, after

the fashion of the Hegelians, a life and strength of its own *qua* concept – without, in other words, according an autonomous reality to knowledge.

Lefebvre makes plain his objections to the "Cartesian model (conceiving of things in their extension as the 'object' of thought) which over time became the stuff of 'common sense' and 'culture'." There is, therefore, little doubt as to how he would have responded to Strawson's invocation of common sense. And Lefebvre explicitly embraces the Leibnizian line:

> Space conceived of in its "purity" ... as Leibniz clearly showed, has neither component parts nor form. Its parts are indiscernible, in which respect it closely resembles "pure" identity – itself empty because of its "purely" formal character. Before any determination can exist here, some content must come into play. And that content is the act which recognizes parts and, within those recognized parts, an order – and hence a time. Otherwise differences could not be *thought* – only thought *about.* (1991: 297)

In his consideration of capitalism, Lefebvre suggests that:

> The commodity world brings in its wake certain attitudes towards space, certain actions upon space, even a certain concept of space. Indeed, all the commodity chains, circulatory systems and networks, connected on high by Gold, the god of exchange, do have a distinct homogeneity. Yet each location, each link in a chain of commodities, is occupied by a thing. ... The space of the commodity may thus be defined as a homogeneity made up of specificities. ... Space thus understood is both *abstract* and *concrete* in character; abstract inasmuch as it has no existence save by virtue of the exchangeability of all its component parts, and concrete inasmuch as it is socially real and as such localized. This is a space, therefore, that is *homogeneous yet at the same time broken up into fragments.* (1991: 341–2)

But it is here that Lefebvre makes his most explicit gesture concerning contradictions. On the one hand "space as actually experienced" prohibits the "expression of conflicts." But on the other:

> Socio-political contradictions are realized spatially. The contradictions of space thus make the contradictions of social relations operative. In other words, spatial contradictions "express" conflicts between socio-political interests and forces: it is only *in* space that such conflicts come effectively into play, and in so doing they become contradictions *of* space. (1991: 365)

In this way, Lefebvre acknowledges on the one hand the regulating force and power of that public time and space which Leibniz saw as necessarily arising out of any condition of "mutual relatedness and connectedness," and, on the other, how struggles within space get transformed into struggles to change space itself. Put another way, as social relations, behaviors and "acts" change within space, so they may entrain radical shifts in the meaning and metric of space. Conflictual social processes are registered as conflictual forms of spatio-temporality.

VII. Conceptions of the Body in Space–Time

So where does this leave us with respect to that "withness" of the body to which Whitehead appealed at the outset to his analyses? Note, first of all, that the physical conception of the body in Leibniz is fundamentally at variance with that of the atomists as well as with that of the Cartesians and this is a necessary corollary of his relational views on space and time. Leclerc (1986: 32–3) describes Leibniz's views as follows:

> All the features which are ascribed as attributes of body – extension, solidity, hardness or impenetrability – are not strictly *attributes* at all but must be analyzed as *relations*. Thus there can be no simple body, as the atomists conceived of it; a body is necessarily a plurality, and the features of body are the relations between the physical existents which are the constituents. Again we see the fundamental status of *relations*. (Leclerc, 1986: 32–3)

The clear distinction often now supposed between "body" used in this physical sense and the human body was not by any means apparent or acceptable to Leibniz who, Martin (1964: 174) suggests, based much of his philosophy, particularly as expressed in *The Mondadology*, on the simple predicate that "I experience myself as something real and in the last resort, therefore reality means being like me." Leibniz is here using a classical figure that understood the human body not as a bundle of enclosed and bounded subjectivities and desires, or of libido and ids and egos, but as a harmonic whose health was measured entirely in terms of its ability to achieve within its microcosm some refracted version of the underlying harmonies of the universe. Not only did Leibniz use the physical body as the leading metaphor in pursuing his scientific aims, but he also accepted the medieval proposition that the macrocosm of the universe is always copresent within the microcosm of the self even though the self is confined in its vision of the macrocosm by virtue of its positionality within it. It is no accident, therefore, that the language of early physics paid so much attention to the idea of "bodies" (heavenly, stationary, or otherwise).

But we cannot go much further without simultaneously conceding the significance of what Whitehead called the "sense-presentation of the body." This is also a historical and social construct, subject to all manner of changes. Rabelais, for example, is generally credited with defining as a fundamental transitional moment in how the human body is to emerge from its intertwining with the natural world to assert its independent identity in space and time:

> the predominance ... of a "somatic fundament" of protuberances and orifices which cancel its localisation and limitation and link it with the rest of nature: exaggeration of the anal–erotic and gastric functions, emphasis on the metamorphosis of birth and death, aging and rejuvenation, and on aspects of fertility, the productive forces of nature. All of this meant the demotion of what was lofty and ideal to what was earthy and material. The grotesque body was represented as non-individualized, incomplete and constantly intertwined with the earth which gives it birth and swallows it up again. (Gurevich, 1985: 53)

This grotesque body contrasts radically with the pure lines and clarity of Renaissance perspective and with its associated noble figure of a man (such as that famously depicted by Leonardo da Vinci). But here we begin to see a story of conflict between different social processes surrounding and defining the meaning of the body. Bakhtin (1984) connects both the figure of the grotesque body and the language of Rabelais with the emergence of the market place as a fundamental institution in some ways "outside of" other forms of social control (often physically outside of the wall of the city itself). The profane, scatalogical, earthy, and materialist language of the market begins to cast its own particular shadow over systems of representation and the consequent self-presentation of the body.

Norbert Elias (1978), by way of contrast, proposes an evolutionary and developmental view of the human body in which the civilizing process, dominated by the rise of courtly behaviors, manners, etiquette, dress codes, and the like, shaped and redefined the human body from the Renaissance onwards. Shilling summarizes Elias's account of the "new human body" as follows:

> the civilized body characteristic of modern Western societies is highly individualized in that it is strongly demarcated from its social and natural environments. The civilized body also has the ability to rationalize and exert a high degree of control over its emotions, to monitor its own actions and those of others, and to internalize a finely demarcated set of rules about what constitutes appropriate behaviour in various situations. The civilized body can be contrasted with the "uncivilized" body of early medieval times which was only weakly demarcated from its social and natural environment. The uncivilized body was constrained by few behavioural norms, gave immediate physical expression to emotions, and sought to satisfy bodily desires without restraint or regard for the welfare of others.

A comparison of Bakhtin and Elias suggests that different kinds of bodies are produced/represented by radically different social processes and that class, racial, and gender distinctions get written large upon the human body by virtue of the different processes within which bodies are implicated. In recent years this general point has been made over and over again in a vast literature dealing with the history of the human body [see, for example, Stafford (1991) and the zone series on *Fragments for a History of the Human Body*]. And this, of course, is the fundamental argument that Bourdieu pursues, primarily in *Distinction* where he strives to document how class distinctions become internalized as different forms of physical and cultural capital within the individual body. The notion of civilized behavior, and its contrast with supposed lower class incivility is an incredibly powerful motif in contemporary discourses about the degraded qualities of "underclass" urban life. But even though the human body may be the measure of all things, it is always an unfinished project open to transformation according to the force of the physical and social processes internalized within it and the transformative powers with which it is endowed.

The production of space–time is inextricably connected with the production of the body. "With the advent of Cartesian logic," Lefebvre (1991: 1) complains, "space had entered the realm of the absolute ... space came to dominate, by containing them, all senses and all bodies." Lefebvre and Foucault (particularly in *Discipline and Punish*) here make common cause: the liberation of the senses and the human body from the absolutism of that produced world of space and time becomes central to their emancipatory strategies. And that means challenging the mechanistic and absolute view through which the "withness" of the human body" is contained and enchained under contemporary conditions. This is not an entirely new project; it was, as Eagleton (1990) points out, one aspect of the whole ideology of the esthetic from its very inception.

But here we hit a peculiar conundrum. On the one hand, to return to the human body as the fount of all experience (including that of space and time) becomes a means (increasingly privileged in these times) to challenge the whole network of abstractions (scientific, social, political–economic) through which social relations, power relations, institutions, and material practices get defined, represented, and regulated. But on the other hand, no human body is outside of the social processes of determination of space–time. To return to it may well be to instanciate the space and time of the very social processes being purportedly rebelled against. If, for example, workers are transformed (as Marx suggests in *Capital*) into appendages of capital in both the workplace and the consumption sphere (or, as Foucault prefers it, bodies are made over into *docile bodies* by the rise of a powerful disciplinary apparatus from the eighteenth century on) then how can their bodies be a measure of anything outside of the circulation of capital or of the various mechanisms that discipline them? Or, to take a more contemporary version of the same argument, if we are all now *cyborgs* (as Haraway in her celebrated manifesto on the topic suggests) then how can we measure anything outside of that deadly embrace of the machine as extension of our own body and body as extension of the machine?

The contemporary fascination with the body, and with the return to it as the site of all fundamental experience, can in part be understood as part of the search for a more authentic grounding of the theoretical abstractions that have for too long ruled purely as abstractions (in planning theory as implemented in cities, for example). "Objectivity," Haraway (1991: 190) claims, "turns out to be about particular and specific embodiment and definitely not about the false vision promising transcendence of all limits and responsibility." But the difficulty is that it is only a certain kind of socially produced body that is being returned to. Whose body is it that is to be the measure of all things? And exactly how and what can it measure?

Consider, for example, a recent formulation by Elizabeth Grosz (1992) that goes some way to confronting but also eliding some of these difficulties. Her aim is "to explore the constitutive and mutually defining relations between corporeality and the metropolis." She defines *body* as:

> indeterminate, amorphous, a series of uncoordinated potentialities which require social triggering, ordering, and long-term "administration," regulated [by] "the microtechnologies of power." The body becomes a *human* body, a body which coincides with the "shape" and space of a psyche, a body whose epidermic surface bounds a psychical unity, a body which thereby defines the limits of experience and subjectivity, in psychoanalytic terms, through the intervention of the (m)other, and ultimately, the Other or Symbolic order (language and rule-governed social order). Among the key structuring principles of this produced body is its inscription and coding by (familially ordered) sexual desires (the desire of the other) ... (and) ... its inscription by a set of socially coded meanings and significances.

This definition (which I have abbreviated) parallels the relational and process-based conceptions of self already encountered in Gurevich, Munn, Strathern, and even in the deep ecology of Naess. What the body measures externally is an effect of what it internalizes. Grosz explores:

> the ways in which the body is physically, socially, sexually, and discursively or representationally produced, and the ways, in turn, bodies reinscribe and project themselves onto their sociocultural environment so that this environment both produces and reflects the form and interests of the body.

This, again, is an unexceptionable version of Marx's argument on the dialectics of social and environmental change. The "city" is understood as:

> a complex and interactive network which links together, often in an unintegrated and de facto way, a number of disparate social activities, processes, and relations, with a number of imaginary and real, projected or actual architectural, geographic, civic and public relations. The city brings together economic and

informational flows, power networks, forms of displacement, management, and political organization, interpersonal, familiar, and extra-familial social relations, and an aesthetic/economic organization of space and place to create a semipermanent but ever-changing built environment or milieu.

The city is also a product of processes: it is a "fundamentally disunified series of systems and interconnections, a series of disparate flows, energies, events or entities, and spaces, brought together or drawn apart in more or less temporary alignments." But it is at this point that a slippage suddenly occurs in her argument. Grosz considers the relationship between bodies and cities as a relation between two compatible kinds of *permanences* (entities). No attempt is made to establish the conditions of cogredience (or compossibility) among distinctive processes operating at different scales (if indeed such conditions can be established at all). The city "provides the order and organization that automatically links otherwise unrelated bodies." It "links the affluent lifestyle of the banker professional to the squalor of the vagrant." It is "the condition and milieu in which corporeality is socially, sexually, and discursively produced." This unfortunate slippage in language converts the intertwining of bodily and environmental processes and their distinctive spatio-temporalities and value schemas operating at different scales into a straight relation between two radically different kinds of entities. It makes no sense to talk about the city as the same kind of "thing" as a body (its boundaries are, for example, far more diffuse and while it typically has institutions it has no psyche or even agency of the sort that human beings possess). There is a confusion of scale and of how to understand permanences that mars a potentially interesting analysis of the "coproduction of human bodies and their environments." What this theory of relational coproduction of cities/bodies produces is the extraordinary claim that "if bodies are not culturally pregiven, built environments cannot alienate the very bodies they produce" even if rapid environmental transformations may prove stressful and some built environments prove unconducive to bodily health and well-being. This, I would argue, is a typical situation in which the relational view gets out of hand. There is a prior question, for example, of whose bodies produce the city versus whose bodies inhabit it. If coalitions of landowners, developers, financiers, contractors, architects, planners, and governments have the power to produce the built environment of the city that the rest of us live in, then it is perfectly feasible for them to build cityscapes from which the mass of the population are alienated in an unrecuperable way. The internalization of relations does not imply a nonalienated form of such relations, though it does throw into question any theory of alienation that presupposes some preformed essence of self that gets violated and which needs to be returned to (cf. chapter 8). While the body may internalize the effects of such process it is not by itself able to measure, assess, and understand the dynamics of its own production through urbanization precisely because of its alienation.

Contemporary (postmodern) views of the body as a site of "a play of difference" and of "an internalization of heterogeneity" bear some marks of a similar way of thinking and pose similar dangers (see chapter 12). But what does have to be understood is that the human body is a battleground within which and around which the forces of production of spatio-temporality are perpetually at play. This, for example, is the idea that Goldberg (1991: 188) pursues in his relational analysis of racially marked bodies in racialized urban spaces. The body that is to be the "measure of all things" is itself a site of contestation for the very forces that create it.

VIII. The Body in Cyberspace

This contestation is strongly evidenced in the "virtual world" of "cyberspace." Leibniz:

> is one of the essential philosophical guides to the inner structure of cyberspace. His logic, his metaphysics, and his notion of representational symbols show us the hidden underpinnings of cyberspace. At the same time, his monadological metaphysics alerts us to the paradoxes that are likely to engulf cyberspace's future inhabitants.

Monads, Heim (1991: 67–73) goes on to remark, may "have no windows, but they do have terminals" and they are thereby able to construct their own correspondence principles, breaking free from a bodily existence to build networks, bulletin boards and virtual communities as:

> computer antidotes to the atomism of society. They assemble the monads. They function as social nodes for fostering those fluid and multiple elective affinities that everyday urban life seldom, in fact, supports.

The boundary between bodies and machines becomes even more blurred:

> Penetrating the screen involves a state change from the physical, biological space of the embodied viewer to the symbolic, metaphorical "consensual hallucination" of cyberspace; a space that is a locus of intense desire for refigured embodiment. ... In all, the unitary, bounded, safely warranted body constituted within the frame of bourgeois modernity is undergoing a gradual process of translation to the refigured and reinscribed embodiments of the cyberspace community. ... The discourse of visionary virtual world builders is rife with images of imaginal bodies, freed from the constraints that flesh imposes. Cyberspace developers foresee a time when they will be able to forget about the body. (Stone, 1991: 107–13).

Cyberspace holds out the Utopian vision of being able to live the "Leibnizian conceit" free of material constraints. The "dematerialization of space" – the ultimate annihilation by capitalist technology of space and time – itself becomes the medium through which the ultimate God-trick can be played. We can each voyage forth to the frontiers of cyberspace as mini-deities. We can assume a variety of personas. "The boundaries between the social and the natural and between biology and technology" take on a "generous permeability" and social spaces begin to appear "that are simultaneously natural, artificial, and constituted by inscription." But, Stone goes on to ask: who decides what sort of bodies become inscribed in cyberspace?

> in the process of articulating a cyberspace system, engineers must model cognition and community, and because communities are inhabited by bodies, they must model bodies as well. ... In doing so, they are articulating their own assumptions about bodies and sociality and projecting them onto the codes that define cyberspace systems. ... Many of the engineers currently debating the form and nature of cyberspace are the young turks of computer engineering, men in their late teens and twenties, and they are preoccupied with the things with which postpubescent men have always been preoccupied. This rather steamy group will generate the codes and descriptors by which bodies in cyberspace are represented.

The computer-generated multiracial vision featured on the cover of *Time* is an exemplar of such dreams given real representational form. But behind all of these virtual bodies lurk real bodies, albeit attached to their consoles. "Life is lived through bodies" comments Stone, and virtual community "originates in, and must return to, the physical." We may aspire to live out the Leibnizian conceit in a consciousness jacked into the machine, but there is more than a hint that the irreducible physicality of the human body will bring us back to Whitehead's materialist–empiricist formulations. William Gibson who is generally credited with coining the term cyberspace in his dystopian novel *Neuromancer* (1984: 256) invents an extraordinary moment towards the end of the novel in which the hero Case sees himself through someone else's eyes. He:

> found himself staring down, through Molly's one good eye, at a white-faced, wasted figure, afloat in a loose fetal crouch, a cyberspace deck between his thighs, a band of silver trodes above closed, shadowed eyes. The man's cheeks were hollowed with a day's growth of dark beard, his face slick with sweat. He was looking at himself.

It will take a strong injection of historical–geographical materialism to understand where all this refashioning of space–time might be taking us.

The processes at work on the human body are changing and the differentiation of human bodies is as marked as its homogenization. As a consequence, our "measure of all things" is itself unstable and conflictual. It has always been so. For as Haraway (1991: 195) comments in her search to ground objectivity in embodied and situated knowledges:

> Feminist embodiment ... is not about fixed location in a reified body, female or otherwise, but about nodes in fields, inflections in orientations, and responsibility for difference in material-semiotic fields of meaning. ... I am arguing for politics and epistemologies of location, positioning, and situating, where partiality and not universality is the condition of being heard to make rational knowledge claims. These are claims on people's lives; the view from the body, always a complex, contradictory, structuring and structured body, versus the view from above, from nowhere, from simplicity.

Martin (1992) provides a fascinating case-study of how our sense presentation of the body has been changing through the impacts of medical science. She suggests that we are now witnessing "a dramatic transition in body percept and practice, from bodies suited for and conceived in terms of the era of Fordist mass production to bodies suited for and conceived in the terms of the era of flexible accumulation" (p. 121). She notes that the metaphors used to understand the body have shifted from the centralized and hierarchically structured control system of cell biology (a Fordist-style conception) to depictions of an immune system in which the body is seen as "an engineered communications system, ordered by a fluid and dispersed command–control–intelligence network" to which objectives of specificity, flexibility, and rapid response are attributed (a metaphor grounded in the political-economy of flexible accumulation). But there are two other telling bits of information which Martin elicits in the course of her ethnographic work. First, is the self-conscious view of the cells in the body as if they are separate from consciousness (a separate spatial worlds theme captured by one respondent's statement in her study that "there's no connection between me being a conscious human being and the cell that's inside me"). Secondly, a feeling of the "unimaginably small and the unimaginably large coalesced in the same image, agency residing in cells, the person becoming an observer of the agency of others inside him or herself" captured by one informant who expressed it all in language that Leibniz would surely have recognized: "When you think about the inside of your body I think about outer space. It's like those are the only things that look like this, you know, they are that far away from you. It's weird because outer space is like, way out there, and your body is just right here, but it's about the same, it's the same thing" (cited in Martin, 1992: 125). The relational view seems alive and well here, and it is, perhaps, wise to consider how transitions in the definitions of space and time through changing social processes are effecting changing conceptions of the body and consequently of identity, particularities, and where the human body resides in the scale of things.

IX. Cartographies

In her introduction to an edited collection on *Third World Women and the Politics of Feminism*, Mohanty (1991) develops the idea of a relational cartography to describe the "contours of the world we occupy in the 1990s." The "cartographies of struggle" that she depicts describe a world:

> traversed with intersecting lines of power and resistance, a world which can be understood only in terms of its destructive divisions of gender, color, class, sexuality, and nation, a world which must be transformed through a necessary process of pivoting the center ... for the assumed center (Europe and the United States) will no longer hold.

Mohanty goes on to raise questions of how this world is to be mapped:

> Which/whose history do we draw on to chart this map of third world women's engagement with feminism? ... Who produces knowledge about colonized peoples and from what space/location? What are the politics of the production of this particular knowledge? What are the disciplinary parameters of this knowledge? What are the methods used to locate and chart third world women's self and agency? Clearly questions of definition and context overlap; in fact, as we develop more complex, nuanced modes of asking questions and as scholarship in a number of relevant fields begins to address histories of colonialism, capitalism, race, and gender as inextricably interrelated, our very conceptual maps are redrawn and transformed. How we conceive of definitions and contexts, on what basis we foreground certain contexts over others, and how we understand the ongoing shifts in our conceptual cartographies – these are all questions of great importance. ...

I agree entirely with this sentiment. But I want to reflect on it in terms of a relational theory of space and time. The question of "positionality" and of "location" was first raised explicitly in chapter 3 through examination of the cases of Bell Hooks ("a space on the margin") and Raymond Williams ("on the border"). In neither instance was a map of the world made explicit but it is not hard to reconstruct its contours. For Williams, a huge and almost unbridgeable chasm separates the working-class world of South Wales miners and that of the metropolis (London and Cambridge). That geographical chasm is redolent of a fundamental class divide that Williams struggled with all his life. For his critics, particularly those from the colonized world, this chasm looks like a minor wrinkle on the high plateau of imperial and metropolitan domination. For Bell Hooks, similar ruptures separate the small-town African-American communities of the south and the metropolitanized center, but her map is marked by multiple fractures of class, race, gender, and sexual identity. Williams might have understood that map in principle, but it was not the map of his experiential world. Bell Hooks might understand Williams' map but not its inner meaning. They produce two different maps of the world, situate themselves in particular ways in relation to those maps, and seek modes of political action and alliance formation defined out of that particular situatedness.

The intuitive recognition of this point has in recent years been most strongly articulated in feminist theory. "Positionality," "situatedness," and "standpoint" have become familiar words as means to locate perspectives and power positions in forms of argument (discourses) as well as in the identification of objects of enquiry and the construal of the subject–object relation. But what kind of map of the world is being talked about? No sooner do white North American feminists produce a map of the world which permits them a place from which to challenge white male patriarchy and oppression, than women of color or in postcolonial settings produce entirely different cartographies of oppression in which the white middle-class feminists of North America appear on that same high plateau of imperial power that Williams' critics see. What we are then confronted with are innumerable seemingly incompatible maps of the world drawn from the standpoint of the "withness" of particular bodies in space–time. And different projections (to invoke the term I use in the introduction) create quite different relational constructs. The famous cartoon of "the New Yorker's Map of the World" is everywhere replicated to produce a fragmentation of cartographies, a multiplicity of projections, a break up of the unified map of the world that the mathematicians, geographers, and cartographers strove so hard to create from the Renaissance onwards. So what are we to make of this?

Let me first establish the intimate connection between the "return to the body as the measure of all things" described in the preceding section and the production of all manner of cartographies of struggle. Here, I think Leibniz is particularly helpful. There are two possibilities to be considered. Different perspectives on the same world can be constructed from different positions in exactly the same way "as one and the same town viewed from different sides looks fundamentally different." This is in part what feminist "standpoint" theory achieves. Marx sought to achieve the same effect in his construction of a science from a proletarian rather than a bourgeois perspective. Under this interpretation all cartographies of the world are representations of the same world but each monad (body) necessarily has its own perspective depending on its position in that world. Different things dominate, loom large or look remote and irrelevant according to the perspective embedded in a particular position (consider, once again, the difference between Williams and Hooks). And, if we follow Leibniz to the letter, some monads (bodies) will see and feel the world in a hazy blurry way, while the others will become more discriminating and sharper in their determinations. But the multiple windows on a same reality, like the multiple theorizations available to us, can constitute a way of triangulating in on this same reality from multiple perspectives. Learning to see the world from multiple positions – if such an exercise is possible – then becomes a means to better understand how the world as a totality works. Multiple projections (mathematical and psychological) are in principle transformable into each other. That is how Haraway (1991: 193) visualizes it. Rejecting both relativism and totalization as "god tricks promising vision from everywhere and nowhere equally," she argues that:

> the topography of subjectivity is multidimensional; so, therefore, is vision. The knowing self is partial in all its guises, never finished, whole, simply there and original; it is always constructed and stitched together imperfectly, and therefore able to join with another, to see together without claiming to be another. Here is the promise of objectivity; a scientific knower seeks the subject position not of identity but of objectivity; that is of partial connection.

This technique of conjoining information from different positionalities is a basic principle of all cartographic construction: to make an accurate map (representation) of the world we require at the very minimum a procedure of triangulation that moves across multiple points. We also need to understand the principles of map transformation and projection.

But Leibniz also indicated a more radical possibility. The relational theory of spatio-temporality indicates how different processes can define completely different spatio-temporalities, and so set up radically different identifications of entities, places and relations. For Leibniz this was simply a theoretical exploration of possible worlds and therefore solely confined to the imaginary. But for Whitehead (and Bakhtin as well as Lefebvre), these radically different spatio-temporalities and their associated cartographies are construed as real, dependent upon the nature of the process being examined. Under this interpretation we seem to be confronted with innumerable radically different and totally incommensurate cartographies of the world. We cannot transform one projection (or map) into another. To produce one dominant cartographic image out of all this multiplicity is a power-laden act of domination. It is to force a singular discursive representational exercise upon multiple cartographies, to suppress difference and to establish homogeneity of representation. To engage in this is a typical discursive strategy of hegemonic power, that has the intended effect of curbing the imaginary and shaping material practices and social relations as well as institutions to a dominant mode of production or, as Foucault (1977) prefers it, to a dominant disciplinary power.

Renaissance mapping of the globe was exactly such an exercise in western domination. The "imperial gaze" mapped the world according to its own needs, wants and desires, imposing a map of the world in such a way as to suppress difference. As Shohat (1991) argues, the effect was to dispossess "the subaltern of authority over knowledge and identity." And as we have already seen in

Cronon's account of colonial settlement in New England, the superimposition of spatio-temporal ordering upon another society destroys the conditions of reproduction of that society (see also Mignolo, 1994). Innumerable cartographies of resistance, each with its own peculiar positionality, can then be construed as struggling against a hegemonic map of the world (that still held by, for example, the World Bank and the IMF as well as by major governments and corporations) but then each appears as incompatible with the other as each is with the hegemonic map (in spite of Mohanty's assertion to the contrary). The parallel here would be with the contemporary postmodern extension of Wittgenstein's theory of language games to imply a fragmented world of "interpretive communities" made up of both producers and consumers of particular kinds of knowledge/experience/imaginaries, operating within a particular institutional context, a particular division of labor and pattern of social relations, and within particular places at particular times. Incommunicability between these interpretive communities becomes a permanent feature of a fragmented postmodern sensibility, in much the same way as multiple fragmented mappings and incommensurate (and untransformable) projections arise out of the unique positionalities of bodies in the world.

But what Whitehead's theory also tells us is that processes cannot be construed as totally disconnected. If there is "cogredience" between processes then there must be "cogredience" (compossibilities) between the different spatio-temporalities and cartographies produced. On the one hand, the radically different cartographies have to be respected since they have a real foundation in highly differentiated socio-ecological processes, but on the other it is erroneous to regard them as totally disconnected. Spatiality, however constructed, simultaneously unifies and separates. Working out what the connections (the "cogrediences") are, is as crucial politically (it grounds any sense of militant particularism, for example) as it is to social–scientific and literary theory. This is a problem that erupts again and again. Haraway (1991: 194) in her search for a new definition of objectivity based on embodiment and situatedness argues, for example:

> local knowledges have also to be in tension with the productive structurings that force unequal translations and exchanges – material and semiotic – within the webs of knowledge and power. Webs *can* have the property of systematicity, even of centrally structured global systems with deep filaments and tenacious tendrils into time, space and consciousness, the dimensions of world history.

If this is so, then we need ways to discover and map those systematicities, to locate situated knowledges within the map and find the cogrediences that are necessary to any sort of political alliance formation. But we cannot do so without relying upon differently situated knowledges to reveal the nature of the processes that underpin whatever systematicity exists.

X. Latitudes of Money/Power and Longtitudes of Resistance

Traces of systematicity are not hard to identify. Flows of money, commodities, information, cultural artefacts, technologies, symbolic systems, all are part of daily life, have their effects upon the sense presentation of the body, play their role in defining value relations and provide some sort of common glue of cogredience across a global space and time within which multiple cartographies (embodied understandings) get defined. Money is also a concentrated form of social power that has ramifications for the definition of selfhood, the production of hegemonic discourses, the running of institutions as well as the material practices of production and social relating.

In these times the accumulation of capital provides a set of master-narratives in relation to which innumerable other narratives get defined. Individual, ego, family, community, nation, civil society, and state would have entirely different meanings in the absence of monetization, commodification, and the exchange relations embedded in the circulation of capital. We fail to pay attention to these master narratives at our peril for to ignore them is to ignore a vital set of social processes through which situatedness gets defined. It is salutary to remember, as Simmel (1978: 437–48) long ago pointed out, that the very existence of a class of independent intellectuals engaging in teaching, writing, and conferencing (about different cartographies, for example) as a professional activity depends upon a power-laden system of extraction and mobilization of money surpluses and occurs under the aegis of a highly sophisticated system of exchange of ideas and information through "print capitalism" (the phrase is Benedict Anderson's).

The social processes that define a hegemonic form of spatio-temporality under conditions of continuous capital accumulation therefore provide one common frame – like that of the Mercator map – within and through which other cartographic perspectives get represented, communicated, and contested. But it is vital to appreciate certain characteristics of this framing. To begin with, the spatio-temporal framing is far from homogeneous but exhibits a considerable degree of internalized heterogeneity and sometimes conflictual fragmentation of the sort described in chapter 9. It is for this reason that I prefer the phrase a "set" or "ensemble" of master narratives rather than the singular term "master narrative." The spatio-temporality built into financial markets and international currency coordination is very different from the spatio-temporalities of fixed capital investment in plant and equipment and is radically different from those long-term and massive projects of environmental transformation that have constituted, for example, the settlement of the US west. The problem within capitalism is to establish mechanisms of "cogredience" or "compossibility" between such radically different processes. But, as Munn's careful analysis of the case of Gawa showed, it is perfectly possible to embed different spatio-temporalities existing at different levels (scales) in relation to different facets of the social process in such a way as to achieve some overall structure. Exactly how this occurs under capitalism is infinitely more complicated and potentially conflictual, but the ensemble of spatio-temporalities created is neither disconnected nor chaotic though it is conflictual and dynamic.

The ensemble is not fixed because the processes of capital accumulation are deeply implicated in the continuous alteration and sometimes rapid transformation of spatio-temporalities through phases of rapid time–space compression (cf. chapter 9). Nevertheless, it is precisely because of the transcending possibilities of such a global framing that we can even register other forms of difference. Something may be lost in such a gesture – integrating into a hegemonic map of the world in order to demonstrate a particular cartography of domination and of power relations is no different than having to learn and use the oppressor's language in order to resist oppression (cf. chapter 5). But something is also gained – the bringing to life of hitherto uncommunicated and hitherto uncommunicable differences. This duality should not be surprising: money, after all, has the capacity to unify universality with all manner of particularities varying from the purity of bourgeois egocentric individualism to the social practices of, for example, community, family, and nation predicated, as I argued in chapter 9, on the great diversity of uses to which money power can be put. In like manner socially constructed spatio-temporalities simultaneously unite *and* divide.

Consider, for example how the human self/body internalizes money values and how the produced human self/body inserts itself (as physical and symbolic *capital*) into the schema of money valuations and capital accumulation. I have argued throughout this and the preceding chapter that value is a socially constructed spatio-temporal relation. But the money form – a thing – itself becomes an embodiment of that spatio-temporal social relation and acquires its own fetishistic powers, thereby casting its spell on the self/body with even greater systematicity and power than witchcraft ever did on Gawa.

When slaves, indentured servants, or the lowliest agricultural laborers convert whatever money they can acquire into wealth, then they procure for themselves a genealogy, symbols that use the powers of money to preserve value over time to sustain identity from one generation to the next. The inability of families to part with "the family silver" even in the face of the direst of necessities, has everything to do with a reluctance to convert valued wealth as a symbol of genealogy back into its point of origin in the ephemerality of money as a means of circulation. When recently arrived immigrants from China work "for the money" in totally unregulated sweatshops in New York that pay on average less than $2 an hour for a 12-hour day, with many workers only ten years old (laws against child labor notwithstanding), they submit themselves to a grueling bodily regime that produces not only daily exhaustion but all sorts of special ailments such as "sewer's back" and explosive headaches (Lii, 1995). When Third World women find themselves caught in the ugly tension of using whatever scarce resources they command to produce for market or to preserve traditional practices, ecosystems and their associated social relations, then here, too, the cartographies of money and power are fundamentally drawn up in resistance to a hegemonic map of capital accumulation driving to be sustained in space and time against all odds. When stressed-out bankers, state department and treasury officials, and innumerable CEOs find themselves in the midst of massive fund switches (of the sort that almost destroyed the economy of Mexico in 1995) then they, too, find themselves in the midst of a social process outside of their individual control.

Recall Simmel's (1978: 101) argument:

> society is a structure that transcends the individual, but that is not abstract. Historical life thus escapes the alternative of taking place either in individuals or in abstract generalities. Society is the universal which, at the same time, is concretely alive. From this arises the unique significance that exchange, as an economic–historical realization of the relativity of things, has for society; exchange raises the specific object and its significance for the individual above its singularity, not into the sphere of abstraction, but into that of lively interaction which is the substance of economic value. (p. 101)

The critical investigation of money as a relation, with its particular constructions of valuing through spatio-temporal practices, provides one key starting point for any attempt to understand the contemporary body, identities, and politics. The social power of money forces the body into postures of laboring and work under a particular condition of valuation that only holds out the possibility of realizing desire through money earned and spent. But here, too, the doctrine of rational consumption (rational that is from the standpoint of capital accumulation) constrains desires within a box from which there is no fundamental exit, no matter how hard desires, lust, energy, and the imaginary seek to escape from a bodily prison into a unification with that other which, in the last instance, can never be attained. Yet bodies/selves insert themselves purposively and imaginatively into social life (as we saw in the case of Saccard's vision explored in chapter 6) and thereby have the power, however minute, to change it. Agency, I argued in chapter 5, resides everywhere and the transformative works with which bodies/selves necessarily engage can be managed, orchestrated and pressured but never totally dominated.

Money, spatio-temporality, values and the body are inextricably intertwined within the overall dynamics of capital accumulation. An understanding of each informs the other at the same time as it sheds light on how situatedness and positionality is itself a product of the hegemonic processes of space creation. While this is not the only set of social processes to which we could refer, a thorough understanding of it is a necessary condition for any proper accounting of how distinctive situations, positions and cartographies arise.

But there are other possibilities of cogredience. When Marx and Engels chose to end *The Communist Manifesto* with the famous call to arms:

The proletarians have nothing to lose but their chains. They have a world to win. WORKING MEN OF ALL COUNTRIES, UNITE!

they were precisely trying to identify an alternative form of valuation, an alternative politics of agency and action and a radically different spatio-temporal world defined by a radically different form of the social process. It is, of course, part of the almost folkloric timidity of these (post)modern times, that such statements send shudders of negation if not of revulsion through circles preoccupied with literary and social theory. Yet the longing for some alternative form of cogredience/compossibility (though preferably one that does not lie in the shadow of *The Communist Manifesto*) never disappears. It suffuses the ecological movement, for example, and again and again each social movement in its turn finds itself confronting the problem of how to secure its own objectives through a sufficiently broad network of alliances to confront hegemonic forms of power. What Derrida calls *The Specter of Marx*, will not go away.

Interestingly, in the early years of the International Working Men's Association, before the split between Marxists and anarchists, syndicalists and proletarians, women and men, did its ugly work, the meaning of this socialist project uniting Irish, English, French, Belgian, German, and Swiss men and women workers within the European space of capital traversed the terrain of proletarian unity and national difference with a common-sense appreciation and subtlety that many later internationalist movements (both proletarian and other) have lacked. Conceptualizing this whole problematic right is, clearly, crucial to defining what some kind of alternative mapping of social relations and of values might look like.

Consider, for example, how this theme echoes and reverberates in Haraway's (1991) work. "Feminist embodiment" recall:

is not about fixed location in a reified body, female or otherwise, but about nodes in fields, inflections in orientations, and responsibility for difference in material-semiotic fields of meaning. ... There is no single feminist standpoint because our maps require too many dimensions for the metaphor to ground our visions. (pp. 195–6)

Yet:

The theoretical and practical struggle against unity-through-domination or unity-through-incorporation ironically not only undermines the justifications for patriarchy, colonialism, humanism, positivism, essentialism, scientism, and other unlamented -isms, but all claims for an organic or natural standpoint. I think that our radical and socialist/Marxist feminisms have also undermined their/our own epistemological strategies, and this is a crucially valuable step in imagining possible unities. (p. 157)

So what kind of possible worlds do these unities define and to what should such alliances and effective affinities be addressed and through what kinds of "conversations" and "translations" (to use two of Haraway's favored terms)?

> I do not know of any other time in history when there was greater need for political unity to confront effectively the dominations of "race", "gender", sexuality", and "class". I also do not know of any other time when the kind of unity we might help build could have been possible. (p. 157)

Capitalist accumulation may define a hegemonic system of spatio-temporal practices and valuations and do untold work upon the body, the imagination, and the self. But it does not exhaust all alternative possibilities. Uncovering cartographic affinities and unities within a world of highly expressive difference appears more and more as the key problematic of the times. This is the political mission that any dialectical theory of historical–geographical materialism must address. But it is a mission that depends, as does capital, on the construction of an ensemble of cogredient/compossible spatio-temporalities in active relation to the world of social and material practices, institutions, and power relations.

A materialist relational theory of space and time has a key political as well as scientific role to play. Not only does it permit us to challenge outright the absolutist presumptions and pretensions – the totalizing vision (the view from nowhere) if you will – of the a-historical treatment of space and time incorporated in conventional analyses and narratives, but it also allows us to resist "the view from everywhere" and ask how relations (cogrediences and compossibilities) get established between, for example, monetary, heavenly, and other bodies. The relational view allows for diversity in the social construction of space–time while insisting that different social processes may relate and that, therefore, the space–time orderings and the cartographies of resistance they produce are in some way or other also interrelated. Discovering the nature of such connections and learning to translate politically between them is a problem for detailed research. Theoretically, the cogency and potential power of the materialist version of the relational view appears as remarkable and as exhaustive as it is dialectically consistent.

11
From Space to Place and Back Again

1. The Issue

Just north of the Johns Hopkins University Homewood Campus in Baltimore lies the affluent and prestigious neighborhood of Guilford. The 296-acre area, situated on pleasant rolling terrain where the Piedmont meets the coastal plain (the famous "fall line" on the water courses draining into the Atlantic that stretches from Georgia to New England and which, a mile to the west, became an attraction point for siting several large cotton-duck mills in the nineteenth century) was purchased in 1907 by a syndicate of rich Baltimoreans to preclude speculative tract development. In 1911 the site was turned over to the Roland Park Company (a land development offshoot of surplus British capital on US soil) for development according to the "best and most modern methods of city planning available." This resulted in sophisticated infrastructures, landscaping in the tradition of Frederick Law Olmstead (whose son's architectural firm did the plan and plainly took to heart the idea that the ruralization of the city was the key to relieving the stress of urban living) and, eventually, an eclectic mish-mash of 1920s architectures scattered around the 841 individual building lots. The lots are open plan, largely devoid of fences and walls, and situated on spacious curvilinear streets amid small parks. But the neighborhood lots were also sold with restrictive and exclusionary covenants, specifically excluding non-Caucasians and Jews. From the 1920s onwards, Guilford, along with Roland Park to its west and Homeland to its north (all developed by the same land company) became a secluded residential centre of affluent white Anglo-Saxon and largely protestant power in the city.

In spite of all the trials and tribulations that have beset the Baltimore economy since the mid-1960s, Guilford has managed to retain much of its original character (even after the exclusionary covenants were struck down). Its distinctive ambience has mellowed with age and it remains a peaceful silvan setting to which many Baltimoreans repair particularly in springtime to admire the flowering dogwoods and azaleas. The neighborhood in part retained its character through strict isolation from the less affluent and racially different communities that formed on its eastern edge. As physical mark and symbol of that separation, a solid wall prevents access from the east for much of the neighborhood; the only road to the east is one way heading out.

On Sunday August 14, 1994 a brutal double murder occurred in Guilford. An elderly white couple, both distinguished physicians but now retired in their 80s, were found in their bed bludgeoned to death with a baseball bat. Murder is no stranger to Baltimore (the rate for the city is close to one a day). But in the eyes of the media the Guilford killings were special. The main local newspaper – the *Baltimore Sun* – devoted full-page coverage to them when most other murders receive nominal attention. The media dwelt at length on how this was the third such incident in Guilford in recent months and that something plainly had to be done to protect the community if it was to survive. The solution that had long been pressed by the Guilford Community Association was to turn Guilford into a gated community with restricted access.

In commenting on this proposal, the *Sun* turned to the expert advice of Oscar Newman, whose 1972 book on *Defensible Space* had long been regarded as fundamental to the security problems of cities. Newman, the *Sun* reported:

> said yesterday that he believes Guilford might be a good candidate for such a change. ... "I think we're headed to a point where sections of cities vulnerable to crime will adopt this philosophy. ... Criminals are finding Guilford a great place to pick up change. You can burglarize a car or house, get out of there and use the money to buy drugs." In Dayton, Ohio, a conversion of one neighborhood, Five Oaks, to defensible mini-neighborhoods, each with only one combined entrance and exit, led to a 67 percent drop in traffic and half as many violent crimes, according to a recent report. "Drug dealers, prostitutes, muggers and other criminals are reluctant to enter a neighborhood with limited points of retreat," Mr Newman said.

But, the *Sun* continued, the proposal "raises issues of racial and class divisions," because the proposed barriers, all on the east, would separate Guilford even further from neighborhoods where residents were predominantly black and lower income while the borders with wealthier and whiter neighborhoods on the west and north remained untouched. The whole tenor of the *Sun*'s report implied, however, that crime was an African-American and "underclass" habit and that therefore the construction of barriers against people of color and of low income, however regrettable, might be justifiable as a means to secure a defensible space of "community" for an affluent white middle-class population that might otherwise flee the city. *Place* had to be secured against the uncontrolled vectors of spatiality.

Five days later it was announced that a grandson – not a random intruder – had confessed to the killings. This confession again rated front page extensive coverage in the *Sun*. But this time the tone was completely different. Several prominent African-Americans in the city, including the mayor, were cited as "relieved" (some even said "elated") that the stereotypical association of crime ("the drug dealers, prostitutes, muggers and other criminals" so bizarrely depicted in the *Sun's* earlier report as wandering the streets of Guilford) with blackness had been found wanting. Oscar Newman was nowhere cited and replaced as expert by Patricia Fernandez-Kelly, a research scientist and sociology professor at the Johns Hopkins University. She was quoted as saying:

> What's happened is the word "crime" has become a receptacle for a series of concerns we cannot mention, the unmentionables; class and race. ... [It] has become a euphemism. It is easier to speak about crime, to speak about larceny and burglary and murder than to evoke the images of class and race. That is very, very telling. This is truly Orwellian, a kind of doublespeak. It is an alternative language we have to refer to the problems we see in society. We cannot use the old language of racism. We come up with all sorts of politically correct terms to refer to the same problems. When we say "crime" we're really saying we are afraid of lower-class black people.

Editorializing, the *Sun*, while mainly blaming the police and city officials rather than its own coverage and selection of experts for the unfortunate associations, suggested that all of "us" ought to think about how "we" instinctively react in such circumstances: "while barricades and alarms can alter the ambience of a community, they can't keep evil at bay."

So what kind of *place* is Guilford? It has a name, a boundary, and distinctive social and physical qualities. It has achieved a certain kind of "permanence" in the midst of the fluxes and flows of urban life. Protection of this permanence has become a political–economic project not only for Guilford residents but also for a wide range of institutions in the city (government, the media, and finance in particular). And it has a discursive/symbolic meaning well beyond that of mere location, so that events that occur there have a particular significance, as signified by the response in the press and media to the murders. Guilford plainly fits into cartographies of struggle, power, and discourse in Baltimore city in very special ways. But different maps locate it differently, as the two contrasting reports in the *Sun* clearly indicated.

In what follows, I want always to try and bear in mind examples like Guilford, in order to ensure some sort of grounded feeling for what a word like "place" might mean against a background of a general relational theory of space–time and environment.

II. Some Theoretical Considerations on Place

Place, in whatever guise, is like space and time, a social construct. This is the baseline proposition from which I start. The only interesting question that can then be asked is: by what social process(es) is place constructed? There are two ways to get a fix on that problem. The first is to recapitulate what the relational view of space–time tells us:

> entities achieve relative stability in both their bounding and their internal ordering of processes creating space, for a time. Such permanences come to occupy a piece of space in an exclusive way (for a time) and thereby define a place – their place – (for a time). The process of place formation is a process of carving out "permanences" from the flow of processes creating spatio-temporality. But the "permanences" – no matter how solid they may seem – are not eternal but always subject to time as "perpetual perishing." They are contingent on processes of creation, sustenance and dissolution. (Above, p. 261)

A double meaning can, therefore, be given to a place as (*a*) a mere position or location within a map of space–time constituted within some social process or (*b*) an entity or "permanence" occurring within and transformative of the construction of space–time. The latter argument includes the environmental transformation through which permanences (places) get built. The difference in meanings is between putting down a marker such as 30.03°S and 51.10°W on a map of the globe or naming the city of Porto Alegre in the state of Rio Grande do Sul in Brazil. In the latter case, the named entity indicates some sort of bounded permanence (whether it be of government, social organization, built form, ecological structure, etc.) at a given location. The socio-ecological processes at work within that and other places may change spatio-temporal orderings in such a way as to undermine, enhance or erode the particular permanences that, say, Porto Alegre has achieved. Many different stories can be told about places. Place can be as varied and as multiple as the various "chronotopes" that Bakhtin (1981: 84) attributes to the novel. The "concrete whole" of the novel (analogous to place) is shaped by a fusion of "spatial and temporal indicators" so that "time, as it were, thickens, takes on flesh, becomes artistically visible" while "spaces become charged and responsive to the movements of time, plot and history." This is the way that places are constructed in human historical geography.

The second broad strategy is to return to the cognitive map of the social process outlined in chapter 4 and look at places as the locus of "imaginaries," as "institutionalizations," as configurations of "social relations," as "material practices," as forms of "power," and as elements in "discourse." A full accounting of place in all of these regards would require a book unto itself. In what follows I shall attempt merely to illustrate how all of these elements typically combine. The effect is to understand places as internally heterogeneous, dialectical and dynamic configurations of relative "permanences" within the overall spatio-temporal dynamics of socio-ecological processes. Guilford, to return to my opening example, can be understood from the standpoint of each separate moment in the social process, but what is most interesting is how it internalizes and combines effects from all moments simultaneously.

III. The Political Economy of Place Construction Under Capitalism

Consider, first, capitalism's historical trajectory of geographical expansion through the construction of actual places as relatively permanent physical and social structures on the land. Or, put another way, consider how places get erected as permanences within the flux and flow of capital circulation. Since I have written extensively on this topic elsewhere (Harvey, 1982, 1985a, b) I shall offer only a very abbreviated account here.

Capitalism is necessarily growth oriented, technologically dynamic, and crisis prone. One of the ways it can temporarily and in part surmount crises of overaccumulation of capital (idle productive capacity plus unemployed labor power) is through geographical expansion. This is what I call the "spatial fix" to capitalism's contradictions. There are two facets to this process. Excess capital can be exported from one place (city, region, nation) to build another place within an existing set of space relations (e.g., the export of British surplus capital to fund land development in Baltimore at the end of the nineteenth century or the export of production capital from the United States overseas after World War II). Space relations may also be revolutionized, as described in chapter 9, through technological and organizational shifts. Such revolutions alter relations between places and affect internalized processes of place construction, sustenance, and dissolution (as has happened through the recent history of rapid deindustrialization in many cities of the advanced capitalist world).

In either case, new networks of places arise, constituted as fixed capital embedded in the land and configurations of organized social relations, institutions, etc. on the land. New territorial divisions of labor and concentrations of people and labor power, new resource extraction activities and markets form. The geographical landscape which results is not evenly developed but strongly differentiated. "Difference" and "otherness" are *produced* in space through the simple logic of uneven capital investment, a proliferating geographical division of labor, an increasing segmentation of reproductive activities and the rise of spatially ordered (often segregated) social distinctions (such as those that separate Guilford from its surrounds).

There are tensions within this process. To begin with, it is marked by class struggle in and through the production of space. Furthermore, the speculative element (like all forms of capitalist development) is very strong, often pitting one faction of capital against another. Place construction ventures often go wrong or become mired down in speculative swindles. Charles Dickens used the history of a mythical New Eden in *Martin Chuzzlewit* as a witty denunciation of a process which continues to this day as pensioners head down to their retirement plot in sunny Florida to find it is in the middle of a swamp. Thorsten Veblen (1967) argued that the whole settlement pattern of the United States should be understood as one vast venture in real estate speculation. This thesis has recently reappeared in the work of Mike Davis (1990) on Los Angeles. To say, therefore, that place construction is given in the logic of capitalism's production of space is not to argue that the geographical pattern is determined in advance. The success or failure of speculative investments is largely worked out *a posteriori* through spatial competition between places.

The second difficulty arises out of the inevitable tension between speculative investment in place development and the geographical mobility of other forms of capital. The space–time system constructed through the activities of contemporary finance capital, for example, is characterized by much faster movement across space relative to producers who have necessarily to tie themselves down in place for at least a time, and investors in physical infrastructures and properties whose commitments are even longer lasting. The integration of these different space–time systems is often problematic (see Merrifield, 1993, for an excellent case study). Those who have invested in the physical qualities of place have to ensure that activities arise which render their investments profitable by ensuring the permanence of place. Coalitions of entrepreneurs actively try to shape activities in places for this purpose. Hence the significance of local "growth machine" politics of the sort that Logan and Molotch (1988) describe and of local class alliances to promote and sustain economic development in places. But such conditions cannot always succeed. Competition between places produces winners and losers. The differences between places to some degree become antagonistic.

The tension between place-bound fixity and spatial mobility of capital erupts into generalized crisis, however, when the landscape shaped in relation to a certain phase of development (capitalist or pre-capitalist) becomes a barrier to further accumulation. The geographical configuration of places must then be reshaped around new transport and communications systems and physical infrastructures, new centers and styles of production and consumption, new agglomerations of labor power, and modified social infrastructures (including, for example, systems of governance and regulation of places). Old places (such as Cowley described in chapter 1) have to be devalued, destroyed, and redeveloped while new places are created. The cathedral city becomes a heritage center, the mining community becomes a ghost town, the old industrial center is deindustrialized, speculative boom towns or gentrified neighborhoods arise on the frontiers of capitalist development or out of the ashes of deindustrialized communities. The history of capitalism is, then, punctuated by intense phases of spatial reorganization.

There has been a powerful surge of such reorganization since around 1970, creating considerable insecurity within and between places. The effect has not been, as some theorists contend, to eliminate the significance of place altogether in the contemporary world (see Meyrowitz's *No Sense of Place* for an excellent example of this genre of writing). But it does mean that the meaning of place has changed in social life and in certain respects the effect has been to make place more rather than less important. This probably accounts for the vast outpouring of works over the past ten years or so in which "place" figures prominently in the title. While there are all sorts of reasons behind this (and these will become clearer as we proceed) there are four reasons internal to the political economy of capital accumulation that deserve immediate consideration:

1. Space–time relations have been radically restructured since around 1970 and this has altered the relative locations of places within the global patterning of capital accumulation. Urban places that once had a secure status find themselves vulnerable (think of Detroit, Sheffield, Liverpool, and Lille) and residents find themselves forced to ask what kind of place can be remade that will survive within the new matrix of space relations and capital accumulation in the past (like Cowley) have been abandoned to their fates today. We worry about the meaning of place in general and of our place in particular when the security of actual places becomes generally threatened.
2. When transport costs were high and communication difficult, places were protected from competition by the frictions of distance. Places could depend upon a relatively high degree of monopoly power. But diminished transport costs have made production, merchanting, marketing, and particularly finance capital much more geographically mobile than heretofore. The monopoly power inherent in place is much reduced. This allows much freer choice of location which in turn permits capitalists to take more rather than less advantage of small differences in resource qualities, quantities, costs and amenities between places. Multinational capital, for example, has become much more sensitive to the qualities of places in its search for more profitable accumulation.
3. Those who reside in a place (or who hold the fixed assets in place) become acutely aware that they are in competition with other places for highly mobile capital. The particular mix of physical and social infrastructures, of labor qualities, of social and political regulation, of cultural and social life on offer (all of which are open to construction) can be more or less attractive to, for example, external capital. Residents worry about what package they can offer which will bring development while satisfying their own wants and needs. People in places therefore try to differentiate their place from other places and become more competitive (and perhaps antagonistic and exclusionary with respect to each other) in order to capture or retain capital investment. Within this process, the selling of place, using all the artifices

of advertising and image construction that can be mustered, has become of considerable importance.

4. Profitable projects to absorb excess capital have been hard to find these last two decades and a considerable proportion of surplus capital has found its way into speculative place construction. The lack of wisdom in much of this became clear in the massive default of savings and loan institutions in the United Sates ($300 billion, almost as much as the combined Third World debt) and the shaky position of many of the world's largest banks (including even the Japanese) through overinvestment in real-estate development. The selling of places and the highlighting of their particular qualities (retirement or tourist resorts, communities with new lifestyles, etc.) becomes even more frenetic.

The upshot has been to render the coercive power of competition between places for capitalist development more rather than less emphatic and so provide less leeway for projects of place construction that lie outside of capitalist norms. In earlier periods, the monopoly protection given to place development by high transport costs allowed for much greater diversity in the way places got constructed. Now, the concern to preserve a good business environment for highly mobile capital or to realize a quick profit from speculative development donates. Inter-place competition is not simply about attracting production, however. It is also about attracting consumers (particularly the affluent) through the creation of amenities such as a cultural center, a pleasing urban or regional landscape, and the like. Investment in consumption spectacles, the selling of images of places, competition over the definition of cultural and symbolic capital, the revival of vernacular traditions associated with places as a consumer attraction, all become conflated in inter-place competition. I note in passing, that much of postmodern production in, for example, the realms of architecture and urban design, is precisely about the selling of place as part and parcel of an ever-deepening commodity culture. The result is that places that seek to differentiate themselves as marketable entities end up creating a kind of serial replication of homogeneity (Boyer, 1988).

The question immediately arises as to why people accede to the construction of their places by such a process? The short answer, of course, is that they often don't. The historical geography of place construction is full of examples of struggles fought for socially just reinvestment (to meet community needs), for the development of "community" expressive of values other than those of money and exchange, or against deindustrialization, the despoliation of cities through highway construction, and the like. The upper classes have been just as active (and of course more effective) as the lower classes in this resistance. Appealing to that distinctive bourgeois esthetic sensibility that has arisen since the eighteenth century, the bourgeoisie often try to design and protect places of distinctive qualities (like Guilford) in terms of relations to both nature and to culture. These qualities are powerfully protected as part of their own particular patrimony. And one of the forces that has to be protected against is crass capital accumulation on the land.

Lefebvre (1991) is quite right, therefore, to insist that class struggle is everywhere inscribed in space through the uneven development of the qualities of places. Yet it is also the case that such resistances have not checked the overall process of place construction through capital accumulation (speculative capital when denied the option to build or despoil one city or neighborhood has the habit of quickly finding somewhere else to go). But instances of popular complicity with speculative activities are also plentiful. These typically arise out of a mixture of coercion and cooptation. Cooptation is largely organized around (*a*) dispersed property ownership which provides a mass base for speculative activity (no one wants to see the value of their house tumbling), (*b*) the benefits supposedly to be had from expansion (bringing new employment and economic activities into a place), and (*c*) the sheer power of pro-capitalist techniques of persuasion (growth is inevitable as well as good for you). For these reasons labor organizations often join rather than oppose local growth coalitions. Coercion arises either through inter-place competition for capital investment and employment (accede to the capitalist's demands or go out of business, create a "good business climate" or lose jobs) or, more simply, through the direct political repression and oppression of dissident voices (from cutting off media access to the more violent tactics of the construction mafias – such as the Yakuza in Japan or the Mafia in the United States).

But the purchase of "place" over our thinking, our politics and our social practices cannot simply be attributed to these trends, powerful and persuasive as they may be in many instances. The generalization of civic boosterism, of growth-machine politics, of cultural homogenization through diversification, hardly provides a full accounting for place-bound identities. Nor can it account for the strength of political attachments which people manifest in relation to particular places. So where can we look for other explanations?

IV. Heidegger and Place as the Locus of Being

"Place" said Heidegger, "is the locale of the truth of Being." Many writers – particularly those within the phenomenological tradition – have drawn heavily from him and it is useful to see how his argument unfolds. He begins with a familiar statement:

> All distances in time and space are shrinking. ... Yet the frantic abolition of all distances brings no nearness; for nearness does not consist in shortness of distance. What is least remote from us in point of distance, by virtue of its picture on film or its sound on radio, can remain far from us. What is incalculably far

from us in point of distance can be near to us. ... Everything gets lumped together into uniform distancelessness. ... What is it that unsettles and thus terrifies? It shows itself and hides itself in the *way* in which everything presences, namely, in the fact that despite all conquest of distances the nearness of things remains absent. (Heidegger, 1971: 165)

Notice the sense of terror of "time–space compression," the fear of a loss of identity (understood as identification with place) as the space–time coordinates of social life become unstable. This terror is omnipresent because all mortals "persist through space by virtue of their stay among things" and are therefore perpetually threatened by changing space relations among things. Furthermore, physical nearness does not necessarily bring with it understanding or an ability to appreciate or even appropriate a "thing" (or for that matter another person) properly. Heidegger recognizes that the achieved shifts in space relations are a product of commodification and market exchange and invokes an argument close to Marx's:

the object-character of technological dominion spreads itself over the earth ever more quickly, ruthlessly, and completely. Not only does it establish all things as producible in the process of production; it also delivers the products of production by means of the market. In self-assertive production, the human-ness of man and the thingness of things dissolve into the calculated market value of a market which not only spans the whole earth as a world market, but also, as the will to will, trades in the nature of Being and thus subjects all beings to the trade of a calculation that dominates most tenaciously in those areas where there is no need of numbers. (Heidegger, 1971: 114–15)

Heidegger, however, reacts to all this in a very particular way. He withdraws attention from the world market and seeks ways to uncover the truths of human existence phenomenologically. The concept which he focuses on is that of "dwelling." He illustrates it with a description of a Black Forest farmhouse:

Here the self-sufficiency of the power to let earth and heaven, divinities and mortals enter in simple oneness into things, ordered the house. It places the farm on the wind-sheltered mountain slope looking south, among the meadows close to the spring. It gave it the wide overhanging shingle roof whose proper slope bears up under the burden of snow, and which, reaching deep down, shields the chambers against the storms of the long winter nights. It did not forget the altar corner behind the community table; it made room in its chamber for the hallowed places of childbed and the "tree of the dead" – for that is what they call a coffin there; the Totenbaum – and in this way it designed for the different generations under one roof the character of their journey through time. A craft which, itself sprung from dwelling, still uses its tools and frames as things, built the farmhouse. (Heidegger, 1971: 160)

Dwelling is the capacity to achieve a spiritual unity between humans and things. From this it follows that "only if we are capable of dwelling, only then can we build." Indeed, buildings "may even deny dwelling its own nature when they are pursued and acquired purely for their own sake" (Heidegger, 1971: 156). Although there is a narrow sense of homelessness which can perhaps be alleviated simply by building shelter, there is a much deeper crisis of homelessness to be found in the modern world; many people have lost their roots, their connection to homeland. Even those who physically stay in place may become homeless (rootless) through the inroads of modern means of communication (such as radio and television). "The rootedness, the autochthony, of man is threatened today at its core." If we lose the capacity to dwell then we lose our roots and find ourselves cut off from all sources of spiritual nourishment. The impoverishment of existence is incalculable (cf. the citations from Birringer, above, p. 243). The flourishing of any genuine work of art, Heidegger (1966: 47–8) insists, depends upon its roots in a native soil. "We are plants which – whether we like to admit it to ourselves or not – must with our roots rise out of the earth in order to bloom in the ether and bear fruit." Deprived of such roots, art is reduced to a meaningless caricature of its former self. The problem, therefore, is to recover a viable homeland in which meaningful roots can be established. Place construction should be about the recovery of roots, the recovery of the art of dwelling.

Heidegger's "ontological excavations" have inspired a particular approach to understanding the social processes of place construction. He focuses our attention on the way in which places "are constructed in our memories and affections through repeated encounters and complex associations" (Relph, 1989: 26–9). He emphasizes how "place experiences are necessarily time-deepened and memory-qualified." He creates "a new way to speak about and care for our human nature and environment," so that "love of place and the earth are scarcely sentimental extras to be indulged only when all technical and material problems have been resolved. They are part of being in the world and prior, therefore, to all technical matters." This poses the whole question of the relation to nature. Place and environmental meanings and politics are inseparable because place is the locale of the truth of being in nature (see Buell, 1995).

There are, however, some difficulties with the Heideggerian argument. Like most great philosophers, he remained extraordinarily vague in his prescriptions and his commentators have had a field day elaborating on what all this might mean. For example, what might the conditions of "dwelling" be in a highly industrialized, modernist, and capitalist world? We cannot turn back to the Black Forest farmhouse, but what is it that we might turn to? The issue of authenticity (rootedness) of the experience of place (and nature in place) is, for example, a difficult one. To begin with, as Dovey (1989: 43) observes, the problem of authenticity is itself peculiarly modern. Only as modern industrialization separates us from the process of production and we encounter the environment as a finished commodity does it emerge. Being rooted in place,

Tuan (1977: 198) argues, is a different kind of experience from having and cultivating a sense of place. "A truly rooted community may have shrines and monuments, but it is unlikely to have museums and societies for the preservation of the past." The effort to evoke a sense of place and of the past is now often deliberate and conscious. But herein lies a danger. The quest for authenticity, invented traditions and a commercialized heritage culture. The final victory of modernity, MacCannell (1976: 8) suggests, is not the disappearance of the non-modern world but its artificial preservation and reconstruction.

Nevertheless, there seems to be a widespread acceptance of Heidegger's claim that the authenticity of dwelling and of rootedness is being destroyed by the spread of technology, rationalism, mass production, and mass values. Place is being destroyed, says Relph (1976), rendered "inauthentic" or even "placeless" by the sheer organizational power and depth of penetration of the market. The response is to construct a politics of place which is then held up as the political way forward to the promised land of an authentic existence. Kirkpatrick Sale (1990) writes in a left-leaning journal *The Nation*: "The only political vision that offers any hope of salvation is one based on an understanding of, a rootedness in, a deep commitment to, and a resacralization of, *place.*"

This permits a second cut at why place is becoming more rather than less important in the contemporary world. What Heidegger holds out, and what many subsequent writers have drawn from him, is the possibility of some kind of resistance to or rejection of any simple capitalist (or modernist) logic of place construction. It would then follow that the increasing penetration of technological rationality, of commodification and market values, and capital accumulation into social life (or into what many writers, including Habermas, call "the life world") together with time–space compression, will provoke resistances that increasingly focus on alternative constructions of place (understood in the broadest sense of that word). The search for an authentic sense of community and of an authentic relation to nature among many radical and ecological movements is the cutting edge of exactly such a sensibility. Even Raymond Williams (1979a: 276) saw place as more than "just the site of an event ... but the materialization of a history which is often quite extensively retracted." His novels, as we have seen in chapter 1, explore the political and affective meaning of place as a site of both complicity with and resistance to capital accumulation. There is certainly enough credibility in the Heideggerian argument to make it worthy of careful consideration, even if, as I shall show, there are strong grounds for rejecting it in its original guise.

V. Place as the Locus of Environmental Qualities

Heidegger, in conjuring up a process of presencing things in intimate closeness cultivates immediately an imaginary of an unalienated relation to nature through an intimate sensuous interaction in place. It is, Buell (1995) remarks, almost impossible to consider environmental issues without at some point confronting the idea of place. There is also a rather touching and abiding faith in much of the literature that "by reviving a sense of place we may be able to reactivate the care of the environment" and that "a reawakened sense of beauty of local places may fuel a deeply spiritual concern for the preservation of the ecological diversity and uniqueness of each place" (Lilburne, 1989: 30, 110). This faith can be found not only in the theological literature (Lilburne, 1989: Brueggemann, 1977), but is also strongly evident in bioregionalist, communi-tarian, and anarcho-socialist forms of ecological politics (see chapter 8). It also plays a key role in environmental justice movements (chapter 13). Place is the preferred terrain of much environmental politics. Some of the fiercest movements of opposition to the political–economy of capitalistic place construction are waged over the issue of the preservation or upsetting of valued environmental qualities in particular places.

Much of this rests on the belief that deep experiential understanding of "nature" cannot be had on the run from one place to another. Some of the classics of natural history – such as Gilbert White's *A Natural History of Selbourne* – testify to the importance of such deep local knowledge. A whole genre of ecologically sensitive writing about particular places – some of it peculiarly beautiful and powerful – has sprung up since the Enlightenment in part through the estheticization of a particular place-bound relation to nature as a key component to social life. The evocation of the particular qualities of place becomes a means to explore an alternative esthetic to that offered through the restless spatial flows of commodities and money. This required a deep and often contemplative familiarity with local fauna and flora, soil qualities, geologies, and the like, as well as the intricate history of human occupancy, environmental modification and the embedding of human labor in the land, particularly in the built environment.

The connection between ecological sentiments and place deserves, however, some critical probing. The intimacy of many place-based accounts – Thoreau's famous and influential exploration of Walden being an exemplary case – yields only limited natural knowledge embedded in ecological processes operating at a small scale. Such knowledge is insufficient to understand broader socio-ecological processes occurring at scales that cannot be directly experienced and which are therefore outside of phenomenological reach. Furthermore, the penchant for regarding place as a privileged if not exclusive locus of ecological sensitivity rests on the human body as "the measure of all things" in an unmediated and very direct way. Sensuous interaction between the body and its environs can certainly carry with it a wide range of psychic as well as social meanings. The difficulty is that our relations as organisms embedded in nature extend far further into a chain of commodity production and exchange that reaches into every corner of the globe. In so far as "alienation from nature" is a widely acknowledged problem in contemporary society, then place comes into its own as a locus of some potentially unalienated direct sensuous interaction with environs. But it does so by hiding *within* the fetishism of commodities and ends up fetishizing the human body, the Self, and the realms of human sensation as the locus of all being in the world.

Nevertheless, much of the "militant particularism" to be found within ecological–environmental movements rests on a certain sense of the intimacy of place-based ecological relations. Violation of the integrity of such relations (by capitalist development or state investments, for example) often provokes local protests that can build outwards to a more universal ecological politics (see chapter 13).

VI. Place as the Locus of Collective Memory

It is hard to probe very long in the extensive literature on place without encountering the idea of some strong associations between place, memory, and identity:

> Place is space which has historical meanings, where some things have happened which are now remembered and which provide continuity and identity across generations. Place is space in which important words have been spoken which have established identity, defined vocation, and envisioned destiny. Place is space in which vows have been exchanged, promises have been made, and demands have been issued. (Brueggemann, cited in Lilburne, 1989: 26)

This was one of the strong points upon which Bachelard insisted in his *Poetics of Space*. It is worth following his argument briefly since it provides a powerful phenomenological baseline to understanding the significance of place in relation to memory:

> In the theater of the past that is constituted by memory, the stage setting maintains the characters in their dominant roles. At times we think we know ourselves in time, when all we know is a sequence of fixations in the spaces of the being's stability – a being who does not want to melt away, and who, even in the past, when he sets out in search of things past, wants time to "suspend" its flight.

> all really inhabited space bears the essence of the notion of home. [Here] memory and imagination remain associated, each one working for their mutual deepening. In the order of values, they both constitute a community of memory and image. Thus the house is not experienced from day to day only, on the thread of a narrative, or in the telling of our own story. Through dreams the various dwelling places in our lives co-penetrate and retain the treasures of former days.

... The house is one of the greatest powers of integration for the thoughts, memories and dreams of mankind. ... Without it, man would be a dispersed being.

But is this sense of place confined only to the house as home? Or does it extend to a broader sense of place as homeland, what the Germans refer to as *Heimat*? The latter word, says Edgar Reitz, director of the 1984 film of that name (arguably one of the most important cultural productions of the 1980s), "is always linked to strong feelings, mostly remembrances and longing." It is, comment Morley and Robins (1993: 8), "about conserving the 'fundamentals' of culture and identity" and "sustaining cultural boundaries and boundedness." As such, it appears to point solely to an exclusionary politics of nationalism and communitarianism (see below) precisely because memories built around places cannot easily be shared with outsiders.

To put it in those terms is to cast something rather more fundamental in a purely negative light. Basso's (1984) study of the Western Apache shows, for example, how "geographical features have served the people for centuries as indispensable mnemonic pegs on which to hang the moral teachings of their history." The permanence of places in the landscape coupled with stories told that invoke them provides a means to perpetuate a cultural identity. Appealing to Bakhtin's concept of the *chronotope* (see chapter 10), Basso writes:

> One forms the impression that Apaches view the landscape as the repository of distilled wisdom, a stern but benevolent keeper of tradition, an ever-vigilant ally in the efforts of individuals and whole communities to put into practice a set of standards for social living that are uniquely and distinctively their own. In the world that the Western Apache have constituted for themselves, features of the landscape have become symbols of and for this way of living, the symbols of a culture and the enduring moral character of its people.

We here encounter, in the symbolic dimension, a particular version of that dialectic between the social and environmental that instanciates one within the other. By thinking and comprehending their relationships to the physical world in a particular way, native-Americans engage in a moral act of imagination that constitutes an understanding of the physical world at the same time as it constitutes an understanding of themselves. From this it follows that losing the land is equivalent to losing identity and that processes of modernization, capital accumulation and spatial integration will be profoundly disruptive of such particular markers of cultural identity.

But memory of the past is also about hope for the future. As Mary Gordon (1995: 47) puts it:

> There is a link between hope and memory. Remembering nothing one cannot hope for anything. And so time means nothing.

The preservation or construction of a sense of place is then an active moment in the passage from memory to hope, from past to future. And the reconstruction of places can reveal hidden memories that hold out the prospects for different futures. "Critical regionalism" as it is called in architecture, invoking as it so often does vernacular traditions and icons of place, is considered a basis for a politics of resistance to commodity flows and monetization. "Militant particularism" seizes upon the qualities of place, reanimates the bond between the environmental and the social, and seeks to bend the social processes constructing space–time to a radically different purpose. Some memories can be suppressed and others rescued from the shadows as identities shift and political trajectories into the future get redefined. "Imagination," says Bachelard (1964: xxx) "separates us from the past as well as from reality: it faces the future." Imagined places, the Utopian thoughts and desires of countless peoples, have consequently played a vital role in animating politics.

Time takes on its spatial meaning through the practices of place construction in the imagination, in discourse, as well as in material, social, and institutional forms. But are there principles of place construction that tie together time past with time future while acknowledging the importance of memory, the experience of environment and the capacity for dwelling in the land? This is the thesis that is explored through the idea of the *genius loci*.

VII. The Search for *Genius Loci*

Kirkpatrick Sale's call for the "resacralization of place" hints at how places exist in relation to a completely different space–time world to that given in capital accumulation. The worlds of myth, of religion, of collective memory, and of national or regional identity are space–time constructs that constitute and are constituted by the formation of distinctive places (shrines, places of worship, icons in stories, etc.). Places expressive of distinctive beliefs, values, imaginaries, and social–institutional practices have long been constructed both materially and discursively. The search to perpetuate such processes of place construction continues to this day. Many traditional institutions, such as those of church and nation, depend crucially upon the existence of a whole network of symbolic places to secure their power and express their social meaning. Places, as permanences, become symbolic and redolent of those values (such as fame, authority, identity, and power) constructed through spatio-temporal practices.

Many architects approach this process through Heideggerian channels. They have sought to capture something of the mythic qualities of places through the concept of the *genius loci*. Writes Norberg-Schulz (1980: 18):

> *Genius loci* is a Roman concept. According to ancient Roman belief every "independent" being has its *genius*, its guardian spirit. This spirit gives life to

people and places, accompanies them from birth to death, and determines their character or essence. ... The *genius* thus denotes what a thing *is*, or what it "wants to be". ... [Ancient man] recognized that it is of great existential importance to come to terms with the *genius* of the locality where his life takes place. In the past, survival depended on a "good" relationship to the place in a physical as well as a psychic sense.

In elaborating upon this idea, Norberg-Schulz invokes Heidegger's conception of "dwelling" directly:

When man dwells, he is simultaneously located in space and exposed to a certain environmental character. The two psychological functions involved, may be called "orientation" and "identification". To gain an existential foothold man has to be able to *orientate* himself; he has to know *where* he is. But he also has to *identify* himself with the environment, that is, he has to know *how* he is in a certain place.

Dwelling consequently entails above all "identification with the environment" and from this it follows that the "existential purpose" of building, architecture, and urban design is "to uncover the meanings potentially present in the given environment." To think this way is not to concede anything to environmental determinism, nor is it to insist upon a static conception of place:

The structure of a place is not a fixed, eternal state. As a rule places change, sometimes rapidly. This does not mean, however that the *genius loci* necessarily changes or gets lost. ... First of all we may point out that any place ought to have the "capacity" of receiving *different* "contents," naturally within certain limits. A place which is only fitted for one particular purpose would soon become useless. Secondly it is evident that a place may be "interpreted" in different ways. To protect and conserve the *genius loci* in fact means to concretize its essence in ever new historical contexts. We might also say that the history of a place ought to be its "self-realization." What was there as possibilities at the outset, is uncovered through human action. ... (Norberg-Schulz, 1980: 18)

The keying in on the exploration of possibilities of a place is a familiar theme in Raymond Williams' work (see chapter 1). The invocation of "self-realization" should also alert us to certain parallels to the "deep ecology" position (see chapter 6). Norberg-Schulz also appeals to process-based philosophy and dialectical formulations (outlined in chapter 2). His examination of the dynamics of places makes these points explicit:

Our examples show that economic, social, political and cultural intentions have to be concretized in a way which represents the *genius loci*. If not, the place loses its identity. ... Thus we learn that cities have to be treated as *individual places*, rather than abstract spaces where the "blind" forces of economy and politics may have freeplay. To respect the *genius loci* does not mean to copy old models. It means to determine the identity of the place and to interpret it in ever new ways. Only then we may talk about a *living tradition* which makes change meaningful by relating it to a set of locally founded parameters. We may again remind ourselves of Alfred North Whitehead's dictum: "The art of progress is to preserve order amid change, and change amid order". A living tradition serves life because it satisfies these words. It does not understand "freedom" as an arbitrary play, but as creative participation. (Norberg-Schulz, 1980: 182)

Norberg-Schulz's interpretation of the *genius loci* makes reference to a number of themes already examined. Buildings "internalize" relations to environment, gathering together social, symbolic, psychological, biological, and physical relations in place so as to offer some sort of identity. The "meanings which are gathered by a place constitute its *genius loci*" he avers. Creative interventions in the construction of places as "permanences" are integral to a process of "self-realization," as understood in Whitehead's philosophy of process and change. The dissolution of place amounts, then, to a loss of identity. It suggests a fundamental spiritual alienation from environment and self that demands remedial measures, be it constraints on "freedom" as arbitrary play, or constraints on action through fear of offending the *genius loci*. While such noble and high-sounding sentiments are directed in Norberg-Schulz's work to the Acropolis or St Peter's Square, they can be seen at work in far more ordinary circumstances such as those of Guilford in Baltimore.

There is, at first sight, much to be said in favor of Norberg-Schulz's argument. It has widespread appeal among groups as diverse as deep ecologists, architects, and urban designers. The dialectical language coupled with a strong penchant for internalizing relations indicates a potential consistency with the theses I have been advancing. But the dangers of what I earlier termed "the Leibnizian conceit" are everywhere apparent. Consider, for example, some of the controversies within architecture itself. Rossi (1982: 103–7) complains with respect to the *locus* concept that:

> we continue to grasp at outlines which only evaporate and disappear. These outlines delineate the singularity of monuments, of the city, and of buildings, and thus the concept of singularity itself and its limits, where it begins and ends. They trace the relation of architecture to its location – the place of art – and thereby its connections to, and the precise articulation of, the *locus* itself as a singular artifact determined by its space and time, by its topographical dimensions and its form, by its being the seat of a succession of ancient and recent events, by its memory. All these problems are in large measure of a collective nature; they force us to pause for a moment on the relationship between place and man, and hence to look at the relationship between ecology and psychology.

Rossi, at least, is willing to see the *genius loci* in terms of collective identity, residing at the intersection of singularity and universality. Furthermore, the fluidity of meaning that Norberg-Schulz necessarily admits, is taken by Rossi in a more constructivist vein to mean the ability to explore possibilities in a far more open fashion. Rossi replaces the oppressive and homogenizing concept of "man" by "collectivity" while recognizing that the history of "built urban artefacts is always the history of the architecture of ruling classes" and that "monuments" (key elements of identity in urban contexts) are constituted symbolically and collectively, as sites of memory. But Rossi still insists on some underlying notion of permanence:

> Myths come and go, passing slowly from one place to another; every generation recounts them differently and adds new elements to the patrimony received from the past; but behind this changing reality, there is a permanent reality that in some way manages to elude the action of time. We must recognize the true foundation of this reality in religious tradition. ... I believe that the importance of ritual in its collective nature and its essential character as an element for preserving myth constitutes a key to understanding the meaning of monuments and, moreover, the implications of the founding of the city and of the transmission of ideas in an urban context. I attribute an especial importance to monuments, although their significance in the urban dynamic may at times be elusive. ... For if the ritual is the permanent and conserving element of myth, then so too is the monument, since, in the very moment that it testifies to myth, it renders ritual forms possible. (Rossi, 1982: 24)

Rossi's formulations open up a whole series of questions. Whose identity and which collectivity, for example? And if collective memory acquires a certain instanciation in place, and if that collective memory is vital to the perpetuation of some social order (or to the visualization of some hoped-for alternative in the future), then all essentialist formulations of the *genius loci* fall away to be replaced by a contested terrain of competing definitions. This is exactly the move that Loukaki (1967) makes in her study of competing treatments and visions of the Acropolis over time. Discursive controversies among architects, archeologists, and art historians over how to understand the *genius loci* here fade before the political power struggle coursing through Greek history as to whose *genius* gets to define the qualities of which *loci*. And that contest, as Loukaki shows, is not simply about the proper interpretation of the past, the authenticity of this or that collective memory, but it is also about all hopes for the future. To release a different imaginary concerning the past is to release a different imaginary as to possibilities in the future. The *genius loci* is open to contestation, both theoretically (as to its meaning) and concretely (as to how to understand a particular place). The absence of active political controversy can then be taken only as a sign of the domination of some hegemonic power. What makes the site of the Acropolis so interesting, for example, is that not only are there competing claims based on class, national sentiments, and locale, but also competing claims of outside powers (such as those of Germany, Britain, and the United States) who appropriate the Acropolis as a symbol of the origins of western civilization rather than respect it as a living monument embedded in the history of Greek geopolitical and political–economic struggles. The burden that the Acropolis bears is that it simultaneously "belongs" to radically divergent imagined communities. And the question as to whom it "truly" belongs has no direct theoretical answer: it is determined through political contestation and struggle and, hence, is a relatively unstable determination.

VIII. Place as the Locus of Community

The invocation of Benedict Anderson's phrase "imagined community" links to yet another dimension of what the idea and practice of place might be about. The history of the word "community" is just as fraught and ambivalent as that of the concept of place. The intertwining of the two terms makes for even more complicated layers of meaning. But something has to be said, for places acquire much of their permanence as well as much of their distinctive character from the collective activities of people who dwell there, who shape the land through their activities, and who build distinctive institutions, forms of organization, and social relations within, around or focused on a bounded domain. The collective memory that attaches to places connects to the imaginary of belonging. "Imagined communities" acquire a certain reality through practices that derive as much from imaginary and discursive links between individuals (mediated in our own times through the activities of "print and image capitalism") as from face-to-face contact (see, for example, the earlier discussion of Zizek's analysis of eastern European nationalism in chapter 5). The practical and discursive practices of "bounding" space and creating the permanences of particular places is likewise a collective affair within which all sorts of contested administrative, military, and social practices occur. And this is as true of bounded communities like Guilford as it is of the nation state.

Such bounding activities are nearly always partial in their effects (where does a city or a neighborhood begin and end?) and the socio-ecological processes that constitute space ensure that all places (even those with strictly controlled territorial borders) are to some degree open. This was precisely Whitehead's point about any kind of permanence, and in contemporary socio-ecological life the multiple flows and heterogeneity of processes at work ensure that all places are in a permanent state of flux (with the usual proviso of uneven geographical development that some places are more in flux than others and some more permanent and securely bounded than others).

So how, then, should territorially bounded community be considered both empirically and normatively? Here is how Sandel (1982: 172–3) sees it:

Insofar as our constitutive self-understandings comprehend a wider subject than the individual alone, whether a family or a tribe or a city or a class or nation or people, to this extent they define a community in the constitutive sense. And what makes such a community is not merely a spirit of benevolence, or the prevalence of communitarian values, or even certain "shared final ends" alone, but a common vocabulary of discourse and a background of implicit practices and understandings within which the opacity of persons is reduced if never finally dissolved.

The emphasis on "common discourse and implicit practices" provides a quite distinctive point of entry to the issue of community and nation compared to that given by Zizek (see chapter 5). It defines the commonality of some public realm within which notions of civic virtue, public responsibility, and the like can be defined. But there are plenty of critics of what is in effect a very Enlightenment view of public virtues and civic life. Young (1990a), for example, is critical of both the repressive homogeneity that such a universalism entails as well as the way that "desire for unity or wholeness in discourse generates borders, dichotomies, and exclusions." Indeed, Young reserves her fiercest denunciations for the often narrow, place-based, and intimate versions of communitarianism that now hold center stage. Such a concept of community "often implies a denial of time and space distancing" and an insistence on "face-to-face interaction among members within a plurality of contexts." But there are, she insists, "no conceptual grounds for considering face-to-face relations more pure, authentic social relations than relations mediated across time and distance." This is a crucial issue for an understanding of place. For while it may be true that in modern society the primary structures of value formation as well as of alienation and domination are defined by state power and capital circulation, it does not follow that all mediated relations are necessarily alienating and that the intimacy of place is the only locus of "authentic" socio-ecological relations. By positing "a society of immediate face-to-face relations as ideal, community theorists generate a dichotomy between the 'authentic' society of the future and the 'inauthentic' society we live in, which is characterized only by alienation, bureaucratization and degradation." Young's criticism of the Heideggerian tradition is strong. "Racism, ethnic chauvinism, and class devaluation ... grow partly from the desire for community." In the United States today, she argues (and the Guilford example well illustrates the point), "the positive identification of some groups is often achieved by first defining other groups as the other, the devalued semihuman."

This external oppressiveness, moreover, gets mirrored in internal repressions. The starting point of Young's argument lies in her own experience of the enforced homogeneity of many radical groups. And it is worth remembering that Freud thought that "hysteria was linked to place" (cited in Kristeva, 1986: 191). But the issue is much broader: there is a quite different definition of community that has a dark and repugnant presence. Foucault (1977), for example, highlights not only those sealed communities put under the strictest surveillance – the prison, the panoptican, the hospital, the school, the factory – but zones of control that produce docile bodies totally enclosed and imprisoned in the repressive mechanisms of disciplinary powers. This is the kind of community that Sennett (1970), in *The Uses of Disorder*, so brilliantly dissects as a fundamentally repressive and inhibitory feature of much of contemporary urban life. Place here functions as a closed terrain of social control that becomes extremely hard to break (or break out of) once it achieves its particular permanence. And there are interests involved in building and maintaining such places. In the United States, for example, several isolated ethnic communities (lacking language access to the rest of society, legal status, civil integration, and civil rights) provide docile bodies for the innumerable sweatshops run by the same ethnically distinct capitalist class. Community solidarities promoted by that class, strongly supported by ideologies of ethnic and religious solidarity, are an assured vehicle for capital accumulation founded on some of the worst forms of exploitation. This is, for example, the import of several recent accounts of sweatshops run on indentured or effectively imprisoned labor in New York and Los Angeles [see Lii (1995) and Kwong's (1987) intimate study of how labor exploitation is organized through promotion of ethnic solidarities in New York's Chinatown].

The effect of this is to create dualism within the communitarian argument. On the one hand, repressions and social control produce docile bodies in closed places open to all manner of exploitation and at the other extreme the mobilization of communitarian powers can be the basis of a revolutionary militant particularism that can shake the world. Young's idealist solution to these opposing tendencies is to replace the ideal of face-to-face community with an "unoppressive city" defined as "openness to unassimilated otherness." While this term is naively specified in relation to the actual dynamics of urbanization, the direction to which it points – the celebration of difference and diversity with some overarching unity – is of interest. It seeks to build upon those positive experiences of city life in which differences of all sorts are embodied, negotiated, and tolerated. It presupposes, in effect, the possibility of somehow bridging the Marxian and Heideggerian conceptions within a new kind of radical politics. What that bridge might look like will be taken up later.

The communitarian emphasis upon common discourses and implicit practices has the virtue of demonstrating that communities and places cannot be distinguished in the realms of discourse "by their falsity/genuineness, but [only] by the style in which they are imagined" (Anderson, 1983). This conclusion is fundamentally at odds with the idea of some easily definable distinction between "authentic" and "inauthentic" communities or places. If Marx (1967: 177–8) is right and imagination and representation always precede production, then Heidegger's view (like those of Sandel, Bookchin, Prince Charles, Etzioni, or whoever) becomes just one possible imagined kind of place awaiting a material embodiment. Heidegger may have invoked a long deep past and the seemingly deep permanence of a pristine language, but he also recognized that it was impossible to go back to a world made up of Black Forest farmsteads and that it was necessary to press forward, in ways which national socialism then seemed to promise, to construct a new kind of "authentic" community appropriate to that time and place. Yet it is, paradoxically, the very conditions against which Heidegger revolts that permit the search for an imagined authentic community to become a political possibility, thus opening up the definition of "the authentic" to social construction as a manifestation of power relations and social struggle.

IX. Heidegger Contra Marx: Splitting Differences

Norberg-Schulz (1980: 168) argues that Marxism fails in its refusal to deal with the mythic qualities of places. Marxism, he says, "does not arrive at a full understanding of 'dwelling', and fails in its attempt" to recover from that human alienation which arises from "man's loss of identification with the natural and man-made things which constitute his environment." Since this loss is also "at the root of our actual loss of place," it follows that the insensitivity of Marxism to the diverse qualities of place and the rich range of meanings that can be derived therefrom (including intimate relations with the environment) is one of its most serious political liabilities. There are clear differences, therefore, between the Marxian and Heideggerian traditions with respect to the understanding of place. But are the differences so irreconcilable in principle? Or is there a certain unity within the difference?

For Marx, analysis of the world of material social practices, of money circulation and commodity production, and exchange defines a spatio-temporal world of intricate social relations and universal valuations, within which places necessarily have their being as constitutive elements within the historical geography of capital accumulation. But this spatio-temporal world also defines an equally universal sphere of moral, economic, and political responsibility for our "species being" which, though characterized by alienation and exploitation, has to be rescued by a global political–economic strategy of class struggle. This does not imply that the experiential world which lies immediately at hand is irrelevant. But what we learn from sensuous interaction with the things we touch and the processes we directly encounter is different from what we need to know to understand the processes of commodity production and exchange that put our global breakfast upon our individual tables. This was the distinction that Marx sought to capture in his thesis on "the fetishism of commodities." What we immediately experience is, he argues, not adequate to understand the political–economic realities of our world. But it is precisely Marx's point that immediate experience is *so* authentic as to permanently tempt us to regard it as all there is and so ground our sense of being, of moral responsibility, and of political commitments entirely within its myopic frame. Marx seeks to go beyond and try, as he puts it in his early work, to construct a sense of "species being" by a politics in which individuals realize their full individuality only through free association with others across the surface of the earth. This is notoriously vague and uncertain rhetoric, but it suggests that we cannot go back, that we cannot reject the world of sociability which has been achieved by the interlinking of all peoples and places into a global economy, and that we should somehow build upon this achievement and seek to transform it in socially constructive ways. The network of places constructed through the logic of capitalist development, for example, has to be transformed and used for progressive purposes rather than rejected or destroyed. But place construction is now complicitous (directly or indirectly) with the universalisms of money, commodity, capital, and exchange without in any way challenging the alienation. The instanciation of social relations through specific forms of environmental transformation here comes into play to make the production of place a moment in the consolidation of a capitalist-inspired regime of social relations, institutions and political–economic practices.

Unfortunately, internationalist working-class politics often abstracted from the material world of experience in particular places. It lost some of its credibility and appeal because the promotion of universal considerations drove out sensitivity to the particularities of environment, milieu, collective memory, community, myth, built forms. While it is one thing to articulate a critical line against a politics based only on all of these, it is quite another – as Raymond Williams so effectively argued – to fashion a politics that treats the politics of place as nothing more than a numbing fantasy.

Heidegger, at the other extreme, totally rejects any sense of moral responsibility beyond the world of immediate sensuous and contemplative experience. He rejects any dealings with the world of commodity, money, technology, and production via any international division of labor. He contracts his field of vision to a much narrower experiential world to ask questions about the innate and immanent qualities of experience of things. He insists upon the irreducibility of the experience of dwelling and specificities of place and environment. In so doing he denies the relevance of those processes that put breakfast on his table and evokes the loss of authentic community, of roots and of dwelling in modern life. The former is a gross act of denial but the latter strikes a potent chord with many people. "If," says Relph (1976: 96), "places are indeed a fundamental aspect of man's existence in the world, if they are sources of security and identity for individuals and for groups of people, then it is important that the means of experiencing, creating and maintaining significant places are not lost."

The problem is that such sentiments easily lend themselves to an interpretation and a politics that is both exclusionary and parochialist, contemplative rather than activist, communitarian if not intensely nationalist (hence Heidegger's respect for Nazism). Heidegger refuses to see mediated social relationships (via the market or any other medium) with others (things or people) as in any way expressive of any kind of authenticity. Indeed, mediated relationships of this sort are felt as threatening to identity and any true sense of self, while anything which contributes to or smacks of rootlessness is rejected outright (does this explain his antagonism to the historical diaspora and rootlessness of the Jews?). Experience, furthermore, becomes incommunicable beyond certain bounds because authentic art and genuine esthetic sense can spring only out of strong rootedness in place. This, as we saw, was the case with the Western Apache (see above). This exclusionary vision becomes even more emphatic, however, given his views on the power of language over social life. Places become the sites of incommunicable othernesses. There can be no interlinkage in the world of esthetics or of communicable meanings of the sort that modernism often sought, even in a context of strong interlinkage in the material world of production and exchange. From this standpoint, it is not hard to see how Heidegger figures so often in postmodern thinking as a precursor of ideas concerning the creation of "interpretive communities," fragmented language games, and the like. And it is not hard to see how the crass and commercial side of postmodernism could play upon these sentiments and market the vernacular, simulate the authentic and invent heritage, tradition, and even commercialized roots. Yet, oddly, there persists another commonality with Marx. Heidegger persists in seeing authentic communities as materially and physically rooted in particular places through dwelling, rather than as being constructed solely, as so frequently happens in postmodernist rhetoric, in the realms of discourse. Heidegger is, in the first analysis, just as committed to the vital moment of *production* as a privileged moment of sensual engagement with the world as is Marx.

But if I am correct, and modernism (as it is now generally interpreted) and postmodernism are dialectically organized oppositions within the long history of modernity (Harvey, 1989a: 339), then we should start to think of these arguments not as mutually exclusive but as oppositions which contain the other. For Marx the potential repressions, misconceptions, and exploitation are emphasized as an outcome of a purely place-based politics in a spatially dynamic capitalist world. For Heidegger, the phenomenological realism of a place-based experience of dwelling is the only respite from that world. Marx regards experience *within* the fetishism as authentic enough but surficial and misleading, while Heidegger views that same world of commodity exchange and technological rationality as at the root of an inauthenticity in daily life which has to be repudiated. This common definition of the root of the problem (though specified as peculiarly capitalist by Marx and modernist – i.e., both capitalist and socialist – by Heidegger) provides a common base from which to reconstruct a better understanding of place. What happens, then, when we see the differences as dialectical oppositions?

The simple answer, is that we live in a world of universal tension between sensuous and interpersonal social relations (including those of domination and repression) in place (with intense awareness of the environmental qualities of that place) and another dimension of awareness in which we more or less recognize the material and social connection between us and the millions of other people who have, for example, a direct and indirect role in putting our breakfast on the table. Put more formally, what goes on in a place cannot be understood outside of the space relations which support that place any more than the space relations can be understood independently of what goes on in particular places. This is, in any case, exactly what the abstract theory of place outlined at the beginning of this chapter tells us. While that may sound banal or trivially true, the manner of its conception has major ramifications for political thinking and practice.

X. The Construction of Places Through Socio-spatial Practices

Places are constructed and experienced as material ecological artefacts and intricate networks of social relations. They are the focus of the imaginary, of beliefs, longings, and desires (most particularly with respect to the psychological pull and push of the idea of "home"). They are an intense focus of discursive activity, filled with symbolic and representational meanings, and they are a distinctive product of institutionalized social and political–economic power. The dialectical interplay across these different moments of the social process (see figure 4.1) is intricate and confusing. But it is precisely the way in which all of these moments are caught up in the common flow of the social process that in the end determines the conflictual (and oftentimes internally contradictory) processes of place construction, sustenance, and deconstruction. This may all seem rather daunting, but it is the only way to attack the rich complexity of social processes of place construction in a coherent way. Let me illustrate.

Times Square in New York city was built up as a pure piece of real-estate and business speculation around the creation of a new entertainment district in the 1890s. In the early 1900s the name was pushed through by the *New York Times* which had just relocated in the Square (after all, the *New York Herald*, its big rival, was located in Herald Square further downtown). The *Times* organized the grand new year's eve celebration of fireworks and, ultimately, the celebratory lowering of the ball, as a promotional gimmick. Thousands came not only on that day but throughout the year to sample the entertainments, watch people, eat out, survey the latest fashions, and pick up gossip or information on anything from business and real-estate deals to latest trends in entertainment, fashion, and the private lives of eminent people. And the Square soon became the center of an advertising spectacle which in itself drew in the crowds. Times Square was, in short, created as a representation of everything that could be commercial, gaudy, promotional, and speculative in the political–economy of place construction. It was a far cry from that "authentic" dwelling in the Black Forest and on the surface at least it ought surely to qualify as the most ersatz, or as cultural critics might prefer to call it, "pseudo-place" or "nonplace" on earth. Yet it soon became the symbolic heart of New York city and, until its decline (largely under the impact of television) from the 1950s onwards, was the focus of a sense of togetherness and community for many New Yorkers and even, for a while, for many Americans. Times Square became *the* symbolic place where everyone congregated to celebrate, mourn, or express their collective anger, joy, or fear. Produced and dominated in the mode of political economy it was appropriated by the populace in an entirely different fashion. It became an authentic place of representation with a distinctive hold on the imagination, even though as a space of material social practices it had all the character of a purely speculative and commodified spectacle. How could this happen?

Times Square rose to prominence as the modern metropolitan New York of five boroughs and sprawling suburbs began to take shape. Its rise coincided with an extraordinary boom in real-estate speculation, the coming of mass-transit systems which changed the whole nature of space-relations between people within the city (the subway came to Times Square in 1901), the maturing of new systems of international and national communication (the radio in particular), of information and money flow, of commercialism and the marketing of fashion and entertainment as mass consumption goods. This was a phase of rapid "time–space compression" as Kern (1983) records and even many New Yorkers seemed to lose their sense of identity. The stresses of rapid urban growth kept New Yorkers "on the run," perpetually undermining the fragile immigrant and neighborhood institutions which from time to time gave some sense of security and permanence in the midst of rapid change. What seems to have been so special about Times Square in its halcyon days was that it was a public space in which all classes of society could intermingle and as a classless (or rather a multiclass, multiethnic and even multiracial) place it held out the possibility to be the focus of a sense of community which recognized difference but which also celebrated unity. The *demi-monde* rubbed shoulders with the aristocracy, immigrants of all sorts could share the spectacle and the democracy of money appeared to be in charge. But community in this instance was not shaped by face-to-face interaction. It was achieved by the act of a common presence in the face of the spectacle, a spectacle which was shamelessly about the community of money and the commodification of everything. New York's Times Square certainly represented the community of money but it also became a representation of a quite different notion of community in the minds and affections of millions of New Yorkers who, to this day, continue to contest plans to transform and redevelop this particular public space precisely because of its unique symbolic meaning and place in the collective memory. It is, perhaps, rather too sadly symbolic to note that the rebirth of Times Square is to be led by its Disneyfication.

This same sort of story can be told, from an exactly opposite direction. The search for authentic community, and in particular a form of community which is expressive of values outside of those typically found in a capitalist materialist and highly monetized culture, has frequently led into direct attempts at community and place construction according to alternative visions. Yet all of them that have survived (and that is a very small proportion) have almost without exception done so by an accommodation to the power of money, to commodification and capital accumulation and to modern technologies. The survivors have also exhibited a capacity to insert and reinsert themselves into changing space relations. This is as true for such massive upheavals as the fundamentalist Islamic revolution in Iran (which is now walking the tightrope of how to reinsert itself into the world capitalist economy without appearing too overtly to accommodate to satan) as it was for the innumerable communitarian movements which hived off from capitalism only in many instances to become the cutting edge of further capitalist development – such as the French Icarians that settled in the United States (see Johnson, 1974), the extraordinary wave of communalism and place building (including the Mormons, the shakers, the early feminists) that had its origins in western New York state in the first half of the nineteenth century, the anarchist and syndicalist movements which spawned dispersed settlements as far apart as Patagonia and Siberia and which even inspired the new towns movement of Geddes and Ebenezer Howard (echoes of which can be found even in Guilford). The whole history of place building suggests that a cultural politics has just as frequently been at the root of the inspiration of place construction as simple desire for profit and speculative gain. Yet the intertwining of the two is omnipresent and in some instances the cultural politics seems more like a means to a political–economic end than an end in itself.

Fitzgerald (1986) in *Cities on a Hill*, provides a fascinating picture of precisely this intersection in the context of the United States. The studies of the gay community's appropriation and subsequent domination of the Castro district of San Francisco, of Jerry Falwell's religious empire in Lynchburg and of Sun City, a retirement community in Florida, all illustrate the cultural politics of capital accumulation in different ways. By far the oddest of Fitzgerald's studies is, however, that of Rajneeshpuram. Founded in 1981 in a sparsely populated and semi-arid ranching area of Oregon as a "self-sufficient" commune of the disciples of Bhagwan Shree Rajneesh, it had all the trappings of a "New Age" community from the standpoint of lifestyle, but yet it also was characterized by powerful use of money, high technology, and a worldwide internationalism founded on the network of disciples that Rajneesh had cultivated over the years. The ranch cost $1.5 million and within two years the Rajneeshis had spent more than $60 million in Oregon, by Fitzgerald's account, and had gone a long way to building a whole new settlement replete with airstrip, large reservoir, power station, irrigated fields, housing, and a whole range of facilities which could support more than 3,000 people permanently and offer temporary accommodation for many thousands more. Rajneesh looked down upon Ghandi and Mother Teresa because of their interest in the poor. Money became the means to the good life. "Religion is a luxury of the rich" he argued and had 21 Rolls-Royces to prove it. Yet the commune demanded at least 12 hours hard labor a day from its residents and pulled together some highly educated and often technically talented people who set to work in an overt atmosphere of nonhierarchical social relations and with seeming joy and relish to create a place within which the human potential for personal growth might be realizable. The exclusionary politics of the commune were, however, very strong. Internally it was represented and imagined as an island of virtue and authenticity in a sea of spiritual and material decay. Outsiders saw it as a cancerous foreign body inserted into the heart of rural United States. The dissolution of the commune, the deportation of Rajneesh, and the arrest of some of the leading luminaries who, within a few years had turned the commune from a mecca of personal liberation and human growth into an armed camp (engaging in all kinds of violent acts such as poisoning various officials, the introduction of salmonella into a neighboring community's water supply), detracted little, according to Fitzgerald, from the intense feelings of affection that many who had passed through the commune felt for it. It had provided a place, a home, however temporary, and a range of personal experiences for which people felt grateful. It had met a need, fulfilled desires, allowed fantasies to be lived out in ways that were unforgettable. Yet it had also exhibited all of the intolerance of internal difference, all the subtle hierarchy and exclusionary politics which Young correctly fears is the inevitable end-product of communitarian politics. And for the brief moment of its success, it had all the attributes of a low-wage work camp sustained out of moral fervor and delivering Rolls-Royces by the score to the guru of the establishment. This was not the first, nor will it be the last time that a cultural politics striving to produce an authenticity of place and of social identity was to be coopted and used for narrow financial gain.

The lesson is simple enough. Everyone who moves to establish difference in the contemporary world has to do so through social practices that engage with the mediating power of money. The latter is, after all, global and universal social power that can be appropriated by individual persons (hence it grounds bourgeois individualism as well as a host of collective movements) and any "interpretive" or "political" community which seeks to forge a distinctive identity in place has to accommodate to it. Indeed, in many instances (such as those that Fitzgerald investigated) possession of sufficient money power is a necessary condition for exploring difference through place construction. Rajneesh's comment that "religion is a luxury of the rich" is in this regard rather too close for comfort. It is, in short, precisely the universality and sociality of money power that allows all kinds of othernesses to take on an independent existence and to survive. There is nothing in itself particularly wrong with that (if we have the resources why not be as eclectic as Jencks or Lyotard suggest we should). But it does force us to consider the relation between the production of difference and otherness in the contemporary world and the organization and distribution of political–economic power. The examples illustrate how cultural politics in general (and the search for affective community in particular) and political–economic power intertwine in the social processes of place construction. It is impossible to examine one without the other.

XI. Place and Power

To write of "the power of place," as if places (localities, regions, neighborhoods, states, etc.) possess causal powers is to engage in the grossest of fetishisms; unless, that is, we confine ourselves rigorously to the definition of place as a social process. In the latter case, the questions to be posed can be rendered more explicit: why, by what means, and in what sense do social beings individually and, more importantly, collectively invest places (localities, regions, states, communities, or whatever) with sufficient permanence to become a locus of institutionalized social power and how and for what purposes is that power then used?

The production and reproduction of power differentiations is central to the operations of any economy. Within capitalism there is not only that great divide between the proletariat (reified as "human resources" as if they are more or less substitutable by oil or firewood) and the capitalist class, but there are also the multiple and more nuanced hierarchical divisions which inevitably arise within the detail, social, and territorial divisions of labor (between, for example, line workers, overseers, managers, service workers, designers, etc.) as well as those that factionalize the bourgeoisie (different interests in finance, land, production, merchanting, administration, law, science, and military and police powers). Differences that may have preceded the capitalist order – of race, language, gender, ethnicity, religion, and pre-capitalist forms of social class – have been absorbed, transformed, and reconstructed by a social system that seeks to assure the accumulation of capital through the domination of nature, the exploitation of wage labor, and a sophisticated system of ideological and social controls and state regulation. For example, the bourgeois tactic of depicting some segment of humanity (women or "the natives") as a part of nature, the repository of affectivity and therefore disposed to be chaotic, "irrational," and unruly, allowed those segments to be subsumed as elements requiring domination within the general capitalistic project. The effect has been to transform gender and racial oppressions (as well as resistances) into forms not hitherto experienced (Goldberg's study of *Racist Culture* is a case in point). Furthermore, the revolutionary dynamic of capitalism ensures that such transformations are not once and for all events, but continuous and often contradictory movements within the historical geography of capitalist development.

While *apartheid* may make sense for a while it is not hard to see how corporate capitalism might turn against it at a certain stage of development. Explicit struggle on the part of the oppressed or active engagement in the politics of place construction by otherwise disempowered social groups has played a role in that development. The long history of decolonization and struggles for national self-liberation have dominated the international stage but these struggles have many local manifestations as do the attempts by racially marked minorities and women (see Hayden, 1981) to construct alternative kinds of places for living and working.

In all of these instances, the construction of a secure place has been a funda-mental moment in the struggle to acquire or resist political power. Anderson's (1983) account of the transformation of linguistic diversity through "print capitalism" into the "imagined communities" of nations that ground the modern state, is a useful example. But there is another way to put this. Those who live in any place (be it Guilford or Guatemala), who have pretensions to create an institutionalized locus of social and political power, have to find or invent an imaginary sufficient to achieve some level of social cohesion, solidarity, and institutionalized order. There are many places in the world (think of many of the African states) that were arbitrarily carved out (by colonizing powers) as loci of political and social power but where the imagined community to support the entity has yet to be properly forged. We have therefore to interpret the changing meaning of the production of place amongst all realms of the social order across all moments of the social process. We need to understand not merely how places acquire material qualities (as constellations of productive forces open to capitalistic use or as bundles of use values available to sustain particular cultural ways and qualities of life). The evaluation and hierarchical ranking of places occurs, for example, largely through activities of discourse and representation that connect to deeply held beliefs, values, and desires. Popular understandings of places are organized through the elaboration of often heterogeneous mental maps of the world each of which can be invested with all manner of personal or collective hopes and fears. The wrong side of the tracks and skid row are hardly parallel places in our mind to the gold coasts of Miami Beach. Psychoanalytic theory teaches that the field of representation is not necessarily all that it seems: that there are all manner of (mis)-representations to which places are prone. If individual identity is constituted by fantasy, then can the identity human beings give to places be far behind?

Representations of places have material consequences in so far as fantasies, desires, fears, and longings are expressed in actual behavior. Evaluative schemata of places, for example, become grist for all sorts of policy-makers' mills. Places in the city get red-lined for mortgage finance, the people who live in them get written off as worthless, in the same way that much of Africa gets depicted as a basket-case. The material activities of place construction may then fulfill the prophecies of degradation and dereliction. Similarly, places in the city are dubbed as "dubious" or "dangerous" again leading to patterns of behavior, both public and private, that turn fantasy into reality. Other places are depicted as "authentic" and "beautiful," testimonies to the power of human beings to shape permanences out of environments in such a way as to instanciate powerful cultural and moral meanings in the world around them. The political–economic and symbolic possibilities of place (re)construction are, in short, highly colored by the evaluative manner of place representation.

Discursive struggles over representation are, as a consequence, as fiercely fought and just as fundamental to the activities of place construction as bricks and mortar. And there is much that is negative as well as positive here. The denigration of others' places provides a way to assert the viability and incipient power of one's own. The fierce contest over images and counter-images of places is an arena of action in which the cultural politics of places, the political–economy of their development and the accumulation of a sense of social power in place frequently fuse in indistinguishable ways.

By the same token, the creation of symbolic places is not given in the stars but painstakingly nurtured and fought over precisely because of the hold that place can have over the imaginary. The survival of religion as a major institution within secular societies has been in part won through the successful creation, protection, and nurturing of symbolic places. But imaginations are not easily manipulated or tamed to specific political–economic purposes. People can and do define monuments in ways that relate to their own experience and tradition (as Rossi insists). The places where martyrs fell (like the Mur-des-Fédérées in Père Lachaise cemetery) have long gripped the imagination of working-class movements. If places are the locus of collective memory, then social identity and the capacity to mobilize that identity into configurations of political solidarity are highly dependent upon processes of place construction and sustenance. Yet no amount of formal monument construction (the extraordinary monumental palace that Ceauşecu had constructed in Bucharest, for example) can make a hated dictator beloved.

Materiality, representation, and imagination are not separate worlds. There can be no particular privileging of any one realm over the other, even if it is only in the social practices of daily life that the ultimate significance of all forms of activity is registered (cf. above, chapter 4). Political mobilization through processes of place construction owes as much to the representational and symbolic realms as to material activities (Lefebvre, 1991). But disjunctions and contradictions frequently occur between the different moments of place construction. Loyalty to place can have a powerful political meaning even when the daily practices of people in that place show little commonality or even outright political contradiction. Though the forces that came together to create the uprising of the Paris Commune in 1871, for example, were extraordinarily heterogeneous, they were all bound together by a common loyalty to the place they called Paris and all agreed that the liberation of Paris was a crucial aim.

Less dramatically, the fact that a category like "New Yorkers" can make sense to the polyglot millions who occupy that place testifies precisely to the political power that can be mobilized and exercised through activities of place construction in the mind as well as on the ground.

There is, then, a politics to place construction ranging dialectically across material, representational, and symbolic activities which find their hallmark in the way in which individuals invest in places and thereby empower themselves collectively by virtue of that investment. The investment can be of blood, sweat, tears, and labor (the kind of building of affection through working to build the tangible product of place). Or it can be the discursive construction of affective loyalties through preservation of particular imageries of place, of environment, and of vernacular traditions, or through new works of art and architecture to celebrate and become symbolic of some special place.

It is dangerous to romanticize this process. Places constructed in the imagery of homogeneity of beliefs, values, ideals, and persuasions coupled with a strong sense of collective memory and spatially exclusionary rights can be extraordinarily powerful players upon the world stage. The effect is to convert the dialectic of community solidarity and repression into a quagmire of violence and oppression. And if, as is so often argued, a place divided against itself will fall, then the maintenance of that permanence that grounds politics becomes an end in itself, however self-destructive the ultimate outcome might be. And self-destructive it surely must be, for, as Eric Wolf (1982: 17) so cogently puts it, all attempts to construct places and build imagined communities must "take cognizance of processes that transcend separable cases, moving through and beyond them and transforming them as they proceed."

The production of places of difference continues in a world in which the process of "accumulation for accumulation's sake" continues unabated, no matter what the political, social, or ecological consequences. While the decentralization of political power to places proceeds a-pace (and even more massive decentralizations are threatened by innumerable autonomy movements), there is a powerful simultaneous movement towards reconcentrations of economic and discursive power particularly in multinational corporations, financial institutions, and the media. The exercise of this latter power has meant the destruction, invasion, and restructuring of socially constituted places on an unprecedented scale. The viability of actual places (like Cowley or even whole nation states) has been powerfully threatened through changing material practices of production, consumption, information flow, and communication coupled with the radical reorganization of space relations and of time horizons within capitalist development. The contemporary necessity for place reconstruction has created dilemmas for spatial practices as well as for the way places get represented and become representations. It is in such a context that the febrile attempt to reconstruct places in terms of imagined communities, replete, even, with the building of places of representation (the new monumentalities of spectacle and consumerism, for example) or the forging of imagined communities as a defense against the new material and social practices of capitalist accumulation becomes more readily understandable. But the building of exclusionary walls (such as those proposed for Guilford) implicit in the new communitarian politics, although it may intervene in relations of production, consumption, exchange, and repro-duction, is always porous with respect to the universalizing power of money. At the same time as places are made more and more exclusionary so they become less and less capable of developing a collective capacity to even influence let alone control money flow and capital accumulation.

This condition has profound political implications. Anti-capitalist movements, as I have argued elsewhere (Harvey, 1989a) are generally better at organizing in and dominating "their" places than at commanding space. The "otherness" and "regional resistances" that postmodernist politics emphasize can indeed flourish in a multitude of particular places. But while such movements form a potential basis for that "militant particularism" that can acquire global ambitions, left to themselves they are easily dominated by the power of capital to coordinate accumulation across universal but fragmented space. The potentiality for militant particularism embedded in place runs the risk of sliding back into a parochialist politics. We need always to confront, as Buell (1995: 261) remarks, the "delicate issue of how the sense of place can be kept alert and sensitive rather than left to lapse into dogmatic slumber in some cozy ethnocentric alcove." Place-bound particularisms, it should be acknowledged, do not necessarily give rise to militant politics. They can just as easily be the locus of political passivity or of collaboration and complicity with a dominant social order.

This was, recall, the central problem that Raymond Williams wrestled with for much of his political life. Says one of the characters in *The Fight for Manod* (1979b: 181)

> The whole of public policy ... is an attempt to reconstitute a culture, a social system, an economic order, that have in fact reached their end, reached their limits of viability. And then I sit here and look at this double inevitability: that this imperial, exporting and divided order is ending, and that all its residual social forces, all its political formations, will fight to the end to reconstruct it, to re-establish it, moving deeper all the time through crisis after crisis in an impossible attempt to regain a familiar world. So then a double inevitability: that they will fail, and that they will try nothing else.

Is there, then, no way to break out of that inevitability?

XII. Conclusion

Places, like space and time, are social constructs and have to be read and understood as such. There are ways to provide a materialist history of this literal and metaphorical geography of the human condition and to do it so as to shed light on the production of historical–geographical difference. An understanding of that process makes it possible to ground a critique of both the chimerical ideals of an isolationist communitarian politics and the inevitable insensitivities of any kind of universal emancipatory politics.

The political–economic possibilities of place (re)construction are highly colored by the evaluative manner of place representation. One of the most powerful strands of independent politics within what Daniel Bell (1976: 20) calls "the cultural mass" ("those working in higher education, publishing, magazines, broadcast media, theater, and museums, who process and influence the reception of serious cultural products"), for example, is to focus rather strongly on the meaning and qualities of community, nation, and place. The shaping of place identity and local tradition is very much within the purview of such workers (from the writers of novels and makers of movies to the writers of tourist brochures) and there are strong institutional forms which that shaping takes (everything from universities which keep local languages and the sense of local history alive to museums, cultural events, and the like). As the cultural mass has dropped any strong association with proletarian movements and sought to avoid a directly subservient position to capitalist culture it has become more closely identified with a cultural politics of place. Hence the outpouring of books on precisely that topic over the past 20 years (see, for example, recent works by Agnew and Duncan, 1989; Davis et al., 1990; Lilburne, 1989; Pred, 1990; Probyn, 1990; Tindall, 1991) and the rise of a whole set of supportive political activities within the cultural mass for place-bound cultural movements. The more the cultural mass explores its own interior values, the more it tends to align itself with a political–economy and cultural politics of place even though it is fundamentally subservient as a paid agent for the globalizing culture of capital accumulation. The effect is to produce a contradiction that can only partly be resolved by the selling of geographically embedded and place-specific difference as a commodity for international tourism. Deeper contradictions arise when institutional arrangements like GATT, NAFTA, and the European Union, designed to facilitate capital accumulation, spark their own regional resistances even in the very heart of capitalism. Political parties split and curious concordances of interest arise between, say, the left of the British Labour Party and Le Pen's fascist movement in France.

The reawakening of place-bound politics clearly has its ugly side. The stereotyping of other places is one of the more viscious forms of bloodletting within the media (one only has to read a London tabloid newspaper like *The Sun*'s descriptions of the French to get the point). Defining the "other" in an exclusionary and stereotypical way is the first step towards self-definition. The rediscovery of place, as the case of Heidegger shows, poses as many dangers as opportunities for the construction of any kind of progressive politics. Deconstruction and the postmodern impulse, as Said (1978) demonstrates in his study of *Orientalism*, certainly provide a means to attack the appalling stereotyping of other places, but there is a huge problem of public perspectives, representation, and politics within the overall work of the cultural mass in this regard that desperately needs to be confronted.

The politics of place and of turf, of local identity and nation, of regions and cities, has long been with us. It has also been of great importance within the uneven geographical development of capitalism. The rediscovery of place as an object of discourse within the rhetoric of the cultural mass and, through that, within the rhetoric of politics is what is here significant rather than the fact that the world has changed in some way to make the political–economy or cultural politics of place more important now than in the past. Yet there is indeed a sense in which the latter proposition is also true. In the face of a fierce bout of time–space compression and of all the restructurings to which we have been exposed these last few years, the security of places has been threatened and the map of the world rejigged as part of a desperate speculative gamble to keep the accumulation of capital on track. Such loss of security promotes a search for alternatives, one of which lies in the creation of both imagined and tangible communities in place. The issue of how to create what sort of place becomes imperative for economic as well as political survival. Talk to the mayors of Baltimore, Sheffield, and Lille and you will find that is exactly what they have been preoccupied with these last few years. And it is here, too, that the politics of the cultural mass can take on considerable importance. For if, as Marx insisted, we get at the end of every labor process a result which is the product of our imaginations at the beginning, then how we imagine communities and places of the future and how we talk about them becomes part of the jigsaw of what our future can be. Rajneesh existed in someone's imagination and captured the imaginations of many of those caught up in the human potential movement who worked so hard to make it the temporary place it was. And even if, as in this case, there is many a slip between imagination and realization and a whole host of unintended consequences to be countered and discounted on the path, the question of how we imagine the future of places and with what seriousness we invest in it is always on the agenda.

Our future places are for us to make. But we cannot make them without inscribing our struggles in space, place and environment in multiple ways. That process is on-going and every single one of us has agency with respect to it. The places – material, representational, and symbolic – handed down to us by former generations were also built up through social struggles and strivings to create material, symbolic, and imaginary places to fit their own particular and contested aspirations. A better appreciation of such processes – of the social and political dialectics of space, place, and environment – has much to teach us about how to construct alternative futures. A renewed capacity to reread the production of historical–geographical difference is a crucial preliminary step towards emancipating the possibilities for future place construction. And liberating places – materially, symbolically, and metaphorically – is an inevitable part of any progressive socio-ecological politics.

PART IV

Justice, Difference, and Politics

Part IV Prologue

The struggle for emancipation and self-realization, for personal liberty, freedom, and justice coupled with socio-political struggles to emancipate spaces and to free up time, to liberate places (most paradigmatically in struggles for national self-liberation), and even, in the rhetoric of an ecological group like Earth First, to emancipate nature from the oppressive qualities of human control, have all played a critical role in the evolution of human historical geography most particularly since the movement of the Enlightenment crystallized so many human emotions and desires around those beliefs and discursive themes. Our historical geography is, as Eagleton (1990: 363) puts it, "awash with the desire for justice and well-being, clamoring for judgement day." But what is this quality called justice? And how many past attempts to create a just society have crumbled into tyranny or dissolved into violence, corruption, and injustice? Is it possible ever to talk about justice as anything other than a contested effect of power within a particular place at a given time?

Consider the following excerpt from Tony Hillerman's novel *Sacred Clowns* (1993) set in Navajo country. Says the tribal policeman Chee:

"We're dealing with justice. Just retribution. That's a religious concept, really. We'll say the tribal cop is sort of religious. He honors his people's traditional ways. He has been taught another notion of justice. He was a big boy before he heard about 'make the punishment fit the crime' or 'an eye for an eye, a tooth for a tooth.' Instead of that he was hearing of retribution in another way. If you damage somebody you sit down with their family and figure out how much damage and make it good. That way you restore *hozho*. You've got harmony again between the two families. Not too much difference from the standard American justice. But now it gets different. If somebody harms you out of meanness ... then he's the one who's out of *hozho*. You aren't taught he should be punished. He should be cured. Gotten back in balance with what's around him. Made beautiful again ... on the inside, of course. Back in harmony. So this hypothetical cop, that's the way he's been raised. Not to put value on punishment, but to put a lot of value on curing. So now what are you going to do if you're this cop?" ...

"It's hard to apply normal city-street law-school solutions when you are looking at this," Janet said.

"Maybe the landscape is part of the answer," Chee said. "Maybe it makes the answer a little different."

The landscape (cf. chapter 10) functions as a mnemonic, alive with particular meanings, upon which native-Americans typically hang their sense of collective identity and values; and in this case it speaks for a certain notion of justice that has its own distinctive qualities, integrities, and meanings. Two quite different notions of justice and retribution clash. Does this mean that there can never be a unitary notion of justice to which we can appeal?

The historical–geographical evidence suggests an unequivocal answer to that question. Like space, time, and nature, "justice" is a socially constituted set of beliefs, discourses, and institutionalizations expressive of social relations and contested configurations of power that have everything to do with regulating and ordering material social practices within places for a time. Once constituted, the trace of a particular discursive conception of justice across all moments of the social process becomes an objective fact that embraces everyone within its compass. Once instutionalized, a system of justice becomes a "permanence" with which all facets of the social process have to contend.

To argue for a particular definition of social justice has always implied, however, appeal to some higher order criteria to define which theory of social justice is more just than another (this is Chee's question). An infinite regress of argument then looms as does, in the other direction, the relative ease of deconstruction of any notion of social justice as meaning whatever individuals or groups, given their multiple identities and functions, at some particular moment find it pragmatically, instrumentally, emotionally, politically, or ideologically useful to mean.

There are two ways to go with the argument. The first is to look at how the multiple concepts of justice are embedded in language and this leads to theories of meaning of the sort that Wittgenstein advanced:

> How many kinds of sentence are there? ... There are *countless* kinds: countless different kinds of use to what we call "symbols", "words", "sentences". And this multiplicity is not something fixed, given once and for all: but new types of language, new language games, as we may say, come into existence and others become obsolete and get forgotten. ... Here the term "language-*game*" is meant to bring into prominence the fact that the *speaking* of language is part of an activity, or a form of life. ... How did we *learn* the meaning of this word ("good" for instance)? From what sort of examples? In what language games? Then it will be easier for us to see that the word must have a family of meanings.

From this perspective, social justice has no universal agreed upon meaning but a "family" of meanings which can be understood only through the way each is embedded in a particular language game. But note two things about Wittgenstein's formulation. First, the appeal to a "family" of meanings suggests some kind of interrelatedness and we should presumably pay attention to what those relations might be. Secondly, each language game attaches to the particular social, communicative, experiential, and perceptual world of the speaker. The upshot is to bring us to a point of cultural, linguistic or discourse relativism, albeit based upon the material circumstances of the subject. We should also, then, pay careful attention to those material circumstances.

The second path is to admit the relativism of discourses about justice, but to insist that discourses are expressions of social power and that the "family" of meanings derives its interrelatedness from the power relations pertaining within and between different social formations. The simplest version of this idea is to interpret social justice as embedded in the hegemonic discourses of any ruling class or ruling faction. This is an idea which goes back to Plato who, in the *Republic* (1965) has Thrasymachus argue that:

> Each ruling class makes laws that are in its own interest, a democracy democratic laws, a tyranny tyrannical ones and so on; and in making these laws they define as "right" for their subjects what is in the interest of themselves, the rulers, and if anyone breaks their laws he is punished as a "wrong-doer". That is what I mean when I say that "right" is the same in all states, namely the interest of the established ruling class. ...

Plato advanced the argument in order to refute it, but Marx and Engels, not taken with Plato's idealism, resurrected it as having deep historical force. Engels, for example, wrote:

> The stick used to measure what is right and what is not is the most abstract expression of right itself, namely *justice*. ... The development of right for the jurists ... is nothing more than a striving to bring human conditions, so far as they are expressed in legal terms, ever closer to the ideal of justice, *eternal* justice. And always this justice is but the ideologized, glorified expression of the existing economic relations, now from their conservative and now from the revolutionary angle. The justice of the Greeks and Romans held slavery to be just; the justice of the bourgeois of 1789 demanded the abolition of feudalism on the ground it was unjust. The conception of eternal justice, therefore, varies not only with time and place, but also with the persons concerned. ... While in everyday life ... expressions like right, wrong, justice, and sense of right are accepted without misunderstanding even with reference to social matters, they create ... the same hopeless confusion in any scientific investigation of economic relations as would be created, for instance, in modern chemistry if the terminology of the phlogiston theory were to be retained. (Marx and Engels, 1951: 562–4)

From this it follows that the "situatedness" or "standpoint" of whoever makes the argument is relevant if not determinant to understanding the particular meaning put upon the concept. Sentiments of this sort have been taken much further, as we shall see, in the postmodern literature. But there is a double message within Engels' formulation. While conceptions of justice may vary according to time, place, and the individuals concerned, the acceptance of a particular conception "without misunderstanding" can provide a powerful mobilizing discourse for political action (as, for example, in the French revolution).

Furthermore, projection of particular meanings across the space of the world as if they have universal meaning has been of major significance in shaping global historical geography. Here we find a form of militant particularism gone universal with all sorts of remarkable effects. The United Nations charter, for example, enshrines a declaration of universal human rights, Amnesty International pursues a universalistic politics and the international observance of market contracts imposes the rough justice of the market place wherever capitalism and commodity exchange does business. Notions of rightness, fairness, justice are so firmly entrenched in our vocabularies, that we seem powerless to make any political decision without appealing to them.

The question of justice falls squarely into the middle of the tension between particularity and universalism and does it in such a way as to make it impossible (politically as well as theoretically and empirically) to remain securely lodged at either end of that polarity. The effect is, to put it mildly, deeply curious. Justice appears to be a foundational concept that is quite indispensable in the regulation of human affairs (in translating, for example, the "natural laws" of competition, adaptation, cooperation, and environmental transformation into collective forms of human endeavor, to use the language of chapter 8). Yet the foundational concept is held to have no foundation save as an arbitrary effect of arbitrary power in particular places and times. While, like space, time, place, and environment, justice is open to being socially constituted and produced, there seems no easy way to bridge the gulf between universalism/particularity, between systematicity/arbitrariness and between necessity/contingency.

But to talk of an alternative kind of social order is to explore a possible world in which alternative ways of construing and institutionalizing justice are also possible. We owe the idea of possible worlds to Leibniz how, as was shown in chapter 10, used it to establish the relational theory of space–time. There is a useful parallel here for understanding how a relational theory of justice might work. A Utopianism of spatial form (often taken as the marker of a just society) is just as absolute (and authoritarian) as anything that Newton came up with (and it is interesting to note the parallel languages of Sir Thomas More and Newton with respect to the absolute qualities of space). By the same token, discursive absolutism concerning the nature of justice is likewise authoritarian. So what kind of Utopianism *is* possible or, put more directly, how can the human imaginary concerning a just society play a creative role in anti-capitalist politics? This is the crucial question that Maler (1995) so brilliantly brings back as a central motif in Marx's search for an anti-capitalist politics and an anti-capitalist rhetoric.

In the case-studies that follow I offer thoughts on how this problem might be negotiated in a manner consistent with a relational and dialectical view of the social process. The effect is, I hope, to make it possible to use the mobilizing powers of the quest for justice not as a mere matter of pragmatism or opportunism, but as a principled way in which to talk about the need to regulate human relationships and our collective endeavours so as to achieve a particular set of goals under a given set of ecological, historical, and geographical conditions. But understanding the embeddedness of particular ideals of justice in particular processes is critical to the endeavor. While, therefore, no society can do without a working and workable concept of justice any more than it can dispense with workable concepts of space, time, place, and nature, the way these concepts get constituted through social practices has to be the primary focus of attention. The implication, as I hope to show most clearly in the final essay, is that a Utopianism of process looks radically different from a Utopianism of form. The implication of the dialectical/relational view is that the former deserves to be pursued with all the intellectual powers at our command while the latter must needs be rejected as self-negating.

12

Class Relations, Social Justice, and the Political Geography of Difference

It is hard to discuss the politics of identity, multiculturalism, "otherness," and "difference" in abstraction from material circumstances and of political project. I shall, therefore, situate my discussion in the context of a particular problematic – that of the search for a "socially just" social order – within the particular material circumstances prevailing in the United States today.

I. Hamlet, North Carolina

In the small town of Hamlet, North Carolina (population approximately 6,000), there is a chicken-processing plant that was run in the 1980s by Imperial Foods. Organized on a mass-production basis under low-cost conditions of industrialized management, broiler chicken production has now become big business. For many of the US's poor (hit by declining incomes these last two decades) chicken has become a major source of protein and health concerns have led even the rich to indulge their taste for all manner of chicken dishes. Chicken consumption consequently doubled in the 1980s to equal and then surpass that of beef. Businesses grew rapidly and consolidated even more so; what was once a family farm affair became a vast agribusiness almost overnight in which a mere 20 companies ended up controlling more than three-quarters of the output, now valued at more than $20 billion a year. The broiler chicken industry stretches in a vast arc running from Maryland's eastern shore through the Carolinas and across the deep south into the Texas Panhandle. In this "Broiler Belt," as it is known, agricultural incomes are dominated by the industry and in some states, Arkansas being a prime example, the industry is the leading employer and producer of wealth. With economic clout of that sort political influence cannot be far behind. In the state of Arkansas, the then Governor Clinton lost his first re-election bid largely because he had antagonized Tyson Foods, the biggest chicken producer in the world. His re-election as governor and, some say, his eventual transition to the White House, depended heavily upon compromising if not currying considerable favor with Don Tyson, the self-made king of the broiler business, whose main claim to fame, apart from organizing the slaughter of 29 million chickens a week (twice as many as second-ranked ConAgra) and having a company that ranks 100 in the *Fortune* 500 (Frantz, 1994), is to have provided suspicious support and advice to various influential figures within the Clinton administration.

The conditions prevailing within the chicken broiler industry are less than salubrious. Salmonella contamination is an endemic danger, pollution problems are rife, and descriptions of production conditions are liable to stir the ire of those only mildly sensitive to animal rights. Ancillary to broiler-chicken production, is a chicken-processing industry employing 150,000 workers in 250 or so plants, mostly located in very small towns or rural settings throughout the "Broiler Belt." And while some attempts have been made to make the production process more humane for the chickens, the industry has not managed to do much for its workers.

On Tuesday September 3, 1991, the day after the United States celebrated its "labor day," the Imperial Foods plant in Hamlet caught fire. Many of the exit doors were locked. Twenty-five of the 200 workers employed in the plant died and a further 56 were seriously injured.

It was a cataclysmic industrial accident, at least by the standards of any advanced industrial country, but it also revealed, as Struck (1991), one of the few journalists to investigate discovered, some very harsh truths about the "latest industry of toil to reign in the [US] South." Those employed in the plant start off at minimum wage ($4.25 an hour) and later progress to $5.60 an hour which translates into take-home pay of less than $200 per week which is below the poverty line for a single-headed household with children. But there is little or no alternative employment in Hamlet, and for this particular town, as for many others throughout the "Broiler Belt," the plant is a vital economic asset precisely because "for a lot of people, any kind of job is better than no job at all." Those living in relatively geographically isolated rural towns of this sort are, consequently, easy prey for an industry seeking a cheap, unorganized, and easily disciplined labor force (see Toth, 1993). Struck continues his account thus:

> The workers at the Imperial Foods plant describe demeaning conditions with few benefits and no job security. They were routinely cursed by bosses, the employees say. They were allowed only one toilet break from the processing line. A single day off required a doctor's permission. Any infraction was noted as an "occurrence" and five occurrences would get a worker fired. "The supervisors treated you like nothing, and all they want you to do is get their chicken out," said Brenda MacDougald, 36, who had been at the plant two years. "They

treated people like dogs," said a bitter Alfonso Anderson. Peggy, his wife of 27 years, died in the fire. She had worked there for 11 years, despite her complaints. "Around here, you have to take some stuff and swallow it to keep a job," he said, fighting back tears.

North Carolina as a state has long had the habit of openly touting low wages, a friendly business climate and "right-to-work" legislation which keeps the unions at bay as the bait to pull in more and more manufacturing employment of exactly this sort. The poultry industry as a whole is estimated to add more than $1.5 billion annually to North Carolina's economy. In North Carolina, the "friendly business climate," translates into not enforcing laws on occupational health and safety. North Carolina "has only 14 health inspectors and 27 safety inspectors [ranking] lowest in the nation in proportion to the number of inspectors [114] recommended under federal guidelines." Federal personnel are supposed, under congressional mandate, to make up the difference, but none have visited the plants in North Carolina in recent years. The Hamlet plant had not, therefore, been inspected in its 11 years in operation. "There were no fire extinguishers, no sprinkler system, no safety exit doors." Other plants in the state have rarely been inspected let alone cited for violations, though fires have been common and the occupational injury rate in the industry is nearly three times the national average.

There are a number of compelling reflections which this incident provokes. First of all, this is a *modern* (i.e., recently established) industry whose employment conditions could easily be inserted as a description into Karl Marx's chapter on "The Working Day" in *Capital* (published in 1867) without any one noticing much of a difference. It surely bodes ill for the "free market triumphalism" to which we are currently exposed when looking towards the east that such a miserable equation can so easily be made in the west between nineteenth-century levels of exploitation in Britain and employment conditions in a recently established industry in the most powerful advanced industrial capitalist country in the world. As for the incident itself, the most obvious comparison in the United States is with the Triangle Shirtwaist Company fire of 1911 in which 146 employees died. This led over 100,000 people to march down Broadway in protest and it subsequently became the *cause célèbre* for the labor movement to fight for better workplace protection. Yet, as Davidson (1991) notes, "despite a dizzying matrix of laws, regulations and codes enacted to protect workers, most of the Imperial workers died as the women in New York had: pounding desperately on locked or blocked fire doors."

The second reflection is that we should pay close attention to the industrial structures developing in rural and small-town settings in the United States, for it is here where the decline of agricultural employment (to say nothing of the rash of farming bankruptcies) over the past decade or so has left behind a relatively isolated industrial reserve army (again, of the sort which Marx described so well in *Capital* – see chapter 25 section 5, for example) which is far more vulnerable to exploitation than its urban counterpart. US industry has long used spatial dispersal and the geographical isolation of employees as one of its prime mechanisms of labor control (in industries like chicken processing and meat packing the equation is obvious but this principle is also deployed in electronics and other supposedly ultra-modern industries). But recent transformations in industrial organization, flexible locational choices, and deregulation have here been turned into a totally unsubtle form of coercive exploitation which is pre- rather than post-Fordist in its organizational form. The effect in North Carolina, for example, is to produce a dramatic contrast between the much touted and much researched "Research Triangle Park" of high-tech information-based companies and the radically different and largely ignored world of scattered rural enclaves of the chicken-processing plants an hour or so away.

This leads to a third reflection concerning the dismantling, through deindustrialization and industrial reorganization over the last two decades, of many of the forces and institutions of "traditional" (i.e., blue-collar and unionized) working class forms of power. The dispersal and creation of many new jobs in rural settings has facilitated capitalist control over labor by searching out nonunionized and pliable work forces. The manufacturing sectors of central cities, which have always been more vulnerable to expressions of organized discontent or political regulation, have been reduced to zones of either high unemployment (cities like Chicago, New York, Los Angeles, and Baltimore have seen their traditional blue-collar manufacturing employment cut in half in the last 20 years) or of unorganized sweatshop-style industries. The nonfinancial zones of inner cities, which have quite rightly been the focus of so much attention in the past, have increasingly become, therefore, centers of *un*employment and *oppression* (of the sort which led to the recent explosion in Los Angeles) rather than creatures of labor *exploitation* and working-class political organization of the classic sort.

But the immediate matter I wish to concentrate attention upon here, is the general lack of political response to this cataclysmic event. For while the Triangle Shirtwaist Company fire provoked a massive protest demonstration at the beginning of the twentieth century in New York city, the fire in Hamlet, North Carolina at the end of the twentieth century received hardly any media or political attention, even though some labor groups and political organizations (such as Jackson's Rainbow Coalition) did try to focus attention upon it as a matter of ethical and moral urgency. The interesting contrast in September of 1991, was with the Clarence Thomas Supreme Court nomination hearings which became a major focus for a great deal of political agitation and action as well as of media debate. These hearings, it should be noted, focused on serious questions over race and gender relations in a *professional* rather than *working-class* context. It is also useful to contrast events in Hamlet, North Carolina, with those in Los Angeles, in which *oppression* as expressed in the beating of Rodney King on a highway and the failure to convict the police officers involved, sparked a virtual urban uprising of the underprivileged, while the deaths of 25 people through *exploitation* in a rural factory setting provoked almost no reaction at all.

Those contrasts become even more significant when it is realized that of the 25 people who died in the Hamlet fire, 18 were women and 12 were African-American. This is not, apparently, an uncommon profile of employment structure throughout the "Broiler Belt," though Hispanics would typically substitute for African-Americans in the Texas Panhandle sector in particular. The commonality that cuts across race and gender lines in this instance is quite obviously that of class and it is not hard to see the immediate implication that a simple, traditional form of class politics could have protected the interests of women and minorities as well as those of white males. And this in turn raises important questions of exactly what kind of politics, what definition of social justice, and of ethical and moral responsibility, is adequate to the protection of such exploited populations irrespective of their race and gender. The thesis I shall explore here is that it was raw class politics of an exploitative sort which created a situation in which an accident (a fire) could have the effects it did. For what happened in Hamlet, North Carolina, Struck surmised, was "an accident waiting to happen."

Consider, first, the general history of workplace safety and of regulatory practices and enforcements in the United States. Labor struggles around events such as the Triangle Shirtwaist Company fire put occupational safety and health very much upon the political agenda during the 1920s and it was a fundamental feature of Roosevelt's New Deal coalition, which included the labor unions, to try to satisfy some minimum requirements on his score without alienating business interests. The National Labor Relations Board acquired powers to regulate class conflict in the workplace (including conflicts over safety) as well as to specify the legal conditions under which unions (which would often take on health and safety issues directly) could be set up. But it was not until 1970 that a Democratically controlled congress consolidated the bits and pieces of legislation that had accumulated from New Deal days onwards into the organization of the Occupational Safety and Health Administration (OSHA) with real powers to regulate business practices in the workplace. This legislation was, it should be noted, part of package of reforms which set up the Environmental Protection Agency (EPA), the Consumer Product Safety Commission, the National Traffic Safety Commission, and the Mine and Safety Health Administration, all of which signaled a much greater preparedness of a Democrat-controlled congress in the early 1970s to enact legislation (in spite of a Republican president) that would extend state powers to intervene in the economy.

I think it important to recognize the conditions which led the Democratic Party, a political party which from the New Deal onwards sought to absorb but never to represent, let alone become an active instrument of, working-class interests, to enact legislation of such an interventionist character. The legislation was not, in fact, an outcome of the class and sectional alliance politics which had created the New Deal, but came at the tail-end of a decade in which politics had shifted from universal programs (like social security) to specially targeted programs to help regenerate the inner cities (e.g., Model Cities and federally funded housing programs), take care of the elderly or the particularly impoverished (e.g., Medicare and Medicaid), and target particular disadvantaged groups in the population (Headstart and Affirmative action). This shift from universalism to targeting of particular groups inevitably created tensions between groups and helped fragment rather than consolidate any broader sense of a progressive class alliance. Each piece of legislation which emerged in the early 1970s appealed to a different group (unions, environmentalists, consumer advocacy groups, and the like). Nevertheless, the net effect was to create a fairly universal threat of intervention in the economy from many special interest groups and in certain instances – OSHA in particular – in the realm of production.

The latter is, of course, very dangerous territory upon which to venture. For while it is accepted, even by the most recalcitrant capitalist interests, that the state always has a fundamental role in ensuring the proper functioning of the market and respect for private property rights, interventions in that "hidden abode" of production in which the secret profit making resides, is always deeply resisted, as Marx (1967) long ago pointed out, by capitalist-class interests. This treading on the hallowed ground of the prerogatives of business provoked an immediate political response. Edsall (1984) early on spotted its direction:

> During the 1970s, business refined its ability to act as a class, submerging competitive instincts in favor of joint, cooperative action in the legislative arena. Rather than individual companies seeking only special favors ... the dominant theme in the political strategy of business became a shared interest in the defeat of bills such as consumer protection and labor law reform, and in the enactment of favorable tax, regulatory and antitrust legislation.

In acting as a class, business increasingly used its financial power and influence (particularly through political action committees) during the 1970s and 1980s, to effectively capture the Republican Party as its class instrument and forge a coalition against all forms of government intervention (save those advantageous to itself) as well as against the welfare state (as represented by government spending and taxation). This culminated in the Reagan administration's policy initiatives which centered on an:

> across-the-board drive to reduce the scope and content of the federal regulation of industry, the environment, the workplace, health care, and the relationship

between buyer and seller. The Reagan administration's drive toward deregulation was accomplished through sharp budget cuts reducing enforcement
capabilities; through the appointment of anti-regulatory, industry-oriented
agency personnel; and, finally, through the empowering of the Office of Management and Budget with unprecedented authority to delay major regulations, to
force major revisions in regulatory proposals, and through prolonged cost-benefit
analyses, to effectively kill a wide range of regulatory initiatives. (Edsall, 1984:
217)

This willingness of the Republican Party to become the representative of "its
dominant class constituency" during this period contrasted with the "ideologically ambivalent" attitude of the Democrats which grew out of "the fact that
its ties to various groups in society are diffuse, and none of these groups –
women, blacks, labor, the elderly, Hispanics, urban political organizations –
stands clearly larger than the others" (Edsall, 1984: 235). The dependency of
Democrats, furthermore, upon "big money" contributions rendered many of
them also highly vulnerable to direct influence from business interests.

The outcome was predictable enough. When a relatively coherent class force
encounters a fragmented opposition which cannot even conceive of its interests
in class terms, then the result is hardly in doubt. Institutions like the National
Labor Relations Board (NLRB) and OSHA were crippled or turned around
to fit business rather than labor agendas. Moody (1988: 120 and chapter 6)
notes, for example, that by 1983 it took on average 627 days for the NLRB
to issue a decision on an unfair labor practice which is an impossible time to
wait if the unfair labor practice involves dismissal and the person dismissed
has nothing to live on in the meantime. It was this political and
administrative climate of total disregard for laws governing labor rights and
occupational health and safety which set the stage for that "accident waiting
to happen" at Hamlet, North Carolina.

The failure to register political anger of the sort which followed the Triangle
Shirtwaist Company fire in 1911 in New York city also deserves some
comment. A similar event in a relatively remote rural setting posed immediate
logistical problems for massive on-the-spot political responses (such as the
protest demonstration on Broadway), illustrating the effectiveness of capitalist
strategies of geographical dispersal away from politicized central city locations
as a means of labor control. The only other path to a generalized political
response lay in widespread media attention and public debate – surely, given
modern communications technology, a very real possibility. But here two other
elements to the situation prevailing in 1991 came into play. First, the conditions of media dissemination of political issues has changed, rendering the
graphic video of the beating of Rodney King and the soap-operatic Clarence
Thomas hearings far more powerful as political icons than the static pictures
of the aftermath of the North Carolina fire (we will encounter this issue again
in chapter 13). Secondly, not only were the working-class institutions which

might have taken up the cause greatly weakened, both in their ability to react as well as in their access to the media, but the very idea of any kind of working-class politics was likewise on the defensive (if not downright discredited in certain "radical" circles), even though capitalist-class interests and an increasingly captive Republican Party had been waging a no-holds-barred and across-the-board class war against the least privileged sectors of the population for the previous two decades.

This weakening of working-class politics in the United States from the mid-1970s on can be tracked back to many causes which cannot be examined in detail here. But one contributory feature has been the increasing fragmentation of "progressive" politics around special issues and the rise of the so-called new social movements focusing on gender, race, ethnicity, ecology, sexuality, multiculturalism, community, and the like. These movements often become a working and practical alternative to class politics of the traditional sort and in some instances have exhibited downright hostility to such class politics.

I think it instructive here to note that as far as I know, none of the institutions associated with such new social movements saw fit to engage politically with what happened in Hamlet, North Carolina. Women's organizations, for example, were heavily preoccupied with the question of sexual harassment and mobilizing against the Clarence Thomas appointment, even though it was mainly women who died in the North Carolina fire and women who continue to bear an enormous burden of exploitation in the "Broiler Belt." And apart from the Rainbow Coalition and Jesse Jackson, African-American (and Hispanic) organizations also remained strangely silent on the matter, while some ecologists (particularly the animal rights wing) exhibited more sympathy for the chickens than for the workers. The general tone in the media, therefore, was to sensationalize the horror of the "accident," but not to probe at all into its origins and certainly not to indite capitalist-class interests, the Republican Party, the failures of the state of North Carolina or OSHA as accessory to a murderously negligent event.

II. The Postmodern Death of Justice

According to most common-sense meanings of the word, many of us would accept that the conditions under which men, women, and minorities work in the Hamlet plant are socially unjust. Yet to make such a statement presupposes that there are some universally agreed upon norms as to what we do or ought to mean by the concept of social justice and that no barrier exists, other than the normal ambiguities and fuzziness, to applying the full force of such a powerful principle to the circumstances of North Carolina. But "universality" is a word which conjures up doubt and suspicion, downright hostility even, in these "postmodern" times; the belief that universal truths are both discoverable and applicable as guidelines for political–economic action is nowadays often held to be the chief sin of "the Enlightenment project" and of the "totalizing" and "homogenizing" modernism it supposedly generated.

The effect of the postmodern critique of universalism has been to render any application of the concept of social justice problematic. And there is an obvious sense in which this questioning of the concept is not only proper but imperative – too many colonial peoples have suffered at the hands of western imperialism's particular justice, too many African-Americans have suffered at the hands of the white man's justice, too many women from the justice imposed by a patriarchal order and too many workers from the justice imposed by capitalists, to make the concept anything other than problematic. But does this imply that the concept is useless or that to dub events at Hamlet, North Carolina as "unjust" has no more force than some localized and contingent complaint?

The difficulty of working with the concept is compounded further by the variety of idealist and philosophical interpretations put upon the term throughout the long history of western thought on the matter. There are multiple competing theories of social justice and each has its flaws and strengths. Egalitarian views, for example, immediately run into the problem that "there is nothing more unequal than the equal treatment of unequals" (the modification of doctrines of equality of opportunity in the United States by requirements for affirmative action, for example, have recognized the historical force of that problem). Positive law theories (whatever the law says is just), utilitarian views (the greatest good of the greatest number), social contract, and natural right views, together with the various intuitionist, relative deprivation and other interpretations of justice, all compete for our attention, leaving us with the conundrum: *which* theory of social justice is the most socially just?

Social justice, for all of the universalism to which proponents of a particular version of it might aspire, has long turned out to be a rather heterogeneous set of concepts. Furthermore, "situatedness," "otherness," and "positionality" (usually understood in the first instance in terms of class, gender, race, ethnicity, sexual preference, and community, though in some formulations even these categories are viewed with suspicion) also become crucial elements in defining how particular differentiated discourses (be they about social justice or anything else) arise and how such discourses are put to use as part of the play of power. There can be no universal conception of justice to which we can appeal as a normative concept to evaluate some event, such as the Imperial Foods plant fire. There are only particular, competing, fragmented, and heterogeneous conceptions of and discourses about justice which arise out of the particular situations of those involved.

The task of deconstruction and of postmodern criticism is to reveal how *all* discourses about social justice hide power relations. The effect of this postmodern extension of Engels' line of reasoning (see the Prologue to Part IV) is well described by White (1991: 115–6). Postmodernists argue:

> that we are far too ready to attach the word "just" to cognitive, ethical, and political arrangements that are better understood as phenomena of power and oppress, neglect, marginalize, and discipline others. In unmasking such claims about justice, postmodern thinkers imply that their work serves some more valid but unspecified notion of justice. One sees this in Derrida's declaration that "Deconstruction is justice," but also in his cautioning that one can neither speak directly about nor experience justice. In answering the sense of responsibility to otherness, one serves justice but one does so with a sense of the infinite, open-ended character of the task.

The effect, however, is to produce "a rather simple bipolar world: deconstructionists and other postmoderns who struggle for justice, and traditional ethical and political theorists who are the ideologues of unjust orders." And this in turn produces a serious dilemma for all forms of postmodern argumentation:

> On the one hand, its epistemological project is to deflate all totalistic, universalistic efforts to theorize about justice and the good life; and yet on the other hand, its practical project is to generate effective resistance to the present dangers of totalizing, universalizing rationalization processes in society. In short, the source of much injustice in contemporary society is seen as general and systematic; the response, however, bars itself from normatively confronting the problem on a comparable level by employing a theory of justice offering universally valid, substantive principles. Postmodern reflection thus seems to deny itself just the sort of normative armament capable of conducting a successful fight.

We can see precisely this difficulty emerging in the circumstances that led up to events in Hamlet, North Carolina. When business organized itself as a class to attack government regulation and the welfare state (with its dominant notions of social rationality and just redistributions) it did so in the name of the unjust and unfair regulation of private property rights and the unfair taxation of the proper fruits of entrepreneurial endeavor in freely functioning markets. Just deserts, it has long been argued by the ideologues of free-market capitalism (from Adam Smith onwards), are best arrived at through competitively organized, price-fixing markets in which enterpreneurs are entitled to hang on to the profit engendered by their endeavors. There is then no need for explicit theoretical, political, or social argument over what is or is not socially just because social justice is whatever is delivered by the market. Each "factor" of production (land, labor, and capital), for example, will receive its marginal rate of return, its just reward, according to its contribution to production. The role of government should be confined to making sure that markets function freely (e.g., by curbing monopoly powers) and that they are "properly organized" (which may extend to compensating for clear cases of market failure in the case of unpriced externalities such as environmental pollution and health hazards – see chapter 13.

It does not, of course, take that much sophistication to deconstruct this conception of justice as a manifestation of a particular kind of political–economic power (see, for example, Carlson, 1992). Yet there is widespread, perhaps even hegemonic acceptance of such a standpoint as the numerous "tax revolts" in the United States over the last decades have shown. From this standpoint, the incident in North Carolina can be interpreted as an unfortunate accident, perhaps compounded by managerial error, in a basically just system which (*a*) provides employment where there otherwise would be none at wages determined by the demand and supply conditions prevailing in the local labor market, and (*b*) fills the shops (contrast the former Soviet Union) with a vast supply of cheap protein which poor people can for the most part afford to buy. In so far as this doctrine of just deserts in the market place is ideologically hegemonic, protest in the North Caroline case would be minimized and confined simply to an enquiry into who it was that locked the doors and who should compensate the victims. In the Imperial Foods case, in a "surprise" plea bargain, the owner, Emmett Roe, took the blame and admitted to 25 counts of involuntary manslaughter in return for dropping all criminal charges against the two managers of the plant, one of whom was his son. Roe, 65 years old, nominally sentenced to 20 years, was expected to be released after three years. "I'm confident," said one of the prosecutors, "that the person who's responsible for that locked door policy is in prison." The defense was equally delighted with the plea agreement, and took great pains to praise the way the elderly owner had "sacrificed himself to save his family" (*New York Times*, September 15, 1992). The company itself was forced into bankruptcy by a fine of over $800,000 levied by the state leaving the question of compensation for victims in chaos for more than a year. In November 1992, immediately in the wake of Clinton's electoral victory, the insurance companies that had resisted pay-outs on the grounds that conditions were so bad that the bankrupt owner should be solely liable, finally agreed to pay $16.1 million compensation to be divided (after the lawyers had taken their cut) among the 80 or so families bereaved or injured.

The tempered and entirely legalistic response to the Hamlet case, and the manner of its handling, can be interpreted as an indication of precisely how dominant the market-led conception of justice is in the United States today. That this is the predominant way in which issues are mediated through market mentality and market justice is suggested by a parallel case in Shanghai. Mai Ziwen, "the Taiwan businessman who ran the Fuzhou textile warehouse in Shanghai in which 61 workers, locked in the building died in a fire," received a "lenient" two-year suspended sentence, ostensibly because he had "showed repentance" and "cooperated in the aftermath of the fire." But it was widely acknowledged that China, seeking to encourage foreign investment (even from Taiwan) under something like free-market conditions of wage labor, was most anxious not to send the wrong signals to foreign investors by any harsh reprisals (Sommer, 1994). The point here is not to cavil at the leniency of treatment to guilty parties (though there are plenty of grounds for concern on this score too), but to marvel at the way in which a condition of systematic violence towards workers is translated into a question of individual culpability and negligence before being thrown into a calculus of extenuating circumstances.

The obvious discourse with which to confront this market justice is that of workers' rights deploying the whole rhetoric of class struggle against exploitation, profit making, and worker disempowerment. Neither Marx nor Engels would here eschew *all* talk of rights and justice. While they clearly recognize that these concepts take on different meanings across space and time and according to persons, the exigencies of class relations inevitably produce, as Marx (1967: 235) argues in the case of the fight between capital and labor over the proper length of the working day, "an antinomy, right against right, both equally bearing the seal of the law of exchanges." Between such *equal* rights (that of the capitalist and that of the worker) "force decides." What is at stake here, is not the arbitration between competing claims according to some universal principle of justice, but class struggle over the particular conception of justice and rights which shall be applied to a given situation. In the North Carolina case, had the rights of workers to be treated with dignity under conditions of reasonable economic security and safety and with adequate remuneration been properly respected, then the incident almost certainly would not have happened. And if all workers (together with the unemployed) were accorded the same rights and if the exorbitant rates of profit in broiler chicken processing (as well as in other industries) had been curbed, then the importance of the relatively low-price of this source of protein for the poor would have been significantly diminished.

The problem, however, is that such working-class rhetoric on rights and justice is as open to criticism and deconstruction as its capitalistic equivalent. Concentration on class alone is seen to hide, marginalize, disempower, repress, and perhaps even oppress all kinds of "others" precisely because it cannot and does not acknowledge explicitly the existence of heterogeneities and differences based on, for example, race, gender, sexuality, age, ability, culture, locality, ethnicity, religion, community, consumer preferences, group affiliation, and the like. Open-ended responsibility to all of these multiple othernesses makes it difficult if not impossible to respond to events in North Carolina with a single institutionalized discourse which might be maximally effective in confronting the rough justice of capitalism's political economy at work in the "Broiler Belt."

We here encounter a situation with respect to discourses about social justice which closely matches the political paralysis exhibited in the failure to respond to the North Carolina fire. Politics and discourses both seem to have become so mutually fragmented that response is inhibited. The upshot appears to be a double injustice: not only do men and women, whites and African-Americans die in a preventable event, but we are simultaneously deprived of any normative principles of justice whatsoever by which to condemn or indite the responsible parties.

III. The Resurrection of Social Justice

There are abundant signs of discontent with the impasse into which post-modernism's and poststructuralism's approach to the question of social justice has fallen. And a number of different strategies have emerged to try to resurrect the mobilizing power of arguments about justice in ways which either permit appeal to carefully circumscribed, but nevertheless general, principles or which, more ambitiously, try to build a bridge between the supposed universalisms of modernism and the fragmented particularities left behind by post-structuralist deconstructions. I note, for example, Walzer's (1983) attempt to pluralize the concept of justice as equality so as to respect the cultural creations of others, and Peffer's (1990) attempt to construct principles of social justice which are consistent with Marxist social theory and as an antidote to that wing of Marxism which regards all talk of justice and of rights as a pernicious bourgeois trap. From multiple directions, then, there emerges a strong concern to reinstate concern for social justice and to re-elaborate upon what it takes to create the values and institutions of a reasonably just society.

I think it important at the outset to concede the seriousness of the radical intent of poststructuralism to "do justice" in a world of infinite heterogeneity and open-endedness. Their reasons for refusing to apply universal principles rigidly across heterogeneous situations are not without considerable weight. To begin with, as Derrida (1992a: 35) for one correctly insists, the founding moment of any institutionalized regime of justice rests on an extra-legal moment of violence:

> All revolutionary situations, all revolutionary discourses, on the left or on the right ... justify the recourse to violence by alleging the founding, in progress or to come, of a new law. As this law to come will in return legitimate, retro-spectively, the violence that may offend the sense of justice, its future anterior already justifies it. The foundation of all states occurs in a situation that we can thus call revolutionary. It inaugurates a new law, it always does so in violence.

The trace of that force which is, as Marx has it, always "the midwife of history," ever leaves its stain upon the social order and it is partly Derrida's intent to insist that the trace is always with us, that it can never be erased. This further alerts us to the unfortunate ways in which many social movements in the twentieth century have foundered on the belief that because their cause is just they cannot possibly themselves behave unjustly. The warning goes even deeper: the application of *any* universal principle of social justice entails an injustice to someone, somewhere. But, on the other hand, at the end of a road of infinite regret for any founding act of violence, of questioning the super-imposition of singular rules in a situation of infinite heterogeneity, and insisting upon open-endedness about what justice might mean, there lies at best a void or at worst a rather ugly world in which the needs of the exploiters or oppressors (like Imperial Foods) can be regarded as "just" on equivalent terms with those of their victims (those who died). We shrink from any founding act of justice in which "the expropriators are expropriated" precisely because it is a moment of violence that will forever leave its trace (until expunged by some further act of violence). We refuse the institutionalized arbitrariness of law because it forms as a recalcitrant "permanence" in the face of the fluidity of social change. And, reducing everything to flows, we refuse to contemplate the construction of those "permanences" that can give order to social being and direction to social becoming. Affirming the importance of infinite hetero-geneity and open-endedness in a world of unstructured processes and infinitely complex flows, directly connects to the charge against poststructuralism that it is an "anything goes" way of thinking within which no particular moral or ethical principles can carry any particular weight over any other. "At some point," says White (1991: 133), "one must have a way of arguing that not all manifestations of otherness should be fostered; some ought to be constrain-ed." And this presumes some general principles of right or justice.

There is, White goes on to assert, often a tacit admission of such a problem in some of the poststructuralism's founding texts. Foucault (1980: 107–8), having argued strenuously that we can never disentangle "mechanisms of discipline" from principles of right, ends up raising the possibility of "a new form of right, one which must be anti-disciplinarian, but at the same time liberated from the principle of sovereignty." Lyotard likewise argues explicitly for the creation of a "pristine" but "nonconsensual" notion of justice in *The Postmodern Condition*. And Derrida (1992a) is deeply concerned about ethics. But in no case are we told much about what, for example, a "new form of right" might mean.

Initiatives have consequently emerged to try to resurrect some general principles of social justice while attending to poststructuralist criticisms of universalizing theory which marginalizes "others." There are four particular debates that deserve scrutiny.

1. Breaking Out of the Local

Most poststructuralist critical interventions tend to confine their radicalizing politics to social interactions occurring "below the threshold where the systemic imperatives of power and money become so dominant" (White, 1991: 107). The politics of resistance which they indicate are typically attached to small-scale communities of resistance, marginalized groups, abnormal discourses, or simply to that zone of personal life sometimes termed "the life world" which can be identified as distinct from and potentially resistant to penetration by the rationalizing, commodified, technocratic, and hence alienating organization of contemporary capitalism. It is hard to read this literature without concluding that the objective of reform or revolutionary transformation of contemporary capitalism as a whole has been given up on, even as a topic for discussion, let alone as a focus for political organization. This "opting out" from consideration of a whole range of questions is perhaps best signaled by the marked silence of most postmodern and poststructuralist thinkers when it comes to critical discussion of any kind of political economy [save, of course, to deconstruct it, as Derrida (1992b) does in his examination of money and exchange]. The best that can be hoped for, as someone like Foucault seems to suggest, is that innumerable localized struggles might have some sort of collective effect on how capitalism works in general.

Dissatisfaction with such a politics has led some socialist feminists in particular (see Fraser, 1989; Young, 1990a, b) to seek ways to broaden the terrain of struggle beyond the world of face-to-face communalism and into battles over such matters as welfare state policy, public affairs, political organization via, in Fraser's case, "an ethic of solidarity" and, in Young's case, through explicit statement of norms of social justice.

Young (1990a: 312) complains that the attempt to counter "the alienation and individualism we find hegemonic in capitalist patriarchal society," has led feminist groups "impelled by a desire for closeness and mutual identification," to construct an ideal of community "which generates borders, dichotomies, and exclusions" at the same time as it homogenizes and represses difference within the group. She turns the tools of deconstruction against such ideals of community in order to show their oppressive qualities (cf. above, chapter 11). But she distances herself from Derrida because she thinks it "both possible and necessary to pose alternative conceptualizations" rather than to rest content with the idea that "deconstruction is justice." The first step to her argument is to insist that individuals be understood as "heterogeneous and decentered" (see chapter 10 and below). No social group can be truly unitary in the sense of having members who hold to a singular identity. Young strives on this basis to construct some norms of behavior in the public realm. Our conception of social justice "requires not the melting away of differences, but institutions that promote reproduction of and respect for group differences without oppression" (p. 47). We must reject "the concept of universality as embodied in republican versions of Enlightenment reason" because it sought to "suppress the popular and linguistic heterogeneity of the urban public" (p. 108). "In open and accessible public spaces and forums, one should expect to encounter and hear from those who are different, whose social perspectives, experience and affiliations are different."

The ideal to which she appeals is "openness to unassimilated otherness." This entails the celebration of the distinctive cultures and characteristics of different groups and of the diverse group identities which are themselves perpetually being constructed and deconstructed out of the flows and shifts of social life. But we here encounter a major problem. In modern mass-urban society, the multiple-mediated relations which constitute that society across time and space are just as important and as "authentic" as unmediated face-to-face relations. It is just as important for a politically responsible person to know about and respond politically to all those people who daily put breakfast upon our table, even though market exchange hides from us the conditions of life of the producers (see chapter 8). When we eat chicken, we relate to workers we never see of the sort that died in Hamlet, North Carolina. Relationships between individuals get mediated through market functions and state powers. And we have to define conceptions of justice capable of operating across and through these multiple mediations. But this is the realm of politics which postmodernism and communitarianism typically avoids.

Young therefore proposes "a family" (note the echo of Wittgenstein) "of concepts and conditions" relevant to a contemporary conception of social justice. She identifies "five faces of oppression"; *exploitation* (the transfer of the fruits of the labor from one group to another, as, for example, in the cases of workers giving up surplus value to capitalists or women in the domestic sphere transferring the fruits of their labor to men); *marginalization* (the expulsion of people from useful participation in social life so that they are "potentially subjected to severe material deprivation and even extermination"); *powerlessness* (the lack of that "authority, status, and sense of self" which would permit a person to be listened to with respect), *cultural imperialism* (stereotyping in behaviors as well as in various forms of cultural expression that "the oppressed group's own experience and interpretation of social life finds little expression that touches the dominant culture, while that same culture imposes on the oppressed group its experience and interpretation of social life"); and *violence* (the fear and actuality of random, unprovoked attacks, which have "no motive except to damage, humiliate, or destroy the person").

Such a multidimensional conception of social justice is useful even if it smacks of a mere extension of traditional liberal notions of toleration across a broader spectrum of social affairs than usual. It alerts us to the existence of a "long social and political frontier" of political action to roll back multiple oppressions. It also emphasizes the heterogeneity of experience of injustice – someone unjustly treated in the workplace can act oppressively in the domestic sphere and the victim of that may, in turn, resort to cultural imperialism against others in the neighborhood. Yet there are many situations, such as those in Hamlet, North Carolina, where these multiple forms of oppression coalesce.

Unfortunately, Young leaves in abeyance the question of how and why these different dimensions of injustice intersect in the ways they do in particular places and times. She also avoids the questions of how one discourse on justice can be used politically and discursively to erase and frustrate concerns about another. While it is not, plainly, Young's intent to bury question of exploitation that were so transparent in the Imperial Foods fire under a morass of questions about gender, race, and culture of the sort that dominated the Anita Hill or Rodney King cases, the political effect with respect to the North Carolina fire was, as we have seen, to do exactly that.

But there are chinks in the armor of Young's idealist conception of a just society:

> The danger in affirming difference is that the implementation of group-conscious policies will reinstate stigma and exclusion. In the past, group-conscious policies were used to separate those defined as different and exclude them from access to the rights and privileges enjoyed by dominant groups. ... Group-conscious policies cannot be used to justify exclusion of or discrimination against members of a group in the exercise of a general political and civil rights. A democratic cultural pluralism thus requires a dual system of rights: a more general system of rights which are the same for all, and a more specific system of group-conscious policies and rights. (p. 174)

The double meaning of universality then becomes plain: "universality in the sense of the participation and inclusion of everyone in moral and social life does not imply universality in the sense of adoption of a general point of view that leaves behind particular affiliations, feelings, commitments, and desires" (p. 105). But *nota bene*: universality is no longer rejected out of hand. It is reinserted (perhaps "smuggled back in" would be a more appropriate way of putting it) in a dialectical relation to particularity, positionality, and group difference. But what constitutes *this* universality; who is to determine how it is to be specified and in what ways is it really so different from what liberal theory and the Enlightenment all along maintained? Young provides no answer to these questions but, plainly, the question of social justice awaits exactly such a clarification.

2. On Not Romancing the Geographical Stone

These questions have been posed in another way in the contested and often testy debates on the "politics of recognition" and on "multiculturalism." I begin here with Walzer's (1983: 314) formulation of a "radically particularist" theory in which "every substantive account of distributive justice is a local account." We are "all of us" he says:

> culture-producing creatures; we make and inhabit meaningful worlds. Since there is no way to rank and order these worlds with regard to their understanding

of social goods, we do justice to actual men and women by respecting their particular creations. And they claim justice, and resist tyranny, by insisting on the meaning of social goods among themselves. Justice is rooted in the distinct understandings of places, honors, jobs, things of all sorts, that constitute a shared way of life. To override those understandings is (always) to act unjustly.

This, it seems to me, is Raymond Williams' thesis of "militant particularism" seen through the other end of the telescope. The only permissible form of universality is infinite respect for that particularity founded on historically (and geographically) produced shared ways of life, each with its own distinctive "structure of feeling." Since such structures are often (though not uniquely) implicated in processes of place construction, we find ourselves at the very minimum invited to a veritable feast of geographically fragmented notions of justice that frequently take on territorial expression through the institutions of state, constitutionality and law, and the rituals of custom. But the demand now exists to respect equally *all* forms of cultural achievement. Gutman (1994: 5) points out, however, that "this requirement of political recognition of cultural particularity – extended to all individuals – is compatible with a form of universalism that counts the culture and cultural context valued by individuals as among their basic interests."

The arguments presented in favor of recognizing cultural particularity are now well rehearsed. Many would now accept Taylor's (1994: 60–1) judgment that "the politics of equal respect, as enshrined in a liberalism of rights" has historically proven "inhospitable to difference, because (*a*) it insists on uniform application of the rules defining these rights, without exception, and (*b*) it is suspicious of collective goals." It cannot, therefore, respond to reasonable demands to support collective goals, survival of cultures, preservation of ecological habitats of special significance, and the like. Nor can it be sensitive to the quite disparate notions of justice and of "just retribution" that can arise out of radically different cultural traditions.

But there is, as I argued in chapter 11, a downside to this. To begin with, "the repudiation of all possible standards of evaluation" undermines judgments of equal worth as much as it undermines judgments of inferior worth. It is therefore destructive to the very goals that arguments of respect for particularity are supposed to support (Wolfe, 1994: 78). If we take Walzer at this word, it would be as unjust to try to override the cultural achievements of slavery, apartheid, fascism, or a caste society as it would be to deny the rights to self-determination of native-Americans or Vietnamese peasants. The AFL-CIO, for example, could be accused of injustice when it petitioned the federal government to reclaim regulatory authority over North Carolina employers in the wake of the Imperial Foods fire since North Carolina, judging by its promotional literature, is proud of its particular anti-union way of doing business.

Recognizing this difficulty, leads Taylor (with Walzer's concurrence) to reformulate the idea into a *presumption* of equality of achievement of cultures that may or may not be sustained on further inspection. But this presumes two things. First there is some universal standard of judgment as to when a particular cultural condition is unacceptable. Secondly, it presumes there are valid entities called "cultures" in places that have distinctive "achievements" to be evaluated. This flies in the face of historical–geographical processes of place and community construction and ignores the fact that cultures are just as relationally (and "dialogically") constructed as individuals and a good deal more porous. Not to acknowledge these processes of cultural construction/dissolution and to build a "particularist theory of justice" with respect to cultures as embodied *things* is to advocate a politics that would effectively freeze geographical structures of place for evermore. The effect would be as dysfunctional as it might be oppressive. There is a third objection; the substantive demand to protect a cultural form (or practice) on the basis of a presumption of its worth can be oppressive and unjust to those who do not share its values. Individuals and subgroups might not want their cultural specificity recognized because that specificity is precisely the social prison from which they desire to escape. Women, for example, do not lack recognition or valuation in our society; the problem lies, rather, in the particular way they are recognized and valued. Here the deconstructionist demand to *dissolve* rather than respect the categories (particularly those of race, ethnicity, and gender that have "essentialist" overtones) makes sense. Unfortunately, the absence of *any* cultural or social categories (permanences) upon which respect and recognition might be bestowed (even for a time) is just as damaging as assuming a historical geography of cultural achievement that is set in stone.

The problem with this idealist political argument, is that it fails to understand how places and cultures are constructed, sustained, and dissolved. The fundamental dialectical question of how processes and cultural entities relate in place is averted. The political struggle to protect supposed cultural "permanences" as highpoints of human cultural achievement may be understandable at a historical conjuncture when flows and processes are rapidly shifting through time–space compression, threatening the achieved qualities of all places. But if all societies, as Taylor (1994, 63) observes, "are becoming more multicultural, while at the same time becoming more porous" and if, as Wolf (1982; 17) has it (see chapter 11), all attempts to construct places and build imagined communities must "take cognizance of processes that transcend separable cases, moving through and beyond them and transforming them as they proceed," then considerations of social justice cannot be particularized in the radical way that Walzer initially imagined.

3. The Politics of Scale

There is another dimension to this that goes back to the production of multiple spatio-temporalities and value structures. If, to echo Raymond Williams (see chapter 1), there is a perpetual ambivalence as to what kind of "permanence" we belong to, or if we take a much more ecological view, of biotic community (as Leopold does – see chapter 7), then we must perforce recognize the hierarchical organization of places (permanences) within which we have our being. Neighborhood, city, region, nation, the globe refer to quite different processes of socio-ecological interaction occurring at quite different spatio-temporal scales. Individuals have membership in all of them. Communitarians are forced to define a scale at which to bound their concerns and where the boundaries are drawn makes all the difference. For example, the Commission on Global Governance (1995) pursues a politics in which a "world community" founded on the growth of "international civil society" seeks "to weave a tighter fabric of international norms" expressive of "certain common values" informed by "a sense of common responsibility." The militia movement in the United States, on the other hand, regards this as a manifestation of betrayal of the principles of the founding constitution of the nation but is equally communitarian in its rhetoric. Etzioni (1993) in lauding the new communitarianism as a basis for political solutions ("without puritanism or repression") to economic and social problems, bounds his argument within the ties of the federated United States. But conflictual loyalties and values (including those of social justice) derive from different scales, as the ecological–environmental issue so clearly demonstrates (see chapters 8 and 13). The contemporary emphasis on the local, while it enhances certain kinds of sensitivities, totally erases others and thereby truncates rather than emancipates the field of political engagement and action. While we all may have some "place" (or "places") in the order of things, we can never ever be purely "local" beings, no matter how hard we try. And while membership in one sort of "permanence" defined at a given scale may be more important to each of us than others, such identifications as we do acquire are rarely so singular as to create no conflicting loyalties.

Communication from one spatio-temporal scale to another, or across spaces, languages, imagined communities, nation states, legal entities and systems, etc. is not easy. This is a condition that has preoccupied Habermas, by far the most outspoken critic of postmodern and poststructuralist particularisms and a strong proponent of universalist arguments. While Habermas never seeks to distill universal *principles*, he does insist on a process-based "metanorm" of free and unfettered communication occurring in the public sphere of civil society. His aim is to democratize communicative action to the point where it can be the bearer of powerful ethical principles, such as those pertaining to justice. Howell (1994: 422) considers his argument as:

> a rebuttal of the most drastic of our normative localizations, promoting the development of a revitalized democratic political life; it puts back a normative standard into political theory, and one that reaches out beyond the bounds of

the community, beyond particular interests and specific social contexts. It recovers a universalism that, at least in principle, is extendable historically and geographically. It avoids both the relativism of post-modern political ethics, and the closely allied localism of communitarian political philosophy; nor is it simply an abstract contractarian normative theory. ...

The difficulty here is with the way Habermas believes the "universalism is extendable historically and geographically." For all of his occasional references to material circumstances, he treats of the problem of communicative action as a linguistic discursive problem and consequently provides a very weak understanding of how the discursive "moment" (to recuperate the language of chapter 4) internalizes effects of power, of material practices, of imaginaries, of institutions, and of social relations, all operating in a world of rapidly diversifying spatio-temporalities and valuation systems. Howell (1994: 423) is right to object to Habermas' "inability to think through the realities of differentiated political space" but does not take the criticism far enough: Habermas has, in short, no conception of how spatio-temporalities and "places" are produced and how that process is integral to the process of communicative action and of valuation. What Habermas does hold out is the ideal of a process-based understanding of how norms and values of justice might better become universalized, even on the basis of certain powerful "militant particularisms."

4. Situating "Situated Knowledges"

The fourth debate concerns what it means to say that all knowledges (including conceptions of social justice and of social needs) are "situated" in a heterogeneous world of difference. "Situatedness" can be construed in different ways. What I shall term the "vulgar" conception of it dwells almost entirely on the relevance of individual biographies: I see, interpret, represent, and understand the world the way I do because the particularities of my life history. The separateness of language games and discourses is emphasized, and difference is treated as biographically and sometimes even institutionally, socially, historically, and geographically determined. It proceeds as if none of us can throw off even some of the shackles of personal history or internalize what the condition of being "the other" is all about. In a way it assumes we cannot even learn another's language. It is inevitably associated with an exclusionary politics of the sort that Young rejects. And it is frequently used as a rhetorical device either to enhance the supposed authenticity and moral authority of one's own accounts of the world or to deny the veracity of other accounts ("since she is black and female of rural origins she cannot possibly have anything authentic to say about conditions of life of the white bourgeoisie in New York city" or, more commonly, "because he is a white, male, western, heterosexual he is bound to be tied to a certain vision of how the world works"). Individual biographies do, of course, matter and all sorts of problems arise when someone privileged (like myself) purports to speak for or even about others. This is a difficult issue for contemporary social science and philosophy to confront, as Spivak (1988) shows. But a relativist, essentialist, and nondialectical view of situatedness generates immense political difficulties. I would not be permitted to speak about the experiential horror of the North Carolina fire, for example, because I am not working class, nor a woman, nor an African-American (nor, for that matter, was I killed in it). Economically secure professional white feminists could not, likewise, speak for any woman whose situation is different. No one in fact could assume the right or obligation to speak for "others" let alone against the oppression of anyone whose identity is construed as "other."

There is, however, a far profounder and more dialectical sense of "situatedness" to which we can appeal. Its first, and I think weaker version occurs in Hegel's parable of the master and the slave. Situatedness is not seen as *separate and unrelated* difference, but as a *dialectical power relation* between oppressor and oppressed. Both need the other and both internalize a relation to the other in their own identity. Marx appropriated, radically transformed, and strengthened this Hegelian dialectic in his examination of the relation between capital and labor. His long and critical engagement with bourgeois philosophy and political economy then became the means to define an alternative subaltern and subversive science situated from the perspective of the proletariat. Feminist writers such as Haraway (1990) and Hartsock (1987) examine gender difference and ground their feminist theory in a similar way.

Such a dialectical conception pervades Derrida's view of the individual subject as someone who has no solid identity, but who is a bundle of heterogeneous and not necessarily coherent impulses and desires. Multiple forms of interaction with the world construct individuals as "a play of difference that cannot completely be comprehended" (Young, 1990b: 232). "Othernesses" are necessarily and inevitably internalized within the self in a dialogical mode (Taylor, 1994: 32). "Situatedness" is then taken out of its wooden attachment to identifiable individuals and their biographies and is itself situated as a play of difference. When I eat Kentucky fried chicken, I am situated at one point in a chain of commodity production that leads right back to Hamlet, North Carolina. When I interact with my daughter, I am inevitably caught in a game of the construction of gender identities that have meaning only in terms of the social processes of gendering that also bear their burden of historical–geographical construction. When I refrain from using bait to destroy the slugs that have eaten every flower I have nurtured, then I situate myself in an ecological chain of existence that has a quite different spatio-temporality to that I invoke as I try to economize on energy use out of a fear of global warming.

Individuals are heterogeneously constructed subjects internalizing "othernesses" by virtue of their intricate relations to a highly diversified world. If individuals are, as we have already argued, relationally (or as Taylor, 1994: 32, prefers it "dialogically") constructed entities, then the definition of individual is vacuous without understanding what relations are being internalized. This leads to Spivak's (1988: 294, 308) answer to the whole dilemma of political representation of the other which rests on invoking Derrida's call to render "delirious that interior voice that is the voice of the other in us."

Unfortunately, this does not exhaust the problem for two reasons that derive directly from considerations on the dialectics of spatio-temporality and identity (individuation) laid out in chapter 10. First, we face the danger of the "Leibnizian conceit" with all of its associated hubris (see above, chapters 3 and 10). Even if we, as individuals, can in some sense be construed as monadic entities internalizing everything there is, there is no way in which we can internalize everything equally or sharpen our perceptions so as to be able to speak for all. If we are not monadic entities, but dialogically constructed individuals produced and "individuated" by and therefore sensitive to certain dominant processes of socio-ecological interaction into which we insert ourselves as transformative beings, then what we say on behalf of others depends crucially upon (*a*) who or what we are primarily in sensual contact and communication with and (*b*) how and why we engage in certain transformative activities rather than others. "Rendering delirious that interior voice of the other within us" is, surely, a vital political moment. But what we say still depends on the sensory, material and communicative world in which our imaginaries, our desires, our discourses and our practices get formed.

Secondly, as Ricoeur (1991) notes, our own sense of self-hood and of identity in part gets constructed through the narrative devices which we use to describe our temporal relation to the world, and so assumes relatively durable configurations. While identity does not rest upon sameness or essence, it does acquire durability and permanence according to the stories we tell ourselves and others about our history and our geography, about, in short, our *place* in the order of things. Although identity internalizes othernesses, it nevertheless delimits and renders relatively durable both the (often spatial) field of "othernesses" brought into play and the relation of those others to a particular sense of self-hood. Whites may construct their identity through historical development of a particular relation to blacks, for example; indeed, both groups may use the other to construct themselves. This intertwining of black and white identities in US history was, as Gates (1992) has recently shown, fundamental to James Baldwin's conception of race relations. But it is precisely within such a process of internalization that much of the racial problematic of contemporary culture resides. To break with racism therefore requires that we break with that process rather than with the discursive categories it produces.

Nevertheless, we can, from this dialectical perspective, better appreciate Hartsock's (1987) claim that "attention to the epistemologies of situated knowledges," can "expose and clarify the theoretical bases for political alliance and solidarity" at the same time as it provides "important alternatives to the dead-end oppositions set up by postmodernism's rejection of the Enlightenment." We must pay close attention to the "similarities that can provide the basis for differing groups to understand each other and form alliances." Refusing the postmodern formulation of the problem, Hartsock insists that we engage with dominant discourses precisely because we cannot abstract from the complex play of power relations. That wing of postmodernism which holds to the "vulgar" version of situatedness, cannot engage with the dominant lines of political–economic power at work under capitalism, and thereby typically marginalizes itself. But that wing of postmodernism that reduces everything to undifferentiated multiplicities and infinite flows also encounters difficulties because the capacity for directed action becomes blocked by the sheer confusion of identities. Kaminer (1995) recounts how:

> The children of identity politics ... routinely deconstruct themselves. "As an educated, married, monogomous, feminist, Christian, Africa-American mother, I suffer from an acute case of multiplicity," Sonja D. Curry-Johnson explains. Sometimes the explanations are sad: "I am not just a woman or just an African-American," Cheryl Green writes. "I am also a person with visible disability, and I have also been shaped by my awareness that my beliefs and experiences conflict with those of white, nondisabled women, nondisabled African-Americans and many women and men with disabilities. I identify partially with all these groups, yet at times I feel contempt and exclusion from each of them."

Somewhere between the vulgar essentialist view and the potentially infinite fluidity of multiple and shifting identifications there has to be a sufficient permanence established (however contingent) to give direction (for a time and in a place) to political action. And that means prioritizing which identities are important. This parallels my conclusion in *The Condition of Postmodernity* (1989a: 117):

> while [postmodernism] opens up a radical prospect by acknowledging the authenticity of other voices, postmodernist thinking immediately shuts off those other voices from access to more universal sources of power by ghettoizing them with an opaque otherness, the specificity of this or that language game. It thereby disempowers those voices (of women, ethnic and racial minorities, colonized peoples, the unemployed, youth, etc.) in a world of lop-sided power relations. The language game of a cabal of international bankers may be impenetrable to us, but that does not put it on a par with the equally impenetrable language of inner-city blacks from the standpoint of power relations.

By insisting upon mutually exclusionary discourses of the sort to which narrow or multiple definitions of situatedness gives rise, we would foreclose upon the most obvious implication of the North Carolina fire: that pursuit of working-class politics might protect, rather than oppress and marginalize, interests based on gender and race even if that working-class politics makes no explicit acknowledgment of the importance of race and gender. The failure of a feminist movement strongly implanted within the professions in the United States to respond to events in North Carolina while mobilizing around the nomination of a supreme court judge, either suggests that narrowly construed views of situatedness have rather more practical political purchase than many would care to admit or else it tacitly orders situatedness in such a way that what happened to those "others" in North Carolina was viewed as somehow less important than the nomination of a supreme court judge of highly dubious moral standing. They were not necessarily wrong in this for as Haraway (1990: 202–3) points out: it is not *difference* which matters, but *significant* difference:

> In the consciousness of our failures, we risk lapsing into boundless difference and giving up on the confusing task of making partial, real connection. Some differences are playful, some are poles of world historical systems of domination. Epistemology is about knowing the difference.

But what is this "epistemology" which permits us to know the difference? How should we pursue it? And to what politics does it give rise?

IV. Class Relations, Social Justice, and the Politics of Difference

There are a number of disparate threads to be drawn together in the guise of a general conclusion. On the one hand we find a line of argument about social justice that passes through postmodernism and poststructuralism to arrive at a point of recognition that some kind of (unspecified) universals are necessary and that some sort of epistemology (unspecified) is needed to establish when, how and where difference and heterogeneity are significant. On the other hand, we have a political–economic situation, as characterized by the North Carolina deaths, which indicates a seeming paralysis of progressive politics in the face of class oppression. How, then, are we to link the two ends of this theoretical and political tension?

Consider, first, the obvious lesson of the Imperial Foods plant fire: that effective working-class politics would have better protected the rights of men and women, whites and African-Americans in a situation where those particular identities, rather than those of class, were not of primary significance. This conclusion merits embellishment.

I first need to define the phrase "working-class politics" since the idea it contains is by no means universally acceptable. To go back to basics, I insist that class is not a thing, an entity, or a "permanence" (though under given conditions it can indeed assume such a form) but fundamentally a process. But what kind of process? Marx appears to define class relationally as command (or noncommand) over the means of production. I prefer to define class as *situatedness or positionality in relation to processes of capital accumulation.* All of us who live under capitalism live out our lives under conditions of embeddedness in such processes. But those processes are often disparate and chaotic, also operating at radically different spatio-temporal scales, so that our individual positionality in relationship to those processes can also be as complicated as it is confused. When I think of my pension fund and insurance I situate myself very differently from how I think about the selling of my labor power or my role as purchaser of commodities. But the fact that each of us has multiple roles in relation to different circuits of capital does not mean that coherent class politics is impossible or undesirable. What it does indicate, is that the formation of those "permanences" required for class politics to function (institutions, social relations, discourses, imaginaries, material practices, and power relations) is itself a process that takes time, persuasion, and a good deal of hard work and cunning. And processes of dissolution are always at work, bringing into question the particular "permanences" shaped to bring political pressure to bear upon capital accumulation. This is what the process of class is all about. Certain "permanences" (such as trade unions) form in a given place and time and are more or less effective in relation to processes of capital accumulation across a certain space for a time. But the question that each generation has to answer for itself, given its own situatedness in relation to capital accumulation is: why does it make sense to struggle to form certain "permanences" rather than others as necessary way-stations *en route* to transforming (or revolutionizing) the socio-ecological processes of capital accumulation?

Let me now put this definition to work in relation to feminist politics. Lynn Segal (1991) has recently noted that "despite the existence of the largest, most influential and vociferous feminist movement in the world, it is US women who have seen the least *overall* change in the relative disadvantages of their sex, compared to other Western democracies" over the past 20 years. The huge gains made in the United States by women within "the most prestigious and lucrative professions" have been offset entirely by a life of increasing frustration, impoverishment, and powerlessness for the rest. The feminization of poverty (not foreign to Hamlet, North Carolina) has been, for example, one of the most startling social shifts in the United States over the past two decades, a direct casualty of the Republican Party class-war against the welfare state and working-class rights and interests. "In countries where there have been longer periods of social-democratic government and stronger trade unions," Segal continues, "there is far less pay-differential and occupational segregation (both vertical and horizontal) between women and men, and far greater expansion of welfare services." Given the far superior material conditions of life achieved for women in such social democracies (and I also note parenthetically the savage diminution in many women's rights since 1989 in what was once the Communist bloc), "it seems strange for feminists to ignore the traditional objectives of socialist or social-democratic parties and organised labour," even though such institutions have obvious weaknesses and limitations as vehicles for pursuit of feminism's objectives [see, for example, Fraser's (1989) compelling argument concerning the gender bias implicit in many welfare-state policies]. Nevertheless, Segal continues, "at a time when the advances made by some women are so clearly overshadowed by the increasing poverty experienced so acutely by others (alongside the unemployment of the men of their class and group), it seems perverse to pose women's specific interests *against* rather than *alongside* more traditional socialist goals." Unless, of course, "women's interests" are either construed in a very narrow professional and class-biased sense or seen as part of "an endless game of self-exploration played out on the great board of Identity" (Segal, 1991: 90–1).

Segal here parallels Hartsock's concern for the "bases for political alliances and solidarity." This requires that we identify "the *similarities* that can provide the basis for differing groups to understand each other and form alliances." Young likewise ties the universality criteria she deploys to the idea that "similarity is never sameness." Difference can never be characterized, therefore, as "absolute otherness, a complete absence of relationship or shared attributes." The *similarity* deployed to measure *difference and otherness* requires, then, just as close an examination (theoretically as well as politically) as does the production of otherness and difference itself. Neither can be established without the other. To discover the basis of similarity (rather than to presume sameness) is to uncover the basis for alliance formation between seemingly disparate groups.

But in today's world, similarity largely resides in that realm of political–economic action so often marginalized in poststructuralist accounts, for it is in terms of commodities, money, market exchange, capital accumulation, and the like that we find ourselves sharing a world of similarity increasingly also characterized by homogeneity and sameness. The radical poststructuralist revolt against that sameness (and its mirror image in some forms of working-class politics) has set the tone of recent debates. but the effect has been to throw out the living baby of political and ethical solidarities and similarities across differences, with the cold bathwater of capitalist-imposed conceptions of universality and sameness. Only through critical re-engagement with political–economy, with our situatedness in relation to capital accumulation, can we hope to re-establish a conception of social justice as something to be fought for as a key value within an ethics of political solidarity built across different places.

Although, therefore, the conception of justice varies "not only with time and place, but also with the persons concerned," (as Engels has it), we must also recognize the political force of the fact that a particular conception of it can be "accepted without misunderstanding" in everyday life. Though "hopelessly confused" when examined in abstraction, ideals of social justice can still function (as Engel's example of the French revolution allows) as a powerful mobilizing discourse for political action. We can certainly find plenty of room to deploy it in relation to our situatedness within the dynamics of capital accumulation.

But two decades of postmodernism and poststructuralism have left us with little basis to accept any particular norm of social justice "without misunderstanding," while in everyday life a titanic effort unfolds to convince all and sundry that any kind of regulation of market freedoms or any level of taxation is unjust and that "class" politics is an anachronism. Empowerment is then conceived of (as conservative politicians like John Major and Newt Gingrich avow) as leaving as much money as possible in the wage earners' as well as in the capitalists' pockets; freedom and justice are attached to maximizing market choice; and rights are interpreted as a matter of consumer sovereignty free of any government dictates. Perhaps the most important thing missing from the postmodern debate these last two decades is the way in which this right wing and reactionary definition of market justice and of rights has played such a revolutionary role in creating the kind of political economy which produced the effects of the North Carolina fire. And I think it is particularly instructive in this regard to note that as market capitalism has re-entered into the hitherto protected space of China, so it has brought with it both the employment conditions and discursive attitudes that surrounded events in Hamlet.

Under such circumstances, reclaiming the terrain of justice and of rights for progressive political purposes appears as an urgent theoretical and political task. But in order to do this we have to come back to that "epistemology" which helps us tell the difference between significant and nonsignificant others, differences and situatedness, and which will help promote alliance formation on the basis of similarity rather than sameness. My own epistemology for this purpose rests on a modernized version of historical and geographical materialism, which forms a meta-theoretical framework for examining not only how differences understood as power relations are produced through social action but also how they acquire the particular significance they do in certain places and situations. From this standpoint it is perfectly reasonable to hold on the one hand, that the philosophical, linguistic, and logical critiques of universal propositions about social justice are correct, while acknowledging on the other hand the putative power of appeals to social justice in certain situations, such as the contemporary United States, as a basis for political action. Struggles to bring a particular kind of discourse about justice into a hegemonic position have then to be seen as part of a broader struggle over ideological hegemony between conflicting groups in society.

V. Conclusions

The overall effect is to leave us with some important analytical, theoretical and political tasks, which can be summarized as follows:

1. The universality can never be avoided, and those who seek to do so (as is the case in many postmodern and poststructuralist formulations) only end up hiding rather than eliminating the condition. But universality must be construed in dialectical relation with particularity. Each defines the other in such a way as to make the universality criterion always open to negotiation through the particularities of difference. Universality must, furthermore, be construed as a differentiated construction embedded in processes operating at quite different spatio-temporal scales. It therefore internalizes contradictions between these scales thus ensuring that there can never be some irreducible principle (or, as Lewontin and Levins put it in their consideration of dialectics, "there is no basement" for enquiry – see chapter 2). It is useful here to examine the political–economic processes by which society actually achieves such a dialectical unity. Money, for example, possessed universal properties as a measure of value and medium of exchange at the same time as it permits a wide range of highly decentralized and particularistic decision making in the realm of market behaviors. These feed back to define what the universality of money is all about. Money is also, as we have seen (see above, pp. 236 and 286) a highly fragmented form with uses that relate to quite different spatio-temporal processes. It is precisely this dialectical power of money which gives such strength to right-wing claims concerning individual freedoms and just deserts through market coordinations. While the injustice that derives is plain – the individual appropriation and accumulation of the social power which money represents produces massive and ever widening social inequality – the subtle power of the universality–particularity dialectic at work in the case of money has to be appreciated. The task of progressive politics is to find an equally powerful, dynamic, and persuasive way of relating the universal and particular at different scales in the drive to define social justice from the standpoint of the oppressed.

2. Respect for identity and "otherness" must be tempered by the recognition that though all others may be others, "some are more other than others" and that in any society certain principles of exclusion have to operate. How this exclusion shall be gauged is embedded in the first instance in a universality condition which prevents groups from imposing their will oppressively on others. This negative freedom (in the sense of freedom from the restraints of others) cannot, however, be imposed hierarchically from above: it must be open to constant negotiation, precisely because of the way in which disparate claims may be framed [for example, when the rich

demand that the oppressive sight (to them) of homelessness be cleared from their vision by expelling the homeless from public spaces]. More serious difficulties arise when we try to speak of the "positive freedoms" (of emancipation, education, realization of human potential, pursuit of cultural achievements, etc.) that might be acceptable as collective projects and how we select those that are desirable and those that are not. If, for example, we reduce ethics to a matter of evolutionary biology (see Wilson's statement cited in chapter 7) then what is to prevent rapists from claiming the freedom to perpetuate their genetic heritage as a matter of right? We typically refute such a claim on the grounds that it involves coercion, but since, as Derrida insists, all legal systems are founded in violence we are left with a principled arbitrariness that excludes that particular otherness from inclusion in our conception of a civilized society.

3. All propositions for social action (or conceptions of social justice) must be critically evaluated in terms of the situatedness or positionality of the argument and the arguer. But it is equally important to recognize that the individuals developing such situated knowledge are not themselves homogeneous entities but bundles of heterogeneous impulses, many of which derive from an internalization of "multiple othernesses" within the self. Such a conception of the subject, renders situatedness (their place) itself heterogeneous and differentiated, highly dependent upon social processes operating at quite different spatio-temporal scales. In the last instance, it is the social construction of situatedness (places) at different scales which matters and in that social construction the agency of personal political choice and commitment, of loyalties, brooks large, however embedded individuals may be in macro-processes of capital accumulation on the world stage.

4. The "epistemology that can tell the difference" between significant and insignificant differences or "othernesses" is one which can understand the social processes of construction of situatedness, places, otherness, difference, political identity, and the like. And we here arrive at what seems to me to be the most important epistemological point: the relation between social processes of construction of identities on the one hand and the conditions of identity politics on the other. If respect for the condition of the homeless (or the racially or sexually oppressed) does not imply respect for the social processes creating homelessness (or racial or sexual oppression), then identity politics must operate at a dual level. A politics which seeks to eliminate the processes which give rise to a problem looks very different from a politics which merely seeks to give full play to differentiated identities once these have arisen.

There here exists a peculiar and difficult tension that we have already encountered in chapter 1. The identity of the homeless person, the racially oppressed, the economically deprived, the woman beset by violence, the worker, the colonial subject, is forged out of certain conditions (material, discursive, psychological, etc.) embedded in the social process. Perpetuation of that sense of self and of identity, I argued in chapter 1, may depend on perpetuation of the processes which gave rise to it. This is a pervasive problem. Poor people rehoused after clearance of even the most appalling slums frequently find themselves "grieving for a lost home" (Fried, 1963). Even working-class movements may seek to perpetuate or return to the conditions of oppression that spawned them, in much the same way that those women who have acquired their sense of self under conditions of male violence may return again and again to living with violent men. It may be, as many feminists have argued and many women have shown, possible to break the pattern, to come out of the dependency. But the first step down that path is to recognize rather than deny the problem. Working-class movements can similarly hope to retain their revolutionary impulse while taking on new political identities under transformed conditions of working and living. But it is a long hard process that needs a lot of careful work. A political program which success-fully combats any form of oppression has to face up to the real difficulty of a loss of identity on the part of those who have been victims of that oppression. And there are subtle ways in which identity, once acquired, can, precisely by virtue of its relative durability, seek out the social conditions (including the oppressions) necessary for its own sustenance. It then follows that the mere pursuit of identity politics as an end in itself (rather than as a fundamental struggle to break with an identity which internalizes oppression) may serve to perpetuate rather than to challenge the persistence of those processes which gave rise to those identities in the first place. The same issue arises even within the ideological debates swirling around identity politics in academia. Recall Spivak's (1988: 280) commentary on the French poststructuralists:

> [they] forget at their peril that [their] whole overdetermined exercise was in the interest of a dynamic economic situation requiring that interests, motives (desires), and power (of knowledge) be ruthlessly dislocated. To invoke that dislocation now as a radical discovery that should make us diagnose the economics ... as a piece of dated analytic machinery may well be to continue the work of that dislocation and unwittingly to help in securing "a new balance of hegemonic relations."

Perhaps this is the best of all possible lessons we can learn from the political failure to respond to events in Hamlet, North Carolina and from the lack of a convincing discourse about social justice with which to confront it. For if the historical and geographical process of class-war waged by the Republican Party and the capitalist class these last few years in the United States has feminized poverty, accelerated racial oppression, and further degraded the ecological conditions of life, then it seems that a far more united politics can flow from a determination to check *that* process than will likely flow from an identity politics which largely reflects its fragmented results.

13

The Environment of Justice

The bourgeoisie has only one solution to its pollution problems: it moves them around.
Saying adapted from Frederick Engels

I. The Movement for Environmental Justice

The Economist (September 8, 1992) reported on a leaked World Bank internal memorandum (dated December 12, 1991) from the pen of Lawrence Summers, a Harvard economist of considerable reputation (nephew of Paul Samuelson and son-in-law of Kenneth Arrow, both Nobel prize-winners in economics). Summers, an oft-quoted advisor to Democratic presidential candidates, then chief economist of the World Bank and subsequently Undersecretary of State for Trade in the Clinton administration wrote:

> Just between you and me, shouldn't the World Bank be encouraging more migration of the dirty industries to the LDC's [less-developed countries?] I can think of three reasons:
> 1. The measurement of the costs of health-impairing pollution depends on the foregone earnings from increased morbidity and mortality. From this point of view a given amount of health-impairing pollution should be done in the country with the lowest cost, which will be the country with the lowest wages. I think the economic logic behind dumping a load of toxic waste in the lowest-wage country is impeccable and we should face up to that.
> 2. The costs of pollution are likely to be non-linear as the initial increments of pollution probably have very low cost. I've always thought that under-populated countries in Africa are vastly *under*-polluted; their [air pollution] is probably vastly inefficiently low compared to Los Angeles or Mexico City. Only the lamentable facts that so much pollution is generated by non-tradable industries (transport, electrical generation) and that the unit

transport costs of solid waste are so high prevent world welfare-enhancing trade in air pollution and waste.

3. The demand for a clean environment for esthetic and health reasons is likely to have a very high income elasticity. The concern over an agent that causes one in a million change in the odds of prostate cancer is obviously going to be much higher in a country where people survive to get prostate cancer than in a country where under-5 mortality is 200 per thousand. Also, much of the concern over industrial atmosphere discharge is about visibility of particulates. These discharges may have little direct health impact. Clearly trade in goods that embody esthetic pollution concerns could be welfare enhancing. While production is mobile the consumption of pretty air is a non-tradable.

The Washington office of Greenpeace faxed copies of the memo around the world. Environmental groups had, and continue to have (see, for example, Bullard, 1993; Pepper, 1993) a field day. The World Bank, already a strong focus for criticism for its lack of environmental concerns, was put very much on the defensive at the very moment it was seeking to influence the Rio Summit on the Environment through publication of its 1992 report on "Development and the Environment." Brazil's Secretary of the Environment described Summers' reasoning as "perfectly logical but totally insane." Summers was featured in *People Magazine* in its special "Earth Day" issue as one of the top eight "enemies of the earth" and even the *Financial Times* thought it time to "save planet earth from economists" (Rich, 1993: 246–50). *The Economist*, however, editorialized that his economic logic was indeed "impeccable."

The Summers memo appears to endorse "toxic colonialism" or "toxic imperialism." The final paragraph of the memo points out, however, that the problem with all of these arguments is that they "could be turned around and used more or less effectively against every Bank proposal." This suggests that Summers was not himself endorsing such ideas but trying to point out to his colleagues, steeped in neoclassical economic theory, the logical consequences of their own mode of thought. While this may exculpate Summers somewhat, it broadens the questions the memo raises to a whole mode of discourse about environmental and economic issues.

So what objections can be raised? To begin with, the class situatedness of the argument is transparent. Affluent groups, including most professional economists [median weekly earnings of $889 in the United States in 1994, according to Uchitelle (1995)] do not have to accept toxic wastes on their own doorstep to survive whereas child care workers ($158 per week), janitors and cleaners ($293 per week), and sewing machine operators ($316 per week) do not have the same range of choice. The logic also pays scant attention to questions of distributive justice, except in the narrowest sense that trade in toxics is meant to be "welfare-enhancing" for all. This presumes that one way to raise incomes of the poor is to pay them to absorb toxins (largely generated on behalf of the rich). Any negative health impacts, it should be noted, will then be visited on those least able to deal with them. Since most of the poor and the disempowered are people of color, the impact is racially discriminatory. And if we care to think about it at all, there is a symbolic dimension, a kind of "cultural imperialism" embedded in the whole proposal – are we not presuming that only trashy people can stomach trash? The question of stigmatization of "the other" through, in this instance, association of racially marked others wit pollution, defilement, impurity, and degradation becomes a part of the political equation. If, as Douglas (1984: 3) claims, "some pollutions are used as analogies for expressing a general view of the social order," and if "pollution beliefs can be used in a dialogue of claims and counter-claims to status," then claims about pollution as "matter out of place" cannot be separated from claims about the impurities and dangers of "people out of place."

Questions of how and why "wastes" in general and hazardous wastes in particular are produced in the first place are, of course, never even mentioned in discussions of the Summers' sort. Yet, as Commoner (1990) has, among others, again and again emphasized, the question of *prevention* surely should take precedence over disposal and cure of any side-effects. But posing that question requires a discursive shift to the far more politically charged terrain of critique of the general characteristics of the mode of production and consumption in which we live.

Though the "impeccable economic logic" advanced by Summers is not hard to deconstruct as the characteristic discourse of a particular kind of political–economic power and its discriminatory practices, it unfortunately approximates as a description of what usually happens. The market mechanism "naturally" works that way. Property values are lower close to noxious facilities and that is where the poor and the disadvantaged are by and large forced by their impoverished circumstances to live. The insertion of a noxious facility causes less disturbance to property values in low income areas so that an "optimal" lowest cost location strategy for any noxious facility points to where the poor live. Furthermore, a small transfer payment to cover negative effects may be very significant to and therefore more easily accepted by the poor, but largely irrelevant to the rich, leading to what I long ago referred to (Harvey, 1973: 81) as the "intriguing paradox" in which "the rich are unlikely to give up an amenity 'at any price' whereas the poor who are least able to sustain the loss are likely to sacrifice it for a trifling sum." If, as is usually the case, areas where low-income, disempowered, and marginalized "others" live are also zones of more political organization, and weak political resistance, then the symbolic, political, and economic logic for the location of noxious facilities works in exactly the way that the Summers' memo envisages.

As a consequence, one of the best predictors of the location of toxic waste dumps in the United States is a geographical concentration of people of low-income and color. The dumping of toxic wastes on indigenous Indian reservations or in communities of color (Africa-American or Hispanic) across much of the south and west of the United States is now well documented (Bryant and Mohai, 1992; Bullard, 1990, 1993, 1994; Hoffrichter, 1993). Even more remarkable, are the bidding wars between, for example, different native-American groups or less-developed countries to accommodate the waste in return for money incomes. While that practice might be better understood in the case of dictators or military regimes who receive all the benefits while visiting the costs on their own populations, it is not unknown for reasonably democratic debate to generate a political consensus in favor of accepting toxic waste facilities on the grounds that this generates otherwise unavailable income and employment. In Alabama's "Blackbelt," for example, the question of hazardous land fills in Sumter County is politically contested: those who have most to lose from denying the facility, in terms of jobs and incomes (the poor and people of color), are in this instance at odds with the middle class and often white environmentalists who seek to close such facilities down (see Bailey et al., 1993). The same conflict holds in Mississippi (Schneider, 1993). The political economy of waste creation and circulation under capitalism incorporates Summers' logic, including some of its inherent social contradictions.

The practice of that logic has, however, sparked militant resistance. In the United States, the movement for environmental justice and against environmental racism has become a significant political force. It is a political movement that has been long in gestation, owing its most recent reincarnation to two particular incidents. First, the celebrated case of Love Canal in 1977, when houses built on top of an infilled-canal in Buffalo, New York, found their basements full of noxious liquids with serious health effects on resident children (Gibbs, 1982; Levine, 1982; Szasz, 1994). This led to the formation of a Citizen's Clearing House for Hazardous Waste which, according to Taylor (1993) now works with over 7,000 community and grass roots groups nationwide. The second arose out of the 1982 protests in Warren County, North Carolina, when a mostly African-American community was selected as the site for burial of soil contaminated with PCBs. The vigor of the protests (multiple arrests of well-known civil rights figures) and the involvement of a wide range of organizations focused attention on what soon came to be known as "environmental racism." In 1991, a very dispersed and highly localized movement came together around the First National People of Color Environmental Leadership Summit held in Washington, DC. There it adopted a manifesto defining environmental justice in no less than 17 different clauses (see Grossman, 1994). I select just a few:

Environmental justice:
    affirms the sacredness of Mother Earth, ecological unity and the interdependence of all species, and the right to be free from ecological destruction

mandates the right to ethical, balanced and responsible uses of land and renewable resources in the interest of a sustainable planet for human and other living things

demands the cessation of the production of all toxins, hazardous wastes, and radioactive materials, and that all past and current producers be held strictly accountable to the people for detoxification and the containment at the point of production

affirms the need for urban and rural ecological policies to clean up and rebuild our cities and rural areas in balance with nature, honoring the cultural integrity of all our communities, and providing fair access for all to the full range of resources

opposes the destructive operations of multi-national corporations ... military occupation, repression and exploitation of lands, peoples and cultures, and other life forms

requires that we, as individuals, make personal and consumer choices to consume as little of Mother Earth's resources and to produce as little waste as possible; and make the conscious decision to challenge and reprioritize our lifestyles to insure the health of the natural world for present and future generations.

I shall return to these principles later, though it is not hard to see how many professionals might regard them as just as "insane" as Summer's memo, while lacking the virtue of elementary let alone "impeccable" logic. The militant local struggles for environmental justice that coalesced to advance these theses created sufficient national political ferment, however, to force the EPA, even in its most recalcitrant Reagan–Bush years, to take up the issues of environmental equity. The EPA's 1992 report on that issue conceded that there were problems of unequal exposure of minority and low-income populations to environmental risks, but asserts that there was not enough hard information to substantiate effective discrimination (except in the case of lead poisoning). In February 1994, however, the Clinton administration – responding to its constituencies of environmentalists, minorities, and the poor – issued an executive order to all federal agencies to ensure that programs would not unfairly inflict environmental harm on the poor and minorities. This means that the environmental needs of low-income and minority communities must be fairly addressed and that environmental issues can be adjudicated in terms of civil rights.

That move did not pacify many in the environmental justice movement in part because they recognized that cooptation into such a legal–political quagmire would be the kiss of death. The reason that hardly any new hazardous waste sites have been opened these last ten years has to do precisely with the fact that movements against such sites have been organized outside of "channels." For this reason too, the environmental justice movement has frequently been at odds with the main environmental groups (such as Friends of the Earth,

The Sierra Club, the Environmental Defense Fund, etc. – usually referred to as "the Big Ten"). The division here reflects class, race, and gender. It also reflects an intense politics of place (cf. chapter 11) versus the more abstract politics of the mainstream environmental movement. "People of Color" and working-class women have been most active in the grass roots movement in particular places where the Big Ten are dominated, in membership but more particularly in organization, by white, middle-class professional men, largely concentrated in the centers of political power (such as Washington, DC). Lois Gibbs, organizer of the original Love Canal protest, recalls her attempt to bring these groups together:

> It was hilarious. ... People from the grassroots were at one end of the room, drinking Budweiser and smoking, while the environmentalists were at the other end of the room eating yoghurt. We wanted to talk about victim compensation. They wanted to talk about ten parts per billion benzene and scientific uncertainty. A couple of times it was almost war. We were hoping that, by seeing these local folks, the people from the Big Ten would be more apt to support the grassroots position, but it didn't work out that way. They went right on with the status quo position. The Big Ten approach is to ask: What can we support to achieve a legislative victory? Our approach is to ask: What is morally correct? We can't support something in order to win if we think it is morally wrong. (Cited in Greider, 1993: 214)

This sort of distinction in allegiance and membership has been playfully characterized as follows:

> Citizen's Clearinghouse – "typical member: quit the church choir to organize toxic dump protest," Natural Resources Defense Council – "typical member: Andover '63, Yale '67, Harvard Law '70, Pentagon anti-war marches '68, '69, '70." Environmental Defense Fund – "typical member: lawyer with a green conscience and a red Miata. ..." (Greider, 1993: 214)

This does not imply that all forms of cooperation are ruled out – Greenpeace, for example, helped the Concerned Citizens of South Central Los Angeles (organized primarily by women) to fight off the LANCER mass-burn incinerator (designed to serve 1.4 million people throughout the city) that was to be located in a poor and heavily minority community (Blumberg and Gottlieb, 1989: chapter 6). Nevertheless, the environmental justice movement preserves its fiercely independent "militant particularism" (see chapter 1). It rejects government and broadly "bourgeois" attempts at cooptation and absorption into a middle-class and professional-based resistance to that impeccable economic logic of environmental hazards that the circulation of capital defines.

II. Discourses of Complicity and Dissent

In recent years the "environmental issue" has, as I argued in chapters 7 and 8, generated a vast diversity of antagonistic and mutually exclusive discourses. There are, to be sure, some common underpinnings. Most – apart, of course, from those who enter only to scoff at the whole idea – accept that there exists a class of problems which might reasonably be dubbed "environmental" and many use a language of actual or potential crisis. Most also argue that the difficulties arise out of the particular way we relate to something external to us called "nature" and that some ameliorative or in some instances revolutionary measures must be taken to put us on some more "sustainable" or "harmonious" trajectory of development. Beyond that, the multiplicity of discourses becomes confusing (see chapter 8) and I now want to take a closer look at how and why this might be the case, focusing particularly upon the political and environmental vision incorporated in discourses about environmental justice. In so doing, I shall make active use of the framework constructed in chapter 4: there, I argued that discourses do not exist in isolation from beliefs, social relations, institutional structures, material practices, or power relations. Discourses internalize effects from all of these domains while reciprocally entering in, though never as pure mirror images, to all of the other moments of the social process.

The advantage of construing things thus is that it allows me to look on a discourse about environmental justice not simply as a philosophical and ethical debate, but rather in terms of the "environmental" conditions (beliefs, institutions, social material practices, and relations, forms of political–economic power) that give rise to such a discourse and become internalized within it. It also permits a closer analysis of how a discourse about environmental justice might "do work" within other moments of the social process (affecting beliefs, imaginaries, institutions, practices, power relations, and the like).

All environmental–ecological arguments, I showed in chapter 8, are arguments about society and, therefore, complex refractions of all sorts of struggles being waged in other realms. Aldo Leopold's land ethic, for example, arose out of a fusion of a discourse on national identity (the role of the frontier and encounter with wilderness in shaping US national identity), religion (the epiphany of looking into the eyes of a mountain lion dying from the hunt) and Darwinian science. Garrett Hardin's "tragedy of the commons" is relentlessly built up through fusion of contemporary Darwinian thinking, the mathematical logic of diminishing returns, and a political economy of an individualized, utility-maximizing, property-owning democracy. Animal rights theorists accept the liberal rhetoric about individual rights and seek to extend it to sentient beings or, as Regan prefers to call them "subjects of a life." Ecological modernization theory (see below) forges a unity between doctrines of efficiency in production and the efficient as well as equitable workings of ecological aggregates. Ecofeminism builds a powerful link between traditional liberal humanism and a vision of women's role as close to nature through nurturing and caring. Each one of these composite discourses shapes a unique blend of complicity and dissent with respect to existing beliefs, institutions, material social practices, social relations, and dominant systems of organizing political–economic power. This is their specific virtue: they pose problems of defining relations across different moments in the social process and reveal much about the pattern of social conflict in all realms of social action.

Consider, for example, the general content in which Summers' version of what to do with toxic wastes becomes possible. It is not sufficient here to argue that it is a typical manifestation of neoclassical economic logic – itself an engaging set of particular metaphors – in which welfare-enhancing trade in waste can be envisaged under conditions of resource-scarcity. For there is a prior question to be answered: why is it that neoclassical economics is such a well-accepted discourse in relation to the dominant forms of political–economic power in capitalist society? And what effects does the privileging of neoclassical economic discourse have on beliefs, the functioning of institutions, social relations, material practices, and the like? I shall not attempt to answer these questions directly here, though I believe a strong case could be made for the deep penetration of neoclassical ways of economic thought into all of these realms. Instead, I shall look more closely at some dominant forms of environmental–ecological discourse in an attempt to gain some insights as to why they hold the particular positions they do and how, given their character and their extensive grip upon the public imagination and public institutions, they have created a set of environmental conditions in which the movement for environmental justice has been forced to articulate its oppositional arguments (and to some degree shape its practices) in very particular ways. With this in mind, let me begin by outlining what seem to be the dominant forms of discourse about the environment in the late twentieth century.

III. The "Standard View" of Environmental Management

Capitalism has frequently encountered environmental problems. Over the last two centuries or so institutions, scientific understandings, public policies, and regulatory practices have been evolved to deal with them. These practices have converged over time into something that I will call "the standard view" of environmental management in advanced capitalist societies.

In the standard view, the general approach to environmental problems is to intervene only "after the event." This strategy in part stems from the belief that no general environmental concerns should stand in the way of "progress" (more precisely, capital accumulation) and that any "after the event" environmental difficulties can be effectively cleaned up if need be. This implies no irreversibility problems of the sort that arise with species extinction or habitat destruction and that a "remedial science" exists to cope with any difficulties that do arise. This "after-the-event" emphasis means that environmental issues are essentially regarded as "incidents" – the result of "errors" and "mistakes" (often based on ignorance) – that should be dealt with on a case-by-case (and often place-by-place) basis. The preference is, furthermore, for environmental cleanups of particular sites and "end-of-pipe" solutions (e.g., soil remediation, the installation of scrubbers on smokestacks, catalytic converters in cars, etc.) rather than for pre-emptive or proactive interventions.

The only general problem sometimes admitted under the standard view is so-called "market failure" which occurs because firms (or other economic entities such as governments and households) can "externalize" costs by free use of the environment for procuring resources or for waste disposal. The theory of the firm developed in neoclassical economics effectively describes why it might be economically rational for individual firms to plunder common resources like fisheries (the famous "tragedy of the commons" argument advanced by Hardin), to pollute, to expose workers to toxic hazards and consumers to environmental degradation under conditions of market failure. It then becomes the task of the state to evolve a regulatory framework that either forces firms to internalize the external costs (generate a more perfect market that factors in all real costs including those attributable to environmental degradation) or to mandate standards that firms (or other entities) must meet with respect to resource management, occupational safety and health, environmental impacts, and the like. It also becomes the task of the state to provide those public goods and public infrastructures conducive to environmentally sound conditions of public health and sanitation. Periodically, as was the case in the progressive era (see Hays, 1959) and in the early stages of the New Deal, this leads to the idea of considerable state intervention to ensure the proper conservation and efficient management of national resources, thus challenging the rights of private property in the interest of a state-managed class strategy for capital accumulation. Against this, neoclassical economics has also evolved a defense of private property solutions under the aegis of the so-called Coase (1960) theorem which holds that both the polluter and any injured party can equally be regarded as wrongdoers since the presence of the latter limits the property rights of the former to emit pollutants.

All state interventions, the logical tool of environmental management, are typically limited under the standard view by two important considerations. First, intervention should occur only when there is clear evidence of serious damage through market failure and preferably when that damage can be quantified (e.g., in money terms). This requires strong scientific evidence of connections between, for example, exposure to asbestos in the workplace and cancers developing 20 years later or power plant emissions and acidification of lakes hundreds of miles away. And it also requires careful measurement of costs of pollution and resource depletion because the second constraint is that there is thought to be a zero-sum trade-off between economic growth (capital accumulation) and environmental quality. To be overly solicitous with respect to the latter is to forgo unnecessarily the benefits of the former. This is the domain of monetized cost–benefit analysis which now plays such an important role in shaping environmental politics under the standard view.

Getting to the heart of what the trade-offs might be (theoretically and empirically) requires a particular combination of engineering and economic expertise coupled with scientific understandings of ecological processes. The translation of the environmental problem into the domain of expert discourses permits the internalization of environmental politics and regulatory activity largely within the embrace of the state apparatus or, more loosely, under the influence of corporate and state finance of research and development. This entails an application of bureaucratic–technocratic rationality under the dual influence of the state and corporations. The rough and tumble of democratic politics is generally viewed as getting in the way of proper, rational, and sensible regulatory activities. The preferred strategy, except in those periods of euphoric state strategizing, is to negotiate out solutions between the state and the private sector often on an *ad hoc* and case-by-case basis.

Under the standard view, the basic rights of private property and of profit maximization are not fundamentally challenged. Concerns for environmental justice (if they exist at all) are kept strictly subservient to concerns for economic efficiency, continuous growth, and capital accumulation. The view that capital accumulation (economic growth) is fundamental to human development is never challenged. The right of humanity to engage in extensive environmental modifications is tacitly accepted as sacrosanct (turning the standard view into a doctrine complicitous with the hubristic version of the domination of nature thesis). The only serious question is how best to manage the environment for capital accumulation, economic efficiency, and growth. From this standpoint, negative externality effects (including those on health and welfare) deserve to be countered (provided no serious barriers are created to further accumulation) and serious attention should be given to proper conservation and wise use of resources. Given the framework, ecological issues within the standard view are generally viewed as a concern of the nation state, in some instances devolving powers to lower levels of government. National politics and cultural traditions (for example, with respect to the importance of wilderness or the forest) then typically play an important role in affecting the way in which the standard view gets worked out and presented in different nation states and even in different localities. Put in the prevailing terms of economics, socially based and often locally specific preferences for environmental qualities can be factored into the argument as a particular manifestation of consumer preference.

A powerful and persuasive array of discourses are embedded (sometimes without even knowing it) within this standard view and its associated practices, institutions, beliefs, and powers. Environmental economics, environmental engineering, environmental law, planning and policy analysis, as well as a wide range of scientific endeavors are ranged broadly in support of it. Such discourses are perfectly acceptable to the dominant forms of political–economic power precisely because there is no challenge implied within them to the hegemony of capital accumulation. Financial and logistical support therefore flows from the state and corporations to those promoting such environmental discourses, making them distinctive discourses of power.

This is not to say that there is no contestation within the standard view. There is abundant room for dispute over the scientific evidence of connection between environmental change and social effects, the extent and measure of damage, the designation of liability, where the trade-offs between economic growth and environmental quality (or equity) should lie, how divergent consumer preferences for environmental qualities might be measured and expressed, how far into the long run environmental concerns should be projected (the literature on discount rates and time-preferences is extensive), and how comprehensive state regulation should be. The intensity of debate within this overall discursive frame often precludes general discussion of broader let alone radically different alternatives. But, the debates have sometimes generated contradictions that do prepare the way for discursive shifts into radically different ways of thinking. While, for example, the apparent intent of Summers' memo was to wake up some of his colleagues to a stronger sense of how to negotiate issues of environmental equity and market forces within the standard view, it subsequently became an icon whose shock value could be used to press for an alternative discourse of environmental justice.

The standard view has a considerable history. Beginning with the extensive public health measures in nineteenth-century urban settings and following through to present-day efforts to improve air and water quality in many areas of the advanced capitalist world, the working out of the standard view has not been without a substantial record of successes to its credit. Were this not the case, it would long ago have been abandoned. At its best, even some of its seemingly negative features have a virtuous side; for example, the *ad hoc* and fragmented approach has sometimes permitted a degree of local and particularist sensitivity to consumer preferences and considerable flexibility in environmental interventions. But there are, plainly, serious limitations to the effectiveness of the standard approach and in recent years some of its more glaring internal contradictions have spawned the search for some alternative way to look at environmental issues.

IV. Ecological Modernization

The thesis of "ecological modernization" (see Hajer, 1995) has periodically emerged as one way to structure thinking about the dialectics of social and ecological change. In the United States it became popular during the progressive era (when the name of Pinchot dominated discussions) and remerged during the 1930s in the soil conservation movement and within institutions like the National Resources Planning Board (Hays, 1987). In recent years there are signs of its adoption/cooptation by both environmental pressure groups and certain institutionalized configurations of political–economic power.

Ecological modernization depends upon and promotes a belief that economic activity systematically produces environmental harm (disruptions of "nature") and that society should therefore adopt a proactive stance with respect to environmental regulation and ecological controls. Prevention is regarded as preferable to cure. This means that the *ad hoc*, fragmented and bureaucratic approach to state regulation should be replaced by a far more systematic set of politics, institutional arrangements, and regulatory practices. The future, it is argued, cannot be expected to look after itself and some sorts of calculations are necessary to configure what would be a good strategy for sustainable economic growth and economic development in the long run. The key word in this formulation is "sustainability." And even though there are multiple definitions of what this might mean (and all sorts of rhetorical devices deployed by opponents to make the term meaningless or render it harmless since no one can possibly be in favor of "unsustainability"), the concept nevertheless lies at the heart of the politics of ecological modernization. The rights of future generations and the question of appropriate temporality therefore move to the center of discussion rather than being assumed away within market forces as typically occurs within the standard view (see chapter 7).

This shift in emphasis is justified in a variety of ways. The irreversibility problem, in the standard view, becomes, for example, much more prominent, not only with respect to biodiversity but also with respect to the elimination of whole habitats, permanent resource depletion, desertification, deforestation, and the like. High orders of environmental *risk* are emphasized coupled with a rising recognition that unintended ecological consequences of human activity can be far-reaching, long-lasting, and potentially damaging. Beck's (1992) formulation of the idea that we now live in a "risk society" (largely a consequence of an accelerating pace of seemingly uncontrollable technological change) has proven a useful and influential adjunct to the discursive thrust to define a risk-minimizing politics of ecological modernization. There has also been growing recognition that *ad hoc* and after-the-fact practices can produce unbalanced and ineffective results.

The role of scientists in promoting the discursive shift from the standard view to ecological modernization was important [see Litfin (1994) and Hajer

(1995) for recent case-studies]. It was science that revealed global problems (acid rain, global warming, and ozone holes) demanding wide-ranging collective action beyond nation state borders, thereby posing a challenge (legal, institutional, and cultural) to the closed bureaucratic rationality of the nation state. And some individual scientists pushed the knowledge of ecological systems and interrelatedness to the point where the unintended consequences of human activities could be seen to be far more widespread, irreversible, and potentially serious than had previously been recognized. This made the "business as usual" and "after the fact" approach of the standard view appear more and more inadequate. This kind of science provided crucial support to many environmental pressure groups, many of whom initially viewed scientific rationality with scepticism and distrust. The thesis of ecological modernization has now become deeply entrenched within many segments of the environmental movement. The effects, as we shall see, have been somewhat contradictory. On the one hand, ecological modernization provides a common discursive basis for a contested rapprochement between them and dominant forms of political–economic power. But on the other, it presumes a certain kind of rationality that lessens the force of more purely moral arguments (cf. the comments of Louis Gibbs cited above) and exposes much of the environmental movement to the dangers of political cooptation.

The general persuasiveness of the ecological modernization thesis rests, however, on one other radical discursive shift. This refuses to see the supposed trade off between environmental concerns and economic growth in zero-sum terms. What are known as "win–win" examples of ecological control are increasingly emphasized. Given the power of money, it is vital to show that ecological modernization can be profitable. Environmental care, it is argued, often contributes to efficiency (through more efficient fuel use, for example) and long-term preservation of the resource base for capital accumulation. If, furthermore, pollution is merely being moved around (from air to water to land) under standard practices, then aggregate efficiency is being impaired in the long-run if, as is increasingly the case, there are fewer and fewer empty "sinks" within which pollutants can costlessly be absorbed. And if, to take the parallel case of supposedly "natural" resources, depletion is occurring too fast to allow for smooth market adjustment and measured technological change, then costly disruptions to economic growth may be in the wind. To some degree the search for "win–win" solutions has also been prompted by environmental litigation, environmental impact legislation and, in some sectors, like those directly associated with occupational and consumer safety and health, by extraordinarily high compensation awards for injured parties (as, for example, with the case of asbestos liability that drove firms and some insurers – a group of celebrated "names" of Lloyds of London – into bankruptcy). The costliness of recent clean-up efforts – the "superfund" experience in the United States to clean up hazardous waste sites being perhaps the best example – has also pushed many to take a new look at prevention.

Environmental equity (distributive justice) has a stronger role to play in ecological modernization arguments. This is in part due to the inroads made by the environmental justice movement and various other movements around the world expressive of what Martinez-Allier (1990) calls "the environmentalism of the poor." But leaving these aside, cooperation is required to gain support for proactive environmental initiatives so that the question of environmental justice has to be integrated into the search for long-term sustainability, partly as a pragmatic adaptation to the internationalism of several key contemporary ecological issues: sovereign nation states, including those that are poor, have to agree to a certain regulatory environment on, for example, carbon emissions and CFC use, and, furthermore, enforce its provisions. Negotiating with China and India is politically quite different from negotiating the location of a hazardous waste site in Mississippi. So some sort of configuration has to be envisaged in which ecological modernization contributes both to growth and global distributive justice simultaneously. This was a central proposition in the Brundtland Report [World Commission on Environment and Development (WCED), 1987] for example. How, and if, that can be done is at the heart of deeply contentious debates. There are also signs of a discursive shift, perhaps fashioned as a response to the contentiousness of the distributive justice issue, in which economic *development* (improvement in human capacities and conditions) is seen as quite distinctive from economic *growth* (the increase in output of goods and services). If governments can be persuaded to take the former path then the competitive challenge to the hegemony of the advanced capitalist powers with respect to capital accumulation through economic growth will be lessened.

One side-consequence of these shifts is that environmental management is no longer seen to be the exclusive provenance of governments or the nation state. The nation state, while clearly still important, should be supplemented by strong international organizations as well as local governments. The general import of the Rio conference, for example, was to give far greater powers to international organizations (like the World Bank and the United Nations Environmental Program) and to set up local government mandates for environmental quality. Many layers of government operating at many different scales should be implicated as partners in the search for better paths of environmental management. This move to construct some sort of hierarchy of powers tacitly recognizes the diverse spatial scales at which environmental issues can arise. While very little of this has actually been worked out in practice, a discursive shift away from the nation state towards some sort of recognition of the spatial scalar layering of environmental issues can certainly be detected (see chapters 7 and 8 for further considerations on spatial scaling). A wide range of forces in civil society (nongovernmental organizations, pressure groups, community agents) can then become involved. The public debate over "values" has consequently become much more explicit, preparing the ground for a veritable industry of philosophical reflection devoted to "environmental ethics." And much more open and democratic as well as wide-ranging discussions of environmental issues become possible. It is precisely at this interface that the fine line between incorporation and open contestation again and again gets crossed and recrossed, with legal, scientific and economic discourses, institutions and practices becoming a deeply implicated and contested terrain.

In portraying the general characteristics of the ecological modernization thesis in this systematic way, I am exaggerating both its coherence and its difference from the standard view. The raggedness of the environmental–ecological debate the last 20 years defies any such simple characterization. But the debate in the public realm has been much more open to ecological modernization arguments than was previously the case. And as often happens with a public discourse in formation, all sorts of interventions and openings have occurred, through which quite a bit of radicalization has been achieved. Some radical environmental groups have been partially drawn to the ecological modernization thesis, sometimes as a tactic because it provides convenient and more generally persuasive public arguments with which to pursue other objectives, but sometimes as a matter of deeper conviction, viewing it as the only way to move a deeply entrenched capitalism towards ecological sanity and a modicum of global justice. And there is some evidence that the nascent European bureaucracy in Brussels saw ecological modernization as a means of empowerment against narrower national and corporate interests. Socialists, for their part, could take to the argument as a way of combining traditional commitments to growth and equity with rational planning under socialized control. Commoner's *Making Peace with the Planet Earth* (1990) and Leff's *Green Production: Toward an Environmental Rationality* (1995) can be read, for example, as left-wing versions of this thesis. I shall come back to this particular line of thinking by way of conclusion.

But the discourse would not have the purchase it evidently has had without a significant tranch of support from the heartland of contemporary political–economic power. The rising tide of affluence in the advanced capitalist countries after World War II increased middle-class interest in environmental qualities and amenities, "nature" tourism, and deepened concerns about environmental dangers to health. While this lent an indelible bourgeois esthetic and politics to much of the environmental movement, it nevertheless pushed environmental issues to the political agenda where they could not easily be controlled as a mere adjunct of bourgeois fashion. The health connection, as Hays (1987) points out, became particularly salient and peculiarly open-ended in relation to environmental concerns in the United States after 1950 or so. Systematic environmental concern for everything from landscape despoliation, heritage, and wilderness preservation, control of air and water quality, exposure to toxics, waste disposal, regulation of consumer products, and the like became much easier to voice given middle-class acceptance of such issues as fundamental to its own qualities of life. This aspect to the problem has been strongly emphasized by Beck (1992) who argues that the costs of the contemporary form of a high-environmental risk society are spread across the class spectrum thereby turning the environmental issue into a populist issue (even the bourgeois can get skin cancer and leukemia). *The Limits to Growth* (Meadows et al.) published in 1972, which in many respects was a powerful warning shot to say that the standard view was inadequate, was supported by the Club of Rome (an influential group of bankers and industrialists) and the Brundtland Report (WCED) of 1987, which consolidated the ecological modernization discourse in important ways, bringing the question of "sustainability" to the fore, was an effort supported by many government officials, industrialists, financiers, and scientists. And since that time, major world institutions, such as the World Bank, which previously paid no attention whatsoever to environmental issues, some corporations (like IBM and even Monsanto), and powerful establishment politicians, like Margaret Thatcher and Al Gore, have been converted to some version of the ecological modernization thesis. Even *The Economist* (June 3, 1995: 57) now sees fit to celebrate "a budding romance between greens and business" in an article entitled "How to Make Lots of Money, and Save the Planet Too."

There is a more sinister aspect to this argument, however. The severe recession of 1973–5, the subsequent slow-down in economic growth and rise of widespread structural unemployment, made an appeal to some notion of natural limits to growth more attractive. Scapegoating natural limits rather than the internal contradictions of capitalism is a well-tried tactic. When faced with a crisis, said Marx of Ricardo, he "takes refuge in organic chemistry" (see Harvey, 1974). This particular way of thinking puts particular blame on population growth, again and again raising the specter of Malthus (see chapter 6), thereby reducing much of the ecological–environmental problem to a simple population problem. But this essentially reactionary political approach was paralleled in *The Limits to Growth* and the Brundtland Report by concerns for natural limits to capital accumulation (and, hence, for employment possibilities and rising standards of affluence worldwide). The rhetoric of "sustainable development" could then be attached to the ideal of a growth economy that had to respect natural limits. Demands for higher wages or more rapid economic growth in poorer parts of the world were countered by appeal to certain immutable laws of nature, thus diverting attention from the far more mutable laws of entrenched class and imperialist privilege. The supposed sheer physical inability of the planet to support global populations with aspirations to a living standard of Sweden or Switzerland became an important political argument against even trying to spread the benefits of capitalist growth around.

The evident failures of capitalist modernization and resource management in many developing countries also made the rhetoric of ecological modernization more attractive. In many developing countries this meant a partial return to traditional methods as more ecologically sensitive and hence more efficient. The World Bank, for example, took to blaming the governments of Africa for the failure of its own development projects there and then sought to decentralize the process of development to see if indigenous methods led by indigenous peoples, with women cast in a much more central role, could work so as to pay off the accumulating debts built up precisely through World Bank-imposed western-style development.

Finally, many corporations, like IBM, saw a great deal of profit to be had from superior environmental technologies and stricter global environmental regulation. For the advanced capitalist nations, struggling to remain competitive, the imposition of strong environmental regulations demanding high-tech solutions promised not only a competitive advantage to their own industries but also a strong export market for the more environmentally friendly technology they had developed (the environmental clean-up in eastern Europe has proven particularly lucrative). If only a small fragment of corporate capital thought this way, it was nevertheless a significant dissident voice arguing for ecological modernization from within a powerful segment of the bourgeoisie. Global environmental management "for the good of the planet" and to maintain "the health" of planet earth could also be conveniently used to make claims on behalf of major governments and corporations for their exclusive and technologically advanced management of all the world's resources. So while a good deal of corporate capture of the ecological modernization rhetoric (particularly via "green consumerism") could be found, there are also positive reasons for some segments of corporate capital to align themselves with a movement that emphasized certain kinds of technological change coupled with highly centralized global environmental management practices. The clean-up industry alone now has a value of some $200 billion within the OECD and, being heavily dependent upon proper regulation, forms a significant pressure group for regulatory action and ecological modernization (*The Economist*, June 3, 1995: 57).

As a discourse, ecological modernization internalizes conflict. It has a radical populist edge, paying serious attention to environmental–ecological issues and most particularly to the accumulation of scientific evidence of environmental impacts on human populations, without challenging the capitalist economic system head on. It does imply strict regulation of private property rights, however, and in so far as it leads to action it can *de facto*, through regulatory action, curb the possibilities for uncontrolled capital accumulation. Yet it is also a discourse that can rather too easily be corrupted into yet another discursive representation of dominant forms of economic power. It can be appropriated by multinational corporations to legitimize a global grab to manage all of the world's resources. Indeed, it is not impossible to imagine a world in which big industry (certain segments), big governments (including the World Bank) and establishment, high-tech big science can get to dominate the world even more than they currently do in the name of "sustainability," ecological modernization and appropriate global management of the supposedly fragile health of planet earth. This is precisely the shift that Sachs (1993: xv) fears:

> As governments, business and international agencies raise the banner of global ecology, environmentalism changes its face. In part, ecology – understood as the philosophy of a social movement – is about to transform itself from a knowledge of opposition to a knowledge of domination. ... In the process, environmental-ism ... becomes sanitized of its radical content and reshaped as expert neutral knowledge, until it can be wedded to the dominating world view.

Class forces resolutely opposed to such a reshaping can be found at both ends of the political spectrum. Let us look first at the reaction of the libertarian right.

V. "Wise Use" and the Defense of Private Property

Ecological modernization is anathema to certain segments of capital (includ-ing important segments of the traditional petit bourgeoisie). There is a strong desire to smother it (together with anything other than the minimalist version of the standard view) in many quarters. While some corporations are favorably disposed towards it, most are not. By far the most powerful opposition derives from its impacts upon the rights of private property (particularly owners of raw materials and "natural" resources). The whole idea of ecological mod-ernization, and the planned government-led or collective interventions it presupposes, is anathema to the libertarian wing of conservative politics. And through the "wise use" movement, particularly focused in the US west, it has found a libertarian equivalent of the environmental justice movement with which to attack not only ecological modernization but anything except minimalist appeal to the standard view.

The "wise use" movement draws in fact on a long tradition of environmental activism – though, as we shall see, of a very special sort. The appropriation of the term "wise use" is not merely an opportunistic rhetorical device with which to counter any form of governmental intervention or regulation. The tradition has its origins in classical liberal theories, particularly those generally attributed to Locke, and their translation into political–economic practices most particularly in the United States with its tradition of Jeffersonian democracy. The argument is in part based on the inalienable right of individuals to mix their labor with the land in such a way as to "make the earth fruitful and to multiply." But it is also strongly based on the view that private property owners have every incentive in the world to maintain and sustain the ecological conditions of productivity that furnish them with a living and that, left to their own devices, they will more likely pass on the land to their offspring in an improved rather than deteriorated condition. Arthur Young, an influential commentator on agricultural affairs in late eighteenth-century England, put it this way: "on an annual rental a man will turn a garden into a desert: but give a man a fourteen year lease and he will turn a desert into a garden."

This was, of course, exactly the sentiment that led William Lloyd to propose "the tragedy of the commons" thesis in 1833. And some commentators on Hardin's (1968) influential restatement of that idea have treated it as a plea for private property arrangements as the best protection against those abuses of the commons which governments by their very nature are powerless to prevent. Even if Hardin does not himself follow that line of reasoning, it has not been hard for legal scholars and for theoreticians to argue that the taking away of private property rights without full compensation for environmental reasons is unjustified and that the wisest and best organizational form for ensuring proper use of the land is a highly decentralized property-owning democracy. Von Hayeck, Nozick, and a whole host of contemporary economists and legal scholars (such as Epstein, 1985) would agree.

The "wise use" movement in the United States has its roots in a long tradition of opposition to the powers of the federal government to regulate private property. The so-called "sage-brush rebellion" of western cattle-ranching interests against federal control over extensive tracts of land in the US west was just one incident in that history. It appeals to popular common sense and makes effective use of powerful anecdotes of personal injustice on the part of individuals caught in the regulatory thickets of government action. In treating the rights of private property as sacrosanct (and the spread of "privatization" and "deregulation" as social goods), the wise use doctrine gathers many powerful adherents from the corporate sector which, when coupled with a populist base, makes for a potent political force (see Echeverria and Eby, 1995). It became dominant in the congress of the United States with the Republican victory of 1994, for example, though there is abundant evidence that it was gathering momentum in the courts as well as within various levels of government in the United States from Reagan's election in 1979 onwards.

The "wise use" movement has two other arguments which it adds to its strong defense of private property against governmental constraints. The first is that the right to jobs (and hence economic development and capital accumulation) must take precedence over the "rights of nature" (however the latter may be construed, if at all). The "wise use" movement thrives on zero-sum arguments of the sort that pitted the fate of the spotted owl in the US northwest against employment opportunities in logging. And the second is that universal land-use rules necessarily do an injustice to local and private determinations. Even the most sophisticated science allied with big government cannot come up with regulations sufficiently sensitive to cover all contingencies in all particulars.

Private property owners are judged in principle much more knowledgeable about their own particulars than state bureaucrats and scientists. In all of these respects, the wise use movement has some strong arguments on its side. Keith Schneider (Echeverria and Eby, 1995: 351), an environmental journalist of some repute, considers it as "maybe one of the most important and interesting movements to arise in environmentalism in a long time" precisely because of its ability to question much of the environmental orthodoxy that has arisen in recent years. So although the movement has been powerfully coopted and funded by corporate, industrial, and, perhaps most important of all, by commercial logging, ranching, and agribusiness interests, it has sufficient of a democratic and populist edge to deserve serious consideration.

The case against the "wise use" movements is strong if not fatal to its pretensions. Even presuming that private property owners are paragons of bourgeois virtue and that they stay in place long enough to become deeply familiar with their local ecological conditions of production (a presumption that hardly applies to most land developers, resource extractors, and speculators), there is no ground to believe in principle that each owner is more knowledgeable than the collective. There is even less ground for believing that the territorial purview of the private owner bears any relationship whatsoever to the spatio-temporal scale of ecological processes varying from the microcosm of the field through regional questions concerning land use, amenities, resource allocations, water and air qualities, to global questions of biodiversity, climate warming, and the like. Since the pattern of property ownership is ecologically chaotic and socially lop-sided, there are absolutely no grounds for believing that appeal to its commensensical wisdoms can allow for any wisdom at all with respect to environmental justice let alone ecologically sustainable development even in its most naked capitalistic form.

VI. Environmental Justice and the Defense of the Poor

The environmental justice movement advances a discourse radically at odds with the standard view and ecological modernization. It is also profoundly at odds with the "wise use" movement though for quite different reasons. Of all the discourses considered here, it has proven far less amenable to corporate or governmental cooptation. Five issues stand out:

1. Inequalities in protection against environmental hazards have been felt in very tangible ways in enough instances, such as Love Canal, to make compensation for and elimination of such inequalities a pressing material (largely health) issue for many. Putting the inequalities at the top of the environmental agenda directly challenges the dominant discourses (be they of the standard, ecological modernization, or "wise use" variety).

2. "Expert" and "professional" discourses have frequently been mobilized by dominant forms of political–economic power to either deny, question, or diminish what were either known or strongly felt to be serious health effects deriving from unequal exposure. The resultant climate of suspicion towards expert and professional discourses (and the form of rationality they frequently espouse) underlies the search for an alternative rationality (even, if necessary, "irrationality") with which to approach environmental hazards. While science, medicine, economics, and the law may remain important ingredients within the discourse of environmental justice, they are not therefore ever permitted to frame the arguments in toto. In this regard there is a similarity of sorts between the "wise use" and the environmental justice movements.

3. The adoption of biocentric discourses that focus on the fate of "nature" rather than of humans on the part of many environmental groups (albeit modified by incorporation of theses of ecological modernization) has prompted its own reaction. As Taylor (1992) notes:

> The more established environmental organizations do fight issues of survival, and they use the survival theme to get the support of their members, but these are survival issues as they pertain to endangered species, national parks and preserves, threatened landscapes. ... These survival debates are not linked to rural and urban poverty and quality of life issues. If it is discovered that birds have lost their nesting sites, then environmentalists go to great expense and lengths to erect nesting boxes and find alternative breeding sites for them; when whales are stranded, enormous sums are spent to provide them food and shelter, when forests are threatened large numbers of people are mobilized to prevent damage; but we have yet to see an environmental group champion the cause of homelessness in humans or joblessness as issues on which it will spend vast resources. It is a strange paradox that a movement which exhorts the harmonious coexistence of people and nature, and worries about the continued survival of nature (particularly loss of habitat problems), somehow forgets about the survival of humans (especially those who have lost their "habitats" and "food sources").

The environmental justice movement therefore puts the survival of people in general, and of the poor and marginalized in particular, at the center of its concerns.

4. The marginalized, disempowered, and racially marked positions of many of those most affected, together with the strong involvement of women as dominant carers for the children who have suffered most from, for example, the consequences of lead-paint poisoning or leukemia, have forced otherwise disempowered individuals to seek empowerment outside of prevailing institutions. The coupling of the search for empowerment and personal self-respect on the one hand with environmentalist goals on the other means

that the movement for environmental justice twins ecological with social justice goals in quite unique ways. In so doing, the movement opens itself to distinctive positionalities from which injustice can differentially be measured. As Krauss (1994: 270) observes:

> women's protests have different beginning places, and their analyses of environmental justice are mediated by issues of class and race. For white blue-collar women, the critique of the corporate state and the realization of a more genuine democracy are central to a vision of environmental justice. ... For women of color, it is the link between race and environment, rather than between class and environment, that characterizes definitions of environmental justice. African American women's narratives strongly link environmental justice to other social justice concerns, such as jobs, housing, and crime. Environmental justice comes to mean the need to resolve the broad social inequities of race. For Native American women, environmental justice is bound up with the sovereignty of the indigenous peoples.

Such different positionalities create, as we shall see, interpretive tensions within the environmental justice movement across the themes of class, race, gender, and national identity. Bullard (1993: 21) summarizes evidence to show, for example, that people of color are much more vulnerable to environmental hazards even when controlling for social status and class and concludes that the injustice is fundamentally a race and not a class problem.

5. Doing battle with the lack of self-respect that comes from "being associated with trash" lends a very emotive symbolic angle to the discourse and highlights the racial and discriminatory aspects to the problem. This ultimately pushes discussion far beyond the scientific evidence on, for example, health effects, cost–benefit schedules or "parts per billion" to the thorny, volatile, and morally charged terrain of symbolic violence, "cultural imperialism" and personalized revolt against the association of "pollution" in its symbolic sense of defilement and degradation with dangerous social disorder and supposed racial impurities of certain groups in the population.

These conditions of production of an environmental justice movement in the United States account for some of its central features. To begin with, the focus on particular kinds of pollution – toxics and dangerous contaminants – loads the discussion towards symbolic questions, making clear that the issue is as much about "claims and counter-claims to status" (cf. Douglas, 1984: 3), as it is about pollution *per se*. This is what gives the movement so much of its moral force and capacity for moral outrage. But the corollary, as Szasz (1994) points out, is that the movement relies heavily upon symbolic politics and powerful media icons of pollution incidents. Toxics in someone's basement at Love Canal in Buffalo, New York is a much more powerful issue from this perspective, even though it involves a very small number of people, than the diffuse cloud of ozone concentrations in major cities that effects millions every summer throughout much of the United States. In the case of Love Canal, there was an identifiable enemy (a negligent corporation), a direct and unmistakable effect (nasty liquids in the basement, sick children, and worried suburban mothers), a clear threat to public trust in government (the Board of Education was clearly negligent), a legal capacity to demand personal compensation, an undefinable fear of the unknown, and an excellent opportunity for dramatization that the media could and did use with relish. In the case of ozone concentration, the enemy is everyone who drives, governments have very little mandate to intervene in people's driving habits, the effects are diffuse, demands for compensation hard to mount, and the capacity for dramatization limited making for very little media coverage. The resultant bias in choice of targets permits critics to charge that the emphases of the environmental justice movement are misplaced, that its politics are based on an iconography and politics of fear, and that the movement has more to do with moral outrage than the science of impacts. Such criticisms – which are frequently made of Greenpeace as well – are often justifiable by certain standards (such as those espoused by mainstream environmentalists), but precisely for that reason are largely beside the point.

The refusal to cast discussion in monetary terms, to take another example, reflects an intuitive or experiential understanding of how it is that seemingly fair market exchange always leads to the least privileged falling under the disciplinary sway of the more privileged and that *costs* are always visited on those who have to bow to money discipline while *benefits* always go to those who enjoy the personal authority conferred by wealth. There is an acute recognition within the environmental justice movement that the game is lost for the poor and marginalized as soon as any problem is cast in terms of the asymmetry of money exchange (and particularly in terms of cost–benefit analysis). Money is always a form of social power and an instrument of discipline in social relations rather than a neutral universal equivalent with which to calculate "welfare-enhancing benefits."

This active denial of the neutrality of the monetary calculus perhaps accounts for the somewhat medieval tone of the declaration on environmental justice adopted at the 1991 conference (though, of course, cast in terms of contemporary technologies and possibilities). The affirmation of "the sacredness of Mother Earth, ecological unity and the interdependence of all species, and the right to be free from ecological destruction" parallels in interesting ways Gurevich's (1985: 274) characterization of medieval justice as:

> at one and the same time a moral and a cosmic principle, to which all human activity must be subordinated. Any departure from this principle is equivalent to transgression of the divine order of things and of natural law ... social justice [is] that by which the harmony of the whole is sustained, and which denies none their due desserts.

I do not present this parallel in order to undermine, but rather to suggest that the principles of environmental justice, though cast in a somewhat unfamiliar mold to many of us, would be familiar to those upon whom what Benton (1993) calls "the liberal illusion" has yet to do its insidious work. This illusion takes the following form:

> In societies governed by deep inequalities of political power, economic wealth, social standing and cultural accomplishment the promise of equal rights is delusory with the consequence that for the majority, rights are merely abstract, formal entitlements with little or no *de facto* purchase on the realities of social life. In so far as social life is regulated by these abstract principles and in so far as the promise is mistaken for its fulfillment, then the discourse of rights and justice is an ideology, a form of mystification which has a causal role in binding individuals to the very conditions of dependence and impoverishment from which it purports to offer emancipation.

The environmental justice movement has, by and large, seen through this illusory state of affairs. But this means that it also has to do battle with the liberal illusion and its pervasive effects as well as with direct forms of ecological harm. In so doing, some have indeed been led into backward-looking praise for the medieval world (a mythical golden age of integration with nature when human societies trod so lightly on the earth that all was well between humans and nature) and sidewards looking admiration for those marginalized peoples who have not yet been fully brought within the global political economy of technologically advanced and bureaucratically rationalized capitalism.

The affirmation of the "sacredness of Mother Earth" and other rhetoric of that sort is, I want to suggest, both problematic and empowering. It is empowering precisely because it permits issues to be judged in terms of moral absolutes, of good and evil, right and wrong. By posing matters in terms of the defilement, violation, or even "rape" of a sacred Mother Earth, the environmental justice movement adopts a nonnegotiable position of intense moral rectitude untouchable by legal, scientific, or other rationalistic discourses. It permits the assertion, in quasi-religious language, of the widespread view that the proper approach is to ask, in Lois Gibbs' words, "what is morally correct?" rather than "what is legally, scientifically, and pragmatically possible?"

It also permits, through the medium of social protest, the articulation of ideas about a moral economy of collective provision and collective responsibility as opposed to a set of distributive relations within the political economy of profit. While the "moral economy" being proposed is definitely not that of the traditional peasant, the very grounding of the discourse in a language of sacredness and moral absolutes creates a certain homology between, say, struggles over exposure to environmental hazards in urban areas, nativist beliefs on the relation to nature and peasant movements throughout the developing world such as that of the Chipko (cf. Guha, 1989: 100) or the Amazon rubber tappers (Hecht and Cockburn, 1990). It is therefore not surprising to find that "the fundamental right to political, economic, cultural and environmental self-determination of all peoples" is asserted as one of the principles of environmental justice.

It is precisely through this discursive strategy that links can then be found between the environmental justice movement as shaped within the specific conditions of the United States, and the broader movements that Martinez-Allier (1990) refers to as "the environmentalism of the poor." These movements fundamentally concern either the defense of livelihoods and of communal access to "natural" resources threatened by commodification, state takeovers, and private property arrangements, or more dynamic movements (both *in situ* and migratory) arising as a response to ecological scarcities, threats to survival and destruction of long-standing ways of life (see Ghai and Vivian, 1995: Sachs, 1993). But, as with the environmental justice movement, the symbolic dimension, the struggle for empowerment, for recognition and respect, and above all for emancipation from the oppressions of material want and domination by others, inevitably has a powerful role to play, making the environmentalism of the poor focus upon survivability in all of its senses.

From this standpoint, it is not hard to understand the fierce critique of "sustainable development" and "ecological modernization" (in its corrupted form) launched by Sachs (1993):

> The eco-cratic view likes universalist ecological rules, just as the developmentalist liked universalist economic rules. Both pass over the rights of local communities to be in charge of their resources and to build a meaningful society. The conservation of nature [should be] intimately related to rights of communal ownership, traditional ways of knowing, cultural autonomy, religious rituals, and freedom from state-centered development.

Doctrines of cultural autonomy and dispersion, of tradition and difference (in short, of place-bound politics with all of its limitations – see chapter 11) nevertheless carry with them a more universal message which permits a loose alliance of forces around alternative strategies of development (or even, in some instances, growth) that focus as much upon diversity of places and geographical difference as upon the necessary homogeneities of global market integrations. What seems to be at work here is the conversion of ideals learned through intense ecologically based militant particularism into some universal principles of environmental justice. The environmental justice movement, like other "militant particularist" movements (see chapter 1):

> has tried to connect particular struggles to a general struggle in one quite special way. It has set out, as a movement, to make real what is at first sight the

extraordinary claim that the defence and advancement of certain particular interests, properly brought together, are in fact the general interest. (Williams, 1989a: 115).

This connection is nowhere more apparent than in the shift from "not-in-my-backyard" politics to "not-in-anyone's-backyard" principles in the United States:

> Environmental philosophy and decision making has often failed to address the justice question of who gets help and who does not; who can afford help and who cannot; ... why industry poisons some communities and not others; why some contaminated communities get cleaned up but others do not; and why some communities are protected and others are not protected. ... The grassroots environmental justice movement ... seeks to strip away the ideological blinders that overlook racism and class exploitation in environmental decision making. From this critical vantage point, the solution to unequal environmental protection is seen to lie in the struggle for justice for all Americans. No community, rich or poor, black or white, should be allowed to become an ecological "sacrifice zone." Saying "NO" to the continued poisoning of our communities of color is the first step in this struggle. Yet our long-range vision must also include institutionalizing sustainable and just environmental practices that meet human needs without sacrificing the land's ecological integrity. If we are to succeed, we must be visionary as well as militant. Our very future depends on it. (Bullard, 1993: 206)

This is not, however, the only leap that the environmental justice movement is prepared to make. The environment itself gets to be redefined (cf. chapter 7) to include "the totality of life conditions in our communities – air and water, safe jobs for all at decent wages, housing, education, health care, humane prisons, equity, justice" (Southern Organizing Committee for Economic and Social Justice, 1992; cited in Szasz, 1994: 151). And this leads straight back to the connection between environmental and social justice. It also leads to a consideration of urban settings since this is where most people now live in the advanced capitalist world.

VII. Environmental Justice and the City

The long-standing hostility of what now passes in the public eye for the environmental movement to the very existence of cities has created a blindspot of startling proportions. Usually depicted as the high-point of the pollution and plundering of planet earth, cities (where nearly half of the world's populations now lives) are either ignored or denigrated in the deep ecology literature as well as in that wing of environmentalism that focuses primarily on "nature" as wilderness, species, and habitat preservation. Theoretically, ecologists may claim that everything is related to everything else, but they then marginalize or ignore a large segment of the practical ecosystem. If biocentic thinking is correct and the boundary between human activity and ecosystemic activities must be collapsed, then this means not only that ecological processes have to be incorporated into our understanding of social life: it also means that flows of money and of commodities and the transformative actions of human beings (in the building of urban systems, for example) have to be understood as fundamentally ecological processes (see chapter 5).

The environmental justice movement, with its emphasis upon marginalized and impoverished populations exposed to hazardous ecological circumstances, freely acknowledges these connections. Many of the issues with which it is confronted are specifically urban in character. Consequently, the principles it has enunciated include the mandate to address environmental justice in the city by the cleaning up and rebuilding of urban environments.

In so doing, the environmental justice movement connects back into a much-neglected facet of environmental politics. Gottlieb (1993: 7) puts it this way:

> Pollution issues are not just a recent concern; people have recognized, thought about and struggled with these problems for more than a century in significant and varied ways. A history that separates resource development and its regulation from the urban and industrial environment disguises a crucial link that connects both pollution and the loss of wilderness. If environmentalism is seen as rooted primarily or exclusively in the struggle to preserve or manage extra-urban Nature, it becomes difficult to link the changes in material life after World War II – the rise of petrochemicals, the dawning of the nuclear age, the tendencies towards overproduction and mass consumption – with the rise of new social movements focused on quality of life issues.

Gottlieb correctly seeks to interpret environmentalism as part of a complex of social movements that arose in response to rapid urbanization and industrialization, accelerating strongly after World War II. He reinscribes in environmental history (and its hegemonic discourses) a whole set of urban environmental concerns that conventional accounts conveniently misplace. In so doing, Gottlieb suggests a way to take the supposed "holism" of the environmental movement at its word and to overcome a long-standing ideological predilection to oppose city and country in ways that denigrate the former and romanticize the latter (see Williams, 1973).

Consider, for example, the case of lead-paint poisoning, an issue that has been of major concern for environmental justice advocates. Lead has been known to be a highly toxic substance for hundreds of years (the Romans understood the problem well, lead featured large in the pioneering work of

Alice Hamilton on industrial toxicology at the beginning of this century and the problems associated with lead-based paints in residential areas were well known by the 1920s). Yet the use of lead continued to expand well into the 1970s (particularly lead-based additives to gasoline) and lead-based paints were banned only in 1978, after repeated and conclusive studies had shown a strong relation between them and serious brain damage in children. But the lead-based paints almost universally deployed in houses before 1950 have remained as a serious environmental hazard. Since its effects were largely concentrated in areas of housing dilapidation and poor maintenance, the lead-paint problem was increasingly seen (incorrectly) as an exclusively inner-city problem. Largely for that reason, the problem did not command the sort of urgency of action that lead-based additives in gasoline commanded through their impacts across all class and race lines. So on an issue where, as early as the 1960s, "the epidemiology was clear, its victims could be predicted, its health effects could be identified, and its treatment was known to the medical profession," little or nothing was done (Gottlieb, 1993: 244–50; Phoenix, 1993; Colpotura and Sen, 1994; Florini et al., 1990).

In Baltimore city, for example, more than 5 percent of the 25,000 or so children under six screened in 1992 suffered from poisoning while 12 percent had elevated lead levels in their blood (see table 13.1). Nationwide, nearly half of all African-American inner-city children are exposed to dangerous levels of lead, compared to 16 percent of white inner-city children (Phoenix, 1993: 78). And the discriminatory impacts are even more startling when race and income are factored together (see table 13.2).

The reason for the lack of action over nearly 20 years goes back to that infernal economic logic that Summers so brilliantly encapsulated: the costs of lead-removal would either drive rents up or render inner-city landlordism for the poor so unprofitable as to exacerbate already serious problems of housing-

Table 13.1 Numbers of children screened diagnosed with lead poisoning or elevated lead levels in their blood contrasting Baltimore city (predominantly poor and African-American) and Baltimore county (white, affluent, and suburban) in 1992

	Children under 6 screened	Percentage of total children	Poisoning cases	Elevated levels	Percentage of units built before 1950
Baltimore city	25,503	37.5	1,295 (5%)	2,794 (11%)	49
Baltimore county	7,600	13.5	69 (0.9%)	143 (1.8%)	19

Source: Baltimore Sun, February 27, 1994.

Table 13.2 Estimated percentages of children 0.5–5.0 years old in US cities over 1 million, with lead blood levels greater than 15 µg/dl, by race and income in 1988

	Income		
Race	Less than $6,000	$6,000–15,000	Greater than $15,000
African-American	68%	54%	38%
White	36%	23%	12%

Source: Bullard (1994: 20).

abandonment in inner-city areas. In either case one consequence is greater homelessness, implying a social choice for the poor between living with lead paint or being on the street. To this is now added another wrinkle – liability suits against landlords after proven exposure of children to lead poisoning (some compensation awards have gone as high as $500,000) have led insurers to deny coverage in many inner-city areas. That leads to even more housing abandonment as landlords prefer to leave a building vacant rather than have it occupied and face personal liability if an occupant suffers from the paint. State government has sought to broker some sort of compromise but again and again agreements break down and legislation falters in the face of the "twin tragedies: childhood lead poisoning and the disappearance of affordable housing" (Wheeler, 1994).

But this irrationality (so characteristic of capitalism) has been long standing. The 1947 housing act in the United States affirmed the *right* of everyone "to a decent house in a suitable living environment." The Report of the National Commission on Urban Problems published in 1968 (US Government, 1968) in the wake of the assassination of Martin Luther King, not only lamented the failure to progress towards such a goal but focused particularly on the failure to define what a "suitable living environment" might mean. In seeking to rectify that omission, the Presidential Commission not only focused on the environment of jobs, racial discrimination, poor social infrastructures (particularly education), and accessibility (particularly transportation) but also inserted a strong chapter on more conventional environmental issues:

> America will surely fail to build a good urban society unless we begin to have a new respect – *reverence* is not too strong a word – for the natural environment that surrounds us. ... None of us can afford to be ignorant or silent about what the despoilers are doing to our environment. We must respond to growing reports of smog-choked cities, air pollution alerts, communities drying up, industries fleeing, people thirsting for lack of water supply, lakes dying, bird species threatened by chemical poisoning, and all life jeopardized by radiation waste hazards.

In seeking solutions to housing questions, the Commission went on to argue that:

> it is impossible to conceive of good housing downwind from a factory spewing ashes and noxious gases, in neighborhoods so poorly served by local government that trash and filth dominate the scene, in sections where open sewers or seepage from septic tanks spread disease, or adjacent to rivers or ponds that would poison or infect anyone who used the water for swimming. (US Government, 1968: 487–8)

But this was a rare historical conjuncture. The dominant forms of power were forced to take a closer look at the wide ranging environmental conditions underlying the political unrest in the inner cities of the United States at the same time as a whole range of esthetic, health, and environmental quality questions were being placed upon the political agenda by the middle class aided and abetted by a restless student movement which, from Paris to Mexico City and from Santa Barbara to Tokyo, was raising profound questions including that of a supposedly "alienated" relation to nature. At that time, therefore, it was a matter of almost common consensus, that social and environmental justice concerns were inseparable from each other in urban settings (see Harvey, 1973: chapter 2). Only since then, has the environmental issue been weaned away from its urban basis (Gottlieb, 1993).

It has, however, taken the multiple and diversified efforts of the environmental justice movement to revive and keep alive such long-standing concerns. Consider, for example, the case of Chicago's notorious southeast side. Home to 150,000 people, mostly African-American or Hispanic, it as "50 active or closed commercial hazardous waste landfills, 100 factories (including seven chemical plants and five steel mills), and 103 abandoned toxic waste dumps." Altgeld Gardens, a segregated African-American community in the area, "is surrounded on all four sides with the most toxic facilities in all of Chicago, and, no surprise, has one of the highest cancer rates in the United States" (Bullard, 1994: 14–15, 279–80). The seriousness of such urban environmental hazards has long been obvious. Various workers associated with The Hull House Settlement organized by Jane Addams in the 1890s recognized then that much of Chicago was nothing short of an urban-environmental catastrophe that demanded immediate and swift remedies if public health was to be protected and a modicum of social justice achieved. They also recognized, as the contemporary environmental justice movement has rediscovered, that the only path to improvement was empowerment of the poor and working classes in the face of a recalcitrant, obdurate, and often corrupt corporate power structure (Gottlieb, 1993: 59–67). Sara Paretsky's novel *Bloodshot*, set in contemporary Chicago, captures the nature of this struggle most graphically.

But the whole question of the link between environmental and social justice in a rapidly urbanizing world does not stop at the borders of communities differentially impacted by exposure to environmental hazards. Urbanizing processes are much more multilayered than that as are the environmental and social justice issues with which they are associated. Changing patterns of urban organization, for example, simultaneously produce configurations of uneven social and economic development at different scales coupled with multiple displacements of environmental issues to different scales. Highly localized urban smogs are reduced at the expense of a regionalized acid deposition problem. Middle-class commuters escape toxic zones and urban heat islands only to contribute to global warming and high metropolitan-wide concentrations of ozone in summer. The health and quality of urban food provision is much improved by resort to packaging practices (an extraordinary growth industry since 1945) that create an immense plastics and paper waste-disposal problem. Battery-driven cars are advocated as a solution to ozone-producing automobiles but there is lead in those batteries. Electrical power contributes to the cleanliness and health of urban environments only at the expense of massive carbon dioxide, nitrous oxides, and sulfur emissions that give rise to acid deposition and global warming. Refrigeration cuts down on food contamination, dysentery, and disease but the CFCs deplete the ozone layer.

In all of these issues, the activities of urbanization pose a distinctive set of environmental problems and foment a wide range of environmental consequences that have uneven social impacts at quite different spatial scales. Furthermore, the immense concentrations of population now occurring throughout the world create their own milieus in which distinctive and often new hazards can all too easily flourish. New diseases emerge and old ones return (see Levins et al., 1994). Measles epidemics occur for the most part only in urban concentrations of more than 250,000 people and outbreaks of plague – such as the pneumonic plague that shattered Surat in India in 1994 and the Ebola virus that hit urban concentrations in Zaire in 1995 – take the course they do in part because of the form that contemporary urbanization takes. Yet only recently has the link between urbanization and environmental questions begun to be explored in any systematic way (Girardet, 1992; and see McCarney, 1995 for a thorough review). How to do that in ways that are sensitive to social justice questions, in the midst of the complex scalar layering of environmental and developmental issues (local, metropolitan, regional, global), has hardly begun to be integrated into any environmental discourse, let alone that of environmental justice. Certainly, the complexity of the issues will make for an abundance of confusion and argument.

But amidst all of the disagreements, both actual and potential, as to how environmental justice might be established, the one solid foundational argument to which all proponents again and again return, is the primacy of social relations and of the justice of those relations. Commoner (cited in Sachs, 1993:

224) summarizes it this way:

> When any environmental problem is probed to its origin, it reveals an inescapable truth – that the real root cause is to be found in how [people] interact with each other; that the debt to nature ... cannot be paid person by person, in recycled bottles or ecologically sound habits, but in the ancient coin of social justice.

But of what metal is that ancient coin?

VIII. Principles of Justice and Environments of Difference

A comparison of environmental discourses and principles of social justice, suggests a crude set of pairings. Utilitarian theories of justice are strongly associated with the standard view. The intermingling of both these discourses in the advanced capitalist societies is fairly evident making this by far the most prevalent and hegemonic mode of thinking for regulating institutional behaviors, political action, and material practices. Ecological modernization, particularly in terms of its concerns for the rights of future generations, seems more compatible with some sort of social contract view and I think it is significant that several attempts to adapt the Rawlsian version of the social contract have emerged in recent years (see Wenz, 1988; de-Shalit, 1995). "Wise use" doctrine appeals directly to libertarian views and draws much of its strength precisely from that association. The environmental justice movement, by contrast, frequently invokes egalitarian principles (sometimes individualistic but more frequently communitarian) in its demands for a more equitable distribution of environmental advantages and burdens.

Each of these broadly anthropocentric theoretical positions has its biocentric analogue. The libertarian view, for example, produces strong doctrines of animal rights when extended onto the terrain of rights accorded to all "subjects of a life" (Regan, 1983). The utilitarian view can be extended to accord rights to as many species as possible in terms of their ability to flourish and to multiply. Radical egalitarianism across all species and habitats characterizes the deep ecology movement while the contractarian view suggests a strong appreciation for rights of the less well-off (endangered species) as well as a conservative approach to habitat transformation (justified only if it is to the benefit of the least advantaged species).

It is on this sort of terrain that we now find an essentially irresolvable debate on the proper form of environmental ethics unfolding. And the arguments can be bitter: for example, concern for whole ecosystems and habitats as against the rights of individual organisms is tantamount to fascism in Regan's view (cited in Benton 1993: 3). We are then left with a case of determining which is the most socially just theory of social justice. In the case of lead-paint poisoning in Baltimore city, for example, the conflict is not between just and unjust solutions but between different conceptions of justice. Libertarian views put the rights of private property owners (and their contractual position *vis-à-vis* consumers of housing services) at a premium and what happens between the parties is a private matter. Utilitarians would treat the problem as a public health nuisance that ought to be cleaned up in so far as it imposes intolerable burdens of long-term losses from mental impairment for life (while leaving open the Achilles' heel that the greatest happiness of the greatest number might be consistent with inflicting damage on a minority, particularly when the cost of doing otherwise is burdensome for the majority). Contractarians of a Rawlsian persuasion would take it more as a question of an inequality of exposure that benefits no one, and most certainly not the least privileged. If none of us knew (and Rawls presumes a "veil of ignorance" as essential to the derivation of his theory) what our location or position in life might be (i.e., whether or not we would be in a lead-paint environment) all parties would presumably choose to eliminate the hazard altogether. Egalitarians would treat differential exposure to lead-paint hazards as an affront to their principles. But the egalitarian principle is not so helpful when it comes to allocating the cost of remediation. Should the poor pay for the clean up of their own rather dirty environments on an equal footing with the rich who live in cleanlier circumstances? Nonfunded federal mandates with respect to clean water and sewage treatment in the United States, for example, will impose enormous financial burdens on older cities where the less affluent live, making this an intractable problem for environmental justice if the raw equality principle is adhered to rigorously.

These are all valid theoretical positions. Each can be subjected to philosophical critique. Benton (1993) thus provides a deep and trenchant analysis of animal rights and social justice theories, de-Shalit (1995) subjects the contractarian theory to a sympathetic critique and Wenz (1988) examines the whole spectrum of possible theories of environmental justice only to decide that "each theory failed when taken by itself." We are therefore confronted with a plurality of theories of justice, all equally plausible and all equally lacking in one way or other. We are, Wenz notes, "attracted to using one theory in one kind of situation and a different theory in a different kind of situation" and in a conflict, such as that surrounding lead-paint poisoning, different groups will resort to different concepts of justice to bolster their position (the property owners use the libertarian rhetoric and the defenders of children typically use a contractarian rhetoric). Wenz's answer to this situation is to abandon the search for coherency among moral judgments and for a singular theory applicable to a diversity of environmental issues arising at different scales. The difficulty with such a solution is evident: why one particular blend of principles rather than another? And what is to prevent the vaunted flexibility of some pluralistic discourse on environmental justice being perverted by acts of power to the material advantage of the already elite and powerful? Trade in toxics, as Summers argued, can indeed be welfare enhancing for all given certain suppositions about how to theorize just outcomes from trade. Class struggle is then over exactly which principles of justice shall prevail (cf. chapter 12).

So while philosophers can operate as sophisticated underlaborers, clearing away much of the underbrush that clutters the way to defining more pristine principles of environmental justice, there is no way to define a philosophical and discursive answer to intense questions of social relations, power, beliefs, and institutions in relation to environmental practices. "Between equal rights, force decides," Marx argued. And so it is with the diversity of currencies to measure that most ancient of all coin, that of social justice. It is therefore vital to move from "a predisposition to regard social justice as a matter of eternal justice and morality, to regard it as something contingent upon the social processes operating in society as whole." The practice of the environmental justice movement has its origins in the inequalities of power and the way those inequalities have distinctive environmental consequences for the marginalized and impoverished, for those who may be freely denigrated as "others" or as "people out of place." The principles of justice it enunciates are embedded in a particular experiential world and environmental objectives are coupled with a struggle for recognition, respect, and empowerment.

But as a movement embedded in multiple "militant particularisms," it has to find a way to cross that problematic divide between action that is deeply embedded in *place*, in local experience, power conditions and social relations to a much more general movement. And like the working-class movement, it has proven, in Williams (1989a: 115) words, "always insufficiently aware of the quite systematic obstacles which stood in the way." The move from tangible solidarities felt as patterns of social bonding in affective and knowable communities to a more abstract set of conceptions with universal meaning involves a move from one level of abstraction – attached to place – to quite different levels of abstraction capable of reaching across a space in which communities could not be known in the same unmediated ways. Furthermore, principles developed out of the experience of Love Canal or the fight in Warren County do not necessarily travel to places where environmental and social conditions are radically different. And in that move from the particular to the general something was bound to be lost. In comes, Williams notes, "the politics of negation, the politics of differentiation, the politics of abstract analysis. And these, whether we liked them or not, were now necessary even to understand what was happening." And in the case of the environmental justice movement the constant search for media attention and an iconography of events around which to build a symbolic politics carries its own negative freight.

But it is exactly here that some of the empowering rhetoric of environmental justice itself becomes a liability. Appealing to "the sacredness of Mother Earth," for example, does not help arbitrate complex conflicts over how to organize material production and distribution in a world grown dependent upon sophisticated market interrelations and commodity production through capital accumulation. The demand to cease the production of *all* toxins, hazardous wastes, and radioactive materials, if taken literally, would prove disastrous to the public health and well-being of large segments of the population, including the poor (Greenpeace's parallel campaign to ban the use of chlorine is an excellent example of the contradictions in such a politics). And the right to be free of ecological destruction is posed so strongly as a negative right that it appears to preclude the positive right to transform the earth in ways conducive to the well-being of the poor, the marginalized, and the oppressed. To be sure, the environmental justice movement does incorporate positive rights particularly with respect to the rights of all people to "political, cultural, and environmental self-determination" but here the internal contradictions within the movement become blatant.

At this conjuncture, therefore, all of those militant particularist movements around the world that loosely come together under the umbrella of environmental justice and the environmentalism of the poor are faced with a critical choice. They can either ignore the contradictions, remain with the confines of their own particularist militancies – fighting an incinerator here, a toxic waste dump there, a World Bank dam project somewhere else, and commercial logging in yet another place – or they can treat the contradictions as a fecund nexus to create a more transcendent and universal politics. If they take the latter path, they have to find a discourse of universality and generality that unites the emancipatory quest for social justice with a strong recognition that social justice is impossible without environmental justice (and vice versa). But any such discourse has to transcend the narrow solidarities and particular affinities shaped in particular places – the preferred milieu of most grass roots environmental activism – and adopt a politics of abstraction capable of reaching out across space, across the multiple environmental and social conditions that constitute the geography of difference in a contemporary world that capitalism has intensely shaped to its own purposes. And it has to do this without abandoning its militant particularist base.

The abstractions cannot rest solely upon a moral politics dedicated to protecting the sanctity of Mother Earth. It has to deal in the material and institutional issues of how to organize production and distribution in general, how to confront the realities of global power politics and how to displace the hegemonic powers of capitalism not simply with dispersed, autonomous, localized, and essentially communitarian solutions (apologists for which can be found on both right and left ends of the political spectrum), but with a rather more complex politics that recognizes how environmental and social justice must be sought by a rational ordering of activities at different scales. The reinsertion of the idea of "rational ordering" indicates that such a movement will have no option, as it broadens out from its militant particularist base, but to reclaim for itself a noncoopted and nonperverted version of the theses of ecological modernization. On the one hand that means subsuming the highly geographically differentiated desire for cultural autonomy and dispersion, for the proliferation of tradition and difference within a more global politics, but on the other hand making the quest for environmental and social justice central rather than peripheral concerns.

For that to happen, the environmental justice movement has to radicalize the ecological modernization discourse. And that requires confronting the fundamental underlying processes (and their associated power structures, social relations, institutional configurations, discourses, and belief systems) that generate environmental and social injustices. Here, I revert to a key moment in the argument advanced in *Social Justice and the City* (Harvey, 1973: 136–7): it is vital, when encountering a serious problem, not merely to try to solve the problem in itself but to confront and transform the processes that gave rise to the problem in the first place. Then, as now, the fundamental problem is that of unrelenting capital accumulation and the extraordinary asymmetrics of money and political power that are embedded in that process. Alternative modes of production, consumption, and distribution as well as alternative modes of environmental transformation have to be explored if the discursive spaces of the environmental justice movement and the theses of ecological modernization are to be conjoined in a program of radical political action. This is fundamentally a class project, whether it is exactly called that or not, precisely because it entails a direct challenge to the circulation and accumulation of capital which currently dictates what environmental transformations occur and why.

There are signs of such a transition occurring. Here, for example, is a recent argument from the Citizen's Clearing House for Hazardous Waste's journal *Everyone's Backyard*:

> Environmental justice is a people-oriented way of addressing "environmentalism" that adds a vital social, economic and political element ... the new Grass-roots Environmental Justice Movement seeks common ground with low-income and minority communities, with organized workers, with churches and with all others who stand for freedom and equality. ... When we fight for environmental justice we fight for our homes and families and struggle to end economic, social and political domination by the strong and greedy. (Cited in Szasz, 1994: 153)

And Szasz (1994) concludes his thorough history of the movement as follows:

> Movements take on greater historical significance when they move from the particular to the universal, when they expand out from their specific issues of origin and embrace a more global social change agenda. They take on greater historical significance when they not only mobilize participants to fight for their

own interests but also provide a broader radicalizing experience. ... The hazardous wastes movement is making explicit gestures in this direction. It increasingly defines its environmental mission in terms of a larger critique of society; it makes common cause with other movements and says that, ultimately, they are all joined in the same struggle. It even envisions a future in which grass-roots environmentalism spearheads the reconstitution of a broad social justice movement.

Those of us who are still somewhat enamored of rather traditional foundational values of socialism will, I think, say "amen" to that. But there is a long and arduous road to travel to take the environmental justice movement beyond the phase of rhetorical flourishes, media successes, and symbolic politics, into a world of strong coherent political organizing and practical revolutionary action.

14
Possible Urban Worlds

I. The Historical Geography of Urbanization

At the beginning of this century, there were just 16 cities in the world with more than a million people. Most were in the advanced capitalist countries and London, by far the largest of them all, had just under seven million. At the beginning of this century, too, no more than 7 percent of the world's population could reasonably be classified as "urban" (Berry, 1990). By the year 2000 there may well be as many as 500 cities with more than a million inhabitants while the largest of them, Tokyo, São Paulo, Bombay, and possibly Shanghai (although the list is perpetually being revised both upwards and downwards), will perhaps boast populations of more than 20 million trailed by a score of cities, mostly in the so-called developing countries, with upwards of ten million. Sometime early next century, if present trends continue, more than half of the world's population will be classified as urban rather than rural.

The twentieth century has been, then, *the* century of urbanization. Before 1800 the size and numbers of urban concentrations in all social formations seem to have been strictly limited. The nineteenth century saw the breach of those barriers in a few advanced capitalist countries, but the latter half of the twentieth century has seen that localized breach turned into a universal flood of massive urbanization. The future of the most of humanity now lies, for the first time in history, fundamentally in urbanizing areas. The qualities of urban living in the twenty-first century will define the qualities of civilization itself.

But judging superficially by the present state of the world's cities, future generations will not find that civilization particularly congenial. Every city now has its share (often increasing and in some instances predominant) of concentrated impoverishment and human hopelessness, of malnourishment and chronic diseases, of crumbling or stressed out infrastructures, of senseless and wasteful consumerism, of ecological degradation and excessive pollution, of congestion, of seemingly stymied economic and human development, and of sometimes bitter social strife, varying from individualized violence on the streets to organized crime (often an alternative form of urban governance), through police-state exercises in social control to occasional massive civic protest movements (sometimes spontaneous) demanding political–economic change. For many, then, to talk of the city of the twenty-first century is to conjure up a dystopian nightmare in which all that is judged worst in the fatally flawed character of humanity collects together in some hell-hole of despair.

In some of the advanced capitalist countries, that dystopian vision has been strongly associated with the long-cultivated habit on the part of those with power and privilege of running as far from the city centers as possible. Fueled by a permissive car culture, the urge to get some money and get out has taken command. Liverpool's population fell by 40 percent between 1961 and 1991, for example, and Baltimore city's fell from close to a million to under 700,000 in the same three decades. But the upshot has been not only to create endless suburbanization, so-called "edge cities," and sprawling megalopoli, but also to make every village and every rural retreat in the advanced capitalist world part of a complex web of urbanization that defies any simple categorization of populations into "urban" and "rural" in that sense which once upon a time could reasonably be accorded to those terms. The hemorrhaging of wealth, population, and power from central cities has left many of them languishing in limbo. Needy populations have been left behind as the rich and influential have moved out. Add to this the devastating loss of jobs (particularly in manufacturing) in recent years and the parlous state of the older cities becomes all too clear. Nearly 250,000 manufacturing jobs were lost in Manchester in two decades while 40,000 disappeared from Sheffield's steel industry alone in just three short catastrophic years in the mid-1980s. Baltimore likewise lost nearly 200,000 manufacturing jobs from the late 1960s onwards and there is hardly a single city in the United States that has not been the scene of similar devastation through deindustrialization.

The subsequent train of events has been tragic for many. Communities built to service now defunct manufacturing industries have been left high and dry, wracked with long-term structural unemployment. Disenchantment, dropping out, and quasi-legal means to make ends meet follow. Those in power rush to blame the victims, the police powers move in (often insensitively), and the politician–media complex has a field day stigmatizing and stereotyping an underclass of idle wrong-doers, irresponsible single parents and feckless fathers, debasement of family values, welfare junkies, and much worse. If those marginalized happen to be an ethnic or racially marked minority, as is all-too often the case, then the stigmatization amounts to barely concealed racial bigotry. The only available response on the part of those left marginalized is urban rage, making the actual state of social and even more emphatically race relations (for all the campus rhetoric on political correctness) far worse now than it has been for several decades.

But is this a universal tale of urban woe I tell? Or is it something rather more confined to the specific legacies of old-style capitalist industrialization and the cultural predilections of the anti-urban Anglo-Saxon way of life? Central cities throughout continental Europe are, for example, undergoing a singular revival. And such a trend is not merely confined to a few centers, like Paris with its long-standing process of embourgeoisement accelerated by all of the *grands projets* for which the French are justly famous. From Barcelona to Hamburg to Turin to Lille, the flow of population and affluence back into the city centers is marked. But, on inspection, all this really signifies is that the same problematic divisions get geographically reversed. It is the periphery that is hurting and the soulless *banlieu* of Paris and Lyon that have become the centers of riot and disaffection, of racial discrimination and harassment, of deindustrialization, and social decay. And if we look more closely at what has been happening in the Anglo-Saxon world, the evidence suggests a dissolution of that simple "doughnut" urban form of inner-city decay surrounded by suburban affluence (made so much of in the late 1960s), and its replacement by a complex checkerboard of segregated and protected wealth in an urban soup of equally segregated impoverishment and decay. The unjustly famous "outer estates" of Glasgow are interspersed with affluent commuter suburbs and the now emerging socio-economic problems of the inner suburbs in many US cities have forced the wealthy seeking security either further out (the urbanization of the remotest countryside then follows) or into segregated and often highly protected zones wherever they can best be set up.

But is there anything radically new in all of this? Or have we, when we look at the parallel conditions of late-nineteenth-century urbanization been here before? The answer is, I fear, both yes and no. Many of the dystopian elements – the concentrated impoverishment and human hopelessness, the malnourishment and chronic diseases, the ecological degradation and excessive pollution, the seemingly stymied human and economic development, and the more than occasional bitter social strife – were all too familiar to our nineteenth-century forebears. Any reading of Mayhew's *London Labour and the London Poor* (1861), Booth's *Life and Labour of the People of London* (1902–3), Mearn's *Bitter Cry of Outcast London* (1883), Jack London's *People of the Abyss* (1903), or Jacob Riis's *How the Other Half Lives* (1890) will immediately disabuse us of the idea that social conditions are now dramatically worse. And in the United States, the speed and heterogeneity of urban social change, that took Chicago from a trading post to a polyglot multicultural emporium of 1.5 million people in two generations, was something quite extraordinary at the time and probably every bit as stressful as anything that has happened since. Indeed, the impression is that contemporary urban ills in at least the advanced capitalist world pale in comparison with what our forebears saw, even allowing for the sometimes exaggerated horror and feigned outrage of the muckrakers and moralists of the day.

But what does seem to have been different then was the reaction of a newly empowered bourgeoisie as it began to swim in the hitherto uncharted waters of large-scale urban sloth and disaffection that seemed to threaten its power, its health, sanity, and economic well-being, as well as its new-found esthetic sensibilities for cleanliness and order. Nineteenth-century thinkers and politicians took the urban problematic very seriously indeed, far more so than is evident today. And the result was not only an outpouring of thoughtful commentary on "general propositions pertaining to urban development and society" and on key urban determinants "of a new way of life" (Lees, 1991: 154), but also a massive movement of urban reform that took moralists like Octavia Hill and Jane Addams into the very heart of urban darkness and bore forward architects, planners, social theorists, and commentators of all political persuasions on a vast wave of energy directed towards finding rational and even "city beautiful" solutions to the problems of the great cities of those days. Olmstead, Haussmann, Geddes, Ebenzer Howard, Daniel Burnham, Camillo Sitte, Otto Wagner, Garnier, Raymond Unwin, all rode forth as saviors of the modern city, bursting with ideas as to what it might mean to the needs of efficiency, cleanliness, and, at least in some respects, to human needs. And while the Utopian and anarchist dreams of writers like Edward Bellamy (whose *Looking Backward* spawned a whole political movement) and Kropotkin were never destined to be realized in any literal sense, they added to the ferment and became a powerful ingredient within a heady brew of progressive bourgeois reformism.

There are plenty of contemporary critics, of course, who, armed with their techniques of deconstruction and of Foucauldian analysis, might look back upon this period with jaundiced eye as a classic case of progressive reformism disguising capitalist plans for capital accumulation and speculative land development, a mask for concealing bourgeois guilt, paternalism, social control, surveillance, political manipulation, deliberate disempowerment of marginaliz-ed but restive masses, and the exclusion of anyone who was "different." But it is undeniable that the aggregate effect was to make cities work better, to improve the lot not only of urban elites but also of urban masses, to radically improve basic infrastructures (such as water and energy supply, housing, sewage, and air quality) as well as to liberate urban spaces for fresh rounds of organized capital accumulation in ways that lasted for much of the twentieth century. Compared to the best of the "gas and water municipal socialism" of those days, one would have to say that the contemporary blasé attitude (to borrow a phrase of Simmel's concerning one of the most powerful mental attributes of modern urban life) towards the degeneration of our cities leaves much to be desired.

But here, the difference between then and now comes more clearly into play. For at the end of the nineteenth century the ideal of some sort of aggregate human progress, though driven by the capitalist passion for "accumulation for accumulation's sake and production for production's sake" (to use Marx's felicitous phrase), seemed to have at least some semblance of a hopeful future attached to it as capitalist industry became more organized and as the political economy of urbanization became seemingly more manageable by reorganizations in urban governance (the London County Council was set up in 1888 and Greater New York in 1898). As the fate of whole metropolitan regions became more closely attached to the fate of successful capital accumulation, so bourgeois reformism in City Hall became integrated into hegemonic strategies for capitalist development. "The large urban centers," Lees (1991: 153) correctly observes, "embodied modernity and the future" and "stood for industry, centralization, and for rationality." For all the populist and often anti-urban rhetoric to the contrary, the coevolution (often dialectical and oppositional) of industrialization and urban politics seemed set fair to dictate a happier future for city dwellers.

Compared to that the contemporary divorce, manifest most dramatically in the dismal history of massive deindustrialization, between highly mobile and compulsively "downsizing" corporate manufacturing interests and urban life, would, therefore, have looked most unusual to our forebears. The corporate enemy has largely moved out of town and corporations don't seem to need cities or particular communities any more. The upshot is to leave the fate of the cities almost entirely at the mercy of real-estate developers and speculators, office builders, and finance capital. And the bourgeoisie, though still mortally afraid of crime, drugs, and all the other ills that plague the cities, is now seemingly content to seal itself off from all of that in urban or (more likely) suburban and ex-urban gated communities suitably immunized (or so it believes) from any long-term threats, secure in the knowledge that urban protests can be repressed by main force and so never become real revolutions. Having lost the fear of imminent revolution that so preoccupied the nineteenth-century bourgeois, all that is left is an occasional shiver of media-instilled fear as the riots taking place on the other side of town play live on television screens in terrifyingly comfortable living rooms. In recent years, the affluent also seem to have shed much of their guilty conscience. The extraordinary impact of Harrington's *The Other America; Poverty in the USA* when it was published in 1962 (and the subsequent "war on poverty" and massive attempts to confront "the urban crisis" in the United States) would not be possible in today's world where tendentious biological explanations of racial differences in IQ and criminality make front-page news and total disillusionment with anything that smacks of redistributive welfarism reigns. The re-emergence of market liberalism here couples with a revival of the Malthusian tradition to deadly effect (see chapter 6). So what if an urban "underclass" (that dreadful term invented as reincarnation of what our forbears often referred to by the much more threatening name of "dangerous classes") kills itself off through crime and drugs and AIDS and all the rest? And just to pile indignity upon indifference, a largish segment of the bourgeoisie now maintains that cities (in the traditional sense) are in any case irrelevant, that the civilization to which we can aspire in the twenty-first century is one "without cities." The "death of the city" (like the supposed "death of the author and the subject") becomes a significant enough trope in contemporary discourse to be a signal of a shift in the human imaginary as well as in institutions and politics. The "city" and "the urban question" disappear from political discourse burying those caught in the maelstrom of urban decay in a politics of contempt and neglect. When attitudes of that sort become current, it is hardly surprising that innovative thinking on urban issues focuses either on how best to escape the consequences of the largely urban concentrations of those poor "that will always be with us," or on how to immunize and secure bourgeois interests from the infectious plague of surrounding urban ills. Oscar Newman (1972), who coined the term "defensible space" as the answer to urban crime (see chapter 11), may well now be one of the most influential of all thinkers about urban design in the United States.

Some astute urban commentators on nineteenth-century urbanizations well understood the limits of what bourgeois reformism could ever be about. The only way the bourgeoisie has to confront its socio-economic problems, Engels observed, is to (*a*) move them around and (*b*) render them as invisible as possible. It is worth in this regard recalling the two key quotes:

> In reality the bourgeoisie has only one method of solving the housing question after *its* fashion – that is to say, of solving it in such a way that the solution continually reproduces the question anew. ... The scandalous alleys disappear to the accompaniment of lavish self-praise from the bourgeoisie on account of this tremendous success, but they appear again immediately somewhere else and often in the immediate neighborhood! The breeding places of disease, the infamous holes and cellars in which the capitalist mode of production confines our workers night after night, are not abolished; they are merely shifted elsewhere! The same economic necessity which produced them in the first place produces them in the next place also. As long as the capitalist mode of production continues to exist, it is folly to hope for an isolated solution of the housing question or of any other social question affecting the fate of the workers. The solution lies in the abolition of the capitalist mode of production. ...

And:

> With the exception of [the] commercial district, all Manchester proper, all Salford and Hume ... are all unmixed working people's quarters stretching like a girdle, averaging a mile and a half in breadth around the commercial district. Outside, beyond this girdle, lives the upper and middle bourgeoisie, the middle bourgeoisie in regularly laid out streets in the vicinity of working quarters ... the upper bourgeoisie in remoter villas with gardens ... in free wholesome

country air, in fine comfortable homes, passed every half or quarter hour by omnibuses going into the city. And the finest part of the arrangement is this, that the members of the money aristocracy can take the shortest road through the middle of all the laboring districts without ever seeing that they are in the midst of the grimy misery that lurks to the left and right. For the thoroughfares ... suffice to conceal from the eyes of the wealthy men and women of strong stomachs and weak nerves the misery and grime which form the complement of their wealth. ...

While the technological, social, political, and institutional context has changed quite radically since Engels' time, the aggregate effective condition has in many respects worsened. The barricades and walls, the segregations and separations, that now mark the living conditions of many advanced capitalist cities hardly deny the truths that Engels depicted. Here is how David Widgery (1991: 219) describes the devastating effects of the urban apartheid recently created by the construction of that fantastic monument to failed financial capital, Canary Wharf in London's east end:

The fortified wall which had once circled the docks was not so much torn down as rearranged as a series of fences, barriers, security gates and keep-out signs which seek to keep the working class away from the new proletarian-free yuppie zones. ... Mrs Thatcher's chosen monument may be the commercial majesty of Canary Wharf topped out only two weeks before her resignation in November 1990, but I see the social cost which has been paid for it in the streets of the East End: the schizophrenic dementing in public, the young mother bathing the newborn in the sink of a B-and-B, the pensioner dying pinched and cold in a decrepit council flat, the bright young kids who can get dope much easier than education, wasted on smack.

And if this urban apartheid seems an oddity just reflect on this: "over 32 million people in the United States currently live in a residential community association" and "more than half of the housing currently on the market in the fifty largest metropolitan areas in the United States and nearly all new residential development in California, Florida, New York, Texas, and suburban Washington, DC is governed by a common-interest community, a form of residential community association in which membership is mandatory." It all sounds innocent enough until the regulatory and exclusionary practices of such community associations are brought under the microscope. When that is done it is hard not to conclude with Knox (1994: 170) that these associations constitute "a web of servitude regimes that regulate land use and mediate community affairs in what often amounts to a form of contracted fascism." All that seems to have changed, then, in the particular manner, institutionalization, and location of that moving around that Engels spotted and the particular strategies of confinement and concealment. The irony here, as Mike

Davis (1990: 224) remarks in *City of Quartz* is that "as the walls have come down in Eastern Europe, they are being erected all over [our cities]." And modern technologies of surveillance, telecommuting, and the construction of cyberspace do not necessarily help. Social justice within the urban form is proving, evidently, as elusive as ever, even for those who still have the temerity to be concerned about it.

But all of these problems of the advanced capitalist world pale into insignificance compared to the extraordinary dilemmas of developing countries, with the wildly uncontrolled pace of urbanization in São Paulo, Mexico City, Cairo, Lagos, Bombay, Calcutta, Seoul, and now Shanghai and Beijing. On the surface there seems to be something different going on here, even more than just that qualitative shift that comes with the quantitative rapidity and mass of urban growth that has Mexico City or São Paulo experiencing in just one generation what London went through in ten and Chicago in three. Air pollution and localized environmental problems, for example, assume a far more chronic character in developing country cities than they ever did even at the most appalling states of threats to public health in the nineteenth-century cities of Europe and North America. Experts far better informed than I believe that "the present situation in Third World large cities is quite different from the one experienced in the course of fast urbanization in Europe and the United States" (Sachs, 1988: 341) and I am inclined to bow to that opinion. But I do so with an important caveat: it is vital for us to understand how, why, and in what ways these differences have arisen for it is, I believe, only in such terms that we will better understand the prospects of urban living in the twenty-first century in *both* the advanced capitalist and the developing world. Sachs is absolutely right, of course, to maintain that "the only progressive interpretation of historical experience is to consider past experiences as antimodels that can be surpassed." But surpassing is not a matter of simple inversion or antidote. It is a matter of dealing with the complex passages from the forces that construct future possibilities and so make the city, as always, a figure of Utopian desire and excitement at the same time as we understand the dystopian complement to the wealth of new possibilities that such social processes create.

We can best get some sort of purchase on these questions by returning to the historical–geographical issue of how cities did or did not grow in the past. What, for example, *were* the constraints to urban growth that kept cities so limited in size and number in the past and what happened sometime before and after 1800, that released urbanization from those limitations?

The answer is, I think, relatively simple in its basics. Up until the sixteenth or seventeenth centuries, urbanization was limited by a very specific metabolic relation between cities and their productive hinterlands coupled with the surplus extraction possibilities (grounded in specific class relations) that sustained them. No matter that certain towns and cities were centers of long-distance trade in luxuries or that even some basic goods, like grains, salt, hides, and timber could be moved over long distances, the basic provisioning (feeding, watering, and energy supply) of the city was always limited by the restricted productive capacity of a relatively confined hinterland. Cities were forced to be "sustainable" to use a currently much favored word, because they had to be. The recycling of city nightsoils and other urban wastes into the hinterland was a major element in that sustainable pattern of urbanization, making medieval cities seem somewhat of a virtuous bioregionalist form of organization for many contemporary ecologists [though what now looks virtuous must have smelled putrid at the time – "the worse a city smelled," notes Guillermé (1988: 171), "the richer it was"]. From time to time the hinterlands of cities got extended by forced trade and conquest (one thinks of north African wheat supply to imperial Rome) and of course localized productivity gains in agriculture or forestry (sometimes a short-run phenomena that lasted until such time as soil exhaustion set in) and the variable social capacity to squeeze surpluses from a reluctant rural population typically made the constraints on urban growth elastic rather than rigid. But the security of the city economy depended crucially upon the qualities of its localized metabolic support system, in which local environmental qualities (the breeding grounds of pestilences, plagues, and diseases of all sorts that periodically decimated urban populations) as well as food, water, and energy supply – particularly firewood – figured large. It is worth remembering in this regard that in 1830 most of the supply of fresh dairy products and vegetables to a city like Paris came from within a relatively restricted suburban zone if not from within the city confines itself. Before 1800, the "footprint" (again to use a currently favored term) of urbanization on the surface of the earth was relatively light (for all the significance cities may have had in the history of politics, science, and civilization): cities trod relatively lightly on the ecosystems that sustained them and were bioregionally defined.

What changed all this, of course, was the wave of new technologies (understood as both hardware and the software of organizational forms) generated by the military–industrial complex of early capitalism. Capitalism as a mode of production has necessarily targeted the breaking down of spatial barriers and the acceleration of turnover time as fundamental to its agenda of relentless capital accumulation (Harvey, 1982, 1989a, b, see also chapter 9). The systemic capitalist rationale behind this distinctive historical geography is important to appreciate along with its contradictions:

- *First*: capitalism is under the impulsion to accelerate turnover time, to *speed up* the circulation of capital and consequently to revolutionize the time horizons of development. But it can do so only through long-term investments (in, for example, the built environment as well as in elaborate and stable infrastructures for production, consumption, exchange, communication, and the like). A major stratagem of crisis avoidance, furthermore, lies in absorbing excess capital in long-term projects (the famous "public works" launched by the state in times of depression, for example) and this *slows down* the turnover time of capital. There is, consequently, an extraordinary array of contradictions that collect around the issue of the time-horizon (the temporalities) within which different capitals function (the time-horizon of finance capital, for example, is hard to match with the requirements of long-term urban and environmental development).

- *Second*: capitalism is under the impulsion to eliminate all spatial barriers, but it can do so only through the production of a fixed space. Capitalism thereby produces a geographical landscape (of space relations, of territorial organization and of systems of places linked in a "global" division of labor and of functions) appropriate to its own dynamic of accumulation at a particular moment of its history, only to have to destroy and rebuild that geographical landscape to accommodate accumulation at a later date. Reductions in the cost and time of movement over space therefore run up against the building of fixed physical infrastructures to facilitate the activities of production, exchange, distribution, and consumption. More and more capital is embedded in space as landed capital, as capital fixed in the land, creating a "second nature" and a geographically organized resource structure that more and more inhibits the trajectory of capitalist development in the midst of greater facility of movement. This tension becomes even more emphatic as the institutions of place become strongly articulated and loyalties to places (and their specific qualities) become a significant factor in political action. The production of territorial organization (the formation of local and metropolitan government systems for example) understood as a process makes territorialization, de-territorialization, and re-territorialization a continuous feature in the historical geography of capitalism.

Many if not all of the major waves of innovation that have shaped the world since the sixteenth century have been built around revolutions in transport and communications – the canals, bridges, and turnpikes of the early nineteenth century; the railroad, steamboat, and telegraph of the mid-nineteenth century; the mass transit systems of the late-nineteenth century; the automobile the radio and telephone of the early-twentieth century; the jet aircraft and television of the 1950s and 1960s; and most recently the revolution in telecommunications. Each bundle of innovations has allowed a radical shift in the way that space is organized and therefore opened up radically new possibilities for the urban process. Breaking with the dependency upon relatively confined bioregions opened up totally new vistas of possibilities for urban growth. Cronon shows, for example, how the rapid urbanization of Chicago in the nineteenth century realized these new possibilities so that the footprint of that city across the whole of the US mid-west and west became ever larger as its metabolic–ecological relations changed and as it itself grew in a few years into one of the largest cities in the world. And within the city, as Platt (1991) so brilliantly shows in his Chicago-based study of *The Electric City*, the progress of electrification allowed the construction of radically new and dispersed urban forms.

Each round of innovation breaking the barriers of space and time has provided new possibilities. The steam engine, to take just one highly significant historical example, liberated the energy supply of cities from relatively inefficient and highly localized constraints, at the same time as it freed local hinterlands from a chronic conflict over whether to use the land for food or firewood (contemporary students now find it very odd, for example, that one of the closer rings of production with which von Thunen surrounded his city in *The Isolated State* of the early nineteenth century is given over to forestry). But the steam engine could only accomplish its revolutionary role to the degree that it was in turn applied to the field of transport and communications: the coal had to be shunted around. It was and is, therefore, the total bundle of innovations and the synergism that binds them together that is really crucial in opening up new possibilities.

And in this, seemingly quite small things can figure large in what created possibilities for city growth. The military engineers and mathematicians of the eighteenth century, for example, in using water flow as a form of fortification learned that networks were far more efficient in moving water than direct pipes and channels: this recognition (and the study of the mathematics of networks that went with it) had immense significance once it was applied to cities in the nineteenth century: a given head of water flowing down one pipe can provision no more than 5,000 people but that same head of water when flowed around a network can provision 20 times that. This is a useful general metaphor for urban growth possibilities: the development of an interrelated and ultimately global network of cities drawing upon a variety of hinterlands permits an aggregate urban growth process radically greater than that achievable for each in isolation.

Since the mid-1960s, to take another example of a phase in which innumerable innovations (including the necessary mathematical knowledges) have bundled together to create a new synergism of urbanizing possibilities, we have witnessed a reorganization in spatial configurations and urban forms under conditions of yet another intense round in the reduction of spatial barriers and speedup in turnover time. The "global village" of which Marshall McCluhan speculatively wrote in the 1960s has become, at least in some senses, a reality. McCluhan thought that television would be the vehicle but in truth it was probably the launching of the sputnik that presaged the break, ushering as it did a new age of satellite communication. But, as in other eras, it is less a single innovation than the total bundle that counts. Containerization, jet-cargo systems, roll-on–roll-off ferries, truck design, and, just as important, highway design to support greater weights, have all helped to reduce the cost and time of moving goods over space, while automatic information processing, optimization, and

control systems, satellite communication, cellular phones, and computer technologies, all facilitate the almost instantaneous communication, collation, and
analysis of information, making the micro-chip as important as the satellite in
understanding the forces that now shape urban life.

These new technological and organizational possibilities have all been
produced under the impulsions of a capitalist mode of production with its
hegemonic military–industrial–financial interests. For this reason I believe it
is not only useful to think of but also important to recognize that we are all
embroiled in a *global process of capitalist urbanization* or *uneven spatio-temporal
development* even in those countries that have nominally at least sought a noncapitalistic path of development and a noncapitalistic urban form. The manner
and particular style of urbanization varies greatly, of course, depending on how
these capitalist possibilities are proposed, opposed, and ultimately realized. But
the context of possibilities is very definitely a capitalist production. And the
sense of new possibilities continually opening up gives rise to that modernist
style of Utopian thinking about technopoles, multifunctionopolizes, and the
like that parallels that dystopian imagery about the city which I began by
invoking.

There are, it seems to me, two basic perspectives from which now to view
the conflicting ways in which such possibilities are being taken up. Firstly, we
can look upon urbanization (and the lures of city construction and destruction) in terms of the forces of capital accumulation (see chapter 9). Capital
realizes its own agenda of "accumulation for accumulation's sake, production
for production's sake" against a background of the technological possibilities
it has itself created. Urbanization in the advanced capitalist countries, for
example, has not in recent history been about sustaining bioregions, ecological complexes, or anything other than sustaining the accumulation of capital.
In the United States, to take the paradigmatic case, capital accumulation
through suburbanization and all that this entailed (from the vast associated
water projects of the US west, the highway systems, the construction complexes, to say nothing of the automobile, the oil and rubber industries, etc.) was
central to the postwar economic success of the United States, even though it
produced its nether side in the form of derelict and deserted central cities. The
point to emphasize here is not so much the technological mix but the active
realization of opportunities for direct capital accumulation by way of that
technological complex of possibilities. The exhaustion of those possibilities (for
example, the relative saturation of the market for new automobiles) makes
capital accumulation more difficult, as every large multinational auto produc-
er now recognizes. The auto industry now looks, therefore, upon those
unsaturated markets in China, India, Latin America, and the deliberately
"underurbanized" world of the former Soviet bloc as its primary realm of future
accumulation. But that means reshaping the urban process in those regions to
the not particularly environmentally friendly (or even economically feasible)

system that for several decades supported economic growth in the United States. While that prospect may send shivers down every mildly ecologically conscious spine, any inability to pursue it will produce even worse *frissons* of horror in the boardrooms of every transnational auto company if not the whole capitalist class.

The particular dialectic of attraction and repulsion that capital accumulation exhibits for different sites within the web of urbanization varies spatio-temporarily as well as with the faction of capital concerned. Financial (money) capital, merchant capital, industrial–manufacturing capital, property and landed capital, statist capital, and agro-business capital – to take the most familiar factional breakdown of the capitalist class configuration (the other being local, national, and multinational capitals) – have radically different needs as well as radically different ways in which to explore the possibilities of exploiting the web of urbanization for purposes of capital accumulation. Tensions arise between the factions because they each have quite different capabilities for and interest in geographical movement – varying from the relatively fixed-in-space capital of property, landed and "local" small-scale capital and the instantaneous capacities for movement of transnational finance. Much of the creative destruction we are now witnessing within the urban process has to be understood in terms of such internal contradictions within the dynamics of overall capital accumulation. But the other part of it comes from the increasingly ruinous competition between places (be they nation states, regions, cities, or even smaller local jurisdictions) as they find themselves forced to sell themselves at the lowest cost to lure highly mobile capital to earth (Harvey, 1989b).

But the other perspective from which to view the recent history of urbanization is in terms of popular (if not "popular") seizure of the possibilities that capitalist technologies have created. To some degree this is about the vast historical migrations of labor in response to capital, from one region to another if not from one continent to another. That formulation basically made most sense in the nineteenth and even the early twentieth centuries (though there were always exceptions such as the flood of Irish overseas in the wake of the potato famine that may have been prompted by conditions of imposed agrarian capitalism but which was hardly a "normal" migration of rural population in search of urban liberties and waged labor). But the flood of people into developing country cities is not fundamentally tied to the pulls of employment attached to capital accumulation or even to the pushes of a reorganizing agrarian capitalism destructive of traditional peasantries (though there are many segments of the world where that process is very strongly in evidence). It is a far more popular search to take advantage of capitalist-produced possibilities no matter whether capital accumulation is going on or not, and often in the face of economic conditions that are just as, if not more appalling than those left behind. And while one of the effects may be to create vast "informal economies" which operate both as proto-capitalist sectors and as feeding grounds for more conventional forms of capitalist exploitation and accumulation (see Portes et al., 1989), the explanation of the movement in itself can hardly be attributed to the machinations of some organized capitalist class action.

The continuing flow of Asiatic and African populations into European countries and the Asiatic and Latino flows into North America exhibit similar qualities producing some wonderfully instructive contrasts right in the heart of capitalist cities. Within earshot of Bow Bells in London, for example, one finds the extraordinary power of international finance capital moving funds almost instantaneously round the world cheek-by-jowl with a substantial Bengali population (largely unemployed in any conventional sense) that has built a strong migratory bridge into the heart of capitalist society in search of new possibilities in spite of rampant racism and increasingly low-wage, informal, and temporary working possibilities. Here, too, the industrial reserve army that such migratory movements create may become an active vehicle for capital accumulation by lowering wages but the migratory movement itself, while it may indeed have been initiated by capital looking for labor reserves (as with guest workers and migrant streams from the European periphery), has surely taken on a life of its own.

The massive forced and unforced migrations of people now taking place in the world, a movement that seems unstoppable no matter how hard countries strive to enact stringent immigration controls, will have as much if not greater significance in shaping urbanization in the twenty-first century as the powerful dynamic of unrestrained capital mobility and accumulation. And the politics that flow from such migratory movements, while not necessarily antagonistic to continued capital accumulation are not necessarily consistent with it either, posing serious questions as to whether urbanization by capital accumulation will be anywhere near as hegemonic in the future as it has been in the past, even in the absence of any major organizing force, such as a powerful socialist or pan-religious (fundamentalist) movement, that seeks to counteract the manifest injustices and marginalizations of the capitalist form of urbanization by the construction of some alternative urban world.

II. Theoretical Reflections

But in all of this I am struck again and again by the difficulty of designing an adequate language, an adequate conceptual apparatus to grasp the nature of the problem we seem to be faced with. I worry that last year's conceptual tools and goals will be used to fight next year's issues in a dynamic situation that more and more requires proactive rather than remedial action. I am not alone in this worry. Nor is this an entirely new dilemma. As Sachs (1988: 343) observes of urban politics and policies in the past:

Urbanists, like economists and generals, were ready for the last battle they won ... the social rhetoric of the charter of Athens served more as a screen to hide their fascination with new building materials, industrialized construction methods, and spatial and architectural aestheticism rather than as a pointer to look at the real person in the streets. ... In their conceptions of society and human needs, most postwar urbanists demonstrated the same mix of naivete, dogmatism, and lack of interest in empirical evidence about people's lifestyles as the protagonists of the discussions held in the Soviet Union in the early 1920s.

Are we, then, in danger of repeating the error that Keynes long ago pointed to when he remarked on how we have a strong penchant for organizing our present lives in accordance with the defunct vision of some long-dead economist?

In thinking through this problem, I think it important first to recognize that as a physical artefact, the contemporary city has many layers. It forms what we might call a *palimpsest*, a composite landscape made up of different built forms superimposed upon each other with the passing of time. In some cases, the earliest layers are of truly ancient origin, rooted in the oldest civilizations whose imprints can be discerned beneath today's urban fabric. But even cities of relatively recent date comprise distinctive layers accumulated at different phases in the hurly burly of chaotic urban growth engendered by industrialization, colonial conquest, neocolonial domination, wave after wave of migration, as well as of real-estate speculation and modernization. Think, for example, of how the migratory layers that occupy even the rapidly expanding shanty-towns of cities in developing countries quickly spawn identifiable physical layers of more and more permanent and solid occupancy.

In the last 200 years or so, the layers in most cities have accumulated ever thicker and faster in relation to burgeoning population growth, massive voluntary and forced relocations of populations, strong but contradictory paths of economic development, and the powerful technological changes that liberated urban growth from former constraints. But it is nevertheless, as Jencks (1993) points out, one of the oddities of cities is that they become more and more fixed with time, more and more sclerotic, precisely because of the way they incrementally add things on rather than totally shedding their skins and beginning all over again. Planners, architects, urban designers – "urbanists" in short – all face one common problem: how to plan the construction of the next layers in the urban palimpsest in ways that match future wants and needs without doing too much violence to all that has gone before. What has gone before is important precisely because it is the locus of collective memory, of political identity, and of powerful symbolic meanings at the same time as it constitutes a bundle of resources constituting possibilities as well as barriers in the built environment for creative social change. There is rarely now a *tabula rasa* upon which new urban forms can be freely constructed.

But the general charge of searching for a future while respecting the past all too frequently internalizes the sclerotic tendencies in urban forms into even more sclerotic ways of thinking. It is precisely here that we need to heed Marx's warning that in moments of crisis we are always in danger of conjuring up the spirits of the past, borrowing "names, battle cries and costumes in order to present the new scene of world history" in a "time-honored disguise," and a "borrowed language." If there is one dominant impression I have of the urban processes that are reshaping cities particularly in developing countries (Seoul or São Paulo, for example), it is simply that of an urban process in which the content transcends the form – social processes literally bursting at the seams of urban form – on a scale never before encountered. How to create the poetry of our urban future in such a situation is the fundamental question.

If I go back to the famous passages of Marx's *Eighteenth Brumaire*, it is because they seem particularly appropriate to this situation. When history repeats itself, Marx observed, it occurs first as tragedy and the second time as farce. How, then, can we, to extend Marx's metaphor somewhat, prevent the modernist tragi-comedy of mid-century urbanization being turned into a late twentieth-century postmodernist farce?

What can the theoretical perspectives of historical–geographical material-ism tell us in this context? From this perspective I take up and rework five conceptual issues essential to understanding contemporary urbanization.

1. Locating the Urban in Fields of Social Action

The "thing" called a "city" is the outcome of a "process" called "urbanization." A dialectical approach (see chapter 2) says that (*a*) processes are more fundamental than things, (*b*) processes are always mediated through the things they produce, sustain and dissolve, and (*c*) the permanences produced (including ways of thought, institutions, power structures, and networks of social relations as well as material objects) frequently function as the solid and immoveable bases of daily material existence. This style of thought initiates a radical break with late-nineteenth-century thinking as well as with much of contemporary architecture and social science, in which the dominant view, in spite of all the emphasis upon social relations and processes, was and is that the city is a thing that can be engineered successfully in such a way as to control, contain, modify, or enhance social processes. In the nineteenth century Olmstead, Geddes, Howard, Burnham, Sitte, Wagner, Unwin, all reduced the problem of intricate social processes to a matter of finding the right spatial form. And in this they set the dominant ("utopic") twentieth-century tone for either a mechanistic approach to urban form, as in the case of Le Corbusier, or the more organic approach of Frank Lloyd Wright.

The difficulty with so-called "high modernism" and the city was not its "totalizing" vision, but its persistent habit of privileging things and spatial forms over social processes. It presumed that social engineering could be accomplished through the engineering of physical form. This is, as Marin (1984) shows, the fundamental posture of all classical forms of Utopianism (beginning with Sir Thomas More): they in effect propose a fixed spatial order that ensures social stability by destroying the possibility of history and containing all processes within a fixed spatial frame. The antidote to such spatial determinism is not to abandon all talk of the city (or even of the possibility of Utopia) as a whole, as is the penchant of postmodernist critique, but to return to the level of urbanization processes as being fundamental to the construction of the things that contain them. A Utopianism of process looks very different from a Utopianism of fixed spatial form.

This debate has interpretive and political significance. Do we attribute the difficulties of contemporary life to the contradictions of capitalism, to modernity (or its chaotic nemesis postmodernity), to the traumas of industrialization (and postindustrialism), to the disenchantment of the world that comes with technological and bureaucratic rationality, to social anomie born of marginalization and alienation, to massive population growth, or to that undefinable but nevertheless potent idea of a decline in religious beliefs and associated social values? Or do we argue that there is something inherent in the city (a thing) or urbanization (the process) that gives a distinctive coloration, form, and content to the structuration of contemporary social, economic and political processes, and pathologies? I have long argued and continue to argue that understanding urbanization is integral to understanding political–economic, social, and cultural processes and problems. But this is true only if we consider urbanization as a process (or, more accurately, a multiplicity of processes) producing a distinctive mix of spatialized permanences in relation to each other. The idea that a thing called the city has causal powers in relation to social life is untenable. Yet the material embeddedness of spatial structures created in the course of urbanization are in persistent tension with the fluidity of social processes, such as capital accumulation and social reproduction. Instanciating social relations through the transformation of material environments, I argued in part II, makes it particularly hard to change either. Thus do the inherently sclerotic qualities of the things we call cities, coupled with the sclerosis that often reigns in planners' heads, effectively check the possibilities of evolving a different urbanization process. The dead weight of conventional spatio-temporal thinking and actual spatio-temporal forms weighs like a practical nightmare on the thoughts and material possibilities of the living.

Traditional thinking about cities is not entirely unaware of this problem. Haussmann and Robert Moses sought to liberate processes of capital accumulation from the constraints of older spatio-temporal structures. The question of urbanization in the twenty-first century similarly becomes one of defining how space–time, environment, and place will be produced with what social processes and with what effects. Continuous capital accumulation, for example, will produce a quite different set of urban forms from those achieved under some regime seeking an emancipatory, egalitarian, and ecologically sensitive politics. Alternative anti-capitalist possibilities are to some degree already present, even though they are the subject of acute contestation and struggle between factions and classes pursuing radically different interests. The issue is not one, therefore, of gazing into some misty crystal ball or imposing some classic form of Utopian scheme in which a dead spatiality is made to rule over history and process. The problem is to enlist in the struggle to advance a more socially just and politically emancipatory mix of spatio-temporal production processes rather than acquiesce to those imposed by finance capital, the World Bank and the generally class-bound inequalities internalized within any system of uncontrolled capital accumulation. Fortunately, the latter powers, however hegemonic they may be, can never entirely control urbanization (let alone the discursive and imaginary space with which thinking about the city is always associated). Intensifying contradictions within a rapidly accelerating and often uncontrolled urbanization process create all sorts of interstitial spaces in which all sorts of liberatory and emancipatory possibilities can flourish. How and where these social movements within the urban process might be mobilized into a more general anti-capitalist politics is then the crucial question – and one that I shall take up shortly.

2. The Place of the City in a Globalizing World

There is a strong predilection these days to regard the future of urbanization as already determined by the powers of globalization and of market competition. Urban possibilities are limited to mere competitive jockeying of individual cities for position within a global urban system. There seems then to be no place within the urbanization process from which to launch any kind of militant particularism capable of grounding the drive for systemic transformations. In the last 20 years in particular, the rhetoric of "globalization" has become particularly important, even replacing within segments of radical thought the more politicized concepts of imperialism, colonialism, and neo-colonialism. The ideological effect of this discursive shift has been extraordinarily disempowering with respect to all forms of local, urban, and even national political action.

Yet, the process of globalization is not new. Certainly from 1492 onwards, and even before (cf. the Hanseatic league system), the globalization of capitalism was well under way in part through the production of a network of urban places. Marx and Engels emphasized the point in *The Communist Manifesto*. Modern industry not only creates the world market, they wrote, but the need for a constantly expanding market "chases the bourgeoisie over the whole surface of the globe" so that it "must nestle everywhere, settle everywhere, establish connections everywhere." They continue:

> The bourgeoisie has through its exploitation of the world market given a cosmopolitan character to production and consumption in every country. ... All old established national industries have been destroyed or are daily being destroy- ed. They are dislodged by new industries, whose introduction becomes a life and death question for all civilized nations, by industries that no longer work up indigenous raw material, but raw material drawn from the remotest zones; industries whose products are consumed, not only at home, but in every quarter of the globe. In place of the old wants, satisfied by the production of the country, we find new wants, requiring for their satisfaction the products of distant lands and climes. In place of the old local and national seclusion and self-sufficiency, we have intercourse in every direction, universal interdependence of nations. And as in material, so also in intellectual production. The intellectual creations of individual nations become common property. National one-sidedness and narrow-mindedness become more and more impossible, and from the numer- ous national and local literatures, there arises a world literature. ...

If this is not a good description of globalization then what is? And from this Marx and Engels derived the global imperative "working men of all nations unite" as a necessary condition for an anti-capitalist and socialist revolution.

The bourgeoisie's quest for class domination has always been and continues to be a very geographical affair. "Globalization" is a long-standing *process* always implicit in capital accumulation rather than a political–economic condition that has recently come into being. This does not preclude saying that the process has changed or worked itself out to a particular or even "final" state. But a process-based definition makes us concentrate on *how* globalization has occurred and is occurring. So what kind of process is it and, more importantly, how has it changed in recent years? Some major shifts stand out. To describe them is to describe some of the key forces at work that have changed within the complex dynamic of urbanization, in particular the extraordinary growth of urbanization in many developing countries.

(*a*) *Financial deregulation* began in the United States in the early 1970s as a forced response to stagflation and the breakdown of the Bretton Woods system of international trade and exchange. Bretton Woods was a global system so this meant a shift from one global system (largely controlled politically by the United States) to another that was more decentralized, coordinated through the market and resting on fluxes and flows of money. The effect was to make the financial conditions of capitalism far more temporally volatile and spatially unstable. The term "globalization" was, I note, largely promoted by the financial press in the early 1970s as a necessary virtue of this process of financial deregulation, as something progressive and inevitable, opening up whole new fields of opportunity for capital. It was a term embedded in the language of money and the commodity that then entered into public and academic discourses (including my own) without too much attention being paid to its class origins and ideological functions. It describes a spatial condition in which a Singapore bank can finance a local development in Baltimore without scarcely any mediation from other levels of territorial control (such as the nation state). The connection between urbanization processes and finance capital has become, as a consequence, much more direct. It is unmediated by other institutional forms of control and much more prone to rapid and ephemeral geographical dispersal across the globe. Ideologically, it makes it appear as if all urban places must submit to the discipline of free-floating finance.

(*b*) *The cost and time of moving commodities, people, and particularly information ratcheted downwards* (cf. above). This brought some significant changes to the organization of production and consumption as well as to the definition of wants and needs. The ultimate "dematerialization of space" in the communication field permitted all sorts of geographical adjustments in the location of industry, consumption, and the like. It is, however, easy to make too much of the so-called information revolution. The newness of it all impresses, but then the newness of the railroad and the telegraph, the automobile, the radio and the telephone in their day impressed equally. These earlier examples are instructive, since each in their own way did change the way globalization worked, the ways in which production and consumption could be organized, politics conducted, and the ways in which social relations between people could become converted on an ever widening scale into social relations between things. Urbanization and the connectivity of urban places through networking across space is indeed changing very rapidly through the use of informational technology.

(*c*) *Production and organizational forms changed.* The effect was an increasing geographical dispersal and fragmentation of production systems, divisions of labor, specialization of tasks, albeit in the midst of an increasing centralization of corporate power through mergers, takeovers, or joint production agreements that transcended national boundaries. The global television set, the global car, became an everyday aspect of political–economic life as did the so-called "global cities." The closing down of production in one place and the opening up of production somewhere else became a familiar story – some large-scale production operations have moved four or five times in the last 20 years. Corporations have more power to command space, making individual places much more vulnerable to their whims but the whole network of urbanization more open to rapid shifts and flows of manufacturing capital.

(*d*) *The world proletariat has almost doubled* in the last 30 years. This occurred in part through rapid population growth but also through mobile capital mobilizing more and more of the world's population (including women) as wage laborers in, for example, South Korea, Taiwan, Africa, as well as most recently in the former Soviet bloc. Much of this huge global proletariat is working under conditions of gross exploitation and political oppression. But it is geographically dispersed across a variety of massive urban concentrations. It is consequently hard to organize even though its conditions would indicate a favorable terrain for widespread anti-capitalist struggle.

(*e*) *The territorialization of the world has changed.* State operations have become much more strongly disciplined by money capital and finance. Structural adjustment and fiscal austerity have become the name of the game and the state has to some degree been reduced to the role of finding ways to promote a favorable business climate, which frequently means exercising strong discipline over the labor force. The "globalization thesis" here functions as a powerful capitalist ideology to beat upon socialists, welfare statists, nationalists, etc. Welfare for the poor has largely been replaced, therefore, by public subventions to capital (Mercedes-Benz recently received one-quarter billion dollars of subventions in a package from the state of Alabama in order to persuade it to locate there).

(*f*) *While individual states lost some of their powers, geopolitical democratization created new opportunities.* It became harder for any core power to exercise discipline over others and easier for peripheral powers to insert themselves into the capitalist competitive game. Money power is a "leveler and cynic" empowering whoever commands it wherever they are. Competitive states could do well in global competition – and this meant low-wage states with strong labor discipline often did better than others. Labor control became, therefore, a vital ideological issue within the globalization argument, again pushing socialist arguments onto the defensive.

All of these quantitative changes taken together have been synergistic enough to transform processes of urbanization. But there has been no revolution in the mode of production and its associated social relations. If there is any real qualitative trend it is towards the reassertion of early nineteenth-century capitalist laissez-faire and social Darwinian values coupled with a twenty-first-century penchant for pulling everyone (and everything that can be exchanged) into the orbit of capital. The effect is to render ever larger segments of the world's population permanently redundant in relation to capital accumulation while severing them from any alternative means of support.

But the political objection to the globalization thesis, is that it denies the possibility for meaningful action within any one of the places of capitalism (be it the nation state or the city as a political milieu for anti-capitalist mobilization). It undialectically presumes the unalloyed powers of spatial processes of capital flow to dominate places. In response, there are many who now try to put the shoe on the other foot.

3. The Communitarian Response

Faced with the innumerable problems and threats that urban life poses, some analysts, rejecting the globalizing thesis, have reached for one simple solution – to try and turn large and teeming cities, so seemingly out of control, into urban villages where, it is believed, everyone can relate in a civil fashion to everyone else in an urbane and gentle environment. In this regard, late nineteenth-century thinking on cities exercises a particularly baleful influence upon present thinking and practices. The Utopian social anarchism of that time has as much to answer for as do the more traditional bourgeois notions that derived as early as 1812 from the Reverend Thomas Chalmers who, in an influential set of writings in Britain, proposed to mobilize "the spirit of community" as an antidote to the threat of class war and revolutionary violence in rapidly urbanizing areas. The merging of these two strains of thought in the work of Patrick Geddes and Ebenezer Howard and its carry over into the planning practices of much of the twentieth century has meant a long continuity in communitarian thinking that is extraordinarily hard to exorcize from any and all thinking about urban processes.

Many contemporary analysts, post-Herbert Gans' study on *The Urban Villagers* (1962), believe that cities are mainly constituted as collections of urban villages anyway. Jencks (1993) thinks that even Los Angeles can be dissolved into 28 townships and Peter Hall, while admitting the whole idea sounds a bit banal, can cheerfully assert the fundamental truth that London is indeed a collection of villages.* In Britain, Prince Charles leads the way on this emotional charger with his emphasis upon the urban village as the locus of urban regeneration. And he is followed in this by a whole host of people across the political and social spectrum, attracting support from marginalized ethnic populations and impoverished and embattled working-class populations as well as from the upper-class nostalgics who think of it all as a civilized form of real-estate development encompassing sidewalk cafes, pedestrian precincts, and Laura Ashley shops. It is never clear of course, where the big and dirty industries might go (or, for that matter, where the great "unwashed and unwanted" might reside). And all of those things that make cities so exciting – the unexpected, the conflicts, and the adrenalin surge that comes with exploring the urban

*Many of the insights on this topic were gained from interviews conducted in researching and narrating three radio programs for BBC Radio 4 entitled "City Lights/City Shadows," broadcast in October, 1993.

unknown – will be tightly controlled and screened out with the big signs that say "no deviant behavior acceptable here."

No matter; the idea of the urban village or of some kind of communitarian solution to urban problems is both attractive and powerful (judging by the innumerable books and articles devoted to the subject). And it is so not only because of nostalgia for some long lost mythical world of intimate village life, ignoring the fact that most of the populist migration out of villages arose precisely because they were so oppressive to the human spirit and so otiose as a form of socio-political organization. It also appeals because some mythical social entity called "community" can perhaps be re-created in an urban village and "community spirit" and "community solidarity" is, we are again and again urged to believe, what will rescue us from the deadening world of social dissolution, grab-it-yourself materialism, and individualized selfish market-oriented greed that lies at the root of all urban ills. The Christian-based community concept, for example, vital brainchild of the now vastly constrained theology of liberation in Latin America, is even brought into Baltimore as the solution to urban problems (McDougall, 1993).

This ideal would not have the purchase it does were there no truth at all to it. My own guess is that the only things stopping riots or total social breakdown in many cities are the intricate networks of social solidarities, the power and dedication of community organizations, and the hundreds of voluntary groups working round the clock to restore some sense of decency and pride in an urbanizing world shell-shocked by rapid change, unemployment, massive migrations, and all of the radical travails inflicted by capitalist modernity passing into the nihilistic downside of postmodernity.

But community has always meant different things to different people and even when something that looks like it can be found, it often turns out to be as much a part of the problem as a panacea. Well-founded communities can exclude, define themselves against others, erect all sorts of keep-out signs (if not tangible walls). As Young pointed out, "racism, ethnic chauvinism, and class devaluation ... grow partly from the desire for community" such that "the positive identification of some groups is often achieved by first defining other groups as the other, the devalued semihuman." The politics of place, as I argued in chapter 11, is by no means irrelevant to the social process, but it cannot be reduced to the simplicities that the communitarians typically espouse.

We encounter here a singular, instructive and very important example of how the *a priori* definition of some theoretical object, construed as a natural entity in absolute space, can mislead. The error arises out of the belief that "community," often understood as a naturally occurring entity, indeed exists or can exist (there is a vast literature on how "communities" get lost and found in the history of urbanization) and that this entity, endowed with causal salving powers, can be put to work as an agent for social change. Even when understood as something socially constructed, communitarianism incorporates mythic beliefs that a "thing" called community can be created as some free-standing and autonomous entity endowed with causative and salving powers, that this "thing" can be internally defined in a manner that can be isolated from "others" and "outsiders," and that external relations of this thing with other things are contingent and occasional rather than integral and continuous. A more dialectical view would have it that entities like communities, while not without significance, cannot be understood independent of the social processes that generate, sustain, and also dissolve them and that it is those socio-spatial processes that are fundamental to social change. I do not mean to assert that the construction of a certain kind of spatio-temporal form designated as "community" has no relevance or interest. Something akin to community can be put in place as a source of comfort and sustenance in the face of adversity, as a zone of political empowerment, as well as a bounded space within which to advance racist, classist, and ethnico-religious exclusionism and powerful mechanisms of internal exploitation. But by abstracting from the dialectic of thing–process relations, our vision of the possibilities for social action becomes so restricted by the rhetoric of community as frequently to be self-nullifying if not self-destructive to the initial aims, however well intentioned (as, for example, in the case of trying to import the ideal of Christian-based communities as panacea for the conditions of deprivation and marginalization experienced by the African-American population in Baltimore). There are far better ways to understand the relations between "community" and social processes by translating the whole issue into one of the dialectics of space–place relations as one aspect of the overall production of spatio-temporality integral to urbanization processes in general. That may sound unduly abstract and complicated, but the idea that the Roman "communitas" or the medieval village can somehow be rebuilt in Bombay or São Paulo appears little less than absurd. This latter is no alternative for the much more tricky problem of creating a politics of heterogeneity and a domain of publicness that stretches across the diverse spatio-temporalities of contemporary urbanized living. While the rhetoric of communitarianism may provide an ideological antidote to the disempowering effects of an unalloyed globalism, it too fails precisely because it abstracts from the dialectics of place and space and treats one side of the antinomy as a self-sustaining entity endowed with causal powers.

4. From Urban Ecology to the Ecology of Urbanization

The pervasive and often powerful anti-urbanism of much of the contemporary environmental–ecological movement often translates into the view that cities ought not to exist since they are the highpoint of plundering and pollution of all that is good and holy on planet earth (see chapter 13). The predominant form of radical solutions proposed for ecological dilemmas is a return to some form of ruralized communitarianism. This predominant anti-urbanism is as odd as it is pernicious. It is almost as if a fetishistic conception of "nature" as something to be valued and worshipped separate from human action blinds a whole political movement to the qualities of the actual living environments in which the majority of humanity will soon live. It is, in any case, inconsistent to hold that everything in the world relates to everything else, as ecologists tend to do, and then decide that the built environment and the urban structures that go with it are somehow outside of both theoretical and practical consideration. The effect has been to evade integrating understandings of the urbanizing process into environmental–ecological analysis.

In this regard, it would at first blush seem as if our nineteenth-century forebears have something to teach us of great significance. Was it not, after all, a central aim in the work of Olmstead and Howard, to try to bring together the country and the city in a productive tension and to cultivate an esthetic sensibility that could bridge the chronic ills of urbanized industrialism and the supposedly healthier pursuits of country life? If would be churlish to deny real achievements on this front. The marks of what were done in those years – the park systems, the garden cities and suburbs, tree-lined streets – are now part of a living tradition that define certain qualities of urban living that many (and not only the bourgeoisie) can and do still appreciate. But it is also undeniable that this ecological vision, noble and innovative though it was at the time, was predominantly esthetic (and very bourgeois) in its orientation and was easily coopted and routinized into real-estate development practices for the middle classes. And there is, to boot, more than a hint that what ought to have been a productive tension between town and country was in fact dominated by a nostalgia for a rural and communitarian form of life that had never existed except in the fertile imaginations of a bourgeoisie seeking to escape the esthetic and social effects of its own capitalistic practices. The ecological tradition within urban thought, even though it ranks such stellar thinkers as Mumford and Geddes in its midst, has little of deep significance to say about the urbanizing dialectics of social and environmental change. While it certainly paid attention to issues of public health and the living environment, it failed to take on board that other thread of environmentalism that focused on conditions of work. Its definition of the ecological was far too limited to match today's concerns.

In recent years, however, some attention has begun to be paid, particularly by environmentalists of a more managerial persuasion, to the question of "sustainable" cities and more environmentally friendly forms of urban growth and change. But the separation of urban from environmental analyses (and a cloying nostalgia for the rural and its supposedly well-balanced sense of community) is still far too marked for comfort. The best that the ecologists (as opposed to the environmental justice movement) seem to be able to offer is either some return to an urbanization regulated by the metabolic constraints of a bioregional world as it supposedly existed in what were actually pestiferous and polluted medieval or ancient times, or a total dissolution of cities into decentralized communes or municipal entities in which, it is believed, proximity to some fictional quality called "nature" will predispose us to lines of conscious (as opposed to enforced) action that will respect the qualities of the natural world around us (as if decanting everyone from large cities into the countrysides will somehow guarantee the preservation of biodiversity, water and air qualities, and the like). And far too much of what passes for ecologically sensitive in the fields of architecture, urban planning, and urban theory amounts to little more than a concession to trendiness and to that bourgeois esthetics that likes to enhance the urban with a bit of green, a dash of water, and a glimpse of sky.

But there are a whole range of ecological issues central to how we should be thinking about our rapidly urbanizing world. The difficulty is that "environment" (see part II), means totally different things to different people, depending not only on ideological and political allegiances, but also upon situation, positionality, economic and political capacities, and the like. When the big ten environmental groups in the United States target global warming, acid rain (issues directly connected with urbanization through automobilization), ozone holes, biodiversity, and the like, they point to serious issues that have relevance at a global scale. Responses to those issues have profound implications for urbanization processes. But these are hardly the most important issues from the standpoint of the masses of people flooding into the cities of developing countries. As a result complaints of bias in the environmental agenda being imposed from the affluent nations are becoming more strident:

> It is in some sense ironic that the immediate, household-level environmental problems of indoor air quality and sanitation are often ignored or given slight treatment by activist environmental groups concerned with the environment. Most of the international attention over the past ten years has been focused on issues of "the commons," or those that threaten global tragedy. But the adverse effects of household airborne and water-carried diseases on child mortality and female life expectancy are of no less global proportions than, say, the destruction of tropical forests, and in immediate human terms they may be the most urgent of all worldwide environmental problems. Certainly, the immediate threats to the urban poor of hazardous indoor air quality and inadequate sanitation exceed the adverse effects of global warming, or even vehicular pollution. (Campbell, 1989: 173)

While Campbell adds that "of course, the world needs action on both these and other fronts" the assignment of priorities and the potentially conflicting consequences of striving to meet different environmental objectives defined at radically different scales is perhaps one of the most singular and unthought through problems associated with the rapid urbanization of the contemporary era. Suffice it to say that the integration of the urbanization question into the environmental–ecological question is a *sine qua non* for the twenty-first century. But we have as yet only scraped the surface of how to achieve that integration across the diversity of geographical scales at which different kinds of ecological questions acquire the prominence they do. And while the environmental justice movement has the potentiality to make political fire by rubbing together questions of social justice and ecological modernization, it carries so much freight of communitarianism and religious mythology as to make its take on the urbanization question somewhat ambivalent and even in some respects potentially backward looking (see chapter 13).

5. Urbanization as Uneven Geographical Development

A conceptual impasse looms. Acceptance of the globalization language is disempowering for all anti-capitalist and even moderately social democratic movements. It denies any relative autonomy for urban development, undermines the capacity within individual cities to define new possibilities of urban living, and makes it impossible to envision the modification, transgression or disruption of the trajectory of capitalist globalization/ urbanization in general. On the other hand, the communitarian response appears either Utopic in the weak nostalgic sense of looking to times past, or else it proposes an illusory isolationist localized politics, supposedly outside of the flux and flow of capitalist accumulation operating across the face of the globe. And while communitarianism often incorporates the dream of ensuring ecological balance and sustainable ecological sanity, it undermines the capacity to face realistically the complex issues of environment as these arise at quite different geographical scales, including that of urbanization.

If the languages of "community" and of "globalization" are both to be rejected, then where is there to go? We find ourselves stranded on a terrain where space–time, place and environment cannot be separated each from the other nor treated as mere abstractions outside of the concrete conditions of history and geography. The theory of historical–geographical materialism is, therefore, ripe for application. This mandates a shift from a language of globalization or communitarianism to a language of "uneven spatio-temporal development" or, more simply, "uneven geographical development."

At its simplest, this concept focuses on the concrete historical–geographical conditions within which socio-ecological action is possible and the way in which human activity in turn transforms socio-ecological conditions. The concept of uneven geographical development captures (*a*) the palimpsest of historically sedimented socio-ecological relations in place, (*b*) the multilayered and hierarchically ordered mosaic of socio-ecological configurations, and aspirations) that order space, and (*c*) the often chaotic motion of socio-ecological (particularly under contemporary conditions capital and migratory) flows that produce, sustain, and dissolve geographical differences in the landscape over time. Urbanization is a manifestation of uneven geographical development at a certain scale.

This is not a particularly new way to understand the world. But it has proven difficult to sustain as a way of thought and politics. Again and again, even when analysts arrive at the moment of understanding the critical ways in which space–time, place, and environment conjoin through the unfolding of socio-ecological processes, they often tend to slip away into a far more simplified and simplistic rhetoric of social processes occurring *in* space and altering an *external* nature. While the tyranny of this latter conception is frequently acknowledged (consider, for example, the way in which theorists like Poulantzas or Giddens dally with the theme) the only major theoretical statement on the production of uneven geographical development is that by Smith (1990). And while he makes it clear that anti-capitalist movements must plan something "very geographical" if they are to succeed, there are all sorts of political problems to be overcome if this is to be effective.

III. Political Perspectives

I suggested in chapter 5 that anti-capitalist agency (and, hence, potentiality for active struggle) is to be found everywhere and amongst everyone. It transpires that there is not a region in the world where manifestations of anger and discontent with the capitalist system cannot be found. In some places anti-capitalist movements are strongly rather than weakly implanted. Localized "militant particularisms" are everywhere, from the militia movements in the Michigan woods (much of it violently anti-corporate and against the capitalist state as well as racist and exclusionary) to the movements of Indian and Brazilian peasants fighting World Bank development projects and the vast array of urban social movements struggling against poverty, oppression, exploitation, and environmental degradation in all parts of the world. There is a veritable ferment of anti-capitalist opposition within the interstices of the uneven spatio-temporal development of capitalism. But this opposition, though militant, often remains particularist (sometimes extremely so), often unable to see beyond its own particular form of uneven geographical development. To say such movements are anti-capitalist is not to say they are pro-socialist (they can just as easily be authoritarian, religious, or neo-fascist). These movements lack coherence and a unified direction. Political moves and actions on one terrain may confound and sometimes check those on another, making it far too easy for capitalist processes and interests to divide and rule. Anti-capitalist struggle is itself unevenly developed, requiring a rather more sensitive approach to wars of position and maneuver than even Gramsci was able to devise.

But while conditions of uneven geographical and historical development may pose particular difficulties for any coherent and international anti-capitalist struggle, they also offer abundant opportunities – an extraordinarily varied and unstable terrain – for political organizing and action. The socialist and anti-capitalist movement has to configure how to make use of such revolutionary possibilities. It has to come to terms with the extraordinarily powerful processes of uneven spatio-temporal development, including those of urbanization, that make organizing so precarious and so difficult. It has to recognize that the traditional objective of socialist movements – the conquest of state power – is insufficient for its purpose and that uniting different factions can never mean suppressing socio-ecological difference. In exactly the same way that Marx saw the necessity that workers of all countries should unite to combat the globalization process at work in his time, so the socialist movement has to find ways to be just as flexible – in its theory and its political practice – over a space of volatile uneven development as the capitalist class has now become.

In this regard, the Marxist movement has considerable historical and geographical strength. At its best it has been able to synthesize diverse struggles with divergent and multiple aims into a more universal anti-capitalist movement with a global aim through a theoretical understanding of its potentialities. The Marxist tradition has an immense contribution to make towards such a work of synthesis in part because it has pioneered the tools with which to find political commonality within multiple differences and to identify primary/secondary/tertiary conditions of oppression and exploitation. I recall, here, Raymond Williams' phrase as to how "the defense and advancement of certain particular interests, *properly brought together*, are in fact the general interest" and emphasize "properly brought together" as the core task to be addressed.

The work of synthesis has to be on-going since the fields and terrains of struggle are perpetually changing as the capitalist socio-ecological dynamic changes. We need, in particular, to understand process of production of uneven spatio-temporal development and the intense contradictions that now exist within that field not only for capitalism (entailing, as it does, a great deal of self-destruction, devaluation, and bankruptcy) but also for populations rendered increasingly vulnerable to the violence of downsizing, unemployment, collapse of services, degradation in work conditions and living standards, destruction of resource complexes, and loss of environmental qualities. It is vital to go beyond the particularities and to emphasize the *pattern* and the systemic qualities of the damage being wrought. "Only connect" is still one of the most empowering and insightful of all political slogans. The analysis has, furthermore, to be extended outwards to embrace a wide array of diverse and seemingly disparate questions. Issues like AIDS, global warming, local environmental degradation, the destructions of local cultural traditions, are inherently class issues and it needs to be shown how building a community in anti-capitalist class struggle can better alleviate the conditions of oppression across a broad spectrum of social action. This is not, I emphasize, a plea for eclecticism and pluralism, but a plea to uncover the raw class content of a wide array of anti-capitalist concerns.

The primary significance of "globalization" for the anti-capitalist struggle in the advanced capitalist countries, for example, is that the relatively privileged position of the working classes has been much reduced relative to conditions of labor in the rest of the world. Conditions of life in advanced capitalism have felt the full brunt of the capitalist capacity for "creative destruction" making for extreme volatility in local, regional, and national economic prospects (this year's boom town becomes next year's depressed region). The free market justification for this is that the hidden hand of the market will work to the benefit of all, provided there is as little state interference (and it should be added – though it usually isn't – monopoly power) as possible. The effect is to make the violence and creative destruction of uneven geographical development (through, for example, geographical reorganization of production) just as widely felt in the traditional heartlands of capitalism as elsewhere, in the midst of an extraordinary technology of affluence and conspicuous consumption that is instantaneously communicated worldwide as one potential set of aspirations. The political terrain for anti-capitalist organizing in advanced capitalism appears more fertile than ever.

This work of synthesis has, however, to reroot itself in the organic conditions of daily life. This does not entail abandoning the abstractions that Marx and the Marxists have bequeathed us, but it does mean revalidating and revaluing those abstractions through immersion in popular struggles, some of which may not appear on the surface to be proletarian in the sense traditionally given to that term. In this regard, Marxism has its own sclerotic tendencies to combat its own embedded fixed capital of concepts, institutions, practices, and politics which can function on the one hand as an excellent resource and on the other as a dogmatic barrier to action. We need to discern what is useful and what is not in this fixed capital of our intellect and politics. And it would be surprising if there were not, from time to time, bitter argument over what to jettison and what to hold. Nevertheless, the debate must take place.

I here take up just one strategic point. The traditional method of Marxist intervention has been via an avant-garde political party. But difficulties have arisen because this has often led to the superimposition of a single aim, a singular objective, an abstract socialist goal upon diverse anti-capitalist movements holding to a multiplicity of objectives appropriate to different historical–geographical conditions. The emancipatory thrust of Marxism here creates the danger of its own negation. This was the difficulty that so troubled Raymond Williams as he reflected on the translation of a language of affective loyalties – "our people" – into that of an abstract political project – "the proletariat." It was in this translation that the politics of negation and abstraction were also to be found (see chapter 1).

Emancipation should mean opening up the production of difference, even opening up a terrain for contestation within and between differences, rather than suppressing them. The production of real rather than commodified cultural divergence should be integral to socialist struggle. One of the strong objections to capitalism is that it has produced a relatively homogeneous capitalist person. This reductionism of all beings and all cultural differences to a common commodified base is the focus of strong anti-capitalistic sentiments. The socialist cause must encompass and seek emancipation from that bland commodified homogeneity. This is not a plea for an unchecked relativism or unconstrained postmodern eclecticism, but for a serious discussion of the relations between commonality/difference, the particularity of the one and the universalism of the other. Socialism has to be understood as a political project, as an alternative vision of how society will work, how socio-ecological relations will unfold, how human potentialities can be realized albeit within a geography of difference.

We badly need a socialist avant-garde movement to express that politics. But it cannot be an old-style avant-garde party that imposes a singular goal. Nor can it function armed only with Derrida's "ultimate post-structuralist fantasy" of a "New International without status, without title and without name ... without party, without country, without national community" (cf. above, p. 8). It will take much more than thought and discourse (however important these may be) to shape socio-ecological and political-economic change in emancipatory ways. That version of avant-gardism, now so entrenched in the academy, in which immersion in the flows of thought and ideality is somehow imagined to be radical and revolutionary in itself has no material purchase.

Organizations, institutions, doctrines, programs, formalized structures and the like simply have to be created. And these political activities must be firmly grounded in and transformative of the concrete historical and geographical conditions through which human action unfolds. Between the traditional avant-gardism of communist parties (the specter of Lenin) and an idealized avant-gardism (the specter of Derrida) there lies a terrain of political organization and struggle that desperately cries out for cultivation.

That general terrain is not empty of possibilities. Many substantive movements claim our attention, some at the margin and some deeply embedded within the structures of advanced capitalism. The difficulty is, as always, to find both a rhetoric and tangible means to link together divergent oppositional forces engaged in anti-capitalist struggle. But consider, for example, the January 30, 1996 call of the Zapatista Army for National Liberation for "A World Gathering against Neoliberalism and for Humanity." They point out how the power of money everywhere "humiliates dignities, insults honesties and assassinates hopes." Renamed as neoliberalism "the historic crime in the concentration of privileges, wealth and impunities democratizes misery and hopelessness." The name "globalization" signifies, they suggest, the "modern war" of capital "which assassinates and forgets." Instead of humanity, this neoliberalism "offers us stock market value indexes, instead of dignity it offers us globalization of misery, instead of hope it offers us emptiness, instead of life it offers us the international of terror." Against this international of terror, they conclude, "we must raise the international of hope."

Now consider the general import of this idea: if only all those touched by the violence of the neoliberal free-market politics of globalization could come together politically, then its days would surely be numbered. While the Zapatista call comes from the margins of advanced capitalism, the struggle for a "liveable wage" in my home town of Baltimore (part of a movement spreading across many US cities) likewise recognizes and rejects the appalling wreckage now being wrought by the Utopian schemes of the neoliberal right in alliance with corporate power. This "brakeless train wreaking havoc wherever it goes" has to be stopped. And the first step, as Wood (1995: 293) concludes from her trenchant analysis, is to draw the obvious lesson from our current economic and political condition: "that a humane, 'social', truly democratic and equitable capitalism is more unrealistically utopian than socialism."

The work of synthesis and of bringing together the multiplicity of anti-capitalist struggles occurring on a variegated terrain of uneven geographical development must proceed a-pace. That is what avant-garde socialist political organization must focus on. But it needs must arm itself with concepts and ideas, ideals and imaginaries, fundamental understandings and "epistemologies that can tell the difference," with foundational beliefs and persuasive arguments, if it is to go about its task effectively. And it is the obligation of those of us who work primarily in realms of discourse and representation to clarify the lessons that historical geography teaches. We cannot rely on poetries drawn from distant places and times even as we learn to appreciate the power and meaning of those poetries in fomenting this or that trajectory of socio-ecological change. We need a poetics fitting for our own times and places and we need to learn how to put this poetics to work in tangible situations so as to shape through collective action the socio-ecological processes of historical and geographical transformation to socialist ends. This means coming to grips with the production of space–time, place, and environments, with the conditions of uneven geographical development that spawn such extraordinarily divergent and widespread oppositional movements to capitalism and multiple possibilities for trans-formative action. And chief among these conditions is the extraordinary socio-ecological reordering defined by contemporary processes of urbanization.

IV. Probing the Frontiers of Possible Urban Worlds

So what sort of stance would a historical–geographical materialism suggest for exploring and probing the possibilities of new urban processes and city forms?

If the famed Utopias of spatial form, those magnificent shining cities on a hill, are judged as not merely wanting but as dangerous, as recipes for authoritarian oppressions in the name of law, stability and order, then how can we even dare to think of future possible urban worlds?

But not to think of them is to evade one of the most important socio-ecological dilemmas that human society now faces. We have already paid a price for such evasions. For urbanization has happened and nobody much has either cared or noticed in relation to the other issues of the day judged more important. It would be an egregious error, even for capitalist interests and most certainly for any socialist project, to enter in upon the twenty-first century making the same mistake. It is, furthermore, vital to understand that what half-worked for the 1890s in Britain or even for the 1950s in the United States and Europe, will not be adequate for the qualitatively different issues to be fought over the nature of a rapidly urbanizing civilization in the twenty-first century.

Coming to terms with what urban living might be about requires a proactive absorption of new ways of thinking into radical politics. The fundamental lesson that a dialectically grounded approach to historical–geographical materialism teaches is that interventions that fetishize processes are empty and that interventions that fetishize things are oppressively full. A politics derived from a dialectical understanding of "process–thing" relations looks fundamentally different from its alternatives. The language of historical–geographical material-ism has much to teach concerning the transformative possibilities embedded in processes of production of space, time, place, and nature. And that teaching carries over directly into approaches to urbanization. So I close with what I consider to be the ten key problems to be worked upon and a parallel set of myths to be exploded as we consider the future of civilization in a rapidly urbanizing world.

The first myth is that cities are anti-ecological ("unnatural," "artificial," or in some way "outside of nature"). Opposing this is the view that high-density urbanized living and inspired forms of urban design are the only paths to a more ecologically sensitive form of civilization in the twenty-first century. We must recognize that the distinction between *environment* as commonly under-stood and the *built, social, and political-economic environment* is artificial and that the urban and everything that goes into it is as much a part of the solution as it is a contributing factor to ecological difficulties. The tangible recognition that the mass of humanity will be located in living environments designated as urban says that environmental politics must pay as much if not more attention to the qualities of those environments as it now typically does to a fictitiously separated and imagined "natural" environment (see chapters 6 and 11). By the same token, urban politics has fundamentally to be about modes of transformation of nature related dialectically to modes of self-realization of a particular form of human nature.

The second myth is that often chaotic and frequently problematic forms of socio-ecological change can be corrected and controlled by finding the right spatial form. Opposed to this is the understanding that all spatializations of Utopias, from Thomas More through Le Corbusier to the Utopic degeneration manifest in Disneyland (with its carry over into much contemporary urban design in the advanced capitalist countries), cannot erase history and process. Emancipatory politics calls for a living Utopianism of process as opposed to the dead Utopianism of spatialized urban form.

The third myth is that a Utopianism of pure process, untrammeled by the materiality of things and permanences, of spatial forms and material constructs, can liberate the human spirit into a dematerialized world – a virtual reality – where self-realization is understood abstractly and ideally as a purely mental act. Opposed to this is an understanding that the dialectics of the imaginary and the material, of spatial forms and temporal processes, constitute the fundamental and inescapable metabolic state of all human being. Becoming without being is empty idealism while being without becoming is death. The dynamic of urbanization and the construct of the city exist in a fundamental creative tension that provides the nexus to explore different modes of species being. The production of different spatio-temporal orderings and structures are active moments within the social process. What we understand by the dialectical relation between urbanization (the process) and the city (the thing) constitutes a critical point of socio-ecological transformation and, consequently, a fundamental point of anti-capitalist and pro-socialist struggle.

The fourth myth is that coming up with the resources and the requisite means to confront urban problems depends on the prior solution of technological, economic development, and population-growth problems. Opposed to this is the idea that cities have always been fundamentally about innovation, wealth creation, and wealth consumption and that getting things right in cities (construed as places) is the only real path towards technological and economic improvement for the mass of the population. Modern technologies produced by the military–industrial complex of capitalism have again and again opened up new and broadly capitalist-oriented possibilities for urbanization. These possibilities and their potential appropriation by progressive forces must be distinguished from the predominant forces (such as capital accumulation or populist appropriation) that realize their own agendas by means of those technologies. Fundamental redefinitions of wealth, well-being, and values (including those that affect population growth and environmental qualities) must be sought in ways that are more conducive to the development of the human potentialities of all segments of the population. Creative forms of socio-ecological change for the many must be explored as opposed to mere capital accumulation for the select few.

The sixth myth is that social problems are curable only to the degree that the decentralized forces of the market are given freer play to produce space, place, and nature in an urbanizing world. Opposed to this is the idea that wealth creation (and redefinition) depends on a mix of social collaboration and cooperation (between all economic entities, including businesses), on adaptations, and on the shaping of environments (the production of space, place, and nature), rather than solely on some individualized Darwinian struggle for existence (see chapter 8). The pursuit of social justice, as explored in chapters 12 and 13, is therefore vital to achieving both improved economic performance and socio-ecological conditions more conducive to feeding the hungry, clothing the naked, ministering to the sick, and relating openly with "others."

The seventh myth is that forces of globalization (spatialization) are so strong as to preclude any relative autonomy for local or particular initiatives to shift the process of urbanization onto a different trajectory. Only a global revolution, so the myth has it, can change anything. Opposed to this is the idea that the space–place dialectic is ever a complicated affair, that globalization is really a process of uneven geographical and historical (spatio-temporal) development that creates a variegated terrain of anti-capitalist struggles that need to be synthesized in such a way as to respect the qualities of different "militant particularisms" (such as those to be found in urban social movements throughout the world) while evolving strong spatial bonds and a global socialist politics of internationalism.

The eighth myth is that community solidarity (often "local") can provide the stability and power needed to control, manage, and alleviate urban problems and that "community" can substitute for public politics. Opposed to this is the recognition that "community," insofar as it exists, is an unstable configuration relative to the conflictual processes that generate, sustain, and eventually undermine it, and that insofar as it does acquire permanence it is frequently an exclusionary and oppressive social form that can be as much at the root of urban conflict and urban degeneration as it can be a panacea for political-economic difficulties.

The ninth myth is that strong order, authority, and centralized control (a state apparatus) – be it moral, political, communitarian, religious, physical, or militaristic – must be reasserted over our disintegrating and strife-prone cities without, however, interfering in the fundamental liberty of the market. Opposed to this is the understanding that the contemporary form of "market stalinism" (and I think it vital we learn to call it by its right name) is self-contradictory and the recognition that urbanization has always been about creative forms of opposition, tension, and conflict (including those registered through market exchange). The tensions born of heterogeneity cannot and should not be repressed. They must be liberated in socially exciting ways – even if this means more rather than less conflict, including contestation over socially necessary socialization of market processes for collective ends. Diversity and difference, heterogeneity of values, lifestyle oppositions and chaotic migrations, are not to be feared as sources of disorder. Cities that cannot accommodate to diversity, to migratory movements, to new lifestyles and to economic, political, religious, and value heterogeneity, will die either through ossification and stagnation or because they will fall apart in violent conflict. Defining a politics that can bridge the multiple heterogeneities, including most emphatically those of geography, without repressing difference is one of the biggest challenges of twenty-first century urbanization.

The tenth myth is that any radical transformation in social relations in urbanizing areas must await some sort of political revolution (communitarian, religious, socialist, communist, authoritarian, fascist) that will then put our cities in sufficiently good order to allow new and preferred social relations to flourish. Opposed to this is the idea that the transformation of socio-ecological relations in urban settings has to be a continuous process of socio-environmental change. From a socialist perspective this means a long urban-based revolution that should have the exploration and construction of alternative social processes and spatial forms as its long-term goal albeit through short-term and often place-based movements and actions.

It will take imagination and political guts, a surge of revolutionary fervor and revolutionary change (in thinking as well as in politics) to construct a requisite poetics of understanding for our urbanizing world, a charter for civilization, a trajectory for our species being, out of the raw materials of this present. We have much to learn from our predecessors, particularly those who worked in the latter part of the last century, for their political and intellectual courage cannot be doubted. They mobilized their imaginations and created their own poetries to confront a task in a certain way that had material consequences – both good and bad – under conditions that are now either superceded or threatened with dissolution. If the current rhetoric about handing on a decent living environment to future generations is to have even one iota of meaning, we owe it to subsequent generations to invest now in a collective and very public search for some way to understand the possibilities of achieving a just and ecologically sensitive urbanization process under contemporary conditions. That discussion cannot trust in dead dreams resurrected from the past. It has to construct its own language – its own poetry – with which to discuss possible futures in a rapidly urbanizing world of uneven geographical development. Only in that way can the possibilities for a civilizing mode of urbanization be thought and imagined. How to translate from this purely discursive moment in the social process to the realms of power, material practices, institutions, beliefs and social relations, is, however, where practical politics begins and discursive reflection ends.

Thoughts for an Epilogue

... it takes a lot of things to change the world:
Anger and tenacity. Science and indignation,
The quick initiative, the long reflection,
The cold patience and the infinite perseverance,
The understanding of the particular case and the understanding of the ensemble:
Only the lessons of reality can teach us to transform reality

Bertolt Brecht *Einverstandnis*

Bibliography

Abbey, E. (1975) *The monkey wrench gang*, New York.

Adorno, T. (1973) *Negative dialectics*, New York.

Agarwal, B. (1992) "The gender and environment debate: Lessons from India," *Feminist Studies*, 18, No. 1, 119–58.

Agnew, J. and Duncan, J. (eds) (1989) *The power of place: Bringing together the geographical and sociological imaginations*, Boston.

Alexander, D. (1990) "Bioregionalism: Science or sensibility," *Environmental Ethics*, 12, 161–73.

Anderlini, L. and Sabourian, H. (1992) "Some notes on the economics of barter, money and credit," in Humphrey, C. and Hugh-Jones, S. (eds) *Barter, exchange and value*, Cambridge.

Anderson, B. (1983) *Imagined communities: Reflections on the origin and spread of nationalism*, London.

Attfield, R. (1991) *The ethics of environmental concern*, Athens, Georgia.

Aurelius, M. (1964) *Meditations*, Harmondsworth, Middlesex.

Aveni, A. (1989) *Empires of time: Calendars, clocks, and cultures*, New York.

Bachelard, G. (1964) *The poetics of space*, Boston, Mass.

Bailey, C., Faupel, C., and Gundlach, J. (1993) "Environmental politics in Alabama's Blackbelt," in Bullard, R. (ed.) *Confronting environmental racism*, Boston, Mass.

Bakhtin, M. (1981) *The dialogic imagination: Four essays*, Austin, Tex.

Bakhtin, M. (1984) *Rabelais and his world*, Bloomington, Ind.

Bakhtin, M. (1990) *Art and answerability*, Austin, Tex.

Basso, K. (1984) " 'Stalking with stories': Names, places, and moral narratives among the Western Apache," *1983 Proceedings of the American Ethnological Society*, American Ethnological Society, Washington, DC.

Bateson, P. (1988) "The active role of behavior in evolution," in Ho. M.-W. and Fox, S. (eds) *Evolutionary processes and metaphors*, New York.

Baudelaire, C. (1981) *Selected writings on art and artists*, London.

Beck, U. (1992) *Risk society: Towards a new modernity*, London.

Bell Hooks (1990) *Yearning: Race, gender, and cultural politics*, Boston.

Bell, D. (1976) *The cultural contradictions of capitalism*, New York.

Bell, J. (1989) "Six possible worlds of quantum mechanics," in Allen, S. (ed.) *Possible worlds in humanities, arts and sciences*, Berlin.

Benedikt, M. (ed.) (1991) *Cyberspace: First steps*, Cambridge, Mass.

Bennett, J. (1976) *The ecological transition: Cultural anthropology and human adaptation*, New York.

Benton, T. (1989) "Marxism and natural limits: An ecological critique and reconstruction," *New Left Review*, 178, 51–86.

Benton, T. (1992) "Ecology, socialism and the mastery of nature: A reply to Reiner Grundmann," *New Left Review*, 194, 55–74.

Benton, T. (1993) *Natural relations: Ecology, animal rights and social justice*, London.

Berman, M. (1982) *All that is solid melts into air*, New York.

Berry, B. (1990) "Urbanization" in Turner, B. et al. (eds) *The earth as transformed by human action*, Cambridge.

Bhaskar, R. (1989) *Reclaiming reality*, London.

Bhaskar, R. (1993) *Dialectic: The pulse of freedom*, London.

Birch, C. and Cobb, J. (1981) *The liberation of life: From the cell to the community*, Cambridge.

Bird, J., Curtis, B., Putnam, T., Robertson, G., and Tickner, L. (eds) (1993) *Mapping futures: Local cultures global change*, London.

Birringer, J. (1989) "Invisible cities/transcultural images," *Performing Arts Journal*, 12, 120–38.

Black, M. (1962) *Models and metaphors*, Ithaca, NY.

Blumberg, M. and Gottlieb, R. (1989) *War on waste: Can America win its battle with garbage*, Washington, DC.

Blumin S. M. (1989) *The emergence of the middle class: Social experience in the American city*, 1760–1900, Cambridge.

Bohm, D. (1983) *Wholeness and the implicate order*, London.

Bohm, D. and Peat, F. (1987) *Science, order, and creativity*, London.

Bookchin, M. (1990a) *Remaking society: Pathways to a green future*, Boston.

Bookchin, M. (1990b) *The philosophy of social ecology: Essays on dialectical naturalism*, Montreal.

Booth, A. and Jacobs, H. (1990) "Ties that bind: Native American beliefs as a foundation for environmental consciousness," *Environmental Ethics*, 12, 27–43.

Borneman, E. (ed.) (1976) *The psychoanalysis of money*, London.

Bourdieu, P. (1977) *Outline of a theory of practice*, Cambridge.

Bourdieu, P. (1984) *Distinction: A social critique of the judgement of taste*, London.

Boyer, C. (1988) "The return of aesthetics to city planning," *Society*, 25, No. 4, 49–56.

Bramwell, A. (1989) *Ecology in the twentieth century: A history*, New Haven.

Braudel, F. (1974) *The perspective of the world*, New York.

Brown, C. (1990) *Leibniz and Strawson: A new essay in descriptive metaphysics*, Munich.

Brueggemann, W. (1977) *The land: Place as gift, promise, and challenge in biblical faith*, Philadelphia, Pa.

Bryant, B. and Mohai, P. (1992) *Race and the incidence of environmental hazards*, Boulder, Col.

Buell, L. (1995) *The environmental imagination: Thoreau, nature writing, and the formation of American culture*, Cambridge, Mass.

Bullard, R. (1990) *Dumping in Dixie: Race, class, and environmental quality*, Colorado.

Bullard, R. (ed.) (1993) *Confronting environmental racism: Voices from the grassroots*, Boston, Mass.

Bullard R. (ed.) (1994) *Unequal protection: Environmental justice and communities of color*, San Francisco, Calif.

Butzer, K. (1982) *Archaeology as human ecology*, Cambridge.

Caffentzis, C. (1989) *Clipped coins, abused words, and civil government: John Locke's philosophy of money*, Brooklyn, NY.

Callicott, J. (1989) *In defense of the land ethic: Essays in environmental philosophy*, Albany, NY.

Callon, M. (1986) "Some elements of a sociology of translation: Domestication of the scollops and fishermen of St. Brieuc Bay." in Law, J. (ed.) *Power, action and belief*, London.

Cameron, D. (1992) *Feminism and linguistic theory*, 2nd edn, New York.

Campbell, T. (1989) "Environmental dilemmas and the urban poor," in Leonard, H. J. (ed.) *Environment and the poor: Development strategies for a common agenda*, New Brunswick, NJ.

Capra, F. (1975) *The tao of physics*, Berkeley, Calif.

Capra, F. (1982) *The turning point: Science, society and the rising culture*, New York.

Carlson, D. (1992) "On the margins of microeconomics," in Cornell, D., Rosenfeld, M., and Carlson, D. (eds) *Deconstruction and the possibility of justice*, New York.

Carlstein, T., Parkes, D., and Thrift, N. (1978) *Timing space and spacing time*, London.

Carter, E., Donald, J., and Squires, J. (eds) (1993) *Space and place: Theories of identity and location*, London.

Cassirer, E. (1943) "Newton and Leibniz," *The Philosophical Review*, 52, 366–91.

Cassirer, E. (1968) *The philosophy of the Enlightenment*, Princeton, NJ.

Castells, M. (1989) *The informational city: Information technology, economic restructuring, and the urban-regional process*, Oxford.

Clark, J. (1989) "Marx's inorganic body," *Environmental Ethics*, 11, 243–58.

Coase, R. (1960) "The problem of social cost," *Journal of Law and Economics*, 3, 1–44.

Coles, R. (1993) "Ecotones and environmental ethics: Adorno and Lopez," in Bennett, J. and Chaloupka, W. (eds), *In the nature of things: Language, politics and the environment*, Minneapolis, Minn.

Collingwood, R. (1960) *The idea of nature*, Oxford.

Colpotura, F. and Sen, R. (1994) "PUEBLO fights lead poisoning," in Bullard, R. (eds.) *Unequal protection*, San Francisco, Calif.

Commission on Global Governance (1995) *Our global neighborhood*, Oxford.

Commoner, B. (1990) *Making peace with the planet*, New York.

Cooke, P. (1989) *Localities*, London.

Cooke, P. (1990) "Locality, structure and agency: A theoretical analysis," *Cultural Anthropology*, 5, 3–15.

Cott, N. (1977) *The bonds of womanhood: "Women's sphere" in New England, 1780–1935*, New Haven, Conn.

Cox, K. and Mair, A. (1989) "Levels of abstraction in locality studies," *Antipode*, 21, 121–32.

Cronon, W. (1983) *Changes in the land: Indians, colonists, and the ecology of New England*, New York.

Cronon, W. (1991) *Nature's metropolis: Chicago and the Great West*, New York.

Crosby, A. (1986) *Ecological imperialism: The biological expansion of Europe, 900–1900*, Cambridge.

Dauncey, G. (1988) *After the crash: The emergence of the rainbow economy*, Basingstoke.

Davidson, O. G. (1991) "It's still 1911 in America's rural sweatshops," *Baltimore Sun*, Saturday, September 7, 1991, p. 7A.

Davis, M. (1990) *City of quartz: Excavating the future in Los Angeles*, London.

David, M. et al. (1990) *Fire in the hearth: The radical political economy of place in America*, London.

Davison, G. (1993) *The unforgiving minute: How Australia learned to tell the time*, Oxford.

Dawkins, R. (1989) *The selfish gene*, Oxford.

De Certeau, (1984) *The practice of everyday life*, Berkeley, Calif.

De-Shalit, A. (1995) *Why posterity matters: Environmental policies and future generations*, London.

Deleuze, G. (1993) *The fold: Leibniz and the baroque*, London.

Derrida, J. (1992a) "Force of law: 'The mystical foundation of authority'," in Cornell, D., Rosenfeld, M., and Carlson, D. (eds) *Deconstruction and the possibility of justice*, New York.

Derrida, J. (1992b) *Given time: 1. Counterfeit money*, Chicago, Ill.

Derrida, J. (1994) *Specters of Marx*, London.

Di Michele, L. (1993) "Autobiography and the 'Structure of Feeling' in *Border Country*," in Dworkin, D. and Roman, L. G. (eds) *Views beyond the border country*, London.

Dickens, P. (1992) *Society and nature: Towards a green social theory*, London.

Dobson, A. (1990) *Green political thought*, London.

Douglas, A. (1977) *The feminization of American culture*, New York.

Douglas, M. (1984) *Purity and danger: An analysis of the concepts of pollution and taboo*, London.

Dovey, K. (1989) "The quest for authenticity and the replication of environmental meaning," in Seamon, D. and Mugerauer, R. (eds) *Dwelling, place and environment: towards a phenomenology of person and world*, New York.

Duncan, J. and Ley, D. (1982) "Structural Marxism and human geography: A critical assessment," *Annals, Association of American Geographers*, 72, 30–59.

Duncan, S. and Savage, M. (1989) "Space, scale and locality," *Antipode*, 21, 179–206.

Durkheim, E. (1915) *The elementary forms of religious life*, London.

Dworkin, D. and Roman, L. (eds) (1993) *Views beyond the border country: Raymond Williams and cultural politics*. London.

Eagleton, T. (ed.) (1989) *Raymond Williams: Critical perspectives*, Cambridge.

Eagleton, T. (1990) *The ideology of the aesthetic*, Oxford.

Eagleton, T. (1995) "Jacques Derrida; Specters of Marx," *Radical Philosophy*, 73, 35–7.

Easterbrook, G. (1995) *A moment on the earth: The coming age of environmental optimism*, New York.

Echeverria, J. and Eby, R. (eds) (1995) *Let the people judge: Wise use and the private property rights movement*, Washington, DC.

Eckersley, R. (1992) *Environmentalism and political theory: Toward an ecocentric approach*, London.

Edsall, T. (1984) *The new politics of inequality*, New York.

Elias, N. (1978) *The civilizing process: The history of manners*, Oxford.

Eliot, G. (1972) *Felix Holt: The radical,* Harmondsworth, Middlesex.

Ellen, R. (1982) *Environment, subsistence and system: The ecology of small-scale social formations,* Cambridge.

Engels, F. (1935) *The housing question,* New York.

Engels, F. (1940) *The dialectics of nature,* New York.

Engels, F. (1947) *Anti-Duhring,* London.

Engels, F. (1952) *The condition of the working class in England in 1844,* Oxford.

Enzensberger, H.-M. (1974) "A critique of political ecology," *New Left Review,* 84, 3–31.

Epstein, R. (1985) *Takings: Private property and the power of eminent domain,* Cambridge, Mass.

Etzioni, A. (1993) *The spirit of community: Rights, responsibilities, and the communitarian agenda,* New York.

Fabian, J. (1983) *Time and the other: How anthropology constructs its object,* New York.

Ferry, L. (1995) *The new ecological order,* Chicago, Ill.

Fisher, S. (ed.) (1993) *Fighting back in Appalachia,* Philadelphia, Pa.

Fitzgerald, F. (1986) *Cities on a hill: A journey through contemporary American cultures,* New York.

Fitzgerald, J. (1979) *Alfred North Whitehead's early philosophy of space and time,* Washington, DC.

Florini, K., Krumbharr, G., and Silbergeld, E. (1990) *Legacy of lead: America's continuing epidemic of childhood lead poisoning,* Washington, DC.

Foltz, B. (1995) *Inhabiting the earth: Heidegger, environmental ethics, and the metaphysics of nature,* Atlantic Highlands, NJ.

Forman, F., with Sowton, C. (eds) (1989) *Taking our time: Feminist perspectives on temporality,* Oxford.

Foster, J. B. (1994) *The vulnerable planet: A short economic history of the environment,* New York.

Foucault, M. (1977) *Discipline and punish,* New York.

Foucault, M. (1980) *Power/knowledge,* Hemel Hempstead.

Foucault, M. (1984) *The Foucault Reader* (edited by P. Rabinov), Harmondsworth, Middlesex.

Foucault, M. (1986) "Heterotopias," *Diacritics,* Spring, 22–7.

Fox, W. (1990) *Toward a transpersonal ecology: Developing new foundations for environmentalism,* Boston, Mass.

Frantz, D. (1994) "How Tyson became the Chicken King," *New York Times,* Business Section, 1 and 6, Sunday August 28, 1994.

Fraser, N. (1989) *Unruly practices: Power, discourse and gender in contemporary social theory,* Minneapolis, Minn.

Fried, M. (1963) "Grieving for a lost home," in Duhl, L. (ed.) *The urban condition,* New York.

Friedan, B. (1963) *The feminine mystique,* New York.

Friedman, S. (1995) "Beyond white and other: Relationality and narratives of race in feminist discourse," *Signs,* 21, 1–49.

Fuss, D. (1989) *Essentially speaking: Feminism, nature and difference,* London.

Gans, H. (1962) *The urban villagers: Group and class in the life of Italian-Americans,* New York.

Gates, H. (1992) "The welcome table: Remembering James Baldwin," paper delivered to *Wissenschaftliche Jahrestagung der Deutschen Gesellschaft fur Amerikastudien,* June.

Gell, A. (1992) *The anthropology of time: Cultural constructions of temporal maps and images,* Oxford.

Gerratana, V. (1973) "Marx and Darwin," *New Left Review,* 82, 60–82.

Ghai, D. and Vivian, J. (eds) (1995) *Grassroots environmental action: People's participation in sustainable development,* London.

Gibbs, L. (1982) *Love Canal: My story,* Albany, NY.

Gibson, W. (1984) *Neuromancer,* New York.

Giddens, A. (1984) *The constitution of society,* Cambridge.

Gilroy, P. (1987) *There ain't no black in the Union Jack,* London.

Girardet, H. (1992) *The Gaia atlas of cities,* London.

Glacken, C. (1967) *Traces on the Rhodian shore,* Berkeley, Calif.

Goldberg, D. (1991) *Racist culture: Philosophy and the politics of meaning,* Oxford.

Goldsmith, E. (1992) *The way: An ecological world view,* London.

Goodin, R. (1992) *Green political theory,* Cambridge.

Gordon, M. (1995) "My mother is speaking from the desert," *The New York Times Magazine,* March 19, 1995, pp. 47–70.

Gosselink, J., Odum, E., and Pope, R. (1974) *The value of the tidal marsh,* Baton Rouge, La.

Gottlieb, R. (1988) *A life of its own: The politics and power of water,* New York.

Gottlieb, R. (1993) *Forcing the Spring: The transformation of the American environmental movement,* Washington, DC.

Goudie, A. (1986) *The human impact,* Oxford.

Gould, S. (1988) *Time's arrow, time's cycle: Myth and metaphor in the discovery of geological time,* Harmondsworth, Middlesex.

Granovetter, M. (1985) "Economic action and social structure: the problem of embeddedness," *American Journal of Sociology,* 91, 481–510.

Gregory, D. and Urry, J. (eds) (1985) *Social relations and spatial structures,* London.

Greider, W. (1993) *Who will tell the people?* New York.

Grossman, K. (1994) "The people of color environmental summit," in Bullard, R. (ed.) *Unequal protection,* San Francisco, Calif.

Grosz, E. (1992) "Bodies-cities," in Colomina, B. (eds.) *Sexuality and space,* Princeton, NJ.

Grundmann, R. (1991a) "The ecological challenge to Marxism," *New Left Review,* 187, 103–20.

Grundmann, R. (1991b) *Marxism and Ecology,* Oxford.

Guha, R. (1989) *The unquiet woods: Ecological change and peasant resistance in the Himalayas,* Berkeley, Calif.

Guillermé, A. (1988) *The age of water: The urban environment in the North of France, A.D. 300–1800,* College Station, Tex.

Gupta, A. and Ferguson, J. (1992) "Beyond 'culture': space, identity, and the politics of difference," *Cultural Anthropology,* 7, 6–43.

Gurevich, A. (1985) *Categories of medieval culture,* London.

Gutman, A. (ed.) (1994) *Multiculturalism and the politics of recognition,* Princeton, NJ.

Habermas, J. (1987) *The philosophical discourse of modernity,* Oxford.

Haila, Y. and Levins, R. (1992) *Humanity and nature: Ecology, science and society*, London.

Hajer, M. (1992) "The politics of environmental performance review: Choices in design" in Lykke, E. (ed.) *Achieving environmental goals: The concept and practice of environmental performance review*, London.

Hajer, M. (1995) *The politics of environmental discourse: Ecological modernization and the policy process*, Oxford.

Hall, E. (1966) *The hidden dimension*, New York.

Hall, S. (1989) "Politics and letters," in Eagleton, T. (ed.) *Raymond Williams*, Cambridge.

Hallowell, A. (1955) *Culture and experience*, Philadelphia, Pa.

Haraway, D. (1989) *Primate visions: Gender, race and nature in the world of modern science*, New York.

Haraway, D. (1990) "A manifesto for cyborgs: Science, technology, and socialist feminism in the 1980s," in Nicholson, L. (ed.) *Feminism/Postmodernism*, London.

Haraway, D. (1991) *Simians, cyborgs, and women: The reinvention of nature*, London.

Hardin, G. (1968) "The tragedy of the commons," *Science*, 162, 1243–8.

Hareven, T. (1982) *Family time and industrial time*, Cambridge.

Hartsock, N. (1983) *Money, sex and power*, London.

Hartsock, N. (1987) "Rethinking modernism: minority versus majority theories." *Cultural Critique*, 7, 187–206.

Harvey, D. (1973) *Social justice and the city*, London.

Harvey, D. (1974) "Population, resources, and the ideology of science," *Economic Geography*, 50, 256–77.

Harvey, D. (1982) *The limits to capital*, Oxford.

Harvey, D. (1985a) *The urbanization of capital*, Oxford.

Harvey, D. (1985b) *Consciousness and the urban experience*, Oxford.

Harvey, D. (1989a) *The condition of postmodernity*, Oxford.

Harvey, D. (1989b) "From managerialism to entrepreneurialism: the transformation in urban governance in late capitalism," *Geografiska Annaler*, 71B, 3–17.

Harvey, D. (1989c) *The urban experience*, Baltimore, Md.

Harvey, D. (1990) "Between space and time: Reflections on the geographical imagination," *Annals, Association of American Geographers*, 80, 418–34.

Hayden, D. (1981) *The grand domestic revolution: a history of feminist designs for American homes, neighorhoods and cities*, Cambridge.

Hays, S. (1959) *Conservation and the gospel of efficiency: The progressive conservation movement, 1890–1920*, Cambridge.

Hays, S. (1987) *Beauty, health and permanence: Environmental politics in the United States, 1955–85*, Cambridge.

Hayter, T. and Harvey, D. (eds) (1993) *The factory and the city: The story of the Cowley auto workers in Oxford*, Brighton.

Hecht, S. and Cockburn, A. (1990) *The fate of the forest: Developers, destroyers and defenders of the Amazon*, New York.

Heidegger, M. (1966) *Discourse on thinking*, New York.

Heidegger, M. (1971) *Poetry, language, thought*, New York.

Heilbroner, R. (1974) *An inquiry into the human prospect*, New York.

Heim, M. (1991) "The erotic ontology of cyberspace," in Benedikt, M. (ed.) *Cyberspace*, Cambridge, Mass.

Helgerson, R. (1986) "The land speaks: Cartography, chorography and subversion in Renaissance England," *Representations*, 16, 51–85.

Hewitt, P. (1974) *Conceptual physics: A new introduction to your environment*, Boston, Mass.

Hiley, B. and Peat, F. (eds) (1987) *Quantum implications: Essays in honour of David Bohm*, London.

Hillerman, T. (1993) *Sacred clowns*, New York.

Hoffrichter, R. (ed.) (1993) *Toxic struggles: The theory and practice of environmental justice*, Philadelphia, Pa.

Holquist, M. (1990) "Introduction" to Bakhtin M., *Art and answerability*, Austin, Tex.

Horkheimer, M. (1947) *The eclipse of reason*, New York.

Horkheimer, M. and Adorno, T. (1972) *The dialectic of Enlightenment*, New York.

Horvath, R. and Gibson, K. (1984) "Abstraction in Marx's method," *Antipode*, 16, 12–25.

Howell, P. (1994) "The aspiration towards universality in political theory and political geography," *Geoforum*, 25, 413–27.

Hugh-Jones, C. (1979) *From the Milk River: Spatial and temporal processes in Northwest Amazonia*, Cambridge.

Humphrey, C. and Hugh-Jones, S. (1992) *Barter, exchange and value: An anthropological approach*, Cambridge.

Ingold, T. (1986) *The appropriation of nature: Essays on human ecology and social relations*, Manchester.

Ingold, T. (1993) "Globes and spheres: the topology of environmentalism," in Milton, K. (ed.) *Environmentalism: The view from anthropology*, London.

Jacks, G. and Whyte, R. (1939) *Vanishing lands*, New York.

Jameson, F. (1984) "Postmodernism, or the cultural logic of late capitalism," *New Left Review*, 146, 53–92.

Jay, M. (1973) *The dialectical imagination: A history of the Frankfurt School and the Institute of Social Research, 1923–50*, Boston, Mass.

Jencks, C. (1993) *Heteropolis: Los Angeles, the riots and the strange beauty of hetero-architecture*, London.

Johnson, C. (1974) *Utopian communism in France: Cabet and the Icarians*, Ithaca, NY.

Joyce, P. (ed.) (1987) *The historical meanings of work*, Cambridge.

Kaminer, W. (1995) "Feminism's third wave: What do young women want?" *New York Times Book Review*, June 4.

Kapp, K. (1950) *The social costs of private enterprise*, New York.

Keith, M. and Pile, S. (eds) (1993) *Place and the politics of identity*, London.

Kern, S. (1983) *The culture of time and space, 1880–1918*, London.

Knorr-Cetina, K. (1994) "Primitive classification and postmodernity: towards a sociological notion of fiction," *Theory, Culture and Society*, 11, 1–22.

Knox, P. (1994) "The stealthy tyranny of community spaces," *Environment and Planning A*, 26, 170–3.

Krauss, C. (1994) "Women of color in the front line," in Bullard, R. (ed.) *Unequal protection*, San Francisco, Calif.

Kristeva, J. (1986) *The Kristeva reader* (edited by Toril Moi), Oxford.

Kuhn, T. (1988) "Possible worlds in history of science," in Akken, S. (ed.) *Possible worlds in humanities, arts and sciences*, Berlin.

Kwong, P. (1987) *The new Chinatown*, New York.

Landes, D. (1983) *Revolution in time*, Cambridge, Mass.

Leclerc, I. (1986) *The philosophy of nature*, Washington, DC.

Lee, D. (1980) "On the Marxian view of the relationship between man and nature," *Environmental Ethics*, 2, 1–21.

Lee, K. (1989) *Social philosophy and ecological scarcity*, London.

Leeds, A. (1994) *Cities, classes, and the social order*, Ithaca, NY.

Lees, A. (1991) "Berlin and modern urbanity in German discourse, 1845–1945," *Journal of Urban History*, 17, 153–80.

Lefebvre, H. (1974) *The survival of capitalism*, London.

Lefebvre, H. (1991) *The production of space*, Oxford.

Leff, E. (1995) *Green production: Towards an environmental rationality*, New York.

Le Goff, J. (1980) *Time, work and culture in the middle ages*, Chicago, Ill.

Le Goff, J. (1988) *Medieval civilization*, Oxford.

Leibniz, G. (1968) *Leibniz: Philosophical writings*, New York.

Leibniz, G. (1991) *G. W. Leibniz's Monadology* (edited by N. Rescher), Pittsburgh, Pa.

Leiss, W. (1974) *The domination of nature*, Boston, Mass.

Leopold, A. (1968) *A Sand County almanac*, New York.

Lévi-Strauss, C. (1963) *Structural anthropology*, New York.

Levine, A. (1982) *Love Canal: Science, politics and people*, New York.

Levins, R. and Lewontin, R. (1985) *The dialectical biologist*, Cambridge, Mass.

Levins, R., Awerbuch, T., Brinkmann, U., Eckardt, L., Epstein, P., Makhoul, N., Albuquerque de Possas, C., Puccia, C., Spielman, A. and Wilson, M. (1994) "The emergence of new diseases," *American Scientist*, January, 52–60.

Lewontin, R. (1982) "Organism and environment," in Plotkin, H. (ed.) *Learning, development and culture*, Chichester.

Lewontin, R., Rose, S., and Kamin, L. (1984) *Not in our genes: Biology, ideology, and human nature*, New York.

Lii, J. (1995) "Life in sweatshop reveals grim conspiracy of the poor," *New York Times*, March 12, p. A1.

Lilburne, G. (1989) *A sense of place: A Christian theology of the land*, Nashville, Tenn.

Litfin, K. (1994) *Ozone discourses: Science and politics in global environmental cooperation*, New York.

Lockwood, M. (1989) *Mind, brain and the quantum: The compound "I"*, Oxford.

Logan, J. and Molotch, H. (1988) *Urban fortunes: The political economy of place*, Berkeley, Calif.

Lomnitz-Adler, C. (1991) "Concepts for the study of regional culture," *American Ethnologist*, 18, 195–214.

Losch, A. (1954) *The economics of location*, New Haven, Conn.

Loukaki, A. (1967) "Whose *genius loci*; competing interpretations of the 'Sacred Rock of the Athenian Acropolis'," *Annals, Association of American Geographers*, forthcoming.

Lovejoy, A. (1964) *The great chain of being*, Cambridge, Mass.

Lovelock. J. (1992) "The earth is not fragile," in Cartledge, B. (ed.) *Monitoring the environment*, Oxford.

Lowe, V. (1962) *Understanding Whitehead*, Baltimore, Md.

MacCannell, D. (1976) *The tourist: A new theory of the leisure class*, New York.

Maler, H. (1995) *Convoiter l'impossible: L'utopie avec Marx, malgre Marx,* Paris.

Malthus, T. (1968) *Principles of political economy,* New York.

Malthus, T. (1970) *An essay on the principle of population and a summary view of the principle of population,* Harmondsworth, Middlesex.

Marin, L. (1984) *Utopics: Spatial play,* Atlantic Heights, NJ.

Marsh, G. (1965) *Man and nature,* Cambridge, Mass.

Martin, E. (1991) "The egg and the sperm: How science has constructed a romance based on stereotypical male–female roles," *Signs,* 16, 485–501.

Martin, E. (1992) "The end of the body," *American Ethnologist,* 19, 121–40.

Martin, E. (1994) *Flexible bodies: Tracking immunity in American culture – from the days of polio to the age of AIDS,* Boston, Mass.

Martin, G. (1964) *Leibniz: Logic and metaphysics,* Manchester.

Martinez-Allier, J. (1990) "Ecology and the poor: A neglected dimension of Latin American history," *Journal of Latin American Studies,* 23, 621–39.

Marx, K. (1963) *The eighteenth brumaire of Louis Bonaparte,* New York.

Marx, K. (1964) *Economic and philosophic manuscripts of 1844,* New York.

Marx, K. (1967) *Capital* (three volumes), New York.

Marx, K. (1972) "On the Jewish question," in McClellan, D. (ed.) *Early texts,* Oxford.

Marx, K. (1973) *Grundrisse,* Harmondsworth, Middlesex.

Marx, K. and Engels, F. (1951) *Selected Works,* Volume 1, Moscow.

Marx, K. and Engels, F. (1952) *Manifesto of the Communist Party,* Moscow.

Marx, K. and Engels, F. (1965) *Selected correspondence,* Moscow.

Marx, K. and Engels, F. (1970) *The German ideology,* New York.

Marx, K. and Engels, F. (1975) *Collected works,* Volume 5, New York.

Massey, D. (1991) "The political place of locality studies," *Environment and Planning A,* 23, 267–81.

Mauss, M. (1990) *The gift: The form and reasons for exchange in archaic societies,* London.

May, R. (1992) "How many species inhabit the earth?" *Scientific American,* October, 18–24.

McCarney, P. (1995) "Urban research in the developing world: Four approaches to the environment of cities," in Stren, E. (ed.) *Urban research in the developing world,* Toronto.

McCay, B. and Acheson, J. (1987) *The question of the commons: The culture and ecology of human resources,* Tucson, Ariz.

McCluhan, M. (1966) *Understanding media: The extensions of man,* New York.

McDougall, H. (1993) *Black Baltimore: A new theory of community,* Philadelphia, Pa.

McEvoy, A. (1988) "Towards an interactive theory of nature and culture: Ecology, production and cognition in the California fishing industry," in Worster, D. (ed.) *The ends of the earth,* Cambridge.

Meadows, D., Meadows, D., Rangers, J., and Behrens, W. (1972) *The limits to growth,* New York.

Merchant, C. (1983) *The death of nature: women, ecology and the scientific revolution,* New York.

Merrifield, A. (1993) "Place and space: a Lefebvrian reconciliation," *Transactions of the Institute of British Geographers,* New Series 18, 516–31.

Meszaros, I. (1970) *Marx's theory of alienation,* London.

450 *Bibliography*

Meyer, R. (1952) *Leibnitz and the seventeenth century revolution*, Cambridge.

Mignolo, W. (1994) *The darker side of the Renaissance: Literacy, territoriality and colonization*, Ann Arbor, Mich.

Mitchell, T. (1991) *Colonizing Egypt*, Cambridge.

Mitman, G. (1992) *The state of nature: Ecology, community, and American social thought, 1900–1950*, Chicago, Ill.

Mohanty, C. (1991) "Cartographies of struggle: third world women and the politics of feminism," in Mohanty, C., Russo, A., and Torres, L. (eds) *Third world women and the politics of feminism*, Bloomington, Ind.

Moody, K. (1988) *An injury to one*, London.

Moore, B. (1986) *Space, text and gender*, Cambridge.

Morley, D. and Robins, K. (1993) "No place like *heimat*: Images of home(land)," in Carter, E., Donald, J., and Squires, J. (eds) *Space and place: Theories of identity and location*, London.

Mungello, T. (1977) *Leibniz and Confucianism: The search for an accord*, Honolulu, HI.

Munn, N. (1986) *The fame of Gawa*, Cambridge.

Naess, A. (1989) *Ecology, community and lifestyle*, Cambridge.

Nash, R. (1989) *The rights of nature: A history of environmental ethics*, Madison, NJ.

Needham, J. (1954) *Science and civilisation in China*, Cambridge.

Newman, O. (1972) *Defensible space: Crime prevention through urban design*, New York.

Norberg-Schulz, C. (1980) *Genius loci: Towards a phenomenology of architecture*, New York.

Norgaard, R. (1985) "Environmental economics: An evolutionary critique and a plea for pluralism," *Journal of Environmental Economics and Management* 12, 382–94.

O'Connor, J. (1988) "Capitalism, nature, socialism: A theoretical introduction," *Capitalism, Nature, Socialism*, 5, No. 1, 1–19.

O'Riordan, T. (1981) *Environmentalism*, London.

Ollman, B. (1976) *Alienation: Marx's conception of man in capitalist society*, Cambridge.

Ollman, B. (1990) "Putting dialectics to work: the process of abstraction in Marx's method," *Rethinking Marxism*, 3, No. 1, 26–74.

Ollman, B. (1993) *Dialectical investigations*, New York.

Ophuls, W. (1977) *Ecology and the politics of scarcity: A prologue to a political theory of the steady state*, San Francisco, Calif.

Osserman, R. (1995) *Poetry of the universe: A mathematical exploration of the cosmos*, New York.

Ozouf, M. (1988) *Festivals and the French revolution*, Cambridge, Mass.

Paehlke, R. (1989) *Environmentalism and the future of progressive politics*. New Haven, Conn.

Palmer, B. (1990) *Descent into discourse: The reification of language and the writing of social history*, Philadelphia, Pa.

Parkes, D. and Thrift, N. (1980) *Times, spaces and places: A chronogeographic perspective*, New York.

Parry, J. and Bloch, M. (eds) (1989) *Money and the morality of exchange*, Cambridge.

Parsons, H. (ed.) (1977) *Marx and Engels on ecology*, Westport, Conn.

Pearce, D., Markandya, A., and Barbier, E. (1989) *Blueprint for a green economy*, London.

Peffer, R. (1990) *Marxism, morality, and social justice*, Princeton, NJ.

Pepper, D. (1993) *Eco-socialism: From deep ecology to social justice*, London.

Perelman, M. (1993) "Marxism and ecology: Marx and resource scarcity," *Capitalism, Nature, Socialism*, 14, 65–84.

Phoenix, J. (1993) "Getting the lead out of the community," in Bullard, R. (ed.) *Unequal protection*, San Francisco, Calif.

Plato (1965) *The Republic*, Harmondsworth, Middlesex.

Platt, H. (1991) *The electric city: Energy and the growth of the Chicago area, 1880–1930*, Chicago, Ill.

Plumwood, V. (1993) *Feminism and the mastery of nature*, London.

Portes, A., Castells, M., and Benton, L. (1989) *The informal economy: Studies in advanced capitalist and less developed countries*, Baltimore, Md.

Pred, A. (1984) "Place as historically contingent process: structuration and the time-geography of becoming places." *Annals of the Association of American Geographers*, 74, 279–97.

Pred, A. (1990) *Making histories and constructing human geographies: The local transformation of practice, power relations, and consciousness*, Boulder, Col.

Probyn, E. (1990) "Travels in the postmodern: making sense of the local," in Nicholson, L. (ed.) *Feminism/postmodernism*, New York.

Rajan, V. (ed.) (1993) *Rebuilding communities: Experiences and experiments in Europe*, Totnes, Devon.

Rawls, J. (1971) *A theory of justice*, Cambridge, Mass.

Redclift, M. (1987) *Sustainable development*, London.

Regan, T. (1983) *The case for animal rights*, Berkeley, Calif.

Relph, E. (1976) *Place and placelessness*, London.

Relph, E. (1989) "Geographical experiences and being-in-the-world: the phenomenological origins of geography," in Seamon, D. and Mugerauer, R. (eds) *Dwelling, place and environment: Towards a phenomenology of person and world*, New York.

Rescher, N. (1979) *Leibniz: An introduction to his philosophy*, Totawa, NJ.

Rescher, N. (1981) *Leibniz's metaphysics of nature*, Dordrecht.

Rich, B. (1993) *Mortgaging the earth: The World Bank, environmental impoverishment and the crisis of development*, Boston, Mass.

Ricoeur, P. (1991) "Narrative identity," in Wood, D. (ed.) *On Paul Ricoeur: Narrative and interpretation*, London.

Roberts, M. (1991) *Living in a man-made world: Gender assumptions in modern housing design*, New York.

Roediger, D. and Foner, P. (1989) *Our own time: A history of American labor and the working day*, London.

Roman, L. (1993) "'On the ground' with antiracist pedagogy and Raymond Williams's unfinished project to articulate a socially transformative critical realism," in Dworkin and Roman (eds) *Views beyond the border country*, London.

Ross, A. (1993) "The Chicago gangster theory of life," *Social Text*, 35, 93–112.

Ross, K. (1988) *The emergence of social space: Rimbaud and the Paris commune*, Minneapolis, Minn.

Rossi, A. (1982) *Architecture and the city*, Cambridge, Mass.

Rousseau, J.-J. (1973) *The social contract and discourses*, London.

Russell, B. (1900) *A critical exposition of the philosophy of Leibniz*, Cambridge.

Sachs, I. (1988) "Vulnerability of giant cities and the life lottery" in Dogan, M. and Kasarda, J. (eds) *The metropolis era: Volume I, a world of giant cities*, Newbury Park, Calif.

Sachs, W. (ed.) (1993) *Global ecology: A new arena of political conflict*, London.

Sack, R. (1980) *Conceptions of space in social thought: A geographic perspective*, Minneapolis, Minn.

Sagoff, M. (1988) *The economy of the earth: Philosophy, law, and the environment*, Cambridge.

Said, E. (1978) *Orientalism*, New York.

Said, E. (1989) (with Raymond Williams) "Appendix: media, margins and modernity," in Williams, R. *The politics of modernism*, London.

Sale, K. (1985) *Dwellers in the land: The bioregional vision*, San Francisco, Calif.

Sale, K. (1990) "What Columbus discovered," *The Nation*, October 22, pp. 444–6.

Sandel, M. (1982) *Liberalism and the limits of justice*, Cambridge.

Sapir, E. (1949) *Selected writings of Edward Sapir on language, culture and personality*, Berkeley, Calif.

Sauer, C. (1956) "The agency of man on earth," in Thomas, W. (ed.) *Man's role in changing the face of the earth*, Chicago, Ill.

Sayer, A. (1985) "The difference that space makes," in Gregory, D. and Urry, J. (eds) *Social relations and spatial structures*, London.

Schivelbusch, W. (1978) "Railroad space and railroad time," *New German Critique*, 14, 31–40.

Schmidt, A. (1971) *The concept of nature in Marx*, London.

Schneider, K. (1993) "Plan for toxic dump pits Blacks against Blacks," *New York Times*, December 13, p. A12.

Schoenberger, E. (1996) *The cultural crisis of the corporation*, Oxford.

Segal, L. (1991) "Whose left: Socialism, feminism and the future," *New Left Review*, 185, 81–91.

Sennett, R. (1970) *The uses of disorder: Personal identity and city life*, New York.

Shilling, C. (1993) *The body and social theory*, London.

Shiva, V. (1989) *Staying alive: Women, ecology and development*, London.

Shohat, E. (1991) "Imaging terra incognita: The disciplinary gaze of empire," *Public Culture*, 3, No. 2, 41–70.

Sibley, D. (1995) *Geographies of exclusion*, London.

Simmel, G. (1978) *The philosophy of money*, London.

Simmel, G. (1994) "Bridge and door," *Theory, Culture and Society*, 11, 5–10.

Simon, K. (1981) *The ultimate resource*, Princeton, NJ.

Smith, N. (1987) "Dangers of the empirical turn," *Antipode*, 19, 59–68.

Smith, N. (1990) *Uneven development: Nature, capital and the production of space*, 2nd edn, Oxford.

Smith, N. (1992) "Geography, difference and the politics of scale," in Doherty, J., Graham, E., and Malek, M. (eds) *Postmodernism and the social sciences*, London.

Smith, N. and Katz, C. (1993) "Grounding metaphor: Towards a spatialized politics," in Keith, M. and Pile, S. (eds), *Place and the politics of identity*, London.

Snedeker, G. (1993) "Between humanism and social theory: The cultural criticism of Raymond Williams," *Rethinking Marxism*, 6, 104–13.

Sommer, J. (1994) "A dragon let loose on the land: And Shanghai is at the epicenter of China's economic boom," *The Japan Times*, Wednesday October 26, p. 3.

Soper, K. (1995) *What is nature?*, Oxford.

Sorokin, P. (1937–41) *Social and cultural dynamics* (four volumes), New York.

Spain, D. (1992) *Gendered spaces*, Chapel Hill, NJ.

Spender, D. (1980) *Man made language*, London.

Spivak, G. C. (1988) "Can the subaltern speak?" in Nelson, C. and Grossberg, L. (eds) *Marxism and the interpretation of culture*, Urbana, Ill.

Spretnak, C. (1985) "The spiritual dimension of Green politics," in Spretnak, C. and Capra, F. (eds) *Green politics*, London.

Spretnak, C. and Capra, F. (1985) *Green politics: The global promise*, London.

Stafford, B. (1991) *Body criticism: Imaging the unseen in Enlightenment art and medicine*, Cambridge, Mass.

Steiner, G. (1991) *Heidegger*, London.

Stevens, W. (1993) "Want a room with a view? Idea may be in the genes," *New York Times*, November 30, pp. C1 and C13.

Stone, A. (1991) "Will the real body please stand up? Boundary stories about virtual cultures," in Benedikt, M. (ed.) *Cyberspace*, Cambridge, Mass.

Stone, J. (1988) "Imperialism, colonialism and cartography," *Transactions Institute of British Geographers*, New Series 13, 57–64.

Strathern, M. (1988) *The gender of the gift*, Berkeley, Calif.

Strawson, P. (1965) *Individuals*, London.

Struck, D. (1991) "South's poultry plants thrive, feeding on workers' needs," *Baltimore Sun*, Sunday September 8, Section A, pp. 1 and 14.

Swyngedouw, E. (1989) "The heart of the place: the resurrection of locality in an age of hyperspace," *Geografiska Annaler*, 71.

Swyngedouw, E. (1992a) "Territorial organization and the space/technology nexus," *Transactions, Institute of British Geographers*, New Series, 17, 417–33.

Swyngedouw, E. (1992b) "The Mamon quest: Globalization, international competition and the new monetary order, the search for a new spatial scale," in Dunford, M. and Kafkalis, G. (eds) *Cities and regions in the new Europe*, London.

Szasz, A. (1994) *Ecopopulism: Toxic waste and the movement for environmental justice*, Minneapolis, Minn.

Taylor, C. (1994) *Multiculturalism: Examining the politics of recognition*, Princeton, NJ.

Taylor, D. (1992) "Can the environmental movement attract and maintain the support of minorities?" in Bryant, B. and Mohai, P. (eds) *Race and the incidence of environmental hazards*, Colorado.

Taylor, D. (1993) "Environmentalism and the politics of inclusion," in Bullard, R. (ed.) *Confronting environmental racism*, Boston, Mass.

Taylor, W. (ed.) (1991) *Inventing Times Square: Commerce and culture at the crossroads of the world*, New York.

Thomas, W. (ed.) (1956) *Man's role in changing the face of the earth*, Chicago, Ill.

Thompson, E. P. (1967) "Time, work discipline, and industrial capitalism," *Past and Present*, 38, 56–97.

Timpanaro, S. (1970) *On materialism*, London.

Tindall, G. (1991) *Countries of the mind: The meaning of place to writers*, London.

Todes, D. (1989) *Darwin without Malthus: The struggle for existence in Russian evolutionary thought,* Oxford.

Toffler, A. (1970) *Future shock,* New York.

Toffler, A. (1980) *The third wave,* New York.

Toth, J. (1993) "Meanwhile, in the other South," *Business Week,* September 27, p. 48.

Tuan, Y.-F. (1977) *Space and place: The perspective of experience,* Minneapolis, Minn.

Turner, B., Clark, W., Kates, R., Richards, J., Mathews, J., and Meyer, W. (eds) (1990) *The earth as transformed by human action: Global and regional changes in the biosphere over the past 300 years,* Cambridge.

U.S. Government (1968) *Building the American City,* Report of the National Commission on urban problems to the Congress and President of the United States, Washington, DC.

Uchitelle, L. (1995) "For many, a slower climb up the payroll pecking order," *New York Times* Sunday May 14, p. F.11.

Veblen, T. (1967) *Absentee ownership,* Boston, Mass.

Volosinov, V. (1986) *Marxism and the philosophy of language,* Cambridge, Mass.

Walzer, M. (1983) *Spheres of justice: A defense of pluralism and equality,* Oxford.

Weale, A. (1992) *The new politics of pollution,* Manchester.

Weber, M. (1991) *From Max Weber: Essays in sociology* (edited by Girth, H. and Wright Mills, C., London.

Wenz, P. (1988) *Environmental justice,* Albany, NY.

Wheeler, T. (1994) "Bill may curb lead poisoning's deadly toll," *Baltimore Sun,* February 27.

White, L. (1967) "The historical roots of our ecological crisis," *Science,* 155, 1203–7.

White, S. K. (1991) *Political theory and postmodernism,* Cambridge.

Whitehead, A. (1916) "La théorie relationiste de l'espace," *Revue de Métaphysique et de Morale,* 23, 423–54 [partially translated in Fitzgerald, J. (1979) *Alfred North Whitehead's early philosophy of space and time,* Washington, DC.

Whitehead, A. (1920) *The concept of nature,* Cambridge.

Whitehead, A. (1922) *The principle of relativity,* Cambridge.

Whitehead, A. (1969) *Process and reality,* New York.

Whitehead, A. (1985) *Science and the modern world,* London.

Whorf, B. (1976) *Language, thought and reality: Selected writings of Benjamin Lee Whorf,* Cambridge, Mass.

Widgery, D. (1991) *Some lives! A GP's East End,* London.

Wigley, M. (1992) "Untitled: The housing of gender," in Colomina, B. (ed.) *Sexuality and space,* Princeton, NJ.

Wilkins, M. H. F. (1987) "Complementarity and the union of opposites," in Hiley, B. and Peat, F. (eds) *Quantum implications,* London.

Williams, R. (1960) *Border country,* London.

Williams, R. (1961) "The achievement of Brecht," *Critical Quarterly,* 3, 153–62.

Williams, R. (1964) *Second generation,* London.

Williams, R. (1973) *The country and the city,* London.

Williams, R. (1977) *Marxism and literature,* Oxford.

Williams, R. (1978) "Problems of materialism," *New Left Review,* 109, 3–18.

Williams, R. (1979a) *Politics and letters,* London.

Williams, R. (1979b) *The fight for Manod,* London.

Williams, R. (1980) *Problems in materialism and culture*, London.

Williams, R. (1983a) *Beyond 2000*, London.

Williams, R. (1983b) *Keywords*, Oxford.

Williams, R. (1985) *Loyalties*, London.

Williams, R. (1989) *People of the Black Mountains: The beginning*, London.

Williams, R. (1989a) *Resources of hope*, London.

Williams, R. (1989b) *The politics of modernism*, London.

Williams, R. (1990) *People of the Black Mountains: The eggs of the eagle*. London.

Wilson, A. (1992) *The culture of nature: North American landscape from Disney to the Exxon Valdez*, Oxford.

Wilson, E. O. (1978) *On human nature*, Cambridge.

Wilson, E. O. and Kellert, S. (1993) *The biophilia hypothesis*, Washington, DC.

Wittfogel, K. (1953) *Oriental despotism*, New Haven.

Wittgenstein, L. (1967) *Philosophical investigations*, Oxford.

Wolf, E. (1982) *Europe and the peoples without history*, Berkeley, Calif.

Wolfe, S. (1994) "Comment" in Gutman, A. (ed.) *Multiculturalism: Examining the politics of recognition*, Princeton, NJ.

Wood, E. M. (1995) *Democracy against capitalism: Renewing historical materialism*, Cambridge.

World Commission on Environment and Development (The Brundtland Report), (1987) *Our common future*, Oxford.

Worster, D. (1985a) *Rivers of empire: Water, aridity and the growth of the American West*, New York.

Worster, D. (1985b) *Nature's economy: A history of ecological ideas*, Cambridge.

Young, I. (1990a) *Justice and the politics of difference*, Princeton, NJ.

Young, I. (1990b) "The ideal of community and the politics of difference," in Nicholson, L. (ed.) *Feminism/Postmodernism*, New York.

Young, R. (1985) *Darwin's metaphor: Nature's place in Victorian culture*, Cambridge.

Zapatista Army for National Liberation (1996) "First declaration of La Realidad against Neoliberalism and for Humanity," *La Jornada*, January 30, 1996.

Zelizer, V. (1994) *The social meaning of money*, New York.

Zerubavel, E. (1985) *Hidden rhythms: Schedules and calendars in social life*, Berkeley, Calif.

Zimmerman, M. (1988) "Quantum theory, intrinsic value, and panentheism," *Environmental Ethics*, 10, 3–30.

Zizek, S. (1993) *Tarrying with the negative*, Durham, NC.

Zola, E. (1891), *Money*, Gloucestershire.

Zone (1989) *Fragments for a history of the human body*, Urzone, NY.

Index

I have always indexed my own books, but in this instance indexing proved peculiarly difficult for reasons that the text itself sheds light on. Indexing entails representing a relational flow of argument by reference to fixed meanings and terms. It is therefore a very undialectical device that is somewhat destructive to the content of what it indexes. This does not mean, I hope, that the index is useless. But it does restrict its appropriateness in ways that perceptive readers should surely appreciate.

(*Note*: Only the names of individuals whose ideas are substantively quoted or considered in the text have been indexed.)